CONQUERORS
OF
THE WEST

STALWART MORMON PIONEERS

VOLUME I

Conquerors of the West: Stalwart Mormon Pioneers Volume I
compiled by National Society of the Sons of Utah Pioneers

For additional copies contact
Sons of Utah Pioneers
3301 East 2920 South
Salt Lake City, Utah 84109-4260

Publisher's Cataloging-in-Publication
(Provided by Quality Books, Inc.)
Conquerors of the West : stalwart Mormon pioneers / edited
        by Florence C. Youngberg. -- 1st ed.
        v. cm.
        Includes index.
        Preassigned LCCN: 98-72414
        ISBN: 1-888106-31-X

        1. Mormons--West (U.S.)--Genealogy. 2. Mormons--West
(U.S.)--Biography. 3. Pioneers--West (U.S.)--Biography
I. Youngberg, Florence C. II. National Society, Sons of
Utah Pioneers.

BX8693.C66 1998   289.3'092'278
                                   QB198-1059

Editor: Florence C. Youngberg
Front drawings courtesy of Sons of Utah Pioneers

Cover Design: John Barnhill

Professionally produced
in the United States of America by

Agreka Books

800 360-5284
www.agreka.com

DEDICATION

"Should we not lift the heroic story of early Mormon pioneering from musty archives and make it live again, that we may better sense the accomplishments of our honored forebears and thereby better understand the requirements of our own times."

Anon

EDITOR'S NOTE

As I determined to write some of the histories of those brave and stalwart men who gave up so very much to leave behind all that meant so much to them–in some cases even their families–to join the migration to a new country not knowing what faced them. With new and often fearsome experiences, with death, birth and marriages, new experiences and perhaps even a new life style, I knew it was a story that needed telling. Individual histories have been written but I wanted to combine as many as I could into a volume that would not only recognize these men but also give credit to their loyal wives and families who accompanied them in this great experience.

I knew there might be some discrepancies in what they sent in and what others of that man's descendants might feel would be right. I have only had the record and information that was sent to me. If, in reading this record you find an error, I hope you will recognize that when we deal with old records we must accept that there will undoubtedly be errors or differences of opinion. I hope you will forgive me if this happens. I only had someone's word that it was right. It would have been impossible for me to research each entry.

I want to thank all those who took the time to contribute their stories to this book. I want to thank the Executive Board of the Sons of Utah Pioneers who showed faith in me in agreeing to let me go ahead with this project .

There are many who helped and encouraged me along the way, but there are several I should mention. Sherrie Held, our secretary in the office, for her knowledge of the computer and her encouragement. Karen Emerson, my daughter, who helped with some of the correcting. Emily Utt who spent many long hours going over the manuscript to catch any errors we had missed. The volunteers at the Family History Center and SUP Library who many times helped people who came in so that I could keep typing. And last, but far from least, my patient and loving husband who has stood by me for so many years and backed me in projects such as this and encouraged me when I wasn't sure I could do it.

I also want to thank Agreka Books who have given me counsel, help and encouragement, especially Laura, Linda, Annette and Rebekah.

I thank you all. My hope is that those who take the time to read from these histories will visit the Family History Center and Library to read further about the courageous lives of these men who made it possible for us to live here in comfort and security.

A NOTE FROM THE NATIONAL SOCIETY OF THE SONS OF UTAH PIONEERS

The National Society of the Sons of Utah Pioneers does not guarantee, warranty, or assume any responsibility for the accuracy of the records contained in these volumes, and will not be held liable for any inaccuracies or descrepancies. While every effort has been made to assure the accuracy of the histories, there will undoubtedly be areas open to dispute. The volumes are comprised of records submitted by descendents of these men. While most of the submitters took great pains to contribute an accurate record, there will always remain some gray areas in the life of man.

FORWARD

QUOTE FROM LOUIS L'AMOUR'S BOOK "SACKETT'S LAND"

"We are all of us, it has been said the children of immigrants and foreigners–even the American Indian–although he arrived here a little earlier. What a man is and what he becomes is in part due to his heritage, and the men and women who came west did not emerge suddenly from limbo. Behind them were ancestors, families, and former lives. Yet even as the domestic cattle of Europe evolved into the wild longhorns of Texas, so the American pioneer had the characteristics of a distinctive type.

Physically and psychologically, the pioneers' need for change had begun in the old countries with their decision to migrate. In most cases their decisions were personal, ordered by no one else. Even when migration was ordered or forced, the people who survived were characterized by physical strength, the capacity to endure, and, not uncommonly, a rebellious nature.

History is not made only by kings and parliaments, presidents, wars and generals. It is the story of people, of their love, honor, faith, hope and suffering; of birth and death, of hunger, thirst and cold, of loneliness and sorrow."

Story by story, generation by generation, these families are moving westward. To freedom, adventure, perhaps to glory. To rewards, some good some not so good, but all to fulfill a need, a desire for something they felt a need for in their lives. These then, are their stories.

CONQUERORS
OF
THE WEST

STALWART MORMON PIONEERS

EDITED BY
FLORENCE C. YOUNGBERG

PETER ABPLANALP, SR.

Born: 2 Mar 1829, Brienzwyler, Bern, Switzerland
Parents: Johannes and Katharina Schild Abplanalp
Died: 28 May 1900, Vernal, Uintah, Utah
Arrived in Valley: 1861

Married: Margaretha Eggler
Date: 30 Nov 1856, Brienzwyler, Bern, Switzerland
Parents: Johannes & Margaretha Schild Eggler
Born: 22 Feb 1835, Brienzwyler, Bern, Switzerland
Died: 25 May 1902, Vernal, Uintah, Utah

Peter, his wife Margaretha, and three children came to New York in 1859 and settled in Pikes Pond, N.Y. for four years. They came by oxen and wagon to the Valley in 1861. They settled in Mound City, later called Midway, Utah until 1886. Peter was a Lieutenant in the Territorial Militia during the Black Hawk War.

The family were all talented in music. Peter was a member of the Andreas-Burgener Band of Midway. Seven more children were born in Midway. They moved to Vernal to homestead in 1886. Peter farmed and worked in the coal mine. He was bishop of Glines Ward from 9 May 1887 to 1889.

Children:

PETER, Md. Mary Jane Alder.
MARGARETHA, Md. Edward Watkins.
ELIZABETH, Md. Jedediah Wardle.

GEORGE, Md. Amanda Wardle.
JOHN, Md. Eva Maybell Wall.
JOSEPH, Md. Hannah Marks Jenkins
EMMA LUELLA, Md. William James Workman
FRANKLIN, Md. Mary Ann Howard
HEINRICH, Md. Margaret Lillian Ross
WILLIAM, Md. Barbara Elizabeth Jenkins.

Submitted by: Elizabeth May A. England

ORSON BENNETT ADAMS

Born: 9 Mar 1815, Alexander, Genessee, New York
Parents: Elisha Bennett and Asenath Camp Adams
Died: 4 Feb 1901, Harrisburg, Washington, Utah
Arrived in Valley: 27 Jul 1847, Morman Battalion Sick
    Detachment

Married 1st: Susan Smith
Date: 20 Mar 1836, Morgan Co., Illnois
Born: 30 May 1819, Glaskow, Kentucky
Parents: Anthony and Sarah Mahuran Smith
Died: 23 Jan 1892, Harrisburg, Washington, Utah

Married 2nd: Charlotte Elizabeth Gingell
Date: 21 Jul 1859, Parowan, Utah
Born: 1 Sep 1841, Sydney, New So. Wales, Australia
Parents: William and Mary Ann Woodhams Gingell
Died: 12 Feb 1879, Evanston, Wyoming

Orson followed the trade of an engineer until he was 21. He married Susan and they moved to Schyler, Illinois where he became a farmer. They were baptized into the Church in 1840 and moved to Nauvoo where he helped build the Temple.

He and his family were one of the first to cross the river when the exodus started. When volunteers were asked to join the Mormon Battalion, he joined. Susan went too as a laundress and nurse. Their little boy, John, was left with another family to come to the Valley. Orson was assigned to guard the sick detachment where his wife was. They spent the winter in Pueblo then journeyed to Salt Lake.

Orson was an explorer for Brigham Young and helped in the settlement of Parowan, Paragonah, Harrisburg and St. George. They lived in Harrisburg for a time until their deaths. While living in Paragona, he ran a sawmill. He had an accident which cut off three of his fingers of his left hand.

He was a devoted and kind father and friend and was always willing to help when Brigham Young or any of the church leaders called on him. The LDS Biographical Encyclopedia states that he married Margaret Jane Carter and Dorothy Frost, but nothing is known of those marriages.

Children of 1st wife:

MARY JANE, b. 11 Apr 1838, Schyler, Illinois. D. 1 Aug 1838, Child.
MARTHA JANE, b. 21 Feb 1841, Schyler, Illinois. D. 1 Mar 1841. Child.
JOHN PAGE, b. 11 May 1844, Macedonia, Illinois. (Adopted) Md. 1st, 3 May 1866, Jane Averett. Md. 2nd, 17 May 1876, Mary E Adair.
SUSAN, b. 30 Jun 1853, Parowan, Washington, Utah. Md. 11 Dec 1870, William Hanes. D. 8 Aug 1931.

Children of 2nd wife:

CAROLINE AUGUSTA, b. 10 Sep 1861, Paragona, Utah. Md.

1st, 10 Dec 1879, William Dennis Dugdale. Md. 2nd, 1866, John B. Wade. D. 30 Jun 1938, Green River, Wyoming.
OLIVER RANDOLPH, b. 29 Sep 1862, Paragonah, Utah. Md. Sarah Eardley. D. 23 Feb 1938.

Submitted by: Carolyn Jensen

WILLIAM HENRY ADAMS, JR.

Christened: 24 Jun 1845, Dover, Kent, England
Parents: William Henry and Martha Jennings Adams Sr.
Died: 4 Nov 1921, Pleasant Grove, Utah
Arrived in Valley: 10 Oct 1848, Willard Richards Co.

Married: Melissa Jane Caldwell
Date: 22 Mar 1869, Salt Lake City, Utah
Born: 7 Apr 1851, Spanish Fork, Utah
Died: 12 Mar 1939, American Fork, Utah

William Henry Jr. was only three years old when his parents brought he and his baby sister from England to the Valley. During the trek across the plains, he was accidentally shot with pepper shot through the knees, the bullet lodging in his left knee. Willard Richards removed it with a knife.

They were one of the first seven families to settle in Pleasant Grove, Utah. As a boy he tended cattle. Later he helped widen the dugway at the Point of the Mountain.

In 1867 he was called to help guard the teams to and from Sanpete as people moved. He was a veteran of the Black Hawk Indian War. He served a mission in 1880-81 to the Southern States in Georgia but was released due to ill health.

William was always active in church organizations. He was an entertainer and very musical. He directed choirs, entertained on stage, called dances. He was often asked to speak and sing.

For a time he and his family lived in Fountain Green. He moved his family back to Pleasant Grove in 1900. He was sent on several missions and was a traveling teacher. He was a student of the bible. He was a farmer and truck gardner and was asked many times to use his talents to administer to the sick and speak, and anything else that was needed.

Children:

MARTHA BARZILLA, b. 13 Jun 1870, Fountain Green, Utah. Md. 4 Dec 1889, Martin Mortensen Lund. D. 13 Jan 1933, Fountain Green, Utah.

ALICE ALMIRA, b. 18 Oct 1872, Fountain Green, Utah. Md. 28 Jun 1893, Jasper Heber Robertson. D. 13 Jan 1923, Fountain Green, Utah.

WILLIAM ALBERT, b. 19 Dec 1874, Fountain Green, Utah. Md. 1 Apr 1903, Virginia Brann. D. 4 Jun 1966, Brigham City, Utah.

DELOS EDGAR, b. 17 Feb 1877, Fountain Green, Sanpete, Utah. Md. 31 Jan 1900, Hannah Christina Peterson. D. 11 May 1960, Ogden, Utah.

MELISSA JANE, b. 4 Sep 1879, Fountain Green, Sanpete, Utah. Md. 15 Jun 1898, Orson Livingston Despain. D. 4 May 1956, Provo, Utah.

ELVA VILATE, b. 28 Mar 1882, Fountain Green, Sanpete, Utah. Md. 23 Mar 1904, David Waldemar West. D. 29 Jun 1961, Provo, Utah.

JOHN MATTHEW, b. 7 Oct 1884, Fountain Green, Sanpete, Utah. D. 25 Mar 1891, Fountain Green, Sanpete, Utah. Child.

GUY WILFORD, b. 25 Mar 1887, Fountain Green, Sanpete, Utah. D. 22 Jan 1891, Fountain Green, Sanpete, Utah. Child.

BURTON HENRY, b. 27 May 1889, Fountain Green, Sanpete, Utah. Md. 21 Apr 1920, Eva May Eldridge. D. 5 Dec 1963, American Fork, Utah.

BYRON LEWIS, b. 25 Aug 1891, Fountain Green, Sanpete, Utah. Md. 10 Jul 1912, Nora Adamson. D. 6 Jun 1981, Sterling, Bingham, Idaho.

Submitted by: Maud Pack

WILLIAM HENRY ADAMS, SR.

Born: 4 Jun 1817, Dover, Kent, England
Parents: John and Mary Nash Adams
Died: 8 Oct 1898, Pleasant Grove, Utah, Utah
Arrived in Valley: 10 Oct 1848, Willard Richards Co.

Married 1st: Martha Jennings
Date: 3 Nov 1839, St. Mary's Parish, Dover, Kent, England
Born: 24 Jul 1808, Dover, Kent, England
Died: 17 Aug 1852, Pleasant Grove, Utah, Utah

Married 2nd: Frances Ann Otten Crossland
Date: Jul 1858, Pleasant Grove, Utah
Born: 8 Feb 1824, Redlion St., London, Middlesex, England
Died: 23 Jan 1903, Pleasant Grove, Utah

William Henry Adams, Sr. was one of the first three settlers of Pleasant Grove on July 19, 1850. With Philo T. Farnsworth and John Mercer, he scouted the area along the Provo River and reported back that there were straight logs for houses and rocks for foundations. These three men surveyed the town site and William set his own stakes for 40 acres for his home. He was a stonemason and assisted in the erection of the first stone and adobe buildings in Salt Lake. He helped erect the Pleasant Grove meeting house which later burned down. In 1858, he worked for $3.50 a day as a mason helping put up the buildings for the army at Camp Floyd. He purchased one of the first wick lamps in Pleasant Grove. He helped build schools and other buildings and did all he could to help the early settlers.

He was self educated and became very good at anything he did. He served eight terms as Treasurer and Tax Collector of Pleasant Grove. He was secretary of the High Priests Quorum for many years. He was well respected for his faith, honesty and willingness to help others. He refused to have trouble with any man. He could converse with anyone on the history of nearly all nations. He was well read and retained the knowledge.

Children of 1st wife:

MARY, b. 1 Feb 1841, Dover, Kent, England. D. 1 Feb 1841. Child.

MARTHA, b. 1 May 1843, Dover, England. D. 19 Sep 1843. Child.

WILLIAM HENRY, JR., chr. 26 Jun 1845, St. Mary's Parish, Dover, Kent, England. Md. 22 Mar 1869, Melissa Jane Caldwell. D. 2 Nov 1921, Pleasant Grove, Utah

ELIZA, b. 6 Oct 1847, Dover, Kent, England. Md. 11 Aug 1865, George Aker Huggins. D. 22 Jan 1913, Fountain Green, Utah

JOHN ALMA, b. 5 Aug 1850, Salt Lake City. Md. 29 Jul 1877, Mary Alice Frampton. D. 4 Aug 1935, Pleasant Grove, Utah.

Children of 2nd wife:

ALICE MARIA, b. 14 May 1859, Pleasant Grove, Utah. Md. 22 Oct 1877, Joseph Ephraim Whiteley. D. 29 Dec 1924.

ANNIE JANE, b. 10 Mar 1861, Pleasant Grove, Utah. Md. 25 Sep 1879, John Henry Newman. D. 17 Aug 1927.

JOSEPH HYRUM, b. 22 Feb 1865, Pleasant Grove, Utah. Md. 4 Jun 1888, Colinda Chrilla Rogers. D. 31 Jul 1950.

Submitted by: Maud Pack

JOHN ADAMSON

Born: 22 Jan 1812, Boreland, Fife, Scotland
Parents: Andrew and Margaret Cunningham Adamson
Died: 10 Jun 1902, Wellsville, Utah
Entered the Valley: 12 Sept 1861, John R. Murdock Co.

Married: Helen Cameron
Date: 31 Dec 1836, Scotland
Born: 6 May 1809, Pathhead, Fife, Scotland
Died: 30 May 1884, Wellsville, Utah

John Adamson was born and reared on the east coast of Scotland. He worked in the mines as a child to help support his family. After his conversion to the Church in 1842/3, along with his wife and parents, he sailed to America on the "Monarch of the Sea," which carried the largest number of saints to cross the ocean in one vessel.

His oldest daughter, Janet, was married on board the ship as it neared New York. Two children, Andrew and Margaret , were professional dancers in Scotland and entertained those on board ship. When they reached Florence, Nebraska, they were met with wagons and teams that Brigham Young had sent to help them get to the valley. They left in July with the John R. Murdock Company.

John took his family to Wellsville in Cache Valley where he lived out his life.

Children:

JANET, b. 25 Apr 1838.

ANDREW, b. 15 Nov 1839.
MARGARET, b. 8 Oct 1841.
ELIZABETH, b. 19 Nov 1846.
ELLEN, b. 25 Nov 1850

Submitted by: LaPrele Hall

JENS PETER AHLSTROM

Born: 15 Apr 1835, Malmo, Sweden.
Parents: Ole Neilson and Ingebarg Bunderson Ahlstrom
Died: 12 Jan 1903, Manti, Utah
Arrived in Valley: 1865.

Married 1st: Inger Marie Larsen
Date: 21 Feb 1857, Burlington, DesMoines, Iowa.
Born: 21 Aug 1836, Hollensgaard, Hfrrng, Denmark.
Died: 22 Jul 1924, Kanosh, Millard, Utah.

Married 2nd: Mary Victor Bunderson
Date: 10 May 1872.
Born: 10 Nov 1854, Borslop, Sweden.
Died: 17 Apr 1907, Junction, Utah.

Jens was a carpenter. He worked on both the St. George and Manti Temples.

After the Manti Temple was dedicated, he became the head custodian. Jens worked on the spiral staircase in that temple.

Jens was a pattern designer.

Children of 1st wife:

ANNA OLENA, b. 12 Feb 1853, Burlington, Des Moines, Iowa.
   D. 22 Feb 1858. Child.
JOHN MICHAEL, b. 24 Mar 1859, Burlington, Iowa. Md. Sarah
   Helah Cherry. D. 23 Aug 1910.
JAMES PETER, b. 6 Sep 1861, Ephraim, Sanpete, Utah. Md.
   Serepta Matilda Jolley.
OLE CHRISTIAN, b. 21 Feb 1864, Ephraim, Utah. Md. Jane
   Stewart. D. 1 Jan 1948.
CHRISTIAN WILLIAM, b. 1 Sep 1867, Ephraim, Utah. D. 9
   Sep 1869. Child.
JOHANNAH MARIE, b. 14 Jun 1870, Ephraim, Utah. Md. 1st,
   George Q. Moffit. Md. 2nd, John P. Weaver. D. 2 Sep 1915.
CHARLES DELBERT, b. 21 Mar 1873, Ephraim, Utah. Md.
   1st, Sariah Elizabeth Campbell. Md. 2nd, Eldora Toles. D. 16
   May 1948.
BENJAMIN FRANKLIN, b. 4 Apr 1875, Ephraim, Utah. Md.
   Rosella Riggs. D. 10 Feb 1952.
SARAH, b. 15 Nov 1877, Ephraim, Sanpete, Utah. Md. Parley
   Pratt Nelson. D. 18 Mar 1945.

Children of 2nd wife:

MATILDA CHRISTINE, b. 7 Sep 1873, Ephraim, Utah. Md.
   Thad L. Buchanan. D. 3 Nov 1952, Manti, Utah.
ENGRI MALINDA, b. 25 May 1875, Ephraim, Utah. Md. E. C.
   Luke. D. 1 Aug 1953, Wyoming.
ELIZABETH, b. 25 Jul 1876, Ephraim, Utah. Md. Nephi Otteson.
   D. 10 Jan 1943, Manti, Utah.
MARY MINNIE, b. 20 Dec 1878, Ephraim, Utah. Md. Lile
   Braithwaite. D. 11 Sep 1951.
ELLEN NORA, b. 2 Apr 1881. D. 15 Nov 1892, Manti, Utah.
ANN GENEVA, b. 4 Apr 1883, Manti, Utah. Md. Archie L.
   Buchanan. D. 7 Apr 1960.
LILA MAY, b. 27 Jul 1885, Manti, Utah. Md. Noah Giles. D. 24
   Jul 1945, Salt Lake City, Utah.
WILLIAM ASPER, b. 31 Aug 1887, Manti, Utah. Md. Elvira

Mortenson. D. 22 Jun 1951, Wyoming.

MYRTLE, b. 23 Mar 1890, Manti, Utah. Md. Heber Clinger. D. 12 Oct 1918, Junction, Utah.

FLORA, b. 26 May 1892, Manti, Utah. Md. Merrell McKinley. D. 4 Apr 1924, Junction, Utah.

PETER VICTOR, b. 7 Dec 1894, Manti, Utah. Md. Ether Sabastian. D. 7 Apr 1952, Salt Lake City, Utah.

RUFUS, b. 7 Apr 1898, Manti, Utah. Md. Ethel Bench. D. 23 May 1951, Manti, Utah.

Submitted by: Clarence Giles

JOHN ALBISTON

Born: 4 Apr 1814, Stockport, Cheshire, England
Parents: John and Hannah Thacker Albiston
Died: 2 Apr 1891, Franklin, Franklin, Idaho
Arrived in Valley: 30 Sep 1854, Darwin Richardson Co.

Married: Elizabeth Mellor Smith
Date: 6 May 1833, Saddleworth, Yorkshire, England
Born: 27 Feb 1812, Silkstone, Yorkshire, England
Parents: John and Hannah Mellor Smith
Died: 18 Aug 1879, Richmond, Cache, Utah

John and his wife were baptized into the Church in August of 1840. Living in England, times were hard for them but they were determined to join the saints in Zion as soon as they possibly could.

They saved their money until they were able to bring their

family with them. How many of their nine children lived to go with them is not known, but it is known that their sixth child, Joseph, and their last child, Ruth, died in America, so undoubtedly others came too.

The trip across the ocean was a stormy, difficult one. Smallpox broke out on the ship, infecting 37 passengers and two crewmen. They were blessed in that only 10 people died. There were six marriages and six babies were born.

After their arrival in the Valley, they settled for a time in Ogden, and their last child, Ruth Agnes was born there. After a time, they moved to Grantsville and then to Franklin, Idaho, where John died.

He was buried in Richmond, Utah.

Children:

JAMES, b. abt 1835 in Staley Bridge, Cheshire, England.

HANNAH, b. 1837, Staley Bridge, England.

CHARLES, b. 11 Apr 1839, Staley Bridge, England. D. 12 Jan 1840, England. Child.

MARTHA, b. 9 Dec 1840, Staley Bridge, England. D. 25 Dec 1840, England. Child.

JOHN, b. 7 Feb 1842, Staley Bridge, England. Md. 3 Dec 1863, Mary Ann Lee. D. 9 Nov 1915, England.

JOSEPH A., b. 7 Jul 1844, Staley Bridge, England. Md. 7 Nov 1869, Christine Almina Christensen. D. 11 May 1907, Soda Springs, Caribou, Idaho.

ELIZABETH ANN, b. 11 May 1847, Staley Bridge, England. D. Child.

MARY PAMELIA, b. abt 1851, Staley Bridge, England. D. Child.

RUTH AGNES, b. 17 Oct 1855, Mt. Ford Ogden, Weber, Utah. Md. Joseph Johnson. D. 30 Jul 1897, Utah.

Submitter: Ralph Littlefield Albiston

ABEL ALEXANDER

Born: 8 Jan 1822, Calne, Wiltshire, England
Parents: Henry and Mary Dolman Alexander
Died: 30 Aug 1897, Woods Cross, Davis, Utah
Entered Valley: 26 Oct 1864, William Hyde Co.

Married 1st: Sara Alexander (maiden name)
Date: abt 1846, England
Died: 3 Dec 1875, Woods Cross, Davis, Utah

Married 2nd: Hannah Kilburn
Date: 1876, Utah

Abel was a farmer. He married Sara with the same surname as he had. They may have been relatives but it is not presently known. He and his wife joined the Church in 1853 and started saving their money to come to the Valley. About this time their two-year-old daughter received some fatal burns from a freshly made pot of tea. She died on December 17, 1853. The cost of her illness took all the funds they had saved. They worked hard another 11 years before they were able to save enough to emigrate in 1864. They were 46 days on the ocean.

After their arrival, Abel and his family moved to Bountiful and Abel hired out to herd sheep. Eventually they moved into a home of their own. Abel owned the first reaper in South Bountiful. He also owned the first mowing machine to cut hay.

Children:

EMMA, b. 14 April 1847, England.

EDNA, b. 1851, D. of burns, age 2, 17 Dec 1853, England. Child.

Submitter: Louise Johnson

RICHARD ALLDRIDGE

Born: 15 May 1815, Floore, Northampton, England
Parents: Robert and Elizabeth Haycock Alldridge
Died: 14 Feb 1896, Cedar City, Utah
Arrived in Valley: 12 Sep 1861, Milo Andrus Co.

Married: Ann Gordon Blunt
Parents: John & Jane Gordan Blunt
Date: 8 Sep 1836, Northampton, Northampton, England

Shortly after their marriage the Alldridges moved to Birmingham, where they lived until immigrating to America in 1861. Richard was a shoemaker and he found that the industrialization of Birmingham enabled him to make a better living for his family.

After arriving in Cedar City, because of his talent for making good boots, he was asked to make boots for the army as well as others. He served as a missionary in England for many years before coming to Utah. Perhaps his greatest mission was his contribution to the hymns of the church. His best known hymns include: "We'll Sing All Hail To Jesus Name," "Lord, Accept Our True Devotion," "Lord Accept Our Songs of Praise," "How Dark and Gloomy Was The Night," and "O, Lord, Preserve Thy Choosen Seed." He loved to sing and was heard singing as he made boots or did other work.

He was active in civil and community affairs and was respected and loved by everyone.

Children:

Elizabeth married David Woolley, and Ann married Thomas Thorley. (daughter)

Submitted by: Howard Thorley

JOHN ALLEMAN

Born: 28 Jun 1808, Middleton, Swatara Twp, Dauphin, Penn.
Parents: John Christopher and Catherine Heppick Alleman
Died: 28 Oct 1883, Springville, Utah, Utah
Entered Valley: 3 Oct 1852, 14th Wagon Co., John B. Walker

Married: Christean Stentz
Date: 11 Dec 1832, Middletown Swatara Twp, Dauphin, Penn.
Born: 28 Nov 1811, Middletown Swatara Twp, Daughin, Penn.
Died: 31 Oct 1886, Springville, Utah, Utah

John Alleman and his family arrived in Nauvoo in 1838 from Pennsylvania with two wagons, 10 horses and personal possessions. He bought farmland and built a brick home. He assisted in building the Nauvoo Temple and served as a cavalryman in the Nauvoo Legion.

In the winter of 1846, when the church members were driven from their homes, they crossed the frozen Mississippi River with

one team of horses and one of oxen, a few cows, and what household goods could be placed in the two wagons. John and his family were part of a group selected to remain at a way station to
plant crops and prepare the way for those who would be following. Eventually he and his family moved to Kanesville and then
Winter Quarters. He served as bishop at one of these places for a
time.

In the spring of 1852, they started for the Salt Lake Valley
arriving in October of that year. He brought nuts and seeds for
planting and he always kept a beautiful and orderly yard and barn.
He furnished nuts and flowers to everyone who desired them.

Children:

ANNA CATHERINE, b. 27 Oct 1833, Middletown, Dauphin,
Penn. Md. 31 Mar 1852, Joseph W. Bissell. D. 16 Mar 1924,
Springville, Utah.
BENJAMIN JORDAN, b. 27 Aug 1835, Mercersburg, Franklin,
Penn. Md. 24 Mar 1861, Sariah Jane Starr. D. 17 Mar 1903.
SUSANNAH, b. 29 Dec 1837, Mercersburg, Franklin, Penn. Md.
Benjamin Thomas Blanchard. D. 26 Dec 1856.
JOHN HENRY, b. 15 Oct 1840 (twin), Nauvoo, Hancock, Ill.
Md. 19 Jun 1871, Zebina Starr. D. 9 Dec 1904.
CHRISTIANA MARY, b. 15 Oct 1840 (twin), Nauvoo, Hancock,
Ill. Md. 3 Feb 1858, William Sumsion. D. 27 Apr 1888.
DANIEL JOSEPH, b. 25 Sep 1843, Nauvoo, Hancock, Ill. Md.
22 Feb 1882, Amanda Elizabeth Starr. D. 13 Oct 1898.
SARAH JANE, b. 19 Feb 1847, Winter Quarters, Nebraska. Md.
8 Apr 1866, Alma Spafford. D. 18 Aug 1920.
MARTHA ELIZABETH, b. 21 Dec 1849, Lake Branch, Iowa.
Md. 3 Aug 1874, Edward Lucian Whiting. D. 4 Jan 1936.
JAMES HYRUM, b. 6 Nov 1852, Springville, Utah, Utah.
Unmarried. D. 10 Jun 1924.
WILLIAM DAVID, b. 7 Apr 1855, Springville, Utah, Utah. Md.
17 Apr 1884, Martha Jane Reynolds. D. 18 Nov 1886.

Submitted by: Royal Oakes

ALANSON DAVID ALLEN

Born: 1 May 1829, Deposit, Tomkins, Delaware, New York
Parents: Albern and Marcia Allen
Died: 3 Mar 1887, Huntsville, Weber, Utah
Arrived in Valley: 27 October 1849, George A. Smith Co.

Married: Chastina Hadlock
Date: 10 Nov 1850

Alanson, with his parents, lived in Nauvoo and knew the Prophet. When the trials with the mobs started, his family started for the Valley but when the call came for the Mormon Battalion, his father Albern and brother Rufus joined them. During the time they were gone, Alanson and his mother and family stayed at Winter Quarters. Realizing their need for supplies, he went back to Eastern Missouri and harvested and bought crops and brought them back to his family. They finally left for the valley in 1848.

After his marriage, they lived in Ogden for a time then moved to Willard. In 1853 they moved to Three Mile Creek (Perry). Four years later they returned to Ogden. In 1866 they were called to go to Hyrum, near Logan. Six years later they moved to Huntsville, where they stayed the rest of their lives.

In 1861 he was made a captain in the Utah Militia and served during the Echo Canyon War. He also served at Salmon River during the problems with the Indians, and suffered from exposure and was never well after that.

He served a mission to Nebraska but was released because of ill health. He was a fine speaker and wrote poetry. He was a kind and generous person to those in need. He was a farmer and also worked on the railroad. He was remembered by his family as a kind and affectionate father.

Children:

EMELINE CLARISSA, b. 26 Aug 1851. Md. Erastus Perry
    Bingham.
ALBERN ALANSON, b. 28 Dec 1852. Md. Louisa Stowell.
ORIN DANIEL, b. 18 Mar 1854. Md. Anna C. Benfrup.
EMILY CHASTINA, b. 30 Nov 1855. Md. John Newy.
MARINDA, b. 15 Feb 1857. Md. John Ingles.
ESTHER, b. 27 Sep 1858. Md. John Tangreen.
AMMON, b. 23 Apr 1860. Md. Isabella Hyslop.
HYRUM, b. 20 Feb 1862. Md. Nancy A. Wilson.
SAMUEL, b. 15 Sep 1863. Md. Louisa C. Dainelson.
SARAH ANN, b. 9 Dec 1865. Md. William G. Moyes.
EMMA ROZINA, b. 18 Jan 1868. Md. John H. Jorgenson.
MARY VILETA, b. 29 Jan 1870. D. 5 Aug 1901.
DAVID ORLO, b. 21 Apr 1872. Md. Emma Lousia Berlin.
ANDREW STEPHEN, b. 23 Feb 1874. Md. Mary Elizabeth
    Hyslop.

Submitted by: Elva Merkley

ANDREW ALLEN

Born: 16 Nov 1849, Near Council Bluffs, Iowa
Parents: Jude and Mary Ann Nicholas Allen
Died: 17 Jan 1904, Salt Lake City, Utah
Came to Valley: 27 Sept 1852, Benjamin Gardner Co.

Married 1st: Elizabeth Lasley
Date: 11 Feb 1868, Salt Lake City, Utah
Parents: John Welton and Elizabeth White Lasley
Died: 27 Mar 1890, Rockland, Idaho

Married 2nd: Marintha Altheria Davis
Date: 6 Jan 1892
Parents: Thomas John and Elizabeth Williams Davis
Born: Gilberton, Pennsylvania

Andrew Allen and his parents joined the Benjamin Gardner Ox Team Company for the trek west in 1852. The children walked most of the way, driving the cattle. They settled in Bountiful, which was then known as the Sessions Settlement. In 1866 they moved to Calls Fort in Box Elder County. Andrew was 17 by then and he helped his father build a two room home. He also became good at farming.

In 1882 Andrew filed homestead papers on some land in Rockland Valley in Idaho, where he had wanted to settle for some time. During his life, Andrew served as County Commissioner, representative, postmaster, and was in the bishopric. He was the first contracted mail carrier between American Falls and Rockland. He operated a general merchandise store as well as running two farms. He was known and respected by everyone who knew him and was known by them as Uncle Andrew.

Children of 1st marriage:

MARY ELIZABETH, b. 27 Mar 1870, Honeyville, Utah. D. 24 Feb 1877. Child.
ANDREW MARTIN, b. 20 Jan 1872, Honeyville, Utah. D. 11 Jul 1885 Rockland, Idaho.
JUDE WILLIAM, b. 2 May 1875, Honeyville, Utah. D. 2 Mar 1877, Honeyville, Utah.
EMILY, b. 11 Jan 1878 Honeyville, Utah. Md. 1st, Henry Boley. Md. 2nd, Ed Kelly. D. 3 Jun 1959, Pocatello, Idaho.
MYRA SUSANNAH, b. 11 Sep 1880. D. 24 Jul 1882, Honeyville, Utah.

HEBER CHARLES, b. 10 Oct 1881, Honeyville, Utah. Md. 21 Feb 1904, Mary Hillhouse. D. 31 Aug 1969, Pocatello, Idaho.

LUCINDA HARRIET, b. 20 Oct 1883, Rockland, Idaho. Md. Robert Hillhouse. D. 1919 American Falls, Idaho.

JOHN WELTON, b. 28 Oct 1885, Rockland, Idaho. Md. 1st, 30 Sep 1907, Jennie Hillhouse. Md. 2nd 5 Feb 1917, Grace Ena McKown. D. 16 Feb 1951, Baldwin Park, California.

Children of 2nd marriage:

MABEL, b. 7 Nov 1892, Samaria, Idaho. D. 12 Sep 1902, Rockland, Idaho.

LEONARD, b. 10 Jun 1894, Samaria, Idaho. Md. 8 Jul 1917, Fern Halling. D. 22 Oct 1918, Rockland, Idaho.

IDA ELIZABETH, b. 6 Nov 1895, Rockland, Idaho. D. 7 Mar 1897, Rockland, Idaho. Child.

VERA, b. 14 Mar 1897, Rockland, Idaho. D. 25 Mar 1898, Rockland, Idaho. Child.

IRENE, b. 4 Mar 1899, Rockland, Idaho. Md. 14 Feb 1936, James Lafayette Young. D. 19 Jul 1972, Logan, Utah.

LLOYD EDWIN, b. 22 Jan 1901, Rockland, Idaho. Md. 1 Sep 1927, Emme Lue Winn. D. 1991, Northridge, California.

AIDA VICTORIA, b. 16 Jan 1903, Rockland, Idaho. Md. John Israel Thomas King Wayman. D. 30 Oct 1969, Logan, Utah.

Submitted by: Darlene Adkins

ANDREW LEE ALLEN

Photograph not available

Born: 24 Nov 1791, Limerick, York, Maine

Parents: Elijah & Mehitable Hall Allen
Died: 14 Aug 1870, Provo, Utah, Utah
Arrived in Valley: 13 Aug 1852, John Higby Co.

Married 1st: Clarinda Knapp
Date: 11 Dec 1824, Cattaraugus Co., New York
Born: 10 Aug 1802, Bethlehem, Litchfield, Connecticut
Died: 7 Dec 1862, Richmond, Cache, Utah

Married 2nd: Martha Christina Johnson
Date: 30 May 1863, Provo, Utah, Utah
Born: 24 Oct 1847, Kalen S., Sweden

Married 3rd: Ann Hughes–No children
Date: 16 Nov 1867, Provo, Utah, Utah

Andrew's mother died when he was nine years old. He went to live with his maternal grandfather and his wife. He learned the blacksmith trade and received a religious training from his grandfather.

At the age of 14, he left home to make his own way. When 21, he joined the War of 1812 for a short time. He moved to Cattaraugus County, New York, where he built a home and at age 33 married Clarinda. After joining the Mormon Church, he sold his home and moved to Kirtland, Ohio. They continued to move west with the saints until they arrived in the Valley in 1852.

The family moved to Provo where Andrew and his sons helped to build the Provo Fort. Andrew was an excellent rope maker and knew how to make dyes from plants.

In 1858 his sons, Charles, James and Andrew, who had moved to San Bernardino, California, did some freighting to Salt Lake. When they returned to California, their mother, a sister, Susan, and brothers Levi and Sidney went with them. In 1862, Clarinda desired to return home. She did not go back to Andrew but went to Richmond and stayed with a son. She died there in 1862

Andrew married Martha in 1863 and adopted her son. They separated in a couple of years. Andrew married Ann Hughes in 1867. She was a good wife to him until his death in 1870.

A granddaughter wrote of him that he was a religious and hard working man. He could split as many rails in a day as any two ordinary men. He loved to fish.

Children of 1st wife:

ELIJAH, b. 7 Feb 1826, Burton, Cattaraugus, New York. Md. 2 May 1852, Eliza Ann Bickmore. D. 21 Apr 1866.

LYDIA JANE, b. 5 Jun 1827, Allegany, Catt, New York. D. 15 Oct 1870, Richmond, Utah. Unmarried.

SOPHRONIA, b. 6 Nov 1828. Md. 1st, 1 Dec 1851, Jacob H. Rose (Div) Md. 2nd, 23 Feb 1863, Abraham Foster. D. 19 Oct 1912, Richmond, Utah.

CHARLES HOPKINS, b. 15 Oct 1830, Allegany, Catt, New York. Md. 1st, 15 Jun 1864, Elizabeth Adelaide Hoopes. Md. 2nd, 29 Oct 1890, Annie Eliza Jones. D. 18 Feb 1922, Mesa, Maricopa, Arizona.

ANDREW LEE, b. 16 Aug 1832, Alegany, Catt, New York. Md. 1st, 4 Mar 1872, Minerva Whittle. Md. 2nd, 8 May 1884, Annie Spackman. D. 8 Jun 1918, Cove, Cache, Utah.

JAMES, b. 12 Oct 1833, Allegany, Catt, New York. Md. 24 Dec 1860, Mary Elizabeth Matthews. D. 17 Jan 1890, Richmond, Utah.

SIDNEY DAVID, b. 12 Aug 1835, Allegany, Catt, New York. Md. 1st, before 1862, Lucretia Winn. Md. 2nd, 31 Jul 1865, Margaret Ann Cooper. D. 1 Jan 1905, Bedford, Lincoln, Wyoming.

SUSAN, b. 31 Dec 1837, Kirtland, Ohio. Md. 4 Jul 1858, John Cornog Goaslind. D. 16 Apr 1924, Logan, Utah.

LEVI KNAPP, b. 1 Apr 1842, Virginia, Cass, Illinois. Md. 11 Dec 1888, Livinia Meriam Henson. D. 18 Feb 1928, Cove, Cache, Utah.

JULIA, b. 8 Jun 1844, Plymouth, Hancock, Illinois. D. 4 Sep 1858, Provo, Utah. Unmarried.

Children of 2nd wife:

CHARLES AUGUST, b. 24 Oct 1847, Kalen, S., Sweden to Johan

Johannas and Martha Christina Johnson. Was adopted
by Andrew Lee Allen. Md. 19 Jan 1873, Elvon Laveria
Stewart. D. 18 Sep 1932, Provo, Utah.

Submitted by: Theda Judd

DANIEL RAPELYEA ALLEN

Born: 2 Aug 1816, Newtown, Long Island, New York
Parents: Robert and Letta Whaley Allen
Died: 23 Jan 1873, Salt Lake City, Utah
Arrived in Valley: 9 Sep 1853, Daniel H. Miller Co.

Married 1st: Eliza Martin
Date: 21 Jan 1837, Jamaica, Queens, New York
Born: 11 May 1823, Brooklyn, New York
Died: 25 Sep 1901, West Jordan, Salt Lake City, Utah

Married 2nd: Eliza Bird Lacy
Date: 2 Apr 1857, Salt Lake City, Utah
Born: 15 Nov 1840, Stocksheath, Worcestershire, England
Died 27 Jul 1918, Shelley, Bingham, Idaho

Married 3rd: Ann Long Didsbury
Date: 25 Jul 1858, Salt Lake City, Utah
Born: 7 Nov 1842, Northampton, England

Married 4th: Margaret Shipley
Date: 16 Feb 1867, Salt Lake City, Utah

Married 5th: Esther Ann Lowder–No children
Date: 1 Apr 1872, Salt Lake City, Utah
Born: 2 Jan 1853, West Jordan, Utah
Died: 2 Sep 1939, Bountiful, Utah

Daniel Rapelyea (or Rapyelle) paid for passage aboard the ship "Brooklyn," but decided to travel by land. He left New York on 1 April 1847, stayed in St. Louis for three years and operated a flour mill, where he employed a number of Utah immigrants. He also operated flour mills at Kanesville and at Perryville, Iowa between 1840 and 1853. He finally left with Daniel H. Miller's Company.

After arriving in the Valley, he settled at West Jordan where he operated a flour mill for Archibald Gardner. During his life he operated flour mills in Flushing, New York, St. Louis, Kanesville, Perryville, Iowa, West Jordan, Utah, American Fork Canyon (along with a saw mill) and American Fork City. He owned the last two.

After several floods that destroyed the canyon mills, he operated Brigham Youngs Midvale and Lower Mill (Liberty Park) in Salt Lake City.

Daniel died at the Lower Mill home of smallpox. He was buried at Wight's Fort (West Jordan) in Salt Lake County.

Children:

MARINDA, b. 21 Jun 1838, Jamaica, Queens, New York. Md. 27 Nov 1854, Samuel Bateman. D. 18 Mar 1919, West Jordan, Utah.

ARMINATA CHURBERRY, b. 14 Feb 1841, Flushing, Queens, New York. Md. 1st, 17 Aug 1856, Samuel Alexander Beckstead. Md. 2nd, 21 Dec 1922, George Washington Beckstead. D. 21 Dec 1922, Midvale, Utah.

THEODORE, b.24 Sep 1842, Flushing, Queens, New York. D. 9 Aug 1843, Flushing, New York. Child.

JULIET, b.30 Mar 1844, Flushing, New York. D. 24 Jul 1848, Flushing, New York. Child.

MARY ELIZA, b. 11 Nov 1845, Flushing, New York. Md. 14

Oct 1860, Joseph Bateman. D.28 Jan 1924, Murray, Utah.

OPHELIA, b. 14 Aug 1848, St.Louis, Missouri. D. 3 Jul 1849, St. Louis, Missouri. Child.

SARAH ANN, b. 2 Sep 1850, Kanesville, Pottawattamie, Iowa. Md. 1863, George Hackett. D. 15 Jan 1930, Salt Lake City, Utah.

JANETTA AMELIA, b. 31 Mar 1853, Kanesville, Pottawattamie, Iowa. D. 14 Aug 1864.

DANIEL RAPALYEA, b. 21 Jan 1855, West Jordan, Utah. D. 15 Sep 1856 West Jordan, Utah. Child.

LYDIA ELIZABETH, b. 13 Apr 1857, West Jordan, Utah. D. 2 Aug 1858, West Jordan, Utah. Child.

FANNIE CAROLINE, b. 10 Apr 1858, West Jordan, Utah. Md. 11 Nov 1872, Franklin Davis Jacobs. D. 28 Feb 1928, Lark, Utah.

ISAAC, b. 26 Dec 1860, West Jordan, Utah. D. 21 Jul 1861, at home at mouth of American Fork Canyon, Utah. Child.

DAVID ROBERT, b. 12 Nov 1862, mouth of American Fork Canyon, Utah. Md. 6 Jul 1882, Leila Smith Merrill. D. 13 Apr 1937, Berkley, California. Bur. Salt Lake City, Utah.

ADA ALETTA, b. 29 Dec 1865, mouth of American Fork Canyon, Utah. Md. Marvin Elmer Pack.

Children of 2nd wife:

ELZADA, b. 27 Oct 1859, West Jordan, Utah. Md. 16 Nov 1874, Andrew Truls Lawrence (Anders Trulsson). D. 25 Jun 1951, Shelley, Bingham, Idaho.

DARIUS HAMILTON, b. 10 Jul 1862, West Jordan, Utah. Md. 10 Nov1890, Sabina E. Robinson. D. 22 Oct 1923. Bur. Shelley, Bingham, Idaho.

ORELLA GENEVA, b. 26 Jun 1864, American Fork, Utah. D. 25 Dec 1866. Child.

GEORGE AUGUSTUS, b. 2 Jan 1866, American Fork, Utah. D. 30 Jun 1875. Child.

DRUSELLA LEONIA, b. 28 Oct 1868, American Fork, Utah. Md. Joshua Adams. D. 25 Jan 1931.

LILLIAN FANELLA, b. 27 Nov 1871, American Fork, Utah. Md. 13 Feb 1888, James Adamson. D. 26 Feb 1933, Shelley, Idaho.

Children of 3rd wife:

ELEANOR MARIA, b. 17 Jan 1860, Salt Lake City, Utah. Md. 19 May 1887, William Morris Newell. D. 7 Jun 1926, Mesa, Maricopa, Arizona.

Submitted by: David L. Walton

ELIHU MARCELLUS ALLEN

Born: 14 May 1791, Cambridge, Washington, New York
Parents: George and Rebecca Allen
Died: 11 Oct 1850, Great Salt Lake, Utah
Arrived in Valley: 2 Oct 1847, Jedediah M. Grant Co.

Married 1st: Laura Foote
Date: abt 1811, Dryden, Tompkins, New York
Born: 23 Apr 1792, Windsor, Broome, New York
Died: 17 Oct 1823, Dryden, Tompkins, New York

Married 2nd: Lola Ann Clawson
Date: abt 1827, New York
Born: 12 Jan 1806, Dryden, Tompkins, New York
Died: 17 Feb 1848, Great Salt Lake, Utah

Elihu Marcellus was raised in Cambridge, New York. After

his first wife's death, he was left with four small children. He married again to his wife's first cousin, Lola Ann Clawson. They were baptized into the Church in 1834/5 and soon moved four miles from Far West, Missouri. They experienced severe persecution while living in Missouri because of the church. In 1839 he executed an affidavit itemizing a bill of damages against the state of Missouri for loss and expenses incurred during the expulsion.

Elihu moved his family east of Burton, Adams, Illinois, for several years. During this period, they lost three of their children. Following this they moved across Iowa to the Missouri River. Shortly before the first group moved out, Elihu's youngest son, Joseph Brigham, was adopted by Brigham Young. Later that same year, Elihu and his family crossed the plains.

His second wife died after their first winter in the valley. Elihu died of inflamation of the lungs three years later.

Children of 1st wife:

LUCINDA, b. Nov 1812, Dryden, Tompkins, New York.
GEORGE, b. 1815, Dryden, New York. Md. Almira. D. 19 Jun
    1838. He drowned in the Missouri River.
FRANKLIN, b. 15 Apr 1818, Dryden, New York. Md. Rebecca
    Myers. D. 16 Dec 1890.
CAROLINE MATILDA, b. 16 Apr 1823, Dryden, New York.
    Md. 11 Jun 1839, William Weeks. D. after 1890, California.

Children of 2nd wife:

HELEN REBECCA, b. 23 Jun 1828, Dryden, New York. Md.
    John Riser.
LAURA ALBINA, b. 19 Sep 1829, Greenwood, Steuben, New
    York. Md. 11 Jun 1849, Cyrus Culver Canfield. D. 2 Jun 1871,
    Santa Clara, California.
PHEBE ANN, b. 17 Dec 1830, Greenwood, New York. Md. Benjamin Blanchard Blackenbury. D. 9 Feb 1902, Almo,
    Cassia, Idaho.
CHARLES WILLIAM, b. 18 Oct 1832, Greenwood, New York.
    Md. Charlotte Mulhall.

WYATT, b. 3 Mar 1834, Greenwood, New York. D. 14 Mar 1834, Greenwood, New York. Child.

ELIHU MORONI, b. 9 Oct 1835, Greenwood, New York. Md. 1854, Mary Elizabeth Graham. D. 22 Nov 1912, Pocatello, Bannock, Idaho.

LOLA ELIZABETH, b. 25 Aug 1837, Far West, Caldwell, Missouri. D. Mar 1849, Great Salt Lake, Utah.

ALMIRA GILBERT, b. 18 Feb 1839. D. 8 Dec 1845, Adams Co, Illinois. Child.

EMMA MELVINA, b. 23 Aug 1840, Burton, Illinois. D. 4 Dec 1845, Adams Co., Illinois. Child.

GEORGE WARREN, b. 23 Apr 1842, Burton, Adams, Illinois. D. 17 Dec 1845, Adams Co, Illinois. Child.

JOHN FERGUSON, b. 18 Feb 1844, Burton, Adams, Illinois. Md. Bernetta Walters Hickman. D.16 Apr 1911, Hagerman, Gooding Idaho.

JOSEPH BRIGHAM, b. 19 Sep 1845, Marquette, Illinois.

Submitted by: Joy Belnap

ELIHU MORONI ALLEN

Born: 9 Oct 1835, Greenwood, Steuben, New York
Parents: Elihu Marcellus and Lola Ann Clawson Allen
Died: 22 Nov 1912, Pocatello, Bannock, Idaho
Arrived in Valley: 2 Oct 1847, Jedediah M. Grant Co.

Married: Mary Elizabeth Graham
Date: abt 1853, Utah
Born: 8 Oct 1836, Laurel Hill, Chester, Pennsylvania

Parents: James and Mary Elizabeth Butler Graham
Died: 2 Jul 1906, Huntsville, Weber, Utah

Elihu Moroni's parents were baptized into the Church about 1834 or 1835. In 1847 the family started their trek to the Valley. They spent the first winter in Salt lake where his mother died. His father died two years later. His youngest brother was adopted by Brigham Young after his mother's death.

At the age of 18, Elihu married 16-year-old Mary Elizabeth Graham. They made their first home in Riverdale, Utah. It is thought that they may have lived for a short time in the 1850's in Huntsville, Utah. Elihu made a lot of the furniture they used. Elihu was a farmer and a good one.

The Indians gave the settlers trouble at first, but later got along with them. They called Elihu "Baldy Allen" and friend. He was active in church and community affairs. He moved to Pocatello, Idaho, where he died.

Children:

CHARLES MARCELLUS, b. 29 May 1854, Riverdale, Utah. D. 17 Jul 1918.

ELIHU MORONI, b. 4 Sep 1858, Riverdale, Weber, Utah. Md. 1st, 18 Oct 1880, Mary Ann Baird. Md. 2nd, Fannie Huntsman. D. 21 Mar 1914, Rupert, Minidoka, Idaho.

MARY LOSINA, b. 23 Aug 1860, Riverdale, Utah. Md. 18 Oct 1879, Hyrum Blanch Pidcock. D.10 Jun 1916, LaGrande, Union, Oregon.

PHOEBE ISADORA, b. 21 Jun 1862, Riverdale, Utah. Md. 9 Nov 1882, Peter Edward Chatelain. D. 11 Jan 1918.

JOHN FRANKLIN, b. 11 Aug 1864, Huntsville, Utah. Md. 27 Mar 1887, Mary Alice Harmon. D. 26 Mar 1944, Burley, Cassia, Idaho.

GEORGE ADELBERT, b.1 Jun 1866, Huntsville, Utah. Md. 23 May 1893, Lydia Musetta Gribble. D. 7 Oct 1931.

LOLA BERNETTA, b. 1 Jun 1868, Huntsville, Utah. Md. 20 Jan 1885/6, Alexander Chatelain. D. 8 Mar 1942, Salt Lake City, Utah.

JOSEPH WILLIAM, b. 7 Mar 1870, Huntsville, Utah. Md. 7 Mar 1895, Helen Adeline Hatton. D. 22 Feb 1925.

ELIZA EMMA, b. 24 Dec 1872, Huntsville, Utah. Md. 1st, 7 Jul 1890, Thomas Wright. Md. 2nd, Jay Grant Crandall. D. 30 May 1949, Ogden, Utah.

DAVID ALLEN, b. 14 Aug 1874, Huntsville, Utah. Md. 28 Jul 1893, Petria Pearl Jensina Jensen. D. 7 Mar 1931, Aberdeen, Bingham, Idaho.

JAMES THOMAS, b. 3 Sep 1876, Huntsville, Utah. D. 11 Jul 1922, Weber Co, Utah.

Submitted by: Joy Belnap

ELIJAH ALLEN

Born: 7 Feb 1826, Burton, Cattaraugus, New York
Parents: Andrew Lee and Clarinda Knapp Allen
Died: 12 Apr 1866, Salt Lake City, Utah
Arrived in Valley: 13 Aug 1852, John Higby Co.

Married: Eliza Ann Bickmore
Date: 3 May 1852, Pottawattamie Co., Iowa
Born: 29 Jan 1830, Madisonville, Illinois
Died: 26 Mar 1901, Cove, Cache, Utah

Elijah's father was a prosperous farmer in New York state. After the family joined the Church, they moved to Kirtland, Ohio, and other towns as the church members moved. They suffered many hardships along with the other members.

As a teen, Elijah left home to try to find work. He went to Brigham Young, who hired him as a teamster. When the saints went west, Elijah went with them, joining the Mormon Battalion enroute.

He became ill and was forced to ride in a wagon, but he eventually recovered. After his discharge, he remained in San Gabriel Mission for a time, hunting gold. He finally returned to Salt Lake, where he traded gold for some land. In 1849 he sold his property, purchased equipment and returned to Kanesville, Ohio, where he found his family. He also found the girl he married. He and his brothers ran a saw mill to get enough funds for the family to go west.

When they arrived in the Valley, they went on to Provo and later they moved north to Fort Herriman. He remained active in church and made his living farming. He died of liver problems at the age of 40, as a result of his illness while with the Battalion.

Children:

ELIJAH, b. 24 Feb 1853, Provo, Utah. D. 2 Nov 1876, Cove, Utah. Unmarried.

WILLIAM, b. 17 Apr 1854, Provo, Utah. D. 21 Jan 1895.

ELIZA ANN, b. 1 Jun 1856, Fort Herriman, Utah. Md. 1 Oct 1877, Manassah Barnes. D. 8 Jul 1912, Cove, Cache, Utah.

JAMES CARSON, b. 21 Mar 1858, Ft. Herriman, Utah. Md. 1st, 1 Mar 1883, Betsy Lowe. Md. 2nd, 11 Sep 1884, Helen (Ellen) Lowe. D. 10 Feb 1935, Cove, Utah.

ANDREW BICKMORE, b. 23 Dec 1859, Ft. Herriman, Utah. Md. 6 Jan 1881, Susanna Elizabeth Preece. D. 14 Apr 1941, Cove, Utah.

HENRY HEBER, b. 11 Mar 1862, Ft. Herriman, Utah. Md. 10 Apr 1882, Elgena Poulson. D. 26 Mar 1941, Logan, Utah.

JOSEPH SMITH, b. 20 Oct 1863, Ft. Herriman, Utah. Md. 9 Dec 1885, Phoebe Anderson. D. 9 May 1933, Santa Ana, California.

Submitted by: Theda Judd

JOSEPH ALLEN

Born: 10 Apr 1843, Parma, Cuyahoga, Ohio
Parents: Jude and Mary Ann Nicholas
Died: 25 Jul 1921, Rockland, Power, Idaho
Arrived in Valley: 25 Sep 1852, Benjamin Gardner Co.

Married 1st: Lucinda Drucilla Lasley
Date: 11 Feb 1867, Calls Fort, Box Elder, Utah
Born: 18 Nov 1850, Pottowattamie, Iowa
Parents: John Welton and Elizabeth White Lasley
Died: 31 May 1937, American Falls, Power, Idaho

Married 2nd: Susan Amelia Perry (widow)
Date: 9 Oct 1879, Calls Fort, Box Elder, Utah
Born: 3 Jun 1849, Pottowattamie Co., Iowa
Parents: Henry E. and Elizabeth Zabriskie Perry
Died: 21 Feb 1925, Perry, Box Elder, Utah

Joseph's parents were early converts to the Church. They moved around quite a bit until 1852, when they joined others to come west. At first they lived on the church farm, then moved to Bountiful, where they lived until his mother died. They then moved to Calls Fort, Box Elder County.

Joseph was one of the teamsters who went east to assist the immigrants. He was also in the freighting business from Corinne to Montana and Idaho. After his marriage, they lived in Calls Fort until 1878, when they moved to Logan. Joseph hauled rock for the Logan Temple while his wife cooked for the men.

Upon his return to Calls Fort, the bishop suggested he take a second wife. He moved his family north to Rockcreek in 1881, where he farmed. He was a big man and very tall. He remained active in church all his life.

Children of 1st wife:

EMILY MARIAH, b. 21 Jul 1868, Calls Fort, Box Elder, Utah. Md. 30 Dec 1886, Augustus Waldamer Thompson. D. 3 Sep 1933, Power Co., Idaho.

JOSEPH JASPER, b. 9 Apr 1870, Calls Fort, Utah. D. 3 Aug 1871. Child.

JUDE WELTON, b. 13 Nov 1871, Calls Fort, Utah. Md. 26 Feb 1892, Betsy Ann Osterhout. D. 9 May 1919, Pocatello, Idaho.

CHARLES WARREN, b. 2 Feb 1873, Calls Fort, Utah. Md. 24 Jun 1918, Lucy Aldous (wid). D. 11 Jul 1927, Rockland, Idaho.

ELIZABETH DESERET, b. 8 Jan 1875, Calls Fort, Utah. Md. 26 Oct 1895, Edwin "Ted" Budge. D. 16 Jul 1930, Twin Falls, Idaho.

GORDON, b. 22 Oct 1876, Calls Fort, Utah. D. 26 Oct 1876. Child.

HARRIETT LOUISA, b. 24 Sep 1878, Logan, Utah. Md. 1st, 11 Feb 1896, Charles Henry Walker. Md. 2nd, 27 May 1909, Isaac Thorne Jr. D. 12 Jun 1955, Pullman, Washington.

ROSALIE ELVIRA, b. 8 Jun 1880, Calls Fort, Utah. Md. 10 Sep 1900, Joseph Frederick Walker. D. 18 Sep 1922, Rockland, Idaho.

ANDREW, b. 24 Sep 1883, Rockland, Idaho. Md. 8 Apr 1908, Rosanna Ina Peck. D. 29 Aug 1958, Pocatello, Idaho.

MARTHA LUCINDA, b. 30 Jan 1887, Rockland, Idaho. Md. 30 Oct 1907, John Willard Potter. D. 29 Jul 1960, Downey, Idaho.

MARTIN WILLIAM, b. 10 Sep 1888, Rockland, Idaho. Md. 4 Jun 1908, Ella Elizabeth Pilkington. D. 5 Dec 1950, Ogden, Utah.

HEBER JOHN, b. 5 Sep 1890, Rockland, Idaho. Md. 1st, abt 1919, Mary Alice Galbraith. Md. 2nd, Ethel. D. 21 Jan 1957, California.

FRANK LASLEY, b. 12 Aug 1892, Rockland, Idaho. Md. 3 Jan 1913, Hazel May Reese. D. 12 Mar 1914, Rockland, Idaho.

Children of 2nd wife:

ISAAC THORNE, b. 28 Aug 1880, Calls Fort, Utah. Md. 26 Jan
1910, Laura May Davis. D. 19 Oct 1951, Brigham City, Utah.
INEZ ELIZABETH, b. 20 Oct 1882, Three Mile Creek (Perry)
Utah. Md. 1st, 25 Jun 1906, Leo Larsen. Md. 2nd, 11 Feb
1918, George William Dicks. D. Jun 1964, Brigham City,
Utah.

Submitted by: Darlene Adkins

JOSEPH STEWART ALLEN

Born: 25 Jun 1806, Whitestown, Oneida, New York
Parents: Daniel and Nancy Stewart Allen
Died: 25 Apr 1889, Huntington, Emery, Utah
Arrived in Valley: 30 Sep 1853, John E. Forsgren Handcart Co.

Married 1st: Lucy Diantha Morley
Date: 2 Sep 1835, Clay Co., Missouri
Born: 4 Oct 1815, Kirtland, Geauga, Ohio
Parents: Isaac Morley
Died: 19 Oct 1908, Orderville, Kane, Utah

Married 2nd: Karen Maria Hansen
Date: 28 Jun 1854, Manti, Utah
Born: 5 Nov 1835, Vester, Marie, Barnholm, Denmark
Parents: Maurice and Christina Ingeborg Jesperson Hansen
Died: 7 Aug 1884, Orderville, Kane, Utah

Joseph and his older brother Daniel were the only ones of the family who joined the Church. They were baptized in 1831. Joseph served a mission in Indiana and was an elder in Zion's Camp. He endured the persecutions in Iowa, Missouri, and Illinois.

Joseph learned the cooper trade from his father-in-law. He was a farmer and shoemaker. He and his family were sent to the Muddy Mission to help colonize there and later moved to Long Valley where they participated in the United Order.

Children of 1st wife:

MARY ELIZABETH, b. 15 Aug 1836.
CAROLINE DELIGHT, b. 15 Sep 1838.
LUCY GUNN, b. 28 Sep 1840.
CORDELIA, b. 31 Jan 1843.
CALISTA, b. 25 Feb 1845.
JOSEPH LORENZO, b.25 Feb 1847.
ISAAC MORLEY, b. 28 Mar 1849.
CHARLES ALBERT, b. 16 Aug 1851.
HYRUM, b. 12 Aug 1853.
HARRIET LENORA, b. 8 Apr 1857.
SIMON MORLEY, b. 6 Oct 1859.
CLARA AMELIA, b. 8 May 1861.

Children of 2nd wife:

ELIZABETH ELIZA, b. 20 Apr 1857.
CHRISTENA MARIE, b. 27 Apr 1859.
JOHN MILLARD, b. 24 Jul 1869.
ELLEN LUCINDA, b. 3 Jan 1864 .
ERASTUS SNOW PETER, b. 15 Jan 1867.
DANIEL SPENCER, b. 20 Jul 1870.
LYDIA JANE, b. 5 Nov 1872.
DIADAMIA, b. 2 Oct 1875.

Submitted by: LaRae McManama

JUDE ALLEN

Born: 12 Oct 1811, Willsborough, Essex, New York
Parents: Andrew and Eunice Miner Allen
Died: 13 Feb 1900, Calls Fort, Box Elder, Utah
Arrived in Valley: 24 Sep 1852, Benjamin Gardner Wagon Co.

Married 1st: Mary Ann Nicholas
Date: 12 Oct 1836, Parma, Cuyahoga, Ohio
Born: 25 Feb 1820, Cincinnati, Ohio
Parents: Jesse and Mary Small Nicholas
Died: 10 Jan 1860, Bountiful, Davis, Utah

Married 2nd: Martha Anglesey–No children
Date: 23 Feb 1859, Salt Lake City, Utah
Born: 20 Feb 1834, Bromborough, Cheshire, England
Parents: John and Catherine Preston Anglesey
Died: 23 Sep 1908, Calls Fort, Box Elder, Utah
    Survivor of Martin Handcart Company

Married 3rd: Sarah Anglesey
Date: 3 Feb 1866, Salt Lake City, Utah
Born: 5 May 1846, Birkenhead, Cheshire, England
Parents: John and Catherine Preston Anglesey
Died: 9 Jan 1923, Honeyville, Box Elder, Utah

Jude Allen was baptized into the Mormon Church in May 1832 in New York. His family moved to Parma, Ohio where in 1836 he was commissioned a captain in the Ohio State Militia.

In October 1843 he moved his family to Nauvoo, where they lived on the corner of Hibbard and Page Streets. He was one of the men who destroyed the Nauvoo Expositor press.

In 1844, Jude and his family joined a group of 150 people who had been recruited by James Emmett for a mission Joseph Smith had given him to explore the West. However, Emmett refused to follow the directions of the Twelve and was disfellowshipped. In Decemer 1844, Brigham Young sent John Lowe Butler to strengthen the Company and was welcomed into the group. By spring, nearly a third of the Company became disheartened and returned to Nauvoo.

In May 1845, the balance of the Company moved west across Iowa to Fort Vermillion in present-day South Dakato. They built cabins, hunted and farmed. In May 1846, Brigham Young directed them to abandon their homes and move south to join the exodus of the saints from Nauvoo at Council Bluffs. It was not until about 1852 that Jude and his family finally met up with the saints in their journey west. He was Captain of Ten in the Benjamin Gardner Company of 1852.

He taught the principles of debate in his home during the 1870's and was active politically in the Peoples Party at Brigham City.

Children of 1st wife:

MARY, b. 13 Apr 1838, Parma, Cuyahoga, Ohio. Md. 23 Apr 1854, JohnCook Dewey. D. 23 Aug 1911, Deweyville, Box Elder, Utah.

MARTHA, b. 26 Sep 1839, Rochester, Lorain, Ohio. Md. 26 Aug 1856, James May. D. 17 Nov 1923, Calls Fort, Utah.

JANE, b. 8 Mar 1841, Parma, Ohio. Md. 5 Jul 1857, John Stoker. D. 5 Aug 1877, Bountiful, Utah.

JOSEPH, b. 10 Apr 1843, Parma, Ohio. Md. 11 Feb 1867, Lucinda Drucilla Lasley. D. 25 Jul 1921, Rockland, Power, Idaho.

EMILY, b. 16 Jun 1845, Fort Vermillion, So. Dakota. Md. 11 Apr 1861, Henry Doctor Lish, Calls Fort, Utah. D. 10 Jan 1936, Rockland, Power, Idaho.

HARRIET, b. 17 Apr 1847, Eastern Nebraska while traveling to join the main body of saints. D. 13 Jun 1858, Springville, Utah.

ANDREW, b. 16 Nov 1848, Pottawattamie, Iowa. Md. 1st, 1 Feb 1868, Elizabeth Louisa Lasley. Md. 2nd, 6 Jan 1892, Marintha Altheria Davis. D. 19 Jan 1904, Rockland, Oneida, Idaho.

JUDE, b. 27 Jun 1851, Pottawattamie, Iowa. D. 31 Jul 1852, Near Ancient Bluffs, Western Nebraska. Child.

CHARLES JOSHUA, b. 31 May 1853, Bountiful, Utah. Md. 23 Jan 1872, Mariah Houston Lish. D. 15 Aug 1937, Wilson, Teton, Wyoming.

EUNICE CLARISSA, b. 26 Oct 1855, Bountiful, Utah. Md. 30 Oct 1871, Heber Cotton Wood. D. 16 Nov 1904, Rockland, Oneida, Idaho.

SARAH, b. 29 Oct 1857, Bountiful, Utah. Md. 19 Jun 1875, Heber Warren Lasley. D. 4 Feb 1934, American Falls, Idaho.

MARY ANN, b. 28 Dec 1859, Bountiful, Utah. D. 18 Oct 1860, Bountiful, Utah. Child.

Children of 3rd wife:

CATHERINE CELESTIA, b. 1 Jan 1867, Calls Fort, Utah. Md. 3 Oct 1883, John Luce Hunsaker. D. 10 Apr 1941, Honeyville, Box Elder, Utah.

NANCY, b. 25 Jul 1868, Calls Fort, Utah. Md. 24 Oct 1885, William Arthur Kelly. D. 18 Mar 1939, Twin Falls, Idaho.

ALBERT AMOS, b. 13 Feb 1870, Calls Fort, Utah. D.15 Sep 1872, Calls Fort, Utah. Child.

MARTHA MATILDA, b. 29 Jul 1872, Calls Fort, Utah. Md. 11 Nov 1891, Hans Peter Hunsaker. D. 9 Dec 1945, Honeyville, Utah.

JOHN ROBERT, b. 31 Jan 1876, Calls Fort, Utah. Md. 24 Aug 1897, Helen Eliza Hunsaker. D. 24 Aug 1956, Tremonton, Utah.

ROSE VILATE, b. 9 Jan 1879, Calls Fort, Utah. Md. 20 Sep 1897, Weldon Hunsaker. D. 9 Jul 1955, Salt Lake, Utah.

JUDE IRA, b. 27 Jun 1881, Calls Fort, Utah. Md. 29 Jun 1905, Nancy Emily Orme. D. 24 Aug 1962, American Falls, Idaho.

Submitted by: Jim Stoker

GEORGE ALLEY

Born: 13 Dec 1792, Lynn, Essex, Massachusetts
Parents: Joseph and Hannah Batchellor Alley
Died: 18 Nov 1859, Salt Lake City, Utah
Arrived in Valley: 20 Sep 1848

Married: Mary Symonds
Date: 15 Sep 1822, Essex Co., Massachusetts

George Alley was an expert shoemaker and had his own shop. Sometime during 1830-1832 the family moved to Salem, Massachusetts, where the family was converted to the Mormon church by Erastus Snow.

Early in the following spring of 1842, George and his family left their home to join with the saints in Nauvoo, Illinois. George made note in his Bible of their move to Nauvoo: "Arrived in Nauvoo, 1842, by virtue of the commandment of the Lord, to gather out of Babylon." They remained there until the trek west to the Valley. They stayed in Winter Quarters until 1848.

Upon their arrival in the valley, they spent the winter in North Canyon, now known as Bountiful, Utah. The following spring they moved to the home George had built on the corner of State Street and Fourth South in Salt Lake, where he died in 1859.

Children:

GEORGE HUBBARD, b.14 Jun 1823, Lynn, Massachusetts.
    Unmarried. D. 6 Apr 1910, Salt Lake City, Utah.
MARGARET MARIA, b. 1825, Md. 1848/49, Brigham Young.
LYDIA ANN, b. 1828.

SUSAN HANNAH, b. 1830.
STEPHEN WEBB, b. 12 Dec 1832.
ELIZABETH ROYCE, b. 1835.
CHARLES HENRY, b.15 Mar 1839.

Submitted by: John Alley

GEORGE HUBBARD ALLEY

Born: 14 Jun 1823, Lynn, Massachusetts
Parents: George and Mary Symonds Alley
Died: 6 Apr 1910, Salt Lake City, Utah
Arrived in Valley: 20 Sep 1848, Brigham Young Co.
 He never married.

 Early in his life, George took an oath which was to govern his conduct the remainder of his life. "I, George Hubbard Alley, do herey swear, before the great and living God, that during an engagement, and while I am an employee of Russell, Majors and Haddell, I will, under no circumstances, use profane language; that I will drink no intoxicating liquor; that I will not quarrel or fight with any other employee of the firm; and that in every respect I will conduct myself honestly, be faithful to my duties, and so direct all my acts as to win the confidence of my employers, So help me God."
 This oath, always kept by George, tells its own story of the character of the man who took it. He took that oath to become a rider of the Pony Express. He was an expert shoemaker by trade, an expert horseman, a gifted artesan of gold. He traveled the pony express route from Sacramento to St. Joseph at various times.

While in San Francisco, he learned to pan for gold. He kept all that he found in panning. He accumulated a large quantity of it and rolled it into balls for storing and future use. It has never been found.

At one time he made two beautiful gold rings and a beautiful mounting for a cameo which he gave his mother. One of the gold rings he gave to his brother, Stephen, with whom he lived after his parents died. He wore the other one.

He was a slight built man, under average height and 125 pounds or less in weight. He didn't know the meaning of fear and he had extraordinary endurance, patience, sound judgement, and a keen, alert intellect.

In his later years he loved to walk with his beautiful companion, a large dog named Old Jack. After the dog was killed in an accident, he became aimless in his wanderings, and the family and neighbors watched over him. He died just a few weeks before his 87th birthday.

Submitted by: John Alley

STEPHEN WEBB ALLEY

Born: 12 Dec 1832, Salem, Essex, Massachusetts
Parents: George and Mary Symonds Alley
Died: 13 Jun 1921, Salt Lake City, Utah
Arrived in Valley: 22 Sep 1848, Brigham Young's Co.

Married: Emma Turner
Date: 3 Oct 1868, Salt Lake City, Utah
Born: Unknown

Parents: George and Hannah Tuner
Died: 27 Jun 1926, Salt Lake City, Utah

Stephen Webb Alley was fortunate in that he attended school until he was 10 years of age. At this time he immigrated with his family to Nauvoo. There he was able to return to school and was baptized with his family.

When the saints left Nauvoo, he with his family left Nauvoo for Winter Quarters where the children were again put in school until they left for the Valley in 1848.

They lived in a log house where the Beehive House now stands. It was the only house outside the fort. Before long they moved to North Canyon which is now called Bountiful, where they spent the winter. In the spring they built a cabin at the corner of 400 South and State Street. It was later replaced by a seven room adobe home where Stephen lived until 1890.

He had a deep interest in music and frequently played the violin at dances in the Social Hall. On opening night at the Salt Lake Theater in 1862, he played in the orchestra.

In 1863 he received a call to serve a mission in England. He returned to the valley three and a half years later. While in England he met his future wife, Emma Turner. She immigrated to the valley in 1868 and was married six weeks after her arrival. They built a home at 941 South 800 East.

Stephen, besides playing the violin, was a farmer and a cooper who was in much demand. He was dearly loved and respected by all who knew him.

Children:

STEPHEN WELLS, b. 16 Aug 1869, Salt Lake City, Utah.
ELLEN MAY, b. 29 Jan 1872, Salt Lake City, Utah.
KATHERINE, b. 31 May 1875, Salt Lake City, Utah.
GEORGE, b. 3 Mar 1878, Salt Lake City, Utah.
DAUGHTER, b. Stillborn.
EDNA EMMA, b. 3 Sep 1888.

Submitted by: John Alley

ISRAEL DODGE ALLPHIN

Born: 8 Sep 1814, Viena, Daviess, Kentucky
Parents: Shelton and Martha Taylor Allphin
Died: 25 Apr 1903, Elba, Cassia, Idaho
Arrived in Valley: Dec 1857, John M. Moody, Missionary

Married 1st wife: Burnetta Collins
Date: 5 Sep 1831, Illinois
Born: 27 Nov 1818, Scott Co., Indiana
Parents: Benjamin and Phoebe Broady Collins
Died: 27 Jul 1871, Illinois

Married 2nd wife: Susan Emaline Damron
Date: 17 Mar 1858, Salt Lake City, Utah
Born: 26 Aug 1833, Dresden, Weakley, Tennessee
Parents: Constantine Ladd and Sarah McCormick Damron
Died: 10 Jan 1879, Panguitch, Garfield, Utah

Married 3rd wife: Christiana Dolbell Riding
Date: 22 May 1885, St. George, Utah
Born: 8 Dec 1857, Provo, Utah
Parents: Christopher Lister and Eliza Adelaide Dolbell Riding
Died: 18 Apr 1925, Lovell, Wyoming

Israel Dodge Allphin was baptized a member of the Church, 25 February 1840, by President Joseph Smith in Payson, Adams, Illinois. His wife was baptized 25 February 1841. The Allphins lived in Walker, Madison, Texas, and it was there that the wagon train was formed from members of the Ellis County, Texas Branch on 11 May 1856. They went north to find the Oregon Trail and encountered snow, death, sickness, and other problems before they reached trail's end. William Coldiron was bitten by a snake and died. His pregnant wife, Susan, was helped along the way by Israel and his wife. Susan delivered a son January 1st, but he died shortly after. In March, Israel was sealed to Burnetta and Susan. Israel was a shoemaker by profession and he kept busy making shoes for his growing family of 14.

Brigham Young called Israel and 300 other families to settle the southern part of the territory which was called Dixie. Seventy-nine families were living there already.

After arriving, Israel, along with several other families, was sent to Pine Valley along the Santa Clara Creek. The men were to establish a lumber-shingle mill near the gulch. In 1866, Mountain Mahogany and yellow pine, which was particularly suited for the construction of pipes for the Tabernacle organ, were discovered. With crude equipment, the huge logs were hauled, cut, and transported by ox team to Salt Lake.

Log cabins were built for Burnetta and Susan's families along the creek. Thirteen years later on 16 July 1863, the residents heard an unfamiliar wild and uproarious noise. Susan, sensing danger, gathered her family and Burnetta's family. Tidal waves raged through the creek and area, destroying everything in its path. Not only were homes destroyed, but four of Susan's children were swept to their death leaving just one child. Susan had now lost six of her seven children.

Susan was a midwife and rode horseback to her patients. She was a kind and loving person. Israel's whole life was dedicated to serving the Lord. He fathered 24 children and raised 7 children who belonged to his last two wives.

At the age of 61, Israel was called to serve a mission in Texas. He baptized his first born son, his mother and some of his brothers and sisters. While there, his companion accidently discharged his pistol, which hit Israel in the leg. He carried the bullet the rest of his life. He was ordained a patiarch at the age of 88 in Bighorn, Wyoming. He died as he had lived, a pioneer who helped everyone.

Children of 1st wife:

BENJAMIN S., b. 1835, Payson, Adams, Illinois. Md. Melissa.

JOHN HENRY, b. 28 Oct 1837, Payson, Adams, Illinois. Md. Elmira Sprouse.

JOSHUA HORTON, b. 16 Jan 1841, Payson, Illinois, Md. Alice Hundley

MARTHA JANE, b. 3 Mar 1844, Payson, Illinois. Md. William Wallace Dameron.

RANSOM WILLIAM, b. 12 Jul 1847, Walker, Madison, Texas. Md. Mary Jane Hendricks.

JASPER, b. 1848, Walker, Madison, Texas. D. 1871.

MARY EMILY, b. 6 May 1850, Walker, Madison, Texas. D. 10 Apr 1851.

SARAH ANN ELIZA, b. 19 Feb 1853, Walker, Madison, Texas. Md. John Mathis Thomas.

ISRAEL DODGE, JR. b. 20 Aug 1857, Big Sandy, Wyo. Md. Amada Clark.

BURNETTA, b. 1859, Salt Lake City, Utah.

Children of 2nd wife:

JOSEPH WARREN, b. 3 Nov 1859, Salt Lake City, Utah. D. 16 Jul 1863. Child.

SUSAN EMALINE, b. 29 Mar 1861, Salt Lake City, Utah. Md. John Harvey Averett.

HYRUM, b. 17 Oct 1862, Pine Valley, Washington, Utah. D. 16 Jul 1863.

DAVID COMFORT, b. 1 Jan 1865, Pine Valley, Utah. Md. Emily Judd.

ANNIE PATIENCE, b. 22 Apr 1866, Pine Valley, Utah. Md. 1st, Francis Riley Owen. Md. 2nd, Charles E. Johnson, Md. 3rd, Charles Joseph Christopherson.

MELISSA JANE, b. 3 Jun 1868, Pine Valley, Utah. D. abt 1870.

CATHERINE LEANOR, b. 15 Sep 1869, Pine Valley, Utah. Md. 1st, Don Carlos Burgess, Md. 2nd Robert Wesley Averett.

PRISCILLA REBECCA, b. 24 May 1871, Pine Valley, Utah. Md. Owen William Orton.

EMMA MAY, b. 8 Dec 1872, Panaca, Nevada. Md. 1st John William Gilson, Md. 2nd George Franklin Price.

SAMUEL TAYLOR, b. 5 Aug 1875, Panaca, Nevada, Md. Lucy
 Hepworth.

Children of 2nd wife:
By 1st Husband - William Henry Coldiron.

WILLIAM HENRY HARRISON, b. 3 Mar 1851, Tennessee. D.
 1857 on plains. Child.
SARAH ELLEN, b. 4 Oct 1853, Joseph, Missouri. D. 16 Jul 1863,
 Pine Valley, Utah.
MARTHA MATILDA, b. 23 Oct 1855, Ellis Co., Texas. D. 16
 Jul 1863, Pine Valley, Utah.
WILLIAM WESLEY, b. 1 Jan 1858, Salt Lake City, Utah. D.
 1858, Salt Lake City, Utah. (abt 1 month old)

Children of 3rd wife:

GEORGE KERRY, b. 6 Mar 1886, Panguitch, Utah. Md. Myra
 Assay.
REUBEN LISTER, b. 5 Dec 1887, Panguitch, Utah. Md. Ella
 Elvina Asay.
OWEN LEE, b. 28 Jul 1889, Panguitch, Utah. Md. 1st, Mary
 Lydia Johnson. Md. 2nd, Grace Alexander.
DONOVAN J., b. 31 Jul 1895, Panguitch, Utah. Md. 1st, Pearl
 Hockins. Md. 2nd, Leta Cline.

Children of 3rd wife by her 1st husband:

FRANKLIN RIDING, b. 29 May 1875, Utah. Md. Angnetta
 (Clara) Allred.
EDWIN, b. 18 Aug 1876, Mt. Carmel, Utah. D. Mar 1877. Child.
ELIZA ADELAIDE, b. 7 Jun 1878, Mt. Carmel, Utah. Md. John
 Cooper Houston.
SARAH ANN, b. 10 Feb 1880, Mt. Carmel, Utah. D. Mar 1880.
 Child.
ADEBERT (twin), b. 8 Jun 1881, Mt. Carmel, Utah. Md. Delilah
 Mae Boice.

ALBERT (twin), b. 8 Jun 1881, Mt. Carmel, Utah. D. 21 Apr 1893.

RUTH, b. 15 Jun 1883, Springville, Utah. Md. Fielding Burns Tebbs.

Submitted by: Cliff Spendlove

ISAAC ALLRED

Born: 27 Jan 1788, Pendleton, South Carolina/Georgia
Parents: William and Elizabeth Thrasher Allred
Died: 3 Nov 1876, Spring City, Sanpete, Utah
Arrived in Valley: 16 Oct 1849, Redick Allred drove lead wagon.

Married 1st: Mary Calvert
Date: 14 Feb 1811.
Born: Unknown
Parents: John and Mary McCurdy Calvert
Died: 16 Sep 1851, Holladay, Salt Lake City, Utah

Married 2nd: Matilda Stewart (wid-Park)
Date: 5 Nov 1852
Born: 9 Sep 1808, West Gallantine, Sumner, Tennessee
Died: 23 Jan 1900, Spring City, Sanpete, Utah

Isaac Allred was the second son and fifth child in a family of eight children. Little is known of his early life. He married Mary Calvert and they moved near Nashville, Tennessee, where his brother James lived.

Apparently their first child, Elizabeth, was born while they were on the road, as she was born in Bedford County, Tennessee. They remained there until about 1830, when they moved north about 500 miles to Monroe County, Missouri. Isaac had a difficult time providing for his family, which by 1831 numbered 11 children.

About this time, the Mormon elders came into the life of Isaac and his family. He soon opened his home to them and meetings were held. Isaac was soon baptized on 10 September 1832 in the Salt River with other members of his family.

In 1832 or 1833, Isaac sold his farm for an intended move to Jackson County, but when the saints were expelled, he rented his home back from the buyer and remained there for a time. In 1835 he moved his family to Clay County, Missouri at the request of the Prophet. They suffered much because of persecution and exposure. Soon they moved to Quincy, where they settled down.

When the exodus from Nauvoo came, Isaac left with his family and had to wait on the Iowa side of the Mississippi River until his son Reddick returned from helping other saints move. Then he helped them move to Council Bluffs. Reddick and William, two sons, joined the Mormon Battalion. Isaac and family remained at Council Bluffs until the return of Reddick, then they moved to the Valley.

Isaac continued to have difficulty supporting his family. They lived in Cottonwood, where his wife died. He married again and raised her children plus one of their own. They moved to Kaysville, Utah, where they lived until his death.

Isaac was a convert, father of 14 children, had two wives, was involved in the persecutions of Missouri, crossed the plains, sent two sons with the Mormon Battalion, settled for a time in Spring City, Utah, Cottonwood, and eventually in Kaysville. He died in Spring City.

Children of 1st wife:

ELIZABETH MARTIN, b. 16 Jan 1812, Bedford, Tennessee.
 D. 11 Oct 1819, Nashville, Davidson, Tennessee.
JOHN CALVERT, b. 5 Oct 1813, Bedford, Tennessee. Md. 22
 Aug 1833, Elizabeth Bates. D. 10 Jan 1893.

NANCY WEEKS, b. 4 Nov 1815, Bedford, Tennessee. Md. 26 Feb 1843, Asa C. Earl. D. 9 Apr 1904.

SARAH LOVISA, b. 14 Nov 1817, Bedford, Tennessee. Md. 5 Sep 1833, Allen Taylor. D. 11 Mar 1879, New Harmony, Washington, Utah.

WILLIAM MOORE, b. 24 Dec 1819, Farmington, Bedford, Tennessee. Md. 9 Jan 1842, Orissa Angelia Bates. D. 8 Jun 1901, Fairview, Uinta, Wyoming.

REDICK NEWTON (twin), b. 21 Feb 1822, Farmington, Bedford, Tennessee. Md. 26 Nov 1843, Nauvoo, Hancock, Illinois, Lucy Hoyt. D. 10 Oct 1905, Chester, Sanpete, Utah.

REDDIN ALEXANDER (twin), b. 21 Feb 1822, , Bedford, Tennessee. Md. 21 Dec 1843, Julia Ann Bates. D. 18 Jun 1900, Hubbard, Graham, Arizona.

MARY CAROLINE, b. 9 Dec 1824, Memphis, Bedford, Tennessee. Md. 6 Dec 1840, Joseph Egbert. D. 29 Apr 1880, Kaysville, Davis, Utah.

JAMES RILEY, b. 28 Jan 1827, Bedford, Tennessee. D. 14 Apr 1871, Spring City, Sanpete, Utah.

PAULINUS HARVEY, b. 21 Jan 1829, Farmington, Bedford, Tennessee. Md. 3 Feb 1848, Melissa Isabel Norton. D. 19 Nov 1900, Lehi, Utah, Utah.

JOSEPH ANDERSON, b. 26 Apr 1831, St. Role, Monroe, Missouri. Md. 1 Jan 1851, Rhoda Ann Palmer. D. 29 Sep 1891, Spring City, Sanpete, Utah.

ISAAC MORLEY, b. 22 Jul 1833, Salt River, Monroe, Missouri. Md. 11 Feb 1844, Charlotte Henderson. D. 27 May 1916, Spring City, Sanpete, Utah.

SIDNEY RIGDON, b. 22 Oct 1837, Caldwell, Missouri. Md. 13 May 1860, Lucy Ann Allred. D. 22 Nov 1911, Spring City, Sanpete, Utah.

Children of 2nd Marriage:

MATILDA, b. 12 May 1853, Big Cottonwood, Salt Lake, Utah. Md. 11 Dec 1871, John Robinson.

Submitted by: Merrill Gomm

JAMES ANDERSON ALLRED

Born: 22 Nov 1819, Farmington, Bedford, Tennessee
Parents: William and Sarah Warren Allred
Died: 3 Apr 1904, Spring City, Sanpete, Utah
Arrived in Valley: 2 Jun 1861, Capt. William McKissick's
    Independent Co.

Married 1st: Elizabeth Parkis
Date: 30 Jan 1844, Pike Co., Illinois
Born: 19 Mar 1823, Pike Co, Missouri
Parents: Henry and Jane Shearer Parkis
Died: 25 Feb 1892, Spring City, Sanpete, Utah

Married 2nd: Mary Ann Pollard
Date: 6 Jan 1866
Born: 22 Aug 1846, Detford, Kent, England
Parents: Joseph and Mary Ann Bailey Pollard
Died: 2 Oct 1930, Salt Lake City, Utah

Married 3rd: Elizabeth Ann Brough
Date: 11 Nov 1878
Born: 18 Jul 1861, Spring City, Utah
Parents: George and Elizabeth Hudson Brough

Upon the death of his father, James assumed the support of his mother, brothers, and sisters. Early in his marriage to Elizabeth, he and his wife operated a stage coach inn in Pike County, Illinois. Later they sold the business and invested in some farm land.

James made the decision to join the saints in the Valley. His wife didn't want to go but finally agreed. She joined the Church after arriving. He was called to go to Sanpete County in 1865 to help develop the area. He settled in Spring City, Sanpete County He invested in a farm and stock, but during the Black Hawk Indian War, he lost a great deal of stock.

He was first counselor in a bishopric, ordained a bishop and served 22 years in Spring City. He was active in community affairs and was first mayor of Spring City in 1870. He resigned in 1878 to become Probate Judge. He was on the board of County Commmissioners. He helped organize the Spring City Co-op store which he managed for 29 years. He also served a mission for the LDS Church. He practiced polygamy, having three wives.

In 1874 he built one of the finest homes in Spring City. It was two stories and the material had to be freighted in from Nephi. The house was still standing in 1996.He was approximately six feet tall, weighed about 160 lbs, stood erect, had brown hair, a beard, was an ambitious person and fairly wealthy for the time.

Children of 1st wife:

STEPHEN HENRY, b. 17 Jan 1846, Pike Co., Illinois. Md. 1st, 10 Feb 1867, Hettie Frost. Md. 2nd, 19 Jun 1874, Joanna Bena Petersen.
WILLIAM, b. 19 Oct 1862. D. 19 Oct 1862 (stillborn), Salt Lake City, Utah.

Children 2nd wife:

MARY OPHELIA, b. 4 Jul 1868, Spring City, Utah. Md. 10 Sep 1891, George Sigried Backman. D. 2 Oct 1930, Salt Lake City, Utah.
JAMES CARLOS, b. 23 Sep 1870, Spring City, Utah. Md. 26 Apr 1899, Ruth A. Justesen. D. 28 Jul 1919.
LOLA JANE, b. 6 Jan 1873, Spring City, Utah. Md. 13 Nov 1895, John Frank Justesen. D. 26 Jan 1950.
JOSEPH DELOS, b. 1 Dec 1874, Spring City, Utah. Md. 23 Jul, Letitia Beckstrom. D. 22 Apr 1899.
MARTHA AMELIA, b. 24 Jun 1876, Spring City, Utah. Md. 2 Apr 1897, James William Anderson. D. 1 Dec 1963.

JOHN ARTHUR, b. 30 May 1881, Spring City, Utah. Md. 1st, 7 Jul 1909, Elva Clyde Larsen. Md. 2nd, 11 Nov 1932, Ruth Henderson.

Children of 3rd wife:

WILFORD MILTON, b. 22 Aug 1881, Spring City, Utah. Md. 18 Jun 1902, Virginia Acord. D. 24 Aug 1931.

Submitted by: John Boyd

JOHN FRANKLIN ALLRED

Born: 1 Jan 1851, Council Point, Iowa
Parents: John Franklin Lafayette and Marinda Melvina Knapp Allred
Died: 1 Jul 1918, Spring City, Sanpete, Utah
Arrived in Valley: 8 Oct 1851. Handcart Co.

Married 1st: Mary Keziah Bunnell
Date: 9 Nov 1874, Salt Lake City, Utah
Parents: Samuel Gardner and Eleanor Keziah Zabriskie Bunnell
Born: 21 Apr 1859, Provo, Utah
Died: 19 May 1947, Fairview, Sanpete, Utah

Married 2nd: Sara Ellen Bunnell
Date: 3 Jul 1881, Salt Lake City, Utah
Parents: Samuel Gardner and Eleanor Keziah Zabriskie Bunnell
Born: Dec 1860, Provo, Utah
Died: 5 Nov 1913, Spring City, Sanpete, Utah

John Franklin Allred attended Brigham Young Academy. He taught school 26 years then changed to farming. He served two terms in the State Legislature.

He filled a mission from September 1898 to November 1900. He was set apart as Patriarch for Sanpete Stake September 1916.

Children of 1st wife:

SILAS LAFAYETTE, b. 9 Oct 1875, Spring City, Sanpete, Utah. Md. 7 Dec 1902, Emily Forsyth. D. 8 Feb 1949.

ELLEN MARINDA, b. 16 Jul 1877, Spring City, Sanpete, Utah. Md. 3 Jul 1898, George Henry Osmond Justesen. D. 12 Mar 1917, Salt Lake City, Utah.

JOHN FRANKLIN, b. 11 Apr 1879, Spring City, Sanpete, Utah. D. 14 May 1901.

SAMUEL ORRIN, b. 20 Feb 1881, Spring City, Sanpete, Utah. D. 15 Nov 1902.

LAURA, b. 25 Feb 1883, Spring City, Sanpete, Utah. D. 5 Oct 1890. Child.

MARY KEZIAH, b. 13 Feb 1885, Spring City, Sanpete, Utah. Md. 16 Dec 1903, Chuncey Vail Howell. D. 21 Dec 1962, Gunnison, Utah.

MARTHA, b. 26 May 1887, Spring City, Sanpete, Utah. D. 4 Aug 1887. Child.

HYRUM, b. 20 Sep 1888, Spring City, Sanpete, Utah. D. 2 Oct 1888. Child.

OLIVE, b. 10 Sep 1889, Spring City, Sanpete, Utah. Md. 27 Mar 1912, John Henry Coleman. D. 16 Nov 1966, Salt Lake City, Utah.

ARMINA, b. 4 May 1892, Spring City, Sanpete, Utah. Md. 6 Mar 1918, Henry Mayor Naylor. D. 25 Jul 1960.

AMY ILENE, b. 17 Jun 1894, Spring City, Sanpete, Utah. Md. 26 Jun 1912, Moses Willard Bigelow. D. 27 May 1980, Logan, Cache, Utah.

BESSIE AMELIA, b. 9 Oct 1896, Spring City, Sanpete, Utah. Md. 1st, 11 Apr 1917, James Williams Larsen. Md. 2nd, 9 Oct 1929, John Peterson. Md. 3rd, 3 Jun 1959, Ernest Sheen. Md. 4th, 17 Aug 1960, Henry Mayor Naylor.

DORA BUNNELL, b. 7 Dec 1901, Spring City, Sanpete, Utah. Md. 22 Mar 1922, Darrell Franklin Worthen. D. 3 Jan 1976.

Children of 2nd wife:

AMANDA ROZILLA, b. 8 Jun 1882, Spring City, Utah. Md. 10 Jun 1903, Henry Jackson. D. 5 Aug 1934, Provo, Utah.

COLEMAN, b. 4 Jan 1884, Spring City, Utah. Md. 7 Sep 1904, Jane Moss Forsyth. D. 31 Oct 1955, Provo, Utah.

SARAH LOUISA, b. 7 Oct 1885, Spring City, Utah, Md. 1st, 20 May 1908, Leon Lery. Md. 2nd, 20 Sep 1921, Anton Joseph Fechtel. D. 25 Apr 1969.

MATTHIAS, b. 24 Nov 1887, Spring City, Utah. Md. 1st, 9 Dec 1914, Audrey Bailey. Md. 2nd, 5 Jun 1918, Dora Rowena Jacobson. Md. 3rd, 4 Mar 1950, Ida Maude Attrell. D. 30 Sep 1969, Fountain Green, Utah.

LORUS, b. 15 May 1892, Spring City, Utah. Md. 1st, 12 Aug 1914, Margaret Dunham (Div). Md. 2nd, 1943, Grace Ander son (Clawson). D. 6 Jul 1961.

WARREN RADCLIFFE, b. Living. Spouse, living. 1996.

Submitted by: Amy Howell

SILAS LAFAYETTE ALLRED

Born: 31 Aug 1848, Council Point (Bluffs), Iowa
Parents: John Franklin and Marinda Melvina Knapp Allred
Died: 12 Dec 1932, Provo, Utah
Arrived in Valley: 1850-51

Married: Sarah Louisa Turner
Date: 29 Sep 1871, Salem, Utah
Parents: John Wesley Turner and wife
Born: About 1854, Provo, Utah.
Died: July 1947, Provo, Utah.

Silas L. Allred was three years old when his father died. His mother brought him and his younger brother, John Franklin, west in company with her father-in-law, James Allred. They settled in Provo, Utah, where Silas spent most of his life. He never attended school but instead helped support his mother.

All his life he signed his name with an "X." Even though he had a lack of schooling, he was successful. He used his talents in farming and raising livestock.

As a young man, he worked in Montana for a time, then on the railroad, and was present at the driving of the Golden Spike. He worked in mines, but farming and livestock was his main interest. For a time he was involved in freighting, and at one time was water master for Provo.

He eloped with Sarah when she was 17 and they had a very happy and successful marriage.

In 1908 they moved to Southern Idaho to help build a dam near Bellevue and Fairfield. It was known as the Magic Dam. They settled in the Gannett area and built a home, but in 1916 they moved back to Provo. He died there in 1947.

Children: They had fifteen children, three of which were still-born. The rest lived to maturity.

Submitted by: Ross Butler

WILLIAM MOORE ALLRED

Born: 24 Dec 1819, Bedford County, Tennessee
Parents: Isaac and Mary Calvert Allred
Died: 8 Jun 1901, Fairview, Uinta, Wyoming
Arrived in Valley: Aug 1851, Orson Pratt Co.

Married 1st: Orissa Angelia Bates
Date: 9 Jan 1842, Nauvoo, Hancock, Illinois
Died: 29 Jan 1878, St. Charles, Bear Lake, Idaho

Married 2nd: Martha Jane Martindale

Married 3rd: Mary Eleanor Osborn–No children

William was the fifth of 13 children born to his parents. They moved from Tennessee to Monroe County, Missouri, in about 1831. A year later he was baptized into the Mormon Church along with other members of his family. The family moved to Clay County and then to Caldwell County.

While still in his teens, he helped in the resistance movement. He later returned to Far West to help his family move to Nauvoo, Illinois, where, after an illness, he met and married Orissa. He helped build the Nauvoo Temple, and he built a home which he sold for $35 when they left Nauvoo. Having no wagon or equipment, they went to Council Bluffs with Orson Pratt. He found employment and was able to purchase equipment for the move west.

He lived in Tooele and Grantsville on farms and built the first house in St. Charles, Idaho, where he lived the rest of his life.

He was active in the Church and in civic callings, being a Justice of the Peace, County Clerk and County recorder. He was

Ward and Stake Sunday School Superintendent.

He had 14 children altogether. There were 12 children from his first wife. (unlisted)

Children of 2nd wife:

EDGAR MARTINDALE, b. 27 Feb 1858, Grantsville, Utah.
MARTHA JANE, b. 9 Nov 1860, Grantsville, Utah.

Submitted by: Merrill Gomm

THOMAS HILL ALSOP

Born: 1835, Cheddleton, England
Arrived in Valley: 1857

Married 1st: Elizabeth Mollart
Died: 30 Aug 1895.

Married 2nd: Mary Elizabeth Roberts

Thomas Hill Alsop joined the Church 21 January 1856, and then came to the valley in 1857 with his wife, step-daughter and sister-in-law. Upon their arrival they were sent by Brigham Young to Provo. Later Thomas was sent to help guard Johnston's Army. In Provo, he planted a large vineyard and orchard. Later he moved to South Jordan, leaving his vineyard and orchard for others. They lived in a dugout until he was able to fashion enough adobe bricks for nearly all the families homes.

Later he moved to West Jordan, then to Midvale, and finally

to Sandy where he homesteaded 240 acres. He was an ambitious man, helping establish communities wherever he lived. He brought the first fruit and shade trees to Sandy. He was a surveyor for the government.

Thomas with three other men, brought water from Little Cottonwood Creek to Sandy. Those already living along the creek fought them, saying it was their water. To pay for the lawsuit, the four men worked at the smelter. Thomas lost his right arm in an accident during this time. They finally won the lawsuit, brought the water to Sandy, built a reservoir and piped the water not only to his property, but also to the smelter and other families. He started a fish hatchery and planted mulberry trees and supplied worms for the silk he said would be wanted.

He spent time in jail for polygamy and was called on a mission to England after he got out. To keep from being jailed again, he left his family and went to Logan, where he worked in the Temple. Later he worked in the Salt Lake Temple. He was ward clerk for several bishops. He taught school and music. He could play six different instruments, including violin, piano, and organ. He has been honored as a pioneer builder, missionary, teacher, musician, clerk and horticulturist.

Children of 1st wife:

SARAH ANN.
EMMA OLIVE.
MOLLART THOMAS.
JOSEPH HENRY.
ALBERT GEORGE.
FANNIE MARIA.
HENRIETTA .

Children of 2nd wife:

HARRIET ELIZABETH.
WILLIAM.
MARY ELIZABETH.
SAMUEL FRANCIS.

DAVID ARTHUR.

LAURA MINETTA.

OLIVE ANN.

RUBY EXILE, named Exile because she stayed away from her
    husband so he would not be jailed.

Submitted: Clif Alsop

THOMAS ALSTON

Born: 24 Oct 1857, Southport, Lancaster, England
Parents: James and Ann Molyneaux Alston
Died: 31 Mar 1941, Salt Lake City, Utah
Arrived in Valley: Nov. 1865, Independent Co. under Capt. Walker

Married: Mary Ellen Holt
Date: 26 Dec 1878, Salt Lake City, Utah
Parents: LeRoy and Ellen Lowe Holt
Born: 22 Oct 1858, No. Ogden, Utah
Died: 21 Aug 1954, Inglewood, California

Thomas, his widowed mother, and two sisters Elizabeth and
Margery immigrated to the Valley in 1865. They lived in Sugar
House until his mother married John Israel Prye. Thomas was
baptized 21 March 1867. They later moved to Pleasant View (on
the north side of Parley's Hollow on the bench lands.

In December 1875, Thomas was asked to teach school in
Hoytsville in Summit County. The students ranged in age from
four to 22 years of age. He was there and in Wanship for one
year. He taught in Sugar House. In 1878 he married one of his

former students, Mary Ellen Holt.

He became an mechanical engineer, and was County and Probate Clerk of Summit County. They later moved to Coalville, and then to Salt Lake in 1888. He filled a mission to England and was gone five years. He was Stake Clerk in Granite Stake in 1900. He worked at various jobs until his retirement.

Children:

ELLEN MAY, b. 10 Dec 1879, Salt Lake City, Utah. D. 29 Jul 1881. Child.

JAMES LEROY, b. 10 Oct 1881, Hoytsville, Utah. Md. 25 Jan 1900, Lilly Josephine Darnell. D. 26 Dec 1918.

CLARENCE HOLT, b.23 May 1883, Hoytsville, Utah. D. 17 Mar 1884. Child.

THOMAS ALSTON, b. 31 Mar 1885, Hoytsville, Utah. Md. Alice Leona Goddard. D. 18 Sep 1967.

EARL, b. 24 Jan 1887, Coalville, Utah. D. 5 Mar 1888. Child.

ANNIE, b. 20 Jul 1888, Coalville, Utah. Md. 9 Oct 1912, Murray Mowry Bywater. D. 3 Dec 1971.

MARY LEONE, b.19 Dec 1891, Salt Lake City, Utah. D. 2 Sep 1914.

PEARL, b. 25 Apr 1893, Salt Lake City, Utah. Md. 12 Dec 1917, Elmer Francis Parry. D. 18 Sep 1965.

WALNE MOLYNEUX, b. 4 Jul 1894, Salt Lake City, Utah. Md. 19 Jun 1914, Sophie Augusta Rohlfing. D. 26 Nov 1994.

RAY LESTER, b. 22 Sep 1895, Salt Lake City, Utah. Md. 25 May 1928, Hannah Pearl Southwick. D. Living in 1996.

LILLIAN, b. 29 Mar 1897, Salt Lake City. Md. 19 Sep 1923, Charles Kendrick Behring. D. 22 Feb 1960.

EMMA AMELIA, b. 2 Jan 1899, Salt Lake City. Md. 12 Dec 1917, William Lester Lutz. D. Jan 1989.

MARTHA, b. 16 Mar 1901, Salt Lake City, Utah. D. 13 Sep 1901. Child.

Submitted by: Joann Killpack

NIELS ANDERSEN (NELS JEPPSEN)

Born: 14 Dec 1834, Monge, Vejby, Frederiksborg, Denmark
Parents: Anders Jeppsen (son of Jeppe Larsen and Bodil
    Andersen) and Inger Larsen (dau of Lars Nielsen and Maren
    Larsen)
Died: 24 Nov 1921, Mantua, Box Elder, Utah
Arrived in Valley: 22 Sep 1861, Capt. Samuel A. Woolley, ox team

Married 1st: Dorthea Magdalena Nichols
Date: 8 Oct 1862, Brigham City, Utah
Came to Valley: 22 Sep 1861, Capt Woolley.
Born: 12 Apr 1840, Majenfelde, Holstein-Schlweiz Schieswig
    Holstel, Prussia
Parents: Adolph August and Johanna Christina Art (Ault-Ort)
    Nichols
Died: 7 May 1871, Mantua, Box Elder, Utah

Married 2nd: Elsie Marie Eskelsen
Date: 1873/74, Mantua, Box Elder, Utah
Parents: Andreas and Maren Eskelsen
Born: 1 Nov 1847, Juland, Denmark
Died: 23 Oct 1874, Box Elder, Utah

Married 3rd: Anna Katherina Jacobsen
Date: 27 Oct 1877, Brigham City, Box Elder, Utah .
Parents: Christen and Maran Johansen Jacobsen

Niels Andersen was baptized into the Church 27 April 1860
in Denmark. He lived with his mother's parents for a time. Not
much is known about his early years. On 9 May 1861, Niels and

his mother sailed from Copenhagen Liverpool where they boarded the ship "Monarch of the Sea." According to family legend, his grandfather, and many of his relatives who had joined the church in Denmark, made their way to the Valley.

The day after his marriage to Dorthea, they walked to their farm. She carried a basket of dishes in one hand and with the other helped Niels carry a large box with the rest of their goods. For a time they lived in Bear River City, but most of their lives were lived in Mantua, until the death of Dorothea in 1872.

His next wife, Elsie, had one son and she died shortly after his birth. Niels felt he needed a wife so he married a third time. They spent many good years together and had three children. During polygamy problems, officers asked him how many wives he had and he said three. They arrested him. When he told them two of them were dead, they were going to make him walk home, but he refused and they had to take him home.

For many years he led the ward choir and was very musical. He had a nice voice. He gave the town of Mantua the ground for its cemetery.

Children of 1st wife:

HANNAH DORTHEA, b. 16 Oct 1862, Harper Ward, Box
    Elder, Utah Md. 16 Sep 1878, Abraham Hunsaker. D. 6 Jun
    1944, Honeyville, Utah.
INGER CHRISTINE, b. 7 Jul 1864, Mantua, Utah. Md. 8 Dec
    1881, Anders Julius Keller. D. 28 Oct 1949, Mantua, Utah.
ADOLFHIN NICOLINE, b. 8 May 1866, Mantua, Utah. D. 12
    May 1866. Child.
NIELS A., b. 17 Oct 1867, Bear River, Utah. Md. 10 Feb 1892,
    Mary Ann Anderson. D. 23 Jul 1930, Arco, Butte, Idaho.
ELISABETH, b. Feb 1870, Bear River, Utah. D. Feb 1870. Child.

Children of 2nd wife:

ANDREAS ANDERSEN, b. 19 Oct 1874, Mantua, Utah. D. same
    year. Child.

Children of 3rd wife:

NIELS CHRISTIAN, b. 3 Apr 1879, Mantua, Utah. D. 10 Sep
 1879. Child.
ADOLPHUS N. ANDERSEN, b. 27 Jun 1880, Mantua, Utah.
 Md. 8 Nov 1900, Victoria Sophia Smith. D. 18 Feb 1943, ,
 Box Elder, Utah.

Submitted by: Ivolene Allen

RASMUS PETER ANDERSEN

Born: 24 Sep 1823, Grenaa-Gammelsogn, Randers, Denmark
Parents: Anders Christensen and Maren Andersen
Died: 12 Apr 1902, Elsinore, Sevier, Utah
Came to Valley: 1866, Co. unknown

Married 1st: Jensine Severine Petrine Jensen
Date: 2 Oct 1857, Denmark (Div)

Married 2nd: Anne Marie Larsen
Date: 4 Feb 1885, St. George, Utah
Died: 7 Aug 1923, Elsinorc, Utah

   Rasmus Peter Andersen and his first wife had four children
before they were divorced. The last one died on the way to
America. Rasmus was baptized 12 April 1864 in Denmark.
   He brought twenty-five people with him to the valley and
paid their way from Denmark to Utah. He first lived in Levan,

Juab County, and later moved to Aurora, Utah. He received his citizenship in 1876. He was a farmer.

Children of 1st wife:

ANDERS PETER, b. 1857, Skinderberg, Denmark.
ANE MARGRETHE, b. 1859.
ANTON, b. 1861.
MARTHINUS, b. 1865.
JENS SEVERINE, b. 1865 or 1866 and died on the ocean enroute
    to America.

Children of 2nd wife and 1st husband. Rasmus adopted them:

MARTINE MARIE, b. 11 Oct 1872, Estrup, Hjorring, Denmark.
    Md. 1889 John Marius Johnson. D. 12 May 1956.
JULIAN PETER, b. 7 Jan 1875, Estrup, Jhorring, Denmark. Md.
    Maria Jacobsen. D. 22 Dec 1934.
CHRISTEN MARIEUS, b. 11 Jul 1877, Estrup, Hjorring, Den-
    mark. Md. 1897, Caroline Jensen. D. 6 Aug 1965.
ALICE, b. 6 Feb 1886, Aurora, Sevier, Utah. Unmarried. D. 19
    Feb 1953.
ALBERT, b. 19 Jan 1889, Aurora, Sevier, Utah. Unmarried. D.
    23 Oct 1921.
JOSEPH, b. 9 Sep 1892, Aurora, Sevier, Utah. Md. 8 Sep 1919,
    Ruby Tenora Hansen. D. 27 Jul 1978.

Submitted by: Rosalie J. Bown

HANS ANDERSON

Born: 3 Mar 1806, West Odarslov, Odarslov, Malmohus, Sweden
Parents: Anders Carlson and Hanna Pehrsson
Died: 19 Jan 1897, Millville, Utah
Arrived in Valley: 25 Sep 1868, John G. Holman Co.

Married 1st: Hanna Jonsson
Date: abt 1837
Born: 17 May 1808
Parents: Jons Jeppson and Malene Andersdotter
Died: 8 Nov 1838 (died of dropsy)

Married 2nd: Karna Nilsson
Date: 15 Nov 1839, Odarslov, Malmohus, Sweden
Born: 19 Jan 1813, Getinge, Gardstanga, Malmohus, Sweden
Parents: Nils Olsson and Hanna Akesson
Died: 30 Nov 1881, Utah

Hans worked as a laborer during his entire life. He joined the Church in 1864 and Karna had joined two months earlier. Four years later, Hans and his family and his sister-in-law and her husband left for America to join other family members who had emigrated earlier. They crossed America by train, steamboat, the railroad, and finally ox team and wagon.

Upon their arrival in Salt Lake, they went on to Millville where they settled.

Children of 1st wife:

ANDREW, b. 19 Jan 1841, Sweden.

HANNAH, b. 10 Apr 1843, Sweden.
CAROLINE, b. 5 Apr 1845, Sweden.
HANS, b. 24 Sep 1847, Sweden. D. Child.
ELNA, b. 13 Jan 1850, Sweden. D. Child.
NIELS, b. 24 Sep 1853, Sweden.

Children of 2nd wife:

HANNA

Submitted by: Thais Carlson DeGrey

NEIL ANDERSON

Born: 4 May 1836, Svedala, Malmohus, Sweden
Parents: Pehr and Sissa Olsson Anderson
Died: 1 Jul 1910, Midvale, Utah
Arrived in Valley: 1861.

Married: Hannah Pehrson Anderson
Date: 25 Oct 1862, Salt Lake City, Utah

Neil Anderson joined the Mormon Church in Sweden, 27 August 1859. He came to America in 1861 and settled in West Jordan, Utah.

He met his wife when she came to the Valley. He picked her out of the Company and said she would be his wife. They lived in a dugout just north of the West Jordan Cemetery. Later they were asked to move to Fairview in Sanpete County, where they had problems with the Indians. Neil fought in the Black Hawk Indian War. After the war, Hannah often invited indians in to eat a meal with her family even though she was afraid to turn her back on them.

Neil farmed, worked on the railroad, and became a citizen on 16 August 1865. In 1885 he served a mission in Sweden for two years. When he left he could not write, but while on his mission he learned to write.

He told Hannah the church officials had said he could take another wife, whereupon she told him "All right, if you do I will walk out." He decided to keep the wife he had.

When the Jordan Stake was organized, Neil was made second Counselor in the presidency. He died of cancer when he was 74.

Children:

MARIA ANN, b 27 Oct 1863, Midvale, Utah. D. Infant.

EMMA, b. 30 Nov 1864, Mt. Pleasant, Utah. Md. 22 Mar 1894, Andrew Larson. D. 30 Sep 1940.

NEIL, b. 29 Apr 1867, Mt. Pleasant, Utah. Md. 22 Mar 1892, Blanche Bishop. D. 7 Jul 1953.

SARAH JANE, b. 4 Mar 1870, West Jordan, Utah. Md. 28 Aug 1889, John Jenson. D. 19 May 1932.

ELIZABETH HARRIET, b. 30 Apr 1872, West Jordan, Utah. Md. 22 May 1893, Eli Mitchell. D. 17 Jun 1941.

HANNAH AMANDA, b. 4 Oct 1874, West Jordan, Utah. Md. 4 Jan 1905, Olf Olson. D. 16 Mar 1944.

ELLEN MARIE, b. 16 Sep 1877, West Jordan, Utah. Md. 1st, 1905, Archie Ernest Borst. Md. 2nd, Carl Lemke. D. 18 Nov 1957.

LAURA MATILDA, b. 29 Dec 1879, West Jordan, Utah. Md. 12 Dec 1907, Thomas Brinley. D. 23 Nov 1960.

MAUD MARINDA, b. 19 Sep 1882, West Jordan, Utah. Md. 16 Jan 1907, Henry Bringhurst. D. 12 Jun 1964.

Submitted by: Dixie Fredrickson

AMOS BETTS ANDREWS

Born: 4 Mar 1800, Whitestown, Oneida, New York
Parents: James and Betsy (Elizabeth) Betts Andrews
Died: 12 Mar 1865, Huntsville, Weber, Utah
Arrived in Valley: 1848, Capt. Snow Co.

Married: Keturah Eliza Button
Date: 1824, Otisco, Onandago, New York
Born: 10 Dec 1810, Ostisco, Onandago, New York
Died: 15 Dec 1887, Willard, Box Elder, Utah

Amos and his wife and three children moved to Kirtland, Ohio, in 1835 and were soon converted to the Church and baptized in the Ohio River. When the saints left Nauvoo, the Andrews family left too. They were apparently living in Nauvoo at the time. They remained in Winter Quarters a year before making the trek west. Amos helped by making friends with the Indians.

They lived in Ogden for a short time and then went south with the saints in 1857-58. They lived in Provo for a short time and then moved to Huntsville. He was called on a mission to Holland where he served for three years.

Children:

LOVISA, b. 19 Mar 1830, Newbury, Chautauqua, New York.
    Md. 25 Sep 1850, Clinton D. Bronson. D. 17 Jul 1912, Ogden,
    Weber, Utah.
ZEBULON, b. 1831, Harmony, Chautauqua, New York.
OLIVIA (ELIZABETH), b. 27 Sep 1833, Harmony, New York.

Md. 27 Mar 1850, Wilmer Wharton Bronson. D. 29 Nov 1864, Ogden, Utah.

JANE ROSETTA, b. 25 Sep 1836, Harmony, New York. Md. 19 Feb 1855, George J. Marsh. D. 1 Mar 1908, Ogden, Utah.

MARY, b. abt 1838, Chautauqua Co, New York. Md. 2 Sep 1860, James W. Duther.

SARAH, b. abt 1840, Chatauqua Co., New York.

AMOS MONTGOMERY, b. 1848, Salt Lake City, Utah. Md. 23 Jun 1879, Caroline Matilda Brackenbury. D. 23 Feb 1922, Thatcher, Utah.

AMOS BETTS, b. 22 Sep 1849, Ogden, Utah. Md. Caroline Graham. D. 12 Feb 1916.

HARRIET CHALISTA ALWIDA, b. 19 May 1853, Willard, Utah. Md. 11 Jan 1875, Andrew Jackson Shupe II. D. 12 Feb 1916, Ogden, Utah.

Submitted by: Daleen Bryant and Garry Bryant

MILO ANDRUS, JR.

Born: 30 Sep 1848, Liverpool, England
Parents: Milo and Sarah Ann Miles Andrus, Sr.
Died: 20 Mar 1938, Utah
Arrived in Valley: 31 Aug 1851, Milo Andrus Co.

Married: Elizabeth Boyes
Date: 4 Dec 1871, Salt Lake City , Utah

Milo was born in Liverpool, England, while his parents were

there serving on a mission. His mother died shortly after they returned home, leaving Milo motherless at the age of three years.

In 1851, his father moved the family to Holladay. As a young boy, he herded cows for his father and some neighbors.

He didn't receive much education because he was always being called on to work and supervise his father's land. He was a member of the Utah Militia by the time he was 19. He engaged in farming most of his life.

Milo worked for the railroad for a time grading and preparing the railroad beds. He built the salt ponds for the Inland Crystal Salt Company, graded and dug three canals. His sons worked with him.

He served in many callings in the Church, including that of a bishop and he was ordained a patriarch in 1911. He spent his last years doing temple work.

Children:

MILO BOYES, b. 4 Oct 1872.
ELIZABETH, b. 4 Apr 1874. Md. Mr. Ritchie.
SARAH, b. 12 Mar 1876. Md. Mr. Brockbank.
MARY, b. 9 May 1878. Md. Mr. Hoagland.
LEONORA B., b. 20 Feb 1880.
GEORGE BOYES, b. 23 May 1881.
ANN ELIZA, b. 22 May 1883. Md. Mr. Jensen.
JOSEPH BOYES, b. 6 Mar 1885.
IDA B., b. 20 Jul 1887.
ELENA, b. 16 Jul 1889. Md. Mr. Erickson.
LAVINA LEONE, b. 11 Feb 1892. Md. Mr. Taylor.
WILLARD OSCAR, b. 26 Apr 1895.
JOHN IVAN, b. 7 Apr 1897.

Submitted by: Ione Andrus Pack

JAMES ARMITSTEAD

Born: 22 Jun 1821, Bentham, Yorkshire, England
Parents: Thomas and Margaret Rawlinson Armitstead
Died: 13 Nov 1905, Pleasant Grove, Utah
Arrived in Valley: 16 Oct 1853, Cyrus H. Wheelock Co.

Married: Mary Coupe
Date: 21 May 1843, Blackburn, Lancs, England
Born: 24 Dec 1821, Haslingden Grane, Lancs, England
Died: 10 Feb 1901, Pleasant Grove, Utah

James emigrated from England in 1851 and arrived in the Valley in 1853. He took his family south to Pleasant Grove where they settled. He was a veterinarian, physician, lawyer, teacher, justice of the peace, school trustee and city councilman. He filled two missions to Illinois during his life.

He was not only active in community and civic affairs but in the Church also.

Children:

THOMAS ELLIS, b. 21 Feb 1845, St. John's Parish, Blackburn, Lancs, England. D. 1 Apr 1845. Child.

MARGARET ANN, b. 15 Jun 1846, St. John's Parish, Blackburn, Lancs, England. Md. 14 Dec 1868, Frederick Thorne. D.15 Dec 1927, Pleasant Grove, Utah.

JAMES NEPHI, b. 31 Oct 1848, St. John's Parish, Blackburn, Lancs, England. D. 27 Mar 1851, near St. Louis, Missouri. Child.

SARAH JANE, b. 21 Mar 1851, on board steamer on Mississippi River between New Orleans and St. Louis. Unmarried. D. 19 Dec 1862, Pleasant Grove, Utah.

WILLIAM HENRY, b. 29 Jan 1854, near Salt Lake City, Utah. Md. 8 Jan 1880, Mary Elizabeth Harper. D. 24 Jun 1923.

JOHN EMER, b. 17 Feb 1856, Pleasant Grove, Utah. Md. 8 Feb 1883, Naomi Bean. D. 25 Jan 1926.

MARY ALICE, b. 29 Dec 1857, Pleasant Grove, Utah. Md. 14 Aug 1877, David Thomas Thorne. D. 17 Dec 1882, Pleasant Grove, Utah.

ADDISON COUPE, b. 23 May 1860, Pleasant Grove, Utah. Md. 20 Oct 1887, Metta Mary Jensen. D. 31 Jan 1898.

ANNIE ELIZA, b. 22 Feb 1863, Pleasant Grove, Utah. Md. 24 Mar 1886, David Thomas Thorne. D. 29 Mar 1932, Pleasant Grove, Utah.

Submitted by: David L. Walton

FRANCIS ARMSTRONG

Born: 3 Oct 1839, Plainmiller, Northumberland, England
Died: 15 Jun 1899, Salt Lake City, Utah
Arrived in Valley: 3 Oct 1839

Married 1st: Isabel Siddoway
Date: 10 Dec 1864, Salt Lake City, Utah
Born: 28 Nov 1849, Sunderland, Durham, England
Died: 11 Dec 1930, Salt Lake City, Utah

Married 2nd: Sarah Carruth Armstrong

Date: 30 May 1870, Salt Lake City, Utah
Born: 8 Jan 1845, Shotts, Lanark, Scotland
Died: 1 Mar 1883, Salt Lake City, Utah

Married 3rd: Mary Hannah Armstrong
Date: 24 Jun 1897, Salt Lake City, Utah
Born: 3 Aug 1875, Salt Lake City, Utah
Died: 16 Feb 1932, Salt Lake City, Utah

Francis or Frank, as he was known, arrived with his parents and family in Canada in 1855. Frank was 18 and wanted to go to Missouri. In 1858 he and two companions left on horseback for the states. He stayed in Richmond when his companions left. He kept hearing about the Mormons, and in 1861 he was baptized and immediately left for Salt Lake City.

Upon his arrival, he worked at Brigham Young's flour mill in Parley's Hollow. He lived with the Robert Siddoway family, fell in love with and married their daughter.

Over the coming years, he bought his own saw mill, a lumber mill, a construction company, a flour mill, several large ranches, developed sugar companies, banks, savings and loan operations, railroads, transfer companies, and eventually electric street cars and the supporting electricity production company.

Despite all this, he felt a deep civic responsibility. He served on the school board, school council, city council, and was mayor plus other positions. He also remained active in the Church holding many positions and helping church leaders when needed. He helped finance construction of the Salt Lake Temple and was an ordained worker in the Endowment House and Temple.

He died at the early age of 59 of stomach cancer. He left an estate second only to that of Brigham Young, plus his family and his testimony of the gospel.

Children of 1st wife:

ELIZABETH DAWSON, b. 18 Nov 1865, Salt Lake City, Utah.
    Md. William S. Bean.
FRANCIS SIDDOWAY, b. 26 Nov 1867, Salt Lake City, Utah.

WILLIAM FRANCIS, b. 19 Mar 1870, Salt Lake City, Utah.
Md. Edythe Moyle.
ISABELLE, b. 8 Dec 1872, Salt Lake City, Utah. Md. Edward
L. Burton
MARY HANNAH, b. 3 Aug 1875, Salt Lake City, Utah. Md.
Richard W. Madsen.
EMMA LOUISE, b. 20 Feb 1878, Salt Lake City, Utah. Md. Wil-
liam M. Armstrong.
FLORENCE GRACE, b. 14 Aug 1880, Salt Lake City, Utah.
Md. Frank E. Bagley.
SARAH ETHEL, b. 13 Mar 1883, Salt Lake City, Utah. Md. Isaac
R. Barton.
HAZEL KIRK, b. 20 Dec 1885, Salt Lake City, Utah.
IRENE LENOIRE, b. 10 Mar 1889, Salt Lake City, Utah. Md.
Elmer Brainard.
ROBERT LEE, b. 20 Aug 1893, Salt Lake City, Utah. Md. Clara
Gillam.

Children of 2nd wife:

FRANCIS JAMES, b. 1873, Salt Lake City, Utah.
JOHN CARRUTH, b. 233 Jun 1874, Salt Lake City, Utah. D.
1874. Child.
ANNIE MENETTA, b. 10 Jan 1875, Salt Lake City, Utah. Md.
Daniel H. Livingston.
FRANCIS MARION, b. 28 Aug 1877, Salt Lake City, Utah. D. 8
Apr 1878. Child.
GEORGE CARRUTH, b. 29 Jun 1879, Salt Lake City, Utah. D.
1907, Utah.
NELLIE, b. 3 Feb 1882, Salt Lake City, Utah. D. 14 Feb 1882.
Child.
JOSEPH FRANCIS, b. 26 Feb 1883, Salt Lake City, Utah. D. 26
Feb.1883. Child.

Submitted by: Francis Madsen, Jr.

THOMAS KIRK ARMSTRONG

Born: 7 Sep 1847, Plenmellor, Haltwhistle, Northumberland,
  England
Parents: William and Mary Kirk Armstrong
Died: 1 Mar 1927, Salt Lake City, Utah
Arrived in Valley: 1 Oct 1867

Married: Margaret Stevenson Hutchinson
Date: 19 Jan 1869, Salt Lake City, Utah
Born: 14 Feb 1848, Rutherglen, Lanark, Scotland
Parents: William and Jane Penman Hutchison
Died: 10 Dec 1938, Salt Lake City, Utah

Thomas was christened Thomas Armstrong and added his mother's maiden name of Kirk later. He left England with his family and came to Canada in 1857. A year after the family's arrival in Canada, an older brother, Francis, left home and went to the States and eventually joined the Church and went west to the Valley.

When Thomas was 20, he left home and followed his brother west to the Salt Lake Valley. He arrived in 1868 and went to work for his brother in the saw mill. He was baptized eight months later in 1868. While working, he met Margaret who was a cook and also a member of the church. They were soon married.

Thomas was a hard worker like his brother. He helped develop the Utah territory with his team and wagon, his sawmill work and the sheep ranch he had seven miles east of Park City. During some hard times, he sold his sheep but later became the watchman at the City reservoir at 1300 East and 100 South.

He was a kind man, honest, and big hearted. He loved the church and his family.

Children:

THOMAS HUTCHISON, b. 15 Feb, 1870, Big Cottonwood, Utah. Md. 11 Sep 1895, Emma Jane Welch. D. 7 Apr 1927, Salt Lake City, Utah.

JANE PENMAN, b. 9 Dec 1871, Big Cottonwood, Utah. Md. 9 Aug 1894, James Hunter.

WILLIAM HUTCHISON, b. 9 Feb 1874, Salt Lake City, Utah. D. 28 Aug 1875. Child.

FRANCIS HUTCHISON, b. 16 Mar 1876, Salt Lake City, Utah. Md. 1st, 2 Nov 1897 (Div), Sophia Phillips. Md. 2nd, Sarah Jane Skillings. Md. 3rd, GuMd.a Larson. D. 26 May 1956, Medical Lake, Spokane, Washington.

MARGARET MAY, b. 8 May 1878, Mt. Hope, Glanford, Ontario, Canada. Md. 6 Sep 1905, Frank Bates Hall. D. 15 Jun 1912, Salt Lake City, Utah.

JOHN WILLIAM, b. 9 Aug 1880, Mt. Hope, Glanford, Ontario, Canada. D. 12 May 1882, Salt Lake City, Utah. Child.

MARY ALICE, b. 6 Dec 1882, Salt Lake City, Utah. Md. 29 Aug 1906, James Patrick Meik. D. 12 May 1977, Salt Lake City, Utah.

DAVID GEORGE, b. 8 Apr 1886, Salt Lake City, Utah. Unmarried. D. 3 Feb 1953, Salt Lake City, Utah.

ANNIE EMMA, b. 25 Oct 1888, Salt Lake City, Utah. D. 14 Dec 1888. Child.

CLARA FAMEY, b. 26 May 1892, Salt Lake City, Utah. Md. 24 Jun 1914, Frank Henry (Daniel) Ebert. D. 18 Oct 1957, Salt Lake City, Utah.

Submitted by: Mildred Porter Hunter

NATHANIEL ASHBY

Born: 15 Apr 1805, Salem, Essex, Massachutes
Parents: Benjamin and Mary Young Ashby
Died: 23 Sep 1846, 6 miles west of Bonaparte, Van Buren, Iowa
Arrived in Valley: Died on way west.

Married: Susan Hammond
Date: 30 Nov 1826, Massachusetts
Born: 28 Aug 1808, Marblehead, Essex, Massachusetts
Died: 15 May 1851, Salt Lake City, Utah

Nathaniel's family were seaman and shipwrights until after the war of 1812. Nathaniel, however, was apprenticed to a shoe-maker at an early age, to learn the shoemaking trade. He became expert in making fine shoes.

After his marriage, the couple soon owned not only his shoe shop but also several houses which they rented out. They were introduced to the gospel and baptized in 1841. In 1843 they sold out and moved to Nauvoo. They lived there until the exodus, then started west with the saints. Nathaniel's health was not good and, after reaching camp a few miles from Bonaparte, Iowa, they decided to camp until he felt better. He died there and was buried there. He was only 41 years old.

Children:

ROBERT REED, b. 17 Aug 1827, Salem, Essex, Massachusetts.
    D. 9 Feb 1828. Child.
BENJAMIN, b. 19 Dec 1828, Salem, Massachusetts. Md. 1st, 25
    Oct 1857, Ann Chester. Md. 2nd, 25 Oct 1857, Mary Jane

Collins Dyer. D. 19 Nov 1907, Bountiful, Utah.

SUSAN ANN, b. 1 Feb 1830, Salem, Massachusetts. Md. 21 Mar 1850, Briant Stringham. D. 28 Apr 1896, Salt Lake City, Utah.

ELIZABETH REBECCA, b. 17 May 1831, Salem Massachusetts. Md. 19 Dec 1847, Erastus Snow. D. 12 Jun 1915, Salt Lake City, Utah.

MARTHA ELLEN, b. 28 Aug 1832, Salem, Massachusetts. Md. 1st, 16 Dec 1850, (Alonzo) Alandas Daniel Lafette Bucklin. Md. 2nd, 12 Aug 1856, Briant Stringham. D. 25 Mar 1873, Salt Lake City, Utah.

HARRIET MARIA, b. 8 Apr 1834, Salem, Massachusetts. Md. 20 Apr 1852, Briant Stringham. D. 18 Apr 1921, Pasadena, California.

NATHANIEL, b. 25 May 1835, Salem, Massachusetts. Md. 1st, 11 Feb 1858, Mary Virginia Garr. Md. 2nd, 11 Aug 1870, Martha Ann Truman. D. 11 Feb 1858, at sea.

RICHARD HAMMOND, b. 25 Dec 1836, Salem, Massachusetts. Md. 20 Dec 1862, Ester Ann Busby. D. 2 Jun 1909, Salt Lake City, Utah.

WILLIAM HARDIN, b. 16 Jul 1839, Salem, Massachusetts. Md. 1st, 14 Jan 1865, Nancy Maria Badger. Md. 2nd, 11 Oct 1875, Charlotte Louisa Badget. D. 19 Mar 1925, Holden, Utah.

MARY JANE, b. 20 Oct 1841, Salem, Massachusetts. Md. 3 Mar 1858, George Ammon Stringham. D. 30 Jul 1912, Santa Monica, California.

EMMA SMITH, b. 14 Mar 1843, Salem, Massachusetts. Md. 28 Oct 1861, Benjamin Joseph (Bennie) Stringham. D. 25 May 1877, St. George, Utah.

JOHN JEFRED (JEFFORD), b. 9 Dec 1845 , Nauvoo, Illinois. Md. 1st, 15 Nov 1869, Susan (Susannah) Felshaw. Md. 2nd, 29 Mar 1886, Augusta (Agusta) Perkins. Md. 3rd, 29 Mar 1886, Louisa Deseret Perkins. D. 17 Sep 1893, Lost Creek, Utah.

LOUISA ADELINE NOBLE, b. 13 Dec 1849, Salt Lake City, Utah. Md. 27 Dec 1877, Rodney Carlos Badger. D. 23 Apr 1944, Salt Lake City, Utah.

Submitted by: Donna Bird and Karma Lewis

HENRY ASHCROFT

Born: 30 Nov 1833, Upholland, Lancs, England
Parents: George Lee and Margaret Ashcroft
Died: 9 May 1867, Hyde Park, Utah
Arrived in Valley: 2 Nov 1855, Isaac Allred Co.

Married 1st: Mary Glover
Date: 12 Nov 1854, Wigan, Lancs, England
Born: 28 May 1837, England

Married 2nd: Elizabeth Ann Barton
Date: 26 Oct 1861, Salt Lake City, Utah
Born: 3 Jun 1839, Pemberton, Lancs, England

Henry went by his mother's maiden name because his parents were never married. He was baptized in 1849 at the age of 16. After his marriage to Mary, they saved enough to pay their way to America in 1855, and crossed the plains that fall. They went on to Payson where they stayed until 1860, then moved to Hyde Park.

They lived in a dugout until Henry was able to erect a home for them. Henry helped build a canal to bring water to the area. Henry was a born leader and was able to get other men to work for public projects.

One month after being sealed to Mary, he took Elizabeth as a second polygamist wife. He built a new two-room log cabin where each wife had a room.

To assist needy saints journey westward, Henry sent yoke of cattle and wagon back east. As thanks for this, the people sent him a stove, one of the first in Hyde Park. Henry was also a friend to the Indians and shared and traded with them for their needs. He was gifted in drama and had a beautiful voice and helped with productions in their town.

While getting lumber out of the canyon during the winter of 1864-65, he contracted consumption (pneumonia). In the spring of 1867, he got caught in a drenching rain. He became ill again and died shortly after. Both wives were expecting again at the time. Two children were born following his death.

Henry was a large, sturdy and well built man with large blue eyes, brown hair and a pleasing manner. He was industrious, honest, faithful and kind.

Children of 1st wife:

HENRY WILLIAM, b. 16 Jan 1857.
JAMES ALBERT, b. 6 Nov 1859.
GEORGE FRANKLIN, b. 2 Jul 1861.
MARY ELIZABETH, b. 22 Aug 1863.
MARGARET ANN, b. 10 Feb 1865. Md. Mr. Hurren.
CHARLES ROBERT, b. 4 Dec 1867.

Children of 2nd wife:

JAMES BARTON, b. 28 Mar 1863.
JOSIAH EMER, b. 7 Sep 1865.
WALTER OTTUAL, b. 14 Oct 1867.

Submitted by: Gaylen Ashcroft

EDWARD ASHTON

Born: 22 Aug 1821, Caersus, Montgomeryshire, Wales
Parents: Richard and Elizabeth Savage Ashton
Died: 7 Feb 1904, Salt Lake City, Utah
Arrived in Valley: 29 Sep 1852

Married: Jane Treharne
Date: 6 Feb 1854, Salt Lake City, Utah
Born: Wales
Parents: William and Ann Richards Treharne

Edward's family was very poor and he was required to work in a woolen factory when he was only eight years old. When he was 10, he caught his hand in a machine, crippling him for a long time. After he recovered, he did chores for a family for two years for his board and clothing. He was then apprenticed to a man for three years to learn how to make shoes. The man beat him and mistreated him until finally he ran away. The magistrate cancelled his bonds because of his obvious mistreatment. He finally went south and obtained work as a shoemaker but it was not a pleasant situation so he left. He was approached by a man who offered him work and he remained there for 10 years.

In 1849, at the age of 28, he learned of the gospel and was baptized in 1849. A year later he left for America and lived in St. Louis where he worked until 1852, then joined a company coming west. He worked as a shoemaker for John Taylor's family and met Jane. After their marriage, Edward built a small home for them. As children were added, he enlarged the home.

He was part of the army who went to Echo Canyon, and later was one of those left in the city to guard it when the families went south because of Johnston's Army. He helped build the temple wall and had a small shoe shop in the rear of his home. He later worked on the Utah Central Railroad where he worked until he was 80 years old. He was active in the church during his life and raised a fine family.

Children:

EDWARD TREHARNE, b. 14 Jul 1855.
JEDEDIAH WILLIAM, b. 27 Dec 1856.
BRIGHAM WILLARD, b. 11 Sep 1858.
ELIZABETH ANN, b. 20 Jan 1860.
SARAH JANE, b. 6 Nov 1861.
EMILY TREHARNE, b. 14 Feb 1864.
GEORGE SAVAGE, b. 27 Jul 1870.

Submitted by: Ruth Walton

THOMAS ASHTON

Born: 27 Nov 1813, Parr, Lancs, England
Parents: Joseph and Catherine Sedden (Callis) Ashton
Died: 22 Jann 1903, Lehi, Utah, Utah
Arrived in Valley: 27 Sep 1851, Morris Phelps Co.

Married 1st: Mary Howard
Date: 20 Nov 1836, Prescott, England
Born: 28 Jan 1814, England
Parents: James and Mary Howard
Died: 26 Aug 1849, Pottawattamie Co., Iowa

Married 2nd: Sarah E. Mills
Date: 25 Sep 1849, Pottawattamie, Iowa.
Parents: John Mills and wife
Died: 3 Sep 1850, Pottawattamie, Iowa

Married 3rd: Arminta Miranda Adelia Lawrence
Date: 17 Feb 1851, Council Bluffs, Iowa
Born: 5 Dec 1832, of Ontario, Canada
Parents: John and Rhoda Sanford Lawrence
Died: 10 Jun 1891, Lehi, Utah

Thomas' father was a silversmith. He only had one sister, Eleanor who was 9 years his senor. At the age of 15 he apprenticed to a wheelwright, carriage builder and ship carpenter. Upon completion of his apprenticeship, he worked helping build the Liverpool and London Railway.

He married Mary in Prescott, England where they met the missionaries and were baptized in 1841. Later that same year they emigrated to America and made their home at Skunk River in Iowa. Because of the mobs, they moved to Nauvoo. The family was involved in all the events and work in Nauvoo. He helped construct the wagons used in the trek west.

He lost his first wife in Iowa and remarried a few months later. She died after giving birth to her first child. Thomas then met and married again at Council Bluffs. They crossed the plains together and had 7 children.

Thomas took part in the Church activities and also in community affairs.

Children of 1st wife:

JOSEPH, b. 27 Nov 1837, St. Helena, Lancs, England. Md. 20 Oct 1866, Elizabeth Mathews. D. 3 Jul 1916, Lehi, Utah.
CATHERINE, b. 19 Dec 1840, St. Helens, England. D. 11 Oct 1845. Child.
MARGARET ELIZABETH, b. 21 Feb 1843, Augusta, Iowa. Dd. 23 Nov 1845. Child.
MARY ANN, b. 7 Oct 1846, Pottawattamie Co., Iowa. Md. 1 Jan

1866, Daniel Wight Thomas. D. 11 Dec 1939, Lehi, Utah.

ELIZABETH ELEANOR, b. 13 Aug 1849, Potawattamie, Iowa. D. 5 Oct 1849. Child.

Children of 2nd wife:

JOHN MILLS, b.1950, Pottawattamie Co., Iowa.

Children of 3rd wife:

THOMAS LAWRENCE, b. 27 Nov 1852, Lehi, Utah. D. 20 Sep 1856. Child.

RHODA JANE, b. 3 Sep 1853, Lehi, Utah. Md. 16 Feb 1874, John Peterson. D. Taylor, Bonneville, Idaho.

ESTHER ANN, b. 17 Feb 1856, Lehi, Utah. Md. 24 Jan 1883, Thaddeus Powell. D. 10 Nov 1945, Lehi, Utah.

JAMES, b. 14 Feb 1858, Lehi, Utah. Unmarried. D. 12 Feb 1889, Killed by a horse.

ELEANOR LAWRENCE, b. 23 Apr 1859, Lehi, Utah. Md. 25 Aug 1881, Prime Coleman Jacobs. D. 20 Jun 1828, Lehi, Utah.

EMMA, b. 11 Dec 1860, Lehi, Utah. D. 2 Apr 1861. Child.

HENRIETTA LAWRENCE (twin), b. 27 Aug 1862, Lehi, Utah. Md. 19 Dec 1889, John Stewart Jr.. D. 18 Aug 1921.

HENRY LAWRENCE (twin), b. 27 Aug 1862, Lehi, Utah. Md. 23 Jan 1884, Aldura Marie Hammer. D. 24 Jun 1907, Los Angeles, California.

WILLIAM, b. 5 Feb 1865, Lehi, Utah. Md. Lydia Carter Barratt. D. 3 Jul 1923.

DANIEL, b. 4 Feb 1872, Lehi, Utah. D. 28 Sep 1873. Child.

ORIN, b. 28 Feb 1874, Lehi, Utah. Md. 15 Jul 1902, Elspeth (Elsie) Hunter. D. 10 Feb 1940.

Submitted by: Richard Moyle

GEORGE ATKIN

Born: 12 Mar 1836, Louth, Lincolnshire, England
Parents: Unknown
Died: 3 Jan 1899, Tooele, Utah
Arrived in Valley: 1849, Orson Spencer Co.

Married 1st: Sarah Matilda Utley
Date: 20 May 1856, Tooele, Utah
Born: 25 Dec 1838, Marion, Perry, Alabama
Died: 2 Aug 1905, Randolph, Rich, Utah.

Married 2nd: Emma Johnson
Date: 22 Nov 1883, Salt Lake City , Utah
Born: 12 Mar 1863, Tooele, Utah
Parents: Andrew John and Elna Petronella Pehrson Johnson
Died: 14 Mar 1925, Tooele, Utah

George's father was a carpenter and joiner. He owned and rented some houses, which made him fairly well off financially. George received a good education for the times.

His father and family joined the Church, and George was baptized in 1846. Three years later his family sailed for America. They sailed up the Mississippi and Missouri Rivers before they finally reached Council Bluffs. They purchased the necessary equipment to cross the plains and did so with the Orson Spencer Company in 1847.

The family obtained a lot in Salt Lake and built a home of adobe. In 1851, the family moved to a farm near Settlement Canyon in Tooele. While crossing the plains, George met Sarah and they continued their friendship until they were old enough to marry.

George was good with carpenter work and he helped construct many of the buildings in the area. He did well in a mercantile store. He belonged to the militia and played in Tooele's first band. He was able to play several instruments.

He served in several civic positions, including city marshall, city council, mayor, and he was on the State Legislature. He served in many church callings over the years. He served a mission in England. Upon his return, he took a second wife. He died after a lengthy illness with heart problems.

Children of 1st wife:

MARY ELIZABETH, b. 2 Dec 1857, Tooele, Utah. Md. 14 Feb 1879, Peter Ross Gillispie. D. 17 Apr 1883, Tooele, Utah.

EMILY, b. 3 Dec 1859, Tooele, Utah. D. 24 Feb 1889, unmarried.

GEORGE, Jr., b. 18 Nov 1861, Tooele, Utah. Md. 10 Sep 1885, Annie Lydia Jones. D. 11 Dec 1926.

LITTLE JOHN, b. 1 Jul 1863, Tooele, Utah. Md. Mary Fullenbach. D. 23 Mar 1899.

ALICE UTLEY, b. 18 Jun 1865, Tooele, Utah. Md. 7 Aug 1884, Joseph William De Lamare. D. 26 Dec 1892, Tooele, Utah.

SARAH MATILDA, b. 20 Oct 1867, Tooele, Utah. Md. Charles R. Simpson. D. 21 Jun 1901.

THOMAS HENRY, b. 31 Oct 1870, Tooele, Utah. Md. 1 Nov 1893, Ellen McFaden. D. 7 Jul 1929, Salina, Utah.

WILLIAM THOMPSON, b. 8 Jun 1872, Tooele, Utah. Md. 21 Dec 1898, Ada Eliza Hagell Foulger. D. 25 Jan 1943.

MILDRED, b. 8 Sep 1874, Tooele, Utah. Md. 24 Jun 1897, Robert Henry Hillstead. D. 7 Jul 1917, Fairview, Wyoming.

Children of 2nd wife:

REBECCA PETRO, b. 11 Dec 1886, Salt Lake City, Utah. Md. 20 Oct 1921, Moroni Howarth Ostler. D. 24 Dec 1965, Salt Lake City, Utah.

EFFIE, b. 6 Jan 1889, Salt Lake City, Utah. Md. 1 Mar 1916, John Henry Buchmiller. D. 17 Dec 1960, Rexburg, Idaho.

FLOYD THOMAS, b. 15 Sep 1909, Salt Lake City, Utah. Md. 7 Jun 1933 (Div), Helen Dalton. D. 19 Apr 1965, Salt Lake City, Utah.

Submitted by: Golden Buchmiller

THOMAS ATKIN

Born: 10 Feb 1804, Legsby, Lincolnshire, England
Parents: John and Mary Ashley Atkin
Died: 16 Dec 1888, Tooele, Tooele, Utah
Arrived in Valley: 22 Sep 1849, Orson Spencer Co.

Married 1st: Mary Morley
Date: 13 Feb 1826, St. Mary's Church, Nottingham, Nottingham, England
Born: 24 Feb 1800, Counton, Nottingham, England
Parents: Thomas and Mary Hole Morley
Died: 3 Jan 1882, Tooele, Tooele, Utah

Married 2nd: Hannah Morley Thompson (widow)
Date: abt 1883.
Parents: Thomas and Mary Hole Morely

Thomas was the eighth of ten children. The family were farmers. Thomas had only a limited education but served as a carpenter and builder's apprentice. About the time of their first child's birth, Thomas went to Louth to obtain employment. He built four homes, rented three of them and lived in one. In 1840 Mary became very ill and the doctors were unable to help her. Thomas, who had never been religious, resolved he would be more devoted in serving the Lord if only his prayers would be granted. Mary was healed and they became affiliated with the Methodist Church. In 1843, he was approached by the Mormon elders and was baptized 25 March 1843. Mary and the children were baptized a short time later.

In January of 1849, Thomas and his family left England for America, arriving in the Valley September 22, 1849. They obtained a city lot in the Eleventh Ward and built a small one-room adobe house. In the spring of 1851, Thomas purchased a 40-acre farm near the mouth of Settlement Canyon in Tooele where they constructed a home. Their two boys and their daughter made their homes in Tooele. His son George was his able assistant in his building projects.

Thomas was a religious man and was soon chosen as first counselor to Bishop Eli B. Kelsey. He was called to serve a mission to England from 1860 to 1863. Although a kind man, he was of stern disposition, had a mind of his own and knew how to use it. He continued to farm as well as build.

Children of 1st wife:

ELIZA, b. 15 Jan 1827, Legsby, Lincolnshire, England. D. 5 Apr 1827, Legsby, England. Child.

GEORGE, b. 3 Jan 1828, Louth, Lincoln, England. D. 12 Dec 1828. Child.

EMILY, b. 17 Oct 1830, Louth, Lincoln, England. Md. 25 May 1851, Richard Warburton. D. 12 Feb 1888, Tooele, Tooele, Utah.

THOMAS JR, b. 7 Jul 1833, Louth, Lincoln., England. Md. 20 May 1856, Mary Ann Maughan. D. 18 Apr 1919, Tooele, Tooele, Utah.

GEORGE, b. 12 Mar 1836, Louth, Lincoln, England. Md. 20 May 1856, Sarah Matilda Utley. Md. 2nd, 22 Nov 1883, Emma Johnson. D. 3 Jan 1899, Tooele, Utah.

HANNAH, b. 29 Aug 1839, Louth, Lincoln, England. D. 21 Mar 1840, Louth, Lincoln, England. Child.

Submitted by: Golden Buchmiller

THOMAS ATKIN, JR.

Born: 7 Jul 1833, Louth, Lincoln, England
Parents: Thomas and Mary Morley Atkin
Died: 18 Apr 1919, Tooele, Tooele, Utah
Arrived in Valley: 1849, Orson Spencer Co.

Married: Mary Ann Maughan
Date: 20 May 1856, Tooele, Tooele, Utah
Born: 16 Jan 1839, Alston Moore, Cumberland, England
Parents: Peter and Ruth Harrison Maughan
Died: 6 Feb 1908, Tooele, Tooele, Utah

Thomas Jr. was born into a well-to-do family. His father was a carpenter and owned property. Thomas was baptized in 1843. His parents decided to emigrate to America and then go west, but when they heard of the death of the Prophet, they postponed their departure until 1849. They were awed by some of the things they saw, including buffalo, Indians.

His father purchased property in Salt Lake and the boys were expected to help farm the land. The next year they moved to Tooele. Thomas Jr. married in 1856 and built a cabin. In 1857 he responded to the call to join the militia. He served in Echo Canyon and returned in time to take his family south to Lehi when the army came through. They returned to their home in Settlement Canyon the next spring. He remained active on their farm and in the Church and community until 1865 when he got a bladder infection. From then on he suffered with his health but still was able to serve as a counselor and then bishop for another 24 years. He was ordained as Stake Patriarch in 1909 and served until his death in 1919.

Children:

THOMAS MAUGHAN, b. 7 Jun 1858, Lehi, Utah. Md. 13 Jul 1882, Hannah Rowberry. D. 23 Sep 1924, Twin Falls, Idaho.

RUTH EVELYN, b. 16 Nov 1859, Tooele, Utah. Md. 10 Sep 1877, John Bissett Gordon. D. 3 Mar 1927, Tooele, Utah.

MARY ANN, b. 19 Nov 1861, Tooele, Utah. Md. 9 Sep 1880, Edward Warburton Lougy. D. 1 Jan 1937, Tooele, Utah.

EDWARD MAUGHAN (twin), b. 30 Oct 1864, Tooele, Utah. Md. Ann Janett (Nettie). D. 4 Sep 1926, Tooele, Utah.

EDITH MAUGHAN (twin), b. 30 Oct 1864, Tooele, Utah. Md. 27 Jan 1886, Peter McIntyre Clegg. D. 1 Jul 1890, Tooele, Utah.

PETER MAUGHAN, b. 3 May 1872, Tooele, Utah. D. 25 Jun 1872. Child.

WILLARD GEORGE, b. 25 Aug 1875, Tooele, Utah. Md. 21 Jan 1903, Clara Jane Isgreen. D. 13 Aug 1938, Tooele, Utah.

WILLIAM FRANK, b. 14 Jan 1878, Tooele, Utah. Md. 9 Dec 1908, Annie Maud Tate. D. 31 Oct 1966, Salt Lake City , Utah.

Submitted by: Golden Buchmiller

WILLIAM ATKINSON

Born: 20 Sep 1812, St. John, Sackville, Westmorland, New
    Brunswick, Canada
Parents: Christopher and Nancy Ann Smith Atkinson
Died: 25 Aug 1879, Bountiful, Davis, Utah
Arrived in Valley: 11 Sep 1853, Jesse W. Crosby Co.

Married 1st: Phoebe Campbell
Date: 26 Dec 1833, Sackville, Westmoreland, New Brunswick,
    Canada
Born: 9 Oct 1809, St. John, Westmorland, New Brunswick,
    Canada
Died: 21 Oct 1904, Bountiful, Davis, Utah

Married 2nd: Sarah Tingby

William was baptized into the Mormon Church in 1845. He
soon brought his family to Utah in 1853 and settled in Bountiful.
He was active in the church and eventually was a counselor
in the bishopric. He made a living for his family by farming.

Children:

SARAH ANN, b. 20 Sep 1834, Canada. Md. 10 Nov 1853. D. 16
    Oct 1915 MARRINER, b. 15 Nov 1835, Canada. D. 15 Nov
    1838. Child.
FRANCES ELIZABETH, b. 11 Mar 1837, Canada. Md. 18 Dec
    1854. D. 26 Jun 1928.
MARY JANE, b. 13 Sep 1838, Canada. Md. 2 May 1855. D. 3
    May 1882.

WILLIAM NEWLOVE, b. 2 May 1840, Canada. Md. 18 Dec 1861. D. 14 Mar 1928.

JAMES ISAAC, b. 28 Nov 1841, Canada. Md. 7 Mar 1870. D. 20 Sep 1928

THOMAS P., b. 23 Jul 1843, Canada. Md. 11 Mar 1865. D. 20 Sep 1928.

PETER,(twin) b. Nov 1844, Canada. D. 1844. Child.

MARK,(twin) b. Nov 1844, Canada. D. 1844. Child.

AMOS, b. 11 Nov 1845, Canada. Md. 23 Nov 1868. D. 28 Sep 1893.

PRISCILLA,(twin) b.Feb 1847, Canada. D. 1847. Child.

AQUILLA,(twin), b. Feb 1847, Canada. D. 1847. Child.

PHOEBE, b. 22 Jan 1848, Canada. Md. 15 Jan 1872. D. 30 Apr 1938.

PROFINDA, b. 26 Dec 1850, Canada. D. 19 May 1853. Child.

RHODA, b. 3 May 1856, Canada. Md. 9 Dec 1915. D. 11 Oct 1947.

Submitted by: Thelma Wyss

ELISHA AVERETT

Born: 12 Dec 1810, Maury Co., Tennessee
Parents: John and Jennett Gil Averett
Died: 22 Oct 1890, Glendale, Kane, Utah
Arrived in Valley: between 1846 and 1850

Married 1st: Dorcas Willis (Witt) (widow)
Date: 1838, Caldwell Co., Missouri
Born: 1 Feb 1810, Gallatin, Sumner, Tennessee

Parents: John and Jane Kirkpatrick Willis
Died: 6 Feb 1843, Nauvoo, Illinois

Married 2nd: Sarah Jane Witt (step daughter)
Date:19 Sep 1846, Nauvoo, Hancock, Illinois
Born: 1 Feb 1831, McLeansboro, Hamilton, Illinois
Parents: Robert L. and Dorcas Willis Witt
Died: 31 Dec 1875, Heber City, Wasatch, Utah

Elisha was a twin to Elijah. They knew they had been named for Biblical Prophets and lived their lives accordingly. Elisha loved music, playing the fife all his life. The twins joined the volunteers in the Blackhawk War. After joining the Church, Elisha and his family moved to Missouri with the saints and faced the problems there with them, moving back to Nauvoo when the rest were forced to flee for their lives. In Nauvoo, Elisha was very active in the church, helping the Prophet whenever needed.

His wife, Dorcas, died in childbirth in Nauvoo. Elisha married her daughter Sarah, by Dorcas' first husband. Then Elisha sustained a bad head wound from a sharp stone thrown by one of the mob. Later a metal plate was implanted in his skull to preserve his life. He never suffered any ill effects from it.

When the Mormon Battalion was formed, Elisha volunteered and became an officer. After his tour of duty ended, he went back to get his family and brought them to the Valley. They were called to help settle Dixie and later other places. He helped in the construction of the St. George, Manti and Salt Lake Temples. He also lived in and helped in the construction of Manti, Salt Lake, Cove Fort, Kanab, Pipe Spring Fort, Arizona, Heber City and other places.

Even after his wife Sarah died, he continued to help wherever and whenever called to serve in the church.

Children of 1st wife:

WILLIAM, b. 31 Jul 1839, Quincy, Adams, Illinois. Md. Elizabeth Hicken.
CHILD, b. abt 1841, Nauvoo, Illinois. D. abt 1841. Child.

DAUGHTER, b. 6 Feb 1843, D. 6 Feb 1843, Nauvoo, Illinois. Child.
(Both baby and mother died)

Children of 2nd wife:

DORCAS, b. 14 Dec 1846, Pottawattamie, Iowa. Md. James Madison. D. 22 Feb 1907, Glendale, Utah.

ELISHA, b. 20 Dec 1848, Council Bluffs, Iowa. Md. Annie Catherine Sedarville (Sidervill). D. 4 May 1912.

SARAH JANE, b. 1 Oct 1850, Salt Lake City, Utah. Md. John Smith Adams.

KIZZIE ANN, b. 11 Sep 1852, Salt Lake City, Utah. Md. David Wm. Campbell.

JOHN HARVEY, b. 8 Mar 1854, Salt Lake City, Utah. Md. Susan Emaline Allphin.

ELIJAH, b. 2 Jan 1856, Salt Lake City, Utah. D. 6 Jun 1868.

EMILY, b. 1858, Manti, Utah.

GEORGE, b. 16 Apr 1859, Salt Lake City, Utah. Md. Edith Manala Leithead.

ROBERT WESLEY, b. 6 Apr 1861, Heber City, Utah. Md. Leanor Catherine Allpin.

JAMES LAFAYETTE, b. 10 Apr 1863, St. George, Utah. Md. Laura Anis Maxwell.

LUCY LAVINA, b. 16 Apr 1866, Washington, Utah. Md. Richard Griffin.

JENNETTE ELIZA, b. 25 Jun 1868, Washington, Utah. Md. George William Smith.

BYRON, b. 2 Apr 1871, Washington, Utah. Md. Sonora Elizabeth Averett.

DAVID AVERETT, b. 31 Dec 1875, Heber City , Utah. D. 4 Jan 1876. Child.

Submitted by: Clifton and Jessie Wallace Spendlove

CALEB AYERS

Born: 13 Nov 1806, Stanhope, Sussex, New Jersey
Parents: Levi and Phebe Russell Ayers
Died: 14 Mar 1852, Council Bluffs, Pottawattomie, Iowa
Arrived in Valley: Died on way to Utah.

Married: Lucinda Catherine Haggerty
Date: 11 Jan 1832, Branchville, Sussex, New Jersey

Caleb was the 11th of 12 children. He was the father of seven children, plus one they raised after about 1853, but no adoption papers have been found.

The family joined the Church in 1842 and moved to Nauvoo, where they lived until the exodus. They went to Kanesville where Caleb met with an accident and died. His wife took their children on to the Valley with the saints.

Children:

ALMYRA MURRY, b. 23 Jun 1834, Stanhope, Sussex, New Jersey.
MOREAN, b. 8 Aug 1838, Stanhope, New Jersey.
VICTORIA, b. 8 Nov 1839, Stanhope, New Jersey.
CATHERINE MALINDA, b. 29 May 1844, Nauvoo, Hancock, Illinois.
IRA GEORGE, b. 31 Aug 1845, Nauvoo, Illinois.
MARTHA PETTY,(foster child), b. 31 Aug 1847, Manti, Sanpete, Utah.
HEBER CALEB, b. 23 Apr 1848, St. Louis, Missouri.

LUCINDA ANN, b. 1 Apr 1851, Kanesville, Iowa.

Submitted by: Arline Martindale Scott Brinton

ALMON WHITING BABBITT

Born: 9 Oct 1812, Chesire, Berkshire, Mass.
Parents: Ira and Nancy Crosier Babbitt
Died: 24 Oct 1856, Iowa, Near Council Bluffs
Arrived in Valley: 1848, Wagon train

Married 1st: Julia Ann Johnson
Date: 23 Nov 1833, Ohio
Born: 9 Nov 1808, Vermont
Died: 23 Oct 1857, Iowa

Married 2nd: Delcina Diadamia Johnson
Date: 24 Jan 1846, Nauvoo, Illinois
Born: 19 Nov 1806, Vermont
Died: 21 Oct 1854, Utah

Almon, sometimes called Captain Babbitt, was the father of six children. He was a member of Zion's Camp in 1834, and was named to the 1st Quorum of Seventies in 1835. He went on a mission to Canada and returned in 1838.

He became President of the Kirtland, Ohio Stake, 22 May 1841 to 1843. He was requested to stay in Nauvoo when the saints left to try to sell the LDS property after the exodus. He was a lawyer.

In 1852 he was named Treasurer of the Territory of Utah and in 1853 he was named Secretary of the Territory of Utah. He was elected Delegate to Congress for the provisional State of Deseret.

He was killed by Indians near Council Bluffs, Iowa, on his return to Utah from Washington, D.C. He was a member of the 16th Ward in Salt Lake City.

Children:

DAVID HOMER, b. 31 Jul 1835. D. 29 Nov 1836. Child.
ANNA CAROLINE (twin), b. 15 Aug 1843. D. 24 Oct 1844. Child.
DON CARLOS (twin), b. 15 Aug 1843. Md. 24 Jan 1864, Melissa Almera Johnson. D. 6 Sep 1912.
ALMON WHITING, b. 25 Jan 1847. Md. 10 Apr 1869, Delcina Elvira Johnson. D. 23 Oct 1918.
JULIA ANN, b. 27 Dec 1849. Md. 25 Apr 1870, David William Johnson. D. 27 Feb 1910.
NANCY MARIA, b. 7 Sep 1855. Md. 29 Nov 1875, Charles Hamblin Riggs. D. 9 Feb 1949.

Submitted by: Junith Roberts

DON CARLOS BABBITT

Born: 15 Aug 1843, Macedonia, Hancock, Illinois
Parents: Almon Whiting and Julia Ann Johnson Babbitt
Died: 5 Sep 1912, Mesa, Maricopa, Arizona
Arrived in Valley: 22 Oct 1848, Willard Richards Co.

Married 1st: Melissa Almera Johnson
Date: 24 Jan 1864.
Born: 11 Dec 1843, Illinois
Died: 17 Sep 1926, Mesa, Arizona

Married 2nd: Isabelle Milican Russell–No children
Date: 16 Oct 1876, Salt Lake City, Utah

Don Carlos was the father of 10 children. After his arrival in the Valley, he and his family were called to help settle Springlake, Utah, Utah, in 1876. While there, he was made second counselor to Bishop Johnson. He was a temple worker in St. George in 1874.

In 1880-1890 he was called to help settle St. John's, Arizona. They went to Mesa, Arizona, to help settle that area in 1890. He lived there until his death. He was a farmer.

Children of 1st wife:

GRACE MELISSA, b. 27 Feb 1866. Md. 28 Nov 1884, Alexander Nicoll. D. 20 Dec 1953.
CLARA ADELIA, b. 22 Jan 1868. Md. 13 Nov 1885, James Burns Ramsay. D. 18 Sep 1957.
DON CARLOS, b. 6 Feb 1870. D. Oct 1870. Child.
JULIA ELLISE, b. 6 Apr 1872. Md. 1st, 6 Jun 1894, Sidney Beatty Lamb. Md. 2nd, 24 Mar 1899, Levi Pratt Brizzee. D. 1 Jan 1948.
CAROLINE NANCY, b. 4 May 1874. Md. 1 Aug 1900, Henry Lewis Horne. D. 28 Nov 1954.
ESTHER DELCENA, b. 25 Apr 1876. Md. 1 Aug 1894, Dudley Sanford Lewis. D. 21 Sep 1914.
ALMON WHITING, b. 11 Jan 1878. D. 23 Sep 1881. Child.
RUTH ANNA, b. 27 Jun 1880. Md. 2 Oct 1902, John Franklin Horne. D. 23 Mar 1919.
BENJAMIN FRANKLIN, b. 7 Apr 1883. D. 26 Feb 1890. Child.
ROSEMARY, b. 19 Apr 1887. Md. 7 Apr 1910, Joseph Leonard Standage. D. 28 Jul 1978.

Submitted by: Junith Roberts

OLAUS BACK (OLIVER BACKMAN)

Born: 8 Apr 1824, Vastra Tunhem, Alvsborgs Lan, Sweden
Parents: Anders Hansson and Anna Britta Olofsson Back
Died: 16 Jul 1902, Huntsville, Weber, Utah
Arrived in Valley: 29 Sep 1866, Peter Nebeker Co.

Married: Inga Lena Johannesson or Engelina Ambjornson or
    Johnson.
Date: abt 1847-48. She was 24 when they married.
Born: 31 Mar 1824, Gardhem, Elfsborgs Lan, Sweden
Parents: Johannes and Casja Ericsdotr or Kaysa Ericsson
    Ambjornson
Died: 19 Apr 1911, Huntsville, Weber, Utah

Olaus and Engelina lived in Gardhem, Trollhattan Moder, Alvsborgs Lan, Sweden, where their first child was born. Olaus was a tailor by trade and also a musician.

Their early married life was marred when cholera broke out in the village. Her parents and one of their children and an aunt were there and no one was allowed in to help them. When her parents died, Olaus decided that he would go in anyway. He got a permit and went in and remained until both the child and aunt were dead too. He buried them all and remained in the house several days until the officials decided that he wasn't going to become ill and then he came home.

The highlight of their lives was when the Mormon elders came to their little town. Olaus was invited to the meeting. The sermon brought to mind a dream he had had as a young man. He dreamed he was sailing on the ocean and finally landed on a foreign shore. He had walked some distance when he saw a man with a book under his arm. The man told him he was preaching a new religion and about the new prophet of God, that the Gospel of Jesus Christ had been restored to the earth. The elder spoke of the same things. When Olaus got home, he woke his wife and read to her from a tract and then reminded her about his dream. A few days later they were baptized. They opened their home to the elders and others.

They couldn't afford to go to America but a young man was disowned by his family and said if he could stay with them, he would pay their way to the Valley. In 1865 the two oldest girls left with a family who paid their way. The next spring, 1866, the young man received his money and paid the way for the rest of the family.

On the way across the plains, Olaus played his violin and his daughter Johanna Sophia played the mouth organ and an accordion in the evenings for the weary travelers.

The family moved to Huntsville where they built their home and farmed. Olaus played for all the dances and social gatherings. He was well loved by everyone. He died after a long illness.

Children:

AUGUSTA CHARLOTTA, b. 9 Oct 1848, Gardhem, Trollhattan Parish, Alvsborgs Lan, Sweden. Md. 30 Jul 1867, Gustav Eric Heder. D. 4 May 1939, Utah.

ANNA MARIA, b. 7 Feb 1851, Gardhem, Sweden. Md. a Mr. Hanson. D. 18 Mar 1893, Utah.

EMMA MATILDA, b. 14 Jul 1853, Gardhem, Sweden. Md. 16 Feb 1869, Christian Peterson. D. 24 Aug 1925, Utah.

JOHANNA SOFIA (SOPHIA), b. 26 Jun 1856, Gardhem, Sweden. Md. 24 Feb 1873, Jens Peter Petersen. D. 29 Nov 1934.

JOHAN ALFRID THEODORE, or John Alfred, b. 5 Mar 1859, Gardhem, Sweden. Md. 7 Feb 1884, Dinah/Diane Marie Johnson. D. 26 May 1890.

LORGA, or LAURA OLIVIA, b. 23 Oct 1861, Elfsborgs Lan Sweden. D. 24 Apr 1862, Sweden. Child.

FRANS OSCAR WILHELM, b. 5 Apr 1863. D. 21 Apr 1863, Sweden. Child.

KARL OTTO EDVIN, b. 5 Apr 1864, Trollhattan, Sweden. D.
Aug/Sep 1866, on plains of America on way west. Child.
OLAUS JOSEPH, b. 5 Apr 1867, Salt Lake City, Utah. Md. 1st,
Margrett Hanson and 2nd Alfraetta Taylor.

Submitted by: Dan Dawson

GEORGE BROWN BAILEY

Born: 15 Feb 1833, Bath, Somerset, England
Parents: Joseph Brown and Ann Smith Bailey
Died: 4 Feb 1895, Mill Creek, Salt Lake City, Utah
Arrived in Valley: 16 Oct 1853, Appleton M. Harmon Co.

Married 1st: Elizabeth Young
Date: 10 Feb 1853, Bristol, Gloucester, England
Born: 30 Apr 1833, Bristol, Gloucester, England
Died: 18 Oct 1918, Salina, Sevier, Utah

Married 2nd: Elsie Marie Christensen
Date: 8 Feb 1868, Salt Lake City, Utah
Born: 13 Sep 1852, Horby, Hjorring, Denmark
Died: 5 Feb 1939, Ucon, Bonneville, Idaho

George Brown Bailey received a good education and learned
the carpenters trade. He met his wife Elizabeth at a Mormon
meeting in Bristol. They left for America a month and 10 days
later.

They settled on 10 acres in Millcreek where he walked twice
weekly into the city for work. There was plenty of work but not

much money. In 1855, George made some chairs for a man and received as pay enough adobes to build a two-room home with two fireplaces.

He served with the Militia when Johnston's Army came. After that they moved back to Millcreek where their twins were born. George moved to Spanish Fork in 1860 to help his mother farm, but Indian problems caused George to move his family back to Millcreek. A flood had undermined one room of their home so George rebuilt it.

In 1868, George married a Danish girl as a polygamous wife. Their financial crisis seemed over. He became a beekeeper which brought in good money for the remainder of his life.

In 1878 diphtheria killed five of George and Elizabeth's children. Their son died later that year of the same disease. Two of George and Elsie's children also died.

George was ward clerk for 19 years. He was choir director for many years. He served two terms in the Utah Penitentiary for "unlawful cohabitation."

At the time of his death, he had 11 peacocks, many turkeys, guinea hens, several kinds of ducks, and many kinds of chickens. He also loved flowers and kept a beautiful garden.

Children of 1st wife:

JOSEPH HYRUM, b. 14 Sep 1854, Millcreek, Utah. D. 30 Jul 1878.

ELLEN MARIE, b. 10 Dec 1856, Millcreek, Utah. D. 23 Feb 1951.

GEORGE SMITH (twin), b.13 Apr 1859, Millcreek, Utah. D. 25 Sep 1932.

ELIZABETH DAVIS (twin), b. 13 Apr 1859, Millcreek, Utah. D. 14 May 1948.

ISAAC YOUNG, b. 10 Aug 1861, Millcreek, Utah. D.3 Feb 1878.

ANNA RUSSELL, b. 14 Feb 1863, Millcreek, Utah. D. 14 Feb 1863. Child.

REUBEN JOSIAH, b. 10 Aug 1864, Millcreek, Utah. D. 9 Nov 1934.

DAVID WILLIAM, b. 16 Mar 1867, Millcreek, Utah. D. 23 Feb 1878.

AARON CHARLES, b. 17 Jun 1869, Millcreek, Utah. D. 24 Feb 1878.

CAROLINE ESTHER, b. 30 Jul 1871, Millcreek, Utah. D. 26 Jan 1878. Child.

RHODA ANN, b.10 Apr 1875, Millcreek, Utah. D.15 Feb 1878. Child.

ALICE ELMINA, b. 31 Mar 1877, Millcreek, Utah. D. 4 Aug 1960.

Children of 2nd wife:

MARY ANN, b. 28 Nov 1870, Millcreek, Utah. D. 18 Feb 1878. Child.

EDWARD FRANCIS, b. 6 Feb 1873, Millcreek, Utah. D. 22 Feb 1878. Child.

JAMES ANDREW, b. 21 Dec 1873, Millcreek, Utah. D.30 Jun 1876. Child.

ELSIE VICTORIA, b. 31 May 1880, Millcreek, Utah. D. 23 Nov 1960.

WILLIAM THOMAS, b. 5 Nov 1882, Millcreek, Utah. D.Aug 1938.

JESSE HENRY, b. 13 Mar 1885, Millcreek, Utah. D. 1 Jan 1961.

JOHN ISRAEL, b. 21 Jan 1888, Millcreek, Utah. D. 25 Jun 1933.

EARL FREDERICK, b. 17 Apr 1890, Millcreek, Utah. D. 3 Oct 1941.

Submitted by: Edith Clinger

FRANCIS WILLIAM BAILEY, II

Born: 6 Aug 1840, Fareham, Hamps, England
Parents: Francis William and Eliza Smith Bailey
Died: 25 Dec 1914, Salt Lake City, Utah
Arrived in Valley: 17 Oct 1862, Henry W. Miller Co.

Married: Annie Eliza Ingram
Date: 25 Apr 1862, Southampton, Hamps, England
Born: 15 Nov 1833, Southampton, Hamps, England
Died: 25 Dec 1912, Salt Lake City, Utah

Francis William Bailey attended school for about five years. At the age of ten years, he went to sea with his father, Captain Francis William Bailey I, and his grandfather, Captain William Bailey. During the next 12 years, he visited many foreign lands both by steamer and sailing vessel.

On one of his return trips, he met his future wife. She was a French school governess and a member of the Mormon Church. He was baptized in February 1852 and she in March 1852.

Shortly after their marriage they left for America. As they came through Echo Canyon, they left the Company and he built a dugout where their first child was born. They went on to the valley and settled on the block between 4th and 5th South and 10th and 11th East. Later they lived in Rich Valley and then Stockton, Tooele County, where he worked at farming and mining.

In 1871, Francis decided to return to England and the sea, but this changed when two ships were lost at sea. He operated the conference house for the church where he was responsible for the missionaries. They soon returned to Salt Lake and lived out their lives there.

Children:

FRANCIS TRACY, b. 16 Apr 1863, Peterson, Morgan, Utah. D. 14 Oct 1942.
MARY HARRIET, b. 23 Nov 1865, Salt Lake City, Utah. D. 23 Apr 1946.
OWEN ALBERT, b. 3 Oct 1866, Salt Lake City, Utah.
JACOB RALPH (twin), b. 7 Dec 1870, Salt Lake City, Utah.
WILLIAM ESAW (twin), b 7 Dec 1870, Salt Lake City, Utah.
SAMUEL CHARLES, b. 29 Sep 1874, Southampton, Hamps, England.

Submitted by: Douglas Smith

ROBERT BAIRD, II

Born: 18 Apr 1831, Ballintoy, Antrim, Ireland
Parents: Robert and Agnes McGowan Baird
Died: 9 Jun 1886, Heber City, Utah
Arrived in Valley: 15 Oct 1863, Samuel D. White Co.

Married: Jane Cumming
Date: 8 Jul 1853, Glasgow, Scotland
Born: 18 Jun 1833, Glasgow, Scotland
Died: 4 Nov 1896, Heber City, Utah

When Robert was 14 years of age he moved to Glasgow, Scotland, where he learned the trade of brass mechanic, serving seven years to complete the course. He was the first man to build sugar refinery machinery. One machine went to Cuba, and one to Australia. He helped put the machinery in two large ships, the "Black Prince" and the "Great Eastern," which laid the cable across the Atlantic Ocean.

After his marriage to Jane Cumming, they moved to Greenock, Scotland, where they remained for 10 years. About this time they joined the Church and on 28 May 1863 they left with their four small children for America on the "Sunnyshore."

Because of the Civil War raging at this time, they went from New York to Albany by steamer and then by rail to Montreal, Canada. They traveled from there by box car train and coaches to the Missouri River. There they waited for ox teams to take them to the Valley.

They lived in Salt Lake for 13 months. Robert was unable to make enough to support his family so he went northwest to Virgina City, Montana, to work in the gold fields while his family stayed in Salt Lake. He was gone nine months. He made good money there working the gold fields and doing wood lathe work for the first furniture shop in Virginia City or Banock.

When his work was completed he came back to his family in Heber City. He built a small log house. They took up a homestead of 160 acres. He joined up with Steve Bond and the men built furniture.

During 1865 and 1866, the men were called to join the militia to help protect the town from Indians and wrong-doers.

Children:

ROBERT III, b. 8 May 1854, Greenock, Scotland. Md. 11 Nov 1878, Sarah Alice Nelson. D. 13 Jun 1929.
DANIEL, b. 31 Jul 1856, Greenock, Scotland. Md. 25 Dec 1890, Mary Alice Barnes. D. 11 May 1949.
JOHN, (twin), b. 17 Jul 1858, Greenock, Scotland. D. 4 Jan 1860. Child.
WILLIAM, (twin), b. 17 Jul 1858, Greenock, Scotland. D. 25 Jul 1859. Child.
JAMES, b. 15 Jul 1860, Greenock, Scotland. Unmarried. D. 11 Apr 1933.
JANE, b. 6 Nov 1862, Greenock, Scotland. Md. 4 Jul 1891, Rob-

ert G. Thornton. D. 20 Feb 1897.

WILLIAM GEE, b. 17 Jun 1865, Heber, Utah. Md. 29 Dec 1895, Matilda D. Smith. D. 30 Jun 1944.

AGNES ROBERTSON, b. 26 Apr 1867, Heber, Utah. Md. 11 Jan 1899, Willard Joseph Handberg. D. 24 Jul 1930.

HENRY, b. 18 Oct 1869, Heber, Utah. Md. 26 May 1904, Elizabeth Ann Rasband. D. 14 Jan 1937.

JANETT, b. 20 Nov 1871, Heber, Utah. D. 10 Jun 1874. Child.

DAVID, b. 1 Sep 1873, Heber, Utah. Md. 20 Dec 1916, Mary Emma Giles. D. 28 Jun 1935.

JOHN ALEXANDER, b. 1 Nov 1875, Heber, Utah. Unmarried. D. 5 Apr 1962.

ELIZABETH, b. 8 Oct 1877, Heber, Utah. Md. 23 Dec 1902, Milton Musser Witt. D. 15 Dec 1939.

Submitted by: Virginia Martin

ROBERT BAIRD, III

Born: 8 May 1854, Greenock, Renfrew, Scotland
Parents: Robert Baird II and Jane Cumming
Died: 13 Jul 1929, Cowley, Wyoming
Arrived in Valley: 1862

Married: Sarah Alice Nelson
Date: 11 Nov 1878, Heber City, Wasatch, Utah
Born: Provo, Utah, Utah
Parents: Robert Baird II and Jane Cumming
Died: 2 Jun 1928, Cowley, Wyoming

Robert came to America in 1862 after his parents heard the gospel and joined the Church of Jesus Christ of Latter-day Saints. He was eight years old when they came across the plains and into the valley of the Great Salt Lake. He walked barefoot most of the way, and always said it made him tough and independent. The family settled in Heber City, Utah. The family prospered by farming, raising horses and cattle.

Robert earned enough credits in school to be able to teach, and followed that profession for many years. Robert met Sarah Alice Nelson at school and they married and were later sealed on 3 November 1881. They started their home life in Charleston, Heber Valley.

Shortly before their 11th child was born, Robert was called to serve a mission in the Southern States. He told his children many times of his mission experiences. He was released 9 June 1899.

Soon after his return, Robert and Sarah received a call to sell their home and go settle an area in Northern Wyoming. They arrived in Cowley, Wyoming, and all of the people sent there met and drew lots for the land they could own. Robert soon built a log home and prepared the land for planting. This was 1900 and one of the last calls to go settle land given by church leaders.

Robert worked hard farming his land, and he drove a wagon to Montana for supplies for residents. He planted trees, shrubs and kept bees. He worked on the school board for years. He was appreciated for his honesty, and generosity with his time and means, especially during the flu epidemic. He spent many hours delivering groceries and caring for the animals of those who were ill.

Robert loved animals and couldn't stand to see them abused. Once he saw a neighbor beating a beautiful riding horse and told him to stop or he'd have him arrested. The man stopped and told Robert he was the only man in town with enough nerve to stand up to him. Robert enjoyed camping, fishing, dancing, singing, and games.

In Cowley, Robert was a judge. In the winter months he worked on the railroad.

Sarah died as a result of an automobile accident in 1928. Robert died about a year later after an illness.

Children:

ROBERT, b. 9 May 1880, Heber, Utah. D. 29 Jun 1883. Child.
SARAH ANN, b. 15 Apr 1882, Heber, Utah. D. 27 Apr 1882. Child.
HENRY JAMES, b. 13 May 1883, Heber, Utah. D. 16 May 1883. Child.
ELIZABETH, b. 21 Jan 1885, Heber, Utah. D. 22 Jan 1885. Child.
JANE, b. 5 Mar 1886. D. 5 Mar 1886. Child.
DANIEL CUMMING, b. 16 Aug 1887, Charleston, Utah. Md. 1 Apr 1915, Ona L. Nebel. D. not listed.
ROBERT, b. 21 Jul 1889. D. 21 Jul 1889. Child.
SARAH JANE, b. 19 Jul 1891, Provo, Utah. Md. 2 Nov 1911, Charles J. Welch. D. 14 Aug 1965.
EVERETT, b. 11 Dec 1893, Provo, Utah. Md. 7 mar 1917, Marie Bassett. D.
RUBY, b. 23 Dec 1895, Provo, Utah. Md. 5 Mar 1914, David Martin. D. 28 Dec 1985.
WILLIAM WALLACE, b. 12 May 1898, Charleston, Utah. Md. 22 Mar 1919, Bertha Morrell. D. 25 Jun 1984.
FLORA, 8 Apr 1902, Cowley, Wyoming. Md. 6 Jun 1923, Marvin Beckstrom. D.

Submitted by: Virginia Martin

JAMES HYRUM BAIRD

Born: 5 Feb 1848, Quincy, Adams, Illinois
Parents: Samuel Baird and Matilda Rutledge
Died: 5 Feb 1910
Arrived in Valley: 1863

Married 1st: Fannie Emmorett Sessions
Date: 7 Mar 1870, Salt Lake City, Utah
Born: 25 Oct 1855, Bountiful, Davis, Utah
Died: 25 Feb 1908, Syracuse, Davis, Utah

Married 2nd: Margaret Ellen Randall
Date: 8 Jul 1880, Salt Lake City, Utah
Born: 31 Mar 1858, Salt lake City, Utah
Died: 30 Oct 1931, Provo, Utah, Utah

In the spring of 1864, at Centerville, Utah, James apprenticed himself to Henry Rampton to learn the blacksmith trade. In July 1866, he enlisted as a private in the Utah Territory Militia to fight the Indians. He served until September 1866.

He made two trips back east to assist immigrants crossing the plains. The first trip was to the railroad terminus at Grand Island, Nebraska, and the second to Fort Steele, Wyoming. His blacksmiths' skills were used extensively on these trips. Often he worked as a blacksmith most of the night and then rode in a wagon the next day. B.H. Roberts served as a blacksmith apprentice under James.

James married Fannie in the Salt Lake Endowment House in 1870. Margaret Ellen Randall was chosen by both to be a plural wife in 1880. There was virtually no courtship.

The two families moved many times to avoid prosecution for the practice of polygamy. He was never arrested. The families often resided in different areas or towns. They lived in Centerville, Farmington, Layton, Morgan, Mountain Green, and Woodruff, Utah; Evanston and Rock Springs, Wyoming; and various places in Colorado when he was contracting railroad grades. He made two or more trips to work on construction of the St. George Temple.

In 1894 the families moved to Syracuse, Utah. They resided in two houses across the lane from each other. He was a blacksmith, farmer, sheep and cattle rancher.

Children of 1st wife:

SYLVIA, b. 4 May 1871. D. 5 May 1871. Child.

HYRUM, b. 11 Apr 1873. Md. 25 Jun 1913, Florence L. Billings. D. 25 Jul 1963.

PERRY, b. 6 Aug 1874. D. 21 Apr 1876. Child.

MINNIE, b. 9 Feb 1875. Md. 25 May 1898, Daniel Henry Walker. D. 1 Jan 1935.

CHLOE, b. 10 Aug 1877. Md. 25 Oct 1899, James Alma Lee. D. 14 Apr 1928.

ZINA, b. 10 Jan 1879. Md. 29 Sep 1897, John William Reed. D. 5 Apr 1960.

ASA, b. 24 May 1880. Md. 23 Jun 1909, Winnifred Kirkman. D. 3 Jul 1969

ELIZA JANE, b. 17 Aug 1881. Md. 22 Nov 1916, Darius Sessions. D. 25 May 1962.

WALTER, b. 10 Mar 1883. Md. 13 Nov 1907, Amelia Tree. D. 1 Feb 1945.

EMMORETT, b. 15 Jun 1885. D. 26 Mar 1887. Child.

CHESTER, b. 14 Nov 1887. D. 7 Jan 1892. Child.

CHAUNCY, b. 31 Jan 1890. Md. 28 Jun 1921, LaPriel Smith. D. 23 Feb 1963.

CLARENCE, b.6 Jan 1892. Md. 1 Aug 1917, Afton Louisa Free. D. 22 Apr 1941.

AMELIA, b. 21 May 1893 D. 17 Nov 1893. Child.

SAMUEL, 25 Nov 1894. Md. Arial Waldemar (Div.), Md. 2nd 22 Jan 1942, Mabel Murphy. D. 7 Jun 1961.

JAMES SESSIONS, b. 27 Jun 1897. D. 6 apr 1899. Child.

JOSEPH REESE, b. 4 Aug 1899. Md. 15 Jun 1926, Ruby Arminella Huish. D. 31 Oct 1971.

Children of 2nd wife:

ALICE, b. 31 Jul 1881. D. 1 Aug 1881. Child.

WILFORD, b. 17 Oct 1882. Md. 22 Sep 1909, Gertrude Helene E. Luck. D. 3 Aug 1966.

MARGARET, b. 6 Dec 1884. Md. 29 Jun 1910, George Henry Evans. D. 20 Aug 1935.

MYRON, b. 27 Nov 1886. D. 4 Aug 1887. Child.

ORRIN RANDALL, b. 24 Sep 1888. Md. 25 Nov 1925, Almira Lambert Eldredge. D. 6 Jul 1953.

EDWIN, b. 8 Jan 1892. Md. 1 Sep 1926, Olive London Condie. D. 6 Mar 1988.

MATILDA, b. 8 Oct 1894. D. 26 feb 1896. Child.

ABNER HARLEY, b. 17 Sep 1897. Md. 11 May 1921, Hazel Rebecca Twede. D. 14 Oct 1989.

CHESTINA, b. 14 Nov 1899. Md. 2 Jun 1926, Hyrum Gordon Larsen. D. 13 Oct 1973.

RUBY, b. 4 Mar 1902. Md. 9 Jun 1927, Reuben Andersen. D. 7 Dec 1947.

Submitted by: Frederick Baird

ROBERT ERWIN BAIRD

Born: 15 May 1817, Londonderry, Ulster, Ireland
Parents: James and Elizabeth Erwin Baird
Died: 24 Aug 1875, Lynne, Weber, Utah
Arrived in Valley: 24 Jul 1847, Brigham Young Co.

Married 1st: Hannah Everhart McCullough
Date: 23 Jul 1840, West Goshen Twp, Chester, Pennsylvania
Born: 10 Dec 1817, of West Goshen Twp, Chester, Pennsylvania
Parents: John and Sarah Dunkins Rogers McCullough
Died: 8 Aug 1889, Lynne, Weber, Utah

Married 2nd: Jane Hadley
Date: 2 Oct 1856, Salt Lake City, Utah
Born: 8 Apr 1835, Cradley, Herefordshire, England
Parents: Richard D. and Mary Shooter Hadley
Died: 27 Dec 1911, Lynne, Weber, Utah

Arrived in Valley: 25 Sep 1855, Richard Ballantyne Co.

Married 3rd: Mary Hadley (sister to Jane)
Date: 12 Aug 1858, Salt Lake City, Utah
Born: 20 Apr 1837, Cradley, Herefordshire, England
Parents: Richard D. and Mary Shooter Hadley
Died: 27 Oct 1908, Lynne, Weber, Utah

Robert Erwin's father decided to emigrate to America in 1853, in the hopes of obtaining a more comfortable living. His wife had died, leaving him with eight children. They settled in Philadelphia, Pennsylvania.

Robert became a tailor by trade. He married his first wife in 1840. They were converted to the Church and baptized in August 1842. At an LDS Conference in 1843, Robert was appointed to preside over the branch in Pennsylvania. He had been a member for less than a year.

In 1844, they moved to Nauvoo, Illinois. After the martyrdom of Joseph and Hyrum, the constant persecution of the saints became more than they wanted to endure. When the saints left Nauvoo, Robert and his family left with them. When Brigham Young organized a company of men to go with him to break trail for those who would follow, Robert was one of those chosen. He told Hannah he would come back for her.

On August 16, Robert and some other men set out to return to Winter Quarters. He found Hannah where she had set out with some others to follow him west. The first winter was difficult for them. They settled in Salt Lake and Robert made clothes for the saints. In 1851, Robert moved his family to Bingham's Fort, later called Lynn. He served in many capacities of leadership in the church and community.

When he heard an address on plural marriage in 1855, he soon took Jane Hadley as a plural wife. When Johnston's Army came, he was called as a scout but the constant work weakened him. After he recovered, he took as his third wife, Jane's sister, Mary.

In January 1874, Brigham Young launched the United Order and within a month, a branch of that order was organized in Lynne.

Robert was faithful to his callings in the church and the community all his life. He was a good father and friend to everyone.

Children of 1st wife:

JOHN, b. 2 May 1841, West Whiteland, Chester, Pennsylvania.
Md. 1867, Mary Ann Heath. D. 21 Apr 1905.

JOSEPH, b. 1 Dec 1846, Nauvoo, Illinois. D. 1 Dec 1846. Child.

ELLEN, b. 1 Jun 1848, Great Salt Lake, Utah. Md. 1864, William Franklin Bishop. D. 1 Mar 1911.

ROBERT, b. 27 Dec 1850, Great Salt Lake, Utah. Md. 1 Nov 1875, Emma Jane Taylor. D. 11 Jun 1920, Lewiston, Cache, Utah.

HANNAH, b. 5 Sep 1854, Lynne, Weber, Utah. Md. 11 Apr 1891, Conrad Layman. D. 2 Dec 1933.

Children of 2nd wife:

JAMES, b. 25 Apr 1858, Ogden, Weber, Utah. Md. 4 Nov 1882, Charlotte Lund. D. 16 Feb 1890.

ELIZA, b. 7 May 1860, Lynne, Utah. Md. 6 Jan 1883, Heber "C" Taylor. D. 22 Aug 1941, Far West, Weber, Utah

JANE, b. 28 Mar 1862, Lynne, Utah. Md. 18 Oct 1883, Edward Martin Perkins. D. 26 May 1914, Mapleton, Franklin, Idaho.

JOHN, b. 17 Feb 1864, Ogden, Utah. D. 23 Dec 1920.

HANNAH, b.1 Aug 1866, Ogden, Utah. D. 7 May 1868. Child.

HANNAH MARY, b. 22 Nov 1868, Ogden, Utah. Md. 9 Jan 1895, Samuel Teancum Merrill. D. 13 Dec 1903.

MARY, b. 9 Feb 1871, Ogden, Utah. Md. 13 Mar 1901, Adelbert Owen Merrill. D. 14 Dec 1937, Preston, Franklin, Idaho.

CAROLINE, b. 23 Oct 1873, Slaterville, Utah. Md. 7 Apr 1894, William Layman. D. 27 Nov 1943, Ogden, Utah.

Children of 3rd wife:

MARY ANN, b. 2 Jun 1859, Lynne, Utah. Md. 18 Oct 1880, Elihu Moroni Allen. D. 26 Jan 1888, Weber, Utah.

ELIZABETH, b. 27 Sep 1860, Lynne, Utah. Md. 27 Nov 1880, Isaac Wilson. D. 24 Sep 1905, Byron, Big Horn, Wyoming.

WILLIAM, b. 7 Apr 1862, Lynne, Utah. Md. 1885, Sarah Ellen Hadley. D. 6 Aug 1897.

ELLEN, b. 20 Apr 1864, Lynne, Utah. Md. 1885, Cyrus Kennedy. D. 18 Sep 1887.

JEANETTE, b. 16 Apr 1866, Lynn, Utah. Md. 27 Dec 1886/7, Isaac Watson Allred. D. 14 Jun 1928, Ogden, Utah.

ROBERT ERWIN, b. 22 Sep 1868, Lynne, Utah. D. 23 May 1913, Slaterville, Weber, Utah.

JOSEPH, b. 19 May 1870, Lynne, Utah. Md. 22 Nov 1899, Margaret Helena Field. D. 3 Jan 1936, Slaterville, Utah.

FRANKLIN, b. 5 May 1872, Lynne, Utah. Md. 30 Dec 1894, Beth Zina McBride. D. 1906.

JOSEPHINE, b. 28 Jul 1873, Lynne, Utah. D. 12 Feb 1896.

Submitted by: Brent J. Belnap and Joy Belnap

JOSEPH BAKER

Born: 15 Aug 1839, near Montrose, Lee, Iowa
Parents: Simon and Mercy Young Baker
Died: 25 Oct 1925, Mendon, Cache, Utah
Arrived in Valley: 2 Oct 1847, Jedediah M. Grant, Co.

Married 1st: Lucy Amelia Pack
Date: 10 Jul 1859, Salt Lake City, Utah
Born: 22 Jun 1837, Kirtland, Lake, Ohio
Died: 16 Apr 1874, Mendon, Cache, Utah

Married 2nd: Mary Alice Morgan
Date: 26 Jul 1875

Joseph was not yet eight years old when the family left Winter Quarters for the west. He had neither hat nor shoes but drove a yoke of bulls on the "Old Seven-foot Cannon" most of the way crossing the plains. This cannon is kept as a relic in the Salt Lake Museum. He made himself some shoes from raw buffalo hides, which tightened on his feet and had to be soaked in water to get them off.

In 1859 Joseph married Lucy Amelia Pack. They resided in Salt Lake City for a time. They moved to South Bountiful, living there until 1861, when they moved to Mendon. Joseph joined his brothers who had settled there the preceding year.

Joseph and Lucy were enjoying a happy life when their son Ward Eaton died. Lucy was heart-broken and was sick from that time until she gave premature birth to another son. He died two hours after birth. Lucy died six days later, leaving a family of eight children. Joseph said of this occurrence, "I felt that I would die of grief. But God tempers the breeze to the shorn lamb, and I saw in a dream the woman that was to take her place, although she was in Wales at the time. I knew her when I first saw her, Mary Alice Morgan, and she became my wife."

Joseph Baker held many positions of trust in the Church and community. He was Elder's Quorum president from 1842 to 1866. He was Justice of the Peace of Mendon for 16 years and was Coroner of Cache County from 1894 to 1896. He felled the first tree used to build a log house in Cache Valley, Utah. He built the first stone house in Mendon, Utah. He was the first man in Mendon to sucessfully raise an orchard with choice apples. He secured grafts from choice fruit trees in the Salt Lake Valley and grafted them on to seedlings.

After Mary's death, his son William and his wife, Fern and their family moved in to help care for him. As he grew older he lost some of his hearing and was confined to a wheelchair most of the time.

He was the last of the pioneers of 1847 living in Cache Valley. He was honored at Jubilee Celebration in Salt Lake City, 24 July 1897. Joseph passed away at his home in Mendon.

Children of 1st wife:

JOSEPH LINDEN, b. 22 Mar 1860, Salt Lake City, Salt Lake, Utah. D. 10 Jan 1880.

JESSE MERRITT, b. 11 Nov 1861, Mendon, Cache, Utah. D. 13 Oct 1932.

SIMON PACK, b. 3 Jan 1864, Mendon, Cache, Utah. D. Jul 1888.

JOHN RUPERT, b. 29 Nov 1865, Mendon, Cache, Utah. D. 20 Aug 1956.

LUCY AMELIA, b. 22 Oct 1867, Mendon, Cache, Utah. D. 20 Apr 1927.

CHARLOTTE ELEANOR, b. 16 Jun 1869, Mendon, Cache, Utah. D. 14 May 1957.

TAMSON LOUELLA, b. 23 Feb 1871, Mendon, Cache, Utah. D. 29 Nov 1960.

WARD EATON, b. 15 Jan 1873, Mendon, Cache, Utah. D. 10 Aug 1873.

GEORGE CALEB, b. 10 Apr 1874, Mendon, Cache, Utah. D. 10 Apr 1874.

Submitted by: Veldon Hodgson

SIMON BAKER

Born: 18 Oct 1811, West Winfield, Herkimer, New York
Parents: Benjamin and Rebecca Tiiorn Baker
Died: 22 Oct 1863, Mendon, Cache, Utah
Arrived in Valley: 1 May 1847, Jedidiah M. Grant Co.

Married 1st: Mercy Young
Date: 31 Dec 1829, Winfield, Herkimer, New York
Born: 27 Jan 1807, Foster, Providence, Rhode Island

Died: 4 Mar 1845, Montrose, Lee, Iowa

Married 2nd: Charlotte Leavitt
Date: 8 Apr 1845, Montrose, Lee, Iowa
Born: 5 Dec 1818, Quebec, Quebec, Canada
Died: 19 Nov 1906, Mendon, Cache, Utah

Married 3rd: Elizabeth Staples
Date: 18 Mar 1853, Salt Lake City, Salt Lake, Utah
Born: 8 Jan 1838, Cheltenham, Gloucestershire, England
Died: 26 Jun 1884, Ogden, Weber, Utah

Married 4th: Emma Walker–No children
Date: 25 Mar 1853, Salt Lake City, Salt Lake, Utah
Born: 7 Jan 1837, Coventry, Warwickshire, England
Died: Unknown

Married 5th: Ann Staples
Date: 10 Feb 1857, Salt Lake City, Salt Lake, Utah (Div. 1858)
Born: 3 Apr 1832, Cheltenham, Gloucestershire, England
Died: 10 Mar 1928, Mesa, Maricopa, Arizona

Simon Baker, the third of five children, was the father of 24 children. He was a courageous man whose life was dedicated to family and church. In 1839 he moved to Chautauqua in New York, joined the Church and lived with the saints.

In the spring of 1839 he moved west and settled across the river from Nauvoo. He bought a small farm, lived on it for a year, then bought a large farm–eighty acres of tillable land, and eighty acres timber. When his first wife Mercy died, leaving four children, Simon looked for a wife and married Charlotte Leavitt. When the children saw the new wife, they shouted, "Mother, Mother."

Simon was an ingenious man who could make all kinds of mechanical devices. He always had full command of his senses when an emergency arose. These qualities made him an essential man on the westward trek. He was a devoted follower of Joseph Smith and guarded him while he slept. Simon was a good financier. He accumulated stock and property rapidly.

The fall of 1850, he was called to colonize what is now Parowan. The mountain road pass he found is known to this day as "Baker's Pass"

The following year he was released from this mission and returned to Salt Lake City, where during his next mission eight miles north of Salt Lake, he and his boys worked in a canyon called Baker's Canyon. In 1855, along with Joseph Baker, Brigham Young, Jr, and others, Simon explored Cache Valley and located a church farm where the church could range its cattle. Next he moved south to the Provo bottoms.

About September 21, 1863, Simon and his wife Elizabeth and family moved to Mendon, Utah, to locate a home, but he became sick and remained bedfast in this new home. A team was sent to Salt Lake City for his wife Charlotte so she might see him while he was alive. At the age of 53, he died of inflamation of the bowels.

Children of 1st wife:

JARVIS YOUNG, b. 13 Nov 1830. D. 27 May 1891.
AMENZO WHITE, b. 19 Jun 1832. D. 13 Jul 1907.
ALBERT MOWRY, b. 3 Oct 1833. D. 3 Sep 1909.
BETSY LUCINDA, b. 24 Jan 1835. D. 30 Jan 1912.
GEORGE WASHINGTON, b. 9 Sep 1837. D.28 Oct 1924.
JOSEPH , b. 15 Aug 1839. D. 25 Oct 1925.
LYDIA REBECCA, b. 9 Jun 1841. D. 1 Apr 1934.
MARY (twin), b. 3 Jul 1843. D. 18 Sep 1843. Child.
SARA (twin), b. 3 Jul 1843. D. 3 Dec 1932.

Children of 2nd wife:

ABIGAL LEAVITT, b. 7 Jan 1846. D. 23 Nov 1923.
BENJAMIN LEAVITT, b. 6 Jul 1847. D. 23 Apr 1933.
CHARLOTTE LEAVITT, b. 5 Apr 1849. D. Nov 1935.
SIMON LEAVITT, b. 20 Nov 1850. D. 5 May 1851. Child.
PHOEBE LEAVITT, b. 26 Aug 1852. D. 25 Apr 1870.
WIEAR LEAVITT, b. 20 Jul 1854. D. 23 Apr 1940.

SAMUEL LEAVITT, b. 26 Jun 1856. D. 15 Aug 1935.
HANNAH LEAVITT, b. 29 Dec 1857. D. 13 Apr 1943.
JEREMIAH LEAVITT, b. 18 Jun 1860. D. 10 Sep 1931.

Children of 3rd wife:

SARAH ANN STAPLES, b. 19 Aug 1854. D. 8 Mar 1856.
    Child.
JAMES STAPLES, b. 25 Aug 1856. D. 29 Jul 1934.
ELIZABETH STAPLES, b. 8 Jul 1858. D. 20 Jun 1933.
MARIA STAPLES, b. 8 Nov 1860. D. 28 Nov 1949.
MERCY STAPLES, b. 15 Jul 1863. D. Feb 1865. Child.

Children of 5th wife:

HENRY, b. 2 Jan 1858. D. 6 Aug 1939.

Submitted by: Veldon R. Hodgson

CALEB BALDWIN

Born: 2 Sep 1791, Nobletown, Orange, New York
Parents: Philemon and Esther Baldwin
Died: 11 Jun 1849, Salt Lake City, Utah
Arrived in Valley: 24 Sep 1848, Heber C. Kimball Co.

Married: Nancy Kingsbury
Date: 7 Dec 1814
Born: 14 Sep 1798, Cleveland, Ohio
Died: 12 Sep 1883, Salt Lake City, Utah

Caleb Baldwin served in the War of 1812 as an Ensign. Following the war he married Nancy Kingsbury and they settled in Cleveland, Ohio. In 1830 they were introduced to the gospel and were baptized by Parley P. Pratt.

The Baldwin and Murdock families were among the first converts to the church from Ohio. They stayed in Jackson County from 1831 to 1835, when they were forced to leave. They were so mistreated and beaten that Caleb, among others, carried the scars the rest of his life. They found refuge in Clay County. He accepted a call to Illinois in 1836. His family moved to Ray County in 1836. Persecutions persisted and eventually Caleb was taken prisoner along with others and were sentenced to be shot but it was never carried out. After the trial, Caleb, along with the Prophet and others, were sent to jail in Liberty, Missouri. They eventually escaped while on the way to a trial.

They lived in Nauvoo for a time until the exodus. They were in Heber C. Kimball's Company which arrived in 1848. Caleb died the following year from the hardships and abuse he had suffered from the mob.

He was the 13th person to be buried in the Salt Lake City Cemetery.

Children:

NANCY MARIA, b. 24 Jun 1815, Warrenville, Cuyahoga, Ohio. Md. Morgan L.Gardner. D. Unknown

CALEB CLARK, b. 3 Jun 1817, Warrenville, Ohio. Md. 29 Oct 1837. Ann Eliza Robinson. D. 2 Jan 1905.

JAMES, b. 1820, Warrenville, Ohio.

EUNICE MARY, b. 29 Mar 1820, Cleveland, Ohio. Mar. & Death unknown.

MARY ANN, b. 9 Mar 1823, Warrenville, Ohio. Md. Jun 1848, Robert Wilson. D. 28 Apr 1917.

DIANA, b.1824, Warrenville, Ohio.

WALDO, b. 1825, Warrenville, Ohio.

JAMES KINGSBURY, b. 28 Jan 1826, Warrenville, Ohio. Md. 23 Nov 1868, Martha Dummer. D. 1 Mar 1883.

ABIGAIL SHERMAN, b. 12 Jan 1828/29, Cleveland, Ohio. Md.

10 May 1854, George Washington Boyd. D. 10 Feb 1897/
98.
JULIA MURDOCK, b. 30 Apr 1831, Cleveland, Ohio. Md. 3
Jan 1851, George Washington Boyd. D. 26 Oct 1851.
ELLEN DIANA, b. 29 Aug 1834, Jackson Co., Missouri. Md.
10 May 1852, George Washington Boyd. D. 12 Jun 1864.
ELIZABETH ELMINA, b. 28 Sep 1837, Far West, Missouri. Md.
1855, Samuel Morrison Mecham. D. 12 Feb 1904.

Submitted by: LeRue W. Winget

NATHAN BENNETT BALDWIN

Born: 27 Jan 1812, Canada
Parents: Aaron Munson and Julia Bishop Baldwin
Died: 1 Nov 1891, Fillmore, Utah
Arrived in Valley: 1852/53

Married 1st: Sarah Ann Pine
Died: 11 Nov 1891, Fillmore, Utah
Married 2nd: Margaretta Oler

Nathan's father, Aaron, was pressed into service by the British to fight against his own country. He and a friend decided to
risk an escape across the frozen St. Lawrence River. He left his
family with friends. They successfully made the crossing and eight
months later, Aaron's wife Julia and two children, finally made it
to the American shore after a difficult and harrowing trip.

In 1832, Nathan heard the Mormon missionaries preach. On

28 April 1833, he was baptized. Six months later he was sent on a mission to the Eastern States. While there he received a distinct impression to go west to his brethren. He didn't know why but he went to Kirtland where he met the Prophet Joseph Smith and was asked to be a member of Zion's Camp. When Zion's Camp was disbanded, he made his way home. In 1835 he was ordained a Seventy and sent on a second mission. Later, after his return, he attended the School of Prophets.

In 1838, he and his wife Sarah went to Missouri where they were subjected to the atrocities there. They came back to Nauvoo where he was ordained a President of the 21st Quorum of Seventy.

In 1852, at Kanesville, Iowa, he found the records of the 21st Quorum of Seventy and took them to President Joseph Young in Salt Lake. He was Senior President of the 21st Quorum of Seventy, the previous three having apostatized. He settled in Fillmore and constructed the first flour mill. He was a stone mason and farmer. He helped construct many of the church buildings. He was a faithful member of the church, a good husband and father.

Children of 1st wife:

JUNIUS COLLINS. D. Infant.
JULIA ORLETTA.
NATHAN BENNETT, JR. lived to raise a family but all his sons
    died in infancy.
SARAH JANE.

Children of 2nd wife:

ANDREW VIRGIL, lived to raise a family.
JAMES WILLIAM, lived to raise a family.
GEORGE BENNETT, D. Infant.
CHARLES HENRY, D. unmarried at age 27.
JUNIUS ELI, D. Infant.
NATHANIEL, lived to raise a family.

Submitted by: Jared Baldwin

HENRY BALLARD

Born: 27 Jan 1832, Cold Ash, Thatcham, Berks, England
Parents: William and Hannah Russell Ballard
Died: 26 Feb 1908, Logan, Cache, Utah
Arrived in Valley: 16 Oct 1852, Eli B. Kelsey Co.

Married 1st: Margaret McNeil
Date: 5 May 1861, Logan, Utah
Born: 14 Apr 1846, Tranent, East Lothian, Haddingtonshire, Scotland
Parents: Thomas and Janet Reid McNeil
Died: 21 Jul 1918, Logan, Utah

Married 2nd: Emily McNeil
Date: 4 Oct 1867, Logan, Utah
Born: 19 Jun 1849, Tranent, East Lothian, Scotland
Parents: Thomas and Janet Reid McNeil
Died: 7 May 1903, Cache Junction, Utah

Henry had no education until he was nine years old. Then he was able to gain admission to a charity school, "The Blue Coat School," which he attended for four years, his only schooling. He learned quickly. Following this, he went to work to help his parents. An employee where he worked told him about the Mormon Church. He was baptized in 1849.

He had lived with his brother George, but when George learned about the church, he offered Henry everything a young man could want to give up the church, when Henry refused, George turned him out without anything. Henry returned to his parents and tried to share the church with them with no success.

He got Typhoid Fever about this time. The elders came and administered to him and by the next day he was well. It so impressed his parents that they were soon baptized.

His trip from St. Louis up the river was a harrowing experience. He arrived at Winter Quarters without any money or clothes but was able to work his way west herding sheep for one of the families. He finally arrived in the Valley and met his parents, who had arrived earlier.

He served in the militia for 18 years, and went to Provo with his parents during the Johnston's Army scare. Upon his return, he went to Logan to find a home. In 1860 he and his parents moved to Logan.

He helped haul timber for the Logan Temple. He remained active in the church. In 1864 he went east and guided a group of saints to the valley. He served a term in the State Penitentiary for polygamy. He served a mission in England, was a bishop and later, a patriarch. He served the community, the church, and the people all his life.

Children of 1st wife:

MARGARET HANNAH, b. 18 Jan 1863, Logan, Utah. D. 13 Jul 1874, Logan.

HENRY WILLIAM, b. 20 Sep 1864, Logan, Utah. Md. 2 Oct 1884, Ada Elvira Davidson. D. 11 Nov 1936, Benson, Utah.

THOMAS McNEIL, b. 8 Jul 1866, Logan, Utah. Md. 2 Apr 1890, Phoebe John Smith. D. 9 Jan 1933, Salt Lake City, Utah.

CHARLES JAMES,(twin) b. 15 May 1868, Logan, Utah. D. 28 Sep 1869. Child.

JANET McNEIL,(twin) b. 15 May 1868, Logan, Utah. D. 18 Sep 1869. Child.

GEORGE ALBERT, b. 9 Apr 1870, Logan, Utah. D. 7 Jul 1874. Child.

MELVIN JOSEPH, b. 9 Feb 1873, Logan, Utah. Md. 17 Jun 1896, Martha Annabell Jones. D. 30 Jul 1939, Salt Lake City, Utah.

ELLEN PHOEBE, b. 19 Sep 1875, Logan, Utah. D. 12 Dec 1889.

REBECCA ANN, b. 8 Feb 1878, Logan, Utah. Md. 17 Jun 1896, Louis Samuel Cardon. D. 12 Sep 1972, Logan, Utah.

LETTIE MAY, b. 13 Dec 1881, Logan, Utah. Md. 22 Feb 1899, George Washington Squires. D. 10 Oct 1935, Logan, Utah.

MARY MYRTLE, b. 21 Aug 1885, Logan, Utah. Md. 3 Sep 1908, Daniel Ray Shurtliff. D. 8 Feb 1975, Salt Lake City, Utah.

Children of 2nd wife:

EMILY ELIZABETH, b. 12 Feb 1870, Logan, Utah. D. 30 Jul 1870. Child.

WILLARD RUSSELL, b. 26 Nov 1872, Logan, Utah. Md. 10 Jun 1896, Bessie Treherne Griffin. D. 13 Apr 1929, Logan, Utah.

FRANKLIN HYRUM, b. 28 Nov 1874, Logan, Utah. Md. 8 Jan 1902, Sarah Elizabeth Stevens. D. 15 Feb 1949, Salt Lake City, Utah.

ERNEST REID, b.20 Oct 1876, Logan, Utah. Md. 22 Jun 1904, Amanda Dorthea Miller. D. 12 Dec 1961, Logan, Utah.

LYDIA JANE, b. 9 Sep 1878, Logan, Utah. Md. 9 Jun 1897, William Henry Griffin. D. 25 Dec 1961, Salt Lake City, Utah.

JENNIE LULU, b. 4 Nov 1880, Logan, Utah. Md. 6 Dec 1899, Thomas Franklin Griffin. D. 22 Sep 1959.

AMY EUGENE, b. 13 Jan 1885, Logan, Utah. D. 15 Oct 1901.

Submitted by: Janet Ralph

WILLIAM BALLARD

Born: Feb 1795, Purley, Berks, England
Parents: Barnard and Mary Elms Ballard
Died: 19 May 1885, Logan, Utah

Arrived in Valley: 3 Sep 1852, O. A. Smoot

Married: Hannah Russell
Date: 16 Oct 1820, Berks, England
Born: 9 Apr 1799, Hannington, Hamps, England
Died: 19 Sep 1884, Logan, Utah

William's mother died when he was young and he was raised by his father's second wife, Ann. He wasn't happy in his home so he ran away at an early age. He worked as a farm hand, had no schooling, but kept himself clean and honorable.

William and his wife Hannah joined the Church seven months after their son, Henry. William was a gardner, serving an English Nobleman as caretaker of his large estate. When he and his wife determined to go to America, their son Henry helped them obtain help through the Perpetual Emigration Fund. They crossed the ocean and country one month ahead of their son Henry. They located in Mill Creek, southeast of Salt Lake.

When Johnston's Army came, William and his wife moved south to Santaquin where he built a shanty to shelter them. After the scare, they moved back to Mill Creek.

William and Henry traveled to Logan where they obtained property. While William went back for his wife, Henry built a small house for them. William planted a nice orchard and garden.

They worked in the temple and kept close to the church all their lives. William was ordained a patriarch in 1873. When his parents became too feeble to take care of their home, Henry brought them to live with him. William was always kind and gentle and well liked by everyone, especially his grandchildren.

Children:

CHARLES, b. 10 Jan 1821, Newberry, Berks, England. Md. Rebecca Hatton. D. 28 Jun 1878.
GEORGE, b. 26 Dec 1823, Newberry, England. Md. Elizabeth Green. D. 22 Aug 1864.
JOHN, b. 18 Aug 1826, Newberry, England. Md. Sarah Hawkins. D. 12 Feb 1883.

HENRY, b. 27 Jan 1832, Cold Ash, Thatcham, Berks, England. Md. 1st, 5 May 1861, Margaret McNeil. Md. 2nd, 4 Oct 1867, Emily McNeil. D. 26 Feb 1908, Logan, Utah.

Submitted by: Janet Ralph

CHRISTIAN PETER BARENTZEN (BERNTZEN)
(AKA Christian Barnson)

Born: 17 Aug 1823, Halslev, Maribo, Denmark
Parents: Bernt and Laurentze Tommerup Barentzen
Died: 19 Jul 1880, Manti, Sanpete, Utah
Arrived in Valley: 30 Sep 1853, John E. Forsgren Co.
    Scandinavian saints.

Married: Maria Anderson
Date: 8 Jan 1853, in the Liverpool harbor aboard ship
Born: 30 Sep 1828, Maribo, Maribo, Denmark
Parents: Anders and Maren Wilhelmsen Pedersen (Petersen)
Died: 7 Oct 1873, Manti, Sanpete, Utah

Christian Peter and Maria were baptized on the same day in September 1852. The members of the church were severely persecuted in their town so the family, along with many other members, decided to emigrate to America. There were 256 saints in the group. It was a most difficult journey due to the weather and lack of proper food and water.

They landed in New Orleans, went up the Mississippi River to Keokuk, and from there west by ox team and wagon.

The majority of the Danish saints went on to Spring City, Sanpete, Utah, which was called "Little Denmark." They had been called to go to this area to help strengthen the settlement against the Indians. Things became so bad that President Young told them to move into Manti. After they left, the Indians burned everything.

He was a devoted father, husband and member of the church. He served as Justice of the Peace. After his wife died, he tried to be mother as well as father to his children for seven years. His seven-year-old daughter found him one day, kneeling in a position of prayer where he had died.

Children:

LOURENCE, b. 27 Jun 1854, Manti, Utah. D. Oct 1854. Child.
CHRISTIAN DIDLOW, b. 15 Jul 1855, Manti, Utah. Md. 20 Dec 1883, Naomi Wood. D. 22 Oct 1888.
BERNARD, b. 27 Oct 1857, Manti, Utah. Md. 28 Dec 1882, Elizabeth Hannah Braithwaite. D. 1 Apr 1933.
CARL PETER, b. 1 Dec 1859, Manti, Utah. Md. Feb 1897, Jessie White. D. 4 Mar 1917.
FREDERICK, b. 13 Jan 1861, Manti, Utah. Unmarried. D. 29 Nov 1918
WILLIAM, b. 19 Feb 1863, Manti, Utah. Unmarried. D. 24 Oct 1894.
JOHN, b. 1 Apr 1866, Manti, Utah. Md. 10 Apr 1891, Hannah E. Whitlock. D. 29 May 1929.
THERESA, b. 24 Mar 1868, Manti, Utah. Md. 1st, 19 Jan 1891, Roswell M. Rogers, Md. 2nd, Seraphin Rechnitzer, Md. 3rd Mr. Thomas, Md. 4th William Curry. D. 21 Jul 1945.
ANDREW, b. 12 Mar 1870, Manti, Utah. Md. 1 May 1896, Vivian Smith. D. 6 Nov 1921.
MAY ELIZABETH (twin), b. 1 May 1872. D. 1872. Child.
MARY ANN (twin), b. 1 May 1872, Manti, Utah. D. 1872. Child.
MARIA VICTORIA, b. 16 Sep 1873, Manti, Utah. Md. 25 Mar 1895, Alfonzo Bryant Jolley. D. 16 Sep 1952.

Submitted by: Zella Matheson

ISRAEL BARLOW

Born: 13 Sep 1806, Granville, HeMd.en, Mass.
Parents: Jonathan and Annis Gillette Barlow.
Died: 1 Nov 1883, Bountiful, Davis, Utah
Arrived in Valley: 23 Sep 1848, Brigham Young Co.

Married 1st: Elizabeth Haven
Date: 23 Feb 1840, Quincy, Adams, Illinois
Born: 28 Dec 1881, Holliston Middlesex, Mass.
Parents: John and Elizabeth Howe Haven
Died: 25 Dec 1892, Bountiful, Davis, Utah

Married 2nd: Elizabeth (Betsy) Barton
Date: 28 Jan 1846.

Married 3rd: Lucy Heap
Date: 2 Dec 1855.
Born: 24 Sep 1836, Litchfield, Staffs, England
Parents: James and Sarah Waters Heap
Died: 4 Jul 1901, Afton, Wyoming

Married 4th: Cordelia Maria Dalrymple
Date: 27 May 1865.

Israel Barlow was a very spiritual person, having been taught by his parents and his own convictions that believing in Christ and living a righteous life was essential. His friends made a mockery of him so he decided if he was to be a Christian he would have to go it alone.

His family moved to Mendon, New York, in 1825. In 1831

he heard the missionaries when they visited his home. He soon determined that what they said was what he wanted. He rode 200 miles on his horse to meet the Prophet. Being impressed with what he saw and learned, he returned to Mendon and was baptized. The family moved to Kirkland where they helped build the temple. Israel, being a sixth cousin to the Prophet Joseph, was very close to him.

Israel and his family endured the Missouri problems but fled and found safety in Quincy, Illinois. It was here that Israel and Elizabeth were married, she having joined the Church earlier.

Elizabeth was a college graduate, while Israel had been deprived of much of his early schooling. Elizabeth taught the Prophets and many of the other church leaders' children.

Because of a friendship Israel had made with a Dr. Isaac Galland, the saints were able to purchase much of the land in Commerce, which later became Nauvoo.

When the exodus came, Brigham Young asked him to stay behind and help others prepare to leave. He didn't leave until 1847-8. He filled a mission to England, bringing 584 saints to the States.

Shortly before his death he was ordained Stake Patriarch.

Children of 1st wife:

JAMES NATHANIEL, b. 8 May 1841, Nauvoo, Illinois. D. 8 May 1841. Child.

ISRAEL, b. 5 Sep 1842, Nauvoo, Illinois. Md. 1st, 26 Apr 1863, Annie Yeates. Md. 2nd, 15 Jun 1917, Mary Elizabeth Beebe. D. 24 Nov 1923.

PAMELA ELIZABETH, b. 6 Sep 1844, Nauvoo, Illinois. Md. 10 Sep 1861, David Wilkin Thompson. D. 29 Apr 1925.

IANTHUS HAVEN, b. 1 May 1846, Nauvoo, Illinois. Md. 7 Dec 1867, Hannah Wintle. D.23 Mar 1907.

JOHN HAVEN, b. 27 Jul 1848, Platt Co., Wyo. Md. 24 Oct 1868, Elizabeth Cook. D. 9 Apr 1922.

MARY ANTENETT, b. 13 Nov 1850, Bountiful, Utah. Md. 7 Dec 1868, David Orson Willey. D. 5 Mar 1936.

WILLARD ALBERT (twin), b. 3 Feb 1854, Salt Lake City, Utah. D. 28 Oct 1854. Child.

WILFORD (twin), b. 3 Feb 1854, Salt Lake City, Utah. Md. 24 Jan 1876, Laura Ann Jackson. D. 9 Sep 1926.

Children of 3rd wife:

TRUMAN HEAP, b. 12 Jun 1857, Bountiful, Utah. Md. 1st, 28 Nov 1878, Fanny Call. D. 19 Feb 1913.

SARAH ISABEL, b. 26 Jun 1859, Bountiful, Utah. Md. 26 Jun 1879, Joseph Holbrook Call. D. 14 Oct 1941.

ANNIS JANETTE, b. 30 Sep 1860, Bountiful, Utah. Md. 28 Oct 1880, Chester Vinson Call. D. 23 Jun 1939.

EMMA JANE, b. 19 Aug 1862, Bountiful, Utah. Md. 28 Oct 1880, Ira Call. D. 27 Oct 1929.

HYRUM HEAP, b. 30 Aug 1864, Bountiful, Utah. Md. 1st, 2 Jan 1889, Margaret Burton. D. 14 Feb 1895.

MINNIE RETTE, b. 17 Nov 1865, Bountiful, Utah. Md. 5 Sep 1884, Chester Vinson Call. D. 9 Jan 1901.

GRANVILLE, b. 31 Jul 1867, Bountiful, Utah. Md. 18 Dec 1889, Eliza Ann Burningham. D. 27 Dec 1955.

NATHAN, b. 26 Mar 1869, Bountiful, Utah. Md. 1st, 24 Jun 1891, Dora Matilda Tolman. D. 18 Nov 1946.

Submitted by: Elaine Evans

JOHN MOLYNEUX BARNES

Born: 15 Nov 1830, Manchester, Lancs, England
Parents: Henry and Maria Barnes
Died: 30 Mar 1909, Wellsville, Utah
Arrived in Valley: 26 Sept 1852, Jacob Gates Co.

Married 1st: Eleanor Wilson
Date: 1852, Salt Lake City, Utah
Parents: Elijah and Martha Wilson

Married 2nd: Angeline Jenkins
Date: (after death of Eleanor)

John Molyneux Barnes came to America with his oldest sister Margaret, who had married Joseph Woodward. He was 12 years old at the time. His mother sent him with the request that when he was old enough, he should do the work in the temple for all the family he was leaving behind. His parents had embraced the gospel early in his life.

The group came to America in 1842, remaining in the Eastern States for a time. When the saints settled in Nauvoo, John was taken into the home of Joseph Smith where he lived as part of the family. He helped in the fields or wherever he was needed.

He crossed the plains with the Jacob Gates Company. Shortly after his arrival there, and his marriage to Eleanor, they moved to Grantsville. Several of their children were born there. In 1860 they moved to Wellsville, Cache, Utah, where he built a log house. At first it had a dirt roof but later he replaced it with a wooden roof and added a lean-to to make more room for their growing family. They made their living from the land.

After Eleanor's death, he married Angeline Jenkins and had three more children. He died and is buried in Wellsville, Utah.

Children of 1st wife:

EPHRAIM, (twin), D. Infant.
MANASSAH, (twin), Md. Eliza Allen, lived in Richmond, Utah
MARTHA MARIA, D. age 1 year.
MARY ELLEN. Md. Robert Baxter, lived in Mt. Sterling and
    then Hyrum, Utah.
SARAH JANE, Md. John Wyatt, lived in Wellsville, Utah.
JOHN W., Md. Sarah Ann Anderson, lived in Rexburg, Idaho.
HENRY, was supposedly killed in a cattle drive.
HARRIET, D. at age of nine years.

MARGARET ANN, Md. James Bradshaw, lived in Wellsville and Mt. Sterling.
JOSEPH, Md. Inez Miner, lived in Nephi, Utah.
RACHEL, Md. William Garrett. D. at age 33.
JEANETTE, Md. William Jones, widowed after five children.

Children of 2nd wife:

PHOEBE, Md. Thomas S. Bradshaw, lived in Wellsville, Utah.
MARY, Md. Nickoli Jorgenson, lived in Hyrum, Utah.
WILLIAM, Md. Martha Christofferson, lived in Montpelier, Idaho.

Submitted by: John Baxter

WILLIAM BARNES

Born: 17 Oct 1789, Sandy, Bedfordshire, England
Parents: Thomas and Frances Day Barnes
Died: 1880, age 91, Kaysville, Utah
Arrived in Valley: 16 Oct 1853, Appleton Harmon Co.

Married: Elizabeth Jeffries
Date: 4 Nov 1816, Bedfordshire, England

William Barnes and his wife and their family, left England 19 March 1853 on the ship "Falcon." The day after their arrival in the Valley, they went to Kaysville, Utah, where their daughter Ann, who had come earlier, lived. They lived with her until the next summer when they were able to build and move into their own house.

William was a farmer. He was a good man. He is buried in Kaysville, Utah.

Children:

WILLIAM JEFFRIES, b. 20 Aug 1820, Sandy Bedfordshire, England. Md. Frances Fitzjohn Chapman. D. 14 Nov 1893, Kaysville, Utah
JOHN R., b. Bedfordshire, England. Md. Emily Shelton.
ANN, b. Bedfordshire, England. Md. William B. Smith, Oct 1838, Bedfordshire, England. Arrived in Valley, 17 Sep 1850.
SARAH, b. Bedfordshire, England.

Submitted by: Inez Barker

WILLIAM JEFFRIES BARNES

Born: 20 Aug 1820, Sandy, Bedfordshire, England
Parents: William and Elizabeth Jeffries Barnes
Died: 14 Nov 1893, Kaysville, Utah
Arrived in Valley: 16 Oct 1853, Appleton Harmon Co.

Married 1st: Frances Fitzjohn Chapman
Date: England

Married 2nd: Mary Simmons
Married 3rd: Sarah Sugden

William was a farmer. He later developed a freighting business. He was also a stock man. He helped build the Old Fort wall, helped dig ditches and canals, helped build the meeting house, and was an active member of the church.

He took an active part in the move south when Johnston's Army came to the valley. In 1870 he filled a mission to the Muddy in Dixie, returning to Kaysville after.

He was a large man of light complexion and a sunny dispostion. He was honest and generous to a fault. On the church records, he was listed as one of the largest doners to the building of the school and meeting house and in giving food to help the emigrants. He was very genial. He had a host of friends.

He was killed in a freighting accident.

Children of 1st wife:

Frances had eleven children.

Children of 2nd and 3rd wives:

They had 12 children between them.

Submitted by: Inez Barker

JAMES BARNETT

Photograph not available

Born: Chr. 6 Dec 1812, Eckington, Worcester, England
Parents: William and Elizabeth Fouch Barnett
Died: 22 Oct 1894, Bountiful, Davis, Utah, bur. Kaysville, Utah
Arrived in Valley: 15 Sep 1866, William Henry Chipman Co.

Married 1st: Elizabeth Moseley

Date: 14 Dec 1837, England
Died: 21 Oct 1850, England

Married 2nd: Mary Ann Lacey Green (widow)
Date: abt 1852, England
Arrived in Valley: 1871
Died: 18 Jun 1913, Bountiful, Utah, bur. Kaysville, Utah

James Barnett lived at Crowle and Stoke Prior, Droitwich Dodderhill Parish, Worcester, England. Some of his children were born there. He was baptized into the Church in 1842.

James not only raised his own children but cared for the children of his second wife's first husband.

In 1866 James, son John, and step-daughter Sarah Ann, came to America, leaving his wife Mary Ann, and the other children to come later. After arriving in the Valley 15 September 1866, they went on to West Jordan to live, where they stayed about three years. Sarah had married on the plains.

James and his son were sent to Wanship, Summit County to help settle the area. Between then and 1871, the rest of the children came over, and in 1871, Mary Ann and a daughter, Eliza, came. In 1875, they moved their family to "Sandridge," later called West Layton, Utah, where they homesteaded 160 acres. Mary Ann was a midwife and nurse and was called many times to help others.

In 1877, James was ordained a high priest and as such was given the calling to gather the fast offerings and deliver them to the poor. While performing this duty one day, his horse ran away and James was badly injured, resulting in his death sometime later.

Children of 1st wife:

ANN, b. 26 Apr 1839.
WILLIAM, b. 2 Apr 1841.
EDWIN, b. 22 Mar 1843.
GEORGE, b. 24 May 1845. Died young.
JAMES, b. 30 Oct 1847. Died young.
HARRIET, b. 29 Jul 1850.

Children of 2nd wife by 1st husband:

SARAH ANN GREEN, b. 25 May 1843.
EMILY GREEN, b. 8 Oct 1845.
JOSEPH GREEN, b. 1847.
MARK GREEN, b. 14 Sep 1850.

Children by James Barnett:

THOMAS, b. 25 May 1853.
LUCY, b. 14 Mar 1856.
JOHN, b. 20 Oct 1858.
ELIZA, b. 15 Mar 1861.
EPHRAIM, b. 27 Jul 1863.

Submitted by: Bertha O'Reilly

ALMA BARNEY

Born: 14 Jul 1848, Springfield, Sangamon, Illinois
Parents: Henry and Marcy Lucas Barney
Died: 27 Dec 1930, Parowan, Iron, Utah, Bur. Panguitch, Utah
Arrived in Valley: 1850

Married 1st: Alice Ann Gardner (or Bone)
Date: 22 Sep 1871, Kanarra, Utah
Born: 15 Aug 1850, Oving, Sussex, England
Parents: Henry and Harriett Ingram Bone (or Gardner)
Died: 1 Apr 1926, Panguitch, Garfield, Utah

Married 2nd: Mary Ardella Gibson–No children
Date: 1 Jul 1927
Born: 10 Dec 1869
Parents: George H. and Ann Newman Gibson
  Widow of William Isom

Alma Barney's parents brought their family across the plains arriving in the valley in 1850. They helped settle Provo, Manti, Parowan, Harmony, Virgin City, and Grafton, Utah. Alma always had a loyalty to the church and taught his children the value of the gospel.

When they first married, the town of Panguitch was being settled, so Alma and Alice became some of the first settlers. They lived in a log cabin for nine years after which they built a substantial brick home and raised their eight children.

Alma was a hard worker and it was said no weeds ever grew on Alma's farm. He had one of the first automobiles in Garfield County, a 1912 Chalmers, which he won in a national catalog contest by selling the most farm equipment.

He was active in local theatrical productions. He was superintendent of the Sunday School for 23 years after which he was called to the high council. It has been said that before the advent of the radio, he told a congregation that the time would come when they would be able to sit in their seats in their own remote chapels, not only hear, but also see the general conference from Salt Lake City.

Children of 1st wife:

ALMA Jr., b. 25 Jun 1872, Panguitch, Utah. D . 18 Sep 1873.
HARRIET, b. 10 Jun 1874, Panguitch, Utah. D. 15 Aug 1874.
GEORGE HENRY, b. 19 Jan 1876, Panguitch, Utah. Md. 1st, 28 Apr 1897, Susan Ellen Tebbs. Md. 2nd, 14 Jul 1906, Edith Porter. Md. 3rd, 1 Dec 1920, Adeline Gottfredson. D. 27 Dec 1930, Centerfield,Sanpete, Utah.
MARY ALICE, b 17 Jan 1878, Panguitch, Utah. Md. 20 Jan 1904, Clarence Woodson Showalter. D. 22 Sep 1954.

SARAH ELIZABETH, b. 3 Jun 1880, Panguitch, Utah. Md. 26 Nov 1913, John Arthur Evans. D. 13 Apr 1948.

EDGAR LAWRENCE, b. 10 May 1882, Panguitch, Utah. Unmarried. D. 20 Dec 1898.

JOSEPHINE, b. 13 Jul 1884, Panguitch, Utah. Md. 17 Jun 1908, William Delbert Smith. D. 14 Mar 1976.

JESSE NEWTON, b. 2 May 1887, Panguitch, Utah. Unmarried. D. 24 Jan 1924.

GRACE ODELIA, b. 11 Jan 1890, Panguitch, Utah. Md. 7 Sep 1910, Dudley D. Tebbs. D. 6 Mar 1941.

AVA DELILAH, b. 3 Feb 1893, Panguitch, Utah. Unmarried. D. 10 Jan 1926.

Submitted by: Pat Grey

CHARLES BARNEY

Born: 23 Mar 1783, Manchester, Bennington, Vermont
Parents: Luther and Abigail Winship Barney
Died: 28 Feb 1865, Spanish Fork, Utah
Arrived in the Valley: 12 Sep 1852, Bryant Jolley Co.

Married 1st: Mercy Yeoman
Date: 1805, New York
Born: Oct 1785, Connecticut
Parents: Stephen and Abigail Fountain Yeoman
Died: 25 Oct 1825, near Good Hope, Fayette, Ohio

Married 2nd: Deborah Riffle Street
Date: 21 Sep 1826, Ohio

Born: 22 Sep 1808
Parents: George and Margaret Helmick Riffle, adopted by step-
father William Street.
Died: 18 Sep 1888, Spring City, Sanpete, Utah

Charles Barney, with his parents, moved to New York about
1795. After his marriage they moved to Knox County, Ohio, where
Charles served for a time in the War of 1812.

In 1825, his wife died after the birth of their eighth child.
Charles and his older boys went to Illinois to prepare for the family to follow. When he returned for the rest of the children, the
neighbor asked to go with them. He agreed only if they would
marry. He was 42 and she was 18. It was a good marriage.

From Illinois they moved to Iowa where they came in contact
with Mormon missionaries and were converted. In 1841, Charles
sold his farm and moved to Carthage where he was active in the
church. They were forced out with the other saints and spent some
years in the Council Bluffs area before finally migrating to Utah
in 1852. They lived in Provo, Spanish Fork (Palmyra) and Spring
City, Utah. He is buried in Spanish Fork.

Children of 1st wife:

LUTHER, b. 8 Sep 1806, Niagara, New York.
LEWIS, b. 8 Sep 1808, Niagara, New York. Md. 1st, 11 Apr
1833, Elizabeth Turner. Md. 2nd Elizabeth Beard Tippets.
D. 5 Nov 1895.
LUCIEN, b. Mar 1811, Niagara New York.
LURINDA, b. 1813, Knox Co., Ohio.
HENRY, b. 1 Jun 1815/16, Winchester, Knox, Ohio. Md. 1st, abt
1847, Marcy Lucas. Md. 2nd, 10 Oct 1863, Mary Powell. D.
Cannonville, Garfield, Utah.
WALTER, b. 7 Jan 1819, Wayne, Fayette, Ohio. Md. 1st, 1849,
Caroline Haws. Md. 2nd, Susan Zabrisca or Zabriskie. D. 14
Apr 1917.
JOHN, b. 15 Apr 1823, Wayne, Fayette, Ohio. Md. Abigail Wiley
or Washburn. D. 3 Jun 1879.
LUCINDA, b. 1825, Paint Creek, Highland, Ohio.

Children of 2nd wife:

EMERINE, b. 12 Aug 1828, Lake Fork, Logan, Illinois. Md. Benjamin Leland.

BETSEY or ELIZABETH , b. Mar 1830, Lake Fork. Md. Benjamin Leland.

LOUISA, b. 1831, Lake Fork. D. Infant.

BENJAMIN FRANKLIN, b.12 Mar 1832, Springfield, Sangamon, Illinois. Md. 1st, 27 Apr 1849, Caroline Beard. Md. 2nd 2 Apr 1856, Priscilla Ann Shepherd. Md. 3rd, 7 Dec 1865, Caroline Neilson. D. 7 Dec 1904.

MARGARET, b. 8 Nov 1834, Springfield, Illinois. Md. Joseph Gilbert. D. 30 Oct 1915.

THOMAS JEFFERSON, b. 25 Dec 1836, Springfield, Illinois. Md. Lucinda Box. D. 8 Dec 1865.

WILLIAM STREET, b. 30 Mar 1841, Nauvoo, Illinois. Md. 26 Feb 1865, Hannah Stoddard. D. 3 May 1875.

SARAH JANE, b. 13 May 1845, Nauvoo, Illinois. Md. 14 Nov 1860, Joseph Smith Black. D. 23 May 1934.

Submitted by: Pat Grey

EDSON BARNEY

Born: 30 Jun 1806, Ellisburg, Jefferson, New York
Parents: Royal and Rachel Marsh Barney
Died: 5 Feb 1905, Provo, Utah
Arrived in Valley: 4 Jul 1850, Capt Edward Hunter's Co.

Married 1st: Lillis Ballou Comstock (widow)

Date: 1 Jan 1831, Amherst, Lorain, Ohio
Born: 20 Apr 1805, Litchfield, Herkimer, New York
Parents: Seth and Sophia Ballou
Died: 22 Dec 1892, Provo, Utah

Married 2nd: Louisa Walker
Date: 10 May 1847, Little Pigeon, Ohio
Born: 14 Jul 1822, Ohio
Died: 15 Apr 1888, Annabella, Sevier, Utah

Edson Barney worked at farming with his father in the summer until 1831, when he married Lillis. Shortly after on 10 May
1831, he and his family joined the Church. He worked in a saw
mill and as a stone cutter. He went to Missouri with the Prophet
to redeem the land, and returned home in time to see his young
son, Olney, die.

He was called on a mission to Ohio, Pennsylvania, and New
York, and returned home in the fall. He did carpenter work on the
temple and helped build a carpenter shop for the church. During
the winter he studied the Hebrew language.

While starting to move to Nauvoo, he was arrested and put in
jail. After bearing his testimony to some who had come to talk to
him, he was released and proceeded to Nauvoo with his family.

He joined the Nauvoo Legion and was made Captain. In 1844,
he was called on a mission to Ohio where he labored until the
death of the Prophet. They moved to Iowa for a year and then left
in 1848 for Council Bluffs. He and his family stayed in the area
for over a year working. They finally were able to leave for the
Valley in the Orson Hyde Company. They arrived in August 1852.

He helped build several saw mills in Salt Lake and Provo. In
the spring of 1856 he was again called on a mission to, Las Vegas, to help with some construction. After his return home, he
farmed, was a member of the City Council, Captain of the Silver
Greys, and served for a time as Justice of the Peace in Provo.

In 1858 he was called on an exploring mission to Las Vegas
area and south of Provo, which he directed. He was in charge of
several other men. He moved his family south to St. George. In
1905, Edson Barney was believed to be the oldest man in the

157

state and oldest in church membership. He was 98 when he died.

Children of 1st wife:

DANIELSON BUREN, b. 14 Sep 1831, Amherst, Lorain, Ohio.
    Md. 1st, 23 Apr 1857, Laura Matthews. Md. 2nd, 6 Jan 1885,
    Sophia Arkansas Hulsey. D. 12 Jan 1922, Thatcher, Graham,
    Arizona.
OLNEY AMMON, b. 19 Mar 1833, Amherst, Ohio. D. 12 Aug
    1834. Child.
ALICE MALENA, b. 25 May 1835, Kirtland, Lake, Ohio. Md. 11
    Dec 1853, Alexander Wilkins. D. 13 Nov 1916, Provo, Utah.
ELIZA ARABELL, b. 10 Dec 1837, Ruthland, Lake, Ohio. Md.
    7 Feb 1857, D. 9 May 1906, Coalville, Utah.
ALICE CELINDA, b. 14 Aug 1839, St. Joseph, Berrien, Mis-
    souri. Md. Horace Knewell or Nevil. D.7 Nov 1874.
EDSON ALROY, b. 4 Apr 1843, Nauvoo, Illinois. Md. Jul 1865,
    Sarah Ann Smith. D. Jul 1865.
JOSEPH SETH, b. 16 Aug 1845, Nauvoo, Illinois. Md. 14 Nov
    1883, Lucy Ellen Heaps. D. 26 Dec 1939, Escalante, Utah.

Children of 2nd wife:

LUCY MATILDA, b. 10 Mar 1848, Winter Quarters, Nebraska.
    D. 10 Dec 1848. Child.
PARTHA ANN, b. 17 Jun 1850, Pottawattamie, Iowa. Md. 9
    Oct 1866, Isaac Hunt. D.8 Apr 1928, St. George, Utah.
LILLIS LOUISA, b. 29 Sep 1852, Provo, Utah. Md. 30 Jan 1871,
    Elisha Burns Keyes. D. 3 Aug 1917, Annabella, Utah.
ROYAL HYRUM, b. 12 Aug 1854, Provo, Utah. Md. 15/17 Apr
    1878, Martha Sophia Jacobsen. D. 5 Jun 1925, Annabella, Utah.
JAMES ALEXANDER, b. 26 Aug 1856, D. 16 Oct 1859. Child.
RACHEL MARSH, b. 29 Aug 1857, Provo, Utah. D. 25 Sep
    1857. Child.
MARTHA ROSETTA, b. 2 Nov 1859, Provo, Utah. Md. 2 Dec
    1875, John Eugene Davis or Willia. D. 15 Nov 1932,
    Annabella, Utah.

EMMA JANE, b. 9 Aug 1859, Provo, Utah. D. 24 Sep 1867.
ELLEN URSELENA, b. 26 Jul 1862, Parowan, Utah. Md. 1st, 2
    Jul 1879, Edwin Thore Thurston. Md. 2nd, 29 Sep 1938,
    Thomas H. Wilson. D. 14 Nov 1951, Holladay, Utah.

Submitted by: Donna Bird

HENRY BARNEY

Born: 1 Jun 1816, Winchester, Knox, Ohio
Parents: Charles and Mercy Yeoman Barney
Died: after 1887, Cannonville, Utah
Arrived in Valley: 1850

Married 1st: Marcy Lucas
Date: abt 1847, Illinois
Born 25 Dec 1814, Clinton Co., Ohio
Parents: Thomas and Sarah Hoblet Lucas
Died: 20 Nov 1896, Escalante, Utah

Married 2nd: Tiptoe, Indian woman–No children
Date: about 1858, for short time.

Married 3rd: Mary Powell
Date: 10 Oct 1862, Salt Lake City, Utah
Born: 10 Mar 1847, London, Middlesex, England
Parents: James Thomas Henry and Sarah Brittle Powell
    She married 2nd Joseph James Cooper.
Died: 15 Oct 1932, Bexley, Franlin, Ohio

Married 4th: Mary Bramall
Date: 21 Dec 1882, St. George, Utah.
Born: 17 Jan 1849, Manchester, England

Henry Barney, with his family, moved to Illinois and then to Iowa, where they joined the Church. They settled in Nauvoo, Illinois, where he married a young widow with six children. They had a son in Springfield, Illinois, and shortly after, made the trek to the Valley. They lived in Provo and Manti where two more children were born, and then they went south to help settle several communities, New Harmony, Grafton, and Virgin City. He served as a bishop's counselor for a time.

Henry was reputed to be an adopted son of John D. Lee. They lived in New Harmony at the time of the Mountain Meadow Massacre. He was not directly involved but remained behind to take the water turns of those who went. He is listed as receiving some of the spoils.

He operated the first molasses mill in Dixie. He took to wife an Indian girl amid some controversy. Some time later, his first wife, Marcy, took the children and went to Kanarra.

In 1863 he married Mary Powell and they helped settle the "Muddy Mission," and later Monroe, Utah. Henry spent his last years in Cannonville, Utah, where he died in a cave-in while digging an irrigation canal.

Children of 1st wife:

ALMA, b. 14 Jul 1848, Springfield, Sangamon, Illinois. Md. 22 Sep 1871, Alice Ann Gardner. D. 27 Dec 1931, Parowan, Utah.
JACOB HENRY, b. 12 Feb 1851, Provo, Utah. D. 14 Oct 1851, Provo, Utah. Child.
MARCY JANE, b. 8 Feb 1854, Manti, Utah. Md. William Henry Deuel. D. Mar 1926.

Children of 3rd wife:

MARY AMELIA, b. 16 Dec 1864, Minersville, Beaver, Utah. Md. Mr. Smith.

GEORGE HENRY, b. 25 Nov 1866, St. Thomas, Clark, Nevada. Md. Kate Baylis.

JAMES WILLIAM, b. 22 Oct 1869, St. Thomas, Nevada. D. 20 Aug 1904.

DAVID, b. abt 1871.

THOMAS AMMON, b. 30 Dec 1872, Monroe, Utah. Md. Mary Anderson

SARAH JANE, b. 1873. Md. Im Maloney.

CURTIS, b. 24 Jul 1874, Monroe, Utah. D. 1895.

Children of 4th wife:

One son supposedly born.

Submitted by: Pat Grey

SAMUEL BARNHURST

Born: 24 Aug 1827, Philadelphia, Pennsylvania
Parents: Joseph Jonah and Priscilla Underhill Barnhurst
Died: 30 Mar 1890, Hatch, Garfield, Utah
Arrived in Valley: Fall of 1857

Married 1st: Ann Elizabeth Thompson
Date: abt 1846, probably Pennsylvania
Born: about 1824
Parents: Broadus Thompson

Married 2nd: Anna Marie Petersen Jensen
Date: 29 Nov 1857, Salt Lake City, Utah

Born: 23 Sep 1833, Rybjerg, Viborg, Denmark
Parents: Jens Christian and Sophia Christensen Peterson
Died 23 Jul 1906, Hatch, Garfield, Utah

Samuel Barnhurst was born in Philadelphia and lived there until he married Ann Elizabeth. After they had four children, he heard the Mormon elders and was baptized. He left his family and moved to the Valley to be with the saints.

He married Anna Marie Jensen and they had nine children. He and his family helped to colonize Circleville. He taught school in Cedar City, Kanarrah, and Belview, Utah. He also operated a grist mill in Cedar City and ran a farm as well. He ran the salt works. He worked for many years in the St. George Temple.

Children of 1st wife:

WILLIAM, b. abt 1847, Pennsylvania.
JOHN HENRY, b. abt 1849, Pennsylvania.
JOSEPH, b. abt 1851, Pennsylvania.
MARY EMMA, b. abt 1853, Pennsylvania.

Children of 2nd wife:

ANNA MARY (twin), b. 18 Nov 1858.
MARY ANNA (twin), b. 18 Nov 1858.
SAMUEL JAMES, b. 25 Nov 1860.
PRISCILLA SOPHIA, b. 6 May 1863.
JENS CHRISTIAN, b. 18 Aug 1865.
ANNIE ELIZABETH, b. 4 Mar 1868.
JULIA ANN MARIE, b. 15 Apr 1872.
JANE, b. 11 Jul 1876.
JOSEPH ERASTUS, b. 8 May 1878.

Submitted by: LaRae McManama

EDWIN BARTHOLMEW

Born: 8 Apr 1851, Salt Lake City, Utah
Parents: Noah Willis and Mary Altaina Catlin Bartholmew
Died: 24 Feb 1920, Fillmore, Millard, Utah
Arrived in Valley: Born in Salt Lake

Married 1st: Lelia Deseret Lyman
Date: 25 Dec 1871, Fillmore, Millard, Utah
Parents: Amasa Mason and Maria Louisa Tanner Lyman

Married 2nd: Sarah Powell Payne Warner
Date: 14 Aug 1909, Fillmore, Utah
    Called Aunt Sadie by Edwins grandchildren

Edwin's parents joined the Church in 1844 and were among the first settlers to arrive in the Valley in 1848. Edwin and his parents lived in a log house inside the old Fillmore Fort. When he was just a small boy, he was an acrobat in his half-brothers circus, which toured all over the country. The Bartholomews raised pure bred horses, which they trained to perform in the circus.

After his marriage to Lelia, they lived in a log cabin in Fillmore. Later they built a substantial two-story brick home for their family. Edwin owned many acres of fertile fields where he planted and produced grains, alfalfa, vegetables, and fruits. He was an excellent gardner and superior craftsman.

After his wife died, he married Sarah or as she was lovingly called, "Aunt Sadie." They had a happy life together. Edwin eventually turned over the farm to Gay and her husband, and Edwin and Sarah moved into a lovely home in Fillmore.

Edwin had a skin cancer removed from his face while visiting his son in California. Later he had a growth removed from his abdomin. He died at 68.

He was a fine looking man about five feet nine inches tall and weighing about 165. He had a fair skin and wore a mustache.

Children of 1st wife;

LILLIE GAY, b. 6 Oct 1872, Fillmore, Utah.
VERNE, b. 4 Jan 1874, Fillmore, Utah.
EDDA CLARE, b. 31 Dec 1875, Fillmore, Utah.
RETTA LU, b. 3 Aug 1878, Fillmore, Utah.
MARK DANTAS, b. 18 Jan 1883, Fillmore, Utah.

Submitted by: Arline Martindale Scott Brinton

GEORGE MARSTON BARTHOLOMEW

Born: 5 Nov 1851, Cainsville, Iowa
Parents: Joseph and Polly Benson Bartholomew Sr.
Died: 12 Sep 1925, Fayette, Utah
Arrived in Valley: 14 Sep 1852, Family says Orson Hyde or
    Claudius Spencer.

Married: Salena Roper
Date: 2 Nov 1880, Utah
Born: 23 Nov 1862, Gunnison, Utah
Died: 26 Dec 1948, Gunnison, Utah

George Marston Bartholomew was one year old when he came

to the Valley with his parents. The family settled in Springville, Utah. In 1861 the family moved to Warm Springs (later changed to Fayette), Utah.

George was a cattle rancher and trapper. He was a veteran of the Black Hawk Indian War. He was present at the meeting and was one of the signers of the Manti Temple Articles of Incorporation.

Children:

GEORGE MARSTON, b. 29 Jul 1884, Fayette, Utah. D. 18 May 1950.
HENRY, b. 19 Jun 1886, Fayette, Utah. D. 19 Jun 1886. Child.
ELLA, b. 5 Nov 1887, Fayette, Utah. D. 6 May 1891. Child.
FLOYD, b. 26 Nov 1890, Fayette, Utah. D. 18 Feb 1964.
SARAH, b.29 Mar 1893, Fayette, Utah. D. 29 Mar 1893. Child.
VERNA LLOYD, b. 14 Nov 1895, Fayette, Utah. D. 16 Nov 1970.
EFFIE, b. 23 Oct 1898, Fayette, Utah.
JUNIUS BLAINE, b. 5 Jul 1906, Fayette, Utah. D. 26 Nov 1984.

Submitted by Miriam Mitchell

JOSEPH BARTHOLOMEW, SR.

Born: 16 Jan 1820, Charleston, Clarke, Indiana
Parents: John and Nancy McNaught Bartholomew Sr
Died: 28 May 1901, Fayette, Sanpete, Utah
Arrived in Valley: 14 Sep 1852. Claudius V. Spencer Co.

Married 1st: Polly Benson

Date: 10 Dec 1843
Born: 12 Feb 1816, Bath, Stuben, New York
Died: 19 Dec 1912, Fayette, Utah

Married 2nd: Electa Benson–No children
Date: 6 Apr 1857
Born: 1812
Died: 1887, Fayette, Utah

Joseph Bartholomew, Sr. originally settled at Springville, Utah. In 1861 he was sent to settle the Gunnison-Fayette area of Sanpete County, Utah. He was a farmer by occupation.

The first school in Fayette was held at night in his home. He was a merchant in the early days of Fayette. He participated in the Black Hawk Indian War at the Salina Canyon and Grass Creek Indian engagements.

Children of 1st wife:

JOSEPH SMITH, (twin) b. 20 Aug 1844. D. 20 Aug 1844. Child.
HYRUM SMITH, (twin) b. 20 Aug 1844. D. 21 Aug 1844. Child.
JOHN, b. 11 Sep 1845. D. 23 Sep 1914.
MARY KEZIA, b. 29 Apr 1847. D. 8 Nov 1937.
JOSEPH JR., b. 5 Jan 1850. D. 19 Apr 1912.
GEORGE MARSTON, b. 5 Nov 1851. D. 12 Sep 1925.
ELIZABETH ALMIRA, b. 25 Jul 1854, Springville, Utah. D. 29 Jul 1934.
ELIZA ELVIRA, b. 25 Jul 1854, Springville, Utah. D. 10 May 1912.
WILLIAM ORANGE, b. 6 Sep 1856, Springville, Utah. D. 24 Oct 1873.
JAMES ORSON, b. 29 Dec 1858, Springville, Utah. D. 14 Jan 1917.

Submitted by: Miriam Mitchell

NOAH WILLIS BARTHOLOMEW

Born: 1 Apr 1808, Dryden, Tompkins, New York
Parents: Jehiel and Jerusha Maltbie Bartholomew
Died: 1 Aug 1876, Fillmore, Millard, Utah
Arrived in Valley: Among the first settlers to arrive in Valley.

Married 1st: Miranda Catlin
Date: 1 Jan 1828
Born: 17 Sep 1806, Otsego Co., New York

Married 2nd: Mary Altaina (Altoona) Catlin, sister to Miranda
Born: 11 Jul 1821, Otsego Co., New York
Died: 20 Feb 1908, Fillmore, Utah

Noah Willis Bartholomew, with his family, moved from Erie County, New York, to Coldwater, Michigan, where he joined the Church in 1844. He determined to move his family to the Valley and they were one of the first families there.

Late in the fall of 1849, Parley P. Pratt led an exploring party to Southern Utah. Noah was part of that group. They had a rough time during part of the trip, not being prepared for the winter snows. They were the first known white men to that part of the country.

Meanwhile, his family lived in Salt Lake. When he returned to Salt Lake, President Young asked him to help settle Fillmore. He was the first bishop of that ward. On the first Sunday, religious services were held in the tent of Bishop Bartholomew. They soon built a fort for protection. Noah and both his families lived in a log house inside the fort.

Eventually he felt the need of a larger home and learned how to make bricks. He was able to erect a three-level house, which came to be known as the Bartholomew Castle. Many years later, the home was transformed into an Inn or Hotel.

In 1855 Noah deeded all his property to the church and joined the United Order.

He was always trying to better things whether it was to make a carding machine or improve the corrals and homes. They raised fine horses, which were used by Noah's son George in a circus which toured Utah. George's brother Noah was the acrobat and his sister Matilda was a bare-back rider.

They were one of the most revered families in Fillmore and did much to help build up the city and church.

Children of 1st wife:

EMILY.
GEORGE W.
LEWIS NELSON.
WILLIS.
LYMAN.
MIRANDA.

Children of 2nd wife:

MATILDA, b. 3 Aug 1850, Salt Lake City, Utah.
EDWIN, b. 8 Apr 1851, Salt Lake City, Utah.
NOAH WILLIS, b. 5 Sep 1853, Fillmore, Utah.
LAURA ALVIRA, b. 1 Jun 1857, Fillmore, Utah.
DON ALONZO, b.16 Nov 1861, Fillmore, Utah.

Submitted by: Arline Martindale Scott Brinton

JOHN BARTON

Born: 22 Jun 1808, West Sunbury, Northumberland, Pennsylvania
Parents: Noah and Mary Cooley Barton
Died: 16 May 1887, Mt. Pleasant, Utah
Arrived in Valley: 20 Sep 1848, Brigham Young's second company

Married: Susannah Wilkinson
Date: 21 Dec 1835
Born: 16 Mar 1814, Northumberland, Pennsylvania
Died: 7 Apr 1887, buried, Mt. Pleasant Cemetary, Utah

John Barton and his family heard the gospel and were converted to the Mormon Church. They were opposed by their families. In 1841 they took their two children and traveled to Nauvoo
and made their home there. They were subjected to much persecution and when Brigham Young ordered the families to leave,
John and his family were among the first to go.

They had only been in the Valley a short time when they were
asked to help settle the area now known as Bountiful. They lived
there about ten years.

In 1856, John and others were chosen to go out and meet the
handcart companies and help them on to the valley.

Upon the marriage of their eldest daughter and the urging of
her husband, John and his family moved to Mt. Pleasant where
he farmed about twenty acres of land.

John was a quiet man of medium size and complexion. He
went gray and lost most of his hair early in life. He was a hard
worker and one of the best farmers in Mt. Pleasant.

Children of 1st wife:

MARY CATHERINE, b. 30 Jun 1837. Md. 16 May 1832, John
     Lehi Ivie. D. 24 Dec 1888, Ketchum, Idaho.
WILLIAM GILBERT.
ELIZABETH JANE, b. 1842, Nauvoo, Illinois. D. 1844. Child.
PHEBE ELEN, b. 1845, Nauvoo, Illinois. D. 1847. Child.
JOHN OSCAR. b. 1847, Pottawattamie Co., Iowa. Md. Emiline
     Seely.
KEMBUR.
SYLVESTER.
ELISHA KEMMER.

Submitted by: Grant Ivie and Noel Barton

JOHN BARTON

Born: 23 Feb 1806, Winstanley, Laancashire, England
Parents: William and Elizabeth Winstanley
Died: 26 Aug 1874, Salt Lake City, Utah
Arrived in Valley: 5 Oct 1862, Ansel P. Harmon Co.

Married 1st: Margaret Webster
Died: early

Married 2nd: Elizabeth Bell
Date: 6 Sep 1835, Haigh Church near Wigan, Lancashire, England

     John Barton's first wife died shortly after the birth of their
daughter Mary Ann. He later married Elizabeth in 1835. They

lived in Wigan until 1837 when they moved to St. Helens. John worked at a large iron foundry where he soon became head foreman. John had an inventive mind and put it to good use. He invented the lantern valve and was one of the first to advocate high pressure and high speed engines.

He was baptized a member of the Church in 1851, four years after his wife, Elizabeth. Because of his job and his boss, he was unable to attend meetings regularly. Shortly before leaving for America, he renewed his covenants by being rebaptized.

Part of his family had already immigrated to the Valley in 1860-61. In 1862, John and the rest of his family followed, arriving in the valley in October 1862. The family remained in the Mill Creek area for three weeks and then moved to Kaysville, where they spent the first winter in a dugout. The next year they built a home of logs and adobe. Later they built the first brick home in Kaysville. Sometime after 1864, they moved to Salt Lake where John died in 1874 and was buried in the Salt Lake City Cemetery.

Children of 1st wife:

MARY ANN, b. abt 1834

Children of 2nd wife:

WILLIAM BELL, b. 21 Jul 1836, Wigan, Lancs, England. Md. 1st, 1860, Ellen Birchall. Md. 2nd, 1867, Sarah Foster. D. 1923.
JAMES, b. 21 Jul 1836, Wigan, Lancs, England. Md. 1863, Eliza Barton. D. 1919.
ELIZABETH, b. 30 Nov 1838, St. Helens, Lancs, England. D.1839. Child.
JOHN, b. 24 Jul 1840, St. Helens, Lancs, England. Md. 1st, 1863, Sarah Flint. Md. 2nd, 1892, Frances Catharine Geeves Stevenson. D. 1916.
ISAAC, b. 11 Dec 1842, St. Helens, Lancs, England. Md. 1870, Agnes Ellen Parr. D. 1916.
PETER, b. 21 Mar 1845, St. Helens, Lancs, England. Md. 1st, 1870, Ellen Ann Beazer. Md. 2nd, 1878, Mary Elizabeth Beesley. D. 1912.

JOSEPH, b. 25 Jul 1848, St. Helens, Lancs, England. Md. 1st, 1869, Mary Ann Allen. Md. 2nd, Hattie Elizabeth Follansbee. Md. 3rd, 1921, Margaret Emily Jones. D. 1932.

HYRUM, b. 13 Jun 1852, Eccleston, Lancs, England. Md. 1st, 1880, Georgina Calder Crabb. Md. 2nd, 1885, Lora Jane Bowdidge Berry. D. 1901.

BERTHA, b. 23 Feb 1855, Eccleston, Lancs, England. Md. 1875, William Graham Irvine. D. 1926.

Submitted by: Grant Ivie

PETER BARTON

Born: 21 Mar 1845, St. Helens, Lancs, England
Parents: John and Elizabeth Bell Barton
Died: 28 Nov 1912, Salt Lake City, Utah
Arrived in Valley: 5 Oct 1862, Ansel P. Harmon Co.

Married 1st: Ellen Ann Beazer
Date: 1870, Salt Lake City, Utah

Married 2nd: Mary Elizabeth Beesley
Date: 1878, Salt Lake City, Utah

Peter Barton was baptized in 1853 by his brother James. He honored his membership and was appointed to various offices in the church including the clerk in the St. Helens' Branch. At the age of 12, he got a job with the London Northwestern Railway in the ticket office. When he turned 14, he was placed in charge of the ticket department. He attended school in St. Helens and later worked as a clerk in an auditor's office.

Peter crossed the ocean with his parents and family in the ship "Manchester" and then went by boat and train to Nebraska, seeing many of the Union and Confederate troops along the way. At Florence they started out in a wagon train to cross the plains. Peter walked the entire distance. Soon after arriving in the Valley, the family moved to Kaysville.

He helped his father and others with farming and also worked for Christopher Layton keeping books, writing letters, etc. He taught school even though many of his pupils were older than he was.

In 1864 he joined the Kaysville Brass Band and played the E flat base. In 1865 he received his endowments and served as a ward clerk. In 1870 he married Ellen Beazer. Four years later he was called on a mission to Britain. While there he served as president of the Sheffield Conference. He returned in 1876 and served as president of the YMMIA in Kaysville. Six months later he was made bishop of the Kaysville ward. Shortly after, he married the second time.

He served two consecutive terms in the Legislature. He served six months in the prison for unlawful cohabitation. His discription was given as being six foot three in height, weighing 195 pounds. His hair and eyes were brown and he had a medium dark complexion.

He worked with his brothers in the merchandising business and was vice-president and director of the Barnes Banking Company. He moved to Salt Lake in 1909 and died on Thanksgiving Day in 1912. He is buried in Kaysville.

Children of 1st wife:

OSCAR CHARLES, b. 13 Nov 1871, Kaysville, Utah. Md. 1906, Nora Vest. D. 1937.
LAURA MARIA, b. 20 Aug 1873, Kaysville, Utah. D. 1873. Child.
NELLIE HANNAH, b. 15 Oct 1874, Kaysville, Utah. Md. 1913, Ezra John Howell. D. 1946.

LILLY, b. 9 Sep 1877, Kaysville, Utah. Md. 1905, Arnold David Miller. D. 1947.

PETER HERBERT, b. 8 Nov 1879, Kaysville, Utah. D. 1880. Child.

ELIZABETH BELL, b. 18 Aug 1881, Kaysville, Utah. Md. 1909, David James Davis. D.1964.

ALBERT BEAZER, b. 29 Oct 1883, Kaysville, Utah. Md. 1911, Mary Layton. D. 1944.

CLARA EUNICE, b. 2 Oct 1885, Kaysville, Utah. Md. 1919, Heber William Perry. D. 1937.

DORA BEATRICE, b. 10 Sep 1888, Kaysville, Utah. Md. 1921, Glen Bennion Cannon. D. 1964.

BERTHA LUELLA, b. 9 May 1896, Kaysville, Utah. D. 1896. Child.

Children of 2nd wife:

ALLOTA, b. 14 Aug 1881, Kaysville, Utah. Md. 1903, Joshua Frederick Conrad. D. 1956.

AMELIA, b. 15 Oct 1884, Kaysville, Utah. Md. 1906, Walter Cottrell. D. 1968.

ROBERT HENRY, b. 2 Feb 1888, Kaysville, Utah. Md. 1916, Jenness Elizabeth Wiggill. D. 1958.

SPENCER JAMES, b. 17 Jan 1892, Salt Lake City, Utah. Md. 1916, Effie Annie Andersen. D. 1943.

Submitted by: Noel Barton

JOEL ALMON BASCOM

Born: 27 Mar 1832, Brookfield, Madison, New York
Parents: Ezekiel and Sarah Pate Bascom
Died: 18 May 1912, Vernal, Uintah, Utah
Arrived in Valley: 13 Aug 1856, Philemon C. Merrill Co.

Married: Alice Jane Bell
Date: 6 Dec 1857, Carterville, (later known as Provo), Utah
Born: 15 Apr 1840, Westgate, New Castle, N., England
Died: 7 Apr 1917, Vernal, Utah

John moved to Nauvoo with his sister Elzina, where he was baptized. He came west driving cattle as a "Bullwhacker," being held responsible to help get Brigham Young's livestock to the Valley.

He was sent to Carterville (Provo), where he was later made Chief of Police. He moved to Mona where he was made a constable. He ran cattle, mined gold, and worked his ranch.

He disliked living too close to people, so in later years he built a cabin in the mountains where he stayed much of the time. It was on the trail of the Indians and outlaws going to Colorado. He was on friendly terms with both even though he fought in the Indian Wars.

He was active in the church and was a leader in the community and a model of the true pioneer. His last words were, "The frontier is gone, I might as well go too."

Children:

ELZINA ANN, b. 1 Dec 1858, Provo, Utah.

IDA JANE, b. 8 Feb 1860, Provo, Utah.
JOEL ALMON, Jr., b. 22 Oct 1862, Provo, Utah.
MARY EMMA, b. 20 Jul 1864, Provo, Utah.
JOHN WATSON BELL, b. 19 Apr 1869, Mona, Juab, Utah.
HANNAH BELL, b. in 1871, Mona, Utah.
IRA KIMBALL, b. 26 Mar 1873, Mona, Utah.
WILLIAM HENRY, b. 21 Feb 1876, Mona, Utah.
CHARLES ANDREW, b. 21 Apr 1878, Mona, Utah.
ALICE JANE LODEMA, b. in 1882, Mona, Utah.
JAMES OREN, b. 23 Jan 1883, Mona, Utah.
MARY ELLEN DYSON, b. 26 May 1884, Mona, Utah.
(Stillborn son), no date.

Submitted by: George Bascom

JOSEPH BATEMAN

Born: 9 Dec 1837, Pendleton, Lancs, England
Parents: Thomas and Mary Street Bateman
Died: 17 May 1890, West Jordan, Utah
Arrived In Valley: 15 Sep 1850, James Pace Co.

Married: Mary Eliza Allen
Date: 14 Oct 1860, West Jordan, Utah
Born: 11 Nov 1845, Flushing, Queens, New York

Joseph Bateman was a farmer and sheepman. He raised a large family of six girls and seven boys. He was an asset to the community as well as to the church. He was known as an honest, trustworthy man.

Children:

ESTELLA JENNETTE, b. 27 Apr 1862, West Jordan, Utah. Md.
    24 Jul 1882, John Mayne. D.16 Nov 1919, Salt Lake City,
    Utah.
JOSEPH SAMUEL, b. 17 Feb 1864, West Jordan, Utah. Md. 29
    Feb 1888, Elsina Morthina Johnson. D. 3 Sep 1922, Lehi,
    Utah.
THEODORE ALLEN, b. 14 Sep 1865, West Jordan, Utah. Md.
    17 May 1894, Christena Johansen. D. 6 Dec 1942, Lehi, Utah.
MARY ELIZA, b. 5 Dec 1867, Alpine, Utah. Md. 17 Jan 1884,
    Thomas Heber Walton. D. 4 Dec 1944, Salt Lake City, Utah.
MARGARET ALLETTA, b. 25 Mar 1870, Alpine, Utah. Md.
    1st, 11 Oct 1898, John Thomas Bateman. Md. 2nd, 30 Mar
    1914, James S. Ferrell. D. 1 Mar 1941, Cardston, Alberta,
    Canada.
DAVID WILLIAM, b. 27 Nov 1872, Alpine, Utah. Md. 17 Aug
    1898, Angelia Grace Clark. D. 21 Sep 1926, Alpine, Utah.
ROYAL JAMES, b. 25 Jun 1875, Alpine, Utah. Md. 18 Jan 1905,
    Maud Elizabeth Brown. D. 19 Jul 1959, Murray, Utah.
JOHN FRANKLIN, b. 22 May 1878, Alpine, Utah. D. 27 Feb
    1881, Alpine, Utah. Child.
CHARLES CLARENCE, b. 8 May 1880, Alpine, Utah. Md. 20
    Sep 1905, Amy Balmforth Burnham. D. 21 Sep 1961, Idaho
    Falls, Idaho.
MERINDA VILATE, b. 26 Oct 1882, Alpine, Utah. D. 17 Apr
    1883. Child.
ETHEL MAUD, b. 14 Apr 1884, Alpine, Utah. Md. 10 Feb
    1917, Henry S. Watts. D. 20 Feb 1960.
CLARA LEILA, b. 15 Apr 1888, Alpine, Utah. Md. 9 Jun 1909,
    Edward Malmstrom. D. 24 Jan 1960.
STEPHEN MARTIN, b. 30 Jun 1890, Alpine, Utah. D. 26 Jul
    1912, Lagoon Amusement Park, Farmington, Utah.

Submitted by: David Walton

SAMUEL BATEMAN

Born: 1 Jul 1832, Manchester, Lancs, England
Parents: Thomas and Mary Street Bateman
Died: 23 Jan 1911, West Jordan, Utah
Arrived in Valley: 15 Sep 1850, James Pace Co.

Married 1st: Marinda Allen
Date: 1854,
Born: 21 Jun 1838, Jamacia, Long Island, New York
Parents: Daniel R. and Eliza Marten Allen
Died: After 1911

Married 2nd: Harriet Egbert
Date: 27 Feb 1871
Born: 18 Sep 1854, West Jordan, Utah
Parents: Samuel and Margaret Mariah Beckstead Egbert
Died: After 1911

Samuel Bateman and his parents accepted the gospel after hearing the missionaries, in about 1836. The family emigrated to America in 1839. They spent the winter in New Orleans and then proceeded to Nauvoo in the spring, arriving the same day the corner stone of the temple was laid. They stayed about four months and then moved to Augusta, Iowa. Samuel and his father returned to Nauvoo and worked in the brick yard and on the temple. They would take goods from Nauvoo to sell in Iowa.

They moved back to Augusta where they worked on the Lowry farm. They purchased a farm, but in 1849 Samuel's father sold this farm and made preparations to leave for the Valley. They spent that winter also in Pidgeon because Samuel's father let George A.

Smith take his best yoke of oxen so he could get to the valley. While staying there, he and his father made brick. They finally left for the valley in 1850 and obtained work in the adobe yard.

In December 1850, Samuel, 18 years old, requested that he be allowed to take his father's place in settling Iron County. While there he became fluent in the Indian language. He fenced and cleared property. He returned home in 1851. His father, Thomas, had gone back to England to dispose of some of his property there. On the return voyage, he was drowned at sea.

Samuel decided to settle in West Jordan where he married his first wife. During an Indian uprising, he was in charge of a group of men to stand guard. Later during the Johnston's Army scare, Samuel was asked to raise a platoon of calvary to harass the army. They burned wagons and supplies.

In the spring of 1861, he traveled with Brigham Young visiting some of the settlements in Southern Utah and Nevada. In 1863 he traveled with Porter Rockwell to help capture horse thieves.

In 1871, he took a polygamous wife, Harriet Egbert. He eventually served some time and paid a fine for it. He spent many years serving the church, government, the people, and Indians.

He became accomplished as a brick and adobe maker and layer, miller, farmer, bee and stock raiser, tax collector, water master, carpenter, blacksmith, trustee, machine man, caller at dances, cook, constable, nurse. Near the close of his life, he was ordained a patriarch.

Children of 1st wife:

SAMUEL ALLEN, b. 27 Dec 1855, West Jordan, Utah. D. 20 Oct 1856. Child.
DANIEL RAPALYEA, b. 21 Feb 1857, West Jordan, Utah. Md. Ellen Malmstrom.
JOSEPH THOMAS, b. 4 Oct 1858, West Jordan, Utah. Md. Clara Strong.
MARINDA PARTHENIA, b. 29 Sep 1861, West Jordan, Utah. Md. Hyrum Goff. D. 5 Oct 18—.
ARAMINTA ELIZA, b. 4 Dec 1862, West Jordan, Utah. Md. John A.Egbert D. 27 Aug 1938.

EDWARD ALONZO, b. 29 Jan 1864, West Jordan, Utah. Md.
Alice Glover. D. 13 Feb 1918.

ALBERTO DELOS, b. 8 Nov 1866, West Jordan, Utah. Md.
Rebecca Goff.

ELIZA JANETTA, b. 5 Mar 1869, West Jordan, Utah. D. abt
1870. Child

MARY JANETTA, b. 3 Oct 1870, West Jordan, Utah. Md. Robert Pixton.

ELZADA OPHELIA,(twin), b. 15 Mar 1874, West Jordan, Utah.
D. Child

ELZINA AMELIA, (twin), b. 15 Mar 1874, West Jordan, Utah.
Md. Hugh Buckley.

ADA LAURELDA, b. 12 Nov 1876, West Jordan, Utah. Md.
George Goodridge.

JULIAETTA, b. 31 Dec 1878, West Jordan, Utah. Md. Christen
Jensen.

Children of 2nd wife:

ORELLA MARIAH, b. 16 Feb 1875, West Jordan, Utah. Md.
Harry Nichols. D. 9 Nov 1955.

MARGARET ELIZA, b. 1 Mar 1877, West Jordan, Utah. Md.
William Walton Irving. D. 11 Jun 1904.

SAMUEL WALLACE, b. 27 Nov 1878, West Jordan, Utah. Md.
Eudora Evelyn Swenson. D. 25 Jan 1958.

HARRIET ELNORA, b. 9 Nov 1880, West Jordan, Utah. D. 13
Mar 1883. Child.

GEORGE ALBERT, b. 28 May 1883, West Jordan, Utah. Md.
Ivy Myrtle Garside. D. 19 May 1970.

BERTHA ELNORA, b. 23 Sep 1886, West Jordan, Utah. D. 29
Jul 1908.

VERA MAUD, b. 14 Dec 1888, West Jordan, Utah. D. 13 Jan
1889. Child.

CORA MAY, b. 23 Feb 1891, Bountiful, Utah. Md. Lester
Harrison Garner. D. 24 Aug 1971.

Submitted by: Ruth Costley

THOMAS BATEMAN

Born: 17 Sep 1808, Bolton, Lancs, England
Parents: Thomas and Elizabeth Armstrong Bateman
Died: 29 Nov 1852, while crossing Atlantic Ocean for third time
Arrived in Valley: 15 Sep 1850, James Pace Co.

Married: Mary Street
Date: August 1829, Manchester, Lancs, England
Born: 12 May 1810, Manchester, Lancs, England
Died: 4 Mar 1891, West Jordan, Utah

Thomas Bateman was a brickmaker and bricklayer. When he heard the Mormon missionaries, he was impressed and shortly after in 1836, he and his family were baptized. They emigrated to America in 1839, staying in New Orleans that first winter. They arrived in Nauvoo in the spring where they stayed about four months before moving across the river to Augusta, Iowa, where they purchased a farm. Thomas and his son, Samuel, returned to Nauvoo where they worked in the brick yard. Later they had a brickyard in Augusta.

Thomas sold this home in 1849 and made preparations to move with the saints to the Rocky Mountains. They left in 1850 with the James Pace Company, arriving in the Valley in the fall.

In December 1850, Brigham Young called Thomas to go to Iron County. Samuel, being 18 years old, asked if he could go in his father's place. His request was granted.

Thomas continued to make bricks and lay them and also took care of his farm until he took a trip to England to dispose of some of his property. On the return trip, he died and was buried at sea.

Children:

HARRIET, b. 4 Nov 1830, Manchester, Lancs, England. Md. 7
    May 1848, Lyman Wight. D. 23 Mar 1907, Brigham City,
    Utah.
SAMUEL, b. 1 Jul 1832, Manchester, Lancs, England. Md. 1st,
    27 Nov1854, Marinda Allen. Md. 2nd, 27 Feb 1871, Harriet
    Egbert. D. 23 Jan 1911, West Jordan, Utah.
ELIZABETH, b. 16 Feb 1834, Manchester, Lancs, England. Md.
    21 Apr 1857, Philip Margetts. D. 11 Jun 1896, West Jordan,
    Utah.
THOMAS, b. 27 Jan 1836, Manchester, Lancs, England. Md. 15
    Sep 1861, Mary Lavender. D. 10 Oct 1868, Cottonwood, Salt
    Lake, Utah.
JAMES ROAME (twin), b. 9 Dec 1837, Pendleton, Lancs, En
    gland. D. 1 Mar 1838, England. Child.
JOSEPH (twin), b. 9 Dec 1837, Pendleton, Lancs, England. Md.
    14 Oct 1860, Mary Eliza Allen. D. 17 May 1890, West Jor-
    dan, Utah.
MARY, b. 27 Feb 1840, Manchester, England. D. May 1847.
    Child.
JAMES MORGAN, b. 3 Mar 1842, Augusta, Lee, Iowa. Md. 1
    Nov 1869, Maria Lovisia Watkins. D. 18 Jun 1904, West Jor-
    dan, Utah.
WILLIAM LEHI, b. 1 Jan 1844, Augusta, Lee, Iowa. Md. 26
    Dec 1870, Sophronia Watkins. D. 2 Aug 1916, Sandy, Utah.
JOHN, b. 21 Feb 1846, Nauvoo, Illinois. D. 29 November 1846.
    Child.
MARTHA ANN, b. 15 Sep 1847, Augusta, Iowa. Md. 1st, 13
    Feb 1865, Samuel M. Jenkins. Md. 2nd, George Moses. D.
    4 Jun 1916, Midvale, Utah.
MARGARET, b. 30 Jun 1849, Council Bluffs, Pottawattamie,
    Iowa. Md. 2 Oct 1872, Alfred Oxenbold Davis. D. 3 Mar
    1917, Murray, Utah.

Submitted by: David Walton

JOHN BATES

Born: 30 Oct 1816, Linton, Derby, England
Parents: William and Mary Robinson Bates
Died: 25 Feb 1887, Wanship, Summit, Utah
Arrived in Valley: 1 Sep 1860

Married 1st: Hannah Draycott
Date: 16 May 1837, Stapenhill, England
Born: 10 Feb 1816, Newhall, Derby, England
Parents: Thomas and Mary Farmer Draycott
Died: 26 Dec 1863, Wanship, Utah

Married 2nd: Rachel Eliasen (Ragnille Tollevsen)
Date: 1864, probably Salt Lake
Born: abt 1832, Norway
Arrived in Valley: 1863, walking entire way

Married 3rd: Orline Dorthea Christianson
Date: Aug 1865, Salt Lake City, Utah
Born: 1823, Norway

Married 4th: Margaret Brooks (widow - R. Williams)
Date: 24 Nov 1866, Salt Lake City, Utah
Born: abt 1845, England
Arrived in Valley: 1866, Thompson Handcart Co.

Married 5th: Hedvig Charlott Youngquist–No children
Born: 16 Aug 1835, Colmar, Sweden

Married 6th: Sarah Edwards (Div)–No children
Date: 31 Oct 1870

According to tradition, John was a stable keeper of the King's horses and hounds. He loved horses and had a special talent working with them.

John was baptized in 1850 in England. His wife was baptized two years later. After his wife's baptism, they made the decision to leave England for America, taking five of their six children. The second daughter remained in England for several more years.

They lived in Pennsylvania where John undoubtedly worked. They had heard of the unsettled conditions in the Valley because of Johnston's army, so many of the immigrants stayed back East until Brigham Young said they could come. In 1859, the word came that all Mormons should come as soon as possible.

Soon after their arrival in the valley in 1860, John was called to help colonize the Weber River country. They homesteaded a place near what is now Wanship. The area was high and the growing season short, which made for difficult times. They had to share with the Indians to keep peace. Soon their rations were pig weeds, greens and sego lilies. They were glad when the new crops came on.

John Bates was musically inclined. He was one of the school trustees. He was a good provider for his large family. He was a very religious man, espousing the idea of polygamy because church leaders said it was right. He retained his love of horses and was a farmer.

After his death, his two wives, Rachel and Charlott, continued to live in Wanship in separate houses but remained friends.

Children of 1st wife:

EMMA.
ELIZA, (stayed in England and came later).
JOHN JR.
MARY ANN.
HYRUM.

HARRIET, all born in England.
SAMUEL DANIEL, b. 4 Jul 1861, Wanship, Utah.

Children of 2nd wife:

THOMAS.
EDWARD, b. 1864.
EPHRAIM.
ANTHONY.
HANNAH.
RACHEL.
ROSEY.
(Rosa) MAY, b. 1873, d. abt 1874. Child. All these children
    born in Wanship, Utah.

Children of 4th wife:

JOSHUA, b. Apr 1869, Wanship, Utah.

Submitted by: Sharon Rae Huff

JOHN CHRISTMAN BAUM

Born: 18 Mar 1804, Alexander, Moreland, Pennsylvania
Parents: John Jacob and Elizabeth Amerlong Baum
Died: 19 Jan 1883, Provo, Utah
Arrived in Valley: Sep 1851, Independant Co.

Married 1st: Hannah Crisman
Date: 3 May 1827, Chester, Pennsylvania

Born: 8 Sep 1808, Brandywine, Chester, Pennsylvania
Parents: John and Jane Mcloughlin Crisman
Died: 12 Sep 1902, Heber, Wasatch, Utah

Hannah was baptized in 1839, and John a year later in 1840. Their first five children were born in Pennsylvania. After they joined the Church, they moved to Nauvoo where the next three were born. Their last child was born at Winter Quarters. They finally made it to the Valley in 1851.

While in Nauvoo, John was a member of the Nauvoo Legion. After he reached the valley, he was sent to help settle Provo. He was a farmer and owned mill property.

Children:

JANE ELIZABETH, b. 15 Sep 1827, Yuklon, Chester, Pennsylvania. Md. John Bennett.
GEORGE, b. 2 Nov 1829, Brandywine, Chester, Pennsylvania. Md. Hannah Jane Cloward.
ISAAC, b. 7 Mar 1833, Brandywine, Pennsylvania. Md. 6 May 1856, Melline Sessions. D. 18 Nov 1920.
MARY ANN, b. 19 Jul 1835, Brandywine, Pennsylvania. Md. James Mason Cloward.
SUSANNAH, b. 5 Nov 1837, Yuklon, Pennsylvania. D. 6 Mar 1842. Child.
MARIAH, b. 6 Mar 1840, Nauvoo, Illinois. Md. 3 Nov 1856, Warren Stone. D. 4 Oct 1922.
RACHEL, b. 6 Mar 1842, Nauvoo, Illinois. D. 16 Nov 1846. Child.
JOHN JAMES, b. 18 Nov 1844, Nauvoo, Illinois. Md. 2 Dec 1867, Susan Ann Davis. D. 27 Aug 1923.
RACHEL ANN, b. 18 Mar 1850, Winter Quarters, Nebraska. Md. Henery Lewis Davis. D. 16 Sep 1870.

Submitted by: Melea Allan

JOHN JAMES BAUM

Born: 18 Nov 1844, Nauvoo, Hancock, Illinois
Parents: John Christman and Hannah Crisman Baum
Died: 27 Aug 1923, Price, Carbon, Utah
Arrived in Valley: 1851, Independent Co.

Married 1st: Susan Ann Davis (Div)
Date: 2 Dec 1867, Provo, Utah
Born: 31 Dec 1852, Provo, Utah
Parents: Joshua and Susan Ann Cole Davis
Died: 20 Apr 1920, Provo, Utah

Married 2nd: Mary Lavernia (Mollie) Epperson
Born: 28 Jul 1858
Parents: Sidney and Mary Jane Robey Epperson

John James Baum, along with his father and brothers, George and Isaac, left Nauvoo on 15 December 1850 to go west. They finally joined an independent wagon train which arrived in the Valley in 1851.

He made several trips back to Nauvoo as a scout with a team and wagon to help others get to the valley.

John was a veteran of the Black Hawk War. He helped to settle Provo, Midway, and Price, Utah.

Children:

SUSSANER, b. 20 May, 1869, Provo, Utah. Md. 17 Jan 1888, George Albert Ferrie. D. Dec 1948.

ALVA JOHN, b. 28 May 1871, Provo, Utah. Md. 23 Mar 1892, Julia Maria Myler (Div). D. 17 Mar 1922.

ALMEDA MEDORA, b. 30 Nov 1872, Provo, Utah. Md. 19 Jul 1889, Milton Leo Scott. D. 26 Aug 1903.

FRANK, b. 21 Apr 1874, Provo, Utah. Md. Nome McCarol. D. 4 Feb 1934.

WILBERT ROY, b. 30 Nov 1875, Provo, Utah. Md. 24 Sep 1901, Margaret Epperson. D. 7 Jun 1932.

ROLLIE GUY, b. 7 Jul 1884, Provo, Utah. Md. 13 Mar 1906, Cora Ann Street. D. 1 Jun 1922.

Submitted by: Melea Allan

ROBERT (LOVE) BAXTER

Born: 2 Nov 1848, Greenock, Renfrewshire, Scotland
Parents: Robert W. and Jane Love Baxter
Died: 14 May 1929, Wellsville, Utah
Arrived in Valley: 25 Sep 1855, Richard Ballantyne Co.

Married: Mary Ellen Barnes
Date: 13 Dec 1875, Utah
Born: 9 Feb 1856, Grantsville, Utah
Parents: John and Elinor Wilson Barnes
Died: 5 Apr 1929, Wellsville, Utah

Robert Baxter came to the Valley with his parents and brothers and sisters. When they got to the valley in 1855, the crickets had destroyed the crops so they lived on bark and roots for a year.

Robert's father was sent to Echo Canyon in 1858 to keep Johnston's Army harrassed, which left ten-year-old Robert the task of gathering sagebrush in order to maintain a fire.

Robert had very little education, as he was kept working to help his family.

In 1868 he went as a teamster across the plains to help the emigrants. On that trip he brought back the first carding machine to the valley.

In 1877, Robert moved to Mt. Sterling as the first settler there. He worked hard to improve the land. He helped with all the development in the community. For a time he was postmaster. He donated the first school house. He started the first free rural delivery. He acted as the first school trustee, the first road supervisor, the first justice of the peace and president of the Wellsville Canal and Irrigation Company. He was the first mail carrier in Cache County. Wherever there was a need, he was there.

Robert was faithful to the church and was well loved and respected by all who knew him.

Children:

MARY JANE, b. 21 Nov 1876, Wellsville, Utah.
ELLENOR, b. 25 Dec 1877, Wellsville, Utah.
MARTHA, b. 26 Jul 1880, Wellsville, Utah.
ROBERT LEROY, b. 14 Jul 1882, Wellsville, Utah.
ARCHIBALD McFAIL, b. 3 Jul 1884, Wellsville, Utah.
HARRIET, b.31 Mar 1886, Wellsville, Utah.
JOHN, b. 22 Oct 1888, Wellsville, Utah.
WILLIAM SANDFORD, b. 21 Aug 1891, Wellsville, Utah.
JOSEPH MERRILL, b. 30 Aug 1893, Wellsville, Utah.
MILTON, b. 14 Jul 1898, Wellsville, Utah.

Submitted by: John Baxter

ROBERT WRIGHT BAXTER

Born: 2 Feb 1820, Parish of Ballyvester, County Down, Ireland
Parents: John and Margaret Baxter
Died: 31 May 1913, Wellsville, Utah
Arrived in Valley: 26 Sep 1855, Richard Ballantyne Co.

Married 1st: Isabella Gray
Date: 31 Jan 1845, Scotland
Died: 4 Jun 1847, Greenock, Scotland

Married 2nd: Jane Love
Date: 1 Feb 1848, (Scotland Ward records indicate Mar. 27th)
Died: 28 Nov 1898, Wellsville, Utah

Married 3rd: Jane McKinnon McPhail, widow
Date: 18 Dec 1856

Married 4th: Marion Stuart
Date: 11 Oct 1868, Utah

As a youth, Robert was apprenticed to learn the shoemaking trade. While living in Girvan in the spring of 1844, he attended a religious service where he learned from the missionaries, the principles of the gospel. He believed what he heard even though he was ridiculed by his friends and discharged from his job. He was baptized in 1845.

He married Isabella and a year later she had a baby girl who lived only six months. Isabella only lived for another year. He married a year later, Jane Love, a member of the church.

Robert did missionary work in Port Glasgow where they lived. One of the men he baptized was promised some money if he would care for a man until he died. When Mr. McQuarrie joined the church the man withdrew his promise. Later Mr. McQuarrie got the money and gave it to Robert so he could take his family to America. Robert and his family and Mr. McQuarrie left on 13 February 1855. When they arrived in the Valley in September, the grasshoppers had eaten the crops and food was scarce.

Robert married Jane McKinnon when her husband died as a result of illness from being a member of the Martin Handcart Company. However, the two Jane's did not get along so Jane McKinnon moved out. She eventually moved to Randolph with her son.

In the spring of 1860 Robert took his family and moved to Cache Valley and settled in Wellsville, where they lived in a dug-out for awhile. Robert was called on a mission. Later, after his return, he, along with several other men, left for old Mexico to escape the punishment for polygamy. Finally in 1887, Robert and one of the other men decided to return home regardless of what happened. On July 25th, 1888, he was arrested.

Robert was ordained High Priest and Patriarch and served in that position until his death in 1913 at age 93 years.

Children of 1st wife:

DAUGHTER, b. 16 Jan 1846, Kilmarnock, Scotland. D. 29 Jun 1846. Child.

Children of 2nd wife:

ROBERT, b. 2 Nov 1848, Kilmarnock, Scotland.
ARCHIBALD McPHAIL, b. 18 Jun 1850. Scotland. D. 27 Oct 1873, Ogden Canyon, Utah.
JANE, b. 31 Oct 1851, Scotland.
WILLARD SNOW, b. 9 Nov 1853, Port Glasglow, Scotland.
STEPHEN GOLDING, b. 17 Oct 1856, Salt Lake, Utah.
JERUSHA GOLDING, b. 1 Jan 1859, Salt Lake, Utah.
LILLIE LYONS, b. 19 Sep 1861, Salt Lake, Utah.

MARGARET, b. 17 Feb 1864, Wellsville, Utah.
JOHN LOVE, b. 1 Nov 1866.

Children of 3rd wife:

JOHN M., b. 3 Jun 1859, Salt Lake, Utah.

Children of 4th wife:

CATHERINE, b. 20 Oct 1870.
SON, D. Infant.
SON, D. Infant.

Submitted by: John Baxter

WILLARD SNOW BAXTER

Born: 9 Nov 1853, Port Glasglow, Scotland
Parents: Robert Wright and Jane Love Baxter
Died: 8 Dec 1920, Salt Lake City, Utah
Arrived in Valley: 25 Sep 1855, Richard Ballentyne Co.

Married: Lydia Christina Hopkins
Date: 12 Sep 1878, Salt Lake City, Utah
Born: 10 May 1865, Lehi, Utah
Died: 28 Feb 1932, Logan, Utah

   Willard Snow Baxter at age two made the voyage to America
and then to the Valley with his parents, two brothers and a sister.

After arriving in Salt Lake, they made a home there for five years and then moved north to Cache Valley, where they lived in Wellsville.

Willard was one of the sturdy pioneers who helped blaze the trail and build homes for those who were to follow. He drove long freight teams of mules through the states of Utah, Idaho, Montana, and Nevada, to transport commodities over the trackless plains, often having problems with the Indians.

In Wellsville, he homesteaded a section of land later called Baxter School District. The land for the Mt. Sterling School, erected in 1893, was donated by Willard Snow Baxter. His brother, Robert Love Baxter, donated the materials for the building. Willard was involved in civic affairs as well as religious.

He was called as first counselor in the first bishopric of Mt. Sterling. In December 1896 he received a mission call to serve a mission in Manitoba, Canada. When he left, his oldest son took over the responsibility for the family. Willard arrived home in March 1898. Again in October 1899 he was called on another mission, this time to Pocatello, Idaho. After his return, he drove the school bus for many years. He was a man of great warmth and love of his family and the church.

Children:

WILLARD HOPKINS, b. 19 Apr 1879, Wellsville, Utah. Md. 20 Feb 1901, Elizabeth Cooper. D.28 Feb 1949, Salt Lake City, Utah.

ROBERT LAURENCE, b. 13 Dec 1880, Wellsville, Utah. Md. 15 Mar 1905, Sarah Haslam. D. 25 Jun 1949, Logan, Utah.

JAMES PARK, b. 9 Nov 1882, Wellsville, Utah. Md. 10 Jun 1908, Sarah Darley. D. 12 May 1934, Wenatchee, Washington.

JANE, b. 9 Mar 1885, Wellsville, Utah. Md. 17 Jun 1904, David W. Murray. D. 31 Mar 1926, Logan, Utah.

STEPHEN HOPKINS, b. 12 May 1888, Wellsville, Utah. Md. Edith Woffinden. D. 1 Dec 1931, Los Angeles, California.

EARL EZEKIEL, b. 9 Aug 1890, Wellsville, Utah. Md. 9 Mar 1917, Esther Hansen. D. 18 Aug 1935, Salt Lake City Utah.

SARAH, b. 13 Jan 1893, Wellsville, Utah. Md. 14 Sep 1926, Samuel Lorenzo Spencer. D. 19 Dec 1956, Salt Lake City, Utah.

ARCHIE LEVON, b. 22 Dec 1896, Wellsville, Utah. Md. 6 Mar 1918, Effie Glenn. D. 6 Jun 1935, Boise, Idaho.

Submitted by: Dean Baxter

JAMES BEAN

Born: 3 Mar 1804, Elkton, Christian, Kentucky
Parents: William and Anna Bucalew Bean
Died: 29 Jun 1882, Provo, Utah
Arrived in Valley: 14 Sep 1848, Daniel Miller Independent Co.

Married: Elizabeth Lewis
Date: 27 Jul 1824,
Born: 22 Sep 1803, Lincoln Co., Missouri
Parents: James and Sarah McCoy Lewis
Died: 16 Oct 1864, Provo, Utah

James and Elizabeth had two children before they moved to Golden Point, Illinois, to be with the Church. It was five miles below Nauvoo. After building a log cabin, he helped work on the Nauvoo Temple. Eventually they moved to Nauvoo and rented a home on Mulholland Street, until he was able to build them a brick home two blocks south of the temple. He worked a farm of 80 acres northeast of the city. The chief crop was corn.

When the saints had to leave Nauvoo, James and Elizabeth

outfitted their wagon with all the things necessary to start a new home in the west. Before they left, their provisions and goods were stolen and they were delayed for a time. They joined with a son-in-law, William W. Casper, and were able to put together three wagons with ox teams, a few horses, cows and sheep, and some parched corn plus their personal belongings. On May 1 1846, they crossed the Mississippi River and caught up with the main body of saints.

At Mt. Pisgah, they broke ground and planted some of the corn for those who would follow. William joined the Mormon Battalion and James and his family continued on to the Valley. James received the call to take care of the money and property that came from the Mormon Battalion volunteers.

After arriving in the valley, James and his family continued on to Provo where they made their home and farmed and worked hard to provide for their family.

Children:

WILLIAM, b. 29 Jul 1829, Pike Co., Missouri. D. 17 Feb 1842.

NANCY, b. 14 Dec 1826, West Troy, Lincoln, Missouri. Md. 1st, (Div) William J. Thomas. Md. 2nd, 5 Feb 1845, (Div) John Doyle Lee. Md. 3rd, 4 Oct 1849, Zachariah Bruyn Decker. D. 3 Mar 1903.

SARAH ANN, b.31 Oct 1828, Mendon, Adams, Illinois. Md. 29 Aug 1844, William Wallace Casper. D. 24 Apr 1882.

GEORGE WASHINGTON, b. 1 Apr 1831, Quincy, Adams, Illinois. Md. 1st 6 Jan 1853, Elizabeth Baum. Md. 2nd, 10 Dec 1856, Emily Haws. Md. 3rd, 15 Dec 1856, Mary Jane Wall. D. 9 Dec 1897.

JAMES ADDISON, b. 11 Mar 1834. Md. 10 Feb 1853, Harriet Catherine Fausett. D. 20 Jan 1917.

MARY ELIZABETH, b. 17 Apr 1837. Md. 27 Dec 1855, Amos Whitcomb Haws D. 25 Sep 1895.

CORNELIA, b. 15 Apr 1841 (adopted). D. 1846.

Submitted by: Moroni Marchant

STEPHEN BEARD

Born: 16 Mar 1839, Duckinfield, Cheshire, England
Parents: Thomas and Ellen Elizabeth Platt Beard
Died: 14 Jan 1905, Henefer, Summit, Utah
Arrived in Valley: Sept 1861, either Samuel Wooley or John
  Murdock Co.

Married 1st: Emma Lee
Date: 6 Feb 1859
Born: of Ashton-under-Lyne, England
Parents: John and Emmaline Arrandale Lee
Died: 1861, On the plains. A brother Thomas, says in his journal,
  "My brother's wife died. She was buried on Sand Nobe in a
  blanket for boards could not be found."

Married 2nd: Mary Ann Roberts
Date: abt 1863, Utah
Born: From Corwen, Merionethshire, Wales
Died: 4 Oct 1900, Hennefer, Utah
Arrived in Valley: With Joseph Dawson Co.

Married 3rd: Jane Carter
Date: 19 Jun 1901, Salt Lake City, Utah
No children

Stephen went to work in the mines to help support the family
when he was just a boy. His father worked on the Woodhead
Tunnel. Families and the men lived where they could and it was
a rough life. They were paid every six to eight weeks but they
were given tickets redeemable for food and necessities. The fam-

ily tolerated this condition for about six or seven years and then Thomas, the father, decided to move to a place where his children could attend church. It was here that Stephen learned to read.

Shortly after this, the family met the elders from the Mormon Church. The parents and Stephen and his brother, Thomas, were baptized. Stephen married shortly after and he became the first of the family to leave England. He left his family and said he would make a place for them to come in the new world. He came to the Valley in 1861.

His wife and children left England with Stephen's brother Thomas and his family. Crossing the plains, Stephen's wife, Emma, became ill and died, as did his oldest daughter and baby daughter. They were buried on the plains. When he met the wagon train, the news was almost more than he could bear.

In 1863, Stephen married again and they made their home in Henefer, Utah. Tragedy befell the family many times. Two of his sons were killed, and his home was burned to the ground.

In 1862 he joined the U.S. Army and served from 1862 through 1867. He was in the Black Hawk war. He filled a mission to the Southern States from 1885-1887. He was very musical and was choir leader for many years. He was a devout, God-loving man. He served wherever he was needed. He was a strong man and enjoyed helping his friends and neighbors.

He became a citizen 9 April 1873.

Children of 1st wife:

ELLEN, b.10 May 1859, England. Died young.
PREMATURE BABY, lived one day.
CHARLOTTE, b. 18 Jul 1860, England. D. 18 May 1862 aboard ship. Child.
MARY ANN, b. 30 Oct 1861, England. D. On plains after mother died. Child.

Children of 2nd wife:

JOHN ROBERTS, b. 24 Feb 1864, Utah. D. 12 May 1899.
WILLIAM HENRY, b. 22 Nov 1865, Utah. D. 7 Dec 1936.

IRA ALMA, b. 1867, Utah. D. 1872, Utah. Child. Fell off wagon and was run over.

GEORGE THOMAS, b. 1870, Utah. D. 5 Jan 1902.

JEREMIAH JAMES, b. 28 Nov 1872, Utah. D. 1882.

DAVID EDGAR, b. 4 Mar 1875, Utah. D. 18 Mar 1894. Killed by train.

OCTAVUS SERENUS, b. 8 Jun 1877, Utah. D. 30 Sep 1950.

Submitted by: Margery Louise Beard Bitter

THOMAS BEARD

Born: 3 Oct 1814, Caulir Firth, Derbyshire, England
Parents: Aaron and Sarah E. Clayton Beard
Died: 7 Dec 1881, Coalville, Summit, Utah
Arrived in Valley: 21 Sep 1868, John G. Holman and E.T. Mumford Co.

Married: Ellen Elizabeth Platt Clark.
Date: 12 Oct 1836, Taxal Church, Caulir Firth, Derby, England
Died: June 1868, buried at sea.

Thomas Beard was a miner. There was a turnout of all workmen throughout England. This caused much suffering among the working class. He finally found work building a tunnel. The family lived there among very poor conditions for several years.

Finally the Mormon elders came and brought hope and happiness to the downtrodden people. In 1852, Thomas, Ellen, Thomas Jr., and Stephen were baptized. They determined they would take their families and emigrate to the Valley as soon as possible. Stephen was first to leave. He left his family in the care of his brother and went to make a home in the valley for his family.

When Thomas Sr. and the rest of the family left England, they had much sorrow on the journey when several died and were buried at sea. Eventually they were able to start west in a wagon train. On the way, Stephen's wife and her youngest child died. They had many hardships on the ship as well as crossing the plains.

After they reached the valley, they decided to settle in Coalville, Utah.

Children:

THOMAS, b. 14 Dec 1836, Cheshire, England. Md. 1st, Mary Ann Openshaw. Md. 2nd, Mahaleth Tanner. D. 23 Dec 1917, Utah.

STEPHEN, b. 16 Mar 1839, Cheshire, England. Md. 1st, Emma Lee. Md. 2nd, Mary Ann Roberts. Md. 3rd Jane Carter. D. 18 Jan 1905.

JOHN, b. 23 Apr 1841, Cheshire, England. Md. Mary Vernon. D. 2 Oct 1876, Utah.

AARON, b. abt 1843, England. D. Infant.

WILLIAM, b. abt 1844, England. D. Infant.

MARY ANN, b. 23 May 1846, England. Md. Thomas Copley. D. 19 Jun 1931.

SARAH, b. 30 Apr 1849, England. Md. Edward Richins. D. 9 Mar 1913.

ELIZABETH, b. 27 Jun 1852, England. Md. 1st, George Crompton. Md. 2nd, James Stones. Md. 3rd, Edward Richins. D. Jan 1935.

GEORGE, b. 21 Dec 1855, England. Md. Sarah Lovinia Bullock. D. 3 Oct 1944.

Submitted by: Margery Louise Beard Bitter

FRANCIS BEARDALL

Born: 20 Feb 1833, Mansfield, Nottingham, England
Parents: John and Mary Chambers Beardall
Died: 29 Jan 1911, Springville, Utah
Arrived in Valley: 4 Oct 1863, John W. Woolley Co.

Married 1st: Emma Gabbitas
Date: 25 Jun 1853, Sheffield, Yorkshire, England
Born: 9 Feb 1833, Mansfield, Nottingham, England
Died: 12 May 1911, Springville, Utah

Married 2nd: Mary Peaslend
Date: 19 Aug 1865, Salt Lake City, Utah

As a young man, Francis worked as an apprentice in an iron foundry for eight years and became an iron moulder. After his marriage, they lived in Mansfield where several children were born. About 1859, they met the LDS missionaries and attended some of their meetings. They determined to go to America and the Valley so Francis worked hard to save the money. They sailed from Liverpool on the "Cynosure" and arrived in New York 19 July 1863.

They joined the John W. Woolley wagon train and set out. Several days after wading the Platt River, Emma gave birth to a son. They arrived in the valley 4 October 1863. They went to Springville to live and moved into a one-room adobe granary. Francis found work and friends helped them to survive that first year.

Francis became the first butcher in Springville, where he had his own store for about twenty-five years. He served as County

Road Supervisor and was Marshall of Springville. He was a veteran of the Black Hawk Indian War. He used to wash and prepare for burial nearly all the men who died in Springville and never charged for his services. He and his wife were spiritual giants in the community and served whenever called upon.

He and his wife had beautiful voices and sang in the ward choir and participated in any musical events. They died only a few months apart.

Children:

ELIZABETH, b. 25 Dec 1853, Mansfield, Nottingham, England. Md. 22 Feb 1875, Oscar Middleton Mower. D. 13 Jul 1917, Springville, Utah.

CHARLOTTE, b. 2 Jan 1856, Mansfield, England. D. 15 Sep 1859. Child.

ELLEN, b. 15 Oct 1858, Mansfield, England. Md. 14 Oct 1880, Marion Moroni Johnson. D. 8 Jun 1896, Springville, Utah.

FRANK, b. 18 May 1861, Mansfield, England. Md. 1st, 16 Dec 1878, Mary Ann Herbert. Md. 2nd 20 Dec 1893, Emma Jemima Watts. D. 14 Apr 1942, Salt Lake City, Utah.

GEORGE, b. 14 Aug 1863, on plains after crossing Platte River. Md. 17 Jan 1885, Rhoda Bird. D. 9 Sep 1909, Springville, Utah.

WILLIAM HENRY, b. 17 Feb 1866, Springville, Utah. Md. 9 Mar 1887, Clara Viola Packard. D. 9 Mar 1936, Springville, Utah

JOHN THOMAS, b. 1 May 1868, Springville, Utah. Md. 23 Jan 1890, Lettie Mae Houtz. D. 7 Feb 1927, Springville, Utah.

MARY CHARLOTTE, b. 11 Nov 1870, Springville, Utah. Md. 23 Jan 1890, Charles Drayson Bramall. D. 28 May 1935, Provo, Utah.

WALLACE EUGENE, b. 30 Jul 1873, Springville, Utah. Md. 17 Oct 1895, Viola Clyde. D. 23 Oct 1922, Salt Lake City, Utah.

EMMA ELIZABETH, b. 1 Sep 1875, Springville, Utah. Md. 21 Dec 1898, Cornelius Anson Van Leuven. D. 4 Nov 1957, Spanish Fork, Utah.

Children of 2nd wife, 1 child.

Submitted by: Marie Twitchell and Marie Boren

WILLIAM BEARDSHALL

Born: 12 Aug 1825, Sim Hill, Silkstone, Yorks, England
Parents: David and Hannah Cauldwell Beardshall
Died: 10 Aug 1893, Salt Lake City
Arrived in Valley: Oct 1851, James W. Cummings Co.

Married 1st: Catherine Clegg
Date: 20 Mar 1862.

Married 2nd: Mary Clegg–No children
Date: 10 Feb 1865.

Married 3rd: Alice Chippendale
Date: 24 Mar 1881

William's mother died when he was three years old. He had a brother who was seven, a sister, two, and another sister one month old. Because of such a young family, his father remarried.

When he was twenty-three years old, he met the Mormon missionaries, was convinced they were right and was baptized. At the time, he was a miner. He worked in the peat bogs, which is wet, marshy ground where peat is the beginning of coal.

In 1851, he and some friends booked passage on the "SS Ellen" for America and eventually got to the Valley. When he was 30, William, with 15 men, were sent to explore Cedar Valley in Utah County, with the idea of establishing settlements there. In 1855, Fairfield was settled there on the west side of Utah Lake.

In 1857 General Albert Sidney Johnston settled on the south side of the irrigation canal on part of William's property. It was there that the army settled down until 1861, when the base was closed.

William was able to purchase army wagons, horse blankets, saddles, bedding from the Army Commissary. He moved the building across the creek and used it as a home which his third wife, Alice, made into an attractive home. This is now the Museum and headquarters for Camp Floyd Utah State Park.

William was a member of the school board, Treasurer of Cedar Fort Ecclesiastical Society, and invested in Lehi Sugar Mill, Provo Woolen Mills, Fairfield Co-op, and Zions Cooperative Mercantile Institution. He was active in community and church affairs.

Children of 1st wife:

JOSEPHINE PEARL THORNTON, Adopted her grandniece,
   daughter of Joseph Thorton and Sarah Cornelia Brown.
HANNAH, b. 28 Dec 1881.
DAVID HENRY, b. 15 Jan 1884.
BERTHA ELIZABETH, b.22 Mar 1886.

Children of 3rd wife:

She brought four children with her from her first marriage to James Duckworth. One died as an infant.
JAMES.
ANN.
ALICE.
WILLIAM.
They with their mother Ann, left Over Darwin, Lancs, England and arrived in Salt Lake, 11 Nov 1880

Submitted by: LaVerne A. Diehl

PETER JACOBSEN BECK

Born: 10 Oct 1850, Torup Simested, Viborg, Denmark
Parents: Stephan Jensen Jacobsen and Inger Kirstine Jacobsen
    Beck
Died: 28 Feb 1927, American Fork, Utah, Utah
Arrived in Valley: 23 Sep 1862, Ola N. Liljenquist Co.

Married 1st: Isadora Jameson
Date: 29 Dec 1873,(Div) Salt Lake City, Utah
Born: 19 May 1855, Provo, Utah
Parents: Alexander and Pirene Brown Ewell Jameson
Died: 17 Sep 1919, Rock Point, Vernal, Utah

Married 2nd: Margaret Boddison
Date: 15 Apr 1886, Salt Lake City, Utah
Parents: Henry and Emma Deane Boddison
Died: 26 Dec 1928, Magna, Utah

Peter Beck was only twelve years old when his parents brought
their children to the Valley. He remembered how hard it was when
his mother gave birth to a son who died and was buried at sea.
The trek west was one of the larger ones with 400 immigrants in
80 wagons.

When they reached the Valley, they stayed for a short time in
Salt Lake and then went to Lehi and then to Alpine in the American Fork area where they settled.

Peter had been baptized at the age of eight in Denmark when
his folks joined the Church. His inability to understand or speak
the language was a drawback to making friends. However, he
soon became friends with a young man who helped him learn the

language. As a youth he herded sheep but by the time he was 18, he had his own herd of cattle and he prospered. He carried the mail for the U.S. Government between the years of 1914 and 1917

He was a quiet, retiring person but he made many friends and people liked and respected him. He was active in the church, and was a good father, husband and friend.

Children of 1st wife:

PETER STEPHEN, b. 6 Dec 1874, Alpine, Utah. Md. 21 Sep 1899, Rosella Corline Freestone. D. 14 Oct 1938.
PIRENE FLORENCE, b. 10 Oct 1877, Goshen, Utah. Md. 28 Sep 1905, William Alexander. D. 13 Sep 1959, Salt Lake City, Utah.
ALEXANDER AVERY, b. 16 May 1878, Alpine, Utah. Md. 26 Jul 1896, Hannah Margaret Thunneson. D. 22 May 1953, Centerfield, Utah.
ISADORA (twin), b. 13 Oct 1879, Alpine, Utah. D. child.
LENORA, (twin), b. 13 Oct 1879, Alpine, Utah. D. 22 Oct 1879. Child.
MARTHA ANN, b. 25 May 1881, Alpine, Utah. Md. 29 Dec 1897 (Div), Alvin Azro Weeks. D. 17 Jul 1957, Provo, Utah.
WILLIAM JAMESON, b. 24 Feb 1883, Alpine, Utah. D. 27 Aug 1901.

Children of 2nd wife:

HANNAH LAURA, b. 27 Jan 1887, American Fork, Utah. Md. 18 Jul 1907, Sidney David Huish. D. 6 Nov 1951, Magna, Utah.
EMMA GENEVA, b.28 Dec 1889, American Fork, Utah. Md. 11 Jan 1912, Murray Kesler. D. 15 Nov 1967, Salt Lake City, Utah.
INFANT, b. 1890, American Fork, Utah. D. Infant.
BYRON LEONARD, b.30 Jul 1891, Highland, Utah. Md. 15 Dec 1915, Margaret Ann Bushman. D. 25 Oct 1962, Magna, Utah.

EDNA TRESSA, b. 21 Feb 1893, Highland, Utah. Md. 22 Oct 1910, Douglas Hindley. D.14 Feb 1957 American Fork, Utah.

KNORD, b. 16 Nov 1894, Highland, Utah. Md. 20 Dec 1916, Carrie Elizabeth Spencer. D. 6 Apr 1968, American Fork, Utah.

CALVERT HENRY, b. 25 Nov 1896, Highland, Utah. Md. 2 Jun 1920, Lillian Greenwood. D. 11 Jan 1963, American Fork, Utah.

MARGARET ETHEL, b. 23 Feb 1899, Highland, Utah. Md. Arnold Andrew. D. 18 Oct 1968, Salt Lake City, Utah.

DANIEL HAROLD, b. 16 Feb 1903, Highland, Utah. D. 16 Nov 1918.

MILTON "Q", b. 19 Feb 1905, American Fork, Utah. Md. Archalous Tavoian. D. 10 Nov 1930, Utah.

Submitted by: Mella Bedell

STEPHEN JENSEN JACOBSEN BECK

Born: 16 Nov 1818, Saltum, Praestegaard, Hjorring, Denmark
Parents: Jacob Stephansen and Dorthea Marie Christensen Beck
Died: 13 Oct 1903, Alpine, Utah, Utah
Arrived in Valley: 23 Sep 1862, Ola N. Liljenquist Co.

Married: Inger Kirstine Jacobsen
Date: 9 Apr 1848, Durup, Aalborg, Denmark
Born: 15 Feb 1827, Alstrup, Aalborg, Denmark
Parents: Peder and Kirstine Marie Jensen Jacobsen
Died: 11 May 1911, American Fork, Utah, Utah

Stephen Beck learned the carpenter trade when he was a youth and was especially good at cabinet making and finishing woodwork. After he came to the Valley, he was called on to make many coffins for the people. At the close of his life he made his own casket.

In 1856 in Denmark, they were contacted by the missionaries. They readily accepted the gospel and were baptized in February 1857. They often told of having to walk four miles in the cold and then cut a hole in the ice to be baptized. Stephen did well in his carpenter trade but the desire to go to Zion was so strong that they saved all they could and made plans to leave for America. They took five children with them. Inger gave birth to a son while crossing the ocean. She often said she didn't have enough to eat to support the baby. He died and was buried at sea.

The Beck family remained in Salt Lake but a short time later they were sent to Lehi where they remained about two years. They were often hungry during this time. They had a difficult time getting enough to eat and refused to ask for help. They moved to Alpine where Stephen built them a lovely home. It didn't take long for people to discover what a fine carpenter he was. He and his two brothers pooled their talents and became known as- farmer Beck, mason Beck, and carpenter Beck. They built many of the homes in the area.

Stephen was very community minded. For many years he carried the mail from American Fork to Alpine. He saw that his children all received a good education plus the opportunity to learn music. He was very strict and insisted that his children do what was right. He remained true to the gospel all his life.

Children:

JACOB STEPHANSEN, b. 20 Jul 1848, Lisentorp, Durup, Aalborg, Denmark. Md. 2 Oct 1878, Elizabeth Healey. D. 5 Sep 1921, American Fork, Utah.
PETER JACOBSEN, b. 10 Oct 1850, Torup, Simested, Viborg, Denmark. Md. 29 Dec 1873 (Div), Isadora Jameson. D. 28 Feb 1927, American Fork, Utah.
CHRISTIAN MATHIAS, b. 23 Jun 1855, Aalborg, Denmark.

Md. 27 Feb 1889, Zilpha Ann Chipman. D. 14 Jun 1923, American Fork, Utah

STEPHEN, b. 24 May 1857, Aalborg, Hjorring, Denmark. Md. Ada. D. 14 Jul 1943, Huntington, Baker, Oregon.

THEODORE, b. 22 Sep 1859, Aalborg, Aalborg, Denmark Md. 27 Dec 1882, Elizabeth Ann Smithies. D. 26 Nov 1931, Idaho Falls, Idaho.

AUGUST, b. 24 May 1862, Crossing Atlantic. D. 29 May 1862, Buried at sea.

JOHN, b. 31 Jan 1865, Lehi, Utah. Md. 5 Jul 1886, Evelyn Elizabeth Bates. D. 5 Dec 1940, American Fork, Utah.

DANIEL, b. 24 Sep 1867, Apine, Utah. Md. Hellena Robinson. D. 2 Nov 1897.

LAURA KIRSTINE, b. 24 Nov 1871, Alpine, Utah. Md. Samuel Hootin. D. 28 Mar 1949, Sandy, Utah.

Submitted by: Mella Bedell

ALEXANDER BECKSTEAD

Born: 16 Mar 1802, Williamsburg, Ontario, Canada
Parents: Francis and Margaret Margaritta Barkley Beckstead Sr.
Died: 20 Feb 1870, West Jordan, Utah
Arrived in Valley: 15 Sep 1849, Reddin Allred Co.

Married 1st: Catherine Lince
Date: 25 Jan 1823, Williamsburg, Ontario, Canada
Born: 6 Jul 1807, Williamsburg, Ontario, Canada
Parents: Bartholomew and Nancy Castleman Lince
Died: 12 Nov 1889, So. Jordan, Utah

Married 2nd: Keziah A. Petty
Date: 18 Nov 1854

Married 3rd: Clarrissa Ann Brown
Date: 1856

Alexander Beckstead was baptized as a young man in Canada when his father joined the Church. They immigrated from Canada to be with the saints in Illinois, but were met with a vicious mob and held prisoner for several days. A fierce rain storm kept the mob from harming them until the Prophet, hearing of their problem, arrived with a company of men who were able to free the prisoners and escort them safely to Nauvoo.

He settled in West Jordan where he resided until his death. He helped dig the first ditch from which water was taken for their use. He helped a great deal in the settling and building up of West Jordan. Many times he helped people in need. Instead of selling his flour at these times, he gave it away.

He helped build the West Jordan old rock meeting house. He was much loved and respected by everyone.

Children of 1st wife:

MARGARET MARIAH, b. 9 Dec 1823, Williamsburg, Ontario, Canada. Md. 18 Apr 1839, Samuel Egbert. D. 1 Jul 1901, So. Jordan, Utah.

GORDON SILAS, b. 25 Nov 1825, Williamsburg, Canada. Md. 1857, Elizabeth Hunsaker. D. 31 Jan 1891, Preston, Idaho.

HENRY, b. 4 Dec 1827, Morrisburg, Canada. Md. 6 Jan 1849 (Div). Lucene Bird Bybee. D. 3 Sep 1889, West Jordan, Utah.

WILLIAM, b. 24 Sep 1829, Morrisburg, Canada. D. 21 Jul 1830. Child.

HARRIET VERNISHA, b. 17 Jan 1831, Williamsburg, Canada. Md. 22 Nov 1850, Abraham Hunsaker. D. 6 Jan 1905, Honeyville, Utah.

THOMAS WESLEY, b. 27 Apr 1833, Williamsburg, Canada. Md. 1st Lydia Maria Rose (and others). D. 21 Sep 1893, Whitney, Idaho.

LUCY ANN, b. 16 Mar 1835, Williamsburg, Canada. D. 21 Jul 1848 on the plains.

EMELINE, b. 4 Apr 1837, Williamsburg, Canada. Md. 4 Jul 1852, William Andrew Bills. D. 1 Jan 1917, Riverton, Utah.

SARAH ELIZABETH, b. 31 Dec 1838, Far West, Caldwell, Illinois. Md. 5 Aug 1854, John William Winward. D. 17 Jul 1890, So. Jordan, Utah.

SAMUEL ALEXANDER, b. 25 Dec 1840, Near Nauvoo, Illinois. Md. 17 Aug 1856, Araminta Churberry Allen. D. 28 Mar 1861, So. Jordan, Utah.

AMANDA, b. 3 Jan 1843, Illinois. D. 6 Sep 1844. Child.

GEORGE WASHINGTON, b. 3 Dec 1845, Hancock, Illinois. Md. 28 Feb 1863, Amaminta Churberry Allen. D. 19 Nov 1912, So. Jordan, Utah.

JOHN ALMA (twin), b. 9 Aug 1848, Kanesville, Iowa. Md. 14 Sep 1867, Sabina Ann Harrison. D. 13 Feb 1927, So. Jordan, Utah.

MARY ELLEN (twin), b. 9 Aug 1848, Kanesville, Iowa. D. 9 Aug 1848. Child.

JOSEPH ALONZO, b. 27 Dec 1850, West Jordan, Utah. Md. 5 Dec 1871, Elizabeth Shields. D. 18 Feb 1923, Preston, Idaho.

ELZINA JANETTE, b. 7 Mar 1860, So. Jordan, Utah. Md. 30 Nov 1874, Gordan Silas Beckstead. D. 26 Nov 1930, So. Jordan, Utah.

Children of 2nd wife:

They had seven boys and three girls

Children of 3rd wife:

They had one boy and six girls

Submitted by: Janell Nichols

FRANCIS BECKSTEAD, JR.

Born: 4 Jul 1810, Williamsburg, Dundas, Ontario, Canada
Parents: Francis and Margaret Barkley Beckstead Sr.
Died: 1848 on the banks of Missouri River

Married: Maria Beckstead
Date: 1829
Born: 15 Sep 1810, Williamsburg, Dundas, Ontario, Canada
Died: abt 1867, Williamsburg, Dundas, Ontario, Canada

Francis Beckstead Jr., his parents, and other family members listened to the missionaries and were baptized in 1836. Immediately they began the preparations to go west with the saints. When they were within a day's journey of Adams County, Illinois, the group was met at the river by a mob who refused to let them cross. Some of the men slipped away to get help. While they were gone, a cloud came up over the area and a terrific downpour filled the creek to overflowing, forcing the mob to flee. In the meantime, the Prophet, with some men, had come to their rescue and escorted them to Nauvoo.

When the saints were preparing to go west, the entire Beckstead family prepared to go with them. By the time they reached Council Bluffs, Iowa, the Mormon Battalion was being called up. Three of the Beckstead boys, brothers of Francis, signed up to go.

Francis Jr. was stricken with cholera while living on a small farm near the Missouri River in 1848, and he died after only a few hours with the illness. He was buried on the banks of the River.

His dream was not fulfilled but numerous members of his posterity did make it to Utah, fulfilling his desire to have his family settle with the saints in the Rocky Mountains.

Children:

ORRIN MORTIMER, b. 2 Feb 1830, Williamsburg, Dundas, Canada.
SIDNEY MARCUS, b. 19 Mar 1832, Williamsburg, Dundas, Canada.
ALEXANDER D.,b. 12 Apr 1834, Williamsburg, Dundas, Canada.
SARAH ANN M., b. 19 Jan 1836, Williamsburg, Dundas, Canada.
JOSEPH E., b. 12 Apr 1838, Williamsburg, Dundas, Canada.
ELTON EFRON, b. 19 May 1840, Carthage, Hancock, Illinois.
WILLIAM I., b. 11 Dec 1842, Warsaw, Hancock, Illinois.
ALMA ALBERT, b. 28 Dec 1846, Bluff City, Potawattomi, Iowa.

Submitted by: Lorna Belnap

FRANCIS BECKSTEAD, SR.

Born: 14 Jun 1773, Schohari County, New York
Parents: John Volckmann and Helena Thomas Beckstead
Died: 1841, Lima, Adams, Illinois
Arrived in Valley: Died enroute to the valley

Married 1st: Margaret Barkley
Date: abt 1794
Born: 24 Sep 1774, Albany, Albany, New York

Married 2nd: Catharine Lang
Date: abt 1817
Born: 23 Feb 1791, Williamsburg, Dundas, Ontario, Canada
Died: 18 Jul 1868, Union, Salt Lake, Utah

Francis Sr., and his brother Alexander, procured large farms near the town of Williamsburg. They worked hard to make their farms the finest in the area. In 1837-38, the Mormon missionaries came into their lives. It is known that Francis and most of his family joined the Church and made the decision to make the journey to be with the rest of the saints. Others joined with them to make the journey, including young children.

After a journey which lasted almost three months and had some problems, the Company reached DeWitt, Missouri, in the latter part of September 1838. During the coming 10 years, they suffered much from persecution. Finally the Prophet, learning of their circumstances, made a trip to see if he could help them. Most had lost their homes and animals and were destitute for food and the necessities of life. They got what things they could gather together, got some wagons and decided to leave the area. Many were sick and weak. They endured much but finally arrived in Caldwell, where some of them stayed while the rest went on to Far West.

It is not known in which place Francis and his family settled, but it is indicated in records that it was Far West, because one of the children was born there in December 1838.

It is believed that Francis later settled in Lima, Illinois. In 1846, they were found in Pottawtamie County, Iowa. It is recorded that Francis Beckstead Sr. died in 1841 in Adams County. His two sons, Francis Jr. and Alexander, brought the family west.

Children of 1st wife:

MARIA, b. about 1795.
HANNAH, b. about 1796.
HELENA, chr. 28 Dec 1798, Schoharie, Rensselaer, New York.
JACOB L., b. 8 Jun 1799, Schoharie, New York.
ALEXANDER, b. 16 Mar 1802, Schoharie, New York.

NELLIE, chr, 16 Oct 1803, Williamsburg, Dundas, Ontario, Canada.

MATHEW, b. 14 Feb 1805, Williamsburg, Dundas, Ontario, Canada.

MOSES, b. 8 Oct 1807, Williamsburg, Dundas, Ontario, Canada.

FRANCIS, JR., b. 4 Jul 1810, Williamsburg, Dundas, Ontario, Canada.

HENRY, b. 1812, Williamsburg, Dundas, Ontario, Canada.

ELIZABETH, b. 1814/16, Williamsburg, Dundas, Ontario, Canada.

Children of 2nd wife:

MARY LOUISE, b. 6 Jul 1818, Williamsburg, Dundas, Ontario, Canada.

SIMON PETER, b. 16 Jan 1822, Prescott, Grenville, Ontario, Canada.

SARAH LOUISA, b. 21 Dec 1823, Williamsburg, Dundas, Ontario.

NANCY, b. abt 1824, Williamsburg, Dundas, Ontario.

CHARLES, b. 1825, Williamsburg, Dundas, Ontario.

ELIZABETH, b. abt 1826, Williamsburg, Dundas, Ontario.

WILLIAM EZRA, b. 13 Mar 1827, Williamsburg, Dundas, Ontario.

EMMA PHOEBE ANN, b. 18 Jul 1829, Williamsburg, Dundas, Ontario.

KEZIAH (DOZIAH), b. 1831, Williamsburg, Dundas, Ontario.

GEORGE WESLEY, b. 23 Apr 1835, Williamsburg, Dundas, Ontario.

Submitted by: Lorna Belnap

SIDNEY MARCUS BECKSTEAD

Born: 19 Mar 1832, Williamsburg, Dundas, Ontario, Canada
Parents: Francis and Mary Beckstead Beckstead Jr.
Died: 7 Aug 1864, 14 miles from the Platt River Bridge in
    Nebraska
Died enroute to Valley

Married 1st: Ann Sophia Rollins
Date: 11 Jun 1850, Bellevue, Sarpy, Nebraska
Born: 5 Mar 1831, Bangor, Penobscot, Maine
Died: 13 May 1885, Annabella, Sevier, Utah

Married 2nd: Anne Susannah Jackson Hill
Date: 8 Mar 1862
Born: Bird, Glouchestershire, England

Sidney Marcus Beckstead was only four years old when the Mormon elders visited his father. Less than two years later, Sidney and his few possessions were packed into a wagon with the rest of the family and their possessions, and then started on their long journey to the west. They were forced to move from place to place and at one point were rescued by the Prophet Joseph. They had arrived in the midst of the persecution of the saints.

When his father died on the way west, he helped his mother by staying with her in Iowa. He married during this time and they stayed behind for two years before they finally made the decision to head west. Sidney and his wife and daughter went on with a relative, George W. Beckstead, while his mother and four brothers stayed behind.

Sidney played the violin and called dances when they would

stop at night. While on the road, his Aunt Sarah Forbush died. Her husband asked Sidney and Ann to take care of his four motherless children. When they arrived in the Valley, they lived with the Forbush family in Union Fort for awhile. Later they moved to West Jordan where Sidney helped another uncle in the blacksmith shop, which trade he learned. He tried to prove on some land which proved worthless.

Sidney finally took Ann to Salt Lake to see her folks and while there, he worked with her father who was a carpenter and wheelwright. They made wagons and did carpenter work. He did a lot of colonizing, living at various times in Weber, Mountain Green, West Jordan, Provo, Riverdale, and Goshen Valley. He learned to make and repair shoes, which helped his family and others. He was always trying to help others. His great disappointment was that his mother stayed in Iowa and never came west after his father's death.

One day Sidney was riding with some other men. One of the wagons broke down and Sidney got off to help fix it. When he mounted again, he forgot his gun and reached down to get it. The hammer of the gun had caught in the brush and discharged, killing him instantly. It was three weeks before the word got to his family.

Children:

MARY LUCETTA, b. abt 1847, St. Louis, Missouri. (Adopted)
SARAH ANN, b. 14 Mar 1851, Traders Point. D. 14 Sep 1944, Payson, Utah.
SABRA JANE, b. 20 Oct 1853, Salt Lake City, Utah. D. 1 May 1946.
LILLIAN SOPHIA, b. 7 Sep 1855, West Weber, Utah. D. 1 Dec 1916.
MARY EMILY, b. 6 Dec 1857, Mountain Green, Utah. D. 2 Jul 1942.
ROSETTA, b. 11 Aug 1859, East Weber, Utah. D. 29 Jan 1863.
LORETTA DELANCY, b. 26 Sep 1861, West Jordan, Utah. D. 28 Jan 1863.
CORDELIA, b. 28 Oct 1863, Provo, Utah. D. 8 Sep 1864.

Submitted by: Lorna Belnap

ELIAS AUGUST BECKSTRAND

Born: 20 Oct 1832, Granstorp, Jon Vilstad, Sweden
Parents: Knut Johan and Ingierd Jacobsson Beckstrand
Died: 26 Feb 1910, Meadow, Millard, Utah
Arrived in Valley: 13 Sep 1861, Joseph Horne Co.

Married 1st: Anna Sofia Hegglund
Date: 24 Jan 1862, Salt Lake City, Utah
Born: 9 Oct 1833, Ryssby, Kalmar, Sweden
Died: 8 Jul 1890, Meadow, Millard, Utah

Married 2nd: Henrietta Cecilia Carlson
Date: 7 Jun 1869, Salt Lake City, Utah
Born: 17 Apr 1851, Malmo, Burlov, Sweden
Parents: Neils Romelhof and Sisse (Cecilla Ellen) Jacobsson
Died: 6 Sep 1923, Meadow, Millard, Utah

Elias August Beckstrand was left an orphan at the age of 15 in Sweden. He then started to earn his own living. He worked as a coachman for a well-to-do family. He received cultural training among aristocrats and was treated with courtesy. He resisted the temptations which were also there.

Later when the gospel came into his life, he was glad that he had no bad habits to overcome. He was baptized 16 February 1859 and in November was called to fill a mission in Sweden.

In 1861, he and his brother and sister emigrated to the Valley, arriving in September 1861. His first work was hauling logs for Joseph Horne. It was there he met his future wife. After they were married, they lived in Salt Lake for a time until they were called by Brigham Young to help settle Deseret.

After two more children were born, Elias met a young lady who agreed to live in his home and help his wife who was ill. The year was 1868. In the spring, he married her. They all made their home in Meadow, Utah.

He served in many positions in the church and on 25 November 1901, he was ordained a patriarch. In 1888 he served four months in the penitentiary for his religious convictions (polygamy).

He homesteaded and farmed some land east of town, known as the Beckstrand Farm.

Children of 1st wife:

ANNA JUDITY (JUDITH), b. 21 Nov 1862, Salt Lake City, Utah. Md. 7 May 1879, J. Duncan.
JOHN AUGUST, b. 19 Mar 1865, Deseret, Utah. Md. 30 Nov 1892, M.E. Stott.
ALBERTINA SOFIA, b. 4 Mar 1867, Deseret, Utah. Md. 6 Dec 1883, J. H. Fisher.
JOSEPH CONRAD, b. 10 Mar 1870, Meadow, Utah. Md. 25 Oct 1893, E. Bennett.
IDA CHRESTINE, b. 3 Apr 1872. D. 6 May 1875. Child.
MARY ELIZABETH, b. 12 Aug 1874, D. 11 May 1875. Child.

Children of 2nd wife:

ELIAS HYRUM, b. 11 Mar 1870, Meadow, Utah. Md. 21 Jul 1908, A. J. Dahlquist.
CHARLES ALFRED, b. 9 Feb 1872. D. 26 May 1872. Child.
HEBER WILLIAM, b. 18 Mar 1873, Meadow, Utah. Md. 23 Aug 1899, M. E. Stewart.
ALMEDA HENRIETTE, b. 16 Feb 1875. D. 11 May 1875, child
RACHEL DINA, b. 11 Apr 1876, Meadow, Utah. Md. 21 Dec 1898, J. J. Bennett.
NEPHI DAVID, b. 1 Nov 1878, Meadow, Utah. Md. 1 Jun 1910, M. H. Adams.
ALMA NEIL, b. 4 Jun 1881, Meadow, Utah. Md. 30 Aug 1911, J. K. Pettit.

EVA ELLEN, b. 16 Jul 1884, Meadow, Utah. Md. 12 Jun 1907,
Lewis Smith.
KNUT, b. 26 Dec 1888. D. 26 Dec 1888. Child.
ARNOLD ASAEL, b. 7 May 1891, Meadow, Utah. Md. 1st, E.
A. Smith. Md. 2nd, B. G. Smith.

Submitted by: Dayle Duncan White

HOGAN BECKSTROM

Born: 8 May 1821, Tarstad, Tirup, Malmohus, Sweden
Parents: Jons and Anna Andersson Hakansson
Died: 27 Nov 1895, Spanish Fork, Utah
Arrived in Valley: 29 Aug 1863, J. R. Murdock Co.

Married: Fredrica Eleonora Bauer or Ekelund
Date: 11 May 1851, St. Petri, Malmo, Malmohus, Sweden
Born: 18 Jul 1824, Caroli, Malmo, Malmohus, Sweden
Died: 26 Jul 1895, Spanish Fork, Utah, Utah

Not much is known of Hogan's early life. The family was
Lutheran before they heard the Mormon missionaries. Times were
difficult before they joined the Church, but afterwards, it became
almost impossible for his father to obtain employment.

They finally gathered together enough money to emigrate to
the Valley in 1863. They came with the Murdock ox wagon train
but there were some in the group who pulled handcarts, and the
Beckstrom Family was one of these. Hogan's wife pulled the
handcart most of the way.

After their arrival in Salt Lake, and a brief stay, they settled in Milton, Weber Valley, Morgan County, Utah, where they lived for seven years. Their first home was a dugout.

In the spring of 1870, they moved to Spanish Fork where, after a couple of years and the death of a child, Hogan built them a nice home. He made most of the furniture himself. He learned so much about carpentering that he became quite skilled at the work. He also kept a farm.

He was a deeply religious man and helped his fellow men whenever possible. He was a fine teacher in the ward and a writer. He was one of two winners in a contest writing about Joseph Smith.

He and his wife taught the children the principles of honesty, obedience, and prayer. The children were forbidden to swear. Fredrica was a fine seamstress and cook, and she and her husband provided a good example for their children.

Children:

JOHN NIELS/NILS JOHAN, b. 4 Jun 1851, St. Petri, Malmo, Malmohus, Sweden. Md. 1st 5 Apr 1875, Mary Christina Hansen. Md. 2nd 1924, Mary Anna Halverson. D. 3 Jun 1928, Spanish Fork, Utah.

ANNA CAROLINA, b. 15 Feb 1854, Caroli, Malmo, Malmohus, Sweden. Md. 27 May 1872, Charles David Johnson. D. 3 Aug 1892, Spanish Fork, Utah.

MARY JOHANNA/MARIA, b. 18 Aug 1856, Caroli, Malmo, Malmohus, Sweden. Md. 13 Feb 1879, Lars Nielsen. D. 23 Jan 1928, Spanish Fork, Utah.

WILLIAM OLIVER/WILHELM, b. 21 Jun 1859, Caroli, Malmo, Malmohus, Sweden. Md. 1 Feb 1883, Phyllis Ann Meason. D. 3 Mar 1918, Lake Shore, Utah.

JOHANNA MATILDA, b. 2 Mar 1862, Caroli, Malmo, Malmohus, Sweden. D. 1863, at sea while coming to Valley. Child.

AUGUSTA ELIZABETH, b. 7 Jul 1864, Milton, Morgan, Utah. Md. 21 Dec 1892, Charles David Johnson. D. 5 Feb 1948, Moore, Butte, Idaho.

NANCY MATILDA, b. 4 Aug 1867, Milton, Morgan, Utah. Md. 1st, 13 Jan 1882, John Erickson. Md. 2nd, 8 Dec 1886, James Henry Hill. D. 24 Oct 1951, Spanish Fork, Utah.

CHARLES/CARL HOGAN, b. 23 Feb 1871, Spanish Fork, Utah. D. 31 Jan 1872, Spanish Fork, Utah.

Submitted by: Helen J. Harris

GEORGE McNIEL BEEMUS

Born: 11 Jan 1837, Louistown, Fulton, Illinois
Parents: Lineus and Martha Amelia Jewel Beemus
Died: 15 May 1906, Gunnison, Utah
Arrived in Valley: 1863, Handcart

Married: Margaret Jones
Date: Aug 1865, Salt Lake City, Utah
Born: 19 Feb 1843, Raglan, Wales
Died: 10 Apr 1890, Gunnison, Utah

George, after his arrival in the valley by handcart, went on to Gunnison where he settled. At first they lived in the fort at Fort Wales. He made three trips back East to bring immigrants to the Valley and then on to Gunnison. He also brought freight and supplies from Council Bluffs.

He built a rock home, being a fine rock mason and stone quarrier. He helped build many of the early homes. He also farmed. He was known as a "water witch," able to locate where to sink a well.

He was well liked by the youth of the area, building a swing and doing other things which endeared him to them.

Children:

MARY MARTHA, b. 6 Sep 1866.
GEORGE THOMAS, b. 25 Aug 1867.
SARAH, b.25 Mar 1869.
HARRIET MATILDA, b.18 Apr 1870.
DIANA ELIZABETH,b. 28 Sep 1872.
JOHN WILLIAM, b. 29 Oct 1874.
IRA LYNUS, b. 20 Aug 1875.
CHARLES DAVID, b. 12 Apr 1877.
ABRAM FRANKLIN, b. 29 Feb 1880.
ISABELL, b. 17 Jul 1882.
MARGARET EMILY (twin), b. 4 Jul 1885 .
JAMES MARTIN (twin), b. 4 Jul 1885.

Submitted by: Orr Hill

WILLIAM BEESLEY

Born: 20 Oct 1833, Walton LeDale, Lancs, England
Parents: George and Elizabeth (Betty) Taylor Beesley
Died: 15 Jul 1903, Kaysville, Davis, Utah
Arrived in Valley: 3 Sep 1855, John Hindley's Co.

Married 1st: Hannah Flint
Date: 11 Apr 1857, Salt Lake City, Utah
Born: 22 Nov 1840, Middleton, Wirksworth, Derby, England
Parents: John and Mary Spencer Flint
Died: 12 Dec 1877, Kaysville, Davis, Utah

Married 2nd: Elizabeth Hibbert
Date: 12 Jun 1879, Salt Lake City, Utah

Born: 4 Jan 1845, Hyde, Cheshire, England
Parents: Walter and Sarah Taylor Hibbert
Died: 11 Apr 1932, Ogden, Weber, Utah

William Beesley didn't get much schooling but worked in a cotton factory as a youth. In his thirteenth year, he did manage to get three months of night school. He studied on his own and managed to develop an unusual ability in mathematics.

He was converted to the Mormon Church and baptized 19 June 1851. He sailed to America three years later, being the only member of his family who came.

After coming to the Valley, he moved to Kaysville, living with George Greenwood. William had driven the oxen team for him across the plains.

After a most difficult winter with much sickness, spring came and William discovered that people wanted combs and there were very few. He took common corset steel and filed out of it a small saw. With this he made combs out of mahogany for the members of the community.

He built one of the first saw mills in Utah in Cottonwood Canyon in Morgan Canyon. He helped build the first road through Weber Canyon. He built a grist mill east of Kaysville. He took over a vacated saw mill and supplied lumber for many years. He was a city councilman for four years. He supplied ice to pack bodies in before funerals. He kept an ice house where the ice was stored in saw dust for the summer months. He was leader of the ward choir for many years and held positions in the ward. He loved to work among the sick and was much loved and respected for all he did.

Children of 1st wife:

WILLIAM GEORGE, b. 14 Feb 1858, Kaysville, Davis, Utah.
MARY ELIZABETH, b. 10 Sep 1859, Kaysville, Utah.
JOHN, b. 21 Dec 1861, Kaysville, Utah.
HANNAH ELIZA, b. 17 Sep 1863, Kaysville, Utah.
ROBERT HEBER, b. 14 Nov 1865, Kaysville, Utah.
THOMAS HENRY, b. 12 Nov 1867, Kaysville, Utah.

DRUCILLA, b. 20 Sep 1869, Kaysville, Utah.
JAMES LAURENCE, b. 24 Mar 1872, Kaysville, Utah.
PHOEBE ELLEN, b. 11 Feb 1875, Kaysville, Utah.
MARGARET, b.4 May 1877, Kaysville, Utah.

Children of 2nd wife:

WILLIAM HIBBERT, b. 4 Mar 1881, Kaysville, Utah.
GEORGE, b. 17 Apr 1883, Kaysville, Utah.
ADAM, (twin), 18 Sep 1885, Kaysville, Utah.
SARAH JANE, (twin), 18 Sep 1885, Kaysville, Utah.

Submitted by: Janet Furgeson

ALFRED BELL

Born: 16 Aug 1794, Rowan County, North Carolina
Parents: William and Sarah McGuire Bell
Died: 17 Feb 1874, Lehi, Utah
Arrived in Valley: 24 Oct 1851, Capt. Horne's Co.

Married 1st: Jane Graham Haynie
Date: 5 Jul 1821, Gallatin, Tennessee.
Born: 8 Jan 1802
Died: 16 Mar 1823

Married 2nd: Martha Louisa Montgomery Elder (widow of David
    Elder)
Date: 8 Sep 1830, Shelby Co., Illinois

Born: 7 Apr 1807, Mecklenburg Co., North Carolina
Died: 20 May 1888, Logan, Utah

Alfred Bell had much sorrow where marriage was concerned. His first wife, Jane G. Haynie, died after only being married two years. His second attempt, Nancy Pierce, died five days prior to their wedding. His third wife brought much happiness into his life. He raised her children by her first husband.

Martha and Alfred were baptized into the Church the 23 May 1839. Alfred ran a ferry on the Mississippi River at Nauvoo and became good friends with the Prophet and Hyrum, and mourned at their deaths.

When the mobs forced the saints from their homes, Alfred and his family of five loaded what they could into their wagon and left with the others. In the spring the family turned off the main road and went down into the state of Missouri in the vicinity of St. Joseph. They remained there while they tried to get an outfit together to cross the plains. By the spring of 1851, the Bells started for the Valley. They were in Captain Horne's Company.

After their arrival, they went to Lehi where they settled. The Walker Indian War was giving problems to the saints. A fort was built for protection and a division of the Nauvoo Legion was formed in Lehi. Soon Brigham Young was able to make a peace treaty with Chief Walker.

Alfred was elected to the city government and served as an alderman, examiner and justice for many years. The family took in emigrants who came to Utah until they found a place to stay.

Children of 2nd wife:

(3 from previous marriage): PLUS:
WILLIAM MILTON, b. 22 Jul 1833, Shelbyville, Illinois. Md. 9
    Apr 1859, Martha K. Benson. D. 12 Nov 1908.
ELI, b. 12 Nov 1834, Shelbyville, Illinois. Md. 18 Aug 1858,
    Louisa Ann McClellan. D. 31 Jul 1895.

Submitted by: Virginia Martin

ELI BELL

Born: 12 Nov 1834, Shelby Co., Illinois
Parents: Alfred and Martha Louisa Montgomery Elder Bell
Died: 30 Jul 1895, Logan, Utah
Arrived in Valley: 24 Oct 1851, Capt. Horne Co.

Married: Louisa Ann McClellen
Date: 18 Aug 1858, Lehi, Utah
Born: abt 1840
Parents: James and Cynthia McClellan
Died: 23 Nov 1916, Logan, Utah

Eli's parents moved to Nauvoo in 1838 after they had joined the Church. In 1851 they arrived in the Valley. In the fall of 1853 Eli was called on a mission to Southern Utah where he also studied the Indian languages. He returned home in the spring in time to attend General Conference.

He was again called on a mission, this time with Joseph F. Smith and 28 others to the South Pacific Islands. They all left together in wagons, working their way to San Francisco. They were able to obtain passage on a ship, and landed in Honolulu. Eli labored on all the islands in Hawaii and learned the language. He worked when necessary to purchase supplies and to save enough to return home. His father met him in Fillmore and rode home with him to Lehi where they arrived 2 June 1858.

Eli married in 1858. They were called in 1860 to help settle Cache Valley, Utah. Eli worked his farm and raised a good crop of potatoes. They built a one-room log cabin. Their first two children died after birth. They were finally blessed with a baby daughter.

In 1865, Eli and his family were called on a mission back to the Hawaiian Islands. His whole family went. Eli helped build the first sugar mill in Hawaii, preached the gospel, baptized and earned a living there. Two boys were born there. Due to poor living conditions and food, Louisa became weak and ill so the mission president released them to return home after six years. Six weeks after returning home another child was born to them.

Eli and his wife began to make another home. Many guests visited them from the Islands, staying with them while attending the temple. Eli built a nice two story home in Lehi.

Eli worked on the Logan temple as a finished carpenter, painter, and furniture maker. He did blacksmith work. He was a well known speaker and conducted many funerals. He was a night watchman and one of the first policemen in Logan, being in charge of the jail. He was also county sheriff. He sang in the Logan Tabernacle choir, served several stake missions and was an ordinance worker in the temple.

Children:

MARTHA JANE, b. 13 Jan 1860, Payson, Utah. D. 13 Jan 1860. Child.

LYLIAN HARRIET, b. 28 Mar 1862, Logan, Utah. D. 24 Mar 1863. Child.

SYLVIA ARMINTA, b. 28 Jun 1864, Logan, Utah. Md. 11 Jan 1888, James H. Davidson. D. 13 Feb 1947.

ELI JASPER, b. 2 Dec 1866, Laie, Oahu, Hawaii. Md. 22 Dec 1898, Elizabeth J. Bywater. D. 18 Jun 1923.

ALFRED JAMES, b. 6 Jan 1869, Laie, Oahu, Hawaii. Md. 27 Dec 1893, Evalyn S. Shirtliff. D. 15 Oct 1952.

EFFIE, b. 23 Jul 1871, Logan, Utah. Md. 22 Dec 1897, Hyrum S. Barson. D. 16 Jul 1955.

GEORGE A., b. 26 Oct 1873, Logan, Utah. Md. 29 Jun 1907, Ruth E. Moench. D. 14 Jun 1964.

ADELBERT, b. 10 Mar 1876, Logan, Utah. Md. 5 Jun 1900, J. Blanche Nelson. D. 26 Jun 1963.

GERTRUDE LOUISA, b. 13 Oct 1878, Logan, Utah. Md. 22 Jun 1898, Robert M. Smith. D. 8 Feb 1940.

SARAH, (twin), b. 22 Mar 1882. D. 22 Mar 1882. Child.
MARY, (twin), b. 22 Mar 1882. D. 22 Mar 1882. Child.
MILTON OLIVER, b. 13 Mar 1883. Md. 7 Jun 1906, Estella M.
  Bernhisel. D. 30 Nov 1973.
ROSE MAE, b. 18 Jun 1886, Logan, Utah. Md. 14 Sep 1910,
  George L. Zundel. D. 27 Apr 1954.

Submitted by: Virginia Martin

JOHN WATSON BELL

Born: 28 May 1805, Wellington, Northumberland, England
Parents: Robert and Alice Rutter Bell
Died: 1877, Mona, Juab, Utah
Arrived in Valley: 7 Sep 1854, Benjamin Clapp Co.

Married: Ann Fish
Date: Oct 1834, England
Born: 21 Jan 1812, England
Died: 1872, Mona, Juab, Utah

John was ordained to the Seventies while still in Nauvoo, Illinois. He made curtains and pulpit covers for the Nauvoo Temple and also helped with the construction.

He served as a guard for U.S. District Judge George Stiles 1854-5. He lived in Salt Lake for four years and in Provo seven years.

He was sent by Brigham Young to help settle Mona, Juab, Utah, in 1867. He lived there until his death. He was a farmer and a tailor by trade.

Children:

ANNA ELIZABETH, b. 22 Mar 1836. Md. 1st, 3 Dec 1856, Henry J. Reynolds. Md. 2nd, 2 Aug 1862, William Lance.
ROBERT MARION, b. 2 Apr 1838. Md. Harriet Ann Compton. D.3 Jan 1925.
ALICE JANE, b. 15 Apr 1840. Md. 6 Dec 1857, Joel Almon Bascom. D. 8 Apr 1918.
JOHN WATSON Jr, b. 23 Jun 1842. Md. 1 Jan 1866, Laura Celestia Roberts. D. 2 Aug 1917.
EMMA DOROTHY, b. 18 Mar 1844. Md. 2 Nov 1861, Ephriam Horace Roberts. D. 9 Jan 1911.
JOSEPH ALMA, b. 6 Oct 1846. Unmarried. D. 1922.
MARY FRANCES, b. 25 Dec 1848. Md. 1 Apr 1866, William James Baldwin D. 22 May 1873.
SARAH EMILY, b.4 Aug 1852. D. 8 Jul 1853. Child.

Submitted by: Junith Roberts

GILBERT BELNAP

Born: 22 Dec 1821, Port Hope, New Castle, Upper Canada. (now Port Hope), Durham, Ontario, Canada.
Parents: Rosel and Jane Richmond Belnap
Died: 26 Feb 1899, Hooper, Weber, Utah
Arrived in Valley: 17 Sep 1850, Warren Foote Co.

Married 1st: Adaline Knight
Date: 21 Dec 1845, Nauvoo, Hancock, Illinois
Died: 10 Jun 1919, Salt Lake City, Utah

Married 2nd: Henrietta McBride
Date: 26 Jun 1852, Great Salt Lake, Utah
Died: 5 Sep 1899, Hooper, Weber, Utah

Gilbert's father raised purebred race horses. Gilbert inherited a great love for horses from his father. Shortly before Gilbert's 11th birthday, his father was killed and three months later, his mother died.

Gilbert had been apprenticed to William C. Moore to learn the trade of wheelwright and wagon maker. In 1834, Mr. Moore took Gilbert with him to New York. He was frequently abused and finally left to try to find his family. He found that his older brother had taken everything so Gilbert took his youngest five-year-old brother and struck out on his own. He found a home with a Christian preacher, where he remained until 1837. His little brother was given to another family.

After hearing about the Mormons, intrigued, he went to Kirtland where he became converted, but was not baptized until 1842. He served a mission in New York and later moved to Nauvoo. He worked closely with the Prophet and church leaders. He eventually married and went west with the saints.

Because of his wisdom and great faith, he was often called on in various capacities to give blessings and serve the church. He was active in community affairs and was loved and respected by everyone who knew him. His life history is filled with events of the strength of this good man and his love for the gospel.

Children of 1st wife:

GILBERT ROSEL, b. 8 Jan 1847, Winter Quarters, Nebraska. Md. 30 Nov 1867. D. 25 Jan 1929, Ogden, Utah
JOHN McBRIDE, b. 11 May 1849, Fremont Co., Iowa. D. 22 Jun 1850, near Salt Creek Ford, Nebraska. Child.
REUBEN, b. 14 Jun 1851, Ogden, Weber, Utah. Md. 11 Jan 1870, Lucien Vilate Hammon. D. 20 Oct 1923, Ogden, Utah.
JOSEPH, b. 26 Jan 1853, Ogden, Utah. Md. 26 Apr 1875, Minerva Permilia Hammon. D.1 Apr 1933, Weber, Utah.

MARTHA JANE, b. 17 Sep 1855, Ogden, Utah. Md. 11 Jan 1870, Levi Byram Hammon. D. 21 Mar 1923, Roy, Weber, Utah.

HYRUM, b. 24 Mar 1858, Ogden, Utah. Md. 1st, 20 Sep 1883, Christiana Rasmussen. Md. 2nd, 7 Feb 1888, Anna Constantia Bluth. D. 18 Sep 1938, Ogden, Utah.

AUGUSTUS WEBER, b. 25 Mar 1860, Ogden, Utah. Md. 21 Apr 1886, Mary Read. D. 15 Mar 1948, Salem, Madison, Idaho.

VOLNEY, b. 17 Feb 1862, Ogden, Utah. D. 14 Mar 1862. Child.

VINSON KNIGHT, b. 26 Jun 1863, Ogden, Utah. Md. 20 Oct 1886, Sarah Emily Hardy. D. 23 Apr 1920, Ogden, Utah.

AMASA, b. 22 Jun 1866, Ogden, Utah. Md. 1st, 20 Oct 1886, Lillian Rosamond Garner. Md. 2nd, 11 Dec 1901, Julia Rosabell (Rose) James. D. 28 Apr 1929, Salt Lake City, Utah.

ADALINE LORINDA, b. 1 Aug 1868, Ogden, Utah. Md. 18 Nov 1891, John Alexander Lowe. D. 9 Jun 1934, Franklin, Idaho.

MARY LOUISA, b. 11 Dec 1870, Hooper, Utah. Md. 1st, 18 Dec 1889, Joseph Heber Lowe. Md. 2nd, 13 Aug 1941, Charles Robert Robbins (Div). D. 2 May 1950, Smithfield, Utah.

LOLA ALMIRA, b. 5 Jun 1874, Hooper, Utah. Md. 8 Aug 1900, David William Coolbear. D. 14 Jun 1921, Salt Lake City, Utah.

Children of 2nd wife:

WILLIAM JAMES, b. 31 Aug 1853, Ogden, Utah. Md. 22 Dec 1873, Eliza Ann Watts. D. 20 Dec 1932, Hooper, Utah.

OLIVER, b. 20 Sep 1855, Springville, Utah. Md. 1st, 6 Jan 1881, Margaret Ann Manning. Md. 2nd, 31 Jul 1895, Emily Desire Shurtliff (Div). Md. 3rd, 6 Jun 1901, Anna Barbara Leuenberger. D. 30 Mar 1929, St. George, Utah.

FRANCIS MARION, b. 5 Jun 1857, Ogden, Utah. Md. 26 Dec 1878, Lillis Subina Robinson. D. 15 Dec 1932, Hooper, Utah.

ISADORA ESTELLA, b. 31 Oct 1860, Farmington, Utah. Md. 14 Aug 1876, John Francis Stoddard. D. 3 Jan 1931, Hooper, Utah.

Submitted by: Joy Belnap

GILBERT ROSEL BELNAP

Born: 8 Jan 1847, Winter Quarters, Nebraska
Parents: Gilbert and Adaline Knight Belnap
Died: 25 Jan 1929, Ogden, Weber, Utah
Arrived in Valley: 17 Sep 1850, Warren Foote Co.

Married: Sarah Jane Cole
Date: 30 Nov 1867, Great Salt Lake, Utah
Born: 19 Oct 1852, Ogden, Utah
Died: 11 Jan 1924, Ogden, Utah

Gilbert Rosel was born shortly after his parents had started their trek west. His mother was only 15 years old when he was born. Her husband had been away on an assignment and didn't return until the baby was six weeks old. His parents remained at Winter Quarters for another three years before leaving for the Valley.

Upon their arrival in the valley, Brigham Young sent them to Ogden to settle. Gilbert learned to shoot at an early age because of problems with the Indians. After his marriage, he and Sarah went to live in Hooper, Utah. He helped with the railroad, was a constable, was sent to help colonize Arizona, and, upon his return, was called on a mission in 1884. At the return from his mission, he was persuaded to accept the position of sheriff of Weber County, whereupon he moved his family to Ogden. Upon his release he entered into the grocery business. Later the building burned to the ground and he returned to farming.

He was trusted and well liked by everyone and remained active in the church. He died at the age of 81.

Children:

SARAH ELIZABETH, b. 14 Jan 1870, Hooper, Utah. Md. 19
    Jun 1901, Parley Pratt Eldredge. D. 1 Jan 1920, Ogden, Utah.
ADALINE, b.27 May 1872, Hooper, Utah. Md. 18 Dec 1890,
    Heber C. Ballantyne. D. 12 Aug 1956, Redmond, Deschutes,
    Oregon.
GILBERT MARTIN, b. 22 Nov 1874, Hooper, Weber, Utah. D.
    20 Jul 1875, Hooper, Utah. Child.
ROSWELL COLE, b. 27 Jan 1881, Hooper, Utah. Md. 16 Aug
    1911, Inez Powell. D. 18 Jan 1961, Salt Lake City, Utah.
WELTHA MAY, b. 27 Jul 1886, Ogden, Utah. Md. 25 Nov 1908,
    Enos Eugene Marriott. D. 18 Jul 1923, Ogden, Utah.
MAUD, b. 7 Oct 1889, Ogden, Utah. Md. 6 Jan 1911, Stanley
    Fielding Kimball. D. 21 Jun 1971, Salt Lake City, Utah.

Submitted by: Joy Belnap

JOHN McBRIDE BELNAP

Born: 11 May 1849, Fremont Co., Iowa
Parents: Gilbert and Adaline Knight Belnap
Died: 22 Jun 1850, Salt Creek, Nebraska
Arrived in Valley: Died crossing the plains

John McBride's parents started west with their family. They
remained in Winter Quarters for a time and then lived in Fremont
County, Iowa, for three years during which time John was born.
    While there they received word that cholera was raging in

some of the companies ahead. They were encamped east of the ford at Salt Creek near present day Ashland, Nebraska, when little 13 month-old John took ill during the evening with cholera. The next morning his father put the little body inside his tool chest and buried him in an unmarked grave.

Submitted by: Joy Belnap

LYNESS BEMUS

Born: 13 Feb 1805, Ohio
Parents: Samuel and Sarah Bemus
Died: 9 Apr 1858, Manti, Utah
Arrived in Valley: between 1848 and 1858

Married: Martha Amelia Juell
Date: 25 Feb 1827
Born: 23 Jan 1808-1810
Parents: Levi and Judith Juell

Martha was a convert to the Mormon Church but her husband never did join. Shortly before his death, he expressed a desire to be baptized but died before it could be done.

When they came west, Lyness wanted to continue on to the gold fields but his wife wanted to stay in Manti, and he was never sorry that he stayed. Martha remained an active member of the church and Lyness got along well with everyone. They built a good home and had the love and respect of their children and everyone in the community.

Children:

IRA, b. abt 1830, Illinois
MARY JUDITH, b. 10 Sep 1832, Lewiston, Illinois. Md. 1854, Mathew Hayes Ivory. D. 29 Jan 1870.
WILLIAM MYRON, b. 17 Jan 1834, Lewiston, Illinois. Md. Harriet Hamilton. D. 18 May 1900.
GEORGE McNEIL, b. 11 Jan 1837, Lewiston, Illinois. Md. 1864 Margaret Jones. D. Jun 1907.
HARVEY FRANKLIN, b. 12 Jan 1839, Lewiston, Illinois. Un married. D. 16 Jun 1906.
FRANCIS MARION, b. 3 Jul 1841, Lewiston, Illinois. Md. Lucinda Woolsey.
HARRIET AMELIA, b. 16 Sep 1844, Lewiston, Illinois. Md. 5 Feb 1858, Robert Braithwaite. D. 10 Feb 1929.
EMILY MATILDA, b. abt 1845 in Illinois. D. Infant.
NORMAN (twin), b. 3 Jul 1849. D. before 1860, past 8 years.
NORRIS (twin), b. 3 Jul 1849.

Submitted by: J. Ralph Brown

ELI BENNETT

Born: 26 Nov 1831, Bedford Co., Tennessee
Parents: Richard and Mary Bell Bennett
Died: 14 Oct 1906, Cedar Fort, Utah, Utah
Arrived in Valley: 18 Oct 1852, Allen Weeks Co.

Married 1st: Louisa Zufelt

Date: 28 Mar 1851, Harris Grove, Pottawattamie, Iowa
Born: 12 May 1834, Ellisburgh, Jefferson, New York
Parents: Henry and Julia Ann Dillabaugh Zufelt
Died: 25 Mar 1867, Cedar Fort, Utah

Married 2nd: Margaret Simmons
Date: 11 Jul 1868, Salt Lake City, Utah
Born: 23 Jun 1848, Bermondsey, London, Middlesex, England
Parents: Henry and Catherine Davis Simmons
Died: 23 Jul 1937, Cedar Fort, Utah
Arrived in Valley: 11 Sep 1857, Capt. Israel Evans Handcart Co.

Eli traveled with his parents and other children to a new home in Bruce, Illinois, where his father died, leaving his wife Mary to take care of eight children. The Mormon missionaries brought their message to the family and Mary and her three daughters were baptized.

Eli, while living in Nauvoo, became acquainted with the Prophet and greatly admired him. Eli was at the meeting after the martyrdom, when Joseph's mantle fell on Brigham Young. He was only 14 at the time.

His mother took her family from Nauvoo when the expulsion came. They lived for a short time at Mt. Pisgah, Iowa then later at Winter Quarters and then Council Bluffs, Iowa. During this time, two of his sisters married and then died within the next three years. Finally his mother moved to Harris Grove, Pottawatamie, Iowa. Her dreams were still of going to the Valley.

It was here that Eli met and married Louisa Zufelt. About a year later, Brigham Young sent word that the people were to come to the valley. Eli built a wagon and used two cows and two steers to draw it. Indians bothered them some and cholera struck the Company.

After arriving in the valley, they located at Cedar Valley. Indians were creating problems there but the law from Salt Lake helped them. They moved to Lehi for protection. In the spring of 1853, several families moved to Cedar Fort which Eli had helped construct. He engaged in farming but a lack of water made it difficult. The establishment of Camp Floyd nearby created some problems, especially when some of the soldiers got drunk and burned a haystack and created problems.

They had their problems with the crickets but outlived that. Eli lost a wife and baby daughter within a few days of each other, leaving him with four children. He asked a young girl to come and help him. After several months he asked her to marry him. She was a good wife and mother to his children.

In 1882 at Provo, Eli was ordained a bishop after having served some time as a counselor. He continued in this position for 25 years until his death.

Children of 1st wife:

ELI, JR., b. 22 Jun 1853, Lehi, Utah. Md. 19 Jan 1873, Maria
  Elizabeth Berry. D. 9 Jul 1937. Charlo Lake, Montana.
CATHERINE LAVINA, b. 26 Apr 1855, Cedar Fort, Utah. D. 18
  Jun 1859, Cedar Fort, Utah. Child.
RICHARD HENRY, b. 24 May 1859, Cedar Fort, Utah. Md. abt
  1885, Athena Augusta Rogers. D. 6 Feb 1937, Lethbridge,
  Alberta, Canada.
WILLIAM DAVID, b. 23 May 1861, Cedar Fort, Utah. Md. 15
  Oct 1885, Emma Neat. D. 24 Oct 1916, Lethbridge, Alberta,
  Canada.
MARY ANN, b. 4 Apr 1863, Cedar Fort, Utah. Md. 7 Apr 1884,
  William Henry Winn. D. 12 May 1950, Salt Lake City, Utah.
LOUISA JANE, b. 12 Mar 1867, Cedar Fort, Utah. D. 21 Mar
  1867. Child.

Children of 2nd wife:

MARGARET ELIZABETH, b 30 Jul 1869, Cedar Fort, Utah.
  Md. 10 Oct 1888, David Alvin Berry. D.28 Sep 1891, Cedar
  Fort, Utah.

Submitted by: Barbara Roach

JOHN BELL BENNETT, SR.

Born: 16 May 1830, Shelbyville, Shelby, Illinois
Parents: William J. and Elizabeth Bell Bennett
Died: 2 Feb 1902, Lehi, Utah, Utah
Arrived in Valley: 7 Oct 1851, Erastus Snow wagon train

Married: Mary Senior
Date: 2 Feb 1863,
Died: 20 May 1891, Provo, Utah

John was five years old when his father joined the Church. His mother joined four years later. After their conversion, the family moved to Nauvoo, Illinois, where his father died during the persecution of the saints. John was baptized when he was 20 while the family was enroute to the Valley.

John hauled wood for fuel from the canyons as well as any other work he could get. He drove a wagon for his brother-in-law back to help the saints migrate. On one of the trips he met his future wife, Mary Senior.

John had made his home in the valley with his mother, Elizabeth, and her other children, until he married. He and Mary made their home in Payson, Utah, for most of their lives.

Their last child was born in Provo where they lived the rest of their lives. Their seventh child, John Bell Jr., contracted spinal meningitis as a child, leaving him totally deaf. Mary taught him to lip read.

After his wife died, John finished raising the boys and later his children said how kind he was. He was a quiet man. He spent much time with his son's wife Alice, and she cared for him when he was sick or needed company. He died in her home in Lehi, Utah.

Children:

MARY CATHERINE, b. 24 Oct 1863. D.1864. Infant.

JOHN WILLIAM, b. 1864. D. Infant

AUSTIN ROBERT, b. 14 Jan 1866, Payson, Utah. Md. 20 Jul 1887, A. E. Harding.

ELLEN ELIZABETH, b. 1867. D. Infant

WILLIAM HYRUM, b. 27 Oct 1869, Payson, Utah. Md. 21 Nov 1894, E. Bushnell.

GEORGE EDWARD, b. 19 Mar 1871, Payson, Utah. D. 3 Jan 1874. Child.

JOHN BELL JR., b. 11 Oct 1872, Payson, Utah. Md. 15 Feb 1905, M. E. Hustler.

DAVID ALFRED, b. 8 Aug 1874, Payson, Utah. Md. 1st, 23 May 1896, M. Reed. Md. 2nd, E. Rowley.

SIDNEY REDFERN, b. 18 Nov 1876, Payson, Utah. D. 27 Dec 1877. Child.

SAMUEL SENIOR, b. 18 Nov 1876, Payson, Utah. Md. 1st, 4 Aug 1901, M. L. Park, Md. 2nd, Mr. Bullock.

JOSEPH McGUIRE, b. 13 SEP 1878, PAYSON, MD. 1st, 10 Jul 1904, L. Besendorfer. Md. 2nd, L. R. Keats.

FRANKLIN TENNYSON, b. 21 Aug 1881, Provo, Utah. Md. 10 Aug 1904, E. Ashworth.

Submitted by: Dayle Duncan White

THOMAS McGUIRE BENNETT

Born: 24 Feb 1816, Bedford Co., Tennessee
Parents: William J. and Elizabeth Bell Bennett
Died: 24 Feb 1894, Franklin, Franklin, Idaho
Arrived in Valley: 9 Oct 1852, James C. Snow

Married: Margaret Wilson
Date: 9 Nov 1837, Illinois
Born: 22 Feb 1815, Bedford Co., Tennessee
Parents: James Alfred and Margaret Graham Wilson
Died: Oct 1907, Franklin, Franklin, Idaho

Thomas McGuire and his wife were converted to the Church after their marriage. Their first child, a girl, was given to them by a friend. The mother had died. They loved the little girl and raised her as their own child.

They crossed the plains with Captain James C. Snow. They settled in Provo, then moved to Cedar Valley, and finally to Franklin, Idaho where they stayed.

Thomas was a farmer.

Children:

ELIZABETH RACHEL (EDWARDS), b. abt 1845, Illinois.
    Raised by Bennetts.
WILLIAM THOMAS, b. 25 May 1849, Illinois.

Submitted by: Dayle Duncan White

JOHN BENNION

Born: 9 Jul 1820, Moor Twnp, Hawarden Parish, Flintshire, Wales
Parents: John and Elizabeth Roberts Bennion.
Died: 1 Sep 1877, Taylorsville, Utah
Arrived in Valley: 5 Oct 1847

Married 1st: Esther Wainwright
Date: 15 Feb 1842, Liverpool, England
Born: 12 Oct 1817, Hawarden, Flints, Wales
Died: 6 Jan 1902, Taylorsville, Utah

Married 2nd: Esther (Ann) Birch, called Esther Ann to differen-
tiate from 1st wife.
Date: 20 Jul 1856 Utah
Born: 7 Jul 1833, Wootton, Kent, England
Parents: William and Mary Rogers Birch
Died: 4 Aug 1909, Vernal, Utah

Married 3rd: Mary Turpin
Date: 19 Apr 1857, Utah
Born: 25 Jan 1841, Berkenshaw, Yorks, England
Parents: William and Elizabeth Tidwell Turpin
Died: 4 Jan 1914, Forest Dale, Salt Lake City, Utah

John moved to Liverpool when he was 16 where he was employed in the iron works. While there he heard the gospel from
John Taylor and Joseph Fielding in 1840 and was baptized 2 May
1841. He went home to help his father and explain the gospel to
him. He returned to Liverpool where he married and sailed for
America in the spring. They went to Nauvoo where his father

joined them in 1844, and his brother Samuel in 1845.

Upon leaving Nauvoo in 1846, they traveled to Garden Grove where they established temporary farms. His father died there. Early in 1847 they left Garden Grove to join the saints going west.

In 1850 John and his family moved "over Jordan" where the brothers established homes, farmed, raised sheep and cattle, helped build canals, helped construct Taylorsville Fort, fought Indians and taught their families the gospel. They lived in Taylorsville.

John, as a member of the Nauvoo Legion, was commissioned a captain in 1857, with the problems of Johnston's Army. When that quieted down, he ran sheep and cattle in Rush Valley, Tooele County. In 1868 he was called to the Muddy Mission. He took Esther Ann and her family with him. Upon his return in 1872, he was called on a six month genealogical mission to his home in Wales. He did much good while there. He returned home and died at the age of 57 years.

Children of 1st wife:

SAMUEL ROBERTS, b. 10 Nov 1842, Md. 1st, 28 Sep 1867, Md. 2nd, 10 Aug 1879. D.16 Nov 1915.

MARY, b. 4 May 1844, Md. 6 Apr 1861. D. 28 May 1933.

ANN, b. 19 Nov 1845, D. Sep. 1847. Child.

ANGELINE ROBERTS, b. 16 Mar 1847, Md. 5 Nov 1865. D. 27 May 1934.

RACHEL, b. 5 Jun 1849, Md. 25 Oct 1868. D. 31 Mar 1933.

JOHN EDWARD, b. 1 Jan 1851, Md. 26 Sep 1870. D. 20 Feb 1930.

MORONI, b. 15 Jun 1853, D. 6 Jun 1855. Child.

ELIZABETH, b. 4 Feb 1855. D.2 Nov 1863.

MARIA, b. 5 Aug 1857. Md. 11 Mar 1886. D. 13 Apr 1925.

HARRIET, b. 18 Dec 1858. Md. 27 Oct 1877. D. 22 Jun 1923.

ESTHER, b. 18 Nov 1862. D. 8 Feb 1863. Child.

IRA WAINWRIGHT, b. 5 Jan 1864. Md. 21 Jul 1887. D. 27 Jan 1929.

KANOSH (adopted), b. 15 Sep 1855, D. 1 Jun 1873. An Indian, left by his mother, adopted by John Bennion.

Children of 2nd wife:

ENOCH, b. 17 Feb 1858, D. 28 Nov 1873.
ISRAEL, b. 2 Jun 1860. Md. 1st, 16 Oct 1884, Md. 2nd Feb 1888. D. 1 Aug 1944.
HARDEN, b. 7 Oct 1862. Md. 31 May 1893, D. 12 Oct 1936.
DAVID, b. 1 Feb 1865, Md. 19 Feb 1891. D. 1 Dec 1937.
JUSTIN, b. 6 Aug 1867. D. 20 Feb 1868. Child.
OWEN, b. 15 Mar 1869, Md. 28 Oct 1893. D. 5 Feb 1946.
WILLARD RICHARDS, b. 2 Dec 1871. D. 2 Feb 1888.
IDA, b. 2 Jan 1873, Md. 9 Dec 1896. D. 16 Feb 1946.
ARCHIE BIRCH, b. 15 Jun 1875. Md. 2 Sep 1903.

Children of 3rd wife:

HEBER, b. 28 Nov 1858, Md. 11 Sep 1885. D. 21 Jan 1932.
ALFRED, b. 20 Dec 1860, Md. 24 Aug 1882. D. 12 May 1906.
WILLIAM, b. 9 Apr 1863, Md. 16 Mar 1887. D. 3 Jul 1906.
MARCUS, b. 10 Jun 1865, Md. 27 Dec 1888. D. 18 Jul 1913.
EDWIN, b. 8 Apr 1868, Md. 12 Oct 1892. D. 3 Apr 1930.
MILTON, b. 7 Jun 1870. Md. 22 Jun 1898. D. 5 Apr 1953.
ZINA, b. 2 Jul 1873. Md. 18 Jul 1893. D. 17 Sep 1954.
JOHN ANGUS, b. 2 Oct 1877. D. Mar 1878. Child.

Submitted by: David Sharp

SAMUEL BENNION

Born: 11 Dec 1818, Hawarden, Flintshire, Wales
Parents: John and Elizabeth Roberts Bennion

Died: 9 Sep 1889, West Jordan, Utah
Arrived in Valley: Oct 1847, Edward Hunters Co.

Married 1st: Mary Bushell
Date: 28 Apr 1839, St. Nicholas Parish, Liverpool, England
Born: 1816, Liverpool, Lancs, England
Died: 1872, Utah

Married 2nd: Sarah Williams–No children
Date: 13 Feb 1853, Salt Lake City, Utah
Born: 1836
Died: 1854, 18 months after marriage

Married 3rd: Rhoda Jones Sargent
Date: 25 Oct 1868, Salt Lake City, Utah
Born: 5 Nov 1840.

Samuel left home at age 11 to live with his uncle, William Bennion in Liverpool, to apprentice as a baker to Robert Farrell. He married when he was 20. He was introduced to the gospel by John Taylor and Joseph Fielding in 1840 and was baptized in 1842. Shortly before leaving, two of his three sons died of scarlet fever, James and William. A month after the death of his sons, Mary gave birth to a daughter. They left and arrived in Nauvoo just in time to see the capstone placed on the Nauvoo Temple. His father was already there. Samuel bought land from Daniel H. Wells. He built a large two-story brick home with six apartments in it. Cost of the house was $1,000.

During the problems in Nauvoo, they lost their daughter. They left Nauvoo in May 1846 after selling their home for $250. The family stayed in Garden Grove for the winter and prepared to go west. Samuel's father died there. In the spring they started west again.

When they arrived in the Valley, they located in what is now downtown Salt Lake. When Brigham Young asked them to move "Over Jordan," Samuel and his brother dismantled their log homes and hauled them over the river early in 1849. Samuel took part in the Echo Canyon expedition of Johnston's Army and was a Minute Man in the battle with Indians under Chief Big Elk.

He built a home in Taylorsville. In 1874 he was called on a mission to England and Wales. He was always active in the church and in the community. He purchased the Gardener Flour Mill. He was a stockholder in Z.C.M.I., Taylorsville Cooperative Mercantile Institution. He was a postmaster, Justice of Peace, county commissioner and served until his death. He was a bishop and leader for 27 years.

Children of 1st wife:

JOHN, b. 1 Feb 1840, West Derby, Liverpool, Lancs, England D. 1899.

JAMES, b. 25 Apr 1841, West Derby, Liverpool, England. D. 1899, Liverpool, England.

WILLIAM, b. 30 May 1842, West Derby, Liverpool, England. D.1844, Liverpool, England. Child.

ELIZABETH, b. 1 Jan 1845, West Derby, Liverpool, England. D. 1846. Child.

HYRUM, b. 13 Jan 1847, Garden Grove, Decatur, Iowa. D. 1926.

MARY ELIZABETH, b. 24 Sep 1848, Great Salt Lake, Utah D.1849. Child.

JOSEPH BUSHELL, b. 14 Feb 1850, Taylorsville, Utah. D. 1888.

NEPHI, b. 1851. (adopted Indian boy)

EMMA, b. 8 Nov 1851, Taylorsville, Utah. D. 1941.

REBECCA ANN, b. 17 Mar 1853, Taylorsville, Utah. D. 1946.

SAMUEL HEBER, b. 20 Jun 1854, Taylorsville, Utah. D. 1910.

ALICE JANE, b. 3 Dec 1856, Taylorsville, Utah. D. 1876.

Children of 3rd wife:

WILFORD, b. 16 May 1870, Taylorsville, Utah. D. 1936.

LEONORA, b.1 Sep 1873, Taylorsville, Utah. D. 1874. Child.

ROBERT WILLIAM, b.10 Aug 1875, Taylorsville, Utah. D. 1875. Child.

RHODA JONES, b. 2 Aug 1876, Taylorsville, Utah. D. 1879. Child.

NAOMI JONES, b. 29 May 1878, Taylorsville, Utah. D. 1878.
   Child.
ARTHUR JONES, b. 9 Feb 1881, Taylorsville, Utah. D. 1945.

Submitted by: Helen Madsen and David Sharp

JOHN MILTON BERNHISEL, M.D.

Born: 23 Jun 1799, Tyrone Twn, Cumberland, Pennsylvania
Parents: Samuel and Susan Bower Bernhisel
Died: 28 Sep 1881, Salt Lake City, Utah
Arrived in Valley: 24 Sep 1848, Heber C. Kimball Co.

Married 1st: Julia Ann Haight Van Orden (widow)
Date: 1845
Born: 6 Oct 1805
Parents: Caleb and Keturah Horton Haight
Died: 23 Jan 1865, Salt Lake City, Utah

Married 2nd: Elizabeth Barker
Date: Nauvoo, Illinois

   Dr. John Milton was a studious young man and was able to
enter the Medical Department of the University of Pennsylvania,
from which he graduated in 1827 with high honors. He practiced
in the Alms Houses and hospitals of Pennsylvania until he moved
to New York, where he succeeded in building an excellent practice.

While in New York, he first heard and accepted the gospel. He left New York and joined the main body of the Church in Nauvoo in 1842. He lived in the Prophet's home until his assassination. At the advice of the prophet, he married Elizabeth Barker as his second wife.

Dr. John as a trustee for the church, and his family remained in Nauvoo until the fall of 1847. He reached the Valley in 1848.

After reaching the valley, Dr. Bernhisel was active in the government of the new territory. He was called on to carry the memorial to Washington D.C. This was passed and approved by Congress 9 September 1850. He was unanimously elected Utah's first delegate to the National Congress where he served five terms, 1851 to 1863. He was intimately associated with Daniel Webster and President Lincoln and others.

He was one of the founders of the University of Deseret, now the University of Utah. He was a member of the first Board of Regents and remained on the board until 1858. After Congress appropriated $5,000 for a new University Library, he selected the books and had them shipped across the plains to Utah.

He was elected a vice president of ZCMI. He was a studious, cultivated man who never waivered from his convictions.

Child of 1st wife:

JOHN MILTON II, b. 21 Dec 1846, Winter Quarters, Nebraska. Md. 3 Jan 1876, Henrietta Harris. D. 13 Jan 1920, Lewiston, Utah.

Children of 2nd wife:

He and Elizabeth had nine children.

Submitted by: Virginia Martin

JOHN MILTON BERNHISEL II

Born: 21 Dec 1846, Winter Quarters, Nebraska in a covered
  wagon
Parents: Dr. John Milton and Julia Ann Haight Van Orden
  Bernhisel
Died: 13 Jan 1920, Lewiston, Utah
Arrived in Valley: 24 Sep 1848, Heber C. Kimball Co.

Married: Henrietta Harris
Date: 3 Jan 1876, Salt Lake City, Utah
Born: 11 Aug 1854, Kaysville, Utah
Parents: Robert and Hannah Maria Eagles Harris, Jr.
Died: 23 Aug 1909, Lewiston, Utah

John was born in a covered wagon at Winter Quarters. He
was the only child of this couple. He came to the Valley with his
parents. Upon their arrival, they lived for a time in the old fort.

He was a student at the University of Deseret. He was a volunteer for the Black Hawk Indian War in Southern Utah. He took
an active part in the building up of Lewiston, Utah, holding many
public positions.

John was Justice of the Peace 1884-1890, road supervisor,
and bridge contractor. He was a representative to the first State
Legislature of Utah. He was involved with Utah Idaho Sugar Company, Lewiston Cooperative Mercantile Institution, Lewiston State
Bank and other enterprises. He planted the first tree in Lewiston,
a cottonwood, and was active in bringing water to the area. He
also witnessed the driving of the Golden Spike.

He was known as a true pioneer and loyal citizen. His kind
acts and generosity to those in need was long remembered.

Children:

JULIA ANN, b. 5 Oct 1876, Lewiston, Utah. Md. 25 Sep 1902, Moroni T. Bcck. D. 13 Apr 1906.

JOHN MILTON III, b. 2 Mar 1878, Lewiston, Utah. Md. 4 Jun 1902, Ruey Pond. D. 11 Feb 1957.

ESTELLA MARIA, b. 26 Jun 1880, Lewiston, Utah. Md. 7 Jun 1906, Milton O. Bell. D. 2 Jun 1957.

JANETTA, b. 9 Jan 1882, Lewiston, Utah. Md. 28 Jun 1905, J. LeRoy Pond. D. 7 Jun 1962.

ROBERT,(twin), b. 11 Aug 1883, Lewiston, Utah. D. 11 Aug 1883. Child.

MARTIN, (twin), b. 11 Aug 1883, Lewiston, Utah. D. 11 Aug 1883. Child.

SARAH LOUISA, b. 4 Feb 1885, Lewiston, Utah. Md. 16 Oct 1919, C. I. Stoddard. D. 10 Feb 1971.

FRANKLIN, b. 23 Jul 1886, Lewiston, Utah. D. 4 Jan 1903.

EVERETT CLARK, b. 29 Mar 1888, Lewiston, Utah. Md. 23 Dec 1916, Jennie Cox. D. 9 Mar 1931.

RALPH, b. 10 Jul 1891, Lewiston, Utah. Md. 13 Sep 1911, Nellie Hendricks. D. 28 Oct 1933.

HARRIS FAY, b. 1 Oct 1893, Lewiston, Utah. Md. 9 Jun 1920, Marie A. Beirdneau. D. 12 Dec 1981.

ASCEL EARL, b. 10 Jan 1896, Lewiston, Utah. D. 5 Jul 1897. Child.

ADELIA, b. 20 Jan 1897, Lewiston, Utah. D. 20 Jan 1897. Child.

Submitted by: Virginia Martin

WILLIAM SAMUEL BETHERS

Born: 18 May 1843, Quincy, Adams, Illinois
Parents: Zadock Stergeous and Sarah Collins Bethards (changed
 to Bethers when parents joined the church)
Died: 7 Oct 1926, Daniel (Heber), Wasatch, Utah
Arrived in Provo: 22 Sep 1852, Capt Joseph Outhouse Co.

Married: Phebe Hannah McMillian
Date: 14 Sep 1866, Heber City, Utah
Died: 7 Apr 1909, Daniel, Wasatch, Utah

When William's father joined the Church, he changed their
name from Bethards to Bethers. They lived in Council Bluffs
when it was only a wildnerness. In 1852 they prepared to cross
the plains. There were only 50 in the Company. The mother, two
daughters and five sons all had the measles while crossing the
plains. They finally arrived in Provo where they were met with
open arms and the help they needed.

William was taught to work hard and endure, and his mother
taught him the value of prayer. William became a freighter as a
young man, helping many come west. He served in the Indian
Wars and was a Blackhawk War veteran. He and his family eventually settled in Wanship and Heber during the time he was working on the railroad, which came into Utah. In 1847 he homesteaded near the mouth of Daniel's Canyon where he built a fine
farm and homes. He acquired one of the first grain binders, horse
powered, and then a steam-powered thresher machine that he and
his sons used to help many people.

He supervised work on the Daniel Canyon Road for 16 years.

He was Trustee and treasurer of the school board, and was a jurist. He had healing power in his hands with his great faith and priesthood. He was in the bishopric and also served in many callings. William and Phebe always had an open door for those in need. They fed and clothed many poor and needy. They were life savers for many in those early years.

Children:

SON, d. 1870. Infant.

MARY JANE, b. 27 Aug 1867, Wanship, Utah. Md. 5 Aug 1884, John O. Oaks, Salt Lake City, Utah. D. 6 Nov 1950, Daniels, Utah.

MAHLON COLLINS, b. 3 Nov 1869, Heber, Utah. D. 26 Sep 1870. Child.

JANETTE, b. 23 May 1871, Heber, Utah. Md. 22 Aug 1890, William Oaks. D. 8 Aug 1921, Provo, Utah.

WILLIAM, b. 14 Oct 1872, Heber, Utah. Md. 16 Jan 1901, Annie Elizabeth McGuire. D. 23 Dec 1949, Daniel, Utah.

SARAH COLLINS, b. 9 Mar 1874, Daniel, Utah. Md. 11 Dec 1901, Charles E. Price. D. 7 Mar 1945, Daniels, Utah.

ZADOCK ALLEN, b. 8 Sep 1875, Daniel, Utah. Md. 30 Jun 1910, Mary Luella Anderson. D. 8 Nov 1961, Salt Lake City, Utah.

NATHAN HENRY, b. 30 Jun 1878, Daniels, Utah. Md. 27 Mar 1918, Hester Almira Duke. D. 3 May 1961, Daniel, Utah.

EPHRAIM, b. 25 Mar 1880, Daniel, Utah. Md. 12 Jan 1904, Edna McGuire, Salt Lake City, Utah. D. 22 Oct 1945, Daniel, Utah.

ALBERT FRANCIS, b. 13 May 1882, Daniel, Utah. Md. 26 Jul 1909, Almira Tiffany. D. 24 Dec 1964, Salt Lake City, Utah.

GEORGE WASHINGTON, b. 30 Sep 1883, Daniel, Utah. Md. 8 Jun 1910, Jane Isabell Carlen. D. 26 Jun 1951, Heber, Utah.

JOHN TAYLOR, b. 17 Aug 1885, D. 15 Aug 1909, Daniel, Utah.

PHEBE ANN, b. and d. 26 May 1887, Daniel, Utah. Child.

ASA ALMA, b. 8 Oct 1890, Daniel, Utah. Md. 20 Apr 1925, Jerome Wall. D. abt 1960, Heber, Utah.

Submitted by: Irene Llewellyn

JAMES BETTS

Born: 22 Dec 1845, Sheffield, Yorkshire, England
Parents: Peter and Eliza Franklin Betts
Died: 26 Mar 1878, Peteetneet (Payson), Utah
Arrived in Valley: 26 Sep 1862, James Warham Co.

Married: Margaret Powell
Date: 3 Apr 1867, Payson, Utah
Born: 12 Mar 1848, Llanover, Wales
Died: 23 Feb 1925, Payson, Utah

James was the last of 11 children. Jame's father was an iron maker and it is said that he was knighted for making the first springs in the Queen's carriage.

When the missionaries visited the family, they soon became converted and all who were old enough were baptized. James was baptized 10 years later by his brother, William in St. Louis.

In 1848 his father was sent to Springfield, Illinois, to work. It took two years before he was able to send for his family. He died in St. Louis, but his wife bravely gathered the necessary equipment. In 1862 they traveled to the Valley. Twice James returned to the Missouri River to help the Mormon immigrants to Utah.

After his marriage, James and his brother, John, leased a shingle and saw mill. James was in charge of making the shingles while John was a wood finisher and painter.

James was a quiet and religious man. He enjoyed taking part in the plays and entertainment of the ward. He served as Marshal for two years. He wasn't interested in farming but loved horticulture. He grew and sold plants. They had only one cow for the family's use.

James and his brother-in-law were killed in a snowslide while cutting ties for the railroad.

Children:

MARGARET ELIZA, b. 28 Dec 1867, Payson, Utah. Md. 14 Apr 1887, William J. Taylor. D. 1 Jan 1935.

JAMES PETER, b. 7 Feb 1870, Payson, Utah. D. 21 Oct 1870. Child.

MARY ELIZABETH, b. 4 Jan 1872, Payson, Utah. Md. 1st, 23 Dec 1891, Colin McMurphy. Md. 2nd, 25 Nov 1942, Stephen W. Walker. D. 21 Jan 1944.

WILLIAM, b. 7 Jan 1874, Payson, Utah. Md. 6 Nov 1901, Martha Ann Bates. D. 7 Jul 1956.

JOHN ALEXANDER, b. 5 Mar 1876, Payson, Utah. Md. 1st, 10 Jul 1894 Helen Ann Cushing. Md. 2nd, 10 May 1922, Katherine Quiley. D. 29 Oct 1952.

DAVID SAMUEL, b. 2 Mar 1878, Payson, Utah. Md. 3 May 1905, Iris Reid. D. 4 Jun 1953, Coalville, Utah.

Submitted by: Janice Betts and Margaret Mayo

WILLIAM M. BICKMORE

Born: 14 May 1799, Friendship, Maine Parents: David and Martha Dixon (or Dickey) Bickmore
Died: 1884, Corralitos, California (near Watsonville)
Arrived in Valley: 3 Oct 1852, John B. Walker Co.

Married: Christena Bagley

Date: Eloped in about 1826, Illinois
Born: 12 Jun 1808, Dutchess Co., New York
Died: 11 Sep 1880.

William lost one eye playing Indians with a bow and arrow when he was young.

He eloped with Christena, tradition says, and stole her from a log cabin. They immediately went to Scott County where William's sister and husband were living. They rented a house where they lived until they were able to save enough to buy a farm in Brown County, Illinois.

In 1841, they moved to Hancock County, where they joined the Church. Later they moved to Des Moines, Iowa, and then to Pottawattamie, Iowa. They moved with members of their family trying to go west with the saints. On the way William's mother and a brother, Isaac, died of cholera.

When they finally got to the Valley, they were sent to live in Millard, Fillmore County. In 1853 they were called to help settle San Bernardino, California. When the saints were recalled from the area in 1857, they chose to stay. They traveled to various parts of California and finally ended up in Santa Cruz County where they camped at first in a side canyon among the redwood trees.

Eventually his sons bought small farms at Corralitos, near Watsonville, California. William and Christena lived there with their sons until they died.

Children:

GILBERT, b. 20 Jul 1827, Madison, Illinois. Md. 12 Mar 1849, Catharine J. Huntsman, Council Bluffs, Iowa. D. 4 Feb 1896.
ELIZA ANN, b. 29 Jan 1830, Madison, Illinois. Md. 3 May 1852, Elijah Allen. D. 26 Mar 1901, Cove, Utah.
MARY JANE, b. abt 1832, Madison, Illinois. Md. Nov 1853, William Huntsman. D. 6 Aug 1891.
PHEDELIA (FIDELIA), b. 5 Feb 1833, Madison, Illinois. Md. 17 Mar 1852, Alexander Kidd. D. 16 Nov 1915, Provo, Utah.
WILLIAM N., b. 14 May 1838, Elkhorn Twn, Brown, Illinois. D. 11 Aug 1847.

LOVINA, b. 27 Nov 1839, Elkhorn Twn., Brown, Illinois. Md. 1st, 9 Sep 1855, Albert Miles Tanner. Md. 2nd, 20 Jun 1888, K. R. Taylor. D. 11 Jan 1913.

THOMAS LOWELL, b. 25 Nov 1841, Elkhorn Twn, Brown, Illinois. Md. 10 May 1866, Martha Jane Cullumber. D. 18 Apr 1918, Corralitos, California.

LOUISA CHRISTINE, b. 20 Mar 1844, Hancock, Illinois. Md. 19 Aug1860, John Boardman Mills. D. 30 Nov 1900.

ORLANDO ALTON, b. 27 Sep 1846, Council Bluffs, Iowa. Md. 5 Sep 1873, Eliza Jane Bauguess. D. 3 Jan 1909.

CATHERINE ANN, b. 16 Jul 1849, Council Bluffs, Iowa. Md. 10 May 1866, Samuel S. McAdams. D. 14 Jun 1928.

JOSEPH HYRUM, (or Hiram Joseph), b. 1851/2, Council Bluffs, Iowa. Md. 20 Apr 1873, Rosa Belle Maule. (Div).

Submitted by: Theda Judd

ASA ELIJAH BIGELOW

Born: 2 Feb 1832, Coles Co., Illinois
Parents: Nahum and Mary Gibbs Bigelow
Died: abt 1910
Arrived in Valley: 1850

Married 1st: Julia Ann Cook
Date: 2 Apr 1853, Provo, Utah
Died: 15 Sep 1911, Wallsburg, Wasatch, Utah

Married 2nd: Elvira Jane Mecham Bigelow (wid. of brother)
Date: 10 Oct 1872, Provo, Utah.

Died: 4 Jan 1920, Salt Lake City, Utah

Married 3rd: Hannah Mosely Johnson
Date: 8 Mar 1899
Died: 22 Apr 1936 (Cancer), Payson, Utah

Asa's parents joined the Church in 1839. They went through the horrible persecutions that so many of the saints did after the martyrdom of the Prophet.

There were two attempts to poison the family but they were able to escape. They made their way to Utah and settled in Provo where they went through the cricket plague with many others.

Asa loved music and dancing and he and a friend were often together. His friend, Francis Marion Ewell, owned a fine Stradivarius violin which Asa truly wanted. He ended up trading his farm, a team of horses, and his house for this instrument. To make a living, he took his family to Kansas for a time where he worked on a ferry. Later they returned to Utah.

Asa loved beautiful things, his garden, music, and flowers. He believed in good manners and saw that his children practiced them. His brother never returned from his mission because of foul play on the returning ship. Asa married his wife, as was often the custom. He built a large brick home for her and her children.

Asa was called to go to Southern Utah to raise dairy cattle for cheese and butter for the saints. He moved Elvira and her children to Gunlock, Utah, where he not only raised the dairy herd, but also helped organize the branch.

He donated much to the church in material things such as the chandlers of the St. George Tabernacle. They enjoyed many community gatherings.

When the children got old enough to attend the academy, Asa returned home to Provo with his wife and children. He later married Hannah and had her children sealed to him. His last child was born when he was 69 years old. At the age of 80, he fell off a scaffold and broke his shoulder. He never got over the accident.

Children of 1st wife:

ASA LIOLA, b. 23 Dec 1853, Provo, Utah. D. 20 May 1868, Kansas.

ROSELLA ANN, b. 21 Dec 1855, Provo, Utah

LOUISE JANE, b. 29 July 1858, Goshen, Utah. D. 19 Aug 1858. Child.

EUDORA LOVINA, b. 8 Sep 1860, Atchison, Kansas.

MARY ELIZABETH, b. 13 Jul 1863, Atchison, Kansas. D. 13 Jul 1863. Child.

WILLIAM DANIEL, b. 6 Feb 1865, Atchison, Kansas.

FRANKLIN DEAN, b. 7 Nov 1869, enroute to Provo, Utah.

Children of 2nd wife by 1st husband. Asa raised these children:

LAYFETTE, b. 29 Jul 1864, Provo, Utah.

JOHN YOUNG, b. 21 Mar 1866, Provo, Utah.

LEO, b. 25 Apr 1869, Provo, Utah.

Children of 2nd wife:

PERRY SCIPIO, b. 12 Nov 1874, Provo, Utah. D. 4 Jan 1919, Alaska.

MOSES WILLARD, b. 1 Jan 1876, Gunlock, Utah.

ELVIRA LILLIAN, b. 27 Aug 1877, Gunlock, Utah.

ELIJAH, b. 8 Oct 1879, Gunlock, Utah.

ALICE, b. 28, Apr 1882, Gunlock, Utah.

Children of 3rd wife:

(All her 8 children from a previous marriage were sealed to Asa)

RALPH, b. 22 Nov 1874.

MARTHA ALICE, b. 5 Jul 1876.

MAY, b. 1 May 1879.

WILDER, b. 6 Mar 1881.

NELL, b. 11 Oct 1883.

BESSIE, b. 16 Apr 1886.

MARY, b. 10 Jun 1888.

SUSAN ELIZABETH, b. 3 Apr 1889. D. 3 Nov 1903.

Child of 3rd wife and Asa:

DAUGHTER, b. 13 Dec 1901.

Submitted by: Valene E. Collings

NAHUM BIGELOW

Born: 9 Feb 1785, Brandon, Vermont
Parents: Simon and Sarah Foster Bigelow
Died: 28 Jan 1851, Farmington, Utah
Arrived in Valley: 1847, Co. unknown

Married: Mary Gibbs
Date: 12 Dec 1826, Lawrenceville, Illinois
Died: 19 Apr 1888, St. George, Utah

Nahum was a farmer and stock raiser. While still a young man he decided to do some traveling, which he did until he met Mary. After their marriage they lived for a time in Illinois where two children were born. They then moved to Coles County where they lived for 10 years.

While there he heard the gospel and after much contemplation and prayer, Nahum, Mary and the two older children were baptized on 1 April 1839.

They moved again to Mercer County, and then to Hancock County in 1843. He was known for his frank, sturdy independence, honesty, generous and affectionate nature, and his quick temper.

He loved to invent things and during his life proved to be a fearless but not reckless man. Several times his life was threatened by the mobs and once he was given a cup of coffee with a deadly poison in it. Only by his strong faith and constant prayer did he live. His constant prayer was that he could live to get his family to the Valley.

He finally was able to move his family to Salt Lake where they decided to settle in Farmington. His daughters Mary Jane and Lucy were married to President Brigham Young.

He fulfilled his desire to be with the church in the mountains and to have his family with him. He eventually died from the effects of the poison and results of a life fighting the mobs and trying to raise his family in righteousness.

Children:

MARY JANE, b. 15 Oct 1827, Lawrenceville, Illinois. Md. Mar 1847, Brigham Young. (Div). Married again, unknown. D. 26 Sep 1868.

HIRUM, b. 20 May 1829, Lawrenceville, Illinois. Md. Martha Mecham. D. probably in Springville, Arizona.

LUCY, b. 3 Oct 1847, Coles County, Illinois. Md. Brigham Young. D. 3 Feb 1905.

ASA ELIJAH, b. 2 Feb 1832, Coles County, Illinois. Md. 1st, 2 Apr 1853, Julia Ann Cook. Md. 2nd, 10 Oct 1872, Elvira Jane Mecham, after the death of her husband (his brother Moroni).

LOVINA, b. 24 Mar 1834, Coles County, Illinois. Md. Mar 1851, John Wesley Witt.

LIOLA, b. 4 Oct 1835, Coles County, Illinois. D. 15 Aug 1845.

SARAH, b. 29 Jan 1838, Coles County, Illinois. Md. Aug 1853, Daniel Dean Cook. D. 11 Jan 1877, Fairfield, Utah.

MORONI, b. 1 Sep 1840, Mercer County, Illinois. Md. Elvira Jane Mecham. D . 13 Apr 1870.

DANIEL, b. 18 Mar 1842, Mercer County, Illinois. Md. 1st, 23 Jul 1866, Permelia Mecham. Md. 2nd, 9 Apr 1882, Emeline Augusta Stevens. Md. 3rd, 9 May 1887, Clara Fredricka Ostenser. D. 22 Oct 1921.

JOSEPH SMITH, b. 18 Mar 1842, Hancock County, Illinois. D. 19 Apr 1845.

Submitted by: Valene Collings

ADAM CUNNINGHAM BIGLER

Born: 17 Dec 1828, Shinnston, Harrison, West Virginia
Parents: Jacob and Sarah Cunningham Bigler
Died: 9 Jan 1915, Daniels, Idaho
Arrived in Valley: 11 Oct 1859, L. G. Rice and J. L. Stoddard Co.

Married 1st: Sarah Anne Compton
Date: 28 Apr 1851, Council Bluffs, Iowa
Born: 31 Aug 1835, Shelby Co., Tennessee
Parents: Allen and Mary Burton Compton
Died: 28 Jan 1867, Farmington, Davis, Utah

Married 2nd: Isabelle Clarinda Miller
Date: 4 Apr 1867, Farmington, Davis, Utah
Born: 21 Jan 1846, Quincy, Hancock, Illinois
Parents: Daniel A. and Hannah Bigler Miller
Died: 4 Jan 1904, Plymouth, Box Elder, Utah

　　Adam was eight to nine years old when his family joined the Church. Shortly after joining the church, the family moved to Nauvoo where the headquarters of the church was located. For eight years, after he married Sarah, he ran the Ferry boat across the Missouri River between Florence and Omaha, Nebraska.
　　In 1859, they decided to move west to Utah to be close to his

parents. Upon their arrival in the Valley they settled in Farmington, where his parents lived. His father died about two months after their arrival.

Adam was a farmer and stock raiser in Plymouth. While living in Farmington, he was road supervisor for four years, and owned a lumber mill. He was a great walker. It was not uncommon for him to cross over the mountains from Plymouth to Afton, Wyoming, or walk to other places he wanted to go.

Distance meant little to him. Shortly before his death, he walked from Plymouth to St. John, Idaho, to visit his children at a family gathering. He returned home and spent the night with his daughter and her husband. The next morning he rode to Elkhorn with a friend, then walked from Elkhorn to Daniels, Idaho, to visit his daughter and her family. In the morning, his daughter went to his bedroom and he was sitting on the side of the bed. He said he wasn't feeling well and laid back on the bed and died. His family shipped his body to Farmington where he was buried in the family plot.

Children of 1st wife:

JAMES ALLEN, b. 18 Jun 1855, Florence, Nebraska. D. Child

MARY FLORENCE, b. 4 Jan 1857, Florence, Nebraska. Md. 5 Nov 1877, Arthur A. Steed. D. 21 May 1931.

MARION FRANCIS., b. 22 Oct 1859, Farmington, Utah. Md. 28 Jul 1875, John W. Hess. D.12 Jul 1927.

JOHN A., b. 13 Sep 1861. Md. 27 May 1905, Lydia Beveridge. D. 4 May 1940.

SARAH ELIZABETH, b. 20 Aug 1863, Farmington, Utah. D. Child.

MARIAH LOUISA, b. 12 Jul 1864, Farmington, Utah. D. Child.

ROBERT BURTON, b. 25 Dec 1866, Farmington, Utah. Md. 19 Sep 1900, Fannie Matilda Reed. D. 1 Jun 1937.

Children of 2nd wife:

JAMES THADDEUS, b. 22 Jan 1868, Farmington, Utah. Md. 20 Dec 1897, Malinda Louisa Stevenson, (Div). (2 other wives). D. 15 Oct 1962.

JACOB WILLIAM, b. 17 Aug 1869, Farmington, Utah. D. 8 Sep 1871. Child

EDWARD, b. 26 Jan 1871, Farmington, Utah. Md. 23 Nov 1903, Behema Bertha Pierson. D. 7 Jun 1957.

HANNAH ISABELLE, b. 5 Oct 1872, Farmington, Utah. Md. 25 Dec 1889, Nephi Levi Wolverton. D. 4 Jan 1952.

LAURA ELIZABETH, b. 19 Oct 1873, Farmington, Utah. Md. 23 Jul 1895, Willard James Stuart Archibald. D. 8 Aug 1963, Pocatello, Idaho.

ADAM, JR., b. 2 Apr 1876, Farmington, Utah. Md. 18 Nov 1900, Rosie Annie Howell. D. 9 Jul 1952.

JOSEPH ARNOLD, b. 14 Nov 1878, Farmington, Utah. D. 16 Dec 1904.

ALVIRA, b. 28 Sep 1881, Farmington, Utah. Md. 7 Dec 1901, Frederick Sylvester. D. 21 Jan 1965, Ogden, Utah.

STANLEY MILLER, b. 30 Sep 1888, Providence, Utah. Md. 31 May 1917, Myrtle Clark. D. 14 Nov 1974.

Submitted by: Jay Whitmore and Isabella Clarinda Miller

JOHN BILLS

Born: 19 Sep 1819, Blairsville, Pennsylvania
Parents: Alanson and Electa Hill Bills
Died: 19 Feb 1850, San Joaquin Valley, California
Arrived in Valley: 20 Sep 1848, Zera Pulsipher's Co. of Brigham Young's First Division

Married 1st: Elizabeth Scott
Date: 7 Jan 1834, Pittsburgh, Allegheny, Pennsylvania

Born: 1 Jan 1817, Horbury, Yorks, England
Died: Summer of 1854, Mountain Meadows, Iron, Utah

Married 2nd: Elizabeth (Eliza) Hall
Date: Jan 1847, Council Bluffs, Iowa
Born: 20 Nov 1820, Saro, Surrey, No. Carolina

John was a tailor by trade and kept a clothing store. After joining the Church, they lost most of what they had due to the persecution of the saints. The family moved to Rushville and then to Commerce. In the spring of 1839 they moved to Nauvoo, Illinois. John joined the Nauvoo Legion and attained the rank of Brigade Major. He used his tailoring skills to sew uniforms for many of his fellow soldiers, including the Prophet Joseph and Hyrum.

Both John and Elizabeth worked hard to help build up Nauvoo. John opened a tailor shop. When the persecution of the saints became unbearable, John moved his family to Winter Quarters. They spent the winter there and when Brigham Young moved out with his group, John and Elizabeth packed their things and joined the first Division under Brigham Young and the second Company under Zera Pulsipher. John was elected captain of ten with 10 wagons and 38 saints.

After arriving in the Valley, they lived in the fort until 1849, when they were able to move out of the fort into a dugout on Little Cottonwood Creek. They raised a crop and after John had made his family as comfortable as possible, he took his eldest son, William Andrew, and commenced a trip to the California gold fields. It was his intent to establish a tailoring business and then send for his family. However, before reaching his destination, he became very ill and died in San Joaquin Valley.

Children of 1st wife:

WILLIAM ANDREW, b. 5 Aug 1835, Pittsburgh, Pennsylvania.
ROBERT, b. 1840, Nauvoo, Illinois.
CHARLES COLSON, b. 1842, Nauvoo, Illinois.
FRANKLIN RICHARD, b. 17 May 1845, Nauvoo, Illinois.
SAMUEL, b. 22 Mar 1848, Council Bluffs, Iowa.

Children of 2nd wife:

MARTHA, b. 18 Feb 1848, Winter Quarters, Nebraska.
THOMAS WESLEY, b. 6 May 1850, Salt Lake City, Utah.

Submitted by: Blaine Crump

WILLIAM ANDREW BILLS

Born: 5 Aug 1835, Pittsburgh, Allegheny, Pennsylvania
Parents: John and Elizabeth Scott Bills
Died: 4 Apr 1915, South Jordan, Utah
Arrived in Valley: 20 Sep 1848, Zera Pulsipher's Co.- Brigham
    Young.

Married 1st: Emeline Beckstead
Date: 4 Jul 1852, Riverton, Utah
Born: 4 Apr 1837, Williamsburg, Ontario, Canada
Died: 1 Jan 1917, Riverton, Salt Lake, Utah

Married 2nd: Annie Eastwood
Date: 6 Feb 1869, Salt Lake City, Utah
Born: 20 Dec 1856, Hudisfield, Yorks, England
Died: 2 Nov 1937, Paul, Idaho

Married 3rd: Matilda Amundsen
Date: 1 Mar 1869 Salt Lake City, Utah
Born: 26 May 1851, Christiania, Norway

Married 4th: Petrenia Amelia Amundsen

Date: 1 Mar 1869, Salt Lake, Utah
Born: 19 Mar 1853, Christiania, Norway
Died: 1879

William Andrew was just a baby when his parents joined the Church and was too young to be much aware of the persecution they underwent. While living in Nauvoo, he grew up and helped build that city. His father, being a tailor, made clothes for the Prophet and Hyrum and others, so William and the family became close friends of these leaders. He delivered some clothes to Joseph's home and was shown the mummies. He was baptized in the spring of 1844.

When they started west in 1848, he drove one of the teams that pulled a wagon. The team consisted of five cows and one ox. Upon reaching the Valley, he taught school for two or three years. He remained active in the church.

After the Johnston's's Army problems, when the saints went south and then returned to the valley, William moved his family to Mount Green, Morgan, Utah, in what is called Weber Valley. He was made president of that branch where he labored for four and a half years. At the end of that time, he moved his family back to South Jordan in April 1863.

The first Sunday there, he was named counselor to James Wood in the branch presidency. In July 1877, he was released and put in as bishop and told to organize the branch into a ward, which he did. He was released from that position in 1900.

His personal records stop in 1902 as he grew more feeble and forgetful. While going to visit some of his children near his home, he never arrived nor did he return home. Sixteen days after his disappearance, the wife of his son David had a dream about him. In it she saw where he was. She told her husband, who organized a search party. His body was where she had seen it. His coat had been caught on a wire under the fast-moving deep water of the Jordan River.

Children of 1st wife:

GORDON SILAS, b. 18 Mar 1854, West Jordan, Utah.

WILLIAM ANDREW JR., b. 4 Sep 1855, West Jordan, Utah.
ALEXANDER, b. 4 Sep 1857, Litte Cottonwood, Salt Lake, Utah.
CATHERINE EMELINE, b. 14 May 1859, Mountain Green, Morgan, Utah.
HARRIET ELIZABETH, b. 18 Feb 1861, Mountain Green, Morgan, Utah.
JOHN ALMA, b. 26 Jun 1863, South Jordan, Utah.
GEORGE WELLINGTON, b. 9 Aug 1864, South Jordan, Utah.
MARY ELLEN, b. 15 Jun 1867, South Jordan, Utah.
MARTHA ANN, b. 27 Jun 1869, South Jordan, Utah.
HENRY, b. 25 Jul 1870, South Jordan, Utah.
DANIEL WALLACE, b. 1 Dec 1872. South Jordan, Utah.
DAVID, b. 13 Apr 1874, South Jordan, Utah.

Children of 2nd wife:

ANNEY BURNETT, b. 13 Jan 1880, South Jordan, Utah.
SARAH ROMANEY, b. 27 Oct 1881, South Jordan, Utah.
WILLIAM LEROY, b. 21 Aug 1883, South Jordan, Utah..
LORENZO E., b. 26 Mar 1886, South Jordan, Utah.
HEBER LOTELLES, b. 22 May 1888, South Jordan, Utah.
WILFORD LESTER, b. 17 Nov 1890, South Jordan, Utah.
BYRAM E., b. 30 Apr 1893, South Jordan, Utah.

Children of 3rd wife:

PARLEY A., b. 10 Feb 1872, South Jordan, Utah.
MARY AMELIA, b. 8 Aug 1874, South Jordan, Utah.
LUTHER MARTIN, b. 22 Nov 1877, South Jordan, Utah.
OLE A., b. 15 May 1880, South Jordan, Utah.
WILLIAM RILEY, b. 9 Jul 1884, South Jordan, Utah.
OLINE, b. 12 Dec 1886, South Jordan, Utah.
NORMAN SCOTT, b. 10 Apr 1889, South Jordan, Utah.
MARTHA JANE, b. 17 Mar 1891, South Jordan, Utah.
IRA PETRENIA, b. 25 Jul 1893, South Jordan, Utah.

Children of 4th wife:

ORSON A., b. 1 Nov 1871, South Jordan, Utah.
SAMUEL ANDREW, b. 6 Jan 1874, South Jordan, Utah.
HOMER L., b. 25 Oct 1876, South Jordan, Utah.

Submitted by: Blaine Crump

ERASTUS BINGHAM

Born: 12 Mar 1798, Concord, Essex, Vermont
Parents: Elisha Warner and Sally (or Sarah) Perry Bingham
Died: 2 May 1882, Lynn, Weber, Utah
Arrived in Valley: 19 Sep 1847, Daniel Spencer's 100

Married 1st: Lucinda Gates
Date: 12 Mar 1820
Born: 19 Sep 1797, Ackworth, Cheshire, New Hampshire
Parents: Thomas and Patty Plumley Gates
Died: 3 Jan 1874, Ogden, Weber, Utah

Married 2nd: Mehitable Sawyer Hall
Date: 11 Sep 1857

Married 3rd: Emma Nye Wilson
Date: Dec 1862

Erastus was baptized in November 1833 at St. Johnsburg, Vermont, as a direct result of early Church missionary work in New England. With his wife and family and others, he traveled to Far West, Missouri, arriving the 4th of November 1836. After the Extermination Order, the Bingham family moved to Hancock County, Illinois, where they rented a farm between Carthage and LaHarpe. They remained there until the spring of 1845. After the martyrdom of the prophet, Erastus moved his family about 20 miles from Nauvoo. After his crops were harvested he worked to help complete the Nauvoo Temple.

In January 1846, Erastus Jr., one of Erastus' older sons, was chosen to go west with an advanced group to make roads and build bridges to prepare the way for the coming saints. The rest of the family set out on the 6th of May.

Erastus Bingham was made Captain of one hundred. When the call came for volunteers for the Mormon Battalion, two sons and a son-in-law volunteered, Erastus Jr., Thomas, and Elijah Norman Freeman. Erastus had the care of the families of these men. They traveled until they arrived at Loop Fork on the Platt River, where they received a message that they should not go further because of the approaching winter and hostile Indians. Bishop Miller, one of the men of the camp, decided to go on anyway because some Indians encouraged them. Erastus tried to deter them. Half the Company remained with him, while Miller pushed on. After loosing much stock and having other problems, they returned.

In the spring, Erastus and his family returned to Council Bluffs. He was choosen to help obtain wagons and supplies for the journey west. They finally started out again.

They arrived in the Valley in September 1847. Erastus built a log house. In the spring he was allotted a farm in the Holladay area.

Later he acquired a grazing permit in Bingham Canyon. In 1851, Erastus was made bishop of North Ward (Weber Stake). He remained here for 17 years. They then moved to a spot north of the Ogden River. He always remained active in the church and community.

Children of 1st wife:

MARY, b. 1 Apr 1820.
SANFORD, b. 3 May 1821.

ERASTUS JR., b. 30 Sep 1822.
THOMAS, b. 19 Jul 1824.
LUCINDA, b. 15 Apr 1826.
MARIA LOUISA, b. 23 Jun 1828.
WILLARD, b. 19 Feb 1830.
EDWIN, b. 5 May 1832.
JACOB, b. 23 Aug 1834.
BRIGHAM HEBER, b. 15 Dec 1841.

Children of 3rd wife:

WARNER, b. 12 Sep 1863.

Submitted by: Kristie Palfreyman and Leilani Grange

ERASTUS BINGHAM, JR.

Born: 30 Sep 1822, Concord, Vermont
Parents: Erastus and Lucinda Gates Bingham
Died: 5 Apr 1906, Tucson, Arizona
Arrived in Valley: 19 Sep 1847, with Second Co. after serving
    with Mormon Battalion

Married 1st: Olive Hovey Freeman
Date: 29 Oct 1843, Illinois
Married 2nd: Susan Green
Date: 15 Nov 1855, Salt Lake, Utah

   Erastus Jr. came west with his parents as far as Far West, Missouri. In 1846 they moved to Illinois, where they lived until 1846.

Erastus Jr. was called to go west and help build roads to prepare the way for the saints. Later he joined the Mormon Battalion.

He and his brother, Thomas, entered the Valley just four days after the original group of pioneers. They helped build some log cabins and the wall around the fort, which is now Pioneer Park. His wife was not well when he finally met his parents and wife somewhere in Wyoming, but he brewed her some herb tea and she got well. They settled in Cottonwood and later in 1850 they moved to Ogden, and finally to Huntsville, Utah.

Children of 1st wife:

OLIVE LOUISA, b. 10 Oct 1844. Md. Mr. Walker. D. 12 Sep 1921.
ERASTUS PERRY, b. 20 Mar 1846. D. 4 Jun 1929.
LUCINDA MARIA, b. Jun 1848. Md. Mr.Foy. D. 27 Feb 1924.
LYDIA ROXENA, b. 6 Jan 1850. Md. Mr. Lish. D. Apr 1936.
ISAAC FARWELL, b. 20 Sep 1852. D. 20 Nov 1853. Child.
MARY ANN, b. 9 Feb 1854. Md. Mr. Geertsen. D. 15 Jan 1941.
LORENZO FREEMAN, b. 7 Dec 1855. D. 1 Nov 1938.
DIANA, b. 17 Jul, 1857. Md. Mr Smith. D. 11 Dec 1935.
OPHELIA CEDENIA, b. 19 Aug 1859. Md. Mr. Foy. D. 29 May 1936.

Children of 2nd wife:

SUSAN MELVINA, b. 23 Nov 1856. Md. Mr. Farr. D. 6 Nov 1903.
NEPHI, b. 9 Apr 1858. D. 2 Aug 1916.
LUCY ANN, b. 5 Mar 1860. Md. Mr. Wheeler. D. 15 Jul 1930.
MARINTHA ATHENA, b. 26 May 1861. Md. Mr. Eccles. D. 12 May 1948.
EDDA, b. 21 Jan 1863. D. 26 Jan 1863. Child.
ENOCH, (twin), b.7 Mar 1864.
DANIEL, (twin), b. 7 Mar 1864. D. 17 Jun 1940.
HARRIET ADELTHA, b. 2 Nov 1865. Md. Mr. Wheeler. D. 6 Jun 1920.
MARY JANE, b. 28 Apr 1867. D. 28 Apr 1867. Child.
ERASTUS ALMA, b. 28 Sep 1868. D. 11 Oct 1955.

VIOLETTA MAY, b. 30 May 1870. Md. Mr. Holt. D. 16 Nov 1946.
BENJAMIN WISDOM, b. 11 Jan 1872. D. 11 Mar 1879. Child.
MYRTLE ADELL, b. 2 Sep 1873. D. 30 Apr 1877. Child.
CLARA ISABELLA, b. 29 Aug 1876. Md. Mr. Woods.
ROZINA DIANTHA, b. 21 Jul 1878. Md. Mr McGee.
JACOB MORONI, b. 4 Nov 1881.

Submitted by: Elva Merkley

JEREMIAH BINGHAM

Born: 15 Jun 1806, Cornwall, Addison, Vermont
Parents: Jeremiah and Mary Ives Bingham
Died: 6 May 1890, Payson, Utah, Utah
Arrived in Valley: 9 Sep 1853, Daniel A Miller & John W. Cooley Co.

Married 1st: Abigail Harrington
Date: 2 Feb 1829, Brockville, Leeds, Ontario, Canada
Born: 25 Jan 1812, Younge, Leeds, Ontario, Canada
Died: 8 Jun 1843

Married 2nd: Sarah Keele
Date: 15 Feb 1846
Born: 10 Apr 1820, Bedford, Bedford, Tennessee
Died: 8 Feb 1852, Council Bluffs, Pottawattamie, Iowa

Married 3rd: Susan Keele
Date: abt 1858

Born: 15 Sep 1832.
Died: 10 Mar 1859, Payson, Utah, Utah

Married 4th: Minerva Dixon
Date: abt 1855
Born: 13 Nov 1826
Died: 2 Oct 1912

Married 5th: Mary Reese
Date: 27 Mar 1857
Born: 4 Sep 1833
Died: 27 Sep 1868

Jeremiah was the youngest of 10 children. After the Revolutionary War, his parents were unable to support their large family so some of the children were "bound out," as it was called. Jeremiah was bound out to a man who was very unkind to him. He remained there until he could no longer tolerate the abuse and he ran away. He went to live with one of his brothers.

After joining the Church, he married Abigail Harrington. She had six children but only two of them lived. He was a close friend of the Prophet, being about the same age. They both enjoyed wrestling together.

When the saints left Nauvoo, Jeremiah and his family left too. His first wife had died so he married again in Iowa. She died after the birth of their fourth child. He later married Susan, a sister to Sarah.

Jeremiah was a blacksmith by trade and each night on the trip west, he would repair the wagons and do other blacksmithing jobs.

After arriving in Utah, they settled first in Ogden, then a year later moved south to Payson where he assisted in building the fort. In 1856 he was called on a mission to help settle Fort Bridger, Wyoming. They stayed there until Johnston's Army came, at which time they returned to Payson.

Shortly before their return to Payson, Alexander Keele, a brother-in-law of Jeremiah, had been killed by the Indians, leaving a small family. When Jeremiah arrived in Payson, the bishop asked him to marry the widow, Minerva, and support her and her children. He lived a long active life, helping others and the church.

Children of 1st wife:

PERRY CALVIN, b. 1830, D. Child.
AMOS OSCAR, b. 1832, D. Child
CLARINDA, b.1834,
LUCINDA, b. 24 Sep 1837. D. 14 Mar 1905.
MARGARET MELVINA, b. 7 Nov 1840. D. 8 Apr 1926.
POLLY, b. 1842. D. Child.
JOHN, b. 1843. D. abt 1843. Child.

Children of 2nd wife:

JEREMIAH, b. 10 Jun 1847. D. 14 Jan 1898.
ABIGAIL, b. 19 Aug 1848.
SARAH ELLENOR, b. 15 Apr 1850. D. 9 Apr 1936.
AUGUSTUS, b. 8 Feb 1852. D. Infant.

Children of 3rd wife:

ALPHEUS, b. 19 Feb 1859. D. 20 Sep 1927.

Children of 4th wife:

JOSEPH HUVVY, b. 8 Jan 1856. D. 14 Jan 1943.
MELINDA SARAH, b. 14 Feb 1859. D. 7 Sep 1902.
MINERVA JANE, b. 22 Sep 1862. D. 24 Mar 1949.
CHARLES RICHARD, b. 10 May 1865. D. 20 May 1910.
MARY LOUISE, b. 30 Jan 1868. D. 10 Oct 1868.
ALONZA, b. 11 Feb 1869. D. 23 Sep 1869.

Children of 5th wife:

HYRUM, b. 19 Feb 1858.

SUSAN COLISTA, b. 6 Feb 1860. D. 3 Jun 1922.
GEORGIANA, b. 19 Oct 1862.
JAMES PERRY, b. 7 Sep 1864. D. 1 Sep 1873.
MARY LARINA, b. 8 Oct 1866.
JAMES, Indian boy, raised by the family.

Submitted by: Elaine Schofield

JEREMIAH BINGHAM, JR.

Born: 10 Jun 1847, Pottawattamie County, Iowa
Parents: Jeremiah and Sarah Keele Bingham
Died 14 Jan 1898, Sanford, Conejos, Colorado
Arrived in Valley: 9 Sep 1853, Daniel A. Miller Co.

Married 1st: Eliza Emeline Roberts
Date: 7 Mar 1869, Utah
Born: 2 Aug 1851, Mill Creek, Salt Lake, Utah
Died: 5 Dec 1882, Burrville, Sevier, Utah

Married 2nd: Margaret Duke
Date: Unknown

Jeremiah was five years old when his mother died giving birth to her fourth child, who also died. The following year his father brought his family to Utah. They lived in Ogden for a year and then moved to Payson.

After Jeremiah was married, they settled in Payson where six of their seven children were born. By 1882 the family had moved to Burrville in Sevier County, Utah. His wife died four days after the birth of their seventh child.

At some point after this, he moved his family to Sanford, Conejos, Colorado, where he married again and had two more children.

Children of 1st wife:

SARAH EMELINE, b. 24 Jun 1870. D. 20 Nov 1906.
JEREMIAH EDWARD, b. 1 Jun 1872. D. 4 Jun 1901.
ELIZABETH, b. 28 Jul 1874. D. 8 Aug 1874. Child.
ETHEL EUPHREMIA, b. 23 Jul 1875. D.25 Jul 1905.
PERRY WILBURN, b. 7 Dec 1877. D. 27 Jul 1918.
OZEMBA IRENE, b. 28 Jan 1880. D. 21 Dec 1965.
JULIA, b. 1 Dec 1882. D. 27 Mar 1956.

Children of 2nd wife:

LORI LONZO, b. 9 Jan 1890.
ANNE A., b. 27 Feb 1892.

Submitted by: Elaine Schofield

SANFORD BINGHAM

Born: 3 May 1821, Concord, Essex, Vermont
Parents: Erastus and Lucinda Gates Bingham
Died: 22 Nov 1910, Ogden, Weber, Utah
Arrived in Valley: 18 Sep 1847, Daniel Spencers Co.

Married: Martha Ann Lewis
Date: 18 Jul 1847, On banks of Platte River, Nebraska
Died: 18 Nov, 1898, Riverdale, Weber, Utah

When Sanford was about three years old his parents moved to Littleton, New Hampshire. In 1830, they moved back to the old farm in New Hampshire. In the spring of 1833, his father first met the missionaries. Later on when the missionaries again returned to the area, after due investigation, his parents and a daughter were baptized. Sanford was baptized a few days later.

In 1836, his father sold their farm and they started west. They arrived in Kirtland, where they stayed until fall. Then they went on to Missouri where he selected a site about 1-1/2 miles from Far West. They lived there until 1839 when they moved not far from Nauvoo. They rented there until 1845 when his father purchased a farm about 20 miles from Nauvoo. They were not long there until persecution became so great that they, along with many others, sold what they could, packed up and left with the other saints.

They wintered in a place called Swift Water, a tributary of the Missouri River. It was shortly after this that he and Martha Ann were married by Parley P. Pratt, on the banks of the Platte River. When they arrived in the Valley, they lived in the fort for a time.

He had club feet, which gave him problems. When he was 24, they started to attempt to straighten them. It was more than two years before he could walk without crutches or a cane. He continued to herd cattle in the area of Bingham Canyon. They eventually moved to Ogden where they remained for awhile before moving back down to the Bingham area .

He was eventually arrested for polygamy and spent time in prison. He did some farming, and was appointed to various community positions. He served as bishop, missionary, and patriarch. He was much loved and respected by everyone.

Children:

SANFORD, b. 1 Sep 1848.
MARTHA ANN, b. 29 Jan 1850.
BENJAMIN FRANKLIN, b. 25 Sep 1851.

JOHN, b. 30 May 1853.
SOPHIA CORDELIA, b.30 Dec 1854.
WILLIAM, b. 16 Oct 1856
IOANNAH, b. 28 Aug 1858.
JOSEPH SMITH, b. 23 Jun 1860.
ELISHA ERASTUS, b. 25 Mar 1862.
REBECCA JANE, b. 7 Nov 1864.
LORIN BEASON, b. 16 Sep 1866.
LUCINDA ELIZABETH, b.27 Nov 1868.
LEONARD RYON, b. 10 Mar 1871.
LEWIS, b. Apr 1872.
MARY FRANCES, b. 18 May 1873.

Submitted by: Kristie Palfreyman and Leilani Grange

JOHN BINNS

Born: 30 May 1806, Colne, Lancs, England
Parents: James and Hannah Dean Binns
Died: 15 Feb 1884, American Fork, Utah
Arrived in Valley: 25 Sep 1854, William Field Co.

Married 1st: Susan Hey
Date: 9 Aug 1829, Lancs, England
Died: 24 Aug 1837, Lancs, England

Married 2nd: Mary Calverley Barton (widow)
Date: 22 Jan 1838
Born: 16 Nov 1814, Waddington, Yorkshire, England
Parents: Robert and Sarah Wilson Calverley

Died: July 1849 of cholera, St. Louis, Missouri

Married 3rd: Jane Creer Snalem (widow)
Date: 21 Mar 1852, St.Louis, Missouri
Born: 18 Oct 1811, Bolton, Lancs, England
Parents: Matthias and Ellen Greenhalgh Creer
Died: 12 Jul 1877, American Fork, Utah

John lost three wives during his lifetime. He was baptized into the church in England. He was a stonemason by trade and made a good living.

John and his second wife, Mary, emigrated to America with their baby and his daughter Ellen, in 1841. His 11-year-old son, Isaac, remained in England. They settled in St. Louis, Missouri. The following year, 1842, Mary and her three youngest children succumbed to cholera.

In the spring of 1854, John, his third wife Jane, and their family started west. Soon after their arrival in the Valley, John purchased a small log cabin in the city. He did some stone work, helping lay the foundation for the Salt Lake Temple.

About 1858, he moved his family to American Fork where he purchased a farm. He worked hard at farming and also did some stone masonary work.

In later years he turned the farm over to his son, Isaac, and moved closer to town. After the death of Ellen, he never remarried. John was a kind, considerate man. He was a good citizen, who was honest in all his dealings. He was a hard worker and expected the same of his children and others.

Children of 1st wife:

ISAAC, b. 25 Feb 1829/30, Lancs, England.
ANN, chr. 1 Jan 1832, d. 12 May 1835. Lancs, England. Child.
ELLEN, chr. 4 May 1835. Lancs, England. Md. 29 Jun 1856,
    Reuben Broadbent.

Children of 2nd wife:

HANNAH, b. 6 Apr 1841. Lancs, England. Md. 30 Mar 1857, John Singleton. She was a midwife.

SARAH, b. 15 Nov 1842, St. Louis, Missouri. Md. 7 Apr 1861, William Henry Chipman.

MARY JANE, b. abt 1845, St.Louis, Missouri. D. Jul 1849. Child.

THOMAS, b. abt 1847, St. Louis, Missouri. D. Jul 1849. Child.

LEWIS, b. Jul 1849, St. Louis, Missouri. D. Jul 1849. Child.

Submitted by: Jean Boyce

ANDREW BIRD

Born: 29 May 1829, Kimble, England
Parents: Richard and Phebe Norton Bird
Died: abt 18 Aug 1868, New York.

Married: Ann Shill
Date: 8 Dec 1850, Syde, Gloucester, England
Arrived in Valley: Oct 1868, Mumford Handcart Co.

Andrew was converted to the Church and was baptized on the 11 November 1849, at Candlegreen, Lancs, England. He met and married Ann Shill at the Parish church in Syde, Gloucester, England. Neither Ann nor Andrew could write. They signed their certificate of marriage with an X.

The family opened their home to the elders whenever they came. One who came more frequently and stayed longer was Charles W. Penrose. He became a good friend.

Their desire to emigrate to America was held up because of

the ill health of Andrew. Finally, the family was able to sail on the ship "Emerald" out of Liverpool. Because of much sickness on the ship coming over, all of Andrew's family were taken right to the hospital. They did not receive good care and contracted cholera. The food was poor and little of it. Ann gave her food to her children.

Finally their youngest child died. About the same time, Ann received a visit from a friend who had come with them on the ship. He gave Ann a watch, chain, knife and a few other articles that had belonged to Andrew.

He had died after finding out that the money for emigrating to the valley had run out and there was none for his family.

Elder Penrose heard of the plight of Ann and her children and helped them get the food they needed. When they recovered, he helped them until the church obtained enough money to aid the saints who were stranded. They suffered a great deal on the journey, but Ann was a strong woman. They settled in Henefer, Utah.

Children:

PRUDENCE ELIZABETH, b. 25 May 1851, Caudlegreen, Gloucester, England. D. 16 Sep 1865 (diptheria).

ANN, b. 13 Aug 1853, Caudlegreen, Gloucester, England.

PHEBE, b. 29 Sep 1855, Caudlegreen, Gloucester, England. D. 8 Sep 1865 (diptheria)

MARY MARRIAH, b. 21 Jan 1859, Caudlegreen, Gloucester, England.

HYRUM, b. 7 Jun 1860, Caudlegreen, Gloucester, England.

EMMA LOUISA, b. 27 Sep 1864. D. 27 Sep 1868, (diptheria) Child.

Submitted by: Renee Call

BENJAMIN FREEMAN BIRD

Born: 19 Jan 1776, Rahway, Essex, New Jersey
Parents: Jeremiah Freeman and Elizabeth Marsh Bird
Died: 23 Feb 1862, Springville, Utah, Utah
Arrived in Valley: 3 Jun 1850, Milo Andrus Co.

Married 1st: Marabah Reeves
Date: 22 Feb 1801 , Morris Co., New Jersey
Born: 8 May 1784, Rahway, Essex, New Jersey
Parents: Phineas and Mary(Polly) Taylor Reeves
Died: 13 Feb 1833, Portsmouth, Chemung, New York

Married 2nd: Margaret Crain Dailey (widow)
Date: 25 Apr 1833, New York.
Born: 2 Jun 1797, Caldwell, Essex, New York
Died: 24 Mar 1865/6, Wellsburg, Chemung, New York

Benjamin Freeman and his wife were visited by a missionary who asked for board and room. Over the next few weeks, after reading the Book of Mormon, they were convinced the Church was true. The elder moved on and when no more elders came, they subscribed to the "Star." They had nowhere else to turn for further information.

In the first edition of the "Messenger and Advocate," Oliver Cowdery published an exerpt from a letter from Benjamin. Before Benjamin received a reply, his beloved wife died. He was ridiculed by former friends for his new beliefs. One woman was kind and believed him. He soon married her.

In June of 1834, some Mormon elders came to the area so Benjamin, his second wife, Margaret, and several of his married children, were baptized.

Shortly after, they moved their family to Kirtland, Ohio, where Benjamin and his family became involved with the church. Many of his father's family were there and pledged their support. They moved to Far West but were eventually driven out. They gathered in Nauvoo as a family and built nice homes. Benjamin and his family lived in a log cabin for three years, but eventually purchased a farm on the outskirts of Nauvoo.

When the saints were driven from Nauvoo, Benjamin and the other Bird families left with them. Because they were weavers, they were asked to remain at Winter Quarters and help outfit the saints so they could go west. They finally left with the Milo Andrus Company. Several members of the Bird family settled in the Springville area where Benjamin lived until his death.

Children of 1st wife:

PHINEAS REEVES, b. 22 Jan 1802, Elizabeth, Essex, New Jersey. Md. Millicent Coalman. D. 25 Jul 1850.

CHARLES, b. 19 Sep 1803, Roxbury Twp, Morris, N.J. Md. 1st 22 Mar 1826, Mary Ann Kennedy. Md. 2nd, 15 Feb 1852, Susie Duston. Md. 3rd, 3 Feb 1853, Sarah Ann Dunsdon. D. 29 Sep 1884, Mendon, Cache, Utah.

SAMUEL, b. 19 Mar 1805, Flanders, Morris, N.J. Md., Casiah Brown. D. 13 Feb 1828.

JAMES, b. 22 Dec 1806, Roxbury , Morris, N.J. Md. 1831, Jane Mott Carpenter. Md. 2nd 3 Feb 1853, Sophia Alcester Fuller. D. 12 Jun 1879, St. George, Utah.

ELIZABETH, b. 8 Feb 1809, Roxbury, N.J. D 16 Jan 1813. Child.

GEORGE, b. 16 Jan 1811, Hector, Seneca, New York. D. 13 Oct 1813. Child.

KELSEY, b. 30 Mar 1813, Hector, New York. Md. Sally Carpenter Allright. D. 9 Jan 1836.

MARY (POLLY), b. 23 Jun 1815, Hector, N.Y. Md. 27 Mar 1832, Joel Matthews. D. 9 Jan 1849.

GEORGE, b. 12 May 1817, Hector, N.Y. D. 24 Feb 1818. Child.

AMANDA ANN, b. 24 Jan 1819, Portsmouth, Tioga, N.Y. Md. 22 Oct 1835, Lawrence Mathews. D. 26 Sep 1869.

RICHARD, b. 13 Oct 1820, Southport, Tioga, N.Y. Md. 1st, 7 Mar 1845, Emeline Crandall. Md. 2nd 6 Mar 1855, Laura Crandall. D. 27 Feb 1895, Springville, Utah.

WILLIAM, b. 16 Jul 1823, Southport, Tioga, N.Y. Md. 28 Sep 1851, Ann Roylance. D. 18 Apr 1894, Paris, Bear Lake, Idaho.

Children of 2nd wife:

MARGARET JANE, b. 9 Apr 1834, Wellsburg, Tioga, N.Y. Md. 12 Jun 1864. Orson Emmet Bird. D. 22 Jun 1912.

BENJAMIN T., b. 20 Jun 1837, Wellsburg, Chemung, N.Y. D. 24 Jun 1864.

MARTHA MARIE, b. 2 Jun 1840, Nauvoo, Illinois. Md. 1st, 19 Apr 1859, Walter Minthorn Farnsworth. Md. 2nd, 20 Jan 1869, Isaac Bennet. Md. 3rd, 22 Feb 1892, Hollis Allen. D. 14 Jan 1903.

Submitted by: Donna Bird, LaPrele Hall and Ephraim Furness

CHARLES BIRD

Born: 19 Sep 1803, Roxbury, New Jersey
Parents: Benjamin Freeman and Marabah Reeves Bird
Died: 29 Sep 1884, Mendon, Utah
Arrived in Valley: 20 Aug 1850, Milo Andrus Co.

Married 1st: Mary Ann Kennedy
Date: 22 Mar 1826
Born: 7 Dec 1807, Great Barrington, Massachusetts
Died: 1 Oct 1867, Mendon, Utah

Married 2nd: Sarah Ann Dunsdon
Date: 3 Feb 1853.
Born: 8 May 1835, Steeple Ashton, England
Died: 5 Dec 1899, Ogden, Utah

Charles joined the Church with his wife and they were baptized in August 1836. After much persecution, he and his wife moved to Far West and eventually to Nauvoo along with his father and family.

They suffered the persecution along with the other saints and eventually crossed the Mississippi heading west. While in Nauvoo, he helped build the Temple. While at Winter Quarters, he helped build homes and secure provisions for the saints.

After arriving in the Valley in 1850, he moved his family to Springville and later made his home in Cottonwood. He was called to help settle Cache Valley and was among the early settlers of Mendon.

Charles was a farmer and the town's first merchant. He had been a weaver and helped establish the woolen mills in Utah. He was Mendon's first elected magistrate. In 1867 he was Justice of the Peace and later served as the second mayor of Mendon.

Children of 1st wife:

JOHN PRATT KENNEDY, b. 24 Aug 1827, Far West, Missouri.
ELIZABETH ANN, b. 30 Oct 1829, Nauvoo, Illinois.
BENJAMIN FREEMAN, b. 19 Jun 1831, Nauvoo, Illinois.
HENRIETTA, b. 7 Jun 1833, Nauvoo, Illinois.
AMANDA SEDILLA, b. 23 Mar 1835, Nauvoo, Illinois. D. 1840.
    Child.
KELSEY, b. 11 Jan 1837, Winterquarters.
CHARLES, b. 13 Jan 1839, d. 1839. Child.
BRADFORD KENNEDY, b. 26 Jan 1840.
ELIZA JANE, b. 7 Feb 1841.
CHARLES, b. 2 Jun 1843.
WILLIAM, b. 6 Apr 1845.
MARTIN LOUIS DAINEY, b. 6 Jan 1847.
GEORGE A. SMITH, b. 26 Jan 1849.

MARY ANN, b. 1851.

Children of 2nd wife:

MORMON, b. 15 Jan 1854.
DELOSS PERLEY, b. 2 Feb 1856.
JAMES DUNSDON, b. 5 Feb 1858, D.1869.
MARY JANE, b. 10 Jun 1860.
PHINEAS REEVES, b. 1 Sep 1862.
JEDDIAH M. GRANT, b. 17 Apr 1865.
ANNA ADELIA, b. 9 Jul 1868.
HESTER MARIAH, b. 31 Dec 1870.
AMANDA LUSINA, b. 19 May 1872.
SARAH ANN, b. 1 May 1873. D. 1873. Child.
HEBER CHARLES. b. 11 Nov 1876.

Submitted by: LaPrele Hall and Ephraim Furness

HYRUM BIRD

Born: 7 Jun 1861, Caudlegreen, England
Parents: Andrew and Ann Shill Bird
Died: 4 Apr 1927 Henefer, Summit, Utah
Arrived in Valley: 24 Sep 1868, Edward T. Mumford Co.

UNMARRIED

Hyrum was the fifth of Andrew and Ann Bird's six children, all born in England. Two of the girls died of diptheria in 1865. They had welcomed the missionaries into their home whenever

285

they needed a place to stay. Elder Charles W. Penrose was especially close to them. They soon determined that they would go to America and then to the Valley where the saints were gathering. They were held back when Andrew's health became worse. Finally Ann's brother, George Shill, sent sufficient money to bring the family to America.

The ship was crowded and food and water was neither sufficient nor good. Many became ill. Upon their arrival in America, Ann and the four children were taken to the hospital on Ellis Island where the treatment was even worse than on board ship. Andrew tried to obtain money and accomodations to go west but was not successful. He died and Ann was left alone. The youngest child, Emma Louisa, died in the hospital. While there, Ann received word that her husband, Andrew, had died.

Eventually, with the help of money raised by the church to help immigrants come west, Ann and her family made it to the valley with the Mumford Handcart Company. They lived in Croydon for several months with some family members and then moved to Henefer.

When Hyrum became older, he worked to support his mother and never married. He built a little cabin on his sister Ann's property. He was beloved by the children and all who knew him.

Submitted by: Renee Call

JAMES BIRD

Born: 22 Dec 1806, Roxbury, Morris, New Jersey
Parents: Benjamin Freeman and Marabah Reeves Bird
Died: 12 Jun 1879, St. George, Washington, Utah

Arrived in Valley: Supposed to be in 1852 but listing says
    Captain Allred came in Nov 1855

Married 1st: Jane Mott Carpenter
Date: 1831, Hester, Tompkins, New York
Born: 31 Dec 1810, Nortford, Hartford, Connecticut
Parents: Joshua and Sally Crane Carpenter
Died: 7 May 1892, Clover Valley, Lincoln, Nevada

Married 2nd: Sophia Alcester Fuller
Date: 5 May 1843
Born: 1806

James was the fourth of 13 children. After his marriage to
Jane Mott Carpenter, they moved to Southport, Chemung, New
York, where their first two children were born. Later they lived
in Hictor, Schmong, New York, and then in Southport, Chemung,
New York. They finally moved to Council Point, Pottawattamie,
Iowa, where their last child was born.

According to his father's history, James may have gone with
his other brothers and sisters first to Kirtland and then to Missouri and finally Nauvoo. He helped build the Nauvoo Temple.

When the move west came, James and his father and brothers
were asked to remain in Council Bluffs for a time to help assist
the saints in getting outfits. The Bird men were weavers by trade.
They set up a woolen mill so they could help the saints.

In one of the histories, it says that James had malaria so bad
that he couldn't work. The family lived on black walnuts and
grew to hate them.

They finally made their way to Utah, where they settled in
Provo. Soon after they were settled, James was ordained to be
the first bishop in the Provo Second Ward from 1852 to 1862.

At October Conference in 1861, James was called to settle in
Southern Utah. He, with his two sons Taylor and Jasper, moved
to St. George, where he helped with the building. He built his
own home one block west of the St. George Tabernacle.

Children of 1st wife:

TAYLOR REEVES, b. 25 Feb 1832, Southport, Chemung, New York. Md. 26 Oct 1862, Alice Stokes. D. 6 Jan 1914, Vernal, Utah.

SARAH JANE, b. 13 Jul 1834, Southport, New York. Md. Lyman Lafayette Woods. D. 12 Jul 1851.

MARIBAH ANN, b. 13 Jun 1837, Hector, Chemung, New York. Md. 13 Jul 1856, Lyman Lafayette Woods. D. 28 May 1907, Clover Valley, Lincoln, Nevada.

JAMES JR., b. 1840, Southport, Chemung, New York.

HARRISON, JR., b. 1843, Southport, New York.

AMANDA ANN, b. 11 May 1846, Southport, Hancock, Ill. D. 20 Nov 1846. Child.

JASPER THOMAS, b. 11 Apr 1849, Council Point, Pottawattamie, Iowa. Md. 12 Oct 1869, Eunice Ann Starr. D. 30 Mar 1901, Provo, Utah.

Submitted by: Donna Bird

JASPER THOMAS BIRD

Born: 11 Apr 1849, Council Point, Pottawattamie, Iowa
Parents: James and Jane Mott Carpenter
Died: 30 Mar 1901, Provo, Utah, Utah
Arrived in Valley: 1852 or 1855, Capt. Allreds Co.

Married: Eunice Ann Starr
Date: 12 Oct 1869, Salt Lake City, Utah
Born: 18 Jul 1850, Ash Hollar, Garden, Nebraska
Parents: Edward William and Amanda Ann Duel Starr
Died: 15 Sep 1905, Provo, Utah, Utah

Jasper Thomas was born at Council Point, Iowa, as his parents were on their way west. The family settled in Provo where they stayed until his father was called on a mission to help settle St. George. It was here that Jasper met his wife. They had ten children but only four grew to adulthood, the others died as infants.

He was engaged primarily in hauling wood for use in the St. George Temple and surrounding area. He made a meager living, and at times they went without shoes. When they had shoes, they were saved for Sundays.

It was about 1888-1889 that the family moved to Clover, Lincoln, Nevada. Jasper couldn't make a living there so when the twins were in their teens, they moved back to Provo. They enrolled the boys in the BY Academy so they could get an education.

Children:

ELLA GERTRUDE, b. 27 Jul 1871, St. George, Washington, Utah. Md. 25 Oct 1890, David Cate Leavitt. D. 17 Jul 1941, Provo, Utah.

JASPER ADELBERT (twin), b. 11 Sep 1875, St. George, Utah. Md. 19 Jun 1907, Mary Ellen Martell. D. 12 Jul 1940, Provo, Utah.

ORSON GILBERT (twin), b. 11 Sep 1875, St. George, Utah. Md. 26 Jun 1901, Mary Jane (Mayme) Wilkins. D. 18 Mar 1927, Los Angeles, California.

EDWARD JAMES, b. 21 Apr 1878, St. George, Utah. D. 13 May 1878. Child.

LORA AMANDA, b. 18 May 1879, St. George, Utah. Md. 1st, 22 Jul 1898, John Andrew Beesley. Md. 2nd 21 Aug 1901, James Henry Yates. Md. 3rd, 20 Sep 1904, Harry Logan. D. 29 Nov 1939, Los Angeles, California.

WILLIS STARR, b. 29 Dec 1881, St. George, Utah. D. 15 May 1882. Child.

ELIZABETH, b. 3 Aug 1883, St. George, Utah. D. 25 Nov 1883. Child.

TAYLOR REEVES, b. 12 Sep 1884, St. George, Utah. D. 16 Dec 1884. Child.

CLAUDIUS, b. 26 Oct 1886, St. George, Utah. D. 30 Jun 1888. Child.

LEONAL (LEON), b. 26 Jul 1889, Clover, Lincoln, Nevada. D. 26 Dec 1890. Child.

Submitted by: Donna Bird

JOHN PRATT KENNEDY BIRD

Born: 24 Aug 1827, Burdette, Hector Twp, Tompkins, New York
Parents: Charles and Mary Ann Kennedy Bird
Died: 9 Mar 1886, Mendon, Utah
Arrived in Valley: 30 Aug 1850, Milo Andrus Co.

Married: Sarah Ann Hoopes
Date: About July or August 1850, along the trail west

John Pratt Kennedy was the oldest of Charles and Mary Ann Bird's children. He was just five years old when the first missionaries came to their home. The family joined the Church and left their comfortable home in New Jersey to move to Kirtland, Ohio, and then to Nauvoo. It was his father's team and wagon that brought Joseph and Hyrum's bodies home from Carthage.

His family remained in Nauvoo to help the saints prepare to go west. When they did leave, they had to cross the river on the ice. So severe was the winter that John's mother's toes were frozen on one foot and had to be amputated without anesthetic.

John and his sweetheart decided not to wait to get married. They were married somewhere along the trail west and sealed in the endowment house when they arrived in Salt Lake. They settled for a time in Little Cottonwood where one child was born. President Young then called them to help settle Springville, where the next five children were born. Later they were again called to move to help settle the beautiful Cache Valley. They lived in Mendon where John became a farmer and died in 1886.

Children:

LEWIS RICHARD, b. 3 Nov 1850, Little Cottonwood, Utah.
ELIZABETH JANE, Springville, Utah.
JOHN WILLIAM, Springville, Utah.
JONATHAN FREEMAN, Springville, Utah.
CHARLES WARNER, Springville, Utah.
ALZADA REBECCA, Springville, Utah.
MARY ANN, Mendon, Utah.
ELIZA SADILLA, Mendon, Utah.
HENRIETTA, Mendon, Utah.
SARAH, Mendon, Utah.
MARIAH LOUISA, Mendon, Utah.
HYRUM HOOPES, Mendon, Utah.
JAMES HOOPES, Mendon, Utah.

Submitted by: Ephraim Furness

JACOB BISCHOFF

Born: 21 May 1837, Vollerup, Soro, Denmark
Parents: Jacob August and Ane Jorgensen Bischoff

Died: 15 Sep 1874, Salt Lake City, Utah, body later interred in
    Fountain Green Cemetery, Sanpete, Utah
Arrived in Valley: Oct 1867, Co. unknown

Married: Maria Jensen
Date: 24 Jun 1862, Vollerup, Soro, Denmark
Born: 10 Aug 1842, Haldegerlille, Soro, Denmark
Died: 28 Apr 1897, Fountain Green, Utah

Jacob was a weaver by trade but was also a traveling sales-man. He was a hunter, faithful member of the church, good hus-band and father. His father had died when he was just six weeks old, and his mother married later the man who had introduced him to weaving and taught him the trade.

Jacob was apprenticed to an expert weaver. The man's or-phaned niece lived with him but she was treated shamefully by him. Jacob tried to help her as much as possible and soon they fell in love and were married. He taught her what love and kind-ness were.

In 1867, after Jacob returned from a war with Germany, they were introduced to the Mormon Church and soon determined to join. They were ostracized by friends and family and decided to journey to America and the West.

They sold their home and business. The first record of them is after they left Omaha, Nebraska. They lost all four of their children in a measles outbreak, but with determination they went on. They lived the first year in Big Cottonwood Canyon.

Because the Scandanavian saints were settling in Sanpete County, Jacob and Maria decided to move there. They lived in Fountain Green where Jacob acquired a fair-sized farm and built a house. He bought a team and wagon, bought produce and sold it to the miners in Nevada and Utah.

Although he provided well for his family, his health was not good and he developed yellow jaundice. He was taken to Salt Lake where he could receive the best care, but he died without ever seeing his family again. Maria had his body brought back to Fountain Green where they are both buried.

Children:

JACOB AUGUST (twin), b. 1 May 1863, Vollerup, Soro, Denmark. D. 25 Jul 1867 on plains near Omaha, Nebraska with measles. Child.

JENS FERDINAND (twin), b. 1 May 1863, Vollerup, Soro, Denmark. D. 17 Jul 1867 on plains. Child.

ANNIE SOPHIE DOROTHEA, b. 30 May 1865, Vollerup, Soro, Denmark. D. 28 Jul 1867 on plains. Child.

LARS HENDRICK, b. 21 Aug 1866, Vollerup, Soro, Denmark. D. 20 Jul 1867 on plains. Child.

ELIZA MARIA, b. 22 Nov 1867, Big Cottonwood Canyon, Utah. Md. 28 Nov 1888, John Anderson. D. 13 Dec 1923, Fountain Green, Utah.

ROBERT JOHN, b. 2 Sep 1869, Fountain Green, Utah. Md. 1st, 12 May 1897, Rose Ann Jensen. Md. 2nd, 20 Aug 1920, Caroline Scholes. D. 4 May 1950, Logan, Utah.

NEPHI DANIEL, b. 25 Dec 1870, Fountain Green, Utah. Md. 9 Mar 1892, Annie Sophia Olson. D. 14 Jan 1931, Lovell, Wyoming.

JOSEPH PETER, b. 22 Oct 1872, Fountain Green, Utah. Md. 3 Sep 1902, Ellamara Christiana Olson. D. 14 Jun 1950, Idaho.

ALBERT FREDERICK, b. 26 Mar 1874, Fountain Green, Utah. Md. 13 Jun 1896, Jeanetta Rebecca Anderson. D. 17 Jun 1956, Idaho.

Submitted by: Rosa Vida Black

FREDERICK JAMES BISHOP

Born: 29 Jun 1832, Nottingham, England
Parents: John and Ann Dennis Bishop
Died: 3 Nov 1891, Murray, Utah
Arrived in Valley: 15 Sep 1861, Ira Eldredge Co.

Married: Eliza Catherine Robinson
Date: 30 Jul 1859, Germantown, Pennsylvania
Born: 15 Apr 1840, England
Died: 2 May 1918, Murray, Utah

Frederick James was a tailor by trade and served in the Crimean War. He was baptized into the Church 14 Aug 1860 in England. During 1861, he and his family crossed the plains along with other members of the Bishop family.

On their arrival in the Valley, the first night was spent in the Pioneer Fort and the next day they were taken to American Fork. They lived in the Tithing room until they were able to provide a dugout home for shelter. After about two years, they moved to the Murray area.

During the winter of 1867-8, while out helping a friend get his wagon out of the mud, Frederick's feet became frozen and the doctor had to amputate a part of Frederick's left foot.

Their first real home was in Murray where they lived out their lives, although in a different home later on. They were active in the church and particularly enjoyed singing in the choir and a mixed quartet. Frederick suffered a sun stroke while working on his farm, which resulted in his death.

Children:

JOHN ROBINSON, b. 17 Jan 1861, Germantown, Pennsylvania. Md. 9 Mai 1882, Emily Stringer. D. 26 Oct 1929, Salt Lake City, Utah.

CLARA ANN, b. 29 Aug 1862, American Fork, Utah. Md. 31 Dec 1882, William Hill Strong. D. 16 Feb 1932, Las Vegas, Nevada.

EDWIN SAMUEL, b. 26 Dec 1863, American Fork. Md. 1884, Bethia Adamson. D. 4 Mar 1903, Murray, Utah.

ELIZA CATHERINE, b. 12 Oct 1865, So. Cottonwood, Utah. Md. 8 Oct 1885, John Abraham Maxfield. D.20 Mar 1948, Salt Lake City, Utah.

MATHEW ROBINSON, b. 5 Mar 1867, So. Cottonwood, Utah. Md. 15 Mar 1888, Aillie Jane Russell. D. 29 May 1938, Salt Lake City, Utah.

LOIS JANE, b. 27 Sep 1868, Cottonwood, Utah. Md. 20 Feb 1888, Alexander Adamson. D. 5 Oct 1942, Murray, Utah.

ANNIE ELIZABETH, b. 11 Jun 1870, Cottonwood, Utah. Md. 18 May 1892, Hyrus K. Meckling. D. 12 May 1933.

AMY LILLIE MAY, b. 27 May 1872, Cottonwood, Utah. Md. Aug 1891, Michael McMillan. D. 17 Jan 1892.

BLANCHE ALBERTA, b. 23 Jan 1875, Cottonwood, Utah. Md. 22 May 1894, Neil Anderson. D. 6 Oct 1959.

MINNIE LOUISE, b. 3 Nov 1876, Cottonwood, Utah. Md. 8 Apr 1896, James Alvin Rassmusson Lindahl. D. 22 Mar 1964, Salt Lake City, Utah.

SARAH JANET, b. 16 Sep 1878, So. Cottonwood, Utah. Md. 8 Dec 1898, David Ezra Greenwood. D. 30 Aug 1965, Salt Lake City, Utah.

FREDERICK JAMES, b. 10 Dec 1881. Stillborn.

Submitted by: Arthur Bishop

JAMES BISHOP

Born: 24 Jun 1831, Shrewsbury, Shropshire, England
Parents: John and Catherine Evans Bishop
Died: 4 Jan 1908, Salt Lake City, Utah
Arrived in Valley: Oct 1853, Appleton Harmon Co.

Married 1st: Sinah Pugh
Date: 24 Dec 1855
Born: 17 Dec 1831, Shrewsbury, England
Died: 24 Dec 1887, Salt Lake City, Utah

Married 2nd: Rachel Sykes
Date: 19 Mar 1864, Draper, Salt Lake City, Utah
Born: 16 Mar 1836, Leicester, Leicester, England
Died: (Bur) 2 Oct 1904, Salt Lake City, Utah

Married 3rd: Ellen Maria (or Marie) Obray. Called Mary Ellen
Date: 26 Feb 1872, Salt Lake City, Utah
Born: 24 Aug 1854, Glamorganshire, Wales
Died: 23 Jul 1900, Salt Lake City, Utah

James was the eighth of nine children. They lived about 20 miles from the Welsh border. He was the first of the family members to be converted to the Mormon Church. He helped with the record keeping in the Branch. When an advertisement appeared in the Millenial Star for mechanics to immigrate to the Valley, he gladly accepted the challenge. He was a pipe fitter.

He married Sinah whom he had known in England, and they settled in Draper, Utah. He did military service in Echo Canyon during the Johnston's War. He also fought in the Bear River Indian Wars. In 1861 he moved his family to Paradise, Cache Valley, where he became known as Jim the plumber. He installed the steam pipes in the Logan Temple. During this time, six of their nine children died very young from diptheria and other illnesses.

With Sinah's encouragement, he entered into polygamy and married Rachel. Her only child died at birth and left her crippled for life. He then married Mary Ellen. Five of her nine children died young. James outlived most of his family.

Children of 1st wife:

JAMES EVAN, b. 20 Jan 1857, Draper, Utah. D. 7 Dec 1861. Child.
HARRIET ELIZABETH, b. 7 Nov 1858, Draper, Utah. D.18 Dec 1861. Child.
THOMAS WILLIAM, b. 2 Sep 1860, Draper, Utah. D. 16 Jul 1863. Child.
JOHN RICHARD, b. 15 Mar 1862, Paradise, Cache, Utah. D. 25 Aug 1862. Child.
MARY CATHERINE, b. 10 Jun 1863, Paradise, Utah. Md. Joseph Summerhays. D.9 Aug 1883.
SINAH PUGH, b. 31 Aug 1865, Paradise, Utah. Md. 20 Aug 1884, John Blackie Reid. D. 8 Oct 1963, Salt Lake City, Utah.
RACHEL ANN, b. 3 Sep 1867, Paradise, Utah. Md. 1st, Augustus Foster Wilcox. Md. 2nd, Walter Fish. Md. 3rd Charles D. Harding. D. 28 Dec 1951.
PRISCILLA JANE, b. abt 1869, Paradise, Utah. D. Infant
CALEB SAMUEL, b. abt 1871, Paradise, Utah. D. Infant

Children of 2nd wife:

DAUGHTER, stillborn.

Children of 3rd wife:

MARY ELLEN OBRAY, b. 23 May 1873, Paradise, Utah. D. 7 May 1883.
JAMES OBRAY, b. 10 Dec 1875, Paradise, Utah. D . 30 Apr 1883. Child.

GEORGE OBRAY, b. 5 May 1880, Paradise, Utah. Md. 3 Mar
1904, Elsie Twitchell Jones. D. 14 Mar 1969, Salt Lake City,
Utah.

ELIZABETH OBRAY, b. 13 Mar 1883, Paradise, Utah. D. 19
Sep 1890. Child.

WILLIAM OBRAY, b. 16 Jun 1886, Paradise, Utah. D. 15 Feb
1891. Child.

KATHERINE OBRAY, b. 1 Aug 1889, Salt Lake City, Utah. Md.
15 Jun 1910, Paul Gay Margetts. D. 6 Nov 1977, Salt Lake
City, Utah.

BENJAMIN OBRAY, b. 1 Sep 1891, Salt Lake City, Utah.

PEARL PRUDENCE, b. 18 May 1893, Salt Lake City, Utah.
Bur. Aug 1894. Child.

JOSEPH OBRAY, b. 28 Mar 1896, Salt Lake City, Utah. Md.
Vivian Lane. D. 7 Mar 1960.

Submitted by: Jay Bishop

WILLIAM EVANS BISHOP

Born: 11 Jun 1828, Shrewsbury, Shropshire, England
Parents: John and Catherine Evans Bishop
Died: 21 May 1921, Paradise , Cache, Utah
Arrived in Valley: 3 Oct 1855, Richard Ballentine Co.

Married 1st: Mary Pocock
Date: 8 Feb 1852, England

Married 2nd: Harriet Morris
Date: 28 Sep 1863, Salt Lake City, Utah

Born: 2 Nov 1839, Hambleton, England
Parents: John and Maria Linney Morris
Died: 24 Dec 1919, Paradise, Utah

William's first memories were of going to day school and Sunday School in his boyhood. He was baptized into the Mormon Church on the 28 July 1848. He lived in England for seven more years, during which time he performed missionary work with his neighbors and friends and also in the surrounding country.

He worked in the gas company in England and also in the coal works, probably in the mines. He also helped build railroads.

They arrived in the Valley the year the grasshoppers first ate the crops. It was very hard for them, especially the newcomers who had used up most of the provisions they had brought with them.

The first year he lived in Provo where they stayed for one and one half years before moving to Draper. William was called to help in the Johnston War. From Draper they moved to Paradise, where he lived out his life.

Children of 2nd wife:

HARRIET LOUISA, b. 12 Jul 1864, Draper, Utah. Md. 13 Nov 1884, Samuel Thomas Kay McMurdie. D. 27 May 1935.

CATHERINE: b. 12 Dec 1865, Paradise, Utah. D. 15 Sep 1875, Paradise, Utah.

WILLIAM JOHN, b. 15 Mar 1867, Paradise, Utah. D.25 Sep 1875, Paradise, Utah.

JAMES MORRIS, b. 10 Feb 1869, Paradise, Utah. D. 7 Sep 1869. Child.

MARIA JANE, b. 22 Jan 1871, Paradise, Utah. D. 8 Sep 1875. Child.

ROBERT MORRIS, b. 15 Dec 1873, Paradise, Utah. Md. 27 May 1913, Josephine Johnson. D. 30 May 1959.

EMMA, b. 6 Mar 1876, Paradise, Utah. Md. 9 Dec 1897, Joseph Terry Lofthouse. D. 24 Feb 1859.

MARY ANNIE, b. 18 Sep 1879, Paradise, Utah. Md. 19 Dec 1906, Hyrum Miles. D. 12 Aug 1949.

RICHARD, b. 29 Jul 1881, Paradise, Utah. Md. 18 Dec 1904, Maria Tams. D. 25 Sep 1946.

Submitted by: Jay Bishop

JOSEPH WADSWORTH BISSELL

Born: 1 Jan 1830, Boston Middlesex, Massachusetts
Parents: Henry and Dorothy Elizabeth Plummer Bissell
Died: 6 Dec 1906, Springville, Utah, Utah
Arrived in Valley: 3 Oct 1852, John B. Walker, Capt.

Married: Anna Catherine Alleman
Date: 31 Mar 1852, Council Bluffs, Iowa
Born: 27 Oct 1833, Middletown, Dauphin, Pennsylvania
Died: 16 Mar 1924, Springville, Utah, Utah

Joseph left Boston in 1850, together with his widowed mother, to join with the Mormons. At Council Bluffs he met his future wife and they were married. In June 1852, their family, together with his wife's family, started across the plains. His mother died in Nebraska of cholera. Arriving in the Valley, they spent their first winter there. The next year they went on to Springville to make their home.

Joseph was a successful business man in Springville. He was superintendent of the Springville Co-op, ran a drug store, was appointed Alderman of Springville in 1861, and later served as Justice of the Peace. He remained active in the community and especially in the church. He was a credit to his family, the community and especially to the church.

Children:

HARRIET ELIZABETH, b. 5 Feb 1853, Salt Lake City, Utah. Md. 26 May 1873, Silas E. Clark. D. 1 Apr 1922.

JOSEPH THEODORE, b. 4 Aug 1855, Springville, Utah. D.11 Jun 1856. Child.

MARY ANN, b. 9 Jun 1857, Springville, Utah. Unmarried. D. 9 May 1902.

ANNA CATHERINE, b. 24 Jan 1860, Springville, Utah. Md. 1 Jul 1880, John James Walton. D. 8 Apr 1930, Salt Lake City, Utah.

ROXA CHRISTIANA, b. 12 Dec 1862, Springville, Utah. Md. 29 Nov1883, Hyrum George White. D. 27 Nov 1936.

JOHN ALLEMAN, b. 27 Oct 1865, Springville, Utah. Md. 21 Dec 1892, Caroline Jensen. D. 3 Jun 1946.

ADALECIA LEUVANE, b. 16 Aug 1868, Springville, Utah. Md. 28 Aug 1889, George William Harrison. D. 27 Jan 1966, Springville, Utah.

PEARL MAY, b. 16 May 1871, Springville, Utah. Md. Jan 1893, Thomas Carter Hanford. D. 30 Sep 1927.

CHARLES EDWARD, b. 28 Jul 1874, Springville, Utah. Md. 1st, 26 Aug 1896, Annie Wignall. Md. 2nd Amelia Rees Stockdale. D. 1 Jul 1940, Salt Lake City, Utah.

Submitted by: Royal Oakes

TRAUGOTT BITTER

Born: 2 Dec 1834, Kreuzburg (Kreutzberg), East Prussia, Prussia
Parents: Gotthardt and Louise Neumann Bitter

Died: 25 Jan 1929, Logan, Cache, Utah
Arrived in Valley: 23 Sep 1861, Joseph W. Young Co.

Married 1st: Rosina Wilhelmina Aust
Date: 27 Sep 1859, Landsberg, East Prussia

Married 2nd: Bertha Anna Grellert
Date: 8 Jul 1887, Logan, Utah

Traugott was a farmer who lived at home until he was 18. He served an apprenticeship to learn the carpenter and cabinet maker trade. When he had completed his apprenticeship he went to Konigsberg where he worked for two years, and then he went to Cranz to work for a man who was building a mill. While visiting a friend in Landsberg, he met and married Rosina. He and his friend decided to leave for America so, taking Rosina, they left a week after the marriage.

Traugott and Rosina stayed in New York for two years because they were short of money. Traugott did carpenter work and Wilhelmina knit wool baby shirts for a store and took in washing.

While in New York, a friend introduced them to the Mormon Church. They were baptized in the East River on 5 Jun 1861. One week after their baptizm, they began their journey west.

Beginning a new life in Utah was not easy. For three days they camped out, having no place to go. They tried living in Lehi for a short time but soon returned to Salt Lake. Because of his skills in carpentry work, Traugott was hired to work on the Salt Lake Theatre, for which he was paid in produce. Life was not easy and there was not much work so when the call came to settle St. George, they went south. He worked at a saw mill and was paid in lumber, which he sold for what he could get.

They decided to return to Salt Lake. Their situation improved considerably. After the birth of their third child, Traugott moved his family to Logan. With his skill, he helped build the Logan Tabernacle and Temple and many other buildings. He was able to obtain some land on which he raised grain and hay, and he built a comfortable house.

Traugott, with the consent of Rosina, took a plural wife. However, there were always bad feelings between the two women so they lived in separate houses. Eventually his second wife and children moved away because of the rising persecution with plural marriage. They lived in several places but finally returned to Providence, which was close to Logan.

Traugott was a talented cabinet maker and loved what he did. He had a great love of music and was of a gentle nature. He always felt that his true wealth and riches were his wives and children. He devoted the last years of his life to genealogical and temple work.

Children of 1st wife:

MARTHA, b. abt 1860, New York. Md. Hyrum Ricks, Sr.
TRAUGOTT WILLIAM, b. 1862, Salt Lake City, Utah. D. 1864. Child.
JOSEPH, b. St. George, Utah. Md. Eliza Clausine Ericksen.
AMELIA, D. unmarried.
ALBERT, D. Infant.
GEORGE, D. Infant.
RICHARD ALFRED, Md. Chloe Alwin Francis.
WILLARD RUDOLF, D. young.
CHARLES, Md. Printha Elizabeth Facer.

Children of 2nd wife:

HYRUM WALTER, Md. Edith Jensen.
EDNA ELIZABETH, Md. Soren Willard Poulsen.
ERMA, D. Infant.
LEONA, Md. Arthur L. Olsen.
KARL, D. Infant.
FRANKLIN, Md. Helen Cyrene Cambell.
HEDWIG LOUISE, Md. Clarence Lehi Petersen.
ALMA, D. Infant.

Submitted by: Grant Bitter

WILLIAM BJORK
(VILHELM JOHANSSON BJORK)

Born: 6 Apr 1837, Brevick, Skaraborg, Sweden
Parents: Johannes Johansson Vall and Catharina Erricksson Bjork
Died: 3 Jun 1928, Pleasant Grove, Utah, Utah
Arrived in Valley: 19 Aug 1868, John R. Murdock Co.

Married 1st: Augusta Gustava Anderson (or Nilson)
Date: 29 Dec 1868, Salt Lake City, Utah
Born: 15 Oct 1836, Brevick, Sweden
Parents: Anders and Anna Maja Anderson (Nilson)
Died: 21 Mar 1904, Pleasant Grove, Utah

Married 2nd: Eva Charlotta Anderson
Date: 12 Aug 1885, Logan, Utah
Born: 31 Mar 1852, Julyta Nu Kopings, Sweden
Parents: Anders and Catharina Anderson Ericson
Died: 20 Dec 1901, Pleasant Grove, Utah

Married 3rd: Mary Mortensen
Date: 26 Jun 1890, Logan, Utah
Born: 5 Jul 1869, Goldbeck, Denmark
Parents: Peder and Anna Dorthea Justsen Mortensen
Died: 30 Oct 1951, Holladay, Salt Lake, Utah

William heard the missionaries along with his parents and was baptized on 22 May 1855 when he was 18. The family wanted to go to Zion but economic conditions delayed them for 14 years. William was the first of the family to leave. It was hard to leave his family but it helped to know his sweetheart was going. They were able to go part way by train because William had agreed to work on the railroad from Echo Canyon to Promontory. From Omaha, Nebraska, to Salt Lake, William drove a wagon. Augusta walked most of the way.

Upon the advice of Brigham Young, they moved to Willow Creek, later called Grantsville, in Tooele County. William built a log house and they settled down. William had been chosen to supervise the building of the last part of the grading so Augusta was also there when the Golden Spike was driven.

While living in Grantsville, a lovely young women visited often and was loved by the family. William, with the consent of Augusta, married Eva Charlotta Anderson.

In 1877 the family moved to Orem and then to Pleasant Grove, where William died. He had made it possible for his parents and some of their children to join him in Utah. William left a heritage of honesty, hard work, and respect, and a love of the gospel that had brought them so far.

Children of 1st wife:

WILHELMINA (Wilhelminnie), b. 9 Sep 1869, Grantsville, Utah.

Children of 2nd wife:

WILMA SOPHIA, b. 5 Jan 1890, Pleasant Grove, Utah.
BEATRICE CHARLOTTA, b. 18 Oct 1892, Pleasant Grove, Utah.
SON, b. Apr 1891. D. Infant. Pleasant Grove, Utah.
SON, b. 19 Apr 1898. D. Infant. Pleasant Grove, Utah.

Submitted by: Dorothy Potter

GEORGE DAVID BLACK, JR.

Born: 18 Feb 1841, Copiah Co., Mississippi
Parents: George David and Mary McRee Black
Died: 7 Apr 1913, Wilford, Fremont, Idaho
Arrived in Valley: 29 Jul 1847, James Brown Co, Mormon Bat.

Married: Mary Hunt
Date: 16 Feb 1861, Ogden, Weber, Utah
Born: 12 Jul 1845, Bear Creek, Nauvoo, Hancock, Illinois
Parents: Jefferson and Celia Mounts Hunt
Died: 29 Sep 1930, St. Anthony, Fremont, Idaho

David, as he was known, and his wife lived in Ogden until 1871. He ran large herds of cattle out on Promontory and was considered a fine judge of cattle. He played the snare drum in the first Marshall band in Ogden. He was also a fine violinist and played for dances. He was the official town cannon shooter, which was fired on special occasions. As he grew older, he lost his hearing as a result.

He moved his family to Huntsville in 1871, and the following spring they moved to Oxford, Idaho. While living in the Oxford Branch, he was made Presiding Elder for three years and then was made 1st counselor to Bishop Fisher. He also served as Justice of the Peace. They lived in Oxford until the Snake River Valley was colonized, at which time he was called to help build up the area in 1883. He served on the High Council, was Sunday School Superintendent and a Lieutenant in the Utah Militia.

He was a real friend to the Indians. His trade was carpenter and plasterer and he helped build many buildings. In 1903, he moved his family to Oregon, but soon returned to Idaho. In 1913, he fell from a wagon and was badly injured and died five days later. Before he died, he told friends to tell his children to always stay true to the church. He was a firm believer in the gospel, a devoted husband, father and friend.

Children:

NANCY JANE, b. 22 Jan 1863, Ogden, Utah. D. 11 May 1865. Child.

GEORGE DAVID JR., b. 24 Oct 1864, Ogden, Utah. Md. 18 Jan 1890. D. 17 Feb 1867, Ogden, Utah.

CHARLES JEFFERSON, b. 24 Nov 1866, Ogden, Utah. Md. 18 Jan 1890, Alice Malona Pratt (Div). D. 18 May 1928.

WILLIAM JESSE, b. 16 Mar 1869, Ogden, Utah. Md. 13 Jun 1895, Elva Sarah Jacobs. D. 25 Jul 1947, Burley, Cassia, Idaho.

HARRIET ERMINNIE, b. 21 Apr 1871, Huntsville, Utah. Md. 18 Jun 1891, Fredrick William Garner. D. 6 Nov 1969, Idaho Falls, Idaho.

JOSEPH WARREN, b. 28 May 1873, Oxford, Idaho. Md. 20 Jul 1899, Sarah Jane Stewart. D. 22 Oct 1954, Salt Lake City, Utah.

JOHN FRANKLIN, b. 28 May 1875, Oxford, Idaho. Md. 15 Jun 1899, Alice Maude Raybould. D. 14 Jul 1958, Boise, Idaho.

MARY ABIGAIL, b. 21 Mar 1878, Oxford, Idaho. Md. 19 Apr 1911, Walter Warren Barney. D. 31 Mar 1939, St. Anthony, Idaho.

GRACE, b. 20 May 1880, Oxford, Idaho. Md. 22 Nov 1901, Frederick Richard Hayes. D. 6 Aug 1904, Sugar City, Idaho.

HENRY HARRISON, b. 22 Feb 1882, Oxford, Idaho. Md. 23 Jul 1903, Lydia Mary Birch. D. 7 May 1951, West Yellowstone, Montana.

CELIA MARGARET, b. 14 Nov 1884, Wilford, Idaho. Md. 14 Jan 1903, Clarence LeRoy Lewis. D. 5 Oct 1956, St. Anthony, Idaho.

WALLACE EDWIN, b. 12 Dec 1885, Wilford, Idaho. Md. 12

Dec 1918, Erma Harris, (Div). D. 16 Dec 1923, Los Angeles, California.
MAUDE ULINE, b. 21 Sep 1890, Wilford, Idaho. D. 28 Mar 1899.

Submitted by: Elaine C. Rowley

WILLIAM BLACK, JR.

Born: 20 Aug 1784, Lisburn, Antrim, Ireland
Parents: William and Mary Gardiner Black, Sr.
Died: 29 Jan 1873, Rockville, Washington, Utah
Arrived in Valley: 20 Sep 1850, James Pace Co.

Married: Jane Johnston
Date: 31 Jul 1822, Ireland
Born: 11 Jun 1801, Lombeg, Antrim, Ireland
Died: 20 Jan 1890

William helped colonize Dixie (St. George). He helped build some of the homes, schools, churches, saw mills, cotton gins, and sugar mills. He was well known and well liked because of his honesty and fine work.

He remained active in the church and community.

Children:

GEORGE, b. 6 May 1823, Lisburn, Ireland. Md. Susan Jacway. D. 13 Nov 1872, Kanosh, Utah.
MARY, b. 25 Apr 1824, Lisburn, Ireland. Md. John McDonald. D. 20 Nov 1845, Nauvoo, Illinois.

WILLIAM VALENTINE, b. 21 Feb abt 1826, Lisburn, Ireland. Md. 1st Almire Murry Ayers. Md. 2nd Victoria Ayers. D. 1 Apr 1927, Deseret, Utah.

JOSEPH SMITH, (Smith added after he joined the church). b. 14 Jul 1836, Lisburn, Ireland. Md. Nancy Cynthia Allred. D. 13 Aug 1910, Deseret, Utah.

Submitted by: Janell Nichols

WILLIAM VALENTINE BLACK

Born: 21 Feb 1836, Lisburn, Antrim, Ireland
Parents: William and Jane Johnston Black, Jr.
Died: 1 Apr 1927, Deseret, Millard, Utah
Arrived in Valley: 20 Sep 1850, James Pace Co.

Married 1st: Almira Murry Ayers
Date: 28 Feb 1854
Born: 23 Jun 1834, Branchville, Sussex, New Jersey
Died: 14 Sep 1872

Married 2nd: Victoria Ayers (sister to Almira)
Date: abt 1857
Born: 8 Nov 1839, Stanhope, Sussex, New Jersey
Died: 1924

William was a good man and father who loved the Church and worked hard to fulfill his obligations to the church and community. He helped settle the Dixie area.

The places he lived and helped develop can be determined by

the births of his children listed below. He lived in Millard the last years of his life.

Children of 1st wife:

JANE LUCINDA, b. 16 Nov 1855, Salt Lake City, Utah. Md. Ezra Tunis Cutler Rappleye. D. 2 Dec 1948, Provo, Utah.
ALMIRA MURRY, b. 25 Jun 1857, Manti, Utah. Md. John Styler. D. 12 Feb 1938.
WILLIAM VALENTINE, Jr., b. 8 Feb 1860, Spring City, Utah. Md. Annie Rotherham. D. 5 Apr 1943.
LUCINDA CATHERINE, b. 19 May 1861, Spring City, Utah. Md. Uriah Curtis.
ELIZABETH, b. 19 Feb 1863, Springdale, Utah. Md. William Broadfield. D. 12 Jun 1937.
ANNIE ALDONA, b. 28 Nov 1864, Springdale, Utah. Md. Homer Hyatt. D. 4 Feb 1952.
FANNY VERENA, b. 24 Aug 1866, Rockville, Utah. Md. Alfred Miksell. D. 22 Jul 1919.
ELEANOR, b. 17 Jul 1869, Rockville, Utah. Md. Hyrum James Walton. D. May 1952.
HEBER MARCELLUS, b. 17 Sep 1871, Kanosh, Utah. Md. Harriet M. Simmons.

Children of 2nd wife:

MARY, b. 25 Nov 1858, Spring City, Utah. D.1860. Child.
GEORGE, b. 3 Mar 1861, Spring City, Utah.
AGNES, b. 11 Feb 1863, Springdale, Utah. D. 14 Apr 1964. Child.
MINERVA, b. 25 Nov 1865, Springdale, Utah. D. 1870. Child.
IRA ADELBERT, b. 10 Feb 1868, Springdale, Utah. D. 11 Apr 1878.
JUSTIN, b. 20 Sep 1870, Kanosh, Utah. D. 14 Jan 1875. Child.
JOSEPH VALENTINE, b. 14 Sep 1873, Kanosh, Utah. D. 20 Mar 1940.
CLARA, b. 27 Sep 1874, Kanosh, Utah. D. 25 Feb 1958.
VICTORIA, b. 27 Jan 1877, Deseret, Utah. D. 24 Jul 1933.
ALBERT CALEB, b. 12 Oct 1878, Deseret, Utah.

MARIETTA (twin), b. 14 Jan 1881, Deseret, Utah.
MARION (twin), b. 14 Jan 1881, Deseret, Utah.
DELORES, b. 26 Apr 1883, Deseret, Utah. D. 31 Jul 1915.
WILLIAM ALONZO, b. 16 May 1886, Deseret, Utah. D. 18 May
    1953.

Submitted by: Janell Nichols

WILLIAM BLACKHURST

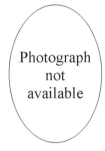

Born: 22 Jun 1807, Longton, Lancashire, England.
Parents: David and Ellen Harrison Blackhurst.
Died: 9 Sep 1864, Salt Lake City, Utah, of pneumonia.
Arrived in Valley: 29 Sep 1847, Edward Hunter Co.

Married 1st: Margaret Stephenson
Date: 1836
Born: 5 May 1804,
Died: 18 Jan 1847, Winterquarters of cholera

Married 2nd: Isabella Meikle
Date: 11 Sep 1857, Salt Lake City, Utah
Born: 6 Apr 1837, Hamilton, Lanark, Scotland

     William and his first wife were baptized into the Church 15
March 1837 in England. They were sealed in the Nauvoo Temple.
He was faithful to the church and active in helping build up the
valley and state. William died as a result of pneumonia.

Children of 1st wife:

ELLEN, b.10 Nov 1837, England. D. 20 Mar 1907, Salt Lake
   City, Utah.
DAVID, b. 3 May 1840, England. D. 1 Mar 1922, Salt Lake City,
   Utah.
JOSEPH BRIGHAM, b. 26 Nov 1845, Nauvoo, Illinois.

Children of 2nd wife:

WILLIAM MEIKLE, b. 17 Jan 1858.
MARGARET MEIKLE, b. 21 Apr 1860.
BRIGHAM MEIKLE, b. 5 Oct 1862.
HYRUM MEIKLE, b.11 Jan 1865. Born after fathers death.

Submitted by: Jay W. Blackhurst

BENJAMIN BLAKE

Born: 27 Jun 1855, Salt Lake City, Utah
Parents: Benjamin Frederick and Harriet Hollis Blake
Died: 2 Jun 1933, St. George, Utah
Arrived in Valley: Born after parents arrival in valley

Married 1st: Ann Elizabeth Ellicock
Date: 29 Jan 1881, St. George, Utah
Born: England
Parents: Mary Ann Bowler Ellicock
Died: 1904, St. George, Utah

Married 2nd: Rosina Eliza Blickenstorfer Gubler (widow)

Date: 22 Dec 1910, St. George, Utah

Benjamin, and his brother Frederick, put up the first sawmill on South Pine Valley Mountain to cut logs into lumber. In 1870 they put up another sawmill on Mount Trumbull. They also ran large herds of cattle.

He narrowly escaped death several times during his life but felt he was saved because of his faith and love of the gospel. His first wife died leaving him with 11 children. He cared lovingly for them but finally married Rosina, a widow with two children. They had three more children.

While Frederick was on a mission to England, Benjamin ran both his and Frederick's cattle herds and also ran both saw mills. He later sold the saw mill because of ill health from cancer.

Children of 1st wife:

BENJAMIN JR., b. 20 Jan 1883. D. 7 Nov 1951.
JOSEPH EDWARD, b. 10 Dec 1884. D. 3 Feb 1958.
NEPHI, b. 31 Jul 1886. D. 5 Oct 1886. Child.
ROWLAND ELLICOCK, b. 3 Apr 1888. D. 3 Jun 1948.
ANNIE ELIZABETH, b. 4 Aug 1889. D.23 Jun 1973.
ROYAL HOLLIS, b. 10 Jul 1891. D. 3 Jun 1963.
ADA, b. 22 Jun 1893. D. 22 Nov 1928.
HERBERT, b. 16 May 1895. D. 16 Dec 1895. Child.
EDITH, b. 26 Jul 1897. D. 12 Oct 1976.
MARY, b. 18 Mar 1899. D. 8 Sep 1934.
MARIE, b. 24 Dec 1901. D. 15 Apr 1977.

Children of 2nd wife:

HAZEL, b. 17 Sep 1911. D. 24 Apr 1993.
INA ELLA, b. 6 Feb 1916.
CECIL, b. 23 Apr 1917.

Submitted by: Roberta Barnum

BENJAMIN FREDERICK BLAKE

Born: 12 Mar 1815, Blandford, Dorset, England
Parents: Isaac and Sophia Wood Blake
Died: 9 Mar 1884, St. George, Utah
Arrived in Valley: Sep 1853, Ten Pound Co.

Married 1st: Harriet Hollis
Date: 31 May 1841, St. Michael's Southampton Parish, England
Born: 11 Dec 1820, Bishopstoke, Hampshire, England
Died: abt 1908, Bur. St. George, Utah

Married 2nd: Mary Ann Bowler Ellicock, widow with four children. Children all took Blake name.

Benjamin Frederick was always a good-natured young man. After his school days, he was apprenticed to the upholstering, carpentry, and paper-handing trade. He later learned to make mattresses, which became his means of livelihood. In England he owned a large furniture store that did well.

He and Harriet lived in England for 12 years before moving to the Valley. In 1851 they first heard the missionaries and accepted the gospel. In 1853 they gave up home, business, loved ones and friends, and immigrated to America.

They lived in the 12th Ward for the next seven years except for the period when they went south because of Johnston's Army. They were called to go to the St. George (Dixie Mission) area to help settle and build up the area. They lived in dugouts until he was able to complete two homes, one of which was for his son Frederick. He also built three carpenter shops. He made most of the beautiful early-day furniture and became known as chairmaker Blake. He made the rare unbrased spiral staircases in the tabernacle. He was in charge of the upholstering in the St. George Temple. His two sons, Frederick and Benjamin, owned two sawmills that provided lumber for his shops, the Temple, Tabernacle, tithing house and homes.

Benjamin was a kind, loving father and husband. He was a faithful member of the church. Their home was always filled with laughter and good times. Benjamin played the violin for dancing, and his wife was a clever story teller. They held spelling matches, played games and even staged dramatics. He was a good and successful businessman and extremely capable in the making of fine furniture.

Children of 1st wife:

FREDERICK, b. 15 Jan 1842, of Salisbury, Wilts, England. D. 4 Feb 1916.

MARIAH SOPHIA, b. 14 Oct 1843, England. D. 20 Jan 1847. England. Child.

CAROLINE LUCY, b. 3 Jul 1845, England. Md. Mr. Hardy and Mr Booth. D. 4 Apr 1893.

EDWARD, b. 2 May 1847, England. D. 22 Jan 1848. Child.

ELIZABETH, b. 28 Jan 1849, England. Md. Mr. Riding. D. 21 Apr 1908.

GEORGE, b. 19 Feb 1851, England. D. 11 Nov 1853. Child.

EMMA, b. 3 Feb 1853, England. D. 18 Mar 1874.

BENJAMIN, b. 27 Jun 1855, Salt Lake City, Utah. Md. 1st, 29 Jan 1881, Ann Elizabeth Ellicock. Md. 2nd Rosina Eliza Blickenstorfer Gubler (widow). D. 2 Jun 1933, St. George, Utah.

JANE, b. 20 Dec 1857, Salt Lake City, Utah. Md. Mr. Branch. D. 22 Mar 1947.

HARRIET, b. 24 Mar 1860. Md. Mr. Sandberg. D. 2 Apr 1926.

ANN ELIZA, b. 4 Aug 1862. D. 24 Oct 1963.

HENRY, b. 28 Nov 1864. D. 10 Aug 1865. Child.

ISAAC, b. 16 Jun 1866. D. 18 Jun 1866. Child.

Children of 2nd wife:

SAMUEL ELLICOCK, b. 11 Dec 1860. D. 11 May 1864. Child.
JOSEPH WANMER ELLICOCK, b. 7 Jun 1862. D. 30 Dec 1944.
ANN ELIZABETH ELLICOCK, b. 11 Feb 1864. Md. Mr. Blake.
    D. 30 Dec 1904.
SARAH JANE ELLICOCK, b. 8 Feb 1866. Md. Mr. Atkin. D.
    10 Jul 1930.
JAMES SAMUEL ELLICOCK, b. 18 Oct 1868. D. 6 Nov 1936.

Submitted by: Roberta Barnum

FREDERICK BLAKE

Born: 15 Jan 1842, Downton, Wiltshire, England
Parents: Benjamin Frederick and Harriet Hollis Blake
Died: 4 Feb 1916, St. George, Utah.
Arrived in Valley: Sep 1853, Ten Pound Co.

Married 1st: Sarah Hardy
Date: (Div. 1866)

Married 2nd: Emily Green
Date: 12 Sep 1868, Salt Lake City, Utah (Div. 1877)

Married 3rd: Eliza Barnett
Date: 10 May 1877 (Div. 13 Jan 1893)

Frederick was only four years old when his family accepted
the gospel and were baptized. When he was 11 years old, he left

316

Liverpool, England with his parents, three sisters and one brother, arriving in northern Utah in 1853. Frederick was 19 when he met and married Sarah.

In 1861, along with his father's family, Frederick was called to help settle the Dixie Mission at St. George, Utah. Two hundred people were called, only 54 stayed, including the Blakes.

Frederick's plan was to go to Dixie, build a home and come back for Sarah. But she changed her mind and refused to go, so they divorced. He married Emily next and they were happy for awhile and had several children, but when it was suggested that he take another wife, Emily left him. He then married for the third time and they had five children, four of whom died young. He had a very bad accident which almost cost him his life and a long hospital stay. After many years of his being a partial invalid, his third wife divorced him too.

Frederick was a hard worker most of his life and tried to provide good homes for his family. He was unlucky in his marriages but tried hard to compensate for his failure by his good life. He ended up living with his brother Benjamin the rest of his life. He died of cancer.

Children of 2nd wife:

SARAH ANN, b. 3 Jul 1869. D. 24 Oct 1959.
FREDERICK BENJAMIN, b. 28 May 1871. D. 3 Mar 1885.
JAMES HENRY, b. 28 Mar 1873. D. 10 Aug 1873. Infant.
GEORGE THOMAS, b. 5 Mar 1875. D. 13 Oct 1876. Infant.
EMILY, b. 31 Jul 1877. D. 8 Jan 1953.

Children of 3rd wife:

MARY, b. 10 Mar 1878. D. 7 Oct 1879. Child.
WALLACE, b. 31 Jan 1880. D. 16 Sep 1960.
LUCY HARRIET, b. 9 Jun 1883. D. 18 May 1885. Child.
MABLE MAE, b. 26 Jul 1885. D. 11 Aug 1887. Child.
FREDERICK BARNETT, b. 22 Apr 1889. D. 15 Sep 1889. Infant.

Submitted by: Roberta Barnum

JOHN REID BLANCHARD, SR.

Born: 18 Jan 1795, Boston, Suffolk, Massachusetts
Parents: John and Molly Holt Blanchard, Jr.
Died: 20 Feb 1882, Logan, Cache, Utah
Arrived in Valley: Between 1847 and 1851

Married 1st: Phoeby Haskell
Date: 1818
Born 1786, Massachusetts
Died: 1820, Vermont.

Married 2nd: Hannah Ann Clark
Date: 21 Jan 1821, Born: 6 Jul 1801, Oppenheim, New York
Died: Spring 1844, Nauvoo, Illinois

Married 3rd: Margaret Cook
Date: Fall 1844
Born: 22 Oct 1811, Pennsylvania
Died: abt 1851, Farmington, Davis, Utah

Married 4th: Eliza Bailey Haggie Potts–No children
Date: 19 Nov 1853, Salt Lake City, Utah
Born: 12 Jun 1798, Gosport, Hampshire, England
Parents: James and Martha Wiggans Bailey
Died: 19 Jul 1877, Logan, Utah

Married 5th: Sarah Potts
Date: 8 Mar 1854, Salt Lake City, Utah (Div 1859)
Born: 14 Jun 1837, Sunderland, Durham, England
Died: 26 May 1909, Logan, Cache, Utah

John Reid tried to live the gospel, including polygamy. But, like some others, apparently he had some problems. His last wife, Sarah, divorced him after only being married about five years. Some of the children went with her and took the name of the second husband, Hendricks.

Apparently John and at least some of his family lived in Logan as that is where John is buried. He apparently was loyal to the church and worked in the community.

Children of 1st wife:

CHILD, b. 1818, Died, 1819.

Children of 2nd wife:

LOIS ANN, b. 18 Jan 1822.
MARY ELIZABETH, b.7 Jun 1823.
GEORGE WASHINGTON, b. 10 Nov 1824.
EMILINE, b. 4 Jul 1826.
HOSIAH LLOYD, b. 6 Jun 1828.
JOHN REID, b. 15 Jul 1830.
SARAH ANN, b. 1 Jun 1832, Oneida, New York.
HENRY, b. Jul 1834, Oneida, New York.
CHARLES.
FRANCIS ANN, b. 15 Apr 1838, Oneida, New York.
CLARK, b. 10 Feb 1841.

Children of 3rd wife:

MORONI, b. 3 Aug 1845, Nauvoo, Hancock, Illinois.
WILLIAM COOK, b. 18 Jun 1848, Council Bluffs, Iowa.
WILLARD RICHARDS, b. 12 Nov 1850, Council Bluffs, Iowa.

Children of 5th wife:

EPHRAIM, b. 24 Dec 1854, Farmington, Davis, Utah.
SARAH, b. 15 Aug 1856, Farmington, Davis, Utah.
THOMAS, b. 9 Jun 1858, Pleasant Grove, Utah.

Some of these children took the name Hendricks.

Submitted: Darwin Salisbury

JAMES GODSON BLEAK

Born: 15 Nov 1829, Southwork, Surrey, England
Parents: Thomas Nelson and Mary Godson Bleak
Died: 29 Jan 1918, St. George, Washington, Utah
Arrived in Valley: 10 Nov 1856, Martin Handcart Co.

Married 1st: Elizabeth Moore
Date: Jun 1849, St. James Church, Bethel Green, London, England
Born: Mar 1828, Twig Folly, London, England
Parents: John and Eunice Holding Moore
Died: 19 Dec 1899, St. George, Utah

Married 2nd: Caroline Blanche Gosnold
Date: 24 Nov 1860, Salt Lake City, Utah
Born: 27 Mar 1830, Westminster, London, England
Parents: William and Mary Martell Gosnold
Died: 1 Dec 1881, St. George, Utah

Married 3rd: Jane Thompson
Date: 26 Oct 1861, Salt Lake City, Utah
Born: 1 Dec 1845, Birmingham, Warws, England
Parents: Joseph Louis and Penelope Thompson
Died: 20 May 1942, St. George, Washington, Utah

Married 4th: Matilda Irene Thompson

Date: 3 Feb 1882
Born: 27 Dec 1861, Rockville, Washington
Parents: William Henry and Matilda Young Thompson
Died: 26 Aug 1937, St. George, Utah

James Godson was the third of six children. He had no formal education after age 14. He kept studying and, being a natural scholar, he became a well educated and widely read man. Following school, he became an expert silversmith.

Shortly after his marriage to Elizabeth, they joined the Mormon Church. They were very active and he was called as the president of the White Chapel Branch in London, England. He was released in 1856 and immediately made ready to come to America.

They crossed the plains in the Martin Handcart Company. His feet became so frozen that the flesh dropped off his heels. He suffered with his feet the rest of his life. His wife and others pulled him in a handcart the rest of the way.

He made his home in North Ogden. He was with the Nauvoo Legion that went to intercept the troops coming to Utah. Shortly after, he moved his family to Lehi for a short time and then returned to Odgen. In 1861, he was called to move his family to help settle Southern Utah.

In 1872 he was called on a mission to England from which he returned in 1873. He was secretary of the United Order in St. George and also private secretary to President Brigham Young. In 1881 he was appointed a temple worker and in 1909 was ordained a patriarch. He later was a clerk in the Tithing Office, clerk in the Co-op store, postmaster, and a critic and coach of the early dramatic clubs of the community.

His self-education served him well during his entire life. His 33 children honored and loved him throughout his 89 years of life.

Children of 1st wife:

RICHARD MOORE, b. 22 Mar 1850, London, MIddlesex, England. Md. 1st, Valeda Rogers. Md. 2nd, 16 Aug 1879, Alice G.E. Wells.

THOMAS NELSON, b. 21 Sep 1851, London, England. Md. 27 May 1872, Elizabeth Olson.

JAMES GODSON, JR., b. 30 Sep 1853, London, England. Md. 11 Jan 1877, Kate Godson Daley.

MARY MOORE, b. 22 Jun 1855, London, England. Md. 10 Jul 1870, Joseph Fordham.

JOHN, b. 22 Jan 1858, No.Ogden, Weber, Utah. Md. 19 Apr 1878, Alice Louisa Barlow.

LILLIE, b. 10 Jun 1860, Salt Lake City, Utah. Md. 1st, 23 Mar 1877, Archibald H. McNeill. Md. 2nd, 18 Feb 1893, Andrew McNeil.

EPHRAIM, b. 30 Jun 1862, St. George, Utah. D. 17 Mar 1898, St. George, Utah.

GEORGE (twin), b. 25 May 1865, St. George, Utah. D. 9 Jun 1865. Child.

EUNICE (twin), b. 25 May 1865, St. George, Utah. Md. 3 Feb 1882, David Walker Sanders.

GRACE, b. 9 Jun 1867, St. George, Utah. D. 10 Jun 1869. Child.

Children of 2nd wife:

JOSEPH GOSNOLD, b. 16 Sep 1861, Salt Lake City, Utah. Md. 1st, 26 Nov 1883, Mary Augusta Brown. Md. 2nd 19 Feb 1912, Mauriba (Mae) Reynolds. D. 27 May 1921, Table Mt. Ranch, Pinal, Arizona.

BLANCH GOSNOLD, b. 31 Dec 1864, St. George, Utah. Md. Harry Siedintoff. D. 1 Nov 1923.

WILLIAM GOSNOLD, b. 15 Feb 1871, St. George, Utah. Md. 1st, Blanch Barton. D. 13 Feb 1931. Md. 2nd, Marry Adell.

Children of 3rd wife:

ALICE, b. 10 Feb 1863, St. George, Utah. D. 3 Oct 1864. Child.

SAMUEL THOMPSON, b. 20 Sep 1865, St. George, Utah. Md. 14 Jul 1887, Lucy Ellen Perkes Calkin. D. 5 Oct 1942, Salt Lake City, Utah.

ROSE THOMPSON, b. 23 Sep 1867, St. George, Utah. Md. 23 Sep 1886, George Jabez Ramsey. D. 21 Nov 1956.

MERCY THOMPSON, b. 8 Sep 1867, St. George, Utah. D. 8 Oct 1869. Child.

OLIVE, b. 29 Nov 1872, St. George, Utah. Md. 22 Mar 1894, Joseph Smith Snow. D. 6 Mar 1935, St. George, Utah.

NELLIE/NETTIE, b. 1 Sep 1874, St.George, Utah. D.1 Sep 1874. Infant.

SARAH THOMPSON, b. 15 Jul 1875, St. George, Utah. Md. 4 May 1893, Frank Bryant Dodge. D.14 Dec 1968.

FRANK NELSON, b. 28 Oct 1877, St. George, Utah. Md. 30 Jan 1902, Mannette Pendleton Church. D. 24 May 1912, Boulder, Utah.

JANE GODSON, b. 9 Feb 1880, St. George, Utah. Md. 25 Apr 1899, William Aaron Nelson. D. 14 Apr 1947.

WILFORD WOODRUFF, b. 3 Aug 1882, St. George, Utah. Md. 14 Sep 1903, Caddie Belle Fullerton. D. 15 Jul 1944, St. George, Ut.

MARONI, b. 1 Dec 1884, St. George, Utah. Md. 2 Aug 1904, Rose May Young. D. 25 Jun 1907, Salt Lake City, Utah.

LEWIS, b. 30 Jun 1887, St. George, Utah. Md. 28 Dec 1910, Maida Fawcett (Twin), (Div). D 12 Jun 1944.

Children of 4th wife:

PENELOPE THOMPSON, b.14 Dec 1883, St. George, Utah. Md. 18 Nov1908, Leo Alva Snow. D. 16 Sep 1910, St. George, Utah.

EMMA THOMPSON, b. 6 Feb 1885, St. George, Utah. Md. 10 Sep 1907, John Allen Humphries. D. 13 Jan 1930, Hurricane, Utah.

KATE, b. 14 Aug 1887, St. George, Utah. Md. 1 Jan 1907, Joseph William McAlister. D. 12 Mar 1957.

MARK, b. 18 May 1890, St. George, Utah. Md. 10 Sep 1913, Annie Cottam. D. 25 Jul 1932, Logandale, Clark, Nevada.

HARRY YOUNG, b. 22 Apr 1895, St. George, Utah. Md. 24 Nov 1915, Ivy Mae Lund. D. 28 Nov 1959, Boulder City, Nevada.

REX JAMES, b. 20 Jul 1898, St. George, Utah. D. 11 Feb 1899. Child.

KARL M., b. 29 Jul 1901, St. George, Utah. Md. 3 times. D. 3
Mar 1961.

Submitted by: Burnyce Powell

THOMAS NELSON BLEAK

Born: 21 Sep 1851, London, Middlesex, England
Parents: James Godson and Elizabeth Moore Bleak
Died: 28 Nov 1924, Salt Lake City, Utah
Arrived in Valley: 30 Nov 1856, Martin Handcart Co.

Married: Elizabeth Olsen
Date: 27 Nov 1872, Salt Lake City, Utah
Born: 9 Dec 1854, Salt Lake City, Utah
Parents: Niels and Anna Maarie Christiansen Olson
Died: 9 Oct 1928, Salt Lake City, Utah

Thomas Nelson crossed the plains with his parents at the tender age of five. The terrible hardships he and the others endured
on this trek are a matter of record and are well known.

While crossing the Green River, his grandfather was pulled
under and was pronounced dead when they pulled him out. Thomas' father asked for some anointed oil, which he used in blessing
his father. The man was returned to life and lived many more years.

Thomas was a good husband and father. He was a painter by
trade. He helped paint the St. George Temple, the Union Pacific
Railroad Depot and many other public buildings as well as homes.
He remained a faithful member of the church and taught his children well. He was a courageous, dedicated pioneer and early set-

tler who left a great heritage for his family.

Children:

JAMES GODSON, b. 9 May 1873, St. George, Utah. Unmarried.
D. 6 Oct 1902.
ANNIE ELIZABETH, b. 7 Nov 1875, St. George, Utah. Md. 23
Jun 1897, John Fredrick Monsen. D. 23 Nov 1921.
ARTEMESIA, b. 9 Aug 1879, St. George, Utah. Md. 21 Jun 1911,
Edward Powell.
GRACE, b. 10 Jan 1882, St. George, Utah. Md. 2 Oct 1912,
Joseph Smith Thompson. D. 17 Mar 1965.
THOMAS NELSON JR., b. 9 Jul 1884, St. George, Utah. Md.
26 Jun 1912, Annie Agnes Holmes. D. 3 Feb 1957.
GEORGE OLSON, b. 10 Feb 1887, Manti, Utah. Unmarried. D.
18 Apr 1912.
EDWARD ERASTUS, b. 8 Jul 1889, Manti, Utah. Unmarried. D
5 Feb 1935.
RALPH MOORE, b. 29 Dec 1891, Manti, Utah. Md. 22 Mar
1916, Erma Smith. D. 5 Feb 1935.
LILA BEATRICE, b. 27 Apr 1899, Salt Lake City, Utah. Md. 2
Sep 1921, Albert Pugsley.

Submitted by: Burnyce Powell

GOTTLIEB BLICKENSTORFER

Born: 31 Jul 1846, Zurich, Switzerland
Parents: Solomon and Anna Barbara Neir Blickenstorfer
Died: 12 Sep 1881, Santa Clara, Washington, Utah

Arrived in Valley: Left Florence, Nebraska 13 Jun 1857

Married 1st: Eliza Knecht
Date: abt 1868, Santa Clara, Utah
Died: 14 Feb 1873, Santa Clara, Utah

Married 2nd: Rosena Stucki
Date: 4 Aug 1873, Salt Lake City, Utah
Died: 2 Jun 1912, Santa Clara, Utah

Married 3rd: Anna Marie (Mary) Knecht–No children
Date: 4 Aug 1873, Salt Lake City, Utah
Died: 1922, Santa Clara, Utah

Gottlieb came to Utah with his parents and some Swiss saints. They settled in Santa Clara, Washington County, Utah, at the request of Brigham Young. His father became ill enroute and was the first death in Santa Clara. Gottlieb took care of and provided for his mother until her second marriage.

This was a very musical family who, after they settled in Santa Clara, formed the Staheli Brass Band. Gottlieb played the lead horn. He was able to play all instruments and earned a living, while crossing the plains, by playing for the saints.

Both his first wife and their first baby died shortly after the birth. He then turned his eyes to a young girl of 16, who married him. He built two homes, one in Santa Clara and the other on the Virgin River. He married his first wife's sister and both his wives got along well.

He owned two farms. In Santa Clara he raised grain, alfalfa, had an orchard of peach, plum, apple and pear trees and grapes. On the Virgin farm he raised cane and cotton.

Gottlieb was a builder, expert carpenter, excellent farmer and a good organizer. He was a kind man who treated his wives fairly. There was a wonderful spirit of love and kindness in his homes.

He was a young man of 35 when he died.

Children of 1st wife:

GOTTLIEB JR., b. abt 1870. Lived 3 weeks, Santa Clara, Utah. Child.

Children of 2nd wife:

ROSENA ELIZA, b. 14 Oct 1875, Santa Clara, Utah.
HENRY, b. 8 Sep 1877, Santa Clara, Utah. D. 5 Oct 1900.
BARBARA SELINA, b. 15 Oct 1879, Santa Clara, Utah. D. 18 Dec 1880. Child.

Submitted by: Velda Gubler

SOLOMON BLICKENSTORFER

Born: 26 Aug 1821, Affoltern, Zurich, Switzerland
Parents: Heinrich and Anna Barbara Schneebeli Blickenstorfer
Died: 9 Apr 1861, Santa Clara, Washington, Utah
Arrived in Valley: 1861

Married: Anna Barbara Meier
Date: 18 May 1846, Affoltern, Zurich, Switzerland
Died: 1880, Santa Clara, Utah

Solomon joined the church in Switzerland and immigrated to the valley in 1861 with other Swiss saints. They were assigned to settle in Santa Clara, Washington, Utah. He was the first man to die in Santa Clara.

Children:

GOTTLIEB, b. 31 Jul 1846, Switzerland. D. 12 Dec 1881, Santa Clara, Utah.

Submitted by: Velda Gubler

JOHN BOOTH

Born: 1 Apr 1837, Middleton, Lancashire, England
Parents: James and Sarah Ann Tetlow Booth
Died: 4 May 1914, West Jordan, Utah
Arrived in Valley: before 1865

Married: Ann Lythgoe
Date: Apr 1856, Pendlebury, Eccles, Lancashire, England
Born: 13 Nov 1836, Leith, Lancashire, England
Died: 5 Sep 1906, Coalville, Utah

John and his wife immigrated to the Valley in about 1865, after having been converted by the missionaries. They settled in Coalville, Utah, where all but the first two children were born and raised. He was a good husband and father and faithful to the church he had chosen to cast his lot with.

Children:

LUCY, b. 23 Nov 1857, Leith, Lancashire, England. D. 14 May 1932 in Henefer, Summit, Utah
ELLEN, b.22 Oct 1859, Pendlebury, Lancashire, England. D. 12 Sep 1918, West Jordan, Utah.

MARY ANN, b. 12 Jun 1865, Coalville, Summit, Utah. D. 20 Mar 1867, Coalville, Utah. Child.

ESTHER, b. 22 Aug 1866, Coalville, Utah. D. 20 Mar 1867, Coalville, Utah. Child.

MARY ELIZABETH EMMA, b. 11 Jan 1868, Coalville, Utah. D. 11 Jun 1875. Child.

RACHEL, b. 1 Dec 1869, Coalville, Utah. D. 10 May 1948.

MARTHA, b. 27 Nov 1871, Coalville, Utah. D. 24 Jun 1875. Child.

ANNIE, b. 15 Dec 1873, Coalville, Utah. D. 23 May 1939.

JOHN THOMAS, b. 22 Aug 1875, Coalville, Utah. D. 15 May 1956, Salt Lake City, Utah.

OLIVE LOVENIA, b. 6 Jan 1877, Coalville, Utah. D. 13 Jan 1924, Standardville, Carbon, Utah.

JAMES WILLARD, b. 23 Sep 1878, Coalville, Utah. D. 20 Mar 1893.

JOSEPH TETLOW, b. 18 May 1880, Coalville, Utah. D. 15 Sep 1946.

Submitted by: Janell Nichols

JOHN EDGE BOOTH

Born: 29 Jun 1847, Bedford Leigh, Lancashire, England
Parents: Richard Thornton and Elsie Edge Booth
Died: 28 Mar 1920, Salt Lake City, Utah
Arrived in Valley: 12 Sep 1857, Jesse Bigler Martin Co.

Married 1st: Maria Josephine Harvey
Date: 1 Oct 1873, Salt Lake City, Utah

Born: 31 Jan 1850, Pottawattamie Co, Iowa
Died: 1 Oct 1884, Provo, Utah

Married 2nd: Hannah Billings–No children
Date: 10 Apr 1876, Salt Lake City, Utah
Born: 12 Mar 1822, Manti, Utah
Died: 18 May 1881, Provo, Utah

Married 3rd: Delia Ina Winters
Date: 22 Jun 1887, Logan, Utah
Born: 16 Mar 1854, Pleasant Grove, Utah
Died: 1 Jun 1940, Provo, Utah

John Edge and his parents immigrated to the Valley after joining the Church in England. They were sent to Alpine, Utah, to help settle the area. They lived in a dugout the first year.

In order to get an education, John walked over the hills from Alpine to Draper to attend the academy, where Dr. John R. Park was the instructor. He carried his shoes until he reached the door so they wouldn't wear out so fast. He learned the law and passed the Utah Bar and went on to hold many municipal offices in the judiciary system in Provo and the state and county, and was a much respected judge. He helped draft the Utah State constitution.

His humor was well known and he was generous with his talents. He and his wife opened their home to students who attended the Brigham Young Academy. He taught at the Academy without remuneration. He filled an honorable mission and was president of the Northern States Mission. While there, his wife Maria died leaving an infant son and three young daughters in his care.

He was a bishop for 28 years and remained faithful to the church throughout his entire life.

Children of 1st wife:

JOHN EDGE, b. 20 Jul 1874, Provo, Utah. D. same day. Child.
JOSEPHINE DIANTHA, b. 16 Mar 1876, Provo, Utah. Md. Mr.
    Woodruff. D. 1 Oct, 19— Provo, Utah.

VIENNA HORTENSE, b. 14 Apr 1878, Provo, Utah. Md. Mr. Kimball. D. 22 Nov 1951, Los Angeles, California.

HANNAH ROWENA, b. 13 Apr 1882, Provo, Utah. Md. Mr.Ray, Mr. Cowan, and Mr. Marks. D. 3 Mar 1954, Hollywood, California.

RICHARD HARVEY, b. 6 May 1884, Provo, Utah. D. 10 Jun 1941, Provo, Utah.

Children of 3rd wife:

JAMES MILTON, b. 21 May 1888, Pleasant Grove, Utah. D. 6 Jan 1939, Los Angeles, California.

DELILAH (LILA) MARIA, b. 7 Jan 1890, Pleasant Grove, Utah. Md. Mr Adams. D. 11 Apr 1973, Provo, Utah.

ELSIE VERNESSA, b. 12 Apr 1894, Provo, Utah. Md. Mr. Brockbank. D. 4 Jun 1978, Provo, Utah.

EDWIN (TED) WINTERS, b. 11 Jun 1896, Provo, Utah. D. 24 Nov 1981, Salt Lake City, Utah.

(The men are probably married but the spouse is not named.)

Submitted by: Elsie Dee A. Florence

RICHARD THORNTON BOOTH

Born: 13 Aug 1821, Turton, near Bolton, Lancashire, England
Parents: James and Jane Pilkington Booth
Died: 27 May 1888, Alpine, Utah (Mountainville)
Arrived in Valley: 12 Sep 1857, James Bigler Martin Co.

Married: Elsie Edge

Date: 13 Aug 1846, Bedford Leigh, Lancashire, England
Born: 21 Dec 1825, Bedford Leigh, Lancashire, England
Died: 10 Jul 1893, Alpine, Utah (Mountainville)

Richard Thornton served as a doctor for Northern Utah County for both physical and dental needs for many years without charging for his services.

He taught school for 18 years and was a member of the City Council. He held the position of Justice of the Peace and was active as the City Recorder for twenty years.

He remained active in the church, holding many positions of responsibility with honor and was much loved and respected by everyone.

Children:

JOHN EDGE, b. 29 Jun 1847, Bedford Leigh, Lancashire, England. D. 28 Mar 1920, Salt Lake City, Utah.
JAMES DAVIS, b. 27 Mar 1850, Bedford Leigh, Lancashire, England.D. 8 Apr 1877.
MARTHA HANNAH, b. 20 Aug 1852, Bedford Leigh, Lancashire, England. D. 3 Mar 1909.
SARAH JANE, b.25 Feb 1855, Bedford, Leigh, Lancashire, England. D. 17 Nov 1950.
ROBERT EBENEZER, b. 31 Aug 1857, Big Sandy, Sublett, Wyoming. D. 27 Jul 1939.
MARGARET ELSIE, b. 1 Sep 1859, Alpine, Utah. D. 29 Jun 1930.
RICHARD THORNTON, b. 6 Jan 1862, Alpine, Utah. D. 23 Nov 1887.
ALFRED LEWIS, b. 17 Jun 1864, Alpine, Utah. D. 3 Jun 1947.
JOSEPH WILFORD, b. 14 Aug 1866, Alpine, Utah. D. 16 Apr 1944.
MERRY MAY, b. 29 Sep 1868, Alpine, Utah. D. 6 Apr 1944.

Submitted by: Elsie Dee A. Florence

JOHN MORRIS BOWEN

Born: 26 Dec 1844, Kidwelly, Carmathenshire, South Wales
Parents: David and Catherine Morris Bowen
Died: 11 Nov 1918, Herriman, Salt Lake, Utah
Arrived in Valley: 15 Oct 1865,

Married 1st: Mariah Adaline Stocking
Date: 22 Feb 1868, Salt Lake City, Utah
Born: abt 1850
Parents: John J. and Harriet Ensign Stocking
Died: 21 Jun 1870, Herriman, Utah, childbirth

Married 2nd: Ann Densley
Date: 26 Feb 1872, Salt Lake City, Utah
Parents: Daniel and Sarah Beech Densley

Married 3rd: Mary Densley
Date: 13 Sep 1883, Salt Lake City, Utah
Parents: Daniel and Sarah Beech Densley

John Morris was converted and baptized into the Church on 18 June 1863. His two brothers, David and Edward, also joined. David sailed to America and John and Edward followed soon after. David had settled in Herriman, Utah, and that was where John and Edward went to build their homes and where John met the young woman whom he married. She died with the birth of their first child. John waited four years before he married again. All their children were born in the rock house John built in Herriman.

John was a stone mason and stone cutter, and he helped with

the construction of the Salt Lake Temple and other church projects. His fertile farm supplied the food for his family.

In 1880 he was called on a mission to Wales. Upon his return home in 1882, he married Ann's sister.

He taught Sunday School, led the choir and held classes in singing and directing. He also was called to other assignments in the church. He was active in the community, acting at various times as Constable and Watermaster and other positions.

He died shortly after receiving word that World War I was over and his two sons would be returning home.

Child of 1st wife:

JOHN DAVID, b.5 Jun 1870. D. 22 Jul 1870. Child.

Children of 2nd wife:

SARAH ANN, b. 18 Feb 1873, Herriman, Utah. D. 28 Dec 1954.
MARIA, b. 10 Nov 1874, Herriman, Utah. D. 14 Sep 1877. Child.
CATHERINE, b. 17 Nov 1876, Herriman, Utah. D 11 Sep 1877. Child.
ABRAM, b. 25 Oct 1878, Herriman, Utah. D. 3 Feb 1947.
MARY ELIZABETH, b. 7 Nov 1880, Herriman, Utah. D. 29 Nov 1957.
JOSEPH WILLIAM, b. 25 Nov 1883, Herriman, Utah. D. 6 Jul 1946.
JOHN HENRY, b. 6 Mar 1886, Herriman, Utah. D. 3 Mar 1920.
GEORGE EDWARD, b. 22 Mar 1888, Herriman, Utah. D 6 Jun 1943.
MARGARET ESTHER, b. 2 Jul 1891, Herriman, Utah.
BENJAMIN BENSEN (twin), b. 21 Oct 1893, Herriman, Utah. D.6 Jun 1954.
INFANT (stillborn twin), b. 21 Oct 1893, Herriman, Utah. Child.
LAURA, b. 27 Dec 1894, Herriman, Utah. D. 6 Mar 1984.
Infant (stillborn), b. 25 May 1898.

Children of 3rd wife:

MARY ANN, b. 26 Oct 1884, Herriman, Utah. D. 2 Jan 1959.

DANIEL, b. 25 May 1887, Herriman, Utah. D. 28 Oct 1958.

HARRIET, b. 12 Sep 1889, Herriman, Utah. D. 18 Aug 1891. Child.

DAVID, b. 7 Feb 1892, Herriman, Utah. D. 28 Nov 1967.

DORA GRACE, b. 24 Feb 1894, Herriman, Utah. D. 21 Nov 1894. Child.

THOMAS ELMER, b. 2 Apr 1896, Herriman, Utah. D.16 May 1961.

LORENZO, b. 11 Jan 1899, Herriman, Utah. D. 15 Dec 1951.

MYRTLE, b. 4 Aug 1901, Herriman, Utah. D. 6 May 1978.

SAMUEL MORRIS, b. 21 Dec 1904, Herriman, Utah. D. 4 Feb 1942.

MOSES (twin), b. 12 Mar 1907, Herriman, Utah. D. 30 Aug 1907. Child.

AARON (twin), b. 12 Mar 1907, Herriman, Utah. D.25 Jun 1985.

Submitted by: Elva Merkley

ISAIAH BOWERS

Born: 21 Apr 1846, Dudley, Stafford, England
Parents: James and Maria Lay Bowers
Died: 18 Nov 1926, Orderville, Kane, Utah
Arrived in Valley: 26 Sep 1856, Edmund Ellsworth Handcart Co.

Married 1st: Harriet Amanda Hoyt
Date: 6 Jun 1868, Salt Lake City, Utah
Born: 16 Oct 1850, Salt Lake City, Utah

Died: 26 Apr 1920, Orderville, Kane, Utah

Married 2nd: Philinda Amanda Sperry
Date: Oct 1884, St. George, Utah
Born: 16 Nov 1849, Salt Lake City, Utah
Parents: Charles and Emily Miller Sperry

    Isaiah joined the Church in England and when he was 20, he joined with other saints in the migration to the Valley in 1856. He came with the first group of saints who pulled handcarts.
    He was involved not only with the church but also with civic and community projects. When he was called to Orderville, he gladly took his family there to help with the settlement. His talents came to good use in helping settle and obey the commandment to live the United Order.

Children of 1st wife:

ISRAEL HOYT, b. 10 Mar 1869.
CLARISSA AMANDA, b. 8 Oct 1871.
ISAIAH LAY HOYT, b. 25 Mar 1874.
MARIA HOYT, b. 5 Oct 1876.
ELLA HOYT, b. 8 Sep 1879.
JONATHAN HOYT, b. 26 Oct 1882.
LILLIAN HOYT, b. 5 Jun 1886.
HARRIET HOYT, b.20 May 1889.

Children of 2nd wife:

WILLIAM S., b 13 Aug 1866.
SARAH E., b. 13 Jun 1890.
JOY S., b. 10 Oct 1893.

Submitted by: LaRae McManama

JACOB BOWERS

Born: 10 Mar 1844, Dudley, Stafford, England
Parents: James and Mary Ann Bowers
Died: A few months after his 90th birthday, Nephi, Utah
Arrived in Valley: 26 Sep 1856, Edmund Ellsworth Handcart Co.

Married: Caroline Goble
Date: Salt Lake City, Utah

Jacob's parents joined the Church in England. Then in 1856, when Brigham Young told them to come with handcarts, his father James and his wife and six children crossed the ocean and joined with the first handcart company to cross the plains. Father James had consumption and died after walking the first 13 miles. He was buried with others on the side of a hill. Jacob's mother and her six children pushed on to the Valley. Jacob was just 10 years old at the time. They didn't stop in Salt Lake but pushed on to Nephi where they made their home.

Jacob worked at all kinds of jobs to help support his mother. One time when he was herding cows, Indians kidnapped him, but after two weeks, he just walked away and came home. He was in the Black Hawk Indian War as the flag carrier.

When he got married, he dug mud and made a two room adobe house. He made their furniture and waxed burlap for the windows.

On his birthday each year he would give a party and a dance. He was a farmer and raised horses. He was friends with the Indians and everyone around called him friend. He had a sense of humor that was contageous.

Children:

MARY MARIA, D. Child.
JAMES, Md. Keterah Price.
JACOB, unmarried.
ETHER, Md. Marietta Pay.
CHARLES, D. Child.
ISABELLA, D. Child.
JOHN HENRY, unmarried.
ADA MAY, Md. Alvin W. Jenkins.
BERTHA LEAH, Md. Leo Bowles.

Submitted by: Jacob Brower

JAMES BOWERS

Born: 27 Jan 1811, Wrexham, Denbigh, Wales
Parents: Joseph Sanson and Isabella Halgren Bowers
Died: 21 Jun 1856, Quarter mile east of Fort DesMoines, Iowa
Arrived in Valley: Family came through after James died enroute
    Came with Edmund Ellsworth Handcart Company, 1856

Married: Mariah Lay
Date: 1 Apr 1831, Tipton Church, Lantz of Stafford, England
Born: 5 Nov 1806, Worcestshire, Dudley, Stafford., England
Died: 8 Nov 1889, Nephi, Juab, Utah

James and his wife and six children joined the saints who crossed the ocean and then the plains with the first handcart company under Edmund Ellsworth. He developed consumption and was only able to make the first few miles (13). He died and was buried on a hill.

James joined the Church and served a mission to England. He was also Branch President. He married Mariah who had been previously married and had one son. Together they had 10 children of their own. Only six of their children came west with them.

Children:

DAVID JOBE, b. 1 Jun 1829 (son by 1st husband).
JOBE, b. 6 Sep 1832.
ISABELL, b. 28 Jul 1834.
JOSEPH, b. 16 May 1836.
SARAH (twin), b. 13 Jul 1837.
HEZEKIAH (twin), b. 13 Jul 1837.
ABRAHAM JAMES, b. 26 Dec 1839.
ISAAC, b. 6 Sep 1841.
JACOB, b. 10 Mar 1844, Dudley, Stafford, England. Md. Caroline
    Goble. D.1934, Nephi, Utah.
ISAIAH, b. 21 Apr 1846.
SHADRACH, b. 25 Jun 1848.

Submitted by: LaRae McManama

WILLIAM BOWN

Born: 7 Oct 1825, Wisbech, Cambridge, England
Parents: William and Jane Batley Bown
Died: 10 Apr 1901, Bur. Fayette, Utah

Arrived in Valley: 11 Oct 1853, Wheelock Wagon Co.

Married: Jane Ann Metcalf
Date: 30 Jan 1853, on board ship by ship's captain
Died: 11 Dec 1894, Fayette, Utah, pneumonia

William's father was a mariner and died at sea before his birth. When he was 13, he became an apprentice to a boat builder. At the end of that time, he went to sea for four years on whaling ships in northern waters.

A boy friend introduced him to the missionaries and he was converted and baptized in 1850. In January 1853 he immigrated to the States. He married, aboard ship, a girl he had met on board.

William and Jane settled in Springville, Utah, where they bought a house and lot for $60.00. In 1862 they were called to go to St. George to help build a community there. They stayed three years, raising cotton and molasses cane. William's health deteriorated in the hot, dry climate.

They went to visit Jane's parents further north and he immediately got better. Her father and brother saw Brigham Young while in Salt Lake and he released William from his mission.

William and Jane and their family settled in Fayette, Utah, where they were active in the church. For 23 years he was Ward Clerk, making the ink he used.

He became a professional gardener. He also made broom cane, which they made into brooms. He was a good carpenter and he and his wife both made and lined caskets. William died as a result of falling into the fireplace.

Children:

WILLIAM JR., b. 9 Nov 1856, Springville, Utah. Md. 1878, Elizabeth Almira Bartholemew. D. 5 Jun 1935.
EDWARD JOHN, b. 20 Dec 1858, Springville, Utah. D. 16 Sep 1859. Child.
LEVI, b. 30 Jun 1860, Springville, Utah. Md. 1st, 1878, Sarah Dack. Md. 2nd, 1884, Annie Mellor. D. 27 Feb 1938.
MARY JANE, b. 11 Jan 1863, St. George, Utah. D. 5 Sep 1874.

HYRUM, b. 2 Feb 1865, St. George, Utah. Md. 20 Jul 1892, Isabella Braithwaite. D. 27 Nov 1936.

JAMES, b. 11 Jul 1867, Gunnison, Utah. Md. 1898, Florence Emma Bartholcmcw. D. 15 Feb 1946.

LAFAYETTE, b. 25 Sep 1869, Fayette, Utah. Md. 1891, Clarissa Jane Dack. D. 29 Nov 1946.

FRANCIS NELSON, b. 28 Feb 1872, Fayette, Utah. Not married. D. 12 Feb 1893.

CHARLES, b. 19 Nov 1873 Fayette, Utah. Not married. D. 19 Jan 1896.

ISABELL, b. 5 Aug 1877, Fayette, Utah. D. 14 Apr 1879. Child.

Submitted by: Rosalie Brown

WILLIAM BOWTHORPE

Born: 30 Sep 1806, Norwich, Norfolk, England
Parents: Thomas and Priscilla Pye Bowthorpe
Died: 15 Apr 1878, Holladay, Salt Lake City, Utah
Arrived in Valley: 16 Oct 1853, Cyrus Wheelock Handcart Co.

Married: Mary Ann Tuttle
Date: 22 Dec 1835, Norwich, Norfolk, England
Born: 14 Jan 1810, Norwich, Norfolk, England
Died: 15 Jun 1884, Holladay, Salt Lake City, Utah

William was a silk weaver by trade. William and his wife joined the Church in England, crossed the ocean, and then crossed the plains by handcart. After arriving in the Valley, they spent that winter in Salt Lake. The following spring they were sent to

Holladay by Brigham Young to settle 11 acres near Spring Creek.

He built a two room adobe house. In the cellar he built a loom on which he wove the yarn into cloth and sold for $1.00 per yard. He taught his daughters how to weave. They were all excellent seamstresss and embroiderers.

He was active in the church all his life.

Children:

VIRTUE ANN, b. 28 Feb 1836, Norwich, Norfolk, England. Md. 1st, 1 Jan 1854, Charles Colebrook, (Div). Md. 2nd, 2 Aug 1857, Preston Lewis. D. 28 Jan 1926, Holladay, Salt Lake, Utah.

GEORGE TUTTLE, b. 5 Sep 1838, Norwich, Norfolk, England. D. 14 Nov 1839. Child.

HANNAH CHARLOTTE, b. 5 Nov 1840, Norwich, Norfolk, England. Md. 13 Feb 1858, George Finley Brooks. D. 29 Oct 1923.

MARIA MARY ANN, b. 6 May 1843, Norwich, Norfolk, England. Md. 1st, 9 May 1861, George Bakcr. Md. 2nd, 7 Oct 1870, Benjamin Barr Neff. D. 13 Mar 1925, Holladay, Utah.

WILLIAM GEORGE, b. 15 May 1846, Norwich, Norfolk, England. D. 19 Jul 1850. Child.

PHOEBE SUSANNAH, b. 23 Oct 1858, Holladay, Salt Lake, Utah. Md. William George Taylor. D. 26 Jun 1924.

WILLIAM JOSEPH, b. 8 Jun 1851, Holladay, Salt Lake, Utah. Md. 13 Feb 1877, Elizabeth C. Reynolds. D. 25 Mar 1920.

NEPHI BRIGHAM, b. 24 Jul 1855, Holladay, Salt Lake, Utah. Md. 22 April 1880, Phylinda Reynolds. D. 27 May 1908.

Submitted by: L. Blake Bowthorpe

LEVI BRACKEN

Born: 14 Mar 1791/2, York, York or Westmoreland, Penn.
Parents: William Bracken and Mary Garrison
Died: July or August 1852, Long Fork or Loup Fork of the Platt
    River, Nebraska
Arrived in Valley: Oct 1868

Married: Elizabeth Clark
Date: about 1810, Hamilton Co, Ohio
Died: 14 Jun 1876, Spring Valley, Lincoln, Nebraska

Levi may have been baptized 10 March 1832 when his wife was. They were endowed 22 January 1846. They settled in Council Bluffs, Iowa. Levi became active in both civil and religious affairs. Levi died on his way to Utah at Long Fork or Loup Fork of the Platt River, Nebraska.

Children:

MARY ANN, b. 26 Oct 1811, Hamilton County, Ohio.
HANNAH MARIE, b. 8 Feb 1814, Hamilton County, Ohio.
JAMES BENNETT, b. 14 Jan 1816, Hamilton County, Ohio.
WILLIAM, b. 1818, Hamilton County, Ohio.
MARTHA RUTH, b. 14 Jan 1820, Colerain, Belmont, Ohio.
SON, 1822, Noble, Rush, Indiana.
LUCRETIA CHARLOTTE, b. 6 Dec 1823, Noble, Rush, Indiana.
MATILDA, b. 19 Apr 1826, Noble, Rush, Indiana.
ELIZABETH ANN, b. 30 Oct 1828, Noble, Rush, Indiana.

Submitted by: Arline Martindale Scott Brinton

EDWARD BRADSHAW

Born: 15 Aug 1827, St. Alkmund, Derby, England
Parents: John and Ann White Bradshaw
Died: 18 Aug 1901, Minersville, Beaver, Utah
Arrived in Valley: Oct 1868

Married: Sarah Bagshaw
Date: 6 Sep 1848, Derby, Derbyshire, England
Born: 19 Mar 1831, Derby, Derbyshire, England
Parents: Thomas and Sarah Redshaw Bagshaw
Died: 12 Jul 1911, Minersville, Utah

Edward's father was a brick and stone mason and Edward learned the trade from him. He became a "master" as a mason.

Edward and Sarah were baptized in 1848. Some of the missionaries stayed at their home and Sarah washed and ironed for them.

In 1868 Edward and his family sailed for America with some of the missionaries on the ship "Constitution." In need of money, Edward and his older daughters found work but soon left to go west. They stayed for a short time in Salt Lake but soon decided to move to Minersville, Utah, where the rest of their children were born.

In about 1883 Edward left home and family to go to Arizona and New Mexico for about 12 years. He left his wife Sarah to provide food and clothing for their family. Eventually he returned but he and Sarah never lived together again. He died at the home of his son George.

Children:

SARAH ANN, b. 23 Aug 1850, Derby, Derbyshire, England.
Md. 21 Mar 1870, Joseph Quimey. D. 10 Mar 1942.

CATHERINE, b. 9 Jun 1852, Derby, Derbyshire, England. Md.
William Smith. D. Feb 1929.

SAMUEL, b. 20 Aug 1854, Derby, England. Md. 8 Feb 1877,
Alice Wood. D. 11 Jul 1942/3.

MARTHA, b. 11 Nov 1856, Birmingham, Warws, England. Md.
21 Nov 1878, Ephriam Oscar Western. D. 18 May 1893.

RACHEL, b. 9 Nov 1859, Birmingham, Warws, England. Md. 9
Nov 1875, Erastus Edwin Myers. D. 25 Aug 1910.

EDWARD, b. 15 Aug 1861, Birmingham, Warws, England. D.
15 Aug 1861. Child.

ELIZA (Elizabeth), b. 10 Jan 1864, Birmingham, Warws, England.
Md. 11 Oct 1880, George Edward Roberts. D. 21 Apr 1953.

JOHN, b. 1866, New Bedford, Bedfordshire, England. D. 20 Oct
1868. Child.

GEORGE, b. 14 Oct 1868, Salt Lake City, Utah. Md. 10 Feb
1892, Rebecca Naylor Eyer. D. 15 Nov 1947.

HARRIET, b. 4 Feb 1872, Minersville, Beaver, Utah. Md. 4 Dec
1890, Moroni Myers. D. 3 Jul 1957.

Submitted by: Darla Rock

JOHN BRADSHAW, SR.

Born: 14 Dec 1795, Cossall, Nottinghamshire, England
Parents: John and Olinda (Melinda) Hazeldine Bradshaw

Died: 27 Aug 1865, Virgin, Utah
Arrived in Valley: 9 Sep 1853, Daniel A. Miller

Married: Ann White
Date: 27 Aug 1817, Heanor, Derbyshire, England
Born: 21 May 1799, Shipley, Derbyshire, England
Parents: George and Mary White
Died: 25 Aug 1875, Virgin, Utah

John's father died when he was only a few months old. His
mother married William Chambers, 27 April 1801. John grew up
in Cossall and became a common laborer.

John and Ann were among the first to be baptized in
Derbyshire. All of his children and their spouses were baptized
within the next year.

John and Ann and two of their unmarried children, Mary and
Samuel, left England in 1851. They spent some time in St. Joseph, Missouri, before going west. When they arrived in the Valley in 1853, there were only two Bradshaws, John and Ann. They
went to Cedar City for awhile and then in 1857/8 they settled in
Virgin City, Utah, where their son, Samuel had settled. He lived
there until his death.

Children:

MARY, b. May 1818, Ilkeston, Derbyshire, England. Md. 28 Dec
1867, William C. Cure.
JOHN WHITE, b. 2 Feb 1819, Ilkeston, Derbyshire, England.
Md. 21 Mar 1857, Harriet Burgess.
SAMUEL, b. 6 Nov 1822, Ilkeston, Derbyshire, England. Sld 21
Mar 1857, Mary Ann Elsey. D. 18 Aug 1897.
RICHARD, b. 28 Oct 1824, St. Alkmund, Derby, England. Md.
12 Aug1847, Emma Dorrington.
EDWARD, b. 15 Aug 1827, St. Alkmund, Derby,England. Sld 6
Aug 1919, Sarah Bagshaw.
CATHERINE, b. 3 Aug 1829, St. Werburg, Derby, England.

Submitted by: Darla Rock

SAMUEL BRADSHAW

Born: 6 Nov 1822, Ilkeston, Derbyshire, England
Parents: John and Ann White Bradshaw
Died: 18 Aug 1897, St. George, Utah
Arrived in Valley: 1851

Married 1st: Mary Ann Elsey
Date: 15 Sep 1852, Salt Lake City, Utah
Born: England
Died: 10 Dec 1871, Virgin, Utah
Children: Ten born, four lived to adulthood

Married 2nd: Mrs. Ballard (widow)
Died: Died not long after their marriage
Children: Had five by first husband

Married 3rd: Ann Bruppacher
Date: 1877, St. George, Utah
Born: Zurich, Switzerland
Children: Had four children, two lived

Samuel came to America with his parents but separated from them after their arrival in America. He was 29 years old. He is later found in Utah in 1851. He did some freighting between Salt Lake and Cedar City where he met his wife. They settled in the fort at Cedar City. They had ten children, of which only four grew to adulthood and only two of them married and raised families.

Samuel was called on to help build a road up LaVerkin Hill. It later became known as "Johnson's Twist." The town of Virgin was settled and Samuel moved his family there, where his wife died.

He married a widow with five children but she died shortly after and her children found homes with friends.

He married a third time to a convert from Switzerland. They were sealed in the St. George Temple. They had four children but only two lived and raised a family.

Throughout the 40 years of living in that area, Samuel had helped shoulder the burder of trying to control the raging waters of the Virgin River in flood season as well as helping build up the area. He remained faithful to the church and was well respected in the community.

Submitted by: Pheobe Sampson

ROBERT BRAITHWAITE

Born: 14 Mar 1830, Kendal, Westmoreland, England
Parents: Rowland and Hannah Askew Braithwaite
Died: 26 Oct 1906, Spanish Fork, Utah
Arrived in Valley: 1854, Daniel McCarthy Co.

Married: Harriet Amelia Bemus
Date: 5 Feb 1858, Manti, Utah
Born: 16 Sep 1844, Lewistown, Illinois
Parents: Lyness and Martha Amelia (Juell) Bemis
Died: 10 Feb 1929, Spanish Fork, Utah

Robert was baptized a member of the Church in 1845. His mother was the first to accept the gospel and was baptized in 1843. His father joined two years later. Robert was determined to save money to take his parents and siblings to Utah, but his father died in England. Robert came alone to the Valley and earned money to send for his family, all but John who came later.

Robert worked in Salt Lake for about a year as a shoemaker. Then he moved to Manti where he settled. He was a shoemaker, a trade learned from his father in England, and a farmer, and he ran a Carding machine shop. He fought in the Black Hawk Indian War. He was well known for the beautiful flowers and good vegetables he raised.

Robert had a good voice and sang in duets and the church choir He also led the choir on many occasions. Robert and Harriet moved to Spanish Fork in 1901 where Robert died a few years later.

Children:

MARTHA HANNAH, b. 17 Sep 1860, Manti, Utah. Md. 1881, James Gordon Cassen Cahoon. D. 24 Feb 1944.

MARY ELIZABETH, b. 10 Sep 1862, Manti, Utah. Md. 1885, James Peterson. D. 3 Feb 1926.

EMILY MATILDA, b. 22 Mar 1865, Manti, Utah. Md. 1882, John Walker. D. 22 Jun 1935.

ROBERT, b. 11 Mar 1867, Manti, Utah. Md. 1889, Ericka Thunell. D. 6 Mar 1951.

HARRIET AMELIA, b. 5 Mar 1870, Manti, Utah. Md. 1889, George Rowe Smith. D. 29 Feb 1916.

ISABELLA, b. 8 Jun 1872, Manti, Utah. Md. 20 Jul 1892, Hyrum Bown. D. 14 Dec 1944.

LYNESS ROWLAND, b. 16 Sep 1874, Manti, Utah. Md. 1898, Anna Larsen. D. 1 May 1949.

ELEANOR, b. 18 Mar 1877, Manti, Utah. Md. 1898, Theodore Dahl Dedrickson. D. 20 May 1952.

CATHERINE, b. 25 May 1879, Manti, Utah. Md. 1897, Albert James Mackley. D. 29 Apr 1949.

JOHN, b. 23 Jan 1882, Manti, Utah. Md. 1903, Ella Chisholm. D.12 May 1962.

WILLARD, b. 3 Feb 1885, Manti, Utah. Md. 1909, Tebeitha Davis. D. 13 Jul 1956.

JESSE, b. 16 Nov 1887, Manti, Utah. Md. 1907, Margaret
Geslison. D. 10 Dec 1932.

Submitted by: J. Ralph Brown and Harold Forbush

WILLIAM BRAMALL

Born: 16 Feb 1824, Plumbly, Cheshire, England
Parents: Samuel and Mary Barlow Bramall
Died: 2 May 1907, Springville, Utah, Utah
Arrived in Valley: 1852, William B. Hodgetts Co.

Married 1st: Ann Drayson
Date: 26 Nov 1849, Leamingtron Priors, Warwicks, England
Born: 20 Apr 1821, Canterbury, Kent, England
Died: 14 Feb 1906, Springville, Utah

Married 2nd: Elizabeth Cranstone Wiscombe
Date: 23 Apr 1864, Salt Lake City, Utah
Born: 9 May 1839, Portfield Oving, Sussex, England
Died: 30 Oct 1899, Springville, Utah

William was 16 when he joined the Church. He served as a
missionary in England from 1845 to 1847 and again in 1849.

He married Ann in England and they sailed from Liverpool
in 1850. Upon their arrival in Pottawatamie County, Iowa, they
stayed for two years. He was a cordwainer (shoemaker) there. In
1852 they started west again, arriving in Salt Lake and then going on to Springville, Utah, where they made their home.

In the 1857 April Conference, William was called, along with 70 elders, to travel by handcart back to Florence, Nebraska, and then to their missions. He went to England where he labored until they were called home because of Johnston's Army. In 1860 he was called on another mission to England. He returned home to Springville in 1863.

He was a farmer and an agent for the *Deseret News*. He was active in the church, serving as a councilor in a bishopric. During the Black Hawk Indian War, he was in charge of the commissary and saw to the needs of those families at home.

In 1878 he returned to England for another mission until 1879. He helped bring many people into the church during his life time.

Children of 1st:

EMMA JANE, b. 21 Aug 1850, Council Bluffs, Pottawatamie, Iowa. Md. 5 Jun 1876, David Wheeler. D. 30 Dec 1898, Springville, Utah.

WILLIAM, JR., b. 15 Jan 1852, Council Bluffs, Iowa. Sld 23 Jun 1873, Sarah Ardilla Warren. D. 1 Jun 1873, Tintic, Juab, Utah.

SAMUEL, b. 14 Jan 1854, Springville, Utah. Md. 1 Nov 1875, Susan Elmina Coffman. D. 14 Sep 1913.

ANN DRAYSON, b. 15 Nov 1856, Springville, Utah. Md. 19 Feb 1880, Thomas Ashton Binks. D. 10 Jul 1943, Springville, Utah.

CHARLES DRAYSON, b. 24 Apr 1859, Springville, Utah. Md. 23 Jan 1890, Mary Charlotte Beardall. D. 2 Dec 1939, Springville, Utah.

Children of 2nd wife:

MARY ANN, b. 5 Jan 1865 Springville, Utah. Md. 28 May 1886, William Daniel Coffman. D. 11 Aug 1927, Salt Lake City, Utah.

CECELIA ELIZABETH, 7 Mar 1869, Springville, Utah. Md. 24 Dec 1891, John Sumison. D. 17 Feb 1927.

Submitted by: Marie Boren

HENRY MALYON BRIDGES

Born: 22 Mar 1809, Birmingham, Warws, England
Parents: George and Jamima Malyon Bridges
Died: 18 Oct 1882, East Millcreek, Salt Lake, Utah
Arrived in Valley: Came west in 1864

Married 1st: Sarah Louisa Lowe
Date: 1829, Birmingham, Warws, England
Born: 26 Dec 1806, London, Middlesex, England
Died: 21 Aug 1864, Cheese Creek, Nebraska

Married 2nd: Barbara Smith
Date: 16 Jun 1866, probably in Utah

Joined the Church in England, married, had six children and came to the Valley prior to the coming of the railroad. His wife died in Nebraska on the way west. He settled in the East Millcreek area, southeast of the city where he farmed. He married 16 June 1866 to Barbara Smith. He remained faithful to the church.

Children of 1st wife:

MARY ANN, b. 12 Feb 1830, Birmingham, Warws, England.
    Md. Patrick Martin.
SARAH ANN, b. 12 Apr 1832, Birmingham, Warws, England.
    D. 29 Jul 1839.
SUSANA JAMIMA, b. 21 Sep 1833, Birmingham, Warws,
    England. Md. 24 Sep 1855. D. 26 Dec 1879.
CHARLES HENRY, b. 9 Aug 1835, Birmingham, Warws,

England. Md. 20 Jun 1860, Frances Elizabeth Pearson. D. 7
Jan 1913.
THOMAS WARNER, b. 11 Apr 1837, Birmingham, Warws,
England. D 9 Aug 1840.
SARAH LOUISA, b. 29 Mar 1839, Birmingham, Warws,
England. Md. 8 Nov 1861, Daniel Augustus Hussey. D. 13
May 1921.

Submitted by: Jay Bishop

GEORGE WASHINGTON BRIMHALL

Born: 14 Nov 1814, South Trenton, Oneida, New York
Parents: Sylvanus and Lydia Ann Guiteau Brimball
Died: 30 Sep 1895, Spanish Fork, Utah
Arrived in Valley: 10 Jul 1850

Married 1st: Lucretia Metcalf
Date: abt 1840-1842, Illinois
Divorced: in 1850

Married 2nd: Rachel Ann Mayer
Date: 2 Feb 1852, Salt Lake City, Utah

George Washington's early years were full of rough and dan-
gerous experiences with Indians, fishing, logging and wild animals. His family ran a saw mill and shipped lumber 500 miles
through Indian country to Pittsburg. Later they moved to Dearborn
County, Indiana, and finally to McHenry County, Illinois.

After his marriage, he became interested in the Mormon religion but his wife would have no part of it. He prayed for direction and comfort and finally saw himself as a young man going west to a beautiful valley. He followed the dream.

He helped organize the settling of Iron County, Utah. He received an appointment to the House of Representatives and moved to Salt Lake. It was at this time that he received a letter from his wife telling of their divorce and her remarriage.

He studied law and was admitted to the bar in 1852. He was a very literary man and taught dancing and music and was expert on the flute. He learned the Indian language until he was able to converse freely.

He, with his brother and John Cox, were instrumental in forming a treaty of peace with the Indians, which ended the Black Hawk War. He was called on several missions to help settle various parts of the country. He was later ordained a patriarch by Lorenzo Snow. Their son, George Henry, was president of Brigham Young University for 21 years.

Children of 1st wife:

They had three children.

Children of 2nd wife:

GEORGE HENRY.
RACHEL EMMA.
EMER M.
ORILLA M.
OMER M.
RUTH R.
PRUDENCE M.
ETHER RECORD.
TRYPHENA M.
GRACE M.

Submitted by: Janice Betts

JAMES BRINKERHOFF, SR.

Born: 22 May 1816, Semprenius, Cayuga, New York
Parents: George and Hannah DeGraff Brinkerhoff
Died: 4 Mar 1875, Glendale, Kane, Utah
Arrived in Valley: 25 Sep 1847, Peregrine Sessions Co

Married 1st: Sally Ann Snyder
Date: 24 Jan 1836, Cayuga Co., New York

Married 2nd: Rebecca Hawk
Date: 28 Sep 1852, Salt Lake City, Utah
Born: 12 Aug 1835, Park Co., Indiana

Married 3rd: Elisa Jane Henderson
Date: 11 Jun 1854, Salt Lake City, Utah
Born: 29 Apr 1831, Jacksonville, Morgan, Illinois

James was among the first converts to the Mormon Church. He was baptized in 1841 and a year later moved to Nauvoo. He was on a mission to Ohio when he was called home because of the martyrdom of the Prophet.

When the saints left Nauvoo, he and his family were among the first to leave. Their son Levi was the first boy born in the Valley.

They lived in Salt Lake about four years when he was called to teach the people of Centerville how to farm. While there, Brigham Young called him to take a second and then a third wife.

After 15 years in Centerville, they were called to go to St. George and help teach the people how to farm in that arid area.

He served there and in the "Muddy Mission" but due to problems with the Indians, they were released and they moved to Glendale, Kane, Utah, where James died of a sun stroke.

Children of 1st wife:

LEVI, b. 3 Nov 1847, Great Salt Lake, Utah.
 Probably more.

Children of 2nd wife:

CLARK.
MARY CAROLINE.
MARGARET.
SAMUEL WILLIAM.
ALONZO.
JESSE.
IRA.
SALLY EDITH.
LORETTA.

Children of 3rd wife:

DAVID.
JOHN.
SILAS.
ELISA ANN.
LUCINDA.
JOSEPH.
MARETTA.
WILFORD.

Submitted by: Kent Leigh

DAVID BRINTON

Born: 29 Dec 1814, Chester Co., Pennsylvania
Parents: John and Priscilla Branson Brinton
Died: 17 May 1878, Big Cottonwood, Utah
Arrived in Valley: 17 Sep 1850, Heber C. Kimball Co.

Married 1st: Sarah Piersol
Date 24 Sep 1836, Pennsylvania
Born: 15 Aug 1819, Chester Co., Pennsylvania
Parents: Daniel and Eliza Lewis Piersol
Died: 15 Jul 1843, Nauvoo, Illinois

Married 2nd: Elizabeth Garrett Hoopes
Date: 22 Feb 1843, Nauvoo, Illinois
Born: 8 Sep 1817,
Parents: George and Albinah Woodward Hoopes
Died: 24 Sep 1846, Winterquarters

Married 3rd: Harriet Wollerton Dilworth
Date: 14 Jan 1848, Winterquarters
Born: 24 Feb 1822, Uwchlan, Chester, Pennsylvania
Parents: Caleb and Eliza Wollerton Dilworth
Died: 19 Nov 1896, Salt Lake City, Utah

Married 4th: Mary Hillhouse
Date: 29 Jan 1857. (Div) No children

Married 5th: Olive Lewis
Date: 14 Oct 1865. (Div) No children

Married 6th: Hilda Matilda Bradesen
Date: 19 Oct 1867
Born: 27 Jan 1848, Solar, Hokkaasen, Norway
Parents: Hans and Oline Olsen Bredesen
Died: 20 Oct 1936. Md. 2nd Antone Ludwig Halsett

David and his wife were baptized in 1840. Soon after they moved to Nauvoo where they lived until the death of Sarah and three of their children. After this David took his small son Evan and went back to their former home in Pennsylvania then he served a mission in the Eastern States. Upon his return, he married his second wife, Elizabeth Hoopes.

When the saints left Nauvoo, David and his family started west with the saints. The cold and conditions resulted in the death of Elizabeth and their infant son. At Winter Quarters he again married. In June 1848, they left with others for the Valley but soon his oxen died. And with other problems, he, with others, turned south to Savannah, Missouri. He worked there two years to rebuild his outfit. They finally reached the valley in 1850 and resided in Salt Lake until December 1850. Then he was called to help establish Parowan. Upon returning, he built a home and blacksmith shop where the Cottonwood Mall is now located.

He was soon called on another mission south of Ft. Bridger in Wyoming. Shortly after his return he was ordained a bishop (1856-1874). Three years after his release, his son was called and served in the same ward for 22 years.

He served as a handcart missionary, served in the defense against Johnston's army, served another mission, helped haul stone for the Salt Lake Temple, and had many other callings. He led a truly examplary life in the church and community. He died suddenly while loading a wagon.

Children 1st wife:

EVANS PIERSOL, b. 16 Aug 1837, Jennersville, Chester, Pennsylvania. Md. Harriet Hudnut Chase. D. 15 May 1915, Springville, Utah.
DANIEL, D. Child.

JOHN, D. Child.
ELIZABETH, D. Child.

Children 2nd wife:

ROBERT H., b. 11 Nov 1845, Nauvoo, Illinois. D. 10 Oct 1846, Winterquarters, Nebraska.

Children of 3rd wife:

CALEB DILWORTH, b. 21 Nov 1848, Savannah, Andrew, Missouri. Md. Emily Elizabeth Maxfield.
DAVID BRANSON, b. 23 Feb 1850, Savannah, Missouri. Md. 1st, Susan Erepta Huffaker. Md. 2nd, Mary Jane McFarlane.
JOSEPH HAMMOND, b. 8 Apr 1852, Salt Lake City, Utah. Md. Mary Webster Howard.
SAMUEL, b. 26 Dec 1853. Md. Joan Helm.
WILLIAM HENRY, b. 22 Sep 1855. D. 14 Sep 1857.
FRANKLIN DILWORTH (twin), b. 21 Nov 1857. Md. Alwilda Nancy Andrus.
HARRIET DILWORTH (twin), b. 21 Nov 1857. Md. Hyrum Alvin Bagley.
SARAH ELIZABETH, b. 8 Mar 1859. Md. Vincent Shurtleff.
ELIZA DILWORTH, b. 30 Mar 1863. Md. Lawrence Henry Young.

Children of 6th wife: 3 sons and 3 daughters born to Hilda and 2nd husband Antone Ludwig Halsett.

HYRUM BRADESEN, b. 23 Apr 1870. Md. 1st, Alice Sophia Maxfield. Md. 2nd, Teenie Olsen.
MINNIE MARJORIE STEWART, b. 6 Jul 1873. Md. George Elias Burbidge.
WILLIAM ROWE, b. 7 Apr 1876. Md. 1st, Cecelia Sharp Burt. Md. 2nd Viola Louisa Smith.
ROBERT NESLIN, b. 26 May 1877. Md. 1st, Martha Pearl Jackson. Md. 2nd, Catherine Mills. Md. 3rd, Bessie Burns.

Submitted by: Sherman Brinton

DAVID BRANSON BRINTON

Born: 23 Feb 1850, Savannah, Andrew, Missouri
Parents: David and Harriet Wollerton Dilworth Brinton
Died: 21 Dec 1929, Salt Lake City, Utah
Arrived in Valley: 17 Sep 1850, Heber C. Kimball Co.

Married 1st: Susan Erepta Huffaker
Date: 20 Apr 1874, Salt Lake City, Utah
Died: 13 Aug 1916

Married 2nd: Mary Jane (Aunt May) McFarlane
Date: 5 Sep 1917, Salt Lake City, Utah
Died: 3 Oct 1965, Salt Lake City, Utah

David Branson came with his parents to the Valley when he was only seven months old. He grew up in Holladay, Salt Lake County.

At the tender age of eight, David drove a wagon load of flour to Lehi, Utah, because his father was on a mission and his mother was involved in moving the family south because of Johnston's Army.

When his father returned, the family moved to the Holladay area to settle. He was a bishop and served another mission in the Eastern States.

He worked making ties for the railroad. He helped his father in his general store although his main work was in construction. He worked hard and expected his men to do the same. He owned much land between Sanpete and Kamas but lost it following World War I. He and his wife Susan helped many arriving immigrants get settled.

Reading, education and the arts were encouraged in their home. They lived for a time in Victor, Idaho, but soon returned to their home in Holladay.

David set a good example for his family and others in working hard, doing good work and getting an education. He served the Lord whenever and wherever called.

Children:

VALERIA EREPTA, b. 13 Dec 1875. Md. Levi Edgar Young. D. 22 Oct 1968. 3 children.

LUCETTA HUFFAKER, b. 7 Feb. Md. William George Wagstaff. D. 12 Jul 1968. 8 children.

ZUA, b. 22 May 1878. Md. Samuel Neff. D. 4 Jun 1940. 10 children.

DORA, b. 17 Apr 1880. Md. Albert Ether Taylor. D. 24 May 1971. 5 children.

DAVID BRANSON, b. 9 Feb 1882. Md. ethel Simons. D. 17 Jun 1956. 5 children.

MELVINA, b. 21 Nov 1884. Md. Chester P. Cahoon. D. 12 Apr 1941. 3 children.

WOLLERTON HUFFAKER, b. 27 Sep 1886. Md. Jane Hamilton. D. 1 Jul 1968. 4 children.

MILTON HUFFAKER, b. 19 May 1888. Md. Sarah Edna Howe. D. 22 Mar 1956. 6 children.

VAN BUREN, b. 5 Jul 1890. Md. Vida Robison Driggs. D 29 May 1971. 8 children.

HAROLD HUFFAKER, b. 10 Dec 1891. Md. Frances Laurene Smith. D. 29 Apr 1967. 4 children.

GENEVE, b. 9 Jan 1893. D. 23 Dec 1915. No children.

EMILY HUFFAKER, b. 17 Jan 1896. Md. Louis Kelly Sims. D. 12 Mar 1968. 4 children.

WILDER HUFFAKER, b. 23 Mar 1899. Md. Bernice Anderson Clark. D. 2 Jan 1974. 2 children.

Submitted by: Sherman Brinton

JOSEPH BROADBENT

Born: 18 Feb 1809, Saddleworth, Yorkshire, England
Parents: John and Sarah "Sally" Winterbottom Broadbent
Died: 28 Oct 1882, Spring City, Sanpete, Utah
Arrived in Valley: Fall of 1863

Married: Elizabeth "Betty" Schofield
Date: 10 Jun (abt 1827)
Born: 8 Jan 1808, Mount Misery, Saddleworth, Yorks, England
Died: Aug 1889, Spring City, Sanpete, Utah

Joseph and his wife joined the Church in England. Joseph was baptized in 1847 and excommunicated in 1859. He was re-baptized in 1862 in Oldham Branch, Lancs, England. He and his wife emigrated to Utah and arrived in the fall of 1863. All of their six infant children died in Oldham, Lancs, England.

Children:

EDWARD, b. 20 Aug 1828, Saddleworth, Yorks, England. Md. abt 1858, Sarah Gledhill. D. 25 May 1863.
SARAH, b. 19 Jul 1833, Saddleworth, England. Md. 23 May 1853, John Nield. D. 10 Jun 1901.
JOHN, b. 26 May 1835, Saddleworth, England. D. 25 Jul 1903.
ANN, b. 2 Jun 1837, Saddleworth, England. D. 24 Sep 1842.
WILLIAM, b. 31 Dec 1838, Saddleworth, England. D. 14 Jun 1839.
JOSEPH, b. 20 Sep 1840, Oldham, Lancs, England. D. 20 Sep 1840.

MARY, b. 26 Aug 1841, Oldham, Lancs, England. D. 24 Sep 1842.

HANNAH, b. 1 May 1844, Oldham, Lancs, England. D. 29 Oct 1847.

SETH, b. 6 May 1846, Oldham, Lancs, England. D. 24 Aug 1846.

Submitted by: Dayle White and Merrill Gomm

ISAAC BROCKBANK, SR.

Born: 17 May 1805, Underbarrow, Westmoreland, England
Parents: Daniel and Agnes Morris Brockbank
Died: 1 Apr 1878, Spanish Fork, Utah, Utah
Arrived in Valley: 3 Sep 1852, Abraham O. Smoot Co.

Married 1st: Elizabeth Mainwaring (Smith)
Date: 1835 England
Born: Jul 1812, Liverpool, England
Died: Jul 1852, on plains near Ft. Laramie, Wyoming

Married 2nd: Sarah Brown
Date: 2 Oct 1852, Salt Lake City, Utah
Born: 25 Nov 1819, Harefield, Middlesex, England
Died: 2 Apr 1888, Spanish Fork, Utah, Utah

Isaac worked on a farm as a youth. When he reached adulthood, he went to Liverpool where he joined the Wesleyan Methodist Church. He learned to manufacture beer and ale. He then worked for a company that furnished water to the ships.

Shortly after hearing Parley P. Pratt preach in 1843, he was baptized. His wife didn't join and was opposed to him joining. He changed his occupation to the meat trade and prepared to leave for America. His wife and children went with him. While crossing the plains, his wife disappeared and was never seen again. He married an acquaintance from the ship and they went to Palmyra Fort for the winter. When they reached the Valley, they settled in Spanish Fork. He remained active in the church as did his children.

Children of 1st wife:

ISAAC JR., b. 13 Jul 1837, England.
ELIZABETH, b. 8 Nov 1839, England. Md. J. Bushnell.
DANIEL, b. 1840, England. D. 1840. Infant.
SUSANA, b. 1842, England. D. 1842. Infant.
JOHN, b. 1845. D. 1845. Infant.
JOSHUA, b. 15 May 1848 AGNES, b. 5 Jun 1851. Md. A. K.
    Thurber.

Children of 2nd wife:

SAMUEL, b. 15 Sep 1853.
WILLIAM, b. Jan 1855,Spanish Fork, Utah. D. Dec 1862,
    Spanish Fork, Utah.
SARAH, b. 27 Oct 1857, Spanish Fork, Utah. D.24 Apr 1868,
    Spanish Fork, Utah.
JOSEPH, b.15 Sep 1859, Spanish Fork, Utah.
MARTHA ANN, b. 5 Sep 1861, Spanish Fork, Utah.

Submitted by: Ross Butler

CLINTON DONERAL BRONSON

Born: 17 Dec 1824, Mentor (Geauga) Lake, Ohio
Parents: Leman and Lucy Brass Bronson
Died: 14 Dec 1906, Soda Springs, Caribou, Idaho
Arrived in Valley: With returning Mormon Battalion members

Married 1st: Lovisa Andrews
Date: 25 Sep 1850, Salt Lake City, Utah
Born: 19 Mar 1830, Newbury, Chatauqua, New York
Died: 17 Jul 1912, Ogden, Weber, Utah

Married 2nd: Orpha Ann Lish

Clinton, his parents and their children were baptized into the Mormon Church between 1842-45 in Brownstown, Wayne, Michigan. His father was prominent and prosperous. Soon the persecution began and the family traveled to Nauvoo where they only remained about three weeks. They then traveled on to Winter Quarters. Clinton enlisted in the Mormon Battalion and his family went on without him.

His experiences with the Mormon Battalion were not pleasant and he was grateful when he was able to return to the Valley. He met Lovisa and after their marriage they moved to Ogden where he was assigned to make and keep peace with the Indians. He served an Indian Mission to Malad Valley. Following that, he was sent to Fillmore, Millard, Utah in 1857.

In 1861 they moved to Huntsville. Clinton was Captain of the Huntsville Scouts, trained to defend the settlement. He saw much action with the Indians. The Indians called him "Inka Pony" because of his red hair. He was known as one of the bravest men who ever walked the earth. He preached that people should never pick a fight with the Indians, but if necessary, to fight back.

They finally settled in Willard, Utah. He died at Soda Springs, Idaho.

Children of 1st wife:

EDWIN HENRY, b. 22 Aug 1851, Ft Ogden, Weber, Utah. Md. 1872, Lydia Ann Cole. D. 22 Jun 1914, Fairview, Franklin, Idaho.

CHARLES AMOS, b. 25 Sep 1852, Ft Ogden, Utah. Md. 20 Dec 1875, Bithiah Minerva Wells. D. 24 Sep 1890, Fairview, Idaho.

JAMES LEWIS, b. 25 Dec 1855, No. Ogden, Weber, Utah. Md. 9 Mar 1882, Susanna Viola Pettingill. D. 12 Jul 1954.

CLINTON DEWITT, b. 22 Jan 1857, No. Ogden, Utah. D. 1908.

WILLIAM BUTTON, b. 22 Sep 1859, No. Ogden, Utah. Md. 17 Nov 1881, Hannah Orinda Pettingill. D. 11 May 1939.

GEORGE MARCH, b. 22 Nov 1862, Huntsville, Weber, Utah. Md. 7 Dec 1884-90, Laura Emily Reid. D. 5 Jan 1946.

KETURAH JANE, b. 6 Dec 1864, Huntsville, Utah. Md. 8 Dec 1890, Charles W. Darby. D. 8 Jan 1937.

ALLIAH DELPHIA ANN, b. 22 Aug 1866, Huntsville, Utah. Md. 10 Apr 1889, Charles Delbert Root. D. 22 Jan 1961.

HARRIET LILLIAN, b. 2 Aug 1868, Huntsville, Utah. Md. 30 Oct 1889, John Alma Woodland. D. Unknown.

BENJAMIN FRANKLIN, b. 23 Dec 1871, Huntsville, Utah. D. Jun 1872.

Submitted By: Dalene and Gary Bryant

LEMAN BRONSON

Born: 15 Jan 1792, Middlebury, New Haven, Connecticut
Parents: Jesse and Esther Osborn Bronson
Died: 1854, Taylor, Michigan
Arrived in Valley: 1 Oct 1847, Jacob Foutz Co.

Married: Lucy Brass
Date: 2 Jan 1817, Mentor, Geauga (now Lake), Ohio
Born: 26 Jun 1795, Chester, Hampden, Massachusetts
Died: Feb 1847, near Ponca, Nebraska

Leman's father and grandfather served in the Revolutionary War. After the war, his parents moved their family to Green County, New York. As a young man, he left there and settled in Mentor, Ohio, where he built a log cabin. In 1825-7, he moved his family to Brownstown, Michigan where his farm became very prosperous, and he became a prominent member of the community.

He resisted the Mormon missionaries for some time but he and his entire family were finally baptized between 1842 and 1845. When the persecution commenced, he moved his family to Nauvoo. After three weeks there, they began their journey west. His son enlisted in with the Mormon Battalion.

The captain, George Miller, was put in charge of a company of saints to find suitable camp sites that would sustain the large companies coming west. After a time, Brigham Young sent a letter telling him to go back to Winter Quarters, but he refused and said nothing to his group. They stopped at a Ponca village but were attacked by a group of Sioux Indians. They commenced to build houses and a make-shift fort, but the entire community was almost entirely destroyed by a fire that burned all the grass. Many died.

In 1847, Elder E.T. Benson came and spoke with Bishop Miller and the group was persuaded to return to Winter Quarters. Leman's wife died during that winter. The following year the Company arrived in the Valley. Leman served a mission in Michigan until he was stricken by an illness. He died at Taylor, Michigan, at his son's home.

Children:

EDWIN RUTHVEN, b. 14 Octt 1817, Mentor, Ohio. Md. Mary
  Clark. D. 19 Mar 1889, Midway, Wasatch, Utah.
TRACY WILLISTTON, b. abt 1819, Mentor, Ohio.
EMERET ORILLA, b. 17 Dec 1824, Mentor, Ohio. D. Young.
CLINTON DONERAL, b. 17 Dec 1824, Mentor, Ohio. Md. 25
  Sep 1850, Lovisa Andrews. D. 14 Dec 1905, Soda Springs,
  Idaho.
HADLEY LAWTON, b. 1827, Brownstown, Wayne, Michigan.
  D. age 8 years.
WILMER WHARTON, b. 20 Oct 1830, Brownstown, Wayne,
  Michigan.
MARTHA ANN, b. 13 Jun 1834, Brownstown, Michigan.
LORINDA ELIZABETH, b. 23 Dec 1836, Brownstown,
  Michigan.

Submitted By: Dalene and Gary Bryant

PHILIP BROKE BROOKS

Born: 13 Oct 1841, Ispwich, Essex, England
Parents: Thomas Philip and Elizabeth Harper Brooks

Died: 13 Jan 1900, Salt Lake City , Utah
Arrived in Valley: 23 Sep 1854, Darwin Richardson Co.

Married: Susan Rebecca Paul
Date: 24 Mar 1866, Salt Lake City, Utah
Born: 27 Jan 1842, Swansea, Glamorgan, Wales
Died: 21 Jan 1925, Ogden, Weber, Utah

Philip Broke joined the Church in England and came to America in 1854 when he was 12 years old. He came down with Mountain Fever while crossing the plains but lived to marry, 12 years after arriving in the valley. He and his wife had seven children. They settled in Salt Lake and remained active in the church and community. He was a carpenter and machinist.

Children:

ELIZABETH EDITH, b. 20 Jan 1867, Salt Lake City, Utah. Unmarried. D. 26 Jan 1893, Salt Lake City, Utah.
PHILIP HENRY, b. 29 Sep 1868, Salt Lake City, Utah. Md. 22 Oct 1891, Minnenetta Clare Crompton. D. 16 Nov 1934, San Francisco, California.
WILLIAM THOMAS, b. 15 Dec 1871, Salt Lake City, Utah. Md. 18 Jan 1893, Theomartha Clays. D. 23 Apr 1962, Salt Lake City, Utah.
PAUL SIDNEY, b. 11 May 1874, Salt Lake City, Utah. Unmarried. D. 12 Jun 1893, Salt Lake City, Utah.
LESLIE ARTHUR, b. Dec 1882, Salt Lake City, Utah. Md. 19 Jul 1906, Anna Marie Lystrup.
ANNA MARIE LYSTRUP, 19 Aug, Salt Lake City, Utah.

Submitted By: Philip Speck

CHRISTIAN BROTHERSON

Born: 14 Jun 1811, Walser, Falster, Denmark
Parents: Bohne and Ann Margrethe Rasmussen Brodersen
Died: 9 Aug 1893, Mt Pleasant, Sanpete, Utah
Arrived in Valley: 13 Sep 1857, Christian Christiansen Handcart Co.

Married 1st: Anne Mortensen
Date: 13 Feb 1846, Denmark
Born: 1824 (age 22 when married)
Parents: Martin Jensen and Dorthea Knudsen Moenbo
Died: 26 May 1851, Denmark

Married 2nd: Else Mortensen (sister to Anne) (Div)
Date: 19 Mar 1852, Denmark
Died: 17 Nov 1891, Moroni, Utah

Christian and Anne had three children. She died from childbirth after her third child. Her sister came in to help with the children and Else and Christian were married about a year later.

They joined the Church and decided to go west with the other saints. Along the way Else became enamored with the man Christian had hired and paid his way to America in exchange for his help. Christian asked her to stay but gave her leave to go if she felt she must. He was left to raise his five children alone. For the rest of her life, Christian sent food to her and helped her when times were rough.

Christian and his children settled in the Sanpete Valley. He had five children under ten years old whom he loved and cared for, instructed and fed. In 1859 he took his family and moved to Hamilton Settlement (Mt. Pleasant) Utah.

He was a kind and loving man and good to everyone. He remained active in the church, teaching his children to be kind and considerate and to remain active in the church. He was loved by everyone who knew him. He died at the age of 82.

Children of 1st wife:

DOROTHEA, b. 18 Dec 1846, Denmark.
HANS, b. 15 Jan 1849, Denmark.
BOHNE, b. 3 Apr 1851, Denmark.

Children of 2nd wife:

MARTIN, b. 30 May 1853, Denmark.
ANN, b. 8 Jan 1856, Denmark.

Submitted By: Mary Baldwin

HANS BROTHERSON

Born: 15 Feb 1849, Bruserip, Falster, Denmark
Parents: Christian and Ane Mortensen Brotherson
Died: 30 Dec 1900, Mt Pleasant, Sanpete, Utah
Arrived in Valley: 13 Sep 1857, Christian Christiansen Handcart
    Co.

Married: Frederickka Andrea Jensen

Date: 18 Oct 1869, Salt Lake City, Utah
Born: 30 Dec 1852, Logstor, Denmark
Parents: Niels and Marie Kirstine Langgaard Jensen Hemmert
    Jensen
Died: 28 Nov 1932, Mt. Pleasant, Utah

Hans' mother died when he was two years old. His father remarried but she left him on the way west. Hans grew up under the loving care and teaching of his father. He walked all the way across the plains in a handcart company with his father and four brothers and sisters. They were often hungry and he was always tired. His feet bled with no shoes.

Upon their arrival in the Valley, they were sent south to Fort Ephraim where other Danish saints had settled. They lived in a fort until his father dug out a home where they lived the first winter. They had little food. Only the faith of their father kept them going.

In 1859 when Hans was 12, his father moved his family to Mt. Pleasant. They lived in the fort for a couple of years while his father worked on a home on property that had been allocated to them. Hans was taught to work, farm and care for the livestock. He was involved in the Black Hawk Indian war.

In 1866, he and other young men were called to go east and help the immigrants from Scandinavia. Upon his return he courted and married. He built a large home for them in Mt. Pleasant. They had 15 children. Their children were well taught and loved. They remained active in the church and were hard workers. Hans died at the age of 51. It was thought he had appendicitis.

Children:

HANS JR., b. 25 Oct 1870. Md. Charlotha Christine Simonsen.
ANNIE MARGARET, b. 9 May 1872. Md. Niels Christian
    Christensen.
CHRISTIAN, b. 1 Nov 1873. Md. Bertha Marie Swensen.
BOHNEY, 23 Jul 1875. Md. Vivian IRrene Olsen.
PARLEY PARKER, b. 19 May 1877. Md. Dorthy Hutchison.
MARIA, b. 9 Sep 1878. Md. John Olof Gunderson.

FREDERICKA, b. 13 Jul 1880. Md. Parley Hansen.
FRANCIS, b. 10 May 1882. Md. Amisena Johansen.
CLEMENTINA, b. 5 Feb 1884. HYrum Sorenson.
LORENZA CHRISTINE, b. 29 Apr 1886.
NELS DOUGLAS, b. 8 Oct 1888. Md. Alice Cecelia Grames.
ORSON HYDE, b. 12 May 1890. Md. Mada Axelsen.
HENRIETTA, b. 9 Nov 1892. Md. Peter Anthony Poulsen.
FERDINAND FLOYD, b. 12 Oct 1894.
VERNON HAMLET, b. 30 Nov 1896. Nora Velma Tidwell.

Submitted By: Mary Baldwin

MARTIN BROTHERSON

Born: 30 May 1853, Bruserip, Falster, Denmark
Parents: Christian and Else Mortensen Brotherson Died: 29 Sep 1931, Boneta, Duchene, Utah
Arrived in Valley: 13 Sep 1857, Christian Christiansen Handcarts

Married: Janet Sterling Rowe
Date: 30 Nov 1874, Salt Lake City, Utah
Born: 24 Aug 1855, Payson, Utah
Parents: Caratat Conderset and Mary Napier Rowe
Died: 22 Feb 1922, Mt Pleasant, Utah

Martin left Denmark with his family to come to America when he was only four years old. He walked barefoot by the side of the handcart. He felt lonely when his mother left his father, while they were enroute, to go with another man. He knew what it was like to hear his father pray that their food would last a little while longer. He learned how to work alongside his father on their farm. While still young, he helped defend their home against the Indian raids. He served in the Black Hawk Indian War. He loved to sing and became very good at it. He loved sports and liked to hunt but didn't have the patience to fish.

He tried living with his mother but his stepfather was mean to him, so eventually his mother told him to go back to his father who loved him and was a good man.

When he married Janet, he found the love and gentleness he had needed in a woman. They worked together to raise and teach their children. At first they lived in Indianola and later moved to Mt. Pleasant Valley, which was known as Meadowville, on the Sanpitch River in Southern Utah. They raised nine of their eleven children.

Martin served a mission in the Northern States. They remained active in the church and made genealogy and their family a big part of their lives.

Children:

MARY JANETTE, b. 14 Nov 1875, Indianola, Utah.
ELSIE THERESA, b. 25 Dec 1877, Mt Pleasant, Utah.
WILLIAM NAPIER, b. 8 Jul 1880, Mt Pleasant, Utah.
CANDACE BLANCHARD, b.10 Sep 1882, Mt. Pleasant, Utah.
MARTIN LAFAYETTE, b. 23 Oct 1884, Mt. Pleasant, Utah.
RUTH HANNA, b. 3 Dec 1886, Mt. Pleasant, Utah. D. 10 Oct
     1895.
JOSEPH CONDERSET, b. 4 Dec 1888, Mt. Pleasant, Utah.
ANNIE, b. 28 Oct 1890, Mt. Pleasant, Utah. D. age 9 months.
GEORGE QUE, b. 25 Jun 1892, Mt. Pleasant, Utah.
JOHN TAYLOR, b. 2 Oct 1894, Mt. Pleasant, Utah.
CHRISTIAN DARWIN, b. 7 Dec 1899, Mt Pleasant, Utah.

Submitted By: Mary Baldwin

ARIAH COATS BROWER

Born: 18 Jan 1817, Phelps, Ontario, New York
Parents: John T. and Fanny Coats Brower
Died: 25 Jun 1884, Goose Creek, near Oakley, Idaho
Arrived in Valley: 29 Sep 1847, Capt Edward Hunter

Married 1st: Margaret Elizabeth Hussey 11
Date: 6 Sep 1838

Married 2nd: Ruth Colbert–No children

Married 3rd: Margaret Thompson

Married 4th: Mary Jane Humphrey
Parents: Henry and Mary Ann Horn Humphrey

Married 5th: Hannah Thompson

Married 6th: Betsy Mason

Married 7th: Anna Sophia Olson–No children
Date: 7 Apr 1884
Born: 28 May 1865, West Venepker, Nynsk, Sweden

Ariah Coats spent his youth on a farm with little opportunity for an education. He determined to learn the art of printing and applied for an apprenticeship in Paineville, Ohio. He was introduced to the Church and was baptized in 1842 in Illinois.

He and his wife and children moved to Nauvoo. After a difficult time trying to obtain work, he finally did find work in the printing office.

Ariah was quite ill several times in his life but survived to marry seven times and raise 29 children. He served a mission in the Central States. He was Mayor of Richmond, Utah. He served in many other positions in the church and community. He was a hard worker. He died of pneumonia after herding some of his sheep.

Children of 1st wife:

ANN ELIZABETH.
VICTORIA ADELAIDE.
WILLIAM HENRY.
ARIAH HUSSEY.
MARGARET ELIZA.
JOSEPH HUSSEY.
JOHN TAYLOR.
GEORGE CANNON.
CORDELIA HUSSEY.
JONATHAN HUSSEY.
JOSHUA HUSSEY.

Children of 3rd wife:

CECELIA THOMPSON.
WILLIAM THOMPSON.
HANNAH THOMPSON.
SARAH THOMPSON.
JANE THOMPSON.
RICHARD THOMPSON.

Children of 4th wife:

MARIA ELIZABETH.
HENRY HUMPHREY.
MARY HUMPHREY.
ARIETTA HUMPHREY.
LUCINDA HUMPHREY.

MINERVA HUMPHREY.
MELISSA HUMPHREY.
GERTRUDE HUMPHREY.

Children of 5th wife:

FANNY THOMPSON.
ALICE THOMPSON.
CLARISSA MAY THOMPSON.

Children of 6th wife:

JAMES MASON.

Submitted By: Merrill Croft

BENJAMIN FRANKLIN BROWN

Born: 22 Feb 1823, Rush, Monroe, New York
Parents: William and Diantha Loveland Brown
Died: 7 Dec 1868, Ogden, Weber, Utah
Arrived in Valley: 27 Aug 1860, Benjamin Franklin Brown,
    Independent Co.

Married: Lucinda Leavitt
Date: 12 Feb 1848, Cambria, Hillsdale, Michigan
Parents: John and Lucy Rowell Leavitt

    Benjamin Franklin joined the church in 1858 at Council Bluffs.

Benjamin and his brother worked with the Michigan Railroad in the summer and followed the trade of shoemaker in the winter. Later he became the first shoemaker in Ogden, Utah.

During their trek west with the Independent Company, which Benjamin had formed, they were able to help two handcart companies who were much in need of food. Upon reaching Echo Canyon, Benjamin and some of the others determined to turn off to Ogden, while the rest went on into the Valley. He built a home in Ogden. He helped with the construction of the railroad near Ogden.

He was a good father and husband, a good provider and a good teacher of values to his children. Most of all he was a good member of the church all his life and taught his children well. He was a violinist and often played for dances and entertainment, and especially to revive the members of the wagon train as they traveled west.

Children:

CHARLES ALBERT, b. 15 Aug 1850, Cambria, Hillsdale, Michigan Md. 28 Aug 1872, Pauline Grover. D. 7 Oct 1924, Loa, Wayne, Utah.

BARNEY ALFRED, b. abt 1853, Cambria, Michigan. D. 1853.

LUCY ADELL, b. 15 Aug 1856, Cambria, Michigan. Md. 5 Jan 1876, Abraham Alonzo Kimball. D. 27 Dec 1904, Kanosh, Utah.

BENJAMIN FRANKLIN, b. 17 Sep 1861, Ogden, Utah. Md. 12 Mar 1890, Phylotte Greene Pack. D. 8 Nov 1911, Loa, Wayne, Utah.

ORILLA, b. 19 Jan 1866, Ogden, Utah. Md. 13 Jun 1894, Nicklas Longworth Sheffield. D. 24 Nov 1935, Kanosh, Millard, Utah. Bur. Loa, Utah.

Submitted By: Joyce Brown Willis

EBENEZER BROWN

Born: 6 Dec 1802, Herkimer County, New York
Parents: William and Hannah Sweet Brown
Died: 26 Jan 1878, Draper, Salt Lake, Utah
Arrived in Valley: Fall 1849, (Mormon Battalion)

Married 1st: Ann Weaver (4 children)
Date: 23 Jul 1823
Died: 24 Jun 1842, Quincy, Illinois

Married 2nd: Phoebe Draper Palmer (widow w/6-7 children)
Date: 26 Aug 1842, Pleasantville, Illinois

Married 3rd: Eliza Samantha Pulsipher
Date: 19 May 1853, Utah
Died: 1850

Married 4th: Mary Elizabeth Wright
Date: 29 Oct 1854, Utah

Ebenezer joined the Church in May 1835 in Pennsylvania at the same time as his sister. He moved his family to Kirtland, Ohio, to be with the saints. They then moved to Far West, Missouri, then back to Pleasantville, Illinois. His first wife died in Quincy, Illinois. He then married a widow with six or seven children. She was a good woman who remained active in the church. When problems started in Nauvoo, Ebenezer moved his family there.

When they heard about the Battalion enlistment call, Ebenezer joined up and Phoebe went with him, leaving her children with Ebenezer's oldest daughter, Harriet and husband, Oliver Stratton.

She endured the hardships alongside her husband for the entire march into California. Their part in the long march is well documented in his history. They were reunited with their children in the fall of 1849.

They settled in the southeast corner of the Valley known as South Willow Creek, later changed to Draper. Ebenezer became a man of substance and was able to help many of the unmarried women in the church, eventually marrying two of them. He was called to help establish a town in Carson Valley, Nevada. He was back in Utah in 1858. He remained active in the church and raised a good family.

Children:

Ebenezer was the father of 22 children; 13 sons and 9 daughters. These probably included the children of Phoebe by her first marriage.

Submitted By: Richard Lee

HENRY WILLIAM BROWN

Born: 10 Oct 1839, Newbury, Berkshire, England
Parents: Jonathan and Sarah Cousins Brown
Died: 9 Jun 1914, Murray, Salt Lake, Utah
Arrived in Valley: 20 Sep 1853, Claudius V. Spencer Co.

Married 1st: Sarah Ann Killpack
Date: 15 Mar 1869, Salt Lake City, Utah
Born: 8 Aug 1851, Banbury, Oxfordshire, England

Parents: John and Frances Sheriff Killpack
Died: 26 Mar 1920, Murray, Utah

Married 2nd: Emily Robinson
Date: 8 May 1884, Utah
Born: 22 May 1862, Great Barrington, Glouchester, England
Died: 1 Oct 1933, Crescent, Salt Lake, Utah

Henry William was the oldest of 10 children. He, with his parents, joined the Church in Liverpool, England. His father died in Utah, and Henry became head of the family and cared for his mother and siblings until they were grown.

He acquired a homestead in Murray where his family lived while he was on a mission to England. A woman convert followed him to the Valley and became his second wife. He lived in comfortable circumstances and provided well for his family. He was held in high esteem by the members of the community. He was a school trustee, Road Supervisor, Deputy Assessor and collector and census taker. He later became a Murray City Councilman. He was active and loyal to the church and held many positions.

In 1912 he suffered a stroke which partially paralyzed him, but he recovered somewhat until 1914 when another stroke took him.

Children:

HENRY JONATHAN, b. 12 Mar 1870, So. Cottonwood, Salt Lake, Utah. Unmarried. D. 20 Aug 1889.
FRANCES SARAH, b. 19 Dec 1871, So. Cottonwood, Utah. Unmarried. D. 22 Sep 1877.
CHARLES, b. 28 Sep 1873. Md. 18 Jan 1899, Hilma Johnson. D. 8 Feb 1943.
ELIZABETH RACHEL, b. 22 Jul 1875, So. Cottonwood, Utah. Md. 23 Oct 1893, James Matthew Dunster. D. 24 Oct 1949.
GEORGE EDWIN, b. 12 Aug 1877, So. Cottonwood, Utah. Md. 7 Nov 1900, Emily May Rawlings. D. 9 Oct 1939.
ARTHUR WILLIAM, b. 24 Jun 1879, So. Cottonwood, Utah. Md. 21 Oct 1903, Ivy May Turner. D. 20 May 1921.

JOHN LOUIS, b. 6 Jul 1881. Md. 2 Sep 1903, Lucy Fisher.
   D. 1 Nov 1945, Salt Lake City, Utah.
LAVENIA LOUISA, b. 20 Apr 1884, So. Cottonwood, Utah. Md.
   20 Jun 1906, James William Cahoon. D. 21 Jan 1961.
ESTHER LILLACE, b. 15 Jun 1886, So. Cottonwood, Utah. Md.
   27 Feb 1907, Melvin Ranck Fisher. D. 2 Apr 1976.
ZINA MERL, b. 7 Jul 1890, So. Cottonwood, Utah. Md. 15 Oct
   1907, Andrew H. Bennion. D. 21 Jan 1972.

Children of 2nd wife:

WILLIAM HENRY.
JOSEPH HYRUM.
TRUMAN RALPH.
HORACE EUGENE.
VIOLA MAY.
GLADYS BROWN.

Submitted By: Linda Erickson

JAMES BROWN, CAPTAIN

Born: 30 Sep 1801, Lich Creek, Rowan, North Carolina
Parents: James and Mary (Polly) Williams Emberson Brown
Died: 30 Sep 1863, Ogden, Weber, Utah
Arrived in Valley: 29 Jul 1847, Member of Mormon Battalion

Married 1st: Martha Stephens
Date: 2 Mar 1823, Rowan, No. Carolina
Born: 12 Oct 1806

Died: 28 Sep 1840

Married 2nd: Susan Foutz
Date: 26 Jan 1841, Adams Co., Illinois
Born: 14 Feb 1823
Died: 18 Aug 1842

Married 3rd: Esther Jones
Date: 20 Nov 1842, Nauvoo, Illinois

Married 4th: Sarah Steadwell (Div)
Date: 10 Jan 1845, Nauvoo, Illinois
Born: 31 Mar 1814
Died: 18 Mar 1893

Married 5th: Abigail Smith
Date: 8 Feb 1846, Nauvoo, Illinois
Born: 11 Sep 1806
Died: 23 Jul 1889

Married 6th: Mary McRee Black, widow
Date: 16 Jul 1846
Born: 17 Oct 1819
Died: 2 Nov 1906

Married 7th: Phoebe Abigail Abbott
Date: 17 Oct 1850
Born: 18 May 1831
Died: 9 Jan 1914

Married 8th: Cecelia Henrietta Cornu
Date: 26 Dec 1854
Born: 17 May 1825
Died: 14 Sep 1882

Married 9th: Mary Woolerton
Date: 7 Feb 1855
Died: 16 Jan 1877, Ogden, Utah

Married 10th: Darthula Catherine Shupe–No children
Date: 17 Feb 1856

Married 11th: Lavina Mitchell–No children
Date: 7 Sep 1856

Married 12th: Harriet Wood–No children
Date: 17 Sep 1859

Married 13th: Maria Mitchell–No children
Date: 22 Sep 1861
Born: 14 Apr 1843
Died: 19 Feb 1923

James, a native of North Carolina, was a convert to the Church, a member of the Mormon Battalion, early pioneer, and founder of Ogden, Utah. He worked on his father's farm as a young man. He was the most studious of the children and acquired sufficient knowledge to qualify for a teacher's certificate at age 18. He was elected to the office of constable and later sheriff.

Upon receipt of a letter from his brother in Illinois, James moved his family to Brown County, Illinois, and later to Adams County. He farmed and sold his produce at markets and became a wealthy man. He and his wife joined the church in 1839. He filled three missions for the church while in Illinois.

After the death of his first wife, he remarried and moved to Nauvoo, where he helped in the building of the Nauvoo Temple. When the saints started west, and volunteers for the Mormon Battalion were called up, James enlisted and was made Captain of Company C. When a group known as the "sick detachment" was sent to Pueblo, Colorado, Captain Brown led them. He arrived in the Valley five days after the main company in 1847.

He was sent to California to collect the pay for the soldiers under his command. He was advised by the brethren to take some of the money and buy out Miles Goodyear, who had established a fort where Ogden now stands.

He served a mission to British Guiana. He was a member of the Ogden City Council, first magistrate, and first legislator from

Ogden. He held many positions in the church and was a stalwart pioneer, caring for and helping others when needed.

Children of 1st wifc:

JOHN MARTIN, b. 29 Jun 1824, No. Carolina.
ALEXANDER, b. 3 Mar 1826, No. Carolina.
JESSE STOWELL, b. 26 Mar 1828, No. Carolina.
NANCY, b. 27 Dec 1830, No. Carolina.
DANIEL, b. 7 Dec 1832, No. Carolina.
JAMES MOORHEAD, b. 17 Nov 1834, Illinois.
WILLIAM, b. 21 Aug 1836, Illinois.
BENJAMIN FRANKLIN, b. 9 May 1838, Illinois.
MORONI, b. 25 Sep 1840, Illinois.

Children of 2nd wife:

ALMA, b. 1842. Lived 3 weeks.

Children of 3rd wife:

ESTHER ELLEN, b. 18 Mar 1849. Md. James Leech Dee. D. 26 Oct 1893.
ALICE, D. age 16 in Ogden.
AUGUST (twin), b. 1843. Lived one day.
AUGUSTA (twin), b. 1843. Lived one day.
AMASA LYMAN, lived two months.

Children of 4th wife:

JAMES HARVEY, b. 8 Oct 1846/7. D. 7 Oct 1912.

Children of 6th wife:

MARY ELIZA, b. 8 Nov 1847, Utah. Md. William F. Critchlow. D. 20 Mar 1903.
MARGARET, b. 17 Dec 1849. D. 6 Feb 1855 - age 5 years.

MARY ANN, b. 5 May 1852. Md. Edward Edwards.

JOSEPH SMITH, b.4 Jan 1856. Md. Sarah Wealthy Patten. D. 22 Mar 1903.

JOSEPHINE VILATE, b. 8 Jan 1858. Md. 25 Oct 1875, Henry James Newman. D. 4 Apr 1917.

Children of 7th wife: (daughter of 1st husband of 5th wife, Abigail Smith.

STEPHEN ABBOTT, b. 22 Aug 1851. D. 22 Dec 1853. Child.

PHOEBE ADELAIDE, b. 24 Oct 1855. Md. Henry Theodore Snyder. D. 11 Jun 1930.

ORSON PRATT, b. 22 May 1863. Md. Martha Dianna Romney. D. 11 Jun 1930.

Children of 8th wife:

CHARLES DAVID, b. 23 Jan 1856 . Md. 26 Jun 1879, Sarah Ellen Dixon D.23 Aug 1926.

JAMES FREDRICK, b. 2 Jul 1859. Md. 27 Mar 1884, Esther AmeliaMarriott. D. 19 Apr 1923.

Submitted By: Belva Moyle

JAMES HARVEY BROWN

Born: 8 Oct 1846, Florence Nebraska (Winter Quarters)
Parents: James and Sarah Stedwell Brown
Died: 7 Oct 1912, Ogden, Weber, Utah

Arrived in Valley: Sep 1848, Heber C. Kimball Co.

Married: Elizabeth Leah Williams
Date: 14 Feb 1870
Born: 8 Sep 1853
Died: 25 Apr 1934

James Harvey was born in a wagon box on the banks of the Mississippi River at Winter Quarters. Despite the difficult winter and sickness, little James and his mother Sarah survived the ordeal and arrived at Brownsville (Ogden) along with his two brothers.

When Harvey, as he was known, was a young child, his mother left his father and married again. Harvey was left with his father and was reared by the other wives. He later went to live with his real mother in Huntsville, Utah.

He learned hard work and early on was obliged to look out for himself. He grew to be a fine religious man. He loved music, played the bass violin, and had a fine tenor voice. He was a farmer and blacksmith as well as cattleman.

He did some prospecting. He worked with the Indians as interpreter and helped them. He set a good example of love and kindness and concern for others. He worked in the church as well as the community. He lived in Ogden much of his life.

Children:

SARAH ELIZABETH, b. 26 May 1872. Md. 20 Sep 1890, William Wallace Richardson. D. 21 Feb 1936.

MARY LEAH, b. 4 Mar 1874. Md. 15 Nov 1893, Daniel Benjamin Rawson. D. 14 Jan 1951.

RACHEL ANN, b. 14 Jun 1876. Md. 18 Jan 1899, Albert Brown. D. 6 Oct 1952.

JAMES HARVEY, b. 22 Jul 1879. Md. 26 Oct 1904, Elsa Sabre Rawson. D. 22 Dec 1966.

NELLIE MAY, b. 28 Oct 1880. Md. 25 Mar 1903, Cyrus Edgar Rawson. D. 22 Nov 1960.

MARGARET JANE, b. 10 Apr 1883. Md. 11 Sep 1907, James I. Kirby. D. 13 Mar 1964.

ETHEL PEARL, b. 17 Dec 1884. Md. 26 Apr 1917, John Riniker.
D. 1 May 1968.

THOMAS WILLIAM, b. 22 Nov 1886. Md. 31 Oct 1910, Mabel
Armstrong. D. 16 Oct 1949.

ELLEN LEONA, b. 15 Apr 1889. Md. 20 Sep 1911, Claborn
Joel White. D. 16 Jul 1967.

WEALTHY VIOLA, b. 15 Oct 1890. Md. 23 Sep 1909, Daniel
Bagley Willis. D. 15 Nov 1977.

JESSIE FRANK, b. 9 Sep 1893. Md. 24 Nov 1920, Alice Elizabeth Medell. D. 5 Nov 1961.

ZINA MYRTLE, b. 9 Jul 1896. Md. 24 Oct 1917, Parley Morris
Stoker. D. 18 Aug 1974.

Submitted By: Roger Rawson

JOHN BROWN

Born: 23 Oct 1820, near Castillian Springs, Sumner Co., Tenn.
Parents: John and Martha Chapman Brown
Died: 4 Nov 1896, Pleasant Grove, Utah
Arrived in Valley: 15 Oct 1847, Brigham Young

Married 1st: Elizabeth Crosby
Date: 21 May 1844, Nauvoo, Illinois
Born: 21 Dec 1822
Parents: John and Elizabeth Colman Crosby
Arrived in Valley: 19 Oct 1848, Amasa M. Lyman Co.

Married 2nd: Amy Snyder
Date: 22 Feb 1854, Salt Lake City, Utah

Born: 24 Feb 1834
Parents: Samuel and Henrietta Marin Stockwell Snyder
Died: 25 Mar 1871

Married 3rd: Margaret Zimmerman
Date: 3 Mar 1857, Salt Lake City, Utah
Born: 25 Mar 1836, Pennsylvania
Parents: George Gotleib and Julia Ann Hoke Zimmerman

John was educated in the schools that were available. When he was 18, his mother took him back to Tennessee where he entered the rural academy. Later they moved to Illinois where John taught school. In 1841 he joined the Church and later worked on the temple. He was sent on a mission to the Southern States in 1843. He met Elizabeth Crosby and they were married. After the martyrdom of Joseph and Hyrum, he returned to Nauvoo in 1844. In 1845 he went back to Mississippi and brought his wife back to Nauvoo. When the problems started, he was instructed to take some of the people and start them on the trek west.

Upon his arrival in the Valley, John immediately set about helping to plow and irrigate the fields. He was an explorer of the area, and was involved in the Indian Wars. He was a colonizer, explorer, merchant, mayor, and legislator. He was a missionary for the church, a bishop and a patriarch. He raised a fine family and anyone who takes the time to read his extensive biography soon finds how much this great man did for his church, community, family, and many others. He was a true pioneer. He crossed the plains 13 times helping others come west.

Children of 1st wife:

SAMUEL, D. young.
JOHN CROSBY, b. abt 1848. D. young.
AMASA LYMAN. D. young.
MARTHA ELIZABETH, Md. James Orson Bullock.
PAULINE ELIZA.
SARAH, Md. Joseph S. Staker.

SYTHA, Md. Wilson I. Snyder.

WILLIAM CROSBY, Md. Ada Johnson.

JAMES LEHI, Md. Selena Charlotte Curtis and Ella Larson.

PARILEE, Md. George S. Hayes. Lived in Salt Lake, Lehi and
Pleasant Grove, Utah.

Children of 2nd wife:

HENRIETTA, D. Infant.

LAURA JANE, age 13 (1871). Md. Ezra F. Walker.

ROBERT, D.

MAY ANN, age 11 (1871). Md. Albert Delanna Clark.

ROBERT ALEXANDER, D.

MINETTA PERMELIA, age 5 (1871). Md. James T. Thorne.

Children of 3rd wife:

JULIANA "Anna," b. 11 Jul 1859. D. 25 Sep 1860.

HARRIET ROSEANN, b. 21 Dec 1860. Md. Sep 1888, William
L. Hayes. D. 1862.

JOSEPH (twin), b.27 Jun 1863. D. age 5 weeks.

JOSPHINE (twin), b. 27 Jun 1863. D. 1 year and 7 months old.

LYDIA CHRISTENA, b. 3 May 1865. Md. Louis Warren Lund.

MARGARET, b. Apr 1867. Md. William Lehi Hayes.

SUSAN ELIZABETH, b.22 Apr 1870. Md. May 1895, Swen L.
Swenson.

AMY CASSANDRA, b. 7 Feb 1872. Md. 1896, Richard R.
Lyman.

JOHN ZIMMERMAN, b. 2 Sep 1872. Md. Alice Vivia Driggs.

LAWRENCE HOKE, b. 3 Dec 1875. D. Nov. age eight of Pleasant Grove, Utah.

Submitted By: Emmeline Wirthlin

JONATHAN BROWN

Born: 31 Jul 1818, Spilsby, Lincolnshire, England
Parents: Jonathan and Frances Mary Green Brown
Died: 5 Jul 1860, Mill Creek, Salt Lake City, Utah
Arrived in Valley: 20 Sep 1853, Claudius V. Spencer Co.

Married 1st: Sarah Cousins
Date: 31 Oct 1838
Born: 7 Mar 1819, Thatcham, Berkshire, England
Parents: George and Ann Herridge Cousins
Died: 5 Feb 1898, Murray, Salt Lake, Utah

Married 2nd: Ann Langfield
Date: 22 Nov 1856, Salt Lake City, Utah
Born: 1825, Newbury, Berkshire, England

Jonathan married Sarah in England, where he was a baker. Seven children were born to them while they were there. In 1852, they joined the Church and became very active in the Reading Branch. He was the branch treasurer.

They soon determined to leave for America. Sarah was expecting another child and the trip was quite rough. The child was born in St. Louis, Missouri, just five days after their arrival. The baby girl lived until their arrival in the Valley and then died.

Jonathan and his family settled in South Cottonwood (Murray). He married Ann Langfield but little is known of this marriage. He was sealed to two other women by proxy on 8 February 1894: Eliza Robinson and Elizabeth Neil.

Children of 1st wife:

HENRY WILLIAM, b. 10 Oct 1839, Newbury, Berkshire, England. Md. 1st, 15 Mar 1869, Sarah Ann Killpack. Md. 2nd, 8 May 1884, Emily Robinson. D. 9 Jun 1914, Murray, Salt Lake, Utah.

EDWIN, b. 24 Jun 1841, Newbury, Berkshire, England. Md. 12 Jun 1865, Desdemona Fox. D. 17 Apr 1928, Murray, Salt Lake, Utah

ELIZABETH, b. 28 Jan 1843, Newbury, Berkshire, England. Md. 7 Apr 1868, Chancy Griswold. D. 14 Nov 1870.

CHARLES, b. 14 Jan 1845, Newbury, Berkshire, England. Md. 9 Feb 1894, Martha Warman. D. 24 Jun 1866.

SARAH ANN, b. 1 Sep 1846, Newbury, Berkshire, England. Md. 31 Dec 1865. James Christian Petersen. D. 4 Dec 1893, Fairview, Sanpete, Utah.

EMMA, b. 12 Jan 1850, Newbury, Berkshire, England. Md. 8 Feb 1870, Job Reading. D. 30 Aug 1932, Murray, Salt Lake, Utah.

ELLEN, b. 11 Aug 1851, Newbury, Berkshire, England. D. 30 Apr 1853.

MARIA ELLEN, b. 23 Mar 1853, St. Louis, Missouri. D. 5 Oct 1853.

MARY FRANCES, b. 9 Apr 1857, South Cottonwood, Salt Lake, Utah. Md. James Barnum Henry.

ALBERT GEORGE COUSINS, b. 13 Dec 1859, South Cottonwood, Utah. Md. 24 Apr 1881, Hannah Thompson.

Child of wife #2:

ELIZABETH ANN, b. Sep 1857, Salt Lake City, Utah. Md. Alexander Bowman.

Submitted By: Linda Erickson

JOSHUA WOODS BROWN

Born: 14 Feb 1832, Preston, Lancs, England
Parents: Joseph and Mary Ann Woods Watt Brown
Died: 9 Dec 1903, Wellsvile, Utah
Arrived in Valley: 27 Sep 1855, Jack C. Serist Co. Independent
   Co.

Married: Sarah Robbins Bailey
Date: 3 Apr 1856, Salt Lake City, Utah
Died: 9 Oct 1902

Joshua Woods, the youngest of three children, was the son of Mary Ann Brown, one of the first people baptized in England. At the time, Joshua was only five years old. He was given a name and a blessing, the first given in Europe.

He became a strong and active young man, which served him well during his seven years as a sailor. In 1855 he joined his mother and others who were bound for America. They worked in America to purchase the necessary equipment to go west. A year later, he was married to Sarah. Their first home was in Farmington, Utah. They soon moved to Maughan's Fort (Wellsville, Utah). The winter was very difficult and before spring they lost their first child.

Joshua worked as a teamster and freighter. In 1882 he was called to a mission in England. Joshua enjoyed music and performing. He became a popular actor in some of the productions in Wellsville. He was buoyant, cheerful, and a self-displined man. He became a painter for the Logan Temple and later the Salt Lake Temple. He was an active member of the church and the community in which he lived.

Children:

MARY JANE, b. 1 Sep 1857, Farmington, Utah. D. 1862,
    Wellsville, Utah.
CHARLES BAILEY, b. 1 Jun 1859, Farmington, Utah.
SARAH ANN, b. 23 Sep 1861, Wellsville, Utah.
JOSHUA BAILEY, b. 1 Apr 1863, Wellsville, Utah.
MARGARET ELLEN, b. 17 Oct 1864, Wellsville, Utah.
KATE ETHELINDA, b. 20 Feb 1866, Wellsville, Utah.
SUSAN, b. 12 Nov 1867, Wellsville, Utah.
ROSELIA, b. 20 Nov 1869, Wellsville, Utah.
JOSEPH BAILEY, b. 7 Dec 1871, Wellsville, Utah.
JOHN ARNOLD, b. 4 Dec 1873, Wellsville, Utah.
AGNES MATILDA, b. 13 Jan 1876, Wellsville, Utah.

Submitted By: Charles Smurthwaite

GIDEON BROWNELL

Born: 5 May 1789, Danby, Vermont
Parents: Benjamin and Mary Ann Russell Brownell
Died: 16 Mar 1871, Logan, Cache, Utah
Arrived in Valley: 1849, Captain Miller's Fifth

Married: Betsey Elizabeth Wheeler
Date: 1814, Dartmouth, Massachusetts
Born: 16 Oct 1789, Chesterfield, New Hampshire
Parents: Randil and Experience Alden Wheeler
Died: 5 Sep 1870, Logan, Cache, Utah

Not much is known about Gideon's early life. After his marriage to Betsey, they moved to Quebec, Canada, where twins were born. The next time we hear of them is in 1817 in Montgomery, Ohio, where a baby girl was born. Then to Columbus, Ohio, for the birth of another child. They went back to Montgomery and apparently stayed there for several years where four more children were born to them. The youngest child was born in Dayton, Ohio. It was in Ohio where they were introduced to the Mormon Church by the missionaries. They were converted and were baptized in Ohio and then they moved to Nauvoo.

Nauvoo records show that Gideon was a gunmaker. When the mobs ran the saints out of Nauvoo, Gideon and his family left with the saints. They crossed the river on the ice just ahead of the mobs who were burning everything. They spent the winter in Montrose, Iowa, and with the coming of spring, they traveled on to Winter Quarters. Gideon's son and son-in-law were enlisted in the Mormon Battalion. Gideon and his family lived under a wagon top set on the ground as a shelter. When the boys got back to Winter Quarters from the Mormon Battalion, Gideon and the boys worked to obtain funds to go west. They left in the second company under Heber C. Kimball.

The family settled in Farmington, Utah, where Gideon built a rock house that was still standing in 1995. In 1859 he was asked to help settle Cache Valley where he worked as a gunsmith in Logan. In the records at Logan, Gideon is listed as a doctor.

Children:

MARY ANN (twin), b. 2 Mar 1815, Ascot, Sherbrooke, Quebec. D. 22 Feb 1898.
EXPERIENCE (twin), b. 2 Mar 1815, Ascot, Sherbrooke, Quebec.
ZORA, b. 1817, Montgomery, Ohio. Died young.
RUSSELL GIDEON, b. 17 Jul 1818, Columbus, Ohio. D. 6 Apr 1895.
FANNY ELIZABETH, b. 20 Apr 1820, Union, Montgomery, Ohio. D. 30 Aug 1882.

GLADYS, b. 1821, Union, Montgomery, Ohio. D. young.

HANNAH, b. 1823, Union, Montgomery, Ohio.

CLIFFORD, b. 1 825, Union, Montgomery, Ohio.

JULIA ANN, b. 12 Feb 1826, Dayton, Hamilton, Ohio. Md. 16 Oct 1843, James Myler, Jr. D. 27 Jan 1898, Lewisville, Jefferson, Idaho.

Submitted By: Jessie Thomas

EBENEZER BRYCE

Born: 17 Nov 1830, Dunblanc, Perthshire, Scotland
Parents: Andrew and Janet Adams Bryce
Died: 26 Sep 1913, Bryce, Graham, Arizona
Arrived in Valley: 16 Sep 1850, James Pace wagon train

Married: Mary Ann Park
Date: 16 Apr 1854, Salt Lake City, Utah
Born: 24 Jan 1837, Warwick, Kent, Canada
Died: 10 Apr 1897, Bryce, Graham, Arizona

Ebenezer joined the LDS Church when he was 17 years old, even though his family and friends objected. Shortly after, he sailed for America. He worked in Paduca, Kentucky, for two years as a carpenter aand then joined a wagon train to the Valley. He lived in Salt Lake, helping build mills and buildings. He was a carpenter and millwright.

After his marriage to Mary Ann, they moved to Tooele where he helped build a mill. Then they moved to Rush Valley to help establish the settlement at Clover. In 1861 he was called to build sawmills in the St. George area to supply wood for the temple construction. Following that he moved to Paria near a Canyon that was later named Bryce after him. In 1880 he moved south to the Gila River in Arizona, where he built a ranch and helped others build canals and mills.

He was a jovial individual although stern in the rearing of his children. He remained active in the church and community. He was ordained a patriarch in later life.

Children:

EBENEZER PARK, b. 15 Feb 1855, Tooele, Utah. Md. 26 Dec 1877, Helen Diana Packer. D. 22 Sep 1938, Thatcher, Graham, Arizona.

ANN JEANETTE PARK, b. 19 Jan 1857, Tooele, Utah. Md. 20 Nov 1877, James Brigham Thompson. D. 12 Dec 1919, Ucon, Bonneville, Idaho.

DAVID ANDREW, b. 7 Jan 1858, Salt Lake City, Utah. Unmarried. D. 22 Jul 1887, Bulture, Maricopa, Arizona.

WILLIAM HENRY, b. 1 Feb 1860, Millcreek, Utah. Md. 1st, 16 Dec 1885, Rose Ann Goulding. Md. 2nd, 28 Oct 1891, Malinda Isabella Riggs. D. 1 Oct 1930, Roosevelt, Duchesne, Utah.

ALMA NEPHI, b. 24 Oct 1861, Millcreek, Utah. Md. 1st, 14 Sep 1887, Caroline Jorgensen. Md. 2nd, 25 Jul 1910, Armena Adelaide Oliver Blair. D. 24 Dec 1916, El Paso, Texas.

GEORGE ALVIN (DICK), b. 22 Nov 1863, Pine Valley, Utah. Md. 1 Jan 1886, Sarah Catherine Carter. D. 16 Feb 1940, Bryce, Arizona.

BARBARA ELLEN (NELL), b. 22 Nov 1863, Pine Valley, Washington, Utah. Md. 2 Mar 1883, George Otis Pcck. D. 6 Jun 1936, Bryce, Graham, Utah.

JANE LOUISA, b. 1 Jun 1867, Pine Valley, Utah. Md. 17 Oct 1888, John Warner Mattice. D. 1 Dec 1957, Pima, Arizona.

MARY ISABELLE, b. 11 Jul 1870, Pine Valley, Utah. Md. 16 Oct 1890, James Andrew McBride. D. 1 Dec 1957, Thatcher, Arizona.

JOSEPH WALTER, b. 7 Jul 1872, Pine Valley, Utah. Md. 25 Oct

1894, Nancy Catherine Nelson. D. 17 Jul 1943, Bryce, Arizona.

HEBER BROOKS, b. 30 Nov 1878, Cannonville, Utah. Md. 25 Aug 1894, Dortheia (Dora) Jorgensen. D. 7 Nov 1926, Safford, Arizona.

REUBEN ADAM, b. 11 Sep 1880, Panguitch, Utah. Md. 8 Aug 1904, Mae Keziah Carter. D. 4 Dec 1956, Bryce, Arizona.

Submitted By: Wendall Bryce

SAMUEL COWAN BRYSON

Born: 15 Aug 1815, Banbridge, County Down, Ireland
Parents: John and Margaret Cowan Bryson
Died: 18 Sep 1908, Bountiful, Davis, Utah
Arrived in Valley: 1855, Handcart Co.

Married: Sarah Ann Connery
Date: 1839, Banbridge, Down, Ireland
Born: 16 Oct 1819, Blaris, Down, Ireland
Parents: Samuel and Alice Bradshaw Conery
Died: 21 Mar 1871, Bountiful, Davis, Utah

Samuel and his wife joined the Church in Ireland. In 1855-6, they brought their family across the ocean to America where they joined a handcart company and crossed the plains to the Valley.

Sometime after their arrival, Brigham Young sent them, with others, to settle the town of Woodruff. They later settled in Bountiful. They built a home and lived and raised their family of 11 children in this area.

Children:

THOMAS HENRY, b. 16 Sep 1841, Banbridge, Down, Ireland. D. same day.

MARGARET, b. 25 Aug 1843, Banbridge, Down, Ireland. D. same day.

SAMUEL JR., b. 11 Apr 1845, Bainbridge, Down, Ireland. Md. 25 May 1867, Polly Tryphena Fairchild. D. 3 Sep 1919, Provo, Utah.

JANE, b. 1 Jan 1848, Glasgow, Lanark, Scotland. D. 30 Nov 1854.

SARAH ANN, b. 21 May 1850, Glasgow, Scotland. Md. 29 Sep 1866, Perrigrine Sessions. D. 23 Dec 1934, Farmington, Utah.

HYRUM SMITH, b. 10 Feb 1852, Glasgow,Scotland. Md. 27 Jan 1877, Olivia Algar. D. 23 Jun 1905.

ELIZA SNOW, b. 13 Jun 1854, Glasgow, Scotland. Md. 22 Nov 1869, Jens Christian Nelson. D. 21 Apr 1933, Woods Cross, Utah.

DAVID COWAN, b. 21 Oct 1856, Bountiful, Utah. D. 20 Nov 1874.

JAMES, b. 18 Dec 1858, Bountiful, Utah. Md. 17 Apr 1879, Md. Mary Emma Oliver. D. 15 May 1950, Woodscross, Utah.

JOHN DUNLAP, b. 18 Jan 1861, Bountiful, Utah.. Md. 29 Dec 1881, Hattie Sophia Allen. D. 23 Sep 1919, Bountiful, Utah.

ALICE BRADSHAW, b. 4 Dec 1862, Bountiful, Utah. Md. 2 Oct 1879, Harvey Sessions. D. 6 Mar 1947, Ephraim, Sanpete, Utah.

Submitted By: L. Hoffman

SAMUEL BRYSON, JR.

Born: 11 Apr 1845, Banbridge, Down, Ireland
Parents: Samuel and Sarah Ann Conray Bryson
Died: 3 Sep 1919, Provo, Utah, Utah
Arrived in Valley: 1855

Married: Polly Tryphena Fairchild
Date: 25 May 1867, Salt Lake City, Utah
Born: 11 Dec 1846, Cattaraugus, New York
Parents: John and Tryphena Pomeroy Fairchild
Died: 25 Mar 1943, Paris, Bear Lake, Idaho

Samuel's name is listed as Samuel Cowley on an Endowment record. Samuel was raised in the Mormon Church, his father being one of the early converts and a branch president in Glasgow, Scotland, when Samuel was one year old. His father was a weaver and Samuel loved to help him. The year after his baptism, his family left for America. They settled in Bountiful, which was then known as the Sessions Settlement.

He lived through many difficult times with his parents in the new land. The only schooling he had was when he was in Scotland. He knew what hard work was and hunger. He loved to dance and played the drums in the Martial Band. He worked for a time in the Salt Lake Temple Rock Quarry. When he was 19, he made a trip to Omaha for freight and with his money he bought a saddle. Horses were his love and hobby.

In 1872 he took his family to settle on the banks of Bear River in Rich County, now Woodruff. In 1883 he was called on a mission to the Northern States. All his life he was deeply religious.

He helped the needy and worked in the community, being school trustee, constable, election judge and other responsible positions. He was a member of the High Council and for 25 years was superintendent of the Sunday School.

He was a handsome man, with fiery brown eyes, and lots of jet black hair. He was tall and carried himself straight "as an arrow." He lived to be 97.

Children:

SARAH TRYPHENA, b. 9 Apr 1868, Bountiful, Utah. Md. 18 Sep 1885, William Cook. D. 2 Jan 1953.

JOHN SAMUEL, b. 28 Dec 1869, Bountiful, Utah. Md. 29 May 1889, Agnes Belzora Linford. D. 11 Apr 1935.

ELIZA SNOW, b. 17 Apr 1872, Woodruff, Rich, Utah. Md. 30 Sep 1891, Joseph Wolcott Cook. D. 31 Oct 1955.

CHARLES MELVIN, b. 22 Apr 1874, Woodruff, Utah. Md. 1 Oct 1902, Martha Quibell. D. 8 Jul 1965.

ELLEN, b. 30 Oct 1876, Woodruff, Utah. Md. 18 Dec 1893, Albert Henry Dickson. D. 29 Jan 1928.

DAVID HYRUM, b. 23 Jul 1879, Woodruff, Utah. Md. 8 May 1901, Luella May Eastman. D. 14 Dec 1975.

MARGARET, b. 8 Feb 1882, Woodruff, Utah. Md. 29 Jan 1908, Charles George Longhurst. D. 19 Feb 1980.

WILFORD WOODRUFF, b. 15 Jan 1885, Woodruff, Utah. Md. 1st, 25 May 1904, Lucy Helen Cornia (Div). Md. 2nd 2 Jan 1917, Naomi Hendry (Div). Md. 3rd 12 Aug 1922, Mary Woodbbury. D. 6 Nov 1945.

LUTHER POMEROY, b. 27 Jun 1889, Woodruff, Utah. Md. 13 Feb 1913, Eliza Catherine Walton. D. 25 Nov 1976.

Submitted By: L. Hoffman

ARCHIBALD WALLER OVERTON BUCHANAN

Born: 9 Feb 1830, Lexington, Fayette, Kentucky
Parents: John and Nancy Ann Back-Bach Buchanan
Died: 7 May 1915, Venice, Sevier, Utah
Arrived in Valley: 13 Sep 1852, by wagon

Married 1st: Helen Amelia Whiting
Date: 22 Aug 1854
Died: 7 Aug 1910, Lyman, Wayne, Utah

Married 2nd: Mary Ann Brown
Date: 1 Jan 1860
Died: 15 Feb 1901, Glenwood, Sevier, Utah

Married 3rd: Ane Marie Larsen
Date: 11 Oct 1869
Died: 3 May 1901, Glenwood, Sevier, Utah

Married 4th: Caroline Sophia Sorensen
Date: 27 Sep 1875
Died: 2 May 1928, Venice, Sevier, Utah

Archibald Waller Overton was just a boy when his parents joined the Church. They endured the Missouri persecution and then moved to Lima, Illinois. After his father's death, the family moved to Nauvoo. When the persecuted saints left Nauvoo, the Buchanan family left with them. Archibald assumed the care of the family when his older brother joined the Mormon Battalion.

Upon their arrival in the Valley, they were called to help settle Manti. He was a friend of the Indians and helped bring peace.

In 1869, he moved his families to Glenwood, Utah, where he was made a branch president. They were called to live the United Order. Their family's job was to run the dairy herd and provide milk, cream, cheese and butter for members of the order.

In 1880 Archibald moved to Old Mexico to escape the persecution from polygamy. He returned in 1892 to be at the Salt Lake Temple dedication. At that time, he decided to remain in Utah and only live with one wife to abide by the law. He continued to work with the Indians and was highly respected by them and his family and friends.

Children of 1st wife:

SARAH ELIZABETH, b. 19 Nov 1856, Manti, Utah. Md. 24 Apr 1876, Peter Kimball Lemmon. D. 17 Mar 1926.
ARCHIBALD WALTER, b. 21 Jan 1859, Manti, Utah. Md. 7 Dec 1881, Mary Peterson. D. 2 Jun 1951.
HELEN AMELIA, b. 14 Mar 1861, Manti, Utah. Md. 6 Mar 1878, Harry "M" Payne. D. 1 Jan 1936.
LORENZO DOW, b. 16 Apr 1864, Manti, Utah. Md. 24 Feb 1892, Mary Larson. D. 31 Dec 1939.
THEDA JANE, b. 29 Dec 1867, Manti, Utah. Md. 1st, 3 Mar 1886, Herbert Horace Bell, (Div). Md. 2nd, 23 Apr 1890, Archibald Oldroyd. D. 20 Mar 1954.
EFFIE LOUISA, b. 29 May 1871, Glenwood, Utah. Md. 18 Aug 1891, George Franklin Hackett. D. 7 Mar 1927.

Children of 2nd wife:

EUNICE ROZINA, 11 Mar 1858, daughter of Mary Ann's 1st husband.
JAMES ALONZO, b. 28 Dec 1860, Manti, Utah.
MARY JANE, b. 28 Dec 1862, Manti, Utah.
WILLIAM WALLACE, 26 Feb 1865, Manti, Utah.
EUGENE DELOS, b. 12 Jun 1867, Manti, Utah.
HENRY POMEROY, b. 13 Mar 1871, Glenwood, Utah.
AMY LORETTE, b. 6 Sep 1873, Glenwood, Utah.
CHARLES VERTNER, b. 15 Mar 1877, Glenwood, Utah.

Children of 3rd wife:

OSMOND, b. 26 Sep 1871, Glenwood, Utah.
ARTHUR ADELBERT, b. 28 Jul 1873, Glenwood, Utah.
CASTINA MARIA, b. 16 Oct 1876, Glenwood, Utah.
JAMES CARLOS, b. 8 Apr 1879, Glenwood, Utah.
ETHELYN, b. 10 Feb 1883.
NANCY EDNA, b. 22 Jul 1886.
JACOB JOSEPH, b. 15 Sep 1866, son of Ane Maria by first husband, but sealed to Archibald.

Children of 4th wife:

JOHN LOREN, b. 15 Jan 1879, D. 1 year.
ANNA DELILAH, b. 27 Apr 1881.
MARY ANN, b. 7 Sep 1883, Venice, Utah.
WILLIAM AARON, b. 5 Apr 1885. Venice, Utah D. 3 years.
PARLEY AMMON, b. 10 Feb 1888. Venice, Utah D. 6 months.
CARRIE MYRL (twin), b. 25 Mar 1892, Venice, Utah.
ARCHIE EARL (twin), b. 25 Mar 1892, Venice, Utah.

Submitted By: Dwain Buchanan and Patti Thygerson

JOHN BUCHANAN, IV

Born: 25 Jan 1825, Lexington, Fayette, Kentucky
Parents: John and Nancy Ann Bache Buchanan
Died: 11 Oct 1897, Manti, Sanpete, Utah
Arrived in Valley: With Mormon Battalion, 1847

Married 1st: Adeline Coons
Date: 23 Feb 1851, Glenwood, Mills, Iowa
Died: 11 Apr 1912, Manti, Utah

Married 2nd: Sarah Wilkinson
Date: 21 Apr 1866, Salt Lake City, Utah
Born: 16 Oct 1847, Mount Pisgah, Harrison, Iowa
Died: 16 May 1920, Manti, Sanpete, Utah

John and his family lived in Kentucky until sometime between 1830 and 1833, when they moved to Tazewell County, Illinois. At various times, John's parents and children were all baptized. Records are not complete, but they did go to Caldwell County, Missouri, and were part of the expulsion there. They are found also in Quincy and Lima, Illinois, with the saints. John's father died in Lima, Illinois, and his wife Nancy took their family and moved to Nauvoo. They stayed until the saints were driven from Nauvoo.

They were with the saints in Council Bluffs. John joined the Mormon Battalion and accompanied the sick detachment members who were sent back to Pueblo, Colorado. They arrived in Salt Lake 29 July 1847. After John's arrival in the Valley, they were advised by Brigham Young to help settle Sanpete County. A year later they moved to Manti where John built a grist mill. He lived here with his family, including his wives and children, until his death.

Children of 1st wife:

JOHN, b. Jan 1852, Glenwood, Mills, Iowa.
    Plus ten more children.

Children of 2nd wife:

RAYMOND, b. 3 Feb 1867, Manti, Utah. Md. 20 Nov 1889,
    Annie Margaret Nielsen/Nelson. D. 29 Apr 1919.
ADELBERT, b. 21 Dec 1869, Manti, Utah. D. 21 Aug 1874.
MARY ANN (Molly), b. 29 Jul 1872, Manti, Utah. Md. 17 Jul
    1895, Christian Miller. D. 17 Sep 1928.

RAPHAEL (RAFE) SIMS, b.22 Dec 1875, Manti, Utah. Md. 10 Oct 1900, Margaret May Braithwaite. D. 28 Dec 1948.

MABEL CLARA (May), b. 24 May 1878, Manti, Utah. Md. 28 Jun 1899, Robert Martin Braithwaite. D. 14 Jan 1947.

NELLIE REID, b. 20 Sep 1879, Manti, Utah. Md. 29 Jun 1904, James Peter Christensen. D. 17 Nov 1960.

ARCHIBALD LORENZO, b. 28 May 1882, Manti, Utah. Md. 23 Sep 1903, Ann Geneva Ahlstrom, D. 19 Feb 1964.

ALLEN, b. 12 Aug 1884, Manti, Utah. D. 12 Aug 1884.

SOPHRONIA, b. 1 Oct 1885, Manti, Utah. D. 1 Dec 1885.

Submitted By: Dan Dawson

ALONDUS DE LAFAYETTE BUCKLAND

Born: 11 Dec 1823, Tunbridge, Orange, Vermont
Parents: Joseph Moseley and Hannah Daggett Buckland
Died: 22 Jun 1854, On plains out of Ft. Leavenworth, Kansas on return from mission
Arrived in Valley: Sailed around the Horn on "Brooklyn" with Samuel Brannan. Came to valley in 1849 when Apostle Amasa Lyman requested it

Married 1st: Nancy Laura Aldrich
Date: 10 Oct 1846, Mission Delores, San Francisco, California
Born: 8 Aug 182 8, Gloucester, Providence, Rhode Island
Parents: Silas and Prudence Clark Aldrich
Died: 11 Jan 1905, Bountiful, Davis, Utah

Married 2nd: Martha Ellen Ashby

Date: 16 Dec 1850, Salt Lake City Utah
Born: 28 Aug 1832, Salem, Essex, Massachusetts
Parents: Nathaniel and Susan Hammond Ashby
Died: 25 Mar 1873

Alondus de LaFayette's parents were divorced when he was young and the family endured many hardships. His mother was a school teacher so Alondus received a fair education. She was also a strong religious person, which she passed on to her children.

In 1845, shortly after their baptism, Alondus and his mother sailed on the ship "Brooklyn" with Samuel Brannan. Their faith was tested many times on the trip around the Horn. Upon their arrival in San Francisco, the families settled in the area until Apostle Amasa Lyman came and asked them to move to the Valley, taking their money to help the saints. Alondus had amassed a great deal of money between the gold discovery and a hotel he had built. He sold all he had and equipped a wagon to go to the valley. He and 13 or 14 others left in the "gold train" on 14 July 1849, bound for Salt Lake. They traveled by night because of Indians and the heat. They brought about $40,000. which helped the Utah economy.

He was among the first families to settle Bountiful. He built a beautiful home and acquired a great deal of property and was a prominent member of the community. He was called in 1852 on a mission to Nova Scotia and the British Provinces of America. Upon his release, he organized a company of saints who wanted to come to Utah. There were approximately 200 people in the wagon train. Just outside of Ft. Leavenworth, cholera invaded the Company and Alondus was one of those who died. His sister emptied a trunk, knocked out one end of it, wrapped his body in a sheet and placed it in the makeship coffin. She buried him by the trail.

During his short life of 36 years, he had acquired much wealth, helped many people, brought many more into the church, had two wives and five children. His main love was the gospel.

Children of 1st wife:

ALONDUS LAFAYETTE, b. 17 Sep 1847, New Hope, San
Joaquin, California. Md. 13 Aug 1871, Geneva Harriet Pack.
D.11 Jun 1933, Parkdale, Hood River, Oregon.

NANCY LAURA, b. 19 Nov 1848, San Francisco, California.
Md. 23 Dec 1866, Charlton Marcellis Goldsberry. D. 15 Jun
1936, Paradise, Cache, Utah.

SILAS ALDRICH, b. 18 May 1850, Bountiful, Utah. Md. 2 Sep
1871, Kamelia Luella Pack. D. 3 Mar 1909, Salt Lake City,
Utah.

SAMANTHA JANE, b. 1 Nov 1851, Bountiful, Utah. Md. 24
Jan 1870, Don Carlos Pack. D.10 Apr 1879, Kamas, Summit,
Utah.

Child of 2nd wife:

ELLEN, b. 10 Jun 1852, Bountiful, Utah. Md. 14 Mar 1870,
William Loder. D. 28 May 1912, Bountiful, Utah.

Submitted By: Irene Jorgensen

NEWMAN BULKLEY

Born: 18 Aug 1817, Catherina, Tioga, New York
Parents: Noah Summers and Nancy Ann Newman Bulkeley
Died 19 Sep 1893, Springville, Utah, Utah
Arrived in Valley: 1 Oct 1848, with Mormon Battalion

Married 1st: Jane Draper
Date: 7 Jan 1844, Nauvoo, Hancock, Illinois

Born: 7 Jun 1825, Loborough, Upper Canada
Died: 28 Dec 1883, Springville, Utah

Married 2nd: Lovina Palmer
Date: 5 Mar 1857

Newman joined the Mormon Battalion when the call came, and, after arriving in California, he helped build roads and map the roads from Los Angeles to San Diego, California.

He owned the first molasses mill in Springville, Utah. He was a book canvaser and owned a sawmill in Springville, Utah. He was active in the church and in the community. He was given the honor of having a mountain between Springville and Provo named after him, Bulkley Mountain.

Children of 1st wife:

CECILIA, b. 1841. D. Unknown

NEPHI NOAH, b. 1843, Kanesville, Hancock, Illinois. D. 12 Nov 1850/4, Kanesville, Illinois.

SAMUEL, b. 12 Oct 1846, Kanesville, Pottawatomie, Iowa. D. 25 Mar 1847, Kanesville, Iowa.

SAMUEL, 7 Aug 1849, Kanesville, Iowa. Md. 4 Mar 1872, Louisa Giles. D.25 Jul 1932, Springville, Utah.

ABNER NEWMAN, b. 1 Mar 1852, Utah. Md. 5 Mar 1873, Olive Amanda Fullmer. D. 28 Mar 1915, Utah.

ANNA MARY ANNIE, b. 21 Jan 1854, Springville, Utah. Md. 18 Dec 1871, Edwin Lucius Whiting. D. 10 Jun 1929, Mapleton, Utah, Utah.

CELESTA, b. 6 Dec 1855, Springville, Utah. Md. 10 May 1875, Franklin H. Whitmore. D. 25 Feb 1931.

The rest of the children did not designate which mother.

LOVINA JANE, 13 Feb 1858, Springville, Utah. Md. 5 Jan 1878, Moses Franklin Farnsworth. D. 12 Mar 1913, Manti, Utah.

AARON, b. 9 Jan 1860, Springville, Utah. Md. 26 Nov 1883, Alice Sophia Gledhill. D. 18 Oct 1928, Vermillion, Utah.

WILLIAM SUMMERS, b. 6 Apr 1862, Springville, Utah. D. 5 Jun 1887, Springville, Utah.

GEORGE ALBERT, b. 30 Jul 1864, Springville, Utah. Md. 21 Mar 1896, Amelia Victoria Sorensen. D. 15 Mar 1948, West Jordan, Utah.

CHARLES EDWARD, b. 17 Jan 1868, Springville, Utah. D. 1869, Springville, Utah.

EMMA LEONA, b. 21 Jul 1870, Springville, Utah. Md. 2 Jan 1890, John Henry Tew. D. 22 Dec 1941, Salt Lake City, Utah.

Submitted By: Lowell Parkinson

NOAH SUMMERS BULKLEY

Born: 27 Jun 1776, Trumball, Fairfield, Connecticut
Parents: Aaron and Elizabeth Wakelee Bulkley
Died: 22 Dec 1851, Kanesville, Potowatomie, Iowa
Arrived in Valley: 1848, Isaac Higbee Co

Married: Nancy Ann Newman
Date: 1807, Stratford, Fairfield, Connecticut
Died: 1858, Springville, Utah, Utah

Noah was a wagon master who helped bring some of the saints to the Valley in the Isaac Higbee Company of 1848. He was a frontiersman and farmer. He died in Kanesville, Iowa, on one of his return trips to that state.

Children:

LUCINDA, b. 26 Mar 1808, Catherine, Tioga, New York. Md. 23 Nov1879, Ephraim Woodard. D. 26 Nov, 1879.

LOUSINA, b. 30 Mar 1808, Catherine, Tioga, New York. Md. Ephraim Woodard. D. 23 Nov 1879.

SALLY, b. 30 Apr 1810, Catherine, Tioga, New York. Md. Enos Woodward. D. 10 Jul 1868.

ABNER, b. 22 Oct 1811, Catherine, Tioga, New York. Md. Sarah McArthur. D. 26 Dec 1879.

NANCY, b. 17 Dec 1813, Catherine, Tioga, New York. Md. Frank Lawrence. D. 20 Aug 1850.

IRA, b. 3 Jan 1816, Catherine, Tioga, New York. D. 3 Sep 1816.

NEWMAN, b. 18 Aug 1817, Catherine, Tioga, New York. Md. 1st, 7 Jan 1844, Jane Draper. Md. 2nd, 5 Mar 1857, Jovina Palmer. Md. 3rd, Mar 1872, Mary Nixon. D. 19 Sep 1893, Springville, Hancock, Illinois.

ELMIRA, b. 30 Jan 1820, Catherine, Tioga, New York. Md. 16 Jun 1838, Abraham Day III. D. 24 Dec 1905, Castle Dale, Emery, Utah.

Submitted By: Lowell Parkinson

LOUIS DEMOTT BUNCE

Born: 29 Sep 1827, Walcott, Wayne, New York
Parents: James Aven Ludlow and Ester Bunce
Died: 16 Sep 1899, Price, Utah
Arrived in Valley: 1852

Married: Elmira Voorhees
Date: 28 Oct 1852, Salt Lake City, Utah

Born: Hamilton Co., Ohio
Parents: Elisha and Nancy Ann Leak Voorhees
Died: 23 Dec 1881, Pettyville, Utah

After Louis Demott joined the Church, he came to the Valley in 1852 and married Elmira who had come west with her parents in 1851 in the Erastus Snow Company.

Louis was a veteran of the Blackhawk and Mexican War. He went on a mission to England from 1875 to 1879. He made his living as a farmer and mason. He invented a churn. He married sisters, Sarah Ann and Emma Eliza Sudweeks. There is not a record of all his wives but it is believed that he had seven. There is a record of 16 of his children, the rest are unknown.

Sarah and Emma remarried after seven years he had been gone. They were declared legally deserted. He did return to visit them when he was older. Seven of his children were born in Manti, Utah, four in Parowan, two in Springdale, one in Rockville, and two in Pettyville, Utah. Louis had a set of twins, Rosa Belle and Ara Belle. His daughter, Sarah Delila, had two sets of twins, Roene and Irene Syrett and Clinton and Clara Syrett.

Known Children:

ESTER ANN, b. 20 Sep 1853, Manti, Utah. Md. Jasper Larsen.
LEWIS AVERY, b. 5 Oct 1854, Manti, Utah. Md. Betsy Jeff.
MARY ELIZABETH, b. 8 Nov 1855, Manti, Utah. Md. William
    Dixon.
WARREN ALONZO, b. 14 Jan 1857, Manti, Utah.
AUSTIN MORONI, b. 8 Apr 1858, Manti, Utah. Md. Ella Burns.
JOSEPH DELANEY, b. 16 Sep 1861, Manti, Utah. Md. Emily
    Maretta Johnston.
ALMIRA MATILDA, b. 6 Apr 1860, Manti, Utah. Md. Neils C.
    Christensen.
WILLIAM FRANKLIN, b. 4 Oct 1863, Springdale, Utah. Md.
    Mamie Pollock.
DIANTHA ADELINE, b. 8 Sep 1 865, Springdale, Utah. D. in
    Parawan, Utah.
JANE, b. 23 Jan 1867, Rockville, Utah.

SARAH DELILA, b. 8 Jun 1868, Parowan, Utah.

ROSABELLE, b. 30 Mar 1968, Parowan, Utah.

ARABELLE, b. 30 Mar 1968, Parowan, Utah.

LAURA LUELLA, b. 8 Sep 1870, Parowan, Utah, Md. Peter Christensen

URBEN ROSS, b. 14 Jun 1875, Pettyville, Utah. Md. Ethel Warnick

JOHN HOMER, b. 25 Aug 1880, Pettyville, Utah. Md. Marnie Ann Gallagher.

Submitted By: J. L. Crawford

JAMES LOVETT BUNTING

Born: 5 Oct 1832, Attleboro, Norfolk, England
Parents: Thomas and Early Lovett Bunting
Died: 20 Nov 1923, Provo, Utah
Arrived in Valley: 21 Jun 1858, John Berrey

Married 1st: Harriet Dye
Date: 15 May 1859, Salt Lake City, Utah
Died: 26 Jan 1893, Kanab, Kane, Utah

Married 2nd: Esther Mayers
Date: 1897

James Lovett was apprenticed at the boot and shoe making trade and became very good at it. His parents were devout members of the "John Wesley" church and became very upset when James joined the Mormon Church. He became a missionary and traveled over the Norwich and Manchester conferences for three

413

years. In 1858 he emigrated to Utah with the elders who had been called home because of the Johnston Army problem.

They passed the fortifications erected in the Johnston's Army conflict and arrived in Salt Lake to find a beautiful city empty of inhabitants. They traveled on to Provo where they met President Young. When the saints returned to Salt Lake, James came too and worked for Brigham Young. He was made a special policeman during this time. He started a boot and shoe making business and was able to rent a little cottage, and he was married.

He was called to help with the Indian problems and helped guard Fairview for a time. He built a nice home and did well in his business. He was asked to help settle Kanab. He remained active in the church and did much to help those in need. In 1875 he was appointed an appraiser in the United Order. He served in the stake presidency until called on a mission to England.

Upon his return home, he built and operated the first tannery in Kanab. Not only was he active in the church but took an active part in politics. He was a probate judge of Kane County. In 1893, he went on another short term mission to England and while there he gathered many names of his family for genealogical work.

In 1897 he married Esther Mayers and moved to St. George where he worked in the temple. He and Esther eventually separated. At the age of 89, he was compelled to discontinue his work at the temple due to ill health. He returned to Kanab where he lived with his children until his death.

Children:

HARRIET ELIZA, b. 1 May 1860.
ELLEN ELIZABETH, b. 21 Jan 1861.
JAMES LOVETT, 19 Feb 1864.
ANI, b. 15 Dec 1865.
JOSEPH WILLARD, b. 8 Jul 1868.
JAMES EBENEZER, b. 28 Aug 1870.
ROBERT WILLIAM, b.7 Jan 1873.
CARRIE, b. 23 Sep 1875.
WALLACE OWEN, b. 16 Dec 1876.
ALICE ZINA, b. 10 Feb 1879.

FANNIE, b. 26 May 1881.
ALMO, b. 10 Sep 1883.

Submitted By: Kristie Palfreyman

HARRISON BURGESS

Born: 3 Sep 1814, Putnam, Washington, New York
Parents: William and Vilate Stockwell Burgess
Died: 10 Feb 1883, Pine Valley, Washington, Utah Arrived in Valley: 1 Jun 1850, Aaron Johnson Co.

Married: Sophia Minerva Foster
Date: 1 Jul 1835, Kirtland, Ohio
Born: 12 Apr 1810, Madison, New Haven, Connecticut
Parents: Orrin and Rachel Crampton Foster
Died: 12 Sep 1889, Woodruff, Rich, Utah
Arrived in Valley: 22 Sep 1848, Brigham Young wagon train

Married 2nd: Amanda Melvina Hammond
Date: 6 Feb 1846, Nauvoo, Hancock, Illinois
Born: 6 May 1827, Foxcroft, Penobscot, Maine
Parents: Benjamin and Almeda Longley Hammond
Died: 8 Aug 1882, Pine Valley, Washington, Utah
Arrived in Valley: 22 Sep 1848, Brigham Young wagon train

Harrison first heard the gospel in 1832, accepted it and was baptized. He, and his father's family journeyed to Kirtland in 1834. They met the Prophet and were converted. He went with the saints to Jackson County, Missouri. When they were compelled to leave, he brought his family out and eventually settled in Nauvoo. He was instrumental in helping many others during this time.

He served several missions. At the time of the exodus of Nauvoo, he and Sophia, and a polygamous wife Amanda Melvina Hammond, were sealed in the Nauvoo temple. He took Sophia to Winter Quarters and then returned for Amanda. He was called on a mission to England but felt he should see his family safely out west. Brigham Young felt he should go on the mission, so he prepared his family for the trek west, then left for his mission.

He returned and arrived in the Valley in 1850 to find his family all well. He settled his family in Parley's Park in Summit County where he ran a dairy and built a saw mill. Two years later he was called to help settle St. George. In the spring they settled in Pine Valley where they stayed. He remained active in the church and the community and was blessed and prospered.

Children of 1st wife:

MARY ALMEDA, b. 8 Feb 1849, Salt Lake City, Utah. Md. 10 Oct 1868, William Gardner. D. 29 Dec 1881, Pine Valley, Washington, Utah

HARRISON JOSEPH (twin), b. 13 Jun 1851, Salt Lake City, Utah. Md. 17 Nov 1873, Emma Snow. D. 21 Jun 1931, St. George, Utah.

BENJAMIN HAMMOND (twin), b. 13 Jun 1851, Salt Lake City, Utah. Md. 25 Dec 1874, Erazma Rogers. D. 8 Jan 1931, Burley, Cassia, Idaho.

SOPHIA MINERVA, b. 20 Feb 1853, Salt Lake City, Utah. Md. 2 Mar 1877, Gabriel Utley. D. 13 Mar 1910.

AMANDA MELESSA, b. 19 Apr 1855, Salt Lake City, Utah. Md. 11 Oct 1869, Henry Slade. D. 4 Dec 1929.

ABRAM WILLIAM, b. 16 Jul 1857, Salt Lake City, Utah. Md. 30 Dec 1880, Jane Sarah Rogers. D. 3 Oct 1936.

ISAAC HENRY, b. 23 Apr 1859, Salt Lake City, Utah. Md. 1st, 20 Mar 1878, Penelope Thomas. Md. 2nd, 20 Mar 1896, Elizabeth Joanna Keys. D. 21 Mar 1938.

CLARISSA JANE, b. 20 Jul 1861, Park City, Summit, Utah. Md.

1st, 20 Mar 1878, William Joseph Lillywhite. Md. 2nd, 22 Oct 1884, William Bracken. D. 16 Feb 1944.

SARAH VILATE, b. 15 Feb 1864, Pine Valley, Utah. Md. 4 Oct 1880, William Edward Bunker. D. 6 Jun 1897, Pine Valley, Utah.

JACOB LEANDER, b. 21 Sep 1866, Pine Valley, Utah. D. 23 Jan 1882.

PHILIP JOHN, b. 17 Apr 1870, Pine Valley, Utah. D. 17 Feb 1872.

Submitted By: Barbara Roach

WILLIAM BURGESS, SR.

Born: 21 May 1794, Putnam, Washington, New York
Parents: Christian (Chris John) and Hannah Newland Burgess
Died: 20 Nov 1880, Pine Valley, Washington, Utah
Arrived in Valley: 22 Sep 1848, Brigham Young Co.

Married: Violate Stockwell
Date: 1 May 1813, Chesterfield, Cheshire, New Hampshire
Born: 10 Oct 1794, Windham County, Vermont
Parents: Abraham and Violate Gale Stockwell
Died: 21 Jul 1880, Pine Valley, Washington, Utah
Arrived in Valley: 22 Sep 1848, with husband

William and Violate lived in Punam and Argyle in New York. Their sons were kept constantly at work and had little opportunity for an education. When their son Harrison joined the Church and decided to move to Kirtland, Ohio, William stayed behind to take care of some business, but soon joined his family. They met the

Prophet and were soon convinced and joined the church in 1835.

William was an industrious man, being able to obtain work wherever he went. He was a skillful blacksmith and carpenter. He helped build the Kirtland Temple. He and his family journeyed to Missouri with the saints and were there when they were driven out. William and his family settled in Lima, Illinois, 20 miles from Quincy.

When the saints were driven out of Illinois, William and his sons made a skein for fishing and furnished fish for the Company, as well as hunting for meat. Upon their arrival in Salt Lake, they settled on the Avenues for 10 years before moving to Parley's Park in Park City where they stayed for two years. Then they were called to St George to help with the work there. They settled in Pine Valley outside of St. George, where they remained. William, being the oldest man in the area, was called "Grandad" by everyone. He remained faithful to the church all his life.

Children:

HARRISON, b. 3 Sep 1814, Putnam, Washington, New York. Md. 1st, 1 Jul 1835, Sophia Minerva Foster. Md. 2nd, 6 Feb 1846, Amanda Melvina Hammond. D. 10 Feb 1883, Pine Valley, Utah.

HORACE, b. 23 Jan 1816, Putnam, New York. Md. 1st, 6 Mar 1836, Iona Almira Pulsipher. Md. 2nd, Bolania Pulsipher. D. 17 Jun 1849, Winter Quarters.

ROSINA, b. 29 Mar 1818, Putnam, New York. Md. George Lyman.

HYRUM, b. 5 May 1819, Putnam, New York. D. 7 Jul 1819, Putnam, New York.

ABRAHAM, b. 3 Sep 1820, Putnam, New York. Md. Symanthia Cheney. D.9 Nov 1846, Warren, Henderson, Illinois.

WILLIAM, b. 1 Mar 1822, Putnam, New York. Md. 1st, 17 Sep 1840, Maria Pulsipher. Md. 2nd, 3 Jun 1852, Charlotte Ligette. Md. 3rd, 21 Feb 1858, Catherine Chamberlain. D. 14 Mar 1904.

HANNAH, b. 1 Feb 1825, Hague, Warren, New York. Md. Alonzo Jones. D. 9 Oct 1846, Winter Quarters.

FREDERICK, b. 5 Feb 1827, Hague, New York. D. Oct 1843, Galena, Illinois.

PHILIP, b. 9 Jan 1829, Hague, New York. D. Oct 1843.

MELANGTHON WHEELER, b.14 Jul 1831, Dresden, New York. Md. 10 Apr 1855, Margaret Jane McIntyre. D. 8 Dec 1855.

VILATE, b. 21 Feb 1837, Kirtland, Ohio. Md. Richard C. Gibbons. D. 9 Dec 1913.

Submitted By: Barbara Roach

ALFRED BURNINGHAM

Born: 18 Nov 1838, Farnham, Surry, England
Parents: Thomas and Sarah Elizabeth White Burningham
Died: 26 May 1927, Bountiful, Utah
Arrived in Valley: 27 Aug 1860, by Handcart

Married: Mary Ann Barrett
Date: 9 Sep 1865, Salt Lake City, Utah
Born: 1848, Deptford, Kent, Engand
Died: 12 Aug 1940, Bountiful, Utah

Alfred was introduced to the Church through the missionaries in 1857 and joined with all of his family, except his oldest brother. In 1860, Alfred, with his brother Thomas and sister Sarah, sailed for America. They pulled a handcart all the way to Utah, arriving in 1860. They settled in Bountiful. A year later their parents and other siblings joined them.

In 1867-68 Alfred joined a group of men to lay the railbed for the railroad near Echo Canyon. With his love of music, he composed the song "Echo Canyon," which was sung for many years. Upon his return, he made bricks for a home, the first in Utah. He had a good garden and sold his produce in Salt Lake. He and some friends established the Salt Lake Fruit and Vegetable Market, which ran for many years.

He was a devoted and active member of the church all his life. He remained active in community affairs. He was about six feet tall, and weighed about 180 lbs. Mary Ann was only about five feet tall and weighed about 120 lbs.

Children:

ALFRED, b. 1865. Left home in 1880's. Was never heard of again.
JOHN HENRY, b. 1858. Md. Emma Ann Corbridge. D. 1951.
MARY ELIZABETH, b. 1871. D. 1872.
MARY ANN, b. 1873. Md. Orsen Sessions. D. 1948.
JAMES WILLIAM, b. 1875. D. 1881.
WILLIAM, b. 1878. Md. Hulda Matilda Thomas. D. 1938.
MARTHA, b. 1879. Md. John W. Moss. D. 1932.
DAVID, b. 1881. D. 1884.
HEBER GEORGE, b. 1884. Md. Hannah Sessions. D. 1958.
BRY HENRY, b. 1885. Md. Jennie Turner. D. 1965.
FLORA VICTORIA, b. 1889. Md. Peter Leonard Hepworth. D. 1962.

Submitted By: Mark Nichols

JAMES BURRUP

Born: 14 Apr 1831, Ashfield, Leigh Parish, Worcester, England
Parents: John & Ann Phillips Burrup (James was christened "James Phillips," son of unwed mother, Ann Phillips.)

Died: 15 Mar 1888, Ogden, Utah
Arrived in Valley: 1849, George A. Smith Co.

Married 1st: Mary Ann Bennett (Kay)
Date: 26 Jan 1855, Kaysville, Utah
Born: 26 Apr 1837, Churchstile, Cradley Parish, Hereford,
    England
Parents: Thomas & Mary Twinberrow Wattis (Kay) Bennett
Died: 18 Dec 1863, West Weber, Utah
Arrived in Valley: 1848, Willard Richards Co.

Married 2nd: Mary Cocker Clegg
Date: 9 Feb 1867, Salt Lake City, Utah
Died: 21 Mar 1923, Ogden, Utah

James was christened when he was three days old. When he was 18 months old, his mother married his father, John Burrup, a freight hauler and carpenter from a neighboring parish. He grew up in the West Midlands where the main product was raising of hops for brewing.

James learned to drink alcohol at an early age, a habit that plagued him off and on for the remainder of his life. His mother died when he was young so he was partly raised by his widowed grandmothers. His father remarried in 1839.

In 1840, Wilford Woodruff introduced the gospel to the area where he lived and, before long, members of James family, including his two grandmothers, joining the church. In 1841, 10 year old James, with his two grandmothers and other relatives, sailed for America. James never saw his father and stepmother again.

James was baptized at Nauvoo in 1844. His grandmother Burrup died about this time. Records are incomplete but it is supposed that James accompanied his grandmother Phillips to Utah in 1849. The family settled in the area now known as Kaysville, Utah.

After the Utah War (Johnston's Army), the Burrups and Kays were among the first families to settle in West Weber, where James was appointed constable. He was friendly to the Indians. James

421

moved his family to Ogden in 1864, where he continued farming. He ran a butcher shop, livery stable and freight-hauling business. He was active in the community. He played the bass drum in the Ogden Brass Band. He called dances and, during the winter months, had a dancing school for children and adults.

He applied for citizenship in 1871. In 1877 he moved to Marsh Valley, Idaho, where he established a cattle ranch. He was postmaster, hauled railroad ties and was a juror. In the mid 1880's he and Mary returned to Ogden where he died in 1888.

Children of 1st wife:

MARY ANN, b. 1856. Md. George Edward Hellewell. D. 1939.
JEANNETTA, b. 1858. Md. 1st, Samuel Henry Delamaterf (Div.)
    Md. 2nd, Ferdinand William Cobabe. D. 1893.
JAMES JR., b. 1859. Md. Julia Hellewell (Div). D.1925.
WILLIAM, b. 1861. Md. Hannah Maria Byington. D. 1924.
JOHN, b. 1863. Md. 1st, Mary Elizabeth Quigley. Md. 2nd, Elsie
    Emmagene Shurtliff.
WILLIAM CLEGG (stepson), b.1857. Md. 1st, Mary Van Noy.
    Md. 2nd, Caroline Van Noy. D. 1940.

Submitted By: Jay Burrup

WILLIAM BUSBY

Born: 1 Jul 1820, Old Weston, Huntingdon, England
Parents: John and Ann Chapman Busby
Died: 1 Aug 1898, Woods Cross, Davis, Utah
Arrived in Valley: Jun 1859. Capt. Robert F. Neslin

Married 1st: Mariah Meadows
Date: 23 Oct 1846, Radcliffe, Lancster, England
Born: 19 Apr 1818, Great Staughton, Huntingdon, England
Parents: James and Maria Woodward Meadows
Died: 22 May 1906, Woods Cross, Davis, Utah

Sealed to: Mary, Alice and Hannah Allen
Date: 24 Oct 1868

Married 2nd: Elizabeth Muntz
Date: 17 Jun 1873, Utah
Died: 22 May 1906, Bur. Bountiful City Cemetery, Utah

William was a farmer in England. While he was courting Mariah, he heard the Mormon missionaries and accepted the gospel. William was baptized in 1846 and Mariah in 1847. They had a great desire to immigrate to the Valley. An elderly couple offered to pay their way if William would help them go too. They crossed the ocean and made their way to Winter Quarters. From there they joined Captain Robert F. Neslen's company for the trip west. Their sixth child was born enroute.

They were sent to Paris, Bear Lake, Idaho, to help settle the area, where they remained three years before moving to Meadowville, Utah. While in Paris, they had to feed the Indians to keep them friendly. William did some freighting between Wyoming and Laketown, Utah, when he met his second wife. Brigham Young had asked him previously to be sealed to the three Allen sisters, which he did. Later on, William moved his families to St. David, Arizona, for awhile. As he got older, he and Mariah moved to their youngest daughter's home in Laketown, Utah, and then their final move was to Bountiful, Utah.

He and his family remained active in the church and were active participants in the various communities in which they lived.

Children of 1st wife:
ANNIE MARIA, b. 28 Aug 1847, Birmingham, England. Md. 4 Nov 1863, Charles William Mann. D. 21 May 1974.

JOHN JAMES, b. 29 Aug 1849, Birmingham, England. Md. 27 Oct 1867. Rosannah Taylor. D. 22 Sep 1905.

SARAH JANE, b. 11 Dec 1851, Birmingham, England. D. 11 Feb 1853.

SAMUEL WILLIAM, b. 1 Feb 1854, Birmingham, England. D. 2 Mar 1854.

WILLIAM JOSEPH, b. 15 Nov 1856, Birmingham, England. D. 5 Sep 1858.

MARY ELIZABETH, b. 13 Aug 1859, Sweetwater River, Wyoming.

Children of 2nd wife:

HENRY CONRAD, b. 1875.
EMMA LOUISE, b. 1876.
CHARLES WILLIAM, b. 1880.

Submitted By: L. Hoffman

JOHN BUSHNELL

Born: 19 Apr 1823, Headington, Oxford, England
Parents: John and Elizabeth Collins Bushnell
Died: 29 Jul 1882, Meadow, Millard, Utah
Arrived in Valley: 1 Oct 1850, Joseph & Lorenzo Young Co.

Married: Elizabeth Mainwaring Brockbank
Date: 15 Aug 1854, Fillmore, Utah
Born 8 Nov 1839, Liverpool, Lancs, England

Died: 16 Sep 1926, Meadow, Millard, Utah

John's father was a stone mason and quarryman. John was not interested in learning this trade. He and a friend were more interested in going to America.

Finally, in 1849, they took passage with some saints and arrived in New Orleans in December 1849. Having been exposed to the gospel, John was baptized in 1850 and joined the Lorenzo Young wagon train as a driver.

He lived in Farmington and American Fork but became homesick and wanted to return home. He was promised if he would remain in Utah that he would be blessed. Brigham Young sent him to Fillmore where he met and married Elizabeth.

They ran the first post office and a store. In 1862, he moved his family to Meadow in Millard County where he farmed and made a living. He later took all the sheep in Meadow and went into the sheep business. He remained faithful to the church, his family, and community. He was loved by all.

Children:

JOHN, b. 23 Sep 1856, Fillmore, Utah. Md. Frances Elizabeth Ferguson.
ISAAC, b. 28 Sep 1858, Fillmore, Utah.
EDWARD, b. 22 Jul 1860, Fillmore, Utah.Md. Catherine Hayes Dame.
DANIEL, b. 22 Jun 1862, Fillmore, Utah.Susan Dearden.
HOWARD, b. 12 Jan 1865, Meadow, Utah. Md. Mary Elizabeth Labrum.
JOSHUA, b. 25 Feb 1867, Meadow, Utah. Md. Ann Dearden.
ELIZABETH, b. 11 Apr 1869, Meadow, Utah. Md. William Hyrum Bennett.
ELIZA JANE, b. 25 Dec 1871, Meadow, Utah. Md. Allison Alger Stott.

Submitted by: Dayle White

JOHN LOWE BUTLER

Born: 8 Apr 1808, Simpson Co., Kentucky
Parents: James and Charity Low Butler
Died: 10 Apr 1860, Spanish Fork, Utah, Utah
Arrived in Valley: 16 Oct 1852, Eli B. Kelsey Co.

Married 1st: Caroline Farozine Skeen
Date: 3 Feb 1831, Simpson Co., Kentucky
Born: 15 Apr 1812, Sumner Co., Tennessee
Parents: Jesse and Keziah Taylor Skeen
Died: 4 Aug 1875, Panguitch, Utah

Married 2nd: Charity Skeen–No children
Date: 23 Dec 1844, Nauvoo, Illinois
Born: 15 Mar 1808, Sumner, Tennessee
Died: 7 Jul 1854

Married 3rd: Sarah Lancaster–No children
Date: 28 Feb 1846, Nauvoo, Illinois

Married 4th: Sarah (Briant) Lancaster (Mother to Sarah)
Date: Early March 1846, Nauvoo, Illinois
Didn't cross plains. Said she was too old.

Married 5th: Ann Hughes–No children
Date: 9 Mar 1857, Salt Lake City, Utah
Parents: Robert and Alice Edwards Hughes

Married 6th: Lovisa Hamilton
Date: 9 Mar 1857, Salt Lake City, Utah

Born: 25 Sep 1857, Mendon, Adams, Illinois
Parents: Andrew and Malissa Hamilton
Died: 9 Jul 1924, Smithfield, Cache, Utah.

Married 7th: Ester Emily Hogden
Date: 9 Mar 1857, Salt Lake City , Utah
Div: Aug 1857

Married 8th: Heneretta Seaton Blythe
Date: 6 Sep 1857, Salt Lake City, Utah
Born: 6 Jun 1831, Newton Parish, Scotland.
Parents: Charles and Isabel Brown Blythe
Died: 10 Aug 1924, Cleveland, Bannock, Idaho

John's autobiography written by him says he stood six feet two and one half inches tall and was "stout." He had blond hair and blue eyes. He was baptized in 1835.

In the spring of 1836, a group of the saints in Kentucky moved to Missouri in Ray County. When they were forced to leave, they settled near Far West and then at Adam-on-Diahman. They settled in Quincy in 1839 until they were able to build a home in Nauvoo. John was set apart as a body guard to Joseph Smith.

When the saints started west, President Young asked John and his family to accompany the James Emmett Company because Emmett was a maverick. John was to try to keep the members of the Company from leaving the church. He faced challenges in connection with this calling but eventually brought his family to the Valley in the Eli Kelsey Company. He was the blacksmith for the Company.

The family settled near Palmyra, Utah, where John helped build Fort St. Luke. He served as a bishop of the combined branches, now known as Spanish Fork. He lived there until his death.

Children of 1st wife:

KENION TAYLOR, b. 17 Nov 1831, Simpson, Kentucky. Md. 16 Dec 1854, Olivve Artemeshy Durfey. D. May 1886, Spanish Fork, Utah.

WILLIAM ALEXANDER, b. 20 Apr 1833, Simpson, Kentucky. D. 4 Aug 1833.

CHARITY ARTEMESIA, b. 13 Jul 1854, Simpson, Kentucky. Md. 1st, 4 Oct 1855 (Div), Hamilton Monroe Wallace, Sr. Md. 2nd, 18 Oct 1862, Amos Griswold Thornton. D. 9 Dec 1908, Pinto, Washington, Utah.

KEZIAH JANE, b. 25 Feb 1836, Kentucky Co., Tennessee. Md. 2 Jan 1856, Lemuel Hardison Redd. D. 15 May 1895, New Harmony, Utah.

PHOEBE MELINDA, b. 16 Dec 1838, Kentucky Co, Tennessee. Md. 5 Dec 1854, George Washington Sevy. D. 14 Aug 1892, Panguitch, Utah.

CAROLINE ELIZABETH, b. 29 Dec 1839, Adams, Illinois. Md. 8 Apr 1857, George Wilkins. D. 3 Feb 1866.

SARAH ADELINE, b. 15 Feb 1841, Nauvoo, Illinois. Md. 1st, 9 Mar 1867, Philo Allen. Md. 2nd, 28 Jun 1895, John Henry Tuttle. D. 20 Jun 1 923, Panguitch, Utah.

JOHN LOWE II, b. 20 Feb 1844, Nauvoo, Illinois. Md. 1st, 23 Jun 1873, Nancy Franzetta Smith. Md. 2nd, 10 Apr 1882, Sarah Sariah Johnson. D. 30 Dec 1898, Richfield, Sevier, Utah.

JAMES, b. 5 Feb 1847, Ponca, Dixon, Nebraska. Md. 2 May 1874, Charlotte Elizabeth Topham. D. 27 Mar 1900, Provo, Utah.

LUCY ANN, b. 23 Feb 1849, Potowattamie, Iowa. Md. 9 Oct 1866, Joseph Penn Barton. D. 18 Aug 1935, Paragona, Iron, Utah.

THOMAS, b. 9 May 1851, Potowattamie, Iowa. D. 16 Apr 1892.

ALVERETTA FAROZINE, b. 26 Mar 1854, Spanish Fork, Utah. Md. 2 Oct 1871, James Coupe Robinson. D. 12 Jan 1940, Paragona, Utah.

Children of 6th wife:

LOVISA PATIENCE, b. 24 Dec 1858, Spanish Fork, Utah D. 17 Nov 1924, Clarkston, Utah.

Children of 8th wife:

ISABELLA ELIZABETH, b. 11 Jun 1856, Spanish Fork, Utah. D. 25 Nov 1872.

JOHN WILLIAM, b. 11 Aug 1860, Spanish Fork, Utah. Md. 28 May 1890, Betty Christina Bulow. D. 12 Nov 1939, Newdale, Fremont, Idaho.

Submitted by: Theda Judd, Ross Butler and Lorna Belnap

JOHN LOWE BUTLER, II

Born: 28 Feb 1844, Nauvoo, Hancock, Illinois
Parents: John Lowe and Caroline Skeen Butler
Died: 30 Dec 1898, Richfield, Sevier, Utah
Arrived in Valley: 1852, Eli B. Kelsey

Married 1st: Nancy Francetta Smith
Date: 23 Jun 1873, Salt Lake City, Utah
10 children from this union.

Married 2nd: Sarah Sariah Johnson
Date: 10 Apr 1882, Salt Lake City, Utah

John Lowe was the eighth of 12 children and just a small child when his parents started west. After finally joining the Eli Kelsey Company, they made their way west and finally arrived in the Valley. John was eight years by the time they arrived. He helped herd cattle and sheep as they crossed the plains. They settled in Palmyra (Spanish Fork).

He was a husky young man and worked at farming, hauling timber, caring for cattle, horses and sheep. By the time his father died, he became the head of the house. The older children were married. At the age of 19, he moved the family to Paragonah, near Parowan, Utah. A year later they moved on to Panguitch, becoming the first settlers there. The land was good but there was trouble with the Indians, which resulted in the Black Hawk War. The family left during the war but returned after.

John participated in an exploration mission. Butler Wash was named for him. At a dance one night he was hit on the head, which necessitated an operation to remove part of his skull to relieve the pressure. He recovered.

He moved his family to Joseph, then Jerico, Elsinore, and finally Richfield. He spent six months in prison because of his polygamous marriage. He was a good man and tried to help those around him.

Children of 1st wife:

JOHN III, Md. Bertha Thurber.
ZETTIE, Md. John Christensen.
SADIE, Md. Gomer Morgan Richards.
CAROLINE, Md. Isaac Erin Thurber.
HORACE CALVIN, Md. Ida Gould.
OLIVE, Md. Jesse Loren Smith.
JANE, Md. Elmer Walter Nielson.
KENION TAYLOR, Md. Thelma Neoma Peterson.
EVA, Bailey Allen Dixon.
LELAND THOMAS, Md. Helen Camille (Carter) Phelps.

Children of 2nd wife:

Six children three of whom lived to maturity.
DENISON "DEN."
MARY.
ANN.

Submitted by: Ross Butler

PETER BUTLER (PEHR PHERSON BOTLER)

Born: 28 Sep 1817, Torreberge, Malmohus, Sweden
Parents: Pehr and Elna Hansdotter Larson
Died: 2 Aug 1899, Santaquin, Utah, Utah
Arrived in Valley: Sep 1857

Married: Anna Nelson
Date: 27 Dec 1846, Nevishog, Malmohus, Sweden
Died: 7 Nov 1922, Santaquin, Utah, Utah

Pehr's father was in the navy and was given the name of Bottler which the family used until they came to America, then it was Americanized to Butler.

Pehr was a skilled tailor as a young man. A few years after his marriage to Anna, they were converted to the Church and were baptized in 1853. His mother, who was also a convert, left with Pehr, his wife, and two daughters. Through various experiences, they finally arrived in New Orleans and then up river to St. Louis.

They started out on the plains but their daughter died two days later. Another daughter was born at Mormon Grove. At this point Pehr (Peter) decided they would wait until his brothers and sisters, and their spouses, arrived. In 1857 they arrived and they pooled their resources and purchased a wagon, oxen and some cattle. Because their wagon was too heavily loaded, they had to lighten it by discarding some things.

When they arrived in Salt Lake, they decided to settle in Spanish Fork. They gleaned in the fields to obtain enough grain to make bread for the coming winter.

In 1860 they moved to Moroni but the Indians were such a problem that in 1866, they moved to Santaquin. Peter purchased some land, built a log house, and operated an old flour mill. He raised livestock and did tailoring. They remained active in the church and civic affairs.

Children:

ELNA, b. 29 Dec 1847, Malmohus, Sweden.
KARMA, b. 15 Apr 1852, Malmohus, Sweden. D. Mar 1855, Achism, Kansas.
CAROLINE, b. 10 Sep 1856, Mormon Grove, Kansas.
HETTIE (ETTA), b. 15 Oct 1859, Spanish Fork, Utah.

Submitted by: Louise Johnson

WILLIAM RICHARD BUTLER

Born: 16 May 1848, Merthyr Tydfil, Glamorganshire, Wales
Parents: William and Ann Morris Butler
Died: 19 Oct 1903, Tropic, Utah. Died of stomach cancer.
Arrived: 2 Oct 1856, Edward Bunker Handcart Co.

Married 1st: Eliza R. Snow Alexander
Date: abt 1868, Cottonwood, (Holladay) Utah

Married 2nd: Elizabeth Fischer
Date: 12 Jan 1881, St. George, Utah
Divorced when children were in their teens

Married 3rd: Susan Clarissa Williams Heaton–No children
Date: 12 Jan 1881, St. George, Utah (Div)

William's father and four of his children died of cholera shortly before the sailing date of William's mother and her daughter and William. William was only eight when they left. William's mother made the decision to leave the burial to another daughter as the fare for the trip had already been paid. It was not an easy thing to do. Nine days before they landed, William turned eight.

When they reached Iowa City, the handcarts were not ready so they had to help build them. They were in the third handcart company. William's mother and sister became ill with cholera and were to be left behind, but the family prayed, and they were able to go on with the Company. About a month after their arrival in the Valley, William was baptized.

They settled in what is now the Holladay/Cottonwood area of the valley, where William received some education. His mother was set apart as a midwife. They were sent to Ogden to live. His mother married Ira Rice. They were called to settle the Beaver Dam area, southwest of St. George. Because of difficulties, they were advised to return north. After William's marriage, they settled in Orderville, Utah, where their children were born and raised. When the Order broke up, they moved to Escalante where they lived until 1895, then they moved to Tropic, Utah.

William loved music, which he taught and wrote. He loved to sing and was the choir leader. He and his sons formed a quartet and sang together. He raised potatoes, worked at a lumber mill, and carried the mail. He also painted some pictures. He remained active in the church and community.

Children of 1st wife:

WILLIAM IRA, b. 14 Sep 1869, Washington, Utah.
MYRZA ANN, b. 12 Dec 1872, Panguitch, Utah.
ELIZABETH JANE, b. 9 Jul 1875, Panguitch, Utah.
LAURA MARY, b. 23 Jan 1878, Orderville, Utah.
JOHN RANDOLPH, b. 25 Apr 1880, Orderville, Utah.
HENRY MORRIS, b. 9 Jul 1882, Orderville, Utah. D. age 11.
HYRUM ALEXANDER, b. 1 Nov 1884, Escalante, Utah.
2 UNNAMED CHILDREN, about 1887, Escalante, Utah.
HANNA ELIZA, b. 25 Jan 1887, Escalante, Utah.

MERIAM,(twin) b. 29 Jun 1889, Escalante, Utah. D. same day.
MARY ANN,(twin) b. 29 Jun 1889, Escalante, Utah.
2 UNNAMED CHILDREN, about 1889, Escalante, Utah.
GEORGE ANDREW, b. 2 Sep 1889, Escalante, Utah.
REATHA, b. 15 Sep 1894, Escalante, Utah.

Children of 2nd wife:

ELIZABETH ANN, b. 8 Mar 1882, Orderville, Utah.
JACOB ALMA, b. 14 Jan 1884, Orderville, Utah.
KATHERINE, b. 8 Mar 1886, Escalante, Utah.

Submitted by: Jared Baldwin

HIRAM NORTON BYINGTON

Born: 19 Aug 1800, Wolcott, Connecticut
Parents: Daniel 111 and Susannah Norton Byington
Died: 9 Mar 1888, Menan, Idaho
Arrived in Valley: 1848, Brigham Young Co.

Married 1st: Sarah "Sally" Holkins/Hawkins
Date: 1828, Camden, Oneida, New York
Born: 3 May 1808, Colebrook, New Hampshire
Parents: Joseph and Mehitable Terry Holkins
Died: 27 Jan 1870, Ogden, Utah

Married 2nd: Henrietta Nelson–No known children
Date: 25 Dec 1849, Salt Lake City, Utah (Div)
Born: 4 Aug 1812, Bradford Co., Pennsylvania

Parents: William Oliver and Elizabeth Morris Nelson
Died: 2 Dec 1880

Married 3rd: Ann Walton Clements (widow)–No known children
Date: 1 Jan 1854,
Born: 28 Aug 1817, Carlton, Yorkshire, England
Parents: James and Mary Walton

Married 4th: Julia Phidelia Ferrin–No known children
Date: 20 Jul 1867, Utah
Born 2 Nov 1826, Castile, New York
Parents: Samuel and Olive Fidelia Coon Ferrin
Died: 12 Sep 1900, Weber Co., Utah

Hiram Norton's mother died when he was three years old. He was raised by his father and his second wife, Hannah Alcott Byington.

After Hiram's marriage to Sarah, they moved on to the Western Reserve in Northeastern Ohio. They apparently later moved near Kirtland, Ohio. Sarah and Hiram became interested in the new religion and were baptized in 1836. After moving around some, they finally moved to Nauvoo, Illinois.

When the saints left there, Hiram and his family moved to Winter Quarters and stayed there until 1848, when they traveled to the Valley. Their son Henry, at age 18 years, came west in 1847 with Jedediah M. Grant. He returned to Iowa and, in 1848, brought his parents and siblings with him in Brigham Young's company.

In 1849, Hiram was mustered into the Nauvoo Legion in Salt Lake. He married three more woman, as plural wives. As far as is known, he only had children by his first wife. He lived in Oxford, Idaho, for a short time and then moved to Menan, Idaho, where he died.

Children of 1st wife:

JOSEPH HENRY, b. 25 Jan 1829, Sheffield, Ashtabula, Ohio.
  Md. 1st Nancy Maria Avery. Md. 2nd Hannah Molland. D. 1909.

HIRAM ELLIOTT, b. 1830, Kingsville, Ohio. Md. Hannah
Dyantha Hoff. D. 1901.

CHILD, name, gender and birth date unknown (abt 1833). D. 8
Aug 1838, buried in an orchard in Bath Twnshp, Greene Co,
Ohio.

SUSAN AUGUSTA, b.25 Sep 1840, Exeter, Scott, Illinois. Md.
1st, Stephen King Wilbur. Md. 2nd Thomas Morgan. D. 1919.

Submitted by: Jay Burrup

JOSEPH HENRY BYINGTON

Born: 25 Jan 1829, Sheffield, Ashtabula, Ohio
Parents: Hyrum Norton and Sarah Hawkins Byington
Died: 22 Sep 1909, Neeley, Power, Idaho
Arrived in Valley: 20 Sep 1848, Heber C. Kimball's company

Married 1st: Nancy Maria Avery
Date: 25 Dec 1849, Salt Lake City, Utah
Born: 25 Dec 1830, Branford, McKean, Pennsylvania
Died: 25 Jan 1914, Redrock, Oneida, Idaho

Married 2nd: Hannah Molland
Date: 24 Feb 1864, Salt Lake City, Utah
Born: 21 Jul 1828, Toxeth Park, Liverpool, Lancs, England
Died: 23 Nov 1889, Annis, Fremont, Idaho

Joseph, the oldest son of Hyrum and Sarah, grew up under
the influence of the Church. He, with his parents, were a part of
the church that moved from Kirtland, Ohio, to Nauvoo, Illinois.

They remained active participants all their lives. Joseph crossed the plains before his parents at the tender age of 18. After arriving in the Valley, he returned for his parents and brought them to the valley. He returned three more times to help saints cross the plains.

In 1867, he was asked to pose for a famous pioneer picture taken by photographer Henry Martineau in Logan, Utah. He was a farmer by vocation after his marriage. He remained active in the church all his life.

Children:

JAMES HENRY, b. 4 Apr 1865, Ogden, Weber, Utah. Md. 26 Dec 1890, Sarah Mirah Carr. D. 7 Apr 1939, Lava, Bannock, Idaho.

HANNA MARIA, b. 8 Aug 1866, Calls Fort, Box Elder, Utah. Md. 9 Aug 1883, Salt Lake City, Utah. D. 22 Mar 1931, Logan, Cache, Utah

CHARLES NORTON, b. 19 Mar 1868, Calls Fort, Utah. Md. 1st, 11 Feb 1903, Ettie Sophia Smithies. Md. 2nd, 29 Jul 1936, Margaret A. Potter Price. D. 25 Dec 1953.

SARAH REBECCA, b. 24 Nov 1869, Calls Fort, Utah. D. 15 Sep 1870. Calls Fort, Utah.

MARTHA JANE, b. 25 May 1872, Nine Mile, Downey, Caribou, Idaho. Md. 27 Nov 1894, Francis Alvin Reed. D. 9 Dec 1959, Ririe, Bonneville, Idaho.

MARY ANN, b. 27 Jan 1875, Nine Mile, Bannock, Idaho. D. 14 Jun 1876, Nine Mile, Bannock, Idaho.

SUSAN ELIZABETH, b. 10 Sep 1876, Red Rock, Bannock, Idaho. Md. 5 Dec 1892, Isaiah Martin Fisher. D. 11 Mar 1956, Rigby, Jefferson, Idaho.

JOSEPH HENRY, 18 Nov 1878, Red Rock, Oneida, Idaho. D. 3 Jun 1886, Annis, Fremont, Idaho.

JOHN PARLEY, b.23 Mar 1880, Red Rock, Oneida, Idaho. Md. 20 Feb 1904, Margaret Brennetta Smith. D. 20 Feb 1964, Poplar, Bonneville, Idaho.

CLARENCE SPENCER, b. 19 Dec 1881, Red Rock, Oneida, Idaho. D. 17 Dec 1910.

Submitted by: Roma Duffin

REYNOLDS CAHOON

Born: 30 Apr 1790, Cambridge, Washington, New York
Parents: William and Mehitable Hodge(s) Cahoon Jr.
Died: 29 Apr 1861, So. Cottonwood, Salt Lake, Utah
Arrived in Valley: 23 Sep 1848, Willard Richards Co.

Married 1st: Thirza Stiles
Date: 11 Dec 1810, Newport, Herkimer, New York

Married 2nd: Lucina Roberts Johnson (widow - Peter H. Johnson)
Date: abt 1842, Nauvoo, Illinois

Married 3rd: Mary Hildrath
Date: 16 Jan 1846, Nauvoo, Illinois

Reynolds was probably given his great grandmother's maiden name. It is 20 years later in 1810, before we hear of him again in Newport, New York, where he married Thirza. The following year he and Thirza moved to Harpersfield, Ashtabula, Ohio, where five children were born. He purchased land there.

In 1829 he moved his family to Kirtland, Ohio, and went into the business of tanning leather, making boots and shoes. During this time, the "Golden Bible" was creating quite a stir in the area. Reynolds soon became satisfied that it was of divine origin and was baptized. From that time on, his life was devoted to the church. He served several missions. In early May 1833, he and Hyrum Smith and Jared Carter were appointed to obtain means to build a building for the first presidency, a school house and a "house for printing." It wasn't long until the committee's responsibility included a temple.

Reynold participated in the dedication of the Kirtland Temple. In the spring of 1838, the Cahoon family left Kirtland for Far West, Missouri, where he served in the stake presidency of two stakes.

From Missouri, the family moved to Nauvoo. He was again appointed to a committee to build a temple. In spite of problems and opposition from outsiders, the temple was finally completed and dedicated. During this time he married Lucina in polygamy. He was sealed to all three wives.

In March 1846, the Cahoon families left Nauvoo for the west. After arriving in the Valley, Reynolds was involved in keeping the roads in repair, managing the church farm, and acting as judge or counter of game for the extermination of ravens, hawks, wolves, and foxes, etc. He spoke at general conference and was sustained as first counselor to the High Priest Quorum.

Reynolds sold his property in Salt Lake to the city for the building of the Salt Lake Theater. He moved his family to South Cottonwood, where he lived for a time with his son Andrew.

Children of 1st wife:

WILLIAM FARRINGTON, b. 7 Nov 1813, Harpersfield, Ohio.
LERONA ELIZA, b. 25 Oct 1817, Harpersfield, Ohio.
PULASKI, b. 18 Sep 1819, Harpersfield, Ohio.
DANIEL STILES, b. 7 Apr 1822, Harpersfield, Ohio.
ANDREW, b. 4 Aug 1824, Harpersfield, Ohio.
JULIA AMINA, b. 24 Sep 1830, Kirtland, Ohio. D. 9 Jan 1831.
    Child.
MAHONRI MORIANCUMER, b. 26 Jul 1834, Kirtland, Ohio.

Children of 2nd wife:

LUCINA JOHNSON, b. abt 1843, Nauvoo, Illinois. D. Child.
RAIS BELL CASSON, b. 13 Oct 1845, Nauvoo, Illinois.
TRUMAN CARLOS, b. 18 Jan 1850, Salt Lake, Utah. Unmarried.
    D. 4 Feb 1911, Bur. Pleasant Green, (Magna) Utah.

Submitted by: Helena Page

ALEXANDER CALDERWOOD

Born: 22 Dec 1836, Delmuir, Scotland
Parents: William and Janet Brooks Calderwood
Died: 1 Dec 1883, Coalville, Utah
Arrived in Valley: 29 Oct 1855, Capt. Charles A. Harper

Married: Margaret Salmon
Date: 28 Dec 1862, Salt Lake City, Utah
Born: abt 1843, of Kirkintelloch, near Glasgow, Scotland
Parents: Robert Salmon
Died: 24 Nov 1923, Coalville, Utah
Arrived in Valley: Sept 1862

Alexander was a deeply religious young man and a member of the Presbyterian Church. Shortly after turning 18, he left his home in search of work which he found in a cotton printing factory at Kirkintelloch, near Glasgow, Scotland. His supervisor, Robert Salmon, became impressed with Alexander and invited him to his home. He soon became like a member of the family. He was invited to attend church with them and was soon baptized into the Mormon Church. It wasn't long before he felt the urge to join the saints in America. He returned home to bid his family goodbye and then bid farewell to the Salmons. He promised their 12 year-old daughter, Margaret, he would send for her.

Upon his arrival in the Valley, he worked for Brigham Young for a short time and then obtained employment with Fenimore Little, receiving a pair of boots in pay for the first week's work. They were too small and he gave them away. He determined to search for work in the outlying area. He found work and a home with the Warren Reynolds' family.

He was called by Brigham Young to help build fortifications in Echo Canyon as a defense against Johnston's army. Later he was sent to St. George to help colonize that area. He worked in Cottonwood Canyon cutting cord wood and timber.

He saved his money and sent for Margaret Salmon, seven years after he had left her in Scotland, and they married. In the spring of 1863, they went to Coalville, Utah, where Alexander had obtained employment on the Allen farm. He helped with everything on the farm, eventually freighting supplies to Fort Bridger. He helped bring in immigrants from Wyoming.

They taught their children to read and write, and other subjects. They all loved the gospel and were devoted members of the church. Alexander loved the youth and served in the Young Men's presidency for many years. He was much sought after as a speaker. He was a great whistler and often whistled for dances. He was kind and generous to everyone including the Indians.

He had planned on a mission but was caught in a storm and became ill as a result, and died at age 47 years.

Children:

ALEXANDER, b. 8 Jul 1864, farmer.
WILLIAM ROBERT, b. 12 Apr 1866, medical doctor.
MARY WEIR, b. 29 Jan 1868, dressmaker, homemaker.
ROBERT SALMON, b. 22 Oct 1869, farmer, accountant, office worker.
JOHN M., b. 25 Nov 1871, teacher.
WALTER, b. 1 Feb 1873, farmer.
JAMES SALMON, b. 30 Nov 1874, dentist.
MARGARET JANET, b. 21 Jan 1877, homemaker.
AGNES ELIZABETH, b. 27 Dec 1878, teacher, homemaker.
ISABELLE, b. 23 Oct 1880, sales clerk, homemaker.
JENNIE, b. 17 Oct 1882, office worker, homemaker.

All the children married and died between the ages of 47 years to 100 years.

Submitted by: Helen Hunter Alldredge

MATTHEW CALDWELL

Born: 11 Jun 1822, Mt Vernon, Jefferson, Illinois
Parents: Curtis and Nancy Hood Caldwell
Died: 15 Mar 1912, Dry Fork, Uintah, Utah
Arrived in Valley: 8 Sep 1850, Aaron Johnson Co.

Married 1st: Barzilla Guymon
Date: 17 Oct 1843, Carthage, Hancock, Illinois
Born: 31 Dec 1823, Jackson County, Tennessee
Died: 7 Nov 1869, Fountain Green, Sanpete, Utah

Married 2nd: Synthelia Guymon–No children
Date: 30 May 1852, Salt Lake City, Utah
Born: 15 Feb 1837, Mount Paris, Edgar, Illinois
Died: 27 Mar 1871, Parowan, Iron, Utah

Married 3rd: Nancy Butler
Date: 8 May 1854, Salt Lake City, Utah
Born: 14 Mar 1830, Calhoun Co., Illinois
Died: 8 Dec 1895, Heber, Wasatch, Utah

Married 4th: Amanda Jane Moore Ivie
Date: 20 Dec 1961, Salt Lake City, Utah
Born: 12 May 1824, Georgetown, Brown, Ohio
Died: 18 May 1863, Fountain Green, Sanpete, Utah

Married 5th: Nancy Mariah Lane
Date: 20 Nov 1865, Salt Lake City, Utah
Born: 14 Feb 1838, Bowling Green, Clay, Indiana
Died: 9 Nov 1920, Vernal, Uintah, Utah

Matthew was an early settler of Adams and Hancock Counties in Illinois. He assisted Brigham Young in purchasing lands and later cattle and horses in Hancock County, Illinois. He joined the Mormon Battalion as a private. He assisted in the burial of members of the Donner Party.

He came to the Valley with a wife and two children in 1850 and was captain of the second division of fifty. He survived cholera on the plains and lived to build the first cabin in American Fork, Utah in 1850-51.

He was the first mayor of Spanish Fork, Utah. He was one of the presidents of the 50th Quorum of Seventies, captain in Walker and Black Hawk Indian Wars, colonizer in Nephi, Fountain Green, and Dry Fork, Utah. He was the Deseret agricultural agent at Fountain Green in 1862, and delegate to Utah Legislature. He remained active in the church.

Children:

THOMAS JEFFERSON, b. 17 Jul 1844, Green Plains, Hancock, Illinois. Md. 17 Oct 1864, Mary Ann Peterson. D. 19 Dec 1929.

ALMIRA RACHEL, b. 7 Dec 1846, Council Bluffs, Iowa, Md. George Washington Horace. D. 14 Jan 1919.

CURTIS WASHINGTON, b. 14 Jan 1849, Council Bluffs, Iowa. Md. 10 Sep 1869, Almira Chase. D. 14 Feb 1926, Emery, Utah.

MELISSA JANE, b. 7 Apr 1851, Spanish Fork, Utah. Md. 22 Mar 1869, William Henry Adams, Jr. D. 12 Mar 1939, American Fork, Utah

MATTHEW, b. 9 Mar 1853, Springville, Utah. D. 28 Aug 1854, Springville, Utah.

WILLIAM GUYMON, b. 25 Jun 1855, Springville, Utah. Md. Eleanor Emerett Gillespie. D. 13 Nov 1943, Salt Lake City, Utah.

SARAH ELIZABETH, b. 5 Oct 1857, Spanish Fork, Utah. Md. 19 Dec 1882, Stephen Nathan Daniels. D. 6 May 1934, Menan, Idaho

JOHN EDGAR, b. 31 Jul 1860, Ephraim, Sanpete, Utah. Md. Mary Margaret King. D. 13 Jan 1941.

BARZILLA, b. 28 Mar 1863, Fountain Green, Utah. D. 1 Jun 1863, Fountain Green, Utah.

JAMES MARTIN, b. 19 Nov 1864, Fountain Green, Sanpete, Utah. Md. Mary Anna Montana Abercrombie. D. 13 Dec 1911, Parowan, Utah.

Children of 3rd wife:

NANCY JANE, b. 14 Dec 1855, Spanish Fork, Utah. Md. 29 Jun 1879, James Monroe Gardner Pyper. D. 7 Jul 1929, Heber City, Utah

HARRIET REBECCA, b. 5 Dec 1857, Spanish Fork, Utah. Md. 23 July 1885, Allen Cox. D. 18 Mar 1844, Cornelius, Washington, Oregon.

JULIA ANN, b. 16 Mar 1860, Fountain Green, Utah. Md. 16 Nov 1871, George Albert Chase. D. 19 Mar 1935, Idaho Falls, Idaho.

CHARLES BUTLER, b. 26 Apr 1865, Fountain Green, Utah. Md. 1885, Lydia Ann Stevens. D. 19 Apr 1929, Caldwell, Idaho.

Children of 4th wife:

AMANDA VETURIA, b. 13 May 1863, Fountain Green, Utah. Md. 14 Dec 1882, Thomas Henry Wilson. D. 26 Sep 1936, Payson, Utah.

Children of 5th wife:

MATTHEW LANE, b. 11 Sep 1866, Nephi, Juab, Utah. D. 10 Dec 1939.

NOAH ELLIS, b. 19 Feb 1869, Chicken Creek, Juab, Utah. Md. 25 Jun 1892, Ida Louisa Bradley. D. 17 May 1949, Maeser, Uintah, Utah.

DAVID CLARANCE, b. 27 Oct 1872, Fountain Green, Utah. Md. 23 Mar 1892, Salley Viola Hall. D. 6 Aug 1939, Salt Lake City, Utah.

GEORGE WILDING, b. 25 Jan 1875, Fountain Green, Utah. Md. 25 Sep 1896, Mary Olive Searle. D. 14 Jul 1963, Salt Lake City, Utah.

ERNEST MARCELLOUS, b. 2 Mar 1878, Fountain Green, Utah. D. 14 Aug 1889, near Dry Fork, Uintah, Utah.

BURTON LEE, b. 20 Sep 1880, Fountain Green, Utah. Md. 14 Feb 1900, Unknown. D. 2 Mar 1953, Vernal, Utah.

Submitted by: Maud Pack

ANSON CALL

Born: 13 May 1810, Fletcher, Franklin, Vermont
Parents: Cyril and Sally Tiffany Call
Died: 31 Aug 1890, Bountiful, Davis, Utah
Arrived in Valley: 19 Sep 1848, Brigham Young Co.

Married 1st: Mary Flint
Date: 3 Oct 1833, Madison, Lake, Ohio
Born: 27 Mar 1812, Braintree, Orange, Vermont
Parents: Rufus and Hannah Haws Flint
Died: 8 Oct 1901, Bountiful, Davis, Utah

Married 2nd: Anna Maria Bowen
Date: 15 Apr 1851, Utah
Born: 3 Jan 1834, New York
Died: 26 Jul 1924, Utah

Married 3rd: Margaretta Unwin Clark
Date: 7 Feb 1857, Utah

Born: 28 May 1828, England
Died: 12 Dec 1908, Utah

Married 4th: Emma Summers
Date: 24 Feb 1857, Utah
Born: 5 Aug 1828, England
Died: 22 Sep 1912, Utah

Married 5th: Henrietta Caroline Williams
Date: 9 Apr 1861, Utah
Born: 26 Sep 1826, New York

Married 6th: Ann Clark (Waldrus)
Date: 24 Jan 1870, Utah
Born: 26 Sep 1826, New York
Died: Unknown

After the martyrdom of the Prophet, Anson was called to assist Sheriff Backenstoes in helping prevent the mob from committing outrages against the saints.

He was bishop in three wards in Bountiful, Utah, from 1849-1851, 1874-77. In 1851 he was called to help settle Parowan, Utah, and was Justice of Peace there. He was appointed Probate Judge of Millard County and represented them in the Legislature.

Brigham Young called him to help settle Fillmore and Anson was a postmaster and Deputy Marshall while there. He was then called to help settle Carson Valley, Nevada. With his sons, he took part in the Echo Canyon problem. He founded Calls Fort in Box Elder County. He was a counselor to President William R. Smith at the organization of Davis Stake.

He was an adjutant in the Silver Grays (Mountain Sharps) and helped in the rescue of the Martin Handcart Company. He was a successful merchant and farmer and helped with the construction of the railroad. He was a loyal member of the church.

Children of 1st wife:

ANSON VASCO, b. 9 Jul 1834. Md. 1st, 28 Jan 1853, Charlotte

Holbrook. Md. 2nd 10 Nov 1856, Eliza Catherine Kent. D. 4 Aug 1867.

MARY VASHTA, b. 27 Mar 1836. Md. 10 Apr 1853, Ira Curtis Parke. D. 11 Aug 1920.

CYRIL MORONI, b. 6 Feb 1838. D. 9 Jul 1846.

CHESTER,(twin), b. 13 May 1841. Md. 1st, 12 Jan 1860, Agnes Melissa Loveland. Md. 2nd, 6 Jul 1869, Mary Angeline Packer. Md. 3rd, 9 Dec 1872, Sarah Maria Dickson. Md. 4th, 16 Jun 1886, Pamela Elizabeth Barlow. D. 26 Jan 1908.

CHRISTOPHER,(twin), b. 13 May 1841. D. 13 May 1841. Child.

HYRUM, b. 14 Nov 1845. D. 15 Jun 1846. Child.

RUTH PIEDE, b. abt 13 May 1849. Md. 25 Dec 1864, James Henry Davids. D. 19 Sep 1919. (Bought from the Indians in Fillmore, Utah.

Children of 2nd wife:

VILATE, b. 27 Jul 1852. D. 10 Jun 1862.

ISRAEL, b. 2 Jul 1854, Md. 1st, 21 Dec 1874, Medora White. Md. 2nd, 11 Jun 1880, Jane Lucinda Judd (Knight). D. 23 Nov 1938.

VENTENTIA, b. 14 Feb 1856. D. 19 Apr 1862. Child.

VIOLA, b. 16 Jun 1858. Md. 6 Nov 1879, James George. D. 2 Oct 1929.

ANSON BOWEN, b. 20 Oct 1863. Md. 1st, 4 Nov 1885, Mary Theresa Thompson. Md. 2nd, 13 Dec 1890, Harriet Casier. Md. 3rd, 11 Mar 1898, Dora Pratt. Md. 4th, 21 Jan 1903, Julia Sarah Abegg. D. 2 Jan 1958.

HARRIET LOUISA, b. 8 Apr 1856. Md. 9 Sep 1885, William Charles Mann. D. 16 Nov 1932.

Children of 3rd wife:

MARY, b. 24 May 1858. Md. 28 Jan 1874, Thomas Waddoups. D. 4 Dec 1916.

CYLISTA, b. 4 Apr 1860. Md. 19 Oct 1876, Mark Waddoups. D. 3 Jul 1907.

SAMANTHA EVELINE, b. 25 Nov 1861. Md. 4 Mar 1880, William Charles Mann. D. 28 Apr 1848.

CYNTHIA, b. 20 Feb 1864. Md. 16 Dec 1880, Thomas Waddoups. D. 8 Jan 1946.

WILLARD, b. 25 Apr 1866. Md. 1st, 19 Apr 1886, Adelaide White. Md. 2nd Leah Pratt. D. 18 Jun 1945.

AARON, b. 3 Jul 1868. Md. 24 Sep 1890, Samantha A. Willey.

Children of 4th wife:

ANN, b. 22 Mar 1858. Md. 24 Jan 1876, Keplar Sessions. D. 8 Oct 1926.

FANNY, b. 11 Aug 1860. Md. 28 Nov 1878, Truman Heap Barlow. D. 30 May 1916.

LUCINA, b. 8 Apr 1863. Md. 13 Apr 1882, Jasper Newton Perkins. D. 23 Jul 1957.

DAVID, b. 20 Jun 1868. Md. 2 Dec 1891, Eliza Dittmore. D. 16 Sep 1943.

SARAH, b. 8 Dec 1870. Md. 30 Jun 1887, Truman Heap Barlow. D. 7 May 1944.

Submitted by: Junith Roberts, Amy Howell, and H. L. Roberts

ANSON VASCO CALL

Born: 9 Jul 1834, Madison, Lake, Ohio
Parents: Cyril Anson and Mary Flint Call
Died: 4 Aug 1867, near Rock Creek, Wyoming
Arrived in Valley: 19 Sep 1848, Brigham Young Co.

Married 1st: Charlotte Holbrook
Date: 28 Jan 1853, Madison, Lake, Ohio

Married 2nd: Eliza Cathcrine Kent
Date: 10 Nov 1856, Salt Lake City, Utah
Born: 29 Feb 1836, Suffield, Ohio
Died: 4 Feb 1908/9, Auburn, Lincoln, Wyoming

Anson Vasco remembered all his life the time he viewed the bodies of Joseph and Hyrum Smith after they were murdered. His parents thought it was something that even a young boy should see. It made a deep impression on him, so much so that he remained active in the church all his life.

He served a mission to England in 1864. But he was released early because of ill health and he never returned home because he died on the way in Rock Creek, Wyoming. His body was brought home and buried in Bountiful, Utah.

Children:

CHESTER VINSON, b. 6 Oct 1859, Bountiful, Utah. Md. 1st 28 Oct 1880, Annis Jeanette Barlow. Md. 2nd Minnerette (Minnie) Barlow. D.16 Jan 1943, Salt Lake City, Utah. Bur. Blackfoot, Idaho.

SIDNEY BENAJAH, b. 27 Dec 1861, Bountiful, Utah. Md. 26 Nov 1884, Henrietta Columbia (Nettie) Loveland. D. 21 Sep 1906, Chesterfield, Carbou, Idaho.

IDA, b. 26 Feb 1863, Bountiful, Davis, Utah. Md. 5 Mar 1882, Ptolmus Philadelphus (Dilla) Walton. D. 28 Nov 1934, Evanston, Wyoming.

Submitted by: Amy Howell

CYRIL CALL

Born: 29 Jun 1785, Woodstock, Windsor, Vermont
Parents: Joseph and Mary Sanderson Call
Died: 23 May 1873, Bountiful, Davis, Utah
Arrived in Valley: 27 Oct 1849, Ezra T. Benson Co.

Married: Sarah (Sally) Tiffany
Date: 6 Apr 1806, Cambridge, Franklin, Vermont
Born: 27 Nov 1790,; Cambridge, Franklin, Vermont
Parents: Christopher and Rebecca Ellis Tiffany
Died: 15 Mar 1856, Bountiful, Davis, Utah

Cyril was introduced to the Church early in his life. He was always active, being the first member of the Call family to join the church. On his way west, he lived for a time in Kirtland, Ohio, and contributed aid in the building of the temple at Kirtland.

Cyril followed the saints to Nauvoo and from there to the Valley. He endured the torments and hardships that early members of the church had endured. He willingly brought his family to the valley and settled in Bountiful. He died at the advanced age of 88 years. He had lost the sight in his left eye in an accident at an earlier age.

Children:

HARVEY, b. 6 Sep 1808, Fletcher, Franklin, Vermont. Md. 22 Jan 1841, Mary Ann Lougy. D. 18 May 1849, Leavenworth, Kansas.
ANSON, b. 13 May 1810, Fletcher, Vermont. Md. 1st, 3 Oct

1833, Mary Flint. Md. 2nd, 15 Apr 1851, Anna Maria
Bowen. Md. 3rd, 7 Feb 1857, Margaretta Clark. Md. 4th,
27 Feb 1857, Emma Summers. Md. 5th, 9 Apr 1861,
Henrietta Caroline Williams. Md. 6th, 24 Jan 1870, Ann
Clark. D. 31 Aug 1890, Bountiful, Utah.

SALMON, b. 27 Jul 1812, Fletcher, Vermont. D. 1813, Fletcher,
Vermont. Child.

SAMANTHA, b. 15 Nov 1814, Fairfax, Franklin, Vermont.
Md. 28 Apr 1839, Jeremiah Willey. D. 13 Nov 1905,
Bountiful, Utah.

FANNY, b. 11 May 1816, Fairfax, Vermont. Md. 1st, 15 Feb
1838 Chester Loveland. Md. 2nd, Chester Corless. D. 20
Nov 1899.

LUCINA, b. 29 Sep 1819, Mentor, Lake, Ohio. Md. 28 Jan 1845,
Perregrine Sessions. D. 27 Jun 1904, Bountiful, Utah.

JOSIAH HOWE, b. 12 Aug 1822, Madison, Lake, Ohio. Md.
1st, 1 Mar 1846, Henrietta Caroline Williams. Md. 2nd, 14
Jan 1856, Christiantha Nielsen. D. 7 Oct 1858, Chicken Creek,
near Scipio, Utah.

MARY, b. 21 Feb 1824, Madison, Lake, Ohio. Md. 20 Jan 1846
Perrigrine Sessions. D. 25 Nov 1865.

ROSALINE SONORA, b. 29 Dec 1826, Madison, Lake, Ohio.
Md. 2 Feb 1845, Fortunastus Dustin. D. 5 Mar 1906.

SARAH, b. 19 Dec 1828, Madison, Lake, Ohio. Md. 1st, 1847,
Samuel Mecham. Md. 2nd, 1853, Nathaniel Calander Martin
Hanchett. D. 4 Sep 1886. Bountiful, Utah.

MELISSA, b. 29 Mar 1830. Md. 29 Mar 1846, Russell Gideon
Brownell D. 31 Aug 1888.

OMER,(twin) b. 9 Jan 1834. Md. 1st, 25 Oct 1855, Sarah
Marie Ferrin. Md. 2nd, 30 Mar 1867, Eleanor Jones. D. 14
Sep 1909.

HOMER, (twin) b.9 Jan 1834. Md. 10 Jul 1856, Nancy
Merrell. D. 12 Jul 1908.

Submitted by: Junith Roberts, Amy Howell, H. L. Roberts

WILLIAMS WASHINGTON CAMP

Born: 23 Dec 1800, Warren Co, Georgia
Parents: Cecillous (Cecil) and Margaret Williams Camp
Died: 21 Nov 1875, Brighton, Salt Lake City, Utah
Arrived in Valley: Oct 1850, Orson Hyde/Shadrock Roundy Co.

Married 1st: Diannah Greer
Date: Sealed, 29 Mar 1852, Endowment House, Salt Lake City,
    Utah
Born: 28 Nov 1806, Sampery, Tennessee
Parents: James and Susannah Searcy Greer
Died: 18 Mar 1876, Kimball, Basque, Texas

Married 2nd: Sarah Bradley
Date: Sealed, 9 Jun 1852, Endowment House, Salt Lake City, Utah
Born: 1822

Married 3rd: Elizabeth Brooks
Date: Sealed, 22 Dec 1854, Endowment House, Salt Lake City,
    Utah
Born: 16 Dec 1805, England

Married 4th: Amelia Evans
Date: Sealed 17 Feb 1857, Endowment House, Salt Lake City,
    Utah
Born: 8 Apr 1839, Flintshire, Wales

Married 5th: Ann Quamby
Date: Sealed 24 Feb 1857, later cancelled in 1858
Born: 2 May 1841.

Married 6th: Della Chadwick
Date: Sealed 2 Mar 1857, Endowment House, Salt Lake City, Utah
Born: 25 Mar 1838, Overton, Tennessee

Married 7th: Marion Lindsay McLean, widow
Date: 1865
Born: 22 Jun 1828, Wanlockhead, Dumfrishire, Scotland

Williams was the father of 23 children: Diannah 15, Amelia six, Marion two.

It was while William and Diannah were living in Tuscaloosa, Alabama, that they first heard the teachings of the Mormon missionaries. Wilford Woodruff stayed for a time in their home. Williams was baptized soon after, probably in 1842, and his wife a year later. They were a deeply religious family and had many interesting experiences to strengthen their faith.

When the saints were getting ready to leave Nauvoo, he was asked to furnish some horses and mules to help the saints, which he did. William was a tall, strong man. Once when attacked by some "Mormon haters," he overcame them with a sledge hammer and irons. He owned several slaves as was the custom in the South. When he came west he sold them all except three, one of which was a woman who had taken care of the children.

Three years after their arrival in the Valley, William built a large two story adobe house on what is now known as South Temple, between 2nd and 3rd East. When his wife received an inheritance from her father, they purchased a piano back east. It was one of the first in the valley. Brigham Young had the first. He entered into plural marriage to help support some of the single sisters and widows who had no means of support.

He remained faithful to the church and was a good father, husband, and provider. He was a fine entertainer and loved to play his violin, dance and sing Southern and Negro songs at dances and parties. He was a fine southern gentleman and active member of the church.

His 23 children were not listed.

Submitted by: Ruby Draper

BENONI CAMPBELL

Born: 10 Feb 1800, Deer Park, Orange, New York
Parents: Johnathan and Phoebe Button Campbell
Died: 4 Jul 1850, near North Platt River, Nebraska
Arrived in Valley: He died on the way west

Married: Mary Leonard
Date: abt 1820
Died: 30 Jun 1850 near North Platt River, Nebraska, shortly before her husband. Their children came to the valley with the help of those in the wagon train.

Benoni joined the Church in the 1830's and moved to Kirtland, Ohio, to be with the main body of the church. He helped build the Kirtland Temple. When the saints moved to Nauvoo, he and his family went with them. In 1846 they moved to Mount Pisgah and, then a few years later, they moved to Holt County, Missouri.

In 1850 they went to Kanesville, Iowa, and started west with the Stephen Markham Company. On the way many of the Company were stricken with cholera. Benoni, his wife Mary, their son Heber, and several others in the Company died. Their son, John, wrote "we buried them by the roadside." The children managed to make a home in the Valley.

Children:

ELIZABETH, b. 7 Mar 1822, New York.
MATHEW, b. 25 Dec 1823, New York
SOLOMAN FREDERICK, b. 29 Aug 1825, Hornby, Steuben, New York.

SAMUEL, b. 4 May 1827, Hornby, Steuben, New York.
JOHN, b. 3 Sep 1828, Hornby, Steuben, New York.
DEBORAH, b. 26 Jul 1830, Kirtland, Geauga, Ohio.
GEORGE H., b. 22 May 1832, New York.
HENRY, b. 29 May 1834, New York.
HULDA HENRIETTA, b. 16 Jul 1835, New York.
JOSEPH HYRUM, b. 15 Aug 1837, Kirtland, Ohio.
HARRIET MELISSA, b. 5 Sep 1839, Kirtland, Ohio.
ELISHA LEONARD, b. 22 Mar 1841, Kirtland, Ohio.
HEBER K., b. 7 Mar 1845, Kirtland, Ohio.

Submitted by: Lynn Ottesen

ELISHA LEONARD CAMPBELL

Photograph
not
available

Born: 22 Mar 1841, Kirtland, Geauga, Ohio
Parents: Benoni and Mary Leonard Campbell
Died: 19 Sep 1912, Portneuf, Bannock, Idaho
Arrived in Valley: 1 Nov 1850

Married 1st: Naomi Elizabeth Spicer
Date: 17 Feb 1862, Providence, Utah
Born: 15 Oct 1844, West Sparta, Livingston, New York
Parents: John and Annie Smith Spicer
Died: 9 Dec 1927, Los Angeles, California

Married 2nd: Unknown. She left and went to Oregon with their
   two children.

Elisha was next to the youngest child when his parents died

on the way west to the Valley. He was nine years old. Members of the wagon train helped the young family finish the trip and his older brothers and sisters made a home for them all. Four of the 13 children died young.

According to records, Elisha lived for a short time in Farmington, and then went to Weber County where his brother Samuel lived. He lived with Samuel for a time and then moved to Ogden Hole, later North Ogden. He was listed among the original settlers of Providence, Cache, Utah, when it was settled in 1859. He apparently lived there with another brother, Joseph Hyrum.

After his marriage to Naomi, they moved to Millville, Cache, Utah. By 1868 they had moved again to Hyrum, Utah, where they stayed for the next 20 years.

At the request of church authorities, he took a second wife. On 21 June 1887, he was arrested for violating the Edmunds Act, found guilty, fined $50 and sentenced to six months in prison. After his release from prison, Elisha and Naomi moved their family to Idaho. They lived in Eagle Rock, (later called Idaho Falls.) In 1905, they moved to the Napa-Santa Rosa, California area, where they lived for one year before returning to Shelley, Idaho.

Elisha was a large man, six feet four. He died after falling down a ladder and breaking his back. Naomi passed away in Los Angeles as a result of being hit by an ice truck while crossing the street.

Children:

ELISHA LENARD, b. 4 Jan 1864. D. 27 Nov 1866.
BENONA NELSON, b. 27 Mar 1865. D. 17 Jan 1939.
JOHN ACY, b. 17 Oct 1868. D. 10 May 1936.
ANNA DIANA, b. 10 May 1870. D. 9 May 1961.
MARY ELIZABETH, b. 10 Mar 1875. D. 9 Jun 1911.

Submitted by: Lynn Ottesen

JOHN ACY CAMPBELL

Born: 17 Oct 1868, Hyrum, Cache, Utah
Parents: Elisha Leonard and Naomi Elizabeth Spicer Campbell
Died: 10 May 1936, Huntington Park, California

Married: Lillie Rosebud Ellis
Date: 1 May 1892, Idaho Falls, Bingham, Idaho
Born: 25 Dec 1876, Corinne, Box Elder, Utah
Parents: Wilburn Gaught and Phoebe Ann Skerry Ellis
Died: 10 Nov 1900, Idaho Falls, Idaho

John Acy's childhood was spent in the small farming community of Hyrum, Utah. In 1887, he moved with his family to Idaho Falls, Idaho, where he met and married Lillie Rosebud Ellis. Several months after the birth of their fourth child, Lillie died of pneumonia, being only 23 years old. John Acy took his children to his parents' homestead in Shelley, Idaho, and moved to Salt Lake City where he could take advantage of the growth in building that was going on there. He was a building contractor.

In 1920 he moved briefly to Texas, and then to Los Angeles in 1923, where he remained the rest of his life. He moved around a good deal in the Los Angeles area. He would buy, fix up, and sell homes. He also constructed many of the buildings in south and central Los Angeles. He was highly respected in his trade. He became substantially wealthy prior to the depression, then lost much of it.

He played both the violin and piano. He was five feet eleven with brown eyes. Children especially loved him. Even during the depression, he always managed to have a little candy for them or take them to the cinema.

He worked in the temple all his life. In the later part of his life, this work necessitated a trip to Mesa from Los Angeles by bus or train.

Children:

LILY MAY, b. 19 Nov 1893. D. 5 Nov 1918.
PEARL ELIZABETH, b. 19 May 1895. D. 2 Oct 1983.
JOHN ACY JR., b.14 Nov 1896. D. 21 Aug 1980.
RUTH FLORINE, b. 24 Feb 1900. D. 25 Sep 1985.

Submitted by: Lynn Ottesen

SOLOMON LENORD CAMPBELL

Born: 29 Aug 1825, Hornby, Steuben, New York
Parents: Benoni and Mary Leonard Campbell
Died: 4 Mar 1903, Lake Point, Weber, Utah
Arrived in Valley: About 1851

Married: Mary Lavina Campbell
Date: 18 Dec 1848, Bradford, Pennsylvania
Born: 26 Jun 1829, Hornby, Steuben, New York
Parents: Joel and Mercy Miranda Hill Campbell
Died: 26 Aug 1903, North Ogden, Weber, Utah

Solomon Lenord became a member of the Mormon Church with his parents and endured many of the hardships incident to the early days of the church. He, with his parents, left Ohio in 1845, moving to Nauvoo, Illinois, where they spent the winter.

They moved on to Missouri where Solomon married his second cousin.

In the summer of 1850, Solomon and his family, and his father's family, joined a company of saints who were immigrating to the Valley.

In June, the Company was stricken with the dreaded cholera. Eleven people died including Solomon's parents and his little brother Heber. He and his family continued on west and, upon arriving in Salt Lake, Solomon went north to Ogden where some of his relatives were.

He was instrumental in helping develop the area. He was the father of the first white child born in North Ogden. Actually, there were two, as the baby was a twin.

In 1852, a log school house was built and used also for meetings. There were problems with the Indians. But after President Young instructed them to build a strong fort, including room for the animals, they had little problem with the Indians.

Solomon was a builder and took a prominent part in all town improvements and building. He was much respected and liked by everyone. He remained active in the church, along with his family.

Children:

JOEL, b. 16 Jan 1850, Orange, Holt, Missouri. D. 14 Mar 1922, Corrine, Box Elder, Utah.

SOLOMON BENONI (twin), b. 15 Dec 1851, Ogden, Utah. D. 5 Dec 1917.

MARY (twin), b. 15 Dec 1851, Ogden, Utah. D. 17 Apr 1929.

CHARLOTTE, b. 28 Dec 1853, Ogden, Utah. D. 26 Jul 1914.

LEMUEL, b. 6 Nov 1856, Ogden, Utah. D. 1856. Child.

MILLIE, b. Ogden, Utah. D. 5 Sep 1956.

DAVID WILLIAM, b. 10 Aug 1858, Ogden, Utah. D. 6 Sep 1956.

WARREN, b. 31 Mar 1861, Providence, Utah.

MERCY MIRANDA, b. 10 Feb 1864, Ogden, Utah. D. Jul 1929.

DELITA, b. 12 May 1869, Ogden, Utah. D. 2 May 1937.

ROSANNA, b. 4 Oct 1872, Ogden, Utah.

WELCOME, b. Ogden, Utah.
BASURIA, b. Ogden, Utah.

Submitted by: Clair Williamson

JAMES SHERLOCK CANTWELL

Born: 24 Nov 1813, Dublin, Dublin, Ireland
Parents: Simon and Wilhelmina Sherlock Cantwell
Died: 4 Sep 1887, Smithfield, Cache, Utah
Arrived in Valley: 14 Dec 1856, Willie Handcart Co. in wagon

Married: Elizabeth Cotterell Wilkinson (Hamer)
Date: 27 Apr 1838, Prestwich, Lancashire, England
Parents: John Wilkinson and wife
Died: 2 Apr 1858, Big Cottonwood, Utah

James was sent to school early and could read and write by the time he was four. His father died when James was seven. He never got over the grief he felt at losing his beloved father. His mother died four years later.

James and his brother were raised by an uncle in Lancashire, England. They were sent to the best school, so that they might help their uncle in his cotton factory. His aunt treated the brothers unkindly and eventually James was bound out to a man for five years, to become a tailor. When he became 20, he broke his indenture to his drunken master and returned to Ireland. He moved around, working as a tailor and a school teacher.

In 1836, James went to live with the family of John Wilkinson in Manchester, where James grew to love the daughter. The marriage was met with opposition but the two met, grew close, and eventually married secretly. Three weeks later Elizabeth left a note for her parents and went to take up housekeeping with James. Her parents eventually became reconciled to the idea.

In 1842 James met the Mormon missionaries and was baptized. His wife didn't join until 1849. In 1850 James and his wife and four children started their journey to the Valley. After a hazardous trip including a hurricane, they reached America and lived in St. Louis for a time, where he was president of the ward and also on the Stake High Council.

In June 1856, they joined the Willie handcart company. James had one of the 10 wagons in the Company. When they got to Red Buttes, they camped for several days because of the bad weather and were joined by the Edward Martin handcart company. They suffered greatly but were eventually rescued by a team sent by Brigham Young. Through most difficult circumstances, they eventually arrived in Salt Lake on 14 December 1856. Their story is part of history.

Milo Andrus, an old friend, took the family to his home in Big Cottonwood. They eventually made a home there and James farmed and the boys hired out.

When Brigham Young gave the order for the saints to go south, James was preparing to leave when his wife gave birth to a new son. She died and James was left with seven children, from a new born to 17 years of age. He found a woman who would nurse the baby and they set out. They built a home two miles north of Provo where they lived until a fire burned them out. He placed his children with friends and came back to Big Cottonwood and made his home for a time and would visit his children.

In 1862, James gathered up his children and they moved to Smithfield. James was active in the church and community. He farmed, did tailoring, taught school, was considered a fine orator, and sang in choirs. He spent much time keeping journals. He helped others with records, became ward clerk, married couples, blessed babies, and was postmaster. He never remarried.

Children:

ROBERT SIMON, b. 22 Dec 1838. D. age 1 year.
JOHN, b. 25 Feb 1840. D. age 1 day.
FRANCIS ROBERT, b. 7 Apr 1841.
JAMES, b. 28 Feb 1843.
ALMA, b. 26 Apr 1845. D. age 1 year.
WILLIAM HAMER, b. 21 Apr 1846.
ELLEN, b. 24 Sep 1848.
WILHELMINA, b. 28 Dec 1850. D. 6 months old.
STEPHEN, b. 25 Jun 1852. D. age 3 weeks.
MARY ANN, b. 9 Sep 1853.
ELIZABETH COTTERELL, b. 16 Dec 1855.
LUCIUS SHERLOCK, b. 2 Apr 1858.

Submitted by: Vickie M. Prows

WILLIAM CAPENER

Born: 30 Jul 1806, London, England
Parents: Daniel and Elizabeth Capener Capener (1st cousins)
Died: 24 Jan 1894, Centerville, Utah
Arrived in Valley: 1852, Ox team and wagon

Married: Sarah Verender
Date: 26 Oct 1828, St. George Church, Hanover Square, England
Born: 2 Sep 1804, Painswick, Gloucs, England
Parents: William and Ann Nichols Verender
Died: 27 May 1863, Salt Lake City, Utah

William and Sarah had three children while in England. The family left London for America in 1834. They settled in

Poughkeepsie, New York, where their next two children were born. The next child was born in Dry Brook, Ulster, New York, in 1840.

It was 12 more years before William moved his family to Utah. They arrived in 1852 and settled in Salt Lake. His wife died 11 years later.

William married Ellen Rigby and apparently moved to Centerville, Utah, where apparently he died as he is buried there.

Children of 1st wife:

GEORGE, b. 29 Jul 1829. Md. 1849, Harriet J. Dunn. D. 24 Feb 1912.

WILLIAM, JR., b. 26 Dec 1831. Md. 1852, Harriet Dunn Hill. D. 2 Dec 1914.

LOUISA REBECKAH, b. 17 Jul 1834. Md. 1852, Joseph E. Taylor. D. 6 May 1931.

CHARLES HENRY, b. 1836.

ELIZABETH ANN, b. 22 May 1837, Poughkeepsie, Dutchess, New York. Md. 18 Mar 1854, Augustus Poor Hardy. D. 15 Oct 1918.

JANE MARIE, b. 16 Oct 1840. Md. 1856, Ephraim K. Hanks. D. 6 Jan 1926.

Submitted by: Howard Hardy

WILLIAM VAN ORDEN CARBINE

Born: 17 Feb 1835, Cairo, Green, New York
Parents: Edmond Z. and Adelia Rider Carbine

Died: 11 May 1921, Portland, Multnomah, Oregon
Arrived in Valley: 1848, Newell K. Whitney Co.

Married 1st: Sarah Jane Miller
Date: 30 May 1870, Salt Lake City, Utah
Born: 22 Mar 1849, Council Bluffs, Iowa
Parents: Henry William and Elmira Pond Miller
Died: 22 May 1902, Salt Lake City, Utah

Married 2nd: Susan Hulda Miller
Date: 25 Feb 1861, Portland, Mitnah, Oregon
Born: 11 Sep 1839, Quincy, Adams, Illinois
Parents: Daniel Arnold and Clarissa Pond Miller
Died: 26 May 1867, Farmington, Davis, Utah

    William was 13 years old when he came to the Valley with his parents. His parents joined the Church in 1841 and moved their family to Nauvoo. In 1846, they moved with the saints to the Missouri River where his father died. His mother and her children were obliged to remain at Winter Quarters until 1848 when William was baptized. After their arrival in Utah, William lived in Farmington, Davis, Utah.

    He was in the Walker Indian War, participated in the Echo Canyon Campaign, accompanied Col. C. W. West on an expedition into Marsh Valley, was one of the Salmon River relief party, and served in the Black Hawk Indian War.

    In 1870 he moved to Clarkston, Cache, Utah where he was postmaster for 10 years, constable for two years and justice of the peace for six years.

    He was in the bishopric in Clarkston. He moved to Parker, Fremont, Idaho, where he served in the same capacity for 10 years. He was on the stake high council and in 1902, a patriarch. In that year, he moved to LaGrande, Oregon, where he lived out his life.

Children of 1st wife:

WILLIAM HENRY.
ALMA MILLER.

SARAH LOVINA.
DANIEL ARNOLD.
HORTON DAVID.
ADELIA ELMIRA.
SUSAN MARY.
LUCY EUGENIA.
EVERETT VAN ORDEN.
JULIA ANER.
FRANCIS HYRUM.
CLARISSA JANE.

Children of 2nd wife:

WILLIAM ARNOLD.
EDMUND Z.

Submitted by: Gloria Faucett, Sarah Jane Miller and Jay Whitmore

CYRUS WILLIAM CARD

Born: 28 Jun 1814, Painted Post, Steuben Co., New York
Parents: William and Sarah "Sally" Sabin Card
Died: 4 Sep 1900, Logan, Utah
Arrived in Valley: 1856, Edmund Ellsworth Handcart Co.

Married 1st: Sarah Tuttle
Date: abt 1837, New York
Born: 14 May 1819, Palmyra, New York
Parents: Jesse and Diane Gillette Tuttle
Died: 11 May 1894, Logan, Utah

Married 2nd: Emma Booth
Date: 7 Nov 1859, Farmington, Utah
Born: 16 Sep 1837, Apperley, Gloucs, England
Parents: William and Ann Matty Booth
Died: 11 May 1885, Logan, Utah
Arrived in Valley: George Rowley Handcart Co.

Married 3rd: Ann Booth
Date: 16 Nov 1861, Logan, Utah
Parents: William and Ann Matty Booth

Cyrus William, while yet a youth, was apprenticed to learn the wheelwright trade. He later became an accomplished lumberman.

Cyrus and Sarah were converted to the Mormon Church and baptized in 1843 in the Ossian East Branch of the church in New York. In 1846 they moved to Park Center, Michigan. Cyrus assumed the care of his mother and siblings after his father died. They returned to New York in 1851.

In 1856, President Young authorized the use of handcarts in the journey west, the Card family joined Edmund Ellsworth in the first company, using a wagon and team. After arriving in Utah, the Cards settled in Farmington. In 1859, Cyrus traveled to Cache Valley to stake out a home site. His son Charles Ora remained to build a cabin. Cyrus returned to Farmington for his family.

In 1860 the Cards moved to Logan where they helped with the new settlement. In the meantime, Cyrus had entered into two polygamous marriages. He operated a sawmill that supplied lumber for both the Logan Tabernacle and the Logan Temple. He was on the high council and was a city councilman. He also helped establish the United Order in Logan.

At his funeral, he was praised for his commitment and dedication to the gospel, his honesty, charitable works, peaceful nature, and thrifty character.

Children of 1st wife:

ABIGAIL JANE, b. 1837. D. in 1841. Child.
CHARLES ORA, b. 1839. Md. 1st, Sarah Jane Birdno. 2nd Sarah

Jane Painter. 3rd Zina Young Williams. 4th, Lavinia Rigby. D. 1906.

POLLY CAROLINE, b. 1841. D. Teenager in 1856.

MATILDA FRANCES, b. 1852. Md. William Hyde. D. 1875.

SARAH ANGELINE, b. 1854. Md. David M. Steele. D. 1871.

Children of 2nd wife:

ALTHEA, b. 1860. Md. John Cluley Greaves. D. 1944.

CYRUS WILLIAM, b. 1862. Md. Alice Muir. D. 1943.

MARY ELLEN, b. 1864. Md. Wilford Chatterton. D. 1934.

DEWILTON BOOTH, b. 1867. Md. Sarah Ann Hochstrasser. D. 1955.

MELVIN, b. 1869. D. 1871. Child.

EMMA ANN, b. 1872. D. 1873. Child

ERNEST, b. 1874. Md. Minnie Arta Bell Hamilton. D. 1936.

DAVID BOOTH, b. 1876. Never married. D. 1933.

Submitted by: Jay Greaves Burrup

GEORGE CARLILE

Born: 11 Apr 1836, Mission, Nottingham, England
Parents: Robert and Christiana Spouncer Carlile
Died: 29 Jan 1909, Heber, Utah
Arrived in Provo: late Oct 1852, Capt Jolley Co.

Married 1st: Laura Ann Giles
Date: 25 Nov 1856, Utah
Born: 19 Apr 1837, Newark, Nottingham, England

Parents: Thomas H. and Elizabeth Susannah Moore Giles
Died: 26 May 1907, Heber, Utah

Married 2nd: Susannah Daybell (widow Pollard)–No children
Date: 31 Mar 1894, Utah
Born: 14 Aug 1848, Lincolnshire, England
Parents: Finity and Mary Draper Daybell
Died: 12 Nov 1932

George was the youngest son of Robert and Christiana. He was baptized in 1848 in England along with other members of his family. They immediately began preparations to leave for America. They left London on the ship "Zetland" in late October of 1849. They remained in St. Louis for two months making preparations, then left for Council Bluffs where they stayed until the spring of 1852.

They had their equipment ready and joined the Company for the long and difficult journey west. They arrived in Provo, Utah, in October 1852 where they stayed a month and then moved to Palmyra, later called Spanish Fork, Utah.

George, at 16, was a good worker and a big help to his father in building their home and planting crops. In 1853, Chief Walker tried to cause problems but was driven back. Three years later the Indians came again but were driven back. In 1857, George was called to help build barricades in Echo Canyon. In 1865-67, he was involved in the Black Hawk Indian War.

In 1861, he was called on a five-month mission to help bring immigrants from Missouri to the valley. Sometime after his return and marriage, he and two brothers, John and James, left Provo to establish a new home in Heber Valley. They planted and harvested a large crop of wheat and then returned to Provo to get their families.

George was listed as five feet eight when he was 16, and weighed 160 lbs; he had blue eyes and jet black hair. He had a friendly and caring disposition. He was a farmer, cattleman, and carpenter. He helped built up the towns where he lived, and particularly Heber. He was a quiet, unassuming man who loved and lived the gospel.

Children of 1st wife:

MARIA ANN, b. 3 Jun 1853, Palmyra, Utah. Md. William G.
Rasband. D. 11 Aug 1941, Heber, Utah.
SARAH JANE, b. 30 Sep 1860, Heber, Utah. Md. Caleb Moore.
D. 1 Mar 1939.
LAVINA ELIZABETH, b. 11 Apr 1863, Heber, Utah. Md.
Frederick Buell. D. 4 Jul 1943, Heber, Utah.
GEORGE ROBERT, b. 19 Jun 1865, Heber, Utah. Md. Marion
R. Neil. D. 19 Oct 1938, Heber, Utah.
THOMAS FRANKLIN, b. 26 Oct 1868, Heber, Utah. Md. Emma
Christensen. D. 7 Aug 1933, Heber, Utah.
ALFRED LORENZO, b.30 Sep 1872, Heber, Utah. Md. Jane
Neil. D. 13 May 1935, Pingree, Idaho.
WILLIAM MOORE, b. 9 Apr 1877. D. 21 Apr 1881, Heber, Utah.

Submitted by: Melvin Carlisle

JOHN CARLILE, JR.

Born: 29 Oct 1856, Spanish Fork, Utah
Parents: John and Elizabeth Williamson Carlisle Sr.
Died: 21 Jun 1902, Heber City, Utah
Arrived in Valley: Born here before railroad came.

Married 1st: Sarah Elizabeth Crook
Date: 28 Nov 1878. Salt Lake City, Utah
Born: Heber, Utah. The first white child born in Heber
Parents: John and Mary Ann Giles Crook

John was three years old when his father died. As he grew, he and his sisters helped their mother run the farm as best they could.

When John married Sarah, they came in the wagon with the Rasbands from Spanish Fork. It took a day and a half by wagon to get to Salt Lake.

After their marriage, they lived in a little log house. John raised fine horses. He often furnished teams for parades and celebrations. He brought into the valley the first pure bred stallion and also the first registered shorthorn cattle.

John was co-owner of the first binder in the valley. He directed the building of Wasatch Creamery. He played in the brass band and was constable of peace several times. Aa member of the Town Board for several terms, he helped organize the North Field Irrigation Company and was director and Water Master for several years.

He served six months of a full time mission to the Southern States, but was sent home early because of sickness. He was well liked and respected by everyone. A real contributor to the growth of the area and to the church.

Children:

JOHN WILLIAMSON, b. 16 Sep 1879. Md. 1st Emma Giles.
    2nd Anna Elizabeth Abegglan Burgener.
MARY ELIZABETH, b. 4 Feb 1881. Md. William Shaw
    McNaughton.
ELLEN, b. 12 Feb 1883. D. Mar 1883. Child.
THOMAS HEBER, b. 17 Apr 1884. D. 17 Apr 1884. Child.
ALMA SPOUNCER, b. 3 Apr 1885. Md. Edith Lewis.
FREDERICK GILES, b.17 Nov 1887. Md. Sarah Todd.
CHARLES FRANCIS, b. 13 Jun 1891. Md. Sarah Vivian
    Cummings.
HAZEL KEZIA, b. 16 Feb 1893. Md. Ernest Paul Knight.
EMMA AMELIA, b. 27 Mar 1896. Md. Joseph Alonzo Smith.
SARAH MANILA, b. 4 Sep 1898. Md. Robert Patterson.

Submitted by: Ralph Carlile

JOHN CARLILE, SR.

Born: 25 May 1825, Mission, Lincolnshire, England
Parents: Robert and Christiana Spouncer Carlile
Died: 16 Sep 1859, Heber, Utah
Arrived in Valley: Arrived in Provo in 1852

Married: Elizabeth Williamson
Date: abt 1843
Born: 22 Nov 1822, Gresburgh, Lincolnshire, England
Died: 23 Jan 1893, Heber, Utah

John was a farmer by trade but owned no land of his own. He worked for others. He loved horses and was much in demand for his work with them.

He and his family left England for America in 1850 and went on to Council Bluffs, where they remained for two years.

Upon their arrival in Utah, they went on to Provo where they made their home. After a short time there, they moved on to Palmyra and then to Spanish Fork, where they lived for a time in the fort due to the Walker Indian War. Later, he moved his family to Heber after being kicked by a horse. He died from those injuries two months later.

Children:

SARAH ANN, b. 21 Jan 1844. Md. William Eastwood.
GEORGE, b. May 1846. D. 18 Apr 1857.
CHRISTIANA, b. 17 Nov 1848. Md. William Giles.
MARY, b. 20 May 1851. Md. Mark William Jeffs.

ELIZABETH, b. 22 Jan 1854. Md. John Nelson Carroll.
JOHN JR., b. 29 Oct 1856. Md. Sarah Elizabeth Crook.
EMMA, b. 2 Mar 1859. D. 6 Oct 1860. Child.

Submitted by: Ralph Carlisle

ROBERT CARLILE

Born: 23 Apr 1789, Coleby, Lincoln, England
Parents: John and Annie Maria Foster Carlile
Died: 15 Oct 1861, Heber City, Utah
Arrived in Valley: Spring of 1852, Capt Jollcy Co.

Married: Christiana Spouncer
Date: 14 May 1817, Goxhill Parish, Lincoln, England.
Born: 1 Feb 1797, Bigby, Lincoln, England
Died: Heber City, Utah after 1861.

On 22 August 1849 most of the family of Robert and Christiana signed up to sail to America. Mary, their oldest child, was married and decided to stay in England. The fare for the family is stated as 14 pounds.

They arrived in the Valley early in 1852 and went immediately to Provo, where they stayed a month and then went on to Palmyra to live. Indian problems forced them to move to Spanish Fork where there was a fort for protection. They lived there for eight years before moving to Heber Valley in the spring of 1860. They lived out their remaining years in Heber.

Children:

MARY, b. 11 Jun 1818, England. Md. Joseph Cooper. Remained in England.

ISAAC, b. 20 Aug 1820, England. Md. Jane Priest.

JOHN, b. 16 Scp 1822. D. 30 Sep 1823, England. Child.

JOHN, b. 25 May 1825, England. Md. Elizabeth Williamson. D. 16 Sep 1859, Heber, Utah.

JAMES, b. 31 Jan, 1829, England. Md. Emily Ann Giles, Md. 2nd, Fanny Lee, Md. 3rd, Eliza Durnell and Md. 4th, Anna Rachel Moser.

ROBERT, b. 28 Jun 1832, England. D. Dec 1833, England. Child.

GEORGE, b. 11 Apr 1836, England. Md. Laura Ann Giles.

Submitted by: Ralph Carlile

JAMES CARLSON

Born: 19 Sep 1853, Ronneberga, Asmundtorp, Malmohus, Sweden

Parents: Swen and Bengta Larsson Carlson

Died: 13 May 1926, Logan, Utah (Heart problems)

Arrived in Valley: 5 Oct 1860, William Budge Co.

Married: Caroline Jenson

Date: 14 Feb 1876, Salt Lake City, Utah

Born: 12 Oct 1856, Getinge, Gardstanga, Malmohus, Sweden

Parents: Jons and Elsa Nilsson Jonsson

Died: 20 Jun 1924, Logan, Utah

James, age six, his parents, a three year old brother and five-week-old sister immigrated from Sweden to America. There was much sickness, including smallpox, aboard ship, but they all got well. When the ship docked, they were vacinated and held for several days until June 20, when they were permitted to land.

His father purchased a wagon and oxen and left in the fifth wagon company of the year. After a few days in Salt Lake, the family moved to Brigham City where they spent the winter. They moved on to Logan the next spring.

James father took a polygamous wife in 1865, then James met a lovely young Swedish girl. After their marriage, they were called, with about two hundred other families, to travel to Southern Arizona where they were to settle and try to teach the Indians. The road was non-existant further south and they made their way with difficulty.

When they arrived, they built a fort for protection. Their food was extremely scarce. They all shared the milk from one cow and finally killed off their cattle. Carolyn became so ill that they were released and went back to Logan to live.

James and his son Ezra hauled wood for one of the families and then would go back and haul some for themselves. It took all day. He farmed and worked to help others, as well as his own family. He died from heart problems.

Children:

EZRA JAMES, b. 25 Dec 1876, Logan, Utah.
IDA CAROLINE.
BETTY ELEASE.
ANNE, D. Infant.
RAYMOND WILFORD.
JOSEPH. D. Infant.

Submitted by: Thais DeGrey

SWEN CARLSON

Born: 16 Feb 1829, Ronneberga, Asmundtorp, Malmohus, Sweden
Parents: Carl and Boel Andersson Carlson
Died: 31 May 1902, Logan, Utah
Arrived in Valley: 5 Oct 1860, William Budge Co.

Married 1st: Bengta Bengtsson
Date: 17 Dec 1852, Asmundtorp, Malmohus, Sweden
Died: 29 Nov 1888, Logan, Utah

Married 2nd: Johanna Hammer
Date: 1 Dec 1865, Salt Lake City, Utah
Died: 5 Aug 1936, Logan, Utah

Swen and his wife Bengta joined the Church in Sweden. They brought their three young children to America with them. Their family was quarantined because they caught smallpox on board ship. They managed the best they could. When they arrived in New York they, were held at the dock for five days along with others, before they were permitted to land.

They traveled by rail to Florence, Nebraska. Swen purchased a wagon and two oxen and they left with the William Budge Company. When he left Sweden, he had considerable money, but traveling expenses, plus purchasing the wagon and equipment to go west, had eaten heavily into it so that by the time they arrived in the Valley, he only had 25-cents left.

The Carlsons stayed in Salt Lake a few days and then went north to Brigham City where they spent the first winter, and then went on further north to Logan the following spring.

Swen married Johanna Hammer as a polygamous wife in 1865 and they had nine children. He took an active part in the growth and development of the new territory.

He helped build roads, bridges, canals, and assisted in the development of the natural resources. He assisted in the construction of the St. George Temple when he received a call.

Children of 1st wife:

JAMES, b. 19 Sep 1853, Ronneberga, Asmundtorp, Malmohus, Sweden. Md. 14 Feb 1876, Caroline Jenson. D. 13 May 1926, Logan, Utah.
NELS, b. 12 Jun 1857, Ronneberga, Sweden.
JOSEPHINE MATILDA, b. 19 Mar 1860, Ronneberga, Sweden.
BETTY MARIE, b. 27 Jan 1863, Logan, Utah.
SWEN WILLARD, b. 28 Jun 1865, Logan, Utah.
JOSEPH, b. 9 Oct 1867, Logan, Utah.

Children of 2nd wife:

NEPHI, b. 10 Feb 1867, Logan, Utah.
CHARLOTTA, b. 13 Jul 1869, Logan, Utah.
CHARLES RICHARD, b. 29 Apr 1872, Logan, Utah.
AMANDA, b. 16 Apr 1875, Logan, Utah.
MOSE HERMAN, b. 23 Nov 1877, Logan, Utah.
GEORGE "B", b. 2 Oct 1881, Logan, Utah.
OLIVER, b. 3 Jun 1883, Logan, Utah.
EDNA, b. 11 Dec 1886, Logan, Utah.
ERNEST, b. 20 Oct 1889, Logan, Utah.

Submitted by: Thais DeGrey

ISAAC CARPENTER

Born: June 1828/29, New York
Parents: Unknown
Died: After 1900, Colorado
Arrived in Valley: Between 1850 and 1852.

Married: Nancy Adaline Perkins
Date: bef 18 Apr 1849, Pleasant Valley, Illinois.
Parents: Absalom Perkins

Little is known of Isaac's birth and early life. It is known that he lived in the area of the Mormon communities of Ramus and Macedonia, and he formed associations with Absalom Perkin's sons, David, Levi, and John, as well as others.

When Isaac Welch and James Welch, some of his friends, decided to go west with the saints, Isaac Carpenter, and others, enlisted in the Mormon Battalion. When the first sick detachment was sent to Pueblo, Colorado, Isaac was assigned to accompany this detachment. Both of the Perkins boys were in this company and died. Issac wintered in Pueblo and in the spring followed the first pioneer company into the Valley.

Two weeks later, Isaac, with David Martin, was called as members of an advance hunting party to return to Winter Quarters. They were to supply an ox team of returning pioneers with meat on the return journey. Isaac is listed as one of the most successful of the hunters. They arrived in Council Bluffs in October and then went on to Pleasant Valley, where he went to the home of Absalom Perkins. He remained there and recuperated, obtained work, and married Adaline Perkins. Their first child was born in Iowa, and they immigrated the same year to the valley.

Isaac was one of 39 men selected to participate in colonizing Fort Supply (Green River). Because of conditions, the extreme cold, inadequate food supply, and morale problems, the men left the mission on March 14, 1854. They returned to Salt Lake.

Because of this experience and being away from his family, he and his family moved to Placerville, California. His wife's relatives were living near there. He worked at mining and with timber until production in the mines dropped off, then he returned with his family to Salt Lake. In 1870, his family moved to Carson City, Nevada.

He was depicted in family tradition as "a rough, old-time, western sheriff who boasted of the number of Indians and bad men who had bit the dust as a result of his quick draw." His death has never been determined.

Children:

SUSAN, b. 1850, Iowa.
ADALINE, b. 20 Jun 1852, Salt Lake, Utah.
CHARLES, b. 1854, Salt Lake, Utah.
FRANCIS, b. 1856, Placerville, California.
ALZADA (twin), b. 1858, Placerville, California.
AWILDA (twin), b. 1858, Placerville, California.
EDGAR, b. 1864, Placerville, California.

Submitted by: Waldo Perkins

JAMES DELEPLANE CARPENTER

Born: 15 Feb 1851, Centerville, New Castle, Delware

Parents: John Steel and Margarett McCullough Carpenter
Died: 3 Nov 1920, Cedar City, Iron, Utah
Arrived in Valley: Fall of 1857, Independent train of John Hoffhein

Married: Catherine Judd
Date: 17 Dec 1871, Glendale, Kane, Utah
Born: 19 Apr 1854, Blue Pitts, Warws, England
Parents: Samuel and Catharine Hines Judd
Died: 27 Dec 1926, Cedar City, Utah

James was the youngest of four children. Erastus Snow was the instrument by which this family was brought into the Church. They were making plans to immigrate to the Valley when James' father, John Steel Carpenter, died leaving his wife with four small children. John's sister Rachael made it possible for the family to come to Utah.

His mother Margarett remarried (her third marriage) and they remained in Salt Lake until 1868, when they were called to help colonize the Muddy Valley. They remained there until 1871. They moved to Glendale, Utah, where James was married to Catherine Judd. They lived there until 1880, when they moved to Kanab.

In 1881, James was called to help settle Gila Valley in Arizona. They first lived in Pema, Graham County. While there, a terrible contagious desease broke out. His wife, who helped nurse many people, was told that if she continued to help, neither she nor her family would suffer from the disease.

A year after the birth of their son Sam, they decided to move back to Utah. They lived in Glendale for several years, then moved to St. George while James worked on the LaVerkin Bench Canal Project. they then moved back to Glendale in 1892.

James and Cathcrine held many different offices in the church and community wherever they lived. James was never too busy to stop what he was doing and administer to the sick or help someone in need. His wife was the same. In 1912 James and Catherine left Glendale for Emmett, Idaho, where they went into partnership with their two sons. When that venture failed, they moved back to Cedar City, Utah, where their three daughters lived. James developed sugar diabetes and soon died.

Children:

MARY JUDD, b. 21 May 1873, Glendale, Utah. Md. 19 Apr
    1893, Thomas James Smith. D. 6 Feb 1934, Cedar City, Utah.
CATHERINE, b. 29 Aug 1875, Glendale, Utah. Md. 4 Jul 1917,
    William Seymour Smith. D. 14 Mar 1917, Cedar City, Utah.
JOHN BOYD, b. 7 Nov 1877, Glendale, Utah. Md. 28 May 1901,
    Vernesa Harris. D. 30 May 1936, Cedar City, Utah.
MARGARETT ELLEN, b. 1 Apr 1880, Kanab, Utah. Md. 27
    Dec 1900, Jacob Nephi Smith. D. 5 Jan 1955, Cedar City,
    Utah.
SAMUEL JAMES, b. 25 Feb 1885, Thatcher, Graham, Arizona.
    D. 4 Jul 1983, Parowan, Iron, Utah.

Submitted by: Dee Smith

DANIEL CARTER

Born: 28 Aug 1803, Benson, Rutland, Vermont
Parents: Jabez and Rebecca Dowd Carter
Died: 10 Apr 1887, Bountiful, Davis, Utah
Arrived in Valley: 12 Sep 1850, Aaron Johnson Co.

Married 1st: Clarissa Amelia Foster
Date: 26 Sep 1829, Benson, Rutland, Vermont
Born: 22 Dec 1813, Madison, New Haven, Connecticut
Parents: Orrin and Rachel Crompton Foster
Died: 12 Feb 1840, Pittsfield, Pike, Illinois

Married 2nd: Sally Sylvia Perry

Date: 23 Dec 1845, Nauvoo, Illinois
Born: 1 Sep 1826, Lewis, Essex, New York.
Parents: Stephen and Rhoby Edwards Perry
Died: 20 Feb 1847, Winter Quarters, Nebraska

Married 3rd: Mary LeGresley Pill–No children
Date: 9 Nov 1855, Salt Lake City, Utah
Born: 26 Mar 1826, Isle of Jersey, England
Parents: John and Victoria Arsene DuFresne LeGresley
Died: 1908, Bountiful, Davis, Utah

Married 4th: Cordelia Harriet Hotchkiss–No children
Date: 2 May 1856, Salt Lake City, Utah
Born: 17 Feb 1808, Bethany, New York
Died: 9 Sep 1903, Bountiful, Davis, Utah

Daniel and his wife Clarissa were baptized into the Mormon Church in 1832. Early in 1836, Daniel, with his family and aged father Jabez, moved to Kirtland where Daniel helped complete the building of the temple. They were called by the Prophet Joseph to go to Far West to help establish a town there. In the spring of 1838, they were again called, this time to help establish Adam-ondi-Aman.

It soon became necessary to leave because of the persecution, and they went back to Far West. In the spring of 1839, they were forced to leave their home again. They moved to Pittsfield, Pike County, Illinois, near Nauvoo.

Due to the many hardships they had to endure, Clarissa soon died. After her death, Daniel took his small family to Nauvoo where they lived with Hyrum Smith, until Daniel was able to purchase land. Then they lived with Ira Ames, a brother-in-law. They were successful in their farming. During the exodus, Daniel piled their belongings in their wagon and left hastily. In Winter Quarters, his second wife died of diptheria.

In June 1850, Daniel and his family left for the Valley, with two wagons, a team each of horses and oxen, and one cow. They settled in Session's Settlement, later known as Bountiful. He was successful in his farming efforts and also had a beautiful orchard. He shared with anyone in need. He built two homes in Bountiful, where his two wives, Mary and Cordelia, lived after his death. He lived a long and uncommonly eventful life. He was sturdy, stalwart, and an obedient son of God.

Children of 1st wife:

HARRIET AMELIA, b. 25 Nov 1831, Benson, Rutland, Vermont. Md. 11 Mar 1849, William Henry Lee. D. 21 Jan 1894, Woodruff, Rich, Utah.

ORRIN DANIEL, b. 3 Mar 1834, Benson, Rutland, Vermont. D. 26 Jul 1836, Kirtland, Geauga, Ohio. Child.

RUTH CLARISSA, b. 2 Nov 1836, Kirtland, Geauga, Ohio. Md. 2 May 1856, Peter Cornia. D. 20 May 1920, Bountiful, Davis, Utah.

JABEZ, b. 22 Dec 1838, Far West, Caldwell, Missouri. D. Jul 1843, Nauvoo, Illinois.

Children of 2nd wife:

MARY, b. 3 Dec 1846, Winter Quarters. She was raised by her Mother's Family after the death of her mother. Md. Edward Stone. She never joined the church.

Submitted by: Mark Redd

DOMINICUS CARTER

Born: 21 Jun 1806, Scarborough, Cumberland, Maine
Parents: John and Hannah Knight Libby Carter
Died: 2 Feb 1884, Provo, Utah, Utah
Arrived in Valley: June 1851

Married 1st: Lydia Smith, 6 children.
Date: 2 May 1829, Newry, Maine.

Married 2nd: Sophronia Babcock, 1 child.
Date: 1838.
Died: 26 Aug 1847. In child birth on plains coming west

Married 3rd: Sylvia Amaret Meacham, 2 children.
Date: 28 Mar 1839. Sylvia left him after the the death of her
    second child. She took her other son with her

Married 4th: Mary Durfee, 13 children.
Date; 2 Jan 1844 (polygamy)

Married 5th: Polly Miner, 9 children.
Date: 9 Oct 1851 (polygamy)

Married 6th: Elizabeth Brown, 8 children.
Date: 20 Jun 1852 (polygamy)

Married 7th: Caroline Hubbard, 2 children.
Date: 27 Oct 1854 (polygamy)

Married 8th: Frances Nash, 8 children.
Date: 6 Jan 1857 (polygamy)

Dominicus was born in poor and humble circumstances. When he was four, his parents moved their family to Newry, Oxford, Maine. He never had the chance for an education. He only knew hard work. He learned the blacksmith trade and between that and his farm, he did fairly well.

In June 1834, Dominicus joined the Mormon Church. His first wife died early so he remarried. She later died while giving birth. He married his first polygamous wife, Sylvia. Later, after Dominicus had taken five more wives, Sylvia took her two small children and left him, saying she could not live in polygamy.

In the spring of 1837, they left Maine and moved to Kirtland, Ohio. In 1838 they moved to Far West and then to Nauvoo where they underwent the persecution that the saints were facing. Brigham asked him to help prepare for the trip by making and strengthening the wagons and other equipment.

After leaving Nauvoo, they settled for a time in Council Bluffs, helping to repair the wagons and equipment of the saints who were going west, and whose equipment had taken a beating. It was 1850 before Dominicus was able to bring his family to the Valley.

The following year he moved his family to Provo where he remained active in civic and church positions, serving in the Utah Stake presidency with George A. Smith. He served as Probate Judge for four years. He was asked to fill a position in the Provo City Council. He played in a Martial Band and helped furnish music for the early militia; he became their leader for 20 years. He had a fine voice and lead the singing in Provo.

For many years he and his sons ran a hostelry as well as his blacksmith shop. He owned a great deal of property in Provo. He was a kindly father and husband, a good neighbor and citizen, and a loyal and active member of the church all his life.

Submitted by: Alfa Jean Carter

ERASTUS FRANCIS CARTER

Born: 24 Jan 1843, Adams Co., Illinois
Parents: Dominicus and Sylvia Amaret Meacham Carter
Died: 26 Nov 1912, Park Valley, Box Elder, Utah
Arrived in Valley: 1851

Married: Alice Elizabeth Green
Date: 12 Nov 1870, Salt Lake City, Utah
Born: 10 Jul 1852, England
Died: 1922, Park Valley, Box Elder, Utah

Erastus Francis spent his boyhood in and around Nauvoo, Illinois, until coming to Utah in 1851. When his mother decided she couldn't live under polygamy, after they had reached the Valley she took Erastus and stayed in Salt Lake, while her husband and his other wives moved to Provo.

She eventually married a widower, John Snyder, who became a good father to Erastus. He saw that Erastus was well educated and taught a good trade. He became a mason and carpenter and helped build many of the early homes in the valley. Erastus had a brother Isaac Morley who died as an infant. Both brothers were sealed to their mother and her second husband, John Snyder.

Erastus acted as body guard for Brigham Young for many years and was chief of police for a time in Salt Lake. He had a beautiful voice and was active in social affairs.

After marriage, they lived in Salt Lake until after the birth of their second child, then they moved to Laketown in Bear Lake County. As sheriff, he did much to bring law and order to the area. After several years, they moved back to Salt Lake and then to Park Valley in Box Elder County. After a time they moved back to Salt Lake, where they stayed until 1883. Then they moved back to Park Valley where they lived out their lives.

At various times he was a Justice of the Peace, sheriff and performed many marriages. He helped build many homes and made caskets. He loved the young folks and often arranged dances. At one time he got gangrene in his leg and it had to be amputated. He never complained but went on with his life as best he could. He was not a church-going man but always taught his family to fulfill their church duties. He was well-loved by young and old alike.

Children:

WILLIAM ERASTUS.
SYLVIA AMARET.
ALICE ELIZABETH.
JOHN MARTIN.
ANN ELIZA.
MARY ALMENA.
FRANCIS EDGAR.
WALTER FLOYD.
JAMES IRWIN.
CLARA EMMA.
RAYMOND.

Submitted by: Alfa Jean Carter

WILLIAM CARTER

Born: 12 Feb 1821, Ledbury, Hereford, England
Died: 22 Jun 1896, St. George, Utah

Arrived in Valley: 22 Jul 1847, Brigham Young Co.

Married 1st: Ellen Benbow
Date: 5 Dec 1843, Nauvoo, Illinois
Born: 1825
Died: 6 May 1901, St. George, Utah

Married 2nd: Harriet Temperance Utley
Date: 23 Nov 1853, Salt Lake City, Utah
Born: 1835
Died: 16 Jul 1925, St. George, Utah

Married 3rd: Sophronia Ellen Lenora Turnbow
Date: 8 Feb 1857, Salt Lake City, Utah
Born: 1842
Died: 5 Feb 1924, St. George, Utah

William was trained as a glassblower and blacksmith. At the age of 19 he was introduced to the Mormon Church and was baptized 27 December 1840. His mother forbade her other children to go to the meetings. An older sister and her family joined the church later. William and his sister and her family determined to leave England and go to Nauvoo, which they did in 1841. William worked on the Nauvoo Temple and Nauvoo House, and became a farmer. It was while having grain ground that he met Ellen Benbow.

They came west with the first company of pioneers and entered the Valley with the advance party on July 22. He plowed the first half-acre of ground at State Street and 3rd East on July 23, 1847. A plaque now stands there.

He entered into polygamy with three wives. They were called to help colonize the area now known as St. George. When the foundation for the St. George Temple was laid, William was given the call to supervise the filling of one corner that was wet and spongy. Through ingenious means, he accomplished this assignment to make the ground firm and dry enough to support that part of the temple foundation.

He filled many church assignments including being in bishoprics. He was assistant cattle marshall, member of a water-ditch survey team, and Quarter master of a military expedition. He was a well known and liked public speaker. He was involved in many irrigation projects for the area. He was one of the superintendents and council members of the St. George United Order. He was instrumental in the conversion and baptism of several of the She-bits Indian Nation. He remained active all his life in church and community.

He was awarded a medal in 1888 by the Territorial Government for being the first plowman in the Salt Lake Valley. The medal plus the plow are often exhibited in the Church History Museum.

Children unlisted.

Submitted by: Bert Carter

JOHN CARVER

Born: 6 Aug 1822, Clifford Parish, Hereford, England
Parents: Catherine Carver
Died: 11 Jan 1912, Plain City, Utah.
Arrived in Valley: September 1853, David Wilkin Co.

Married 1st: Mary Ann Eames
Date: 10 Mar 1850, aboard the ship Josiah Bradlee
Born: 8 Aug 1828, Orcop, Hereford, England
Parents: Samuel and Nancy Ann Castree Eames
Died: 18 Jun 1870, Plain City, Utah

Married 2nd: Rachel Fredrica Tellefsen

Date: 10 Dec 1864, Plain City, Utah
Born: 26 Jun 1839, Kristiansand, Norway
Parents: Peter and Rachel Lovdahl Tellefsen

Married 3rd: Sarah Ann Eames, niece of 1st wife.
Date: 9 Jan 1871, Plain City, Utah
Born: 23 Jan 1848, Garway, Hereford, England
Parents: John and Sarah Elizabeth Powell Eames
Died: Eden, Utah

John heard the gospel preached in 1841, when his mother was baptized. He waited another year to join on 14 May 1842. He moved to South Wales to be near a branch of the Church. In July 1846 he was called to travel and preach the gospel in his native Herefordshire, and served for three years.

On 14 February 1850 he boarded ship with his half brother and a friend, Mary Ann Eames. He married Mary Ann aboard ship.

Upon arriving in St. Louis, John obtained employment as a coal miner to earn money to continue on west. In 1853 they came on to Salt Lake where they settled first in Kaysville. In 1858, during the Johnston Army scare, they moved south to Spanish Fork. The following year they moved on to Plain City, where John helped establish the community. His cabin still stands near the city park. He married his first plural wife, Rachel, in 1839. After the death of his first wife, he married a third time to his first wife's niece.

After living in America for 23 years, John applied for and was granted U.S. citizenship in 1873. He helped organize the United Order in Plain City and served as its vice president. Later he moved his family to Eden, Utah, where he served in the bishopric. He was later ordained a patriarch. In 1886 he was arrested for "unlawful cohabitation," but the charges were dismissed because he was too ill. He eventually recovered.

Children of 1st wife:

SON, b. 1851. D. Infant.

JOHN WILLIAM, b 1852. D. 1930. Unmarried.

GEORGE HENRY, b. 1854. D. 1922. Md. Elizabeth Geddes.

MARY ANN, b. 1857. D. 1955. Md. William Stewart Geddes.

JAMES SAMUEL, b. 1859. D. 1932. Md. Mary Elizabeth Wood and Ina E. Heller.

JOSIAH BRADLEY, b. 1861. D. 1931. Md. Eliza Priscilla Folkman.

NANCY CATHERINE, b. 1863. D. 1874.

WILLARD CHANCY, b. 1865. D. 1947. Md. Cordelia Cora Moyes.

PARLEY PRATT, b. 1867. D. 1953. Md. Elizabeth Ann Pritchett.

ORSON EDWIN, b. 1869. D. 1869. Died an infant.

Children of 2nd wife:

FRANCES RACHEL, b. 1865. D. 1947. Md. Robert Lemuel Moyes.

MARY LOUISE, b. 1869. D. 1928. Md. Stephen Knight.

EMMA JANE, b. 1872. D. 1937. Md. Fredrick J. Palmer.

LOUISE ANN, b. 1874. D. 1874. D. Infant

HEBER CHARLES, b. 1882. D. 1973. Md. Clarinda Christensen.

Children of 3rd wife:

DAVID EDWIN, b. 1871. D. 1928. Md. Emelia Caroline Iverson and Courtney Stallings Burnett.

LEWIS HENRY, b. 1873. D. 1945. Md. Emma Jane Skeen and Alice Afton Freestone.

ALBERT JAMES, b. 1875. D. 1954. Md. Eliza Stevenson.

WALTER ELI, b. 1878. D. 1879. Child.

HYRUM SAMUEL, b. 1880. D. 1961. Md. Maud Geneva Bronson.

ELIZABETH ANN, b. 1882. D. 1937. Md. George Franklin Stallings.

CURTIS ROY. b. 1885. D. 1889. Child.

Submitted by: Jay Greaves Burrup

DUNCAN SPEARS CASPER

Born: 8 Dec 1824, Bellville, Richland, Ohio.
Parents: William and Avarilla Durban Casper.
Died: 20 May 1898, Holladay, Salt Lake, Utah
Arrived in Valley: 3 Sep 1855, John M. Hindley Co.

Married 1st: Matilda Allison
Date: 24 May 1845, Nauvoo, Illinois
Died: 20 Jun 1871, Big Cottonwood, Salt Lake, Utah

Married 2nd: Elizabeth Ann Clark
Date: 9 Sep 1872, Big Cottwood, Salt Lake, Utah
Died: 18 Jul 1911, Big Cottonwood, Salt Lake, Utah

Duncan Spears' parents joined the Church when Duncan was 12 years-old. Thereafter the life of the family revolved around the church. They moved to Richland County, Ohio, and then to Ray County, Missouri.

After Governor Boggs extermination order, they moved first to Fairfield and then to Carthage, Illinois, and then to Nauvoo where his father, William, died. His mother sent word to Duncan and son-in-law John Neel in Missouri to come and get them and take them home. Rather than go back to Missouri, they proceeded on to the Valley. Their movements can be traced by the birth-places of their children. They settled in Big Cottonwood.

Duncan was very active in the church, serving in various capacities. He was called to the "Mission in the Muddy," but because of his wife's poor health, she remained behind and soon died. After her death, Duncan married again and adopted the two children from her first marriage. Duncan and his two wives are buried in the Holladay Cemetery.

Children of 1st wife:

RACHEL LOUISA, b. 12 Mar 1846, Nauvoo, Illinois. D. 30 Jul 1846. Child.
AMANDA ELIZABETH, b. 18 Feb 1848, Lexington, Platt, Missouri. D 18 Sep 1848. Child.
HARRIET MATILDA, b. 9 Nov 1849, Lexington, Platt, Missouri. Md. 17 Feb 1873, Albert George Henry Marchant. D. 24 Oct 1921.
REBECCA AVARILLA, b. 21 Nov 1851, Lexington, Platt, Missouri. Md. 11 Dec 1871, Niles Pearson. D. 17 Feb 1920.
DUNCAN ALONZO, b. 2 Nov 1853, Lexington, Platt, Missouri. Md. 25 Mar 1884, Lucy Elizabeth Card. D.21 Nov 1933.
PETER WILLIAM (twin), b. 2 Aug 1857, Big Cottonwood, Utah. Md. 4 Jun 1888, Margaret Maria Miles. D. 12 Apr 1936.
MARY MALINDA, (twin), b. 2 Aug 1857, Big Cottonwood, Utah. Md. 18 Sep 1876, Edward Gunderson. D. 15 Aug 1930.
CYRENE ROSANNA, b. 18 Aug 1859, Big Cottonwood, Utah. Md. 1st, 10 Jun 1876, James J. Hards. Md. 2nd, Henry Robert Love. Md. 3rd, Charles Henry Lantz. D. 25 Feb 1920.
WELTHEA, b. 6 Aug 1862, Big Cottonwood, Utah. Md. 5 Jan 1882, Arthur Maxwell. D. 10 Jan 1924.

Children of 2nd marriage:

Two adopted children of her first marriage to Charles Jacob. Blackwell.

CHARLES THOMAS, b. 17 Sep 1865, Cheltenham, Gloucester, England.
SARAH ANN, b. 10 Mar 1868, Shrevenham, Berks, England. Md. 15 May 1889, William Herbst. D. 25 Feb 1952.
DAVID ALLISON, b. 24 Oct 1873, Big Cottonwood, Utah. D. 19 Apr 1893.

EMILY CLARK, b. 9 Sep 1875, Big Cottonwood, Ut. Md. 11 Oct 1894, Edgar Samuel Oakley. D. 8 Jan 1925.

ALICE CLARK, b. 5 Jan 1877, Big Cottonwood, Utah. D. 7 Oct 1877. Child.

GEORGE HARVEY, b. 2 Jul 1879, Big Cottonwood, Utah. D. 20 Jul 1886. Child.

ARTHUR CLARK, b. 13 Sep 1881, Big Cottonwood, Utah. Md. 11 Jan 1905, Ailcy Arzell Brady. D. 11 Jan 1936.

BEATRICE ELIZA, b. 25 Nov 1884, Big Cottonwood, Utah. Md. 3 Dec 1903, Henry Rasmussen. D. 21 Mar 1969.

JESSE CLARK, b. 17 Oct 1888, Big Cottonwood, Utah. Md. 25 Jun 1913, Leona May Ashby. D. 20 Jan 1960.

Submitted by: Preston Marchant

WILLIAM NEPHI CASPER

Born: 10 Nov 1848, Millcreek, Salt Lake, Utah
Parents: William Wallace & Sarah Ann Bean Casper
Died: 11 Oct 1932
Arrived in Valley: Born shortly after his parents arrived

Married 1st: Agnes McFarland
Date: 20 Apr 1867, Salt Lake City, Utah
Born: 29 Apr 1948
Parents: James and Sarah Mitchell McFarland

Married 2nd: Lucy Edwards
Date: 29 Nov 1877, Salt Lake City, Utah.
Parents: Philip and Mary Simmons Edwards

William Nephi worked with a group of men cutting railroad ties, which were floated down the Provo River to help build the railroad. He also used his wagon and team to haul milk from the farmers to the Daybell Creamery in Charleston, Utah, and also the Mark Jeffs Creamery. He farmed a great deal of the land around Charleston, Utah. He was a good farmer and worker and taught his children to love the land and farm animals.

He was active in the Church, serving in various capacities. He also served a mission to the Southern States for two years, and a short term mission later in life. He loved the scriptures and tried to help young people understand them. He was a man of integrity and expected others to do the same. He settled in Heber Valley in 1882. The family home was in Charleston.

Children of 1st wife:

JAMES WILLIAM, b. 20 Feb 1868. Died the same day. Child.

MARY JANE, b. 6 Aug 1869. Md. Joseph Everett Nelson.

MARGARET PRISCILLA, b. 4 Jun 1872. Md. John Herbert Noakes.

GEORGE NEPHI, b. 13 Feb 1874. Md. 1st, Eva Maude Miles. Md. 2nd Hannah Wilkins Miles.

AGNES VALERIA, b. 17 Mar 1876. Md. 1st, Ernest Edwin Webb. Md. 2nd, Mr. Johnson.

JOHN RUBEN, b. 7 Sep 1878. Md. Terissie Albertina Carlen.

SARAH CHENNIRA, b. 15 Aug 1880. Md. 1st, John Potter. Md. 2nd, George Amos Jones.

MORONI JEDIDIAH, b. 13 Nov 1882. Md. Leah Charlotte Thacker.

HARRIET LUELLA, b. 13 Oct 1884. Md. Charles William Carlen.

WALLACE DURBIN, b. 7 Feb 1887. Md. Lucy Wagstaff.

Children of 2nd wife:

THOMAS PHILLIP, b. 7 Nov 1879. Md. Mary Elizabeth Carlen.

EMMA MIRIAM, b. 10 Mar 1882. Md. 1st, Ernest Elijah Jacklin. Md. 2nd, Henry Clegg.

ELIZA MATILDA, b. 13 Sep 1884. Md. Owen Wright.
PHOEBE LUCY, b. 18 Apr 1888. Md. John Elmer Wright.
MELLISSA ELVIRA, b. 30 Sep 1890. Md. Dan Street.
RACHEL MELVINA, b 16 Feb 1896. Md. Simon Street.
MABLE JEMIMA, b. 19 Dec 1900. Md. Ray Alva Thacker.
JOSEPH WARREN, b. 13 Nov 1902. Md. Rena Woodard.
WILFORD RAYMOND, b. 18 May 1904. Md. Alice Melvina
    Provost.

Submitted by: Ralph Carlile

WILLIAM WALLACE CASPER

Born: 12 Mar 1821, Bellville, Richland, Ohio
Parents: William and Avarilla Durbin Casper
Died: 17 Jul 1808, Mill Creek, Salt Lake, Utah
Arrived in Valley: 16 Oct 1847, from California, via Fort Hall to
    the valley

Married 1st: Sarah Ann Bean
Date: 29 Aug 1844, Nauvoo, Illinois
Born: 31 Oct 1828, Quincy, Adams, Illinois
Parents: James and Elizabeth Lewis Bean
Died: 24 Apr 1883, Mill Creek, Salt Lake, Utah

Married 2nd: Margaret Mattice, (Polygamy)–No children
Date: 12 Feb 1856, Salt Lake City, Utah
Born: 24 Aug 1836.
Parents: Peter and Margaret Ault Mattice
Died: 1859.

Married 3rd: Elizabeth Ann Erickson
Date: 26 Mar 1864, Salt Lake City, Utah
Born: 7 Dec 1844, Solberga, Goteborg, Sweden
Parents: Anders and Pernilla Bengston Ericsson
Died: 29 Jan 1916, Mill Creek, Utah

William Wallace, and his parents and family, joined the Church and moved to Nauvoo where, shortly after the martyrdom of the Prophet, William married Sarah. Her father was a prosperous farmer in Quincy who provided housing for needy saints. He later moved to Nauvoo near the temple.

When the call came for men to join the Mormon Battalion, William Wallace enlisted and served in Company A under Captain Jefferson Hunt. He left his wife and baby at Winter Quarters. With the help of her brother, George Bean, Sarah was able to join the Jedehiah Grant Company and come west, arriving in 1847. She and her baby lived with the Jefferson Hunt family until her husband arrived from the battalion. They had had no contact since he had left.

They made their home in Mill Creek for the rest of their lives. William entered into polygamy twice, the first, Margaret, died in 1859 with no children. He married again in 1864 to Elizabeth. When the call came for him to help settle Dixie, Elizabeth went with him as she was 16 years younger than Sarah and better able to withstand the hardships.

During the Black Hawk Indian War of 1868, Major William Wallace was in charge of five platoons. He remained active in the church and was involved in the community.

Children of 1st wife:

SARAH JANE, b. 7 Oct 1845, Nauvoo, Illinois. Md. 1st, 22 Jan 1860 Ebenezer Hanks. Md. 2nd, 1888, Henry Matthew Burnell. D. 20 Feb 1920.
WILLIAM NEPHI, b. 10 Nov 1848, Mill Creek, Utah. Md. 1st, 20 Apr 1867, Agnes McFarland. Md. 2nd, 29 Nov 1877, Lucy Edwards. D. 11 Oct 1932.
ELIZABETH ANN, b. 24 Dec 1850, Mill Creek, Utah. Md. 23

Dec 1866, John Marion Cook. D. 14 Apr 1934.

JAMES MORONI, b. 28 Feb 1853, Mill Creek, Utah. Md. 14 Feb 1876, Sarah Jean McFarland. D. 22 Aug 1948.

HARRIET PRISCILLA, b. 29 Oct 1855, Mill Creek, Utah. Md. 16 Dec 1872, Thomas Gunderson, Jr. D. 21 Dec 1923.

JEDEDIAH GRANT, b. 18 Aug 1857, Mill Creek, Utah. Md. 1 Jan 1880, Annie Elmira Merrill. D. 10 Jul 1941.

EMILY MARGARET, b. 23 Jan 1860, Mill Creek, Utah. D. 9 Mar 1866. Child.

GEORGE ETHER, b. 15 Dec 1861, Mill Creek, Utah. Md. 21 Oct 1885, Eliza Wray. D. 4 Mar 1945.

SHEMIAH ELLEN, b. 1 Mar 1864, Mill Creek, Utah. Md. 4 May 1882, George Heber Luck. D. 7 Nov 1945.

JOHN EBENEZER, b. 10 May 1866, Mill Creek, Utah. Md. 18 May 1887, Rhoda Ann Williams. D. 27 Mar 1945.

REUBEN MILLER, b. 4 May 1868, Mill Creek, Utah. Md. 1st, 3 Apr 1891, Elizabeth Arrowsmith. Md. 2nd, 5 Nov 1905, Sarah Elizabeth Twitchell. D. 29 Mar 1953.

Children of 3rd wife:

RACHEL ANN, b. 22 Jan 1865, Mill Creek, Utah. D. 10 Apr 1866. Child.

MARY MALINDA, b. 26 Aug 1867, Mill Creek, Utah. Md. 1st, Edward Gunderson. Md. 2nd, Charles Natcher. D. 5 Mar 1941.

LUELLA VICTORIA, b. 22 Feb 1869, Mill Creek, Utah. Md. 12 Dec 1888, James Arthur Barber. D. 9 Mar 1944.

OSCAR DURBIN, b. 27 Feb 1871, Mill Creek, Utah. Md. Wilhelmina (Minnie) Hintze. D. 1950.

WALLACE HEBER, b. 16 May 1873, Mill Creek, Utah. Md. 1 Jan 1896, Adeline Gould Burgon. D. 26 Feb 1949.

JOSEPH ALBERT (twin), b. 20 Jan 1876, Mill Creek, Utah. Md. 20 Sep 1897, Gertrude Jackson Cook. D. 2 Jan 1958.

DAVID HENRY (twin), b. 20 Jan 1876, Mill Creek, Utah. D. 23 Feb 1876. Child.

ARVILLA (twin), b. 8 Mar 1881, Mill Creek, Utah. D. 8 Mar 1881. Child.

CLEMENCY CASPER (twin), b. 8 Mar 1881, Mill Creek, Utah. D. 8 Mar 1881. Child.

Submitted by: Hazel Marrott and Jay Marchant

JOSEPH CHADWICK

Born: 9 May 1809, Millen or Cava, Yorkshire, England
Died: 10 Apr 1876, Dayton, Idaho. Bur. Franklin, Idaho
Parents: William and Molly Shaw Chadwick
Arrived in Valley: abt 1857 from California gold fields

Married 1st: Mary Whitehead
Date: 19 Nov 1832, England
Born: 20 Mar 1812, England
Died: 26 Mar 1874, Franklin, Idaho

Married 2nd: Sarah Goode (widow Marshall)
Date: 1857, Ogden, Utah
Born: 4 Mar 1822, Mitcheldean, Gloucester, England
Died: 24 Apr 1904, Dayton, Idaho

Joseph was apprenticed in a rope factory as a boy and later worked in the coal mines in England. He met and married Mary Whitehead. Nine children were born to them while they lived in England. Six of them died young.

The family joined the Church in 1841. They saved so they were able to come to America about 1849. For almost three years they lived in Minersville (New Mines), Pennsylvania, where Joseph worked in the coal mines to get enough money to go to the

Valley. While there, two more children were born to them. One died as an infant.

Joseph and his oldest son, Benjamin, went west to California by way of the Isthmus of Panama to work in the gold fields. His wife agreed to meet in Utah in two and a half years. Apparently she lost the money or was defrauded out of it and was unable to make the long trip. She had no way to let Joseph know so when he got to the valley, he was probably told that his wife had died.

Joseph met Sarah Goode Marshall in Ogden, Utah. She was a widow with two boys. They married and had two more boys. In 1860, son Benjamin found out that his mother was still alive so he went to Pennsylvania to get her and the three children. When she got to the valley and found Joseph had married, even though polygamy was practiced, she felt she could not live that way.

Joseph and Sarah, and Benjamin and his mother, moved to Franklin, Idaho where Mary died in 1874. Joseph took his family and moved to Dayton, Idaho, where he raised grain and cattle. He caught cold and died suddenly.

Children of 1st wife:

WILLIAM, b. 1832, Oldham, England. D. 1836. Child.
ELIZABETH, b. abt 1833, Oldham, England. D. 1840-50.
ABRAHAM, b. 1834, Oldham, England. D. 1846.
ELIZA, b. 1835/6, Oldham, England. D. 29 Oct 1849.
BENJAMIN, b. 26 Mar 1837, Saddleworth, England. Md. 31 Aug 1860, Sarah Walker. D. 29 Mar 1917, Slaterville, Utah.
WILLIAM, b. 1840, Oldham, England. D. 1845. Child.
JAMES, b. 23 Jun/Jul 1840-42, Saddleworth, England. Md. 20 Jan 1866, Mary Catherine Candland. D. 5 Mar 1899, Preston, Idaho.
MARY ANN, b. 22 Jan 1844, Oldham, England. Md. 1 Jun 1863, Robert McClellan Hull. D. 3 Oct 1937, Logan, Utah.
SARAH, b. 1847, Oldham, England. D. 1859/61.
ABRAHAM, b. 1849, Minersville, Pennsylvania. D. 1849. Child.
ADAM, b. 10 Aug 1853, Minersville, Pennsylvania. Md. 12 Dec 1882, Eliza Jane Fluitt. D. 9 Apr 1895, Logan, Utah.

Children of 2nd wife:

WILLIAM, b. 6 Oct 1857, Ogden, Utah. Md. 1st, 25 Nov 1879, Lauretta Geneva Neeley. Md. 2nd, after 1899, Nettie Wilson. D. 25 Nov 1909, Franklin, Idaho.
CHARLES FREDERICK, b. 6 Aug 1860, Franklin, Idaho. Md. 2 Jun 1880/81, Luna Nelson. D. 25 Jan 1910, Burley, Idaho.

Submitted by: Theda Judd

JOHN ALLEN CHAMBERLAIN

Born: 16 Jul 1834, Ewelme, Oxford, England
Parents: William and Mary Allen Chamberlain
Died: 30 Mar 1919, Salt Lake City, Utah
Arrived in Valley: 1 Sep 1859, Horton D. Haight Co.

Married 1st: Amanda Susannah Watmough
Date: 29 Dec 1864, Salt Lake City, Utah
Died: 5 Apr 1879, Deseret, Millard, Utah

Married 2nd: Sarah Elizabeth Hartle
Date: 29 Jun 1882, Salt Lake City, Utah
Died: 10 Oct 1897, Wasatch Co., Utah

John Allen was the eldest of seven children born in England. At the age of eight, his family moved to the Cape of Good Hope in South Africa, where his father was a veterinarian for the English government. He also ran the lighthouse there.

It was in south Africa that the family met the Mormon missionaries and were converted and baptized.

John early learned the languages that surrounded him in Africa. His travels took him all over the continent. Later, when his father was transferred to Australia, they did some placer mining and found gold, which enabled them to fulfill their dream of returning to Africa, and from there to America. During his life time, John visited every continent except Asia. People loved to be around him to hear his stories and singing and hear him play his harmonica. The family eventually made their way to Utah and then on to Ruby Valley in Nevada. John remained in Salt Lake where he did some freighting for Brigham Young.

He married Amanda and they were blessed with seven children, four of whom died in infancy. After his wife died, while they lived in Deseret, Utah, his wife's parents sent word for him to bring the children back to Salt Lake. The two boys died and the grandparents raised Carrie.

As John traveled extensively in Utah, he met and married Sarah. He did farming in Charleston, Utah, and raised cattle, sheep, and chickens. When Sarah died, John sold his ranch. He lived with his children in Colorado, Wyoming, and eventually back in Salt Lake where he died.

He loved life and people and was happy entertaining them with his stories and music. He loved the church and remained active.

Children of 1st wife:

WILLIAM HENRY, b. 12 Oct 1865. D. Infant in Deseret, Millard, Utah.
MARY ANN, b. 25 Jun 1867. D. infancy in Deseret, Millard, Utah.
JOHN WATMOUGH, b. 9 Dec 1869, Deseret, Millard, Utah
BENONI, b. 11 Oct 1871, Deseret, Millard, Utah. D. infancy.
CARRIE EMMA, b. 30 Jul 1873, Deseret, Millard, Utah
MERRY ANDER, b. 20 Feb 1875, Deseret, Millard, Utah. D. Infant.
MARK, b. 25 Sep 1877, Deseret, Millard, Utah.

Children of 2nd wife:

EVA, b. 8 Jun 1883, Walsburg Creek, Charleston, Utah. D. Colorado.

HERBERT, b. 20 Nov 1885, Walsburg Creek, Charleston, Utah. D. Wyoming.

CARL, b. 29 May 1887, Walsburg Creek, Charleston, Utah.

ADA, b. 13 Nov 1889, Walsburg Creek, Charleston, Utah. D. Salt Lake City, Utah.

ORSON, b. 12 Mar 1893, Walsburg Creek, Charleston, Utah.

PEARL, b. 4 Sep 1895, Walsburg Creek, Charleston, Utah.

Submitted by: Darro Glissmeyer

WILLIAM CHAMBERLAIN

Born: 27 Oct 1815, Ewelme, Oxford, England
Parents: Joseph and Hannah Pocock Chamberlain
Died: 6 Jun 1868, Bensington, Oxford, England
Arrived in Valley: 16 Sep 1859, Edward Stevenson's 4th Wagon Train Co.

Married: Mary Allen
Date: 12 Nov 1836, Ewelme, Oxford, England
Died: 23 Mar 1900, Charleston, Utah, Utah

William was a shephard in his youth. Later he became a veterinarian and was hired by the government and sent to South Africa to doctor sheep and other animals at Capetown. He also cared for the lighthouse there. He was later transferred to Australia. After being there awhile, he and his family returned to South Africa where he learned of the Church from missionaries.

Eventually they were able to immigrate to Utah. They lived for a time in Kaysville, Utah, but did not stay long. His love of the land and animals led him to purchase land in Ruby Valley (Elko), Nevada.

While working on his ranch, he seriously injured himself lifting rock. He was not able to get the medical help he felt he needed so leaving his family in Nevada, he went first to Boston and then back to his home in England.

Near his birthplace was one of the finest schools of medicine. He probably felt that if anyone could help him, they could. He left his family asking that the children take care of their mother during his absence. His search was in vain, however, as he died there. His death certificate lists the cause as cancer of the liver.

Children:

JOHN, b. 16 Jul 1838, Ewelme, Oxford, England
HENRY, chr 25 Aug 1840, Swyncombe, Oxford, England
ELIZABETH, chr 5 Jun 1842, Ewelme, Oxford, England
JOSEPH, chr 22 Sep 1844, Ewelme, Oxford, England. D. 27 Aug
    1845, Ewelme, England. Child.
ANNA, b. 19 Jul 1846, Cape of Good Hope, South Africa
JAMES, b. 10 Mar 1848, Cape of Good Hope, South Africa
EMMA, b. 23 Feb 1850, Algoa Bay, South Africa

Submitted by: Darro Glissmeyer

WILLIAM SISSON CHAMPLIN

Born: 16 Apr 1792/4, West Green River, New Hampshire.

Parents: Joseph and Mercy Sisson Champlin
Died: 29 Jan 1861, Lehi, Utah, Utah
Arrived in Valley: Came west prior to 1860

Married: Mary Ring
Date: 28 Mar 1816, Hartland, Windsor, Vermont
Born: 27 Jan 1794, Old Salisbury, Essex, Massachusetts
Parents: Reuben French and Anna Ring
Died: 3 Apr 1871, Salt Lake City, Utah

William and Mary were converted to the Church and baptized. They determined to migrate with the other members of the church to the Valley. It is not known exactly when they arrived, but one of their children, Angelina, was married in 1840 while they were in Nauvoo.

Another one, Mary Jane, was married in 1849-50 in Austin, Fremont, Iowa. Margaret was married in 1851 in Kanesville, Pottawatamie, Iowa. Undoubtedly they reached the valley sometime in the 1850's.

It is known that William and Mary survived the Haun's Mill Massacre. When the massacre was over, it was found that William had survived by feigning death while lying surrounded by dead men. The dead body of George Richards fell across him in the blacksmith shop and he played "possum" so well that when one of the mob searched him, he thought he was dead.

From then on he was known as "Possum." Two of his children also survived by running into the tall corn and brush. He remained faithful to the church all his life.

Children:

SAPHRONIA, b. abt 1815.
MARIE LAVERNA, b. 1816, Hartland, Windsor, Vermont. Md. Jonathan Taylor Packer.
SOPHRONIA, b. 1817 in Vermont. Md. Abraham Miller. D. 5 Jun 1877, Yorkshire or Pottowattamie, Iowa.
REUBEN ALONZO, b. 17 Jan 1818, Hartland, Windsor, Vermont. Md. Mary Elizabeth Fisk. D. 12 Mar 1891.

ANGELINA AVILDA, b. 8 Jan 1820, Hartland, Vermont. Md. 1840, Jonathan Taylor Packer. Bur 8 Jan 1893, Juarez, Chihuahua, Mexico.

WILLIAM JEFFERSON, b. 22 Nov 1823, Brooklyn, Pennsylvania. Md. abt 1844, Polly Meachan. D. 16 Sep 1894, Hanford, Kings, California.

JOSEPH ALBERT, b. 1824, Hartland, Vermont.

ALONZO, b. abt 1827, Hartland, Vermont.

AVILDA, b. abt 1828.

MARY JANE, b. 20 May 1830, Brooklyn, Pennsylvania. Md. 27 Aug 1849/50, Stewart (Stuart) Dickson. D. 1 Nov 1906, Chesterfield, Bannock, Idaho.

MARGARET EMMA, b.11 Jun 1833, Brooklyn, Pennsylvania. Md. 25 Feb 1851, Leonidas Clifton Mecham. D. 18 Feb 1909, Preston, Oneida, Idaho.

SARAH, b. abt 1835. Md. Mr. Call.

ERASTUS, b. abt 1836. D. 1841. Child.

MARIA, b. abt 1838. D. Bef. 1852.

Submitted by: L. Hoffman

FRANK CHANDLER

Born: 17 Aug 1828, Oving, Sussex, England
Parents: Thomas and Lucy Foster Chandler
Died: 15 Aug 1889, Wanship, Summit, Utah
Arrived in Valley: 2 Aug 1864, Warren S. Snow Co.

Married 1st: Sara Trower
Date: 7 Nov 1857, Parrish Church of Oving, Sussex, England

Born: 25 Dec 1828, Wisborough Green, Sussex, England
Parents: George Trower
Died: 1864, Nebraska Territory while crossing plains

Married 2nd: Gustavia Sophia Stark
Date: 29 Jun 1866, Coalville, Summit, Utah
Born: 7 Apr 1830, Gamelby, Kalamar, Sweden
Died: 19 Oct 1897, Coalville, Summit, Utah

Frank, with his wife Sara and three children, sailed for America in June 1864. When the ship landed, the oldest child was not listed, so he probably died and was buried at sea. Nine children on board ship died.

They left Council Bluffs in August and those who were healthy had to walk. On the way some Gentiles joined the train, making it five miles long. The Indians were very agressive at that time. Sara crossed the ocean with him but did not make it to the valley, and it is presumed she died on the way west. Frank was a farmer in Wanship, remarried and raised a family devoted to the church.

Children of 1st wife:

GEORGE TROWER, b. 3 Oct 1858, Oving, Sussex, England. Date and place of death unknown.
SARAH, b. 19 Oct 1860, Chichester, Sussex, England. Md. 29 Nov 1878, John George Hallom. D. 14 Jun 1926, Lander, Wyoming.
FRANK, chr 28 Sep 1862, Oving, Sussex, England. D. Unknown.

Children of 2nd wife:

AMANDA, b. 8 May 1867, Hoytsville, Summit, Utah. Md. 1st, 1 Jun 1889, William Samuel Robinson. Md. 2nd, Tobias Rasmussen (Div). D. 6 Feb 1950, Huntington Beach, Orange, California.
EMMA, b. 28 Apr 1869, Wanship, Summit, Utah. Md. 1st, 1886, Thomas Ray (Div). Md. 2nd, 5 Jun 1902, Henry Fister (Div). D. 24 May 1957, Grace, Idaho.

LUCY, b. 23 Aug 1871, Wanship, Utah. D. 2 Aug 1880, Wanship, Utah.

Submitted by: Burnyce Powell

HYRUM CHAPMAN

Born: 3 Oct 1841, Nauvoo, Hancock, Illinois
Parents: Welcome and Susan Amelia Risley Chapman
Died: 22 Jan 1928, Bluewatere, Valencia, New Mexico
Arrived in Valley: 23 Sep 1848, Heber C. Kimball

Married: Rhoda Ann Fullmer
Date: 10 Apr 1871, Salt Lake City, Utah
Born: 15 Mar 1847, Garden Grove, Decatur, Iowa
Died: 28 Jan 1917, Bluewater, Valencia, New Mexico

Hyrum's parents joined the Church in New York and followed the church migration west to Nauvoo. He immigrated to the Valley with his parents in 1848. Within a year they moved to Manti, where they lived for the next 13 years.

Hyrum learned the stone cutter's trade and worked on the Salt Lake Temple for several years, along with his father and brothers. He followed that trade most of his life. He built a rock home after his family moved to New Mexico. He was a veteran of the Black Hawk and Walker Indian Wars.

In 1871, after his marriage to Rhoda, they lived in Salt Lake for a short time and then moved to Parley's Park. They moved to St. John's, Arizona, in 1884 where they lived for 11 years until their house burned down. Apparently after this, they moved to

Bluewater, New Mexico, in 1895, becoming one of the first LDS families to settle that area.

The last few winters of his life were spent at the Old Soldiers Home in Los Angeles, California. In the summer he came back to Utah with his children. He was a temple worker and active in the church all his life.

Children:

RHODA SUSAN, b. 27 Jan 1872, Parley's Park, Utah. D. 24 Jan 1944.

HYRUM DAVID, b. 12 Nov 1874, Salt Lake City, Utah. D. 5 Dec 1937.

WELCOME OCTAVIS, b. 7 Feb 1876, Parley's Park, Utah. D. 22 May 1945.

TROOP EUGENE, b. 24 Mar 1878, Parley's Park, Utah. D. 26 Sep 1930.

ZERA MARVIN, b. 29 Nov 1881, Salt Lake City, Utah. D. 22 Jun 1942.

WINNIE BELLE, b.30 Jul 1885, St. Johns, Arizona. D. 22 Aug 1885. Child.

MINNIE, b. 27 Feb 1887, St. Johns, Arizona. D. 16 May 1963.

DON ARCHIBALD, b. 18 Apr 1891, St. Johns, Arizona. D. 14 Feb 1920.

Submitted by: Elaine Schofield

WELCOME CHAPMAN

Born: 24 Jul 1805, Reedsboro, Bennington, Vermont

Parents: Benjamin and Sibyl Amidon Chapman
Died: 9 Dec 1893, Fountain Green, Sanpete, Utah
Arrived in Valley: 23 Sep 1848, Heber C. Kimball

Married 1st: Susan Amelia Risley
Date: 1831, Madison, Madison, New York
Born: 24 Aug 1807, Madison, Madison, New York
Died: 18 Feb 1888, Fountain Green, Sanpete, Utah

Married 2nd: Ann MacKey
Date: 5 Oct 1855
Born: 8 Oct 1839
Died 24 Apr 1926

Married 3rd: Catherine Ann Stayner
Date: 3 May 1856
Born: 3 Mar 1839
Died: 22 Jan 1920

Welcome spent his boyhood days in Reedsboro where his father had helped settle the town. His poor health as a child was a handicap to his education, but it didn't stop him from learning to read and write, spell, and do arithmetic.

As a young man he wasn't able to do hard labor, but was asked by some fishermen to go on their boat and be their cook. He would spend six months at a time on the ocean doing their cooking. Because of the clean air, he finally regained his health and strength.

He heard about the man Joseph Smith and determined to find him. After going to New York, he found the prophet and stayed for two weeks in their home. He was baptized before returning to Vermont.

After his marriage to Susan, she too, joined the Church. Welcome became a body guard to the prophet until his martyrdom. While in Kirtland, he cut stone for the Kirtland and Nauvoo Temples. The family spent a winter at Winter Quarters. While there, he built a wagon to help them go west. Upon their arrival in the Valley, they stayed in Salt Lake about a year and then were called to go to Manti. In 1854, he became stake president of the Manti Stake. He was a member of the first militia of Manti and helped build the stone fort and Manti Temple and other buildings.

At the end of eight years, he was released as stake president and asked to return to help with the stone work on the Salt Lake Temple. During this time he also cut wood and hauled and sold it to the soldiers at Fort Douglas, to earn a living. After his work on the Salt Lake Temple, he moved his family back to Manti.

Welcome helped everyone who needed help. He was known for his honesty and often said that he owed no man money. His life was dedicated to the church and helping those in need.

Children of 1st wife:

CHESTINA (twin), b. 28 Mar 1833. D. Apr 1833. Child.
ALMINA (twin), b. 28 Mar 1833. Died shortly after birth. Child.
ROSETTA ANISE, b. 4 Sep 1834. D. 3 Nov 1914.
AMELIA, b. 20 Mar 1837. D. 13 Mar 1923.
JOSEPH SMITH, b. 17 Nov 1838. D. 15 Jul 1917.
HYRUM, b. 3 Oct 1841. D. 22 Jan 1928.
BENJAMIN, b. 12 Aug 1843. D. 27 Nov 1843. Child.
LEVI, b. 20 Apr 1845. D. Unknown.
FIDELIA, b. 11 Oct 1846. D. 16 Jul 1909.
WELCOME, b. 2 Oct 1849. D. 20 Feb 1900.

Children of 2nd wife:

PHOEBE ANN, b. 1 Dec 1856. D. 17 Dec 1932.
FANNIE, b. 20 Oct 1858. D. 15 Oct 1861. Child.
SAMUEL WELCOME, b. 3 Dec 1860. D. 23 Jun 1940.
ANTHONY, b. 2 Dec 1862. D. 25 May 1947.
LOIS, b. 27 Nov 1864. d. 28 Apr 1939.
CALANTHIA, b. 24 Oct 1866. D. 31 Oct 1866. Child.
JOHN, b. 19 Apr 1868. D. 25 Nov 1869. Child.
HARRIET AMELIA, b. 8 Nov 1869. D. 18 Oct 1871. Child.
HENRY, b. 7 Jul 1874. D. 22 May 1876. Child.
MAMIE, b. 9 Jan 1878. D. 12 Apr 1947.
LILLIE SARAH, b. 22 Dec 1881. D. 23 Oct 1882. Child.

Children of 3rd wife:

JESSE, b. 22 Feb 1857. D. 26 Apr 1940.
SIBYL MARTHA, b. 21 Feb 1861. D. 27 Apr 1883.
ELIZUR, b. 1 Feb 1862. D. 22 Aug 1936 .
CATHERINE LORELLA, b. 14 May 1863. D. 6 Feb 1867. Child.
JEREMIAH, b. 6 Sep 1865. D. 8 Nov 1866. Child.
WILLIAM, b. 15 Oct 1867. D. 26 Sep 1869. Child.
SARAH FRANCES, b. 17 Aug 1871. D 11 Nov 1949.
ELLEN, b. 2 Mar 1874. D. 11 Jul 1949.
ALLIE ANDREW, b. 21 Jun 1876. D. 30 Jun 1901.
BENJAMIN WELCOME, b. 1 Mar 1881. D. 11 Mar 1925.

Submitted by: Elaine Showfield

ELI CHASE

Born: 9 Nov 1808, Ellisburg, New York
Parents: Stephen and Orryanna Rowe Chase
Died: 20 Feb 1851, Salt Lake City, Utah
Arrived in Valley: 25 Aug 1849, Co. unknown

Married: Olive Hills
Date: 25 Jul 1840, Madison County, New York
Born: 12 Aug 1815, Brookfield, Madison, New York
Died: 1889, Utah

Eli joined the church in 1832 and moved to Jackson Company, Missouri. He was driven out with the rest of the saints and went to Clay Company. He was wounded by the mob but recovered.

He served a mission in Madison, Wisconsin, where he met his future wife. Upon their return to Nauvoo, they were sealed in the temple. They helped with the building of Nauvoo. When the saints left Nauvoo, Eli and his family went too. He died in Salt Lake two years after his arrival. His wife, Olive, married James Green Browning in 1852.

Children:

HARIETT LOUISE, b. 18 Mar 1841, Nauvoo, Illinois.
OLIVE, b. 18 Jul 1846.
FRANCES HELEN, b. 21 Jul 1849, on way west.
ELI, b. 5 Jul 1851, Utah.

Submitted by: LaRue McManama

EZRA CHASE

Born: 4 Feb 1796, Colrain, Franklin, Massachusetts
Parents: Timothy and Sarah Simmons Chase
Died: 24 Oct 1873, Harrisville, Weber, Utah
Arrived in Valley: 1848, Lorenzo Snow Co.

Married: Tirzah Wells
Date: 22 Aug 1818, Greenfield, Franklin, Massachusetts
Born: 29 Jul 1796, Greenfield, Franklin, Massachusetts
Died: 4 Apr 1867, Farr West, Weber, Utah

Ezra was a Quaker in his youth and his teenage years were spent in Bristol, Vermont. After marriage they lived in Bristol. In

1829 they moved to Sparta, Livingston, New York, with his brother Isaac, to live on a farm. While there, they met the Mormon missionaries and joined the Church in 1839. Ezra returned to Bristol as a missionary, and he converted the family of his deceased brother, Abner. Soon after, he and Isaac moved their families to Nauvoo.

In 1842, Ezra led an expedition of 50 men up the Mississippi River to the pine woods of Wisconsin, where they helped operate several saw mills. They returned in October with a huge raft and timber for the Temple and Nauvoo House.

In 1846, the Chase families fled west with the other saints. After arriving in the Valley, they soon moved on to Weber County where they settled in the Mound Fort Area of Ogden.

In 1850, Ezra, his wife Tirzah, and their younger children joined an expedition to California to the gold fields of El Dorado. In 1853, they went south to San Bernardino. They returned to Weber County when San Bernardino was abandoned in 1857/58. Ezra became the great grandfather of George Albert Smith, eighth president of the church.

Children:

EZRA JR., b. 6 Jul 1819, Bristol, Addison, Vermont. D. 6 Sep 1819. Child.
ELIZA, b. 4 Oct 1820, Bristol, Vermont. Md. Apr 1848, Adam C. Hubbard. D. 21 Jan 1891.
NANCY BAILEY, b. 27 Jan 1823, Briston, Vermont. Md. 1 Jan 1846, Lorin Farr. D. 10 Sep 1892, Ogden, Utah.
CHARLOTTE, b. 11 May 1825, Bristol, Vermont. Md. 1st, 10 Oct1844, Heber C. Kimball (Div). Md. 2nd, 1850, Thaddeus C. Hicks. Plus others. D. 15 Dec 1904, Lewisville, Jefferson, Idaho.
DIANA SEVERANCE, b. 25 Jul 1827, Bristol, Vermont. Md. 1st 10 Oct 1844, Brigham Young (Div). Md. 2nd, 1 Jan 1849, William M. Shaw. D. 6 Sep 1886, Ogden, Weber, Utah.
ELISHA WELLS, b. 21 Apr 1830, Sparta, Livingston, New York. Md. 23 Nov 1853, Jane McGary. D. 7 Mar 1917, Ogden, Utah.

HENRY, b. 21 Jul 1832, Sparta, New York. Md. 16 Dec 1860, Mary Ann Baldwin. D. 15 Oct 1910.

DUDLEY, b. 22 May 1835, Sparta, Livingston, New York. Md. 1st 19 Jul 1857, Samantha Crismon., plus others. D. 24 Feb 1906, Idaho Falls, Idaho.

NEWTON, b. 3 Dec 1837, Sparta, New York. Md. 12 Feb 1860, Elsie Elizabeth Tanner. D. 30 Aug 1918.

JULIETT, b. 13 Sep 1841, Nauvoo, Illinois. Md. 13 Aug 1858, Hugh J. McClellan. D. 21 Mar 1911, Loa, Wayne, Utah.

Submitted by: Dell Madsen

SISSON ALAMDOROUS CHASE

Born: 1 Oct 1808, Bristol, Addison, Vermont
Parents: Abner and Amy Scott Chase
Died: 4 Apr 1892, Salt Lake City, Utah
Arrived in Valley: 9 Sep 1853, Daniel Mill and John Cooley's Co.

Married: Miriam Gove
Date: 16 May 1832, Bristol, Vermont
Born: 22 Mar 1813, Lincoln, Addison, Vermont
Died: 4 Nov 1909, Payson, Utah, Utah

Sisson Alamdorous was a good man who was a friend to everyone. He worked hard to furnish his family with a home and food. He remained strong and active in the church and community. His original farm was located where the Salt Lake City Hall now stands.

Children:

HANNAH GOVE, b. 11 Dec 1834, Lincoln, Addison, Vermont. Md. 16 Nov 1856, Barnabas Lothrope Adams. D. 27 Jul 1897, Salt Lake City, Utah.

RACHAEL, b. 10 Jan 1834, Lincoln, Vermont. D. 11 Jan 1834, Lincoln, Vermont. Child.

JANE ANN MASON, b. 15 Jun 1839, Stocksborough, Adams, Vermont. Md. 15 Feb 1862, James Marvin Hicks. D. 5 Jul 1881, Salt Lake City, Utah.

LURANCY, b. 17 May 1842, Lincoln, Vermont. Md. 25 Nov 1860, Heaman Alison Hill. D. 28 Aug 1926, Payson, Utah.

STEPHEN, b.15 Sep 1844, Lincoln, Vermont. D. 15 Sep 1844. Child.

SISSON ALAMDORUS JR., b. 19 Jan 1847, Pottawattamie, Iowa. Md. 27 Jul 1867, Elizabeth Ann Hunt. D. 12 Jan 1918, Salt Lake City, Utah.

MARIAN, b. 3 Mar 1849, Pottawattomie, Iowa. Md. 20 Dec 1869, Creighton Hawkins. D. 3 (or 23) Jul 1878, Salt Lake City, Utah.

AMY, b. 3 Oct 1851, Rupert, Harrison, Vermont. Md. 1st, 20 Dec 1869, Garrett Hyers Conk. Md. 2nd, 7 Apr 1884, German Ellsworth. D. 18 Dec 1940, Salt Lake City, Utah.

Submitted by: Lowell Parkinson

STEPHEN CHASE

Born: 11 Apr 1779, Duchess Co., New York

Parents: Barry and Phoebe Wixon Chase
Died: 11 Feb 1847, 40 miles West of Council Point, Iowa
Arrived in Valley: Died enroute to valley in Iowa

Married: Orryanna Rowe
Date: 12 May 1799, New York
Died: abt 1885, Utah

Stephen joined the Church in 1832 and promptly left with his family for Jackson County, Missouri. They were driven before the mob and endured all the persecutions that were visited upon the saints. They finally settled in Nauvoo for a time and helped that great city grow.

When they were finally forced from Nauvoo, Stephen became ill and died about 40 miles west of Council Point, Iowa. His family came west without him.

Children:

DANIEL, b. 25 Jul 1800.
SILAS, b. 4 Jun 1803.
ASNATH (female), b. 18 Aug 1804.
SOPHIA, b. 9 Apr 1807.
ELI, b. 9 Nov 1808.
ORPHA, b. 27 Jun 1811.
ORRYANNA, b. 30 Apr 1813.
DARWIN, b. 25 Feb 1816.
HARRIET NANCY, b. 27 Oct 1818.
STEPHEN, b. 27 Aug 1821.
HYRUM BARRY, b. 14 Mar 1823.
MARY MARIA, b. 29 Mar 1825.

Submitted by: LaRae McManama

HENRY CHATWIN

Born: 30 Dec 1821, Rochdale, Lancaster, England
Parents: Joseph and Christina Gilbert Chatwin
Died: 7 Feb 1908, Heber City, Wasatch, Utah
Arrived in Valley: 1852

Married 1st: Sarah Jeffs
Date: 1851 in England
Married 2nd: Fanny Lee
Date: 7 Jun 1869, Heber City, Utah.

Henry moved with his parents to Bury, Lancaster, England, shortly after his birth. When he was in his teens, it became necessary for him to get a job to support himself. He was not satisfied with menial jobs, so he studied at night to become a school teacher. After some time, he was successful in obtaining a teaching assignment.

He married the same year he was converted to the Church. He and his bride immigrated to the Valley in 1852. He worked on the foundation of the temple until he was injured in a cave-in, but not seriously. His wife died and he moved to Provo in 1856, later he was one of those who opened New London, or Heber City as it is now known. In 1869 he remarried and they made their home in Heber City.

Henry was a school teacher, usually accepting produce from the families in payment for his services. Later he was given $25.00 per month. He volunteered in several of the Indian battles. He took part in many local community projects and was active in church affairs.

Children of 1st wife:

SARAH ANN, b. 23 Mar 1854. D. 30 Aug 1913

Children of 2nd wife:

HENRY DAVID, b. 15 Aug 1870. Unmarried. D. 26 Mar 1938.
ELLEN MARIA, b. 14 Jun 1872. Md. 19 Jun 1891, Henry James
    Clegg. D. 15 Dec 1941.
CHAUNCEY CHARLES, b. 30 Jun 1875. Md. 30 Jun 1896,
    Maria Elizabeth Giles. D. 30 Mar 1957.
NEPHI, b. 25 Nov 1879. Md. 17 Jan 1900, Sarah Clegg. D. 28
    Jun 1959.

Submitted by: Hazel Hall

CARL CHRISTIAN ANTON CHRISTENSEN

Born: 28 Nov 1831, Copenhagen, Copenhagen, Denmark
Parents: Mads and Dorothea Christiana Christensen
Died: 3 Jul 1912, Ephraim, Sanpete, Utah
Arrived in Valley: 13 Sep 1857, 7th Handcart Co., Christian
    Christiansen

Married 1st: Elise Rosalia Haarbye
Date: 1857
Born: 13 Nov 1834, Fredrickshald, Norway

Married 2nd: Maren Fredrikke Petterson

Date: 30 Nov 1868, Salt Lake City, Utah
Born: Norway

Carl Christian Anton, or C.C.A. as he was known, had three younger brothers, Niels, Mads, and Otto. Because of his father's love of drink, the family lost everything and were reduced to poverty.

His mother worked doing washing and other household tasks while Carl took care of the children and the home. He loved his mother dearly and did the best he could to care for the children and the house. His mother taught him to read and write, and at an early age his talent for painting and as a writer showed up. His mother encouraged him as best she could.

She had a dream in which she was encouraged to make application for Carl in the State school for worthy poor. So she did. At 11 he did well. He could only visit his family on holidays, if his behavior was good. He was known only by a number. At 14 he was apprenticed to a carpenter in a manual training school.

Through the interest of a lady, he was accepted at King's Royal Academy of Arts. He remained there for six or seven years.

In 1850 his mother heard the missionaries and was baptized. Shortly after, Carl heard and accepted the gospel. When it became known at school that he was a Mormon, he suffered much persecution. He kept going until he graduated with honors.

After graduation he was sent as a missionary. Thus began many years of missionary service. During this time, his family began to immigrate to the Valley. In 1853 he bade his mother goodbye, not knowing he would never see her again.

His work as an artist is well known, as are his poems and songs. Upon his arrival in the valley, Carl and his wife settled first in Fairfield, then moved to Fairview, then Mt. Pleasant and finally to Ephraim. During this time, he served another mission and took a second wife.

He painted many pictures in the temples at Manti, St. George, and Logan. He served two more missions, meanwhile working on his hymn book and paintings. In 1900 he was ordained Stake Patriarch. In 1901 he was called to work in the Church Historian's office as writer, translator, and compiler of material on the history of the Scandinavian saints and mission. He died at the age of 80.

Children of 1st wife:

ELIZA VIRGINIA, b. 16 Feb 1859. Md. Otto G. Olsen. D. 13 Apr 1925. The first woman baptized in Fredrickshald, Norway.

CHARLES JOHN, b. 21 Mar 1861. Md. Marie Elizabeth Frost. D. 13 Jan 1929.

FREDERICK WILLIAM, b. 25 Aug 1863. Md. Amelia Jensen. D. 5 May 1912.

ANDREA DOROTHEA, b. 29 Nov 1865. Md. Niels L. Christensen. D. 1 Feb 1928.

NIELS ERASTUS, b. 28 Nov 1869. D. 24 Jun 1889.

CANUTE EPHRAIM, b. 27 Apr 1872. Md. Clara Augusta Johansen. D. 9 Mar 1929.

TEKLA PAULINE, b. 7 Sep 1874. Md. A.C. Nielsen. D. 13 Sep 1935.

Children of 2nd wife:

MARY ANN, b. 8 Jun 1870. Md. Peter R. Jensen, D. 25 Oct 1953.

JULIA ELEONORA, b. 5 Dec 1871. Md. Andrew Christian Nielsen. D. 25 Sep 1899.

CAROLINE MARIA, b. 17 Dec 1873. D. 10 May 1874. Child.

JOHN CARLOS, b. 17 Jun 1875. D. 5 Feb 1943.

GEORGE PARLEY BRIGHAM, b. 21 Aug 1877. Md. Olena Olsen Hansen. D. 11 Oct 1918, Argonne Forest, France.

JOSEPH ANTHONY, b. 29 Jan 1880. D. 9 Sep 1881. Child.

HYRUM MORONI, b. 14 Oct 1882. Md. Jonetta Blom Langseth. D. 11 Nov 1946.

Submitted by: Margery Louise Bitter

CHRISTIAN CHRISTENSEN

Born: 16 Oct 1820, Sindal, Hjorring, Denmark
Parents: Christian and Karen Olsen Christensen
Died: Nov 1872, Ephraim, Sanpete, Utah
Arrived in Valley: 1868

Married: Ane Marie Nielsen
Date: 12 Dec 1847, Taars, Hjorring, Denmark
Born: 17 Dec 1820, Taars, Hjorring, Denmark
Parents: Niels and Johanne Pedersen Mikkelsen
Died: 11 Mar 1884, Ephraim, Sanpete, Utah

Christian's home in Ugilt, Denmark, was always open to the Mormon missionaries. They joined the Church in 1862 but because of the ridicule of their former friends and neighbors, they saved their money and were able to emigrate. They didn't all come at once.

In 1867 they sent the two older girls. In 1868 Christian brought nine-year-old Ane. A year later his wife came, and the following year, 1870, son Niels completed the family. Niel came by train. Six of their ten children were buried in Denmark.

They settled among other Danish immigrants in Ephraim, Sanpete, Utah. Christian's health began to fail him and he died four years later. They always remained true to the church and did whatever they were asked to do. They were good neighbors and parents.

Children:

JOHANNE SINA FREDERIKA PEDERSON (adopted), b. 30

Sep 1843, Taars, Denmark to Ane Marie Nielsen and Petter Andersen. Md. 19 Jan 1869, Gustave Walfred Soderberg. D. 20 May 1920.

CAROLINE, b. 5 Sep 1848, Ugilt, Hjorring, Denmark. Md. 15 Dec 1868 Niels Peder Nielsen. D. 24 May 1928.

ELSE MARIE, b. 5 Aug 1850, Ugilt, Denmark. Unmarried. D. 1 Aug 1866.

NIELS CHRISTIAN, b. 24 Jan 1853, Ugilt, Denmark. Md. 19 Aug 1873, Mette Marie Jorgensen. D. 23 Aug 1937.

MICHAEL (twin), b. 10 Jul 1855, Ugilt, Denmark. D. 11 Dec 1855. Child.

KARL (twin), b. 10 Jul 1855, Ugilt, Denmark. D. 27 Nov 1855. Child.

KARL, b. 8 Oct 1856, Ugilt, Denmark. Unmarried. D. Nov 1869.

ANE KATRINE, b. 18 Apr 1859 (or 10 Apr 1858), Ugilt, Denmark. Md. Andrew Anderson. D. 1884.

NIELS PEDER, b. 10 Aug 1861, Ugilt, Denmark. D. 13 Jul 1866.

ANTINE, b. 8 Mar 1864, Ugilt, Denmark. D. 8 May 1866.

Submitted by: Pat Grey

CHRISTIAN CHRISTENSEN

Photograph not available

Born: 7 Apr 1790, Hindborg, Dolby, Viborg, Denmark
Parents: Christen and Else Kirstine Christiansen Pedersen
Died: 18 Jan 1871, Levan, Utah
Arrived in Valley: 30 Sep 1853, Forsgren Co.

Married 1st: Anne Marie Espersen
Date: 29 Dec 1814, Dalby, Viborg, Denmark

Born: 1 Jun 1784, Dalby, Viborg, Denmark
Parents: Christen and Maren Roersen Espersen
Died: 28 Feb 1858, Salt Lake City, Utah

Married 2nd: Anne Kirstine Pedersen–No children
Date: 22 Jul 1855, probably Utah
Born: 1772 (age 37 in 1809)
Died: 21 Mar 1809, Copenhagen, Denmark

Married 3rd: Johanne Marie Larsen–No children
Date: 28 Mar 1858, Utah
Born: abt 1790

Married 4th: Anne Maria Christensdatter
Born: abt 1802

Christen joined the Church in 1850. He was appointed president of the Copenhagen Branch. He labored as a missionary one and a half years before sailing for America.

He filled a mission to the United States in 1854-57. He labored mostly in St. Louis, Missouri. He completed another mission in Scandinavia in 1865-67. After his return home, he was called to help settle Levan in Juab County. In 1884-85 he filled another mission to Scandinavia.

While in Denmark, he served in the Danish-Prussian war of 1848. He and his first wife were the first Mormon couple married in Denmark. He was the first man to receive the Melchizedek Priesthood in Denmark. Upon his return from his mission to Scandinavia, he headed up a handcart company of Scandinavian saints.

Children of 1st wife:

OLE, b. 25 May 1810, Trustrup, Dalby, Viborg, Denmark. D. 28 Dec 1870.
CHRISTEN, b. 16 Nov 1815, Vester Dalby, Viborg, Denmark. D. 22 Dec 1823.
NIELS, b. 4 Oct 1817, Dolby, Denmark. Md. 28 Oct 1845,

Catherine Mortensen, and 1 other. D. 27 Jan 1899, Ephraim, Utah.

ELSE MARIE, b. 9 Apr 1820, Delby, Denmark. Md. 3 Mar 1843, Iver Johannes Olsen. and 2 others. D. 1 May 1909, Ephraim, Utah.

CHRISTIAN, b. 15 Sep 1822, Trustrup, Dalby, Denmark. D. 8 Aug 1853, Petite Creek, on the plains in Nebraska.

NIELS PETER, b. 5 Nov 1822, Haurbak, Viborg, Denmark. Md. 26 Oct 1852, Ane Marie Jensen and 1 other. D. 29 Apr 1867, Denmark.

CHRISTEN, b. 7 Oct 1824, Trustrup,Virborg, Denmark. Md. 13 Oct 1850, Christina Maria Hedvig Bruhn and 8 others. D. 23 Sep 1900, Manti, Utah.

CHRISTEN, b. 12 Aug 1824, Meilsohus, Thisted, Denmark. Md. 12 Apr 1852, Inger Christine Pedersen and 1 other. D. 23 Dec 1870, Hundborg, Denmark.

ANNE MARIA, b. 25 May 1826, Trustrup, Viborg, Denmark. Md. 25 Jun 1854, Nils Olsson and 3 others. D. 2 Dec 1863, Castle Dale, Utah.

ASMUS CARL, b. 23 Sep 1830, Ruede, Schlho, Prussia. Md. 20 Nov 1912, Catharina Dorothea Erichsen. D. 20 Nov 1912, Schleeswig, Rude, Germany.

2nd and 3rd wives had no children.

Child of 4th wife:

CHRISTEN, b. 7 Oct 1824, Trustrup, Viborg, Denmark. Md. 13 Oct 1850, Christina Maria Hedvigg Bruhn and 8 others. D. 23 Sep 1900, Manti, Utah.

Submitted by: Burnyce Powell

CHRISTEN CHRISTIANSEN (DALBY)

Photograph
not
available

Born: 7 Oct 1824, Trustrup, Dolby, Viborg, Denmark
Died: 23 Sep 1900, Manti, Sanpete, Utah
Arrived in Valley: 1853, John E. Forsgren Co.

Married 1st: Christina Maria Hedvig Bruhn (Bruun)
Date: 13 Oct 1850, Dolby, Viborg, Denmark

Married 2nd: Ana Marie Jensen
Date: 2 May 1868, Salt Lake City, Utah

Married 3rd: Karen Bendtsdatter
SS: 3 Jun 1892 (not married)

Married 4th: Anna Marie Olsen
SS: 12 Oct 1857

Married 5th: Mary Langrus

Married 6th: Christinia Marie Hedevig Brown

Married 7th: Mary Ann Louisa Langrup
SS: 11 Nov 1856

When Christen heard the Mormon missionaries, he joined the Church, becoming the first convert in Denmark. He married Hedvig Bruun, was appointed president of the Copenhagen Branch, and was the first member in Scandinavia to be ordained an Elder.

He was a missionary in Denmark for a year and a half and

then emigrated with his family to Utah in 1852-3. He filled a mission in Missouri and, while returning to Utah, took charge of a handcart company of Scandinavian saints. He filled another mission to Scandinavia in 1865-67. Upon his return he was called to help settle Levan, Juab County, Utah. He was one of the first settlers of Nephi and Ephraim. He filled another mission to Denmark in 1884-85. He moved his family to Manti when the temple was dedicated and worked in the temple the rest of his life.

He took the name of Dalby as his surname. After he joined the church, he immediately gave up his occupation and devoted his entire time to being a missionary. He and Hedwig were the first Mormon couple married in Denmark. Those who came west in his handcart company always blessed him for all he did to help them stand the rigors of the journey.

When he brought his family to the Valley in 1853, they lost twin stillborn children. In Captain John Forsgren's journal of the trip, he mentions the parents and several brothers and sisters of Christian who were in the Company. He also mentions the still-born birth of the twins near Keokuk, Iowa on 29 April 1853.

Children of 1st wife:

TWINS, b. 29 Apr 1853, Near Keokuk, Iowa. Stillborn.

Children of 2nd wife:

ANNE JENSINE KRISTENSDATTER, b. 1852, Ofoten, Nordland, Norge. Md. 28 Jul 1878, Johan Andreas K. N. Ramberg. D. 25 Oct 1878, Norge.
ANTOMINE THOMSEN, b. 27 Jan 1862, Volstrup, Hjorning, Denmark. D. 1867.
EZRA , b. 24 Mar 1869, Ephraim, Utah. Md. 14 Feb 1894, Rosella Anderson. D. 1 Jan 1934, Salt Lake City, Utah.
OLIVER, b. 11 Nov 1870, Levan, Juab, Utah. Md. 1 Jan 1896, Frances Francom. D. 10 Jul 1928.

Children of 3rd wife:

ANE KIRSTINE CRAMER, b. 10 Apr 1860, Ostbirk,
    Skanderborg, Denmark. D. 17 Dec 1865.
JOHN CHARLES (Johan Karl), b. 8 Mar 1862, Traeden,
    Skanderborg, Denmark. D. 17 Jan 1941.

Submitted By: Burnyce Powell

JENS CHRISTENSEN

Born: 1 Jul 1830, Tobberup, Aalborg, Denmark
Parents: Christen and Else Nielsen Pedersen
Died: 17 Feb 1892, Newton, Cache, Utah
Arrived in Valley: Sep 1864, William B. Preston Co.

Married 1st: Karen Anderson
Date: 17 May 1862, Logster, Viborg, Denmark
Born: 4 Jan 1840, Aalborg, Denmark
Died: 9 Sep 1866, Sanpete Co., Utah

Married 2nd: Mary Regastine Jensen
Date: 1867, Salt Lake City, Utah

Married 3rd: Karen (Caroline) Jensen
Date: 21 Dec 1874, Utah
Jens adopted her daughter, Zina

   Jens brought his family to the Valley in 1864. They were immediately called to help settle Sanpete County. He was involved in the Black Hawk Indian War when most of his stock and other property was stolen by the Indians.

When his wife died at the birth of their baby, he moved to Salt Lake. He soon took on two more wives and endured a short term in prison for cohabition. With his second wife he moved to Logan, and later moved to Brigham City and Newton, Cache, Utah.

He left a legacy of faith and honesty and love of the gospel to his children. He believed in education and it showed up in the lives of his children and grandchildren.

Children of 1st wife:

MARY ELIZABETH (twin), b. 3 May 1863, Hobro, Randers, Denmark
CHRISTIAN (twin), b. 3 May 1863. D. 3 May 1863.
CHRISTIAN LARAMIE, b. 22 Aug 1864, Fort Laramie, Wyoming. D. 23 Feb 1924, Logan, Utah.

Children of 2nd wife:

CHARLES MARTINEZ, b. 17 Nov 1867. Md. 20 Dec 1893, Bernice Griffiths Ledingham. D. 1 Dec 1929, Logan, Utah.
JAMES, b. 28 May 1869, Brigham City, Utah. D. 5 Oct 1869, Brigham City, Utah.
JOSEPH ADOLPHUS, b. 17 Apr 1871, Brigham City, Utah. Md. 27 Jun 1900, Helen May Campbell. D. 19 Jul 1904, Logan, Utah.
PETER NEPHI, b. 7 May 1873, Newton, Utah. Md. 15 Jun 1903, Anna Therese Miller. D. 1 Jul 1941, Newton, Utah.
MOSES, b. 26 Apr 1876, Newton, Utah. Md. 21 Nov 1900, Mary Ann Cooley. D. 21 Nov 1900, Logan, Utah.
SON, b 1879, Newton, Utah. Stillborn.
HENRY MORONI, b. 2 Dec 1877, Newton, Utah. D. abt 1882, Newton, Utah.

Children of 3rd wife:

KAREN ELIZABETH, b. 30 Oct 1875, Newton, Utah. Md. 30 Sep 1903, Fred Fredrickson. D. 17 Nov 1961, Logan, Utah.

JAMES WILLIAM, b. 17 Sep 1877, Newton, Utah. Md. 4 Feb 1910, Agnes Christiansen. D. 9 Aug 1937, Downey, Bannock, Idaho.

ANNA CHRISTINE, b. 25 Dec 1879. Md. 27 Jan 1910, George Amos Rigby. D. 28 Jun 1963, Bancroft, Caribou, Idaho.

ADA BOLETTA, b. 25 Oct 1883, Newton, Utah. Md. 21 Jul 1901, Moroni Richard Almond. D.30 May 1979, Preston, Idaho.

DAVID WILFORD, b. 18 Oct 1885, Newton, Utah. Md. 26 Jun 1912, Mary Marie Eilertsen. D. 9 Oct 1961, Bountiful, Utah.

SIGNE (ZINA) JENSEN (adopted. Daughter of wife Karen). b.21 Jul 1870, Silkeborg, Skanderborg, Denmark. Md. 29 Oct 1890, Elmer Ludwick Johnson. D. 17 Feb 1937, Logan, Utah.

Submitted by: Stephen Alley

MADS FREDERICK THEOBALD CHRISTENSEN

Born: 10 Mar 1837, Copenhagen, Denmark
Parents: Mads and Dorthea Christiane Tranum Christensen
Died: 14 Jul 1917, Mt Pleasant, Sanpete Co., Utah
Arrived in Valley: 5 Sep 1854, Hans Peter Olson Co.

Married 1st: Sophia Christina Rasmussen
Date: 3 Jun 1861, Fairview, Sanpete, Utah
Born: 2 Aug 1844, Voium, Sommerstead, Haderslev, Denmark
Parents: Hans Peter and Anne Kristine Ludvigson Kjar Rasmussen
Died: 18 Mar 1906, Utah

Married 2nd: Frederrikka "Rikki" Olson

Date: 26 Dec 1863, Salt Lake City, Utah. (Div)
Born: Danish

Married 3rd: Jensine Serine Larson
Sealed: 2 Jul 1909, Salt Lake Temple, Utah

Fred, as he was known, was a brother to C.C.A. Christensen, the well known pioneer artist. Their father died when he and his two brothers were young. Their mother was determined they should have a good education, so as each reached the age, they attended the "Orphans School." Upon completion, they were apprenticed in a trade. Fred served his apprenticeship as a Saddler.

When his mother became converted by the Mormon missionaries, Fred was the first of his brothers to join the Church. Being anxious to go to "Zion," his youngest brother Niels left first. The next year while CCA was on a mission, Fred and his mother had an opportunity to go. After reaching the Valley, Fred was picked to labor south of Salt Lake. William was working in Springville, so Fred got permission to join him. Times were extremely difficult for the boys, but they struggled through.

Fred married and later decided to try polygamy. When Brigham Young asked for volunteers to settle "the Muddy," Fred moved his two wives and children to St. Thomas. They lived in a dugout until he was able to make enough bricks for a house. During this time, his wives had children, some of which died. It was another difficult time.

Fred worked not only as a farmer, but he and his brother William built a shingle mill. He also worked as a mason, painter, carpenter, paper hanger, and he made fine furniture. Later he ran a harness shop, tuned pianos, and had a photo gallery . He sold Singer sewing machines and organs. In 1877, he and C.C.A. decided to join together in an artist exhibit of C.C.A.'s paintings on the "Mormon Panorama." Later he sold his interest to C.C.A.

He served several missions in Denmark. During the third mission, his wife Sophia died. His children were all grown, so he remained to complete his mission. He was advised to marry again, which he did.

Fred wrote the music for several hymns including "Transport," which was in the LDS Psalmody (1889). In the 1927 hymn book, it is called "Go Ye Messengers of Heaven." John Taylor wrote the music. He also wrote "Join the Children of the Lord."

He left a great legacy to his family.

Children of 1st wife:

FREDERICK CHARLES, b. D. age 19.
ANNIE DOROTHEA, b. 1864, Fairview, Utah.
JOHN WILLIAM, b. 20 Jul 1867, St. Thomas, Utah.
GEORGE FRANKLIN, b. 1 Aug 1870, St. Thomas, Utah.
WARREN OSCAR, b. 6 May 1872, Fairview, Utah.
ELINORA SOPHIA, b. 6 Apr 1874, Fairview, Utah.
EMMA REBECCA, b. 7 May 1876, Fairview, Utah.
SARAH OCTAVIA, b. 6 Dec 1878, Fairview, Utah.
ELIZA MAY, b. 1 May 1881, Fairview, Utah.
JESSIE EDNA, b. 27 May 1883, Fairview, Utah.
LOUISE LORETTA, b. 24 Dec 1886, Fairview, Utah. D. 1888/9.

Children of 2nd wife:

HELEN ELIZABETH, b. 31 Jul 1865, St. Thomas, Utah. D. 1866.
JOSEPH AUGUST, b. 22 Sep 1867, Muddy, Utah. D. 1868 (10 months)
LORENZO PETER, b. 14 Oct 1869. Lived a long life.

Children of 3rd wife:

ELLA ROSALIE, b. 20 Feb 1908, Mt Pleasant, Utah
JENNIE ZINA, b. 24 Feb 1909, Mt. Pleasant, Utah

Submitted by: Ruby Smith

RASMUS PETER CHRISTENSEN

Born: 9 Apr 1821, Tulstrup, Skanderborg, Denmark
Parents: Christen and Maren Rasmussen
Died: 20 Sep 1913, Moroni, Sanpete, Utah
Arrived in Valley: 22 Sep 1961, Samuel A. Woolley Co.

Married 1st: Bodil Kjerstine Sorensen
Date: 1 Aug 1846
Born: 16 Feb 1827, Sorring, Dallerup, Skanderborg, Denmark
Died: 13 Nov 1850, Denmark

Married 2nd: Karen Eskilsen
Date: 14 Jun 1851
Born: 19 Dec 1829, Dallerup, Aarhus, Denmark
Died: 15 Apr 1852, Denmark

Married 3rd: Maria Svensen
Date: 2 Nov 1852
Born: 15 Dec 1824, Balle, Viborg, Denmark
Died: 22 Dec 1905, Moroni, Sanpete, Utah

Married 4th: Sena Peterson (Stark)
Date: 28 Apr 1873
Born: 17 Mar 1838, Serup, Viborg, Denmark
Died: 26 May 1905, Moroni, Sanpete, Utah

Rasmus Peter's name, being the oldest child in the family, was changed to Christensen, according to Danish custom. He was required to work while young to help the family income.

He mourned the loss of two wives who left him with several young children. He married again. He and his third wife joined the Church in 1860. He became a missionary in his area and labored for 16 months before immigrating to the Valley. They brought with them six children. On board ship a measles epidemic broke out, resulting in the death of two children. A third child died in Nebraska.

Upon their arrival in Utah, they settled in Moroni in a dugout. There were so many Peters in Moroni that he became known as "Peter Dane." He was a farmer by trade and was considered well off. He also learned the art of making and firing brick. He financially helped many of the Danish saints immigrate to America. He worked on the St. George and Manti Temples.

After living in Moroni 11 years, he married again. He was a great commedian and people loved having him around, especially at socials where he performed. He loved to sing and was the chorister of a Danish Choir.

In 1888, Rasmus and Sena and their children moved to Sanford, Colorado, where they stayed for seven years before returning to Moroni. He lived with his daughter after his wife died. He was blind the last four years of his life.

Children of 1st wife:

ANE ELIZABETH RASMUSSEN, b. 5 Jul 1846, Denmark
SOREN, b. 18 Feb 1848, Denmark
CHRISTEN, b. 10 Feb 1850. D. 5 Oct 1850

Children of 2nd wife:

CHRISTEN, b. 29 Mar 1852, Denmark. D. 13 Jan 1855

Children of 3rd wife:

KJERSTEN CAROLINE, b. 20 Oct 1853. D. 25 May 1855.
KJERSTINE CAROLINE, b. 14 Feb 1856.
MARIANE, b. 10 Oct 1857, Denmark. D. aboard ship of measles.
SVEND, b. 15 Jul 1859, Denmark. D. 1861, Florence, Nebraska

KAREN MARIE, b. 29 Sep 1860, Denmark. D. aboard ship of
   measles.
PETER, b. 5/6 Sep 1862, Moroni, Utah.
ERASTUS, b. 4 Feb 1865, Moroni, Utah.
JAMES, b. 13 Sep 1867, Moroni, Utah

Children of 4th wife:

MARIA ELIZABETH, b. 27 Jan 1874, Moroni, Utah. D. 16 Mar
   1965
ANNA ROZINA, b. 10 Oct 1875, Moroni, Utah. D 18 Mar 1878,
   drowned.
ERASTUS PETER, b. 6 Jan 1878, Moroni, Utah. D. 21 Oct
   1955
ANNIE ELIZABETH, b. 13 Oct 1880, Moroni, Utah.

Submitted by: Elaine Schofield

NIELS CHRISTIAN CHRISTIANSEN

Born: 4 Oct 1817, Trustrup, Dolby, Viborg, Denmark
Parents: Christian and Anne Maria Christensdatter Christensen
Died 26 Jan 1899, Ephraim, Sanpete, Utah.
Arrived in Valley: 30 Sep 1853, John E. Forsgren Co.

Married 1st: Catherine Mortensen
Date: 18 Oct 1845, Skive, Viborg, Denmark
Born: 14 Jan 1821, Egeris, Skive, Viborg, Denmark
Parents: Frederick and Dorthe Jensen Mortensen
Died: 26 Feb 1893, Ephraim, Sanpete, Utah

Married 2nd: Dorthe Kjerstine (Dahl) Clemmensdatter
Date: 13 Apr 1856 , Salt Lake City, Utah.
Born: 22 Mar 1827, Jegindo, Thisted, Denmark
Died: 27 Jul 1920, Gunnison, Sanpete, Utah

Niels was a mason and stone cutter by trade and worked on the Salt Lake Temple. He was sent to Ephraim to help settle it and work with the Indians. He also worked on the Manti Temple.

He was active as Captain of the Silver Grays in the Black Hawk War. He was active in the community, serving on the City Council and as a school trustee plus other public offices. He was active in the church as a missionary and temple worker. He set a good example for his family and others to follow.

Children of 1st wife:

ANNA MARIA, b. 26 Jan 1845, Skive, Viborg, Denmark. Md. 1865, Rasmus Clausen. D. 16 Feb 1930.

DORTHE MARIE, b. 6 Jan 1848, Skive, Viborg, Denmark. D. 17 Jan 1848.

CHRISTIAN, b. 30 Jun 1850, Skive, Viborg, Denmark. Md. Johanna Marts Madison. D. 7 Feb 1899.

CHRISTINE, b. 21 Jan 1852, Skive, Viborg, Denmark. D. Jul 1852.

JOSEPH, b. 17 Aug 1854, Salt Lake City, Utah. Md. 31 Jan 1874, Hannah Mette Pedersen. D. 6 Mar 1895.

EPHRAIM, b. 24 Aug 1857, Ephraim, Sanpete, Utah. D.1 Oct 1857.

EMMA, b. 17 Jul 1859, Ephraim, Utah. Md. 24 Apr 1884, Ole Olson. D. Jan 1843.

HANNAH, b. 23 Sep 1862, Ephraim, Utah. Md. 8 Apr 1885, Thomas Peter Thomson. D. 17 Jun 1926.

CATHERINE, b. 24 Nov 1865, Ephraim, Utah. Md. 19 Jun 1901, Benjamin Hansen. D. 20 Dec 1920.

Children of 2nd wife:

PARLEY, b. 7 Dec 1857, Salt Lake City, Utah. Md. 19 Apr 1880, Dorthea Christine Scow. D. 13 May 1920.

MARY, b. 6 Apr 1861, Ephraim, Utah. Md. 6 Apr 1861, James William Stevenson. D. 17 Jun 1941.

ELIZABETH, b. 2 Feb 1865, Ephraim, Utah. Md. 10 Mar 1883, John Hardin Whitlock. D. 9 May 1934.

Submitted by: Hazel Marrott and John Christiansen

HADEN WELLS CHURCH, SR.

Born: 29 Aug 1817, Franklin, Williamson, Tennessee
Parents: Abraham and Polly Emmons Church
Died: 27 Sep 1875, Shady Grove, Hickman, Tennessee
Arrived in Valley: 29 Jul 1847, Brigham Young Co.

Married 1st: Sarah Ann Arterbury
Date: 19 Dec 1844, Perry Co., Alabama
Born: 4 May 1824, Dallas, Alabama
Died: 29 Jul 1889, St. George, Washington, Utah
Arrived in Valley: 25 Sep 1847, A.O Smoot Co.

Married 2nd: Emily Jame Powell–No children
Date: Sealed 17 Jul 1853

Married 3rd: Ellen McKennia–No children
Date: Sealed 15 Sep 1852. (Div. 16 Mar 1853
Born: 16 Aug 1833, Cleverton, Hereford, England

Married 4th: Cathern Gardner–No children
Date: Sealed 15 Mar 1857
Born: 17 Nov 1809/10, Wolvereton, Hamps, England

Married 5th: Matilda Rutledge–No children
Date: Sealed 15 Oct 1870
Born: 4 Apr 1813, Lancaster Dist., So. Carolina

Deceased women sealed to Haden Wells Church 30 Apr 1854:
Martha Jane Arterbury, b. 17 Mar 1826, Dallas Co, Alabama
    D. 28 Jun 1845.
Rebecca Caroline Arterbury, b. 12 or 5 Dec 1832, Dallas Co.
    Alabama. D. 22 Feb 1845.
Mary Louisa Arterbury, b. 11 May 1834, Dallas Co., Alabama.
    D. 11 Feb 1845.

Haden Wells grew up near Duck River, Shady Grove, Hickman, Tennessee. He became a school teacher. He was a typical old time school master who spoiled no child by sparing the rod.

Haden met the missionaries and traveled 400 miles to Nauvoo to learn more. He was baptized by the Prophet in 1843. He returned to Alabama to marry Sarah Ann. They returned to Nauvoo but were soon driven out by the mobs. He joined the Mormon Battalion, leaving his wife and son with the saints.

After his release, he arrived in the Valley but left shortly to find his wife. They arrived in the valley Sept. 1847.

Haden served five missions besides being called to the Dixie Cottonwood Mission to help settle the area. He served in the Southern States, British Mission, Mississippi, Alabama and Tennessee Missions. He was one of the first school teachers in St. George. In his final mission in Tennessee, he came down with Typhoid Fever and died there.

Children of 1st wife:

HYRUM SMITH, b. 9 Mar 1846, Nauvoo, Illinois. Md. 3 Oct
    1868, Melissa Ella Elmer. D. 15 Sep 1908, Panguitch, Utah.
HADEN WELLS JR., b.8 Sep 1848, Salt Lake City, Utah. Md. 4
    Oct 1866, Violet Jeffery Pendleton. D 20 Apr 1922, St. George,
    Utah.
ABRAHAM ARTERBURY, b. 25 Feb 1854, Salt Lake City, Utah.

Md. 4 Oct 1877, Martha Ellen Alger. D. 5 May 1916, Panguitch, Garfield, Utah.

PARALEE AMANDA, b. 8 Jul 1857, Salt Lake City, Utah. Md. 25 May 1874, William Gustavus Miles. D. 29 Jul 1929, Salt Lake City, Utah.

ROBERT ROBBINS, b. 27 Oct 1859, Salt Lake City, Utah. Md. 14 Sep 1881, Charlotte Emily Talbot. D. 30 Apr 1881, St. George, Utah.

Submitted by: Walter Church

DANIEL CLARK

Born: 25 Oct 1815, Colchester, Essex, England
Parents: William and Catherine Nichols Clark
Died: 28 Aug 1864, Near Alda, Hall, Nebraska
Died while crossing the plains with the William Hyde Co. 1864.

Married: Elizabeth Gower
Date: 27 Oct 1839, St. Mary Magdalen Parish, Colchester, Essex, England
Born: 20 Feb 1819, Little Badadow, Essex, England
Parents: William and Elizabeth Nunn Gower
Died: 28 Oct 1882, Richville, Morgan, Utah

Daniel's father died when he was two years old and his mother died when he was six. His maternal grandmother raised him and his brother William. Their father was a shoemaker whose father and grandfather were also shoemakers, thus with Daniel it made four generations of shoe makers.

Daniel loved music and developed his talents at every opportunity. He learned to play the concertina, the fife, and several other instruments. He had a good voice and loved to sing.

In 1851, young missionary Charles Penrose entered their lives and Daniel and Elizabeth were converted. They became very active in the Colchester branch of the Church. This brought on much persecution by former friends and acquaintances, even affecting his business. The children were no longer allowed to attend school but were taught at home. They finally left in the middle of the night and went to live with Elizabeth's parents.

They determined to go to America. They sent the three oldest girls first and then saved money to take the rest of them. They finally were able to leave England in 1864. The voyage was extremely difficult. By the time they got to Wyoming, cholera was raging in the companies and Daniel was not immune. He became a victim by the Platte River near Grand Island and was buried there.

Children:

ELIZABETH FRANCES, b. 17 Sep 1840, Colchester, Essex, England. Md. 7 Jun 1862, Caleb Ebenezer Crouch (Div). D. 25 Jun 1872, Ogden, Utah.

SARAH ANNIE, b, 27 Mar 1842, Colchester, England. Md. 24 Dec 1861, Grantsville, Utah. D. 7 Sep 1918, Logan, Utah.

REBECCA ANGELINA, b. 13 Mar 1844, Colchester, England. Md. 22 Nov 1861, Thomas John Stayner. D. 27 Aug 1917, Bountiful, Utah.

DANIEL, b. 13 Jul 1846, Colchester, England. D. Nov 1846.

ELLEN VICTORIA, b. 6 Jan 1848, Colchesteer, England. Md. 19 Aug 1865, Alma Helaman Hale. D. 8 Mar 1940, Groveland, Idaho

WILLIAM GOWER, b. 26 Mar 1850, Colchester, England. D. 26 Apr 1850.

CATHERINE, b. 7 Sep 1851, Colchester, England. Md. 21 Dec 1868, David Coolbear. D. 12 Jun 1922, Morgan, Utah.

ARTHUR BENJAMIN, b. 22 Mar 1854, Barking, Essex,

England. Md. 7 Dec 1874, Helen Margaret Ross. D. 26 Jul
1917, Blackfoot, Idaho.
ROSA EMELINE, b. 14 Jun 1857, Barking, England. Md. 22
Feb 1875, George Hammond. D. 18 Jan 1941, Grantsville,
Utah.
FREDERICK WILLIAM, b. 19 Dec 1859, Barking, England.
Md. 25 Jun 1885, Emma Sophia Robinson. D. 21 Aug 1949,
Richville, Utah.

Submitted by: Janet Ralph

JAMES CLARK(E)

Born: 3 Apr 1806, Clawthrope, Burton in Kendal, Westmoreland,
England
Parents: Abram and Jane Beck Clark
Died: 30 Jun 1881, Cedar Fort, Utah, Utah
Arrived in Valley: 27 Sep 1856, James Pearson Co. who broke
off from John Banks Co.

Married: Elizabeth Pearson
Date: 26 Dec 1829, Burton In Kendal, Westmoreland, England
Born: 29 Mar 1805, Whitehaven, Cumberland, England
Died: 1 Feb 1889, Cedar Fort, Utah, Utah

James was a stone cutter and mason by trade. After their second child, they moved to Preston, Lancashire, England, where
they heard the gospel and were converted, being baptized in 1839.
They sacrificed much so they might come to the Valley. They left
England in 1850, lived in St. Louis for five and a half years to

earn enough money for the journey west. While there their oldest son John died of cholera, and their daughter Jane, married.

They arrived in the valley in 1856 and continued on and settled in Cedar Fort, Utah. James was called to help build the Salt Lake Temple, working without pay. He died before the temple was completed and was buried in Cedar Fort, Utah.

Children:

JOHN, b. abt 1831, Clawathrope, Burton In Kendall, Westmoreland, England. D. 1851, St. Louis, Missouri

JAMES PEARSON, b. 26 Oct 1833, Clawathrope, Burton In Kendall, Westmoreland, England. Md. 7 May 1857, Mary Ann Dobson. D. 18 Mar 1913, Cedar Fort, Utah

THOMAS, b. abt 1835, Preston, Lancashire, England

JANE, b. 21 Feb 1839, Preston, Lancashire, England. Md. 16 May 1856, John Sampson Hacking. D. 3 Mar 1913, Cedar Fort,Utah

ALICE, b. 8 Dec 1841, Holme, Burton in Kendal, Westmoreland, England.

EMMA, b. 25 Jul 1845, Longridge, Stafford, England. Md. 8 Jul 1861 John Drysdale. D. 15 Jun 1919, Salt Lake City, Utah.

Submitted by: Donna Bird

JOHN CLARK

Born: 2 Nov 1804, Lochwinnock, Renfrewshire, Scotland
Parents: David and Elizabeth Wylie Clark
Died: Spring 1854, Bingham's Fort, Ogden, Weber, Utah

Arrived in Valley: 1852, Independent Wagon Co.

Married 1st: Johanna Welsh
Date: Unknown
Died: 1834

Married 2nd: Lillias Barbour
Date: 18 Dec 1837, Abby Paisley, Renfrewshire, Scotland
Born: 12 Jan 1818, Scotland
Died: 8 Oct 1898, North Ogden, Weber, Utah

John's first three children all died of consumption and tuberculois, followed by his wife. Three years later he married his second wife, Lillias, and they lived in Paisley. John worked as a weaver.

They became acquainted with the first missionaries sent to Scotland and were converted in 1840. Soon after the birth of a daughter in 1840, the family began making plans to leave for America. They arrived in 1841 and settled in LaHarpe, Hancock, Illinois, on a farm. His mother-in-law and sister-in-law had come with them.

In 1852 they left for the valley. Soon after arriving, they went to Ogden and settled in Bingham's Fort. John worked hard to make a good home for his family. He and his family remained active in the church, holding many positions. He was also active in the community efforts. He died of tuberculosis not quite two years after arriving in the valley.

Children of 1st wife:

DAVID, b. 1827. D. before 1834, Scotland
MARY, b. 1829. D. before 1834, Scotland
AGNES, b. 1833. D. before 1834, Scotland

Children of 2nd wife:

PETER BARBOUR, b. 6 Oct 1838, Paisley, Scotland. D. 30 May
    1926.

MARGARET CALDWELL, b. 6 Nov 1840, Paisley, Scotland. D. May 1877.

JAMES DOUGLAS, b. 6 Oct 1843, LaHarpe, Hancock, Illinois. D. 2 Nov 1845.

KATE ARABEL, b. 9 Jun 1846, LaHarpe, Illinois. D. 12 Jun 1925.

NANCY MARIA, b. 14 Jan 1849, Council Bluffs, Iowa. D. 23 Jun 1923.

ANDREW ALEXANDER, b. 5 Oct 1851, Council Bluffs, Iowa. D. 11 Nov 1937.

CHARLES EDWARD, b. 23 Dec 1853. D. 9 Jun 1937.

Submitted by: Alice Wyatt

WILLIAM CLARK

Born: 26 Jul 1825, Mitre Oak, Worcestershire, England
Parents: John Wheeler and Mary Hill Clark
Died: 7 May 1910, Lehi, Utah, Utah
Arrived in Valley: 1852.

Married 1st: Emily K. Bryant
Date: 20 Sep 1848, England
Died: 1850, England

Married 2nd: Jane Steverson (widow with 3 children)
Date: Winter 1851, England
Children: 6 girls and 1 boy

Married 3rd: Julia Ann Zimmerman
Date: abt 1854,

Married 4th: Margaret Boardman
Date: 20 Apr 1867, Salt Lake City, Utah
Born: 30 Sep 1840, Preston, Lancs, England
Parents: William and Mary Marshall Boardman
Died: 10 Aug 1894, Lehi, Utah

William married his first wife prior to leaving England. She died following childbirth the next year. In the winter of 1851, he married Jane who was a widow. The following spring they started for the west. He married Julia Ann, and then in 1867, he moved to Lehi and met and married Margaret Boardman.

From all his marriages, he had 10 children plus three he adopted from Jane's first marriage.

He was a plaster by trade and did work for many of the people in Lehi. He was also a successful farmer and sheep man. He was prominent in the community, being at various times involved in the People's Co-op Mercantile Institution, Lehi Irrigation Company, and Lehi Commercial and Savings Bank.

He served several terms in the Lehi City Council, was road supervisor, and Pound Keeper. He went on a mission to England in 1880 and was a counselor in the bishopric in Lehi prior to the division of the ward. He was known as a fair and honest man, and he was a good husband and father.

Three of his children were:

THOMAS HENRY, b. 19 Jan 1868, Lehi, Utah. Md. 22 Feb 1886,
    Margaret Ann Fox. D. 19 Aug 1939, Lehi, Utah.
MARY ANN, b. 18 Sep 1871, Lehi, Utah. D. 14 Jan 1948.
JAMES, b. 18 Jul 1875, Lehi, Utah. D. 11 Aug 1939.

Submitted by: Woodrow Dennett

ROBERT CLARKSON

Born: 17 Jan 1834, Beverly, Yorkshire, England
Parents: Matthew and Elizabeth Lealand Clarkson
Died: 8 Mar 1867, Logan, Utah
Arrived in Valley: 6 Sep 1860, Jesse Murphy Co.

Married: Ann Clegg
Date: 24 Dec 1854, Hull, Yorkshire, England
Born: 13 Feb 1832, Hull, Yorkshire, England
Parents: Nathaniel and Ann Leaf Clegg.
Died: 8 Feb 1862, Salt Lake City, Utah

Married 2nd: Sarah Dowell Rogers
Date: 15 Mar 1862, Salt Lake City, Utah (Div)
Born: 8 Jul 1825, Glouchestershire, England

Married 3rd: Hannah J. Hough (widow)
Date: abt 1863, Salt Lake City, Utah

Robert was baptized a member of the Church on 24 February 1850 at the age of 16. He and his family were very active in the branch for four years until they left for America. He was active in missionary work in England where he would walk to the surrounding area in all kinds of weather to help the saints when needed. He distributed tracts and sang with his beautiful voice in the meetings and took part in many programs.

His wife was baptized in 1851. She was expert in milinery work and dressmaking. She, too, had a lovely voice and they enjoyed singing together.

They sailed for America on the ship "Cynosure" in 1855. When they arrived in the Valley, Robert got work as a cooper. They were faithful to the Church. Robert held many positions in the church. Ann died when she was 30 years old, after the birth of their son.

Due to poor health and the care of small children, Robert married soon after Ann's death, but they were later divorced. He married once more to a Danish widow who had an adopted daughter.

In the fall of 1863, he moved his family to Logan where he built a cooper shop. He made wooden butter kegs, water buckets, washtubs, etc. In February 1867, after pouring dusty wheat into a bin, his lungs, already weakened previously, filled with dust and he started to cough, which started a severe hemorrhage. He died at the young age of 33.

Children of 1st wife:

ANN ELIZABETH, b. 38 Jan 1856, Petersburg, New York. D. 18 Sep 1857, New York.
RUTH, b. 12 Sep 1857, New York City, New York. Md. 26 Dec 1878, Ozro Ozias Crockett. D. 12 May 1947, Preston, Idaho.
IDA CLARISSA, b. 19 Sep 1859, New York City, New York. Md. 17 Nov 1881, Hugh James Adams. D. 1 Feb 1922, Hyrum, Utah.
CHARLES ROBERT, b. 2 Feb 1862, Salt Lake City, Utah. Md. 1st, 18 Sep 1884, Alvira Stout. Md. 2nd, 1925, Mary Araminta North Nielsen. D. 16 Jan 1954, Holladay, Utah.

Child of 2nd wife:

EMILY CLARISSA.

Submitted by: Rosalie Brown

WILLIAM CLAYSON

Born: 9 Feb 1840, Wilby, North Hampton, England
Parents: Thomas and Fanny Essom Clayson
Died: 28 Jul 1887, Payson, Utah
Arrived in Valley: Sep 1861.

Married 1st: Susan Moulton
Date: 16 Dec 1863, Salt Lake City, Utah

Married 2nd: Selina Heaton
Date: Sep 1865.

Married 3rd: Sarah A. Sheffield
Date: 1876

William lost half of his left foot in an accident when he was 10 years old. After his return to health, he apprenticed to learn the shoemaking trade. About this same time, he also learned to play the flute and took lessons from a good teacher.

While working, he learned of the missionaries and became converted, along with his sister Emma. He was baptized in 1855. Later, his parents and the rest of their children were also baptized. Soon after his baptism, he was called to accompany the elders.

In 1859 he was ordained an elder and called to preside over the Wilby branch. He became acquainted with his future wife. Upon his release in 1861, he joined a group of saints who were going to Utah. Soon after arriving in the Valley, he started south with other emigrants for Parowan, where he intended to live. On the way, a friend persuaded him to stop in Payson and help in a shoe shop there. He worked in this trade the rest of his life.

He played the flute in the ward and also for dances and programs. He was the ward chorister from 1865 until his death in 1887. He had a small orchestra that was in great demand for dances and the theater. At times he had to make arrangements for the orchestra and sometimes even compose music. He composed the music for some of the LDS Hymns. He taught the youth of the area and helped music become an important part of their lives. He was also involved in the community.

He died of from Brights disease.

Children of 1st wife:

WILLIAM, Jr., b. 10 May 1863.
FANNY, b. 1 Aug 1867.
CHARLES, b. and d. about 1869/70.

Submitted by: William and Paula Joy Meldrum Davis

JOHN CLEGG

Born: 20 May 1823, Hayride, Shaw, Oldham, Lancashire, England
Parents: John and Sarah Thornton Clegg
Died: 17 Mar 1888, Fairfield, Utah, Utah
Arrived in Valley: 1851, Capt. Moses

Unmarried

The first we know of John is February 1850, when he witnessed the baptism of his nephew, Squire Thornton. John was employed as a warper. He pulled the warp or thread length wise on a loom.

When he was 25, he, his mother and two sisters left England for America. They arrived in the Valley in 1851. At age 30, John was sent with 15 men to explore Cedar Valley in Utah County for possible settlements. They selected the sight later known as Fairfield.

In 1861, John and a friend agreed to drive an ox team to Carson City, Nevada. They were gone three and a half months. He never married but settled in Fairfield. His name is on the Pony Express Monument in Fairfield, Utah.

Submitted by: LaVerne Diehl

EDWARD CLIFF

Born: 7 Sep 1830, Barrowden, Rutland, England
Parents: William and Ursula Wilkinson Cliff
Died: 7 Apr 1906, Mt. Pleasant, Utah
Arrived in Valley: 16 Oct 1858, Cyrus Wheelock's Co.

Married 1st: Eliza Cresswell
Date: 1863, Longton Parish, Staffordshire, England
Born: 14 Oct 1839, Hanley, Staffs, England
Parents: William and Sarah Woolley Cresswell
Died: 225 Feb 1916, Mt. Pleasant, Utah

Married 2nd: Harriet Moore
Date: 12 Jul 1883, Salt Lake City, Utah

Born: 20 Aug 1863, Hanley, Staffs, England
Died: 26 Jan 1951, Salt Lake City, Utah

Edward was called back to England on a mission shortly after arriving in the Valley. At the end of his mission he married Eliza and brought her and her parents back to Utah with him. They lived in Hambleton, later named Mt. Pleasant, Utah.

In 1869 he was again called to serve a mission in England. While there, he met Harriet Moore whom he married after returning to Salt Lake. He was called on another mission in 1876 to the Eastern States but he became ill and had to return home. Again in 1885, he was called on a mission to New Zealand.

He was very active in the church, serving not only as a missionary but also a bishop and in other positions of leadership.

John was a felt monger by trade in England, but after reaching the valley he was a nurseryman and potter. He worked on the Salt Lake, Manti, and St. George Temples. He also was active in the Silk Worm and Bee industry in Utah. For many years he was a reporter for the *Deseret News*. He was a justice of the peace and stake patriarch.

Child of 1st wife:

EDWARD CRESSWELL, b. 26 Aug 1864, Mt. Pleasant, Utah. D. 18 May 1868 (drowned)

Children of 2nd wife:

EDWARD PARLEY, b. 29 Aug 1884, Mt. Pleasant, Utah. D. 18 May 1922, Heber City, Wasatch, Utah.
JOHN THOMAS, b. 18 Feb 1888, Mt. Pleasant, Utah. D. 1 Mar 1975, Ogden, Weber, Utah.
GEORGE WILLIAM, b. 1898, Mt. Pleasant, Utah. D. 6 Jun 1978, Oregon. Bur. Salt Lake.

Submitted by: Gladys Eppich

JAMES CLINGER

Born: 3 Feb 1813, Bedford, Bedford, Pennsylvania
Parents: Henry and Ann R. Askin Clinger
Died: 6 Sep 1884, Pleasant Grove, Utah
Arrived in Valley: 27 Sep 1852, Thomas C. D.Howell Co./

Married: Harriet Chapin
Date: 7 Dec 1845, Illinois
Born: 6 Jun 1828, Bath, Steuben, New York
Parents: Adolphus and Katherine Billings Chapin
Died: 22 Jun 1883, Lake View, Utah, Utah

James was five feet six inches tall and weighed 170 pounds. He had blue eyes and reddish-brown hair.

After his marriage to Harriet, they moved across the Mississippi river to Iowa. Later they moved further west to Little Pigeon Creek, Pottawattamie County, Iowa. James built his own wagon to come west. After their arrival in the Valley, they moved on to Weber County where he helped erect Bingham's Fort.

After Johnston's Army problem was settled, he moved his family to Lake View, Utah. Because of problems with settling there and the hardships they experienced, they were encouraged to leave for fellowship with the Reorganized Church. They moved to Malad, Idaho, where they lived for two years, and then on to Columbus, Platt, Nebraska, in 1868. Their oldest son went east to in 1872 to persuade them to return. They did and were rebaptized in 1880. James died four years later.

Children:

MARTHA ANN, b. 19 Nov 1846, Iowa. D. 3 Feb 1940

JAMES HENRY, b. 10 Feb 1849, Little Pigeon Creek, Iowa. Md. 1st, 9 Feb 1868, Pauline Mary Williamson. Md. 2nd, 18 Sep 1884, Caroline Christensen. D. 22 May 1926, Lake View, Utah

ELMIRA ZALLOTTA, b. 26 Apr 1851, Iowa. D. 5 Jul 1852. Infant. Bur. by Platte River.

MARY JANE, b. 8 Jun 1853, Weber Co, Utah. D. 27 May 1926

WILLIAM CARLOS, b. 24 Nov 1855, Weber Co, Utah. D. 7 Oct 1912

GEORGE FRANCIS, b. 25 Jun 1858, Weber Co, Utah. D. 31 Oct 1902

ELNORA (ELINORE), b. 28 Oct 1860, Lake View, Utah. D. 10 Nov 1941

CHARLES EDWARD, b. 17 Feb 1863, Lake View, Utah. D. 18 Jun 1863. Infant

JOHN RIGGS, b. 28 Nov 1864, Lake View, Utah. D. 8 Dec 1943

LAURA CATHERINE, b. 1 Oct 1867, Malad, Idaho. D. 28 Jun 1930

HARRIET (ELIZABETH), b. 11 May 1870, Columbus, Nebraska. D. 8 Aug 1870. Infant.

LUCY ELIZABETH, b. 6 Sep 1871, Columbus, Nebraska. 8 Nov 1946.

Submitted by: Edith Clinger

JAMES HENRY CLINGER

Born: 10 Feb 1849, Little Pigeon, Council Bluffs, Iowa
Parents: James and Harriet Chapin Clinger
Died: 22 May 1926, Lake View, Utah, Utah

Arrived in Valley: 27 Sep 1852, Thomas C. D. Howell Co.

Married 1st: Pauline Mary Williamson
Date: 9 Feb 1868, Provo, Utah
Born: 15 Sep 1848, Brevik, Telemark, Norway
Died: 19 Apr 1931,Lake View, Utah

Married 2nd: Caroline Christensen
Date: 18 Sep 1884, Salt Lake City, Utah
Born: 4 Dec 1865, Ogerbie, Hjorring, Denmark
Died: 20 Jul 1934, Mayfield, Sanpete, Utah

James Henry spent the first three years of his life in Pottawattamie County, Iowa where his parents had come with the Mormons. After arriving in the Great Salt Lake Valley, they moved on to Weber County and then to the Ogden River. By 1860, they were living in Lake View in Utah County. By the time Henry, as he was known, was 16, his parents moved to Malad, Idaho, but James and his sister Martha Ann stayed in Utah. For two years he worked, and then in 1866, he enlisted in the Utah militia to fight in the Black Hawk Indian War.

He met Pauline the night she arrived in Lake View, and they were married in 1868. Henry worked hard to provide for his family. He was elected constable in Provo in 1880.

He took a second wife in 1884 and was called on a mission to Norway. The two wives lived together while he was gone. While there he adopted a Norwegian boy. He returned in 1886.

His interest was in horses and farm machinery. He was an assistant in the horse department of the State Fair for eight years. He was involved in the church and county affairs all his life.

Children of 1st wife:

MARY, b. 9 May 1869, Lake View, Utah. D. 15 Feb 1874. Child.
JAMES HENRY, b. 9 Sep 1879, Lake View, Utah. D. 10 Oct 1879. Infant
JOHN WILLIAM, b. 3 Dec 1871, Lake View, Utah. D. 15 Feb 1922

MARION, b. 13 Jun 1874, Lake View, Utah. D. 25 May 1934

HENRIETTA, b. 11 Sep 1876, Lake View, Utah. D. 4 Dec 1947

PARLEY BOWERING, b. 5 Apr 1878, Lake View, Utah. D. 3
May 1957.

MARTIN ALBERT, b. 18 Sep 1880, Lake View, Utah. D. 20 Jul
1964.

HARRIET ANN, b. 31 Jan 1883, Lake View, Utah. D. 18 Sep
1953.

LILLIE MAY, b. 14 Sep 1887. Dd. 21 Feb 1963

ALBERT MARTIN (adopted), b. 25 Feb 1877, Norway. D. 23
Feb 1939

Children of 2nd wife:

HEBER CHRISTIAN, b. 31 May 1889, Mayfield, Utah. D. 3
Nov 1918

MYRTLE MARIE ROSETTA, b. 14 Nov 1893, Mayfield, Utah.

Submitted by: Edith Clinger

DAVID CLUFF (CLOUGH)

Born: 20 Jun 1795, Nottingham, Rockingham, New Hampshire
Parents: William and Susannah Runnels Cluff (Clough)
Died: 6 Dec 1881, Pima, Graham, Arizona
Arrived in Valley: 3 Oct 1850, Edward Hunter's Co.

Married 1st: Elizabeth (Betsy) Hall
Date: 11 Jan 1824, Shipton, Quebec, Canada
Died: 5 Jun 1881, Central, Graham, Arizona

Married 2nd: Sarah Pippen
Date: 25 Jul 1851

Married 3rd: Hannah Garlick
Date: 20 Apr 1852

Married 4th: Hannah Chapman
Date 30 Aug 1852
Died: 19 Dec 1928

David and his parents traveled to an unsettled part of Canada called Canada East when he was nine. At the age of 17, he returned to New Hampshire to serve his country in the war of 1812. After the war, he returned to Canada where he met Betsy Hall. Their only daughter was born in Canada. David moved his young family back to New Hampshire, where he took up his trade as a shipbuilder. He became interested in the Church and was baptized in 1832,

In 1837 he served a mission to Canada and the Eastern States. In 1838, he took his family with the intention of going to Jackson County, Missouri. When they arrived in Springfield, Illinois, all the members of the family became ill, except David and his eldest son. Fortunately this prevented them from going to Missouri and enduring the persecution there.

When they were well, they proceeded to Nauvoo where he opened a carpentry shop. He helped build the Nauvoo Temple. David was serving another mission at the time of the martyrdom. When he returned to Nauvoo, a remarkable incident happened that helped him obtain new carpenter tools and get back into business. David and his sons obtained what work they could to obtain the necessary equipment to go west.

Upon their arrival in Salt Lake in 1850, they decided to go further south to Provo, where he built them a home in the new fort.

David again was called on a mission in 1858 to the Eastern States. Upon his return, he farmed and did carpentry work. At the age of 82, he and his family moved once more to Arizona, where he died. He remained faithful to the church.

Children of 1st wife:

LAVINA, b. 17 Oct 1824, Shipton, Canada.
DAVID JR., b. 29 Jul 1826, New Hampshire.
MOSES M., b. 20 Feb 1828, Durham, Strafford, New Hampshire. Md. 1st, 25 Dec 1856, Rebecca Cula Langman. Md. 2nd, 14 Feb 1857, Ann Bond. Md. 3rd, 22 Apr 1857, Margaret Jane Johnston. Md. 4th, 11 Oct 1869, Eliza Langman. Md. 5th, Rebecca Scoular (Schooler). D. 30 Jan 1903, Pima, Graham, Arizona.
BENJAMIN, b. 20 Mar 1830, New Hampshire.
WILLIAM WALLACE, b. 8 Mar 1832, Kirtland, Ohio.
JOSEPH, b. 11 Jan 1834, Kirtland, Ohio.
HARVEY HARRIS, b. 9 Jan 1836, Kirtland, Ohio.
SAMUEL SAMPSON, b. 27 Sep 1837, Kirtland, Ohio.
HYRUM, b. 19 Apr 1841, Nauvoo, Illinois.
HENRY, b. 15 Feb 1843, Nauvoo, Illinois.
ALFRED, b. 1 Nov 1844, Nauvoo, Illinois.
ORSON, b. 17 Aug 1848, Nauvoo, Illinois.

Child by 3rd wife:

JERRY, b. 20 Apr 1856, Provo, Utah.

Submitted by: Anne Faber

MOSES M. CLUFF

Born: 11 Feb 1828, Durham, Strafford, New Hampshire
Parents: David and Elizabeth (Betsy) Hall Cluff

Died: 30 Jan 1903, Pima, Graham, Arizona
Arrived in Valley: Spring 1850, Seth Blair Co.

Married 1st: Rebecca Cula (Culey) Langman
Date: 25 Dec 1856
Died: 1 Oct 1913, Pima, Graham, Arizona

Married 2nd: Ann Bond
Date: 14 Feb 1857

Married 3rd: Margaret Jane Johnston (Johnson)
Date: 22 Apr 1857

Married 4th: Eliza Langman
Date: 11 Oct 1869

Married 5th: Rebecca Scoular (Schooler)

Moses M. was a child when his parents joined the Mormon Church. He was later baptized in 1836. He accompanied his parents from Ohio to Nauvoo. When his family started west, Moses helped earn the money for the equipment they would need. He was noted for his ambition and powers of endurance. At various times he worked in the fields, helped build, worked in a blacksmith shop, and as an engineer in a sawmill.

After his family left Nauvoo, he worked in Nauvoo for a time and was there when the temple was burned. He and his two brothers, David and Joseph, preceded the family to the Salt Lake Valley. They each drove an ox team for Seth Blair. When their parents settled in Provo, they went with them.

Moses was called on a mission to Prussia in 1852, but upon arriving in England, his plans were changed and he labored in the Hull Conference in England. He didn't return until 1856.

After his return home and subsequent marriage, he and his brothers built a two story building, which was called the Home Dramatic Company. The building was used for dramatic and musical entertainment. Moses was the comedian.

He moved his family to Arizona and settled in the Gila Valley. He worked hard and provided a good living for his family. He was working in the fields when he was stricken. He lived only a few more days.

Children of 1st wife:

REBECCA (JOSEPHINE), b. 10 May 1858.
MOSES ALFRED, b. 6 Jan 1860.
SARAH, b. 15 Sep 1862.
JOHN HENRY, b. 18 Jan 1864.
JAMES, b. 7 Oct 1866.
BRIGHAM HARRIS, b. 18 May 1869.
SUSAN ANN, b. 15 May 1871.
ROSILTHY, b. 14 Apr 1874.
ETHLON GENEVIEVE, b. 9 Feb 1877.

Children of 2nd wife:

DAVID WILLIAM, b. 6 Oct 1860.
MORONI ALMA, b. abt 1861.
HEBER MANASSEH, b. 15 Nov 1863.
CHARLES HENRY, b. 25 Nov 1864.
MARY JANE, b. abt 1866.
ORSON WASHINGTON, b. abt 1868.

Children of 3rd wife:

JOSEPH EPHRAIM, b. 3 May 1859.
JANE CELIA, b. 26 Aug 1862.
HYRUM ALBERT, b. 16 Oct 1865.
MOSES HARVEY, b. 11 Dec 1868.
MARY LULA, b. 10 Feb 1871.
CYLINA VILATE, b. 13 Mar 1873.
MARYBELLE, b. 21 Jan 1826.
EFFIE ELLA, b. 6 Jun 1878.
PERHELIAN, b. 16 May 1881.

Children of 4th wife:

WILLIAM SCHOOLER, b. 11 Jun 1872.
NEPHI ALMA, b. 26 Aug 1873.
ELIZA PEARL, b. 30 Jul 1876.
ROBERT THOMAS, b. 8 Sep 1880.

Submitted by: Anne Faber

WILLIAM MARION COFFMAN

Born: 24 Oct 1830, Greene County, Tennessee
Parents: Jacob and Rebecca Matthews Coffman
Died: 12 Jun 1910, Springville, Utah, Utah
Arrived in Valley: Unknown

Married: Margaret Serena Wood
Date: 11 May 1854, Putnam Co., Missouri
Born: 18 Feb 1831, Ripley Co., Indiana
Died: 24 Apr 1915, Springville, Utah

Children:

SUSAN ELMINA.
JACOB EDWARD.
JOHN WOOD.
SYLVESTER MARION.

Submitted by: Daniel Bartholomew

JOHN COLE

Born: 19 May 1820, Parish of Bishops Frome, Hereford, England
Parents: William and Ann Fenner Cole
Died: 20 May 1909, Willard, Box Elder, Utah
Arrived in Valley: 6 Oct 1850, Gardiner Snow, Capt

Married 1st: Charlotte Jenkins
Date: 1843, Nauvoo, Hancock, Illinois
Born: 9 Aug 1824, Mathon, Worcester, England
Died: 13 Oct 1906, Willard, Box Elder, Utah

Married 2nd: Mary Ann Voss (Cordon) widow.
Date: 1873, Willard, Utah
Born: 12 Aug 1842, Rugby, Warws, England
Died: 8 Mar 1884, Willard, Utah

Married 3rd: Helena Gustava Andersson (Danielson) widow
Date: abt 1886.
Born: 5 Apr 1843, Hallingberg, Kalmar, Sweden
Died: 20 May 1929, bur. Willard, Utah1

John first heard the gospel from Wilford Woodruff at the time of his great mission to England. He was baptized with his parents. His education was limited; he only attended school until he was eight. After that, he worked in the fields with his father. At the age of 10, he was apprenticed as a wheelwright until he was 15, often working 12 to 14 hours a day.

He and his family emigrated in the second company to cross the ocean. The family settled in Nauvoo where John married. His father died suddenly and his mother took her three younger children back to England with her.

John and his wife traveled to Winter Quarters in 1846, where they lived for a year. They then moved to Kanesville, Iowa, and lived there four years. Life was difficult for them, but his wife's spiritual strength kept him going. Finally, in 1850, they joined the Snow Company and came west. They settled in American Fork where they helped build a fort.

He fought in the Walker Indian War. In 1856, he answered the call to help the stranded handcart company. He was a guard in Echo Canyon. In the spring of 1859, he moved his family to Willard, Utah, where John became a wealthy farmer. He helped establish the Mercantile Association. He took three more wives. He was a trustworthy citizen and an honest man.

Children of 1st wife:

RACHEL, b. 17 Jul 1844, Nauvoo, Illinois.
CHARLOTTE, b. 6 Oct 1846, Florence, Nebraska.
WILLIAM EDWARD, b. 3 Jul 1848, Nebraska.
JOSEPH J., b. 26 Jun 1850, Nebraska Territory.
MARY ELIZABETH, b. 13 Dec 1852, American Fork, Utah.
LYDIA ANN, b. 5 Oct 1854, American Fork, Utah. Md. 1872,
    Edwin H. Bronson. D. 22 Aug 1916, Preston, Franklin, Idaho.
JOHN HEBER, b. 18 Mar 1857, American Fork, Utah.
THOMAS RICHARD, b. 9 Nov 1859, Willard, Utah.
GEORGE AMOS, b. 19 Nov 1863, Willard, Utah.
SARAH MELISSA, b. 22 Apr 1866, Willard, Utah.
ROBERT FRANKLIN, b. 6 Jun 1868, Willard, Utah.

Children of 2nd wife:

JOHN ALFRED, b. 31 Jan 1874, Willard, Utah. Md. 1st, 28 Feb
    1895, Almyra Ellie Nelson. Md. 2nd, 21 Nov 1901, Jane
    Millington. D. 26 May 1958, Idaho Falls, Idaho.
RICHARD, D. 15 Feb 1875, Willard, Utah.
RICHARD, b. 15 Sep 1876, Willard, Utah. D. 15 Feb 1878,
    Willard, Utah.

EDWIN VOSS, b. 19 Oct 1878, Willard, Utah. Md. 19 Mar 1901, Olla Rebecca Owens. D. 19 Mar 1901, Brigham City, Utah.
ALICE HADDAN, b. 11 Jul 1883, Willard, Utah. Md. 12 Apr 1905, Joseph Emil Poulsen. D. 10 Jan 1957, Idaho Falls, Idaho.

Child of 3rd wife:

ESTHER ELLEN, b. 1 Aug 1887, Willard, Utah. Md. Joseph Young. D. 13 Mar 1907.

Submitted by:Dalene Bryant

WILLIAM RILEY COLE

Born: 22 May 1817, Middlesex, Yates Co., New York
Parents: Owen and Sally Turnbaugh Cole
Died: 27 Nov 1910, Roy, Weber, Utah
Arrived in Valley: 1851

Married 1st: Nancy Sarepta Parrish
Date: 19 Mar 1840, Quincy, Illinois
Born: 18 Dec 1820, Brownville, Jefferson, New York
Parents: Nathan and Rebecca Rhodes Parrish
Died: 26 Oct 1855, Ogden, Utah.

Married 2nd: Mahala Garner/Gardner
Date: 9 Apr 1868, Salt Lake City, Utah
Born: 5 Feb 1833, Washington, Erie, Pennsylvania
Parents: Benjamin and Electa Lamport Gardner
Died: 10 Apr 1915, Ogden, Weber, Utah

William Riley and his parents moved to Copley, Ohio, in 1832, where they first heard the gospel. William was baptized in 1834. He married Nancy and soon they started west. Brigham Young felt William should remain for a time in Winter Quarters and use his talents as a wheelwright to help others prepare for the journey. They remained there until 1851 and then came west.

They settled south of Ogden (Riverdale), where he became Justice of the Peace, one of the first. He and his son-in-law built the first threshing machine in Utah. He was a millwright all his working years. He helped build many of the mills in the valley. He remained true to the church and was loved and respected by everyone who knew him.

Children of 1st wife:

NATHAN OWEN, b. 3 Jan 1841, Quincy, Adams, Illinois. Md. Elizabeth Twaddle. D. 8 Nov 1856.

HYRUM, b. 8 Oct 1842, Nashville, Iowa. D. 8 Oct 1842, Nashville, Iowa.

HENRY STRONG, b. 8 Oct 1842, Nashville, Iowa. D. 8 Oct 1842.

SARAH REBECCA, b. 1 Apr 1844, Nashville, Iowa. Md. 1 Jan 1861, Justin True Grover. D. 31 Jul 1924, McCammon, Bannock, Idaho.

SAREPTA JANE, b. 8 Nov 1846, Iowaville, Van Buren, Iowa. Md. 10 Oct 1863, Myron Barber Child. D. 12 Sep 1882.

ESTHER CELESTIA, b. 28 Jun 1849, Ottumwa, Wapello, Iowa. Md. 8 Mar 1865, William Evans Baker. D. 8 Mar 1915, Ogden, Utah.

WILLIAM RILEY, b. 15 May 1852, Kanesville, Iowa. D. 9 Apr 1888.

EMELINE DIANA, b. 28 Jun 1855, Riverdale, Weber, Utah. Md. David Mark Cole. D. 22 Oct 1948.

Children of 2nd wife:

JAMES ALVA, b. 18 Mar 1869, Riverdale, Utah. D. 28 Nov 1940.

JOHN MARK, b. 1 Oct 1870, Riverdale, Utah. Md. 27 Nov 1895,

Sarah Isabell Gardner. D. 6 Dec 1926, Sterling, Bingham, Idaho.

HANNAH, b. 8 Aug 1872, Riverdale, Utah. Md. 27 Apr 1964, Moroni Shipley. D. 2 Jul 1938, Bell, Los Angeles, California.

JOSEPH ANSEL, b. 25 Jul 1875, Riverdale, Weber, Utah. D. 10 Sep 1964.

MARGARET, b. 28 Jun 1878, Riverdale, Utah. D. 20 Aug 1878.

MARGUERITE, b. 28 Jun 1878, Riverdale, Utah. D. 20 Aug 1878.

Submitted by: Jay Bishop

JOHN COMISH

Born: 9 Dec 1838, Kirk Ochan, Ochan, Isle of Mann, Great Britain
Parents: William and Elizabeth Keig/Kegg Comish
Died: 14 May 1922, Cove, Utah, Bur. Franklin, Idaho
Arrived in Valley: 3 Sep 1855, John Hindley Co.

Married: Esther Elizabeth Stanford
Date: 22 Nov 1862, Salt Lake City, Utah
Born: 20 Feb 1845, Portslade, Sussex, England
Parents: Thomas and Elizabeth Barnett Stanford
Died: 15 Mar 1916, Cove, Utah

John was the fifth of nine children. His father William joined the Church in 1841, and his mother Elizabeth in 1848, over the objections of her parents. They decided the only way to get to the

Valley was for William to take their oldest daughter and then send for his wife and the rest of the children. William and his daughter left in 1849 and found a job in St. Louis, Missouri, where they stayed for two years until he had earned enough to send for his wife and other children. The family stayed two additional years in St. Louis and then joined the John Hindley company to travel to the Valley. John worked to help earn money for the family to go west.

Upon their arrival in the valley, they were sent to help settle Kaysville, Utah. John, age 18, was one of the volunteers sent to help the Martin and Willie handcart companies. He was called to help in the Salmon River Indian problems. He was, at various times, involved in the Echo Canyon problems, and made two trips to help the emigrants. He was an Indian Scout, wagon master and guard on several occasions. He made seven trips across the plains.

John was described as six feet tall, dark brown hair, blue eyes, and weighed about 150 pounds. President Brigham Young said he should get married. He already had his eye on a cute little girl so they came to Salt Lake and got married.

They were among the families called to help settle in what is now Franklin, Idaho, but was then known as Spring Creek, in Cache Valley, Utah. John and Esther lived there, and eight children were born. John and his father and brother were given five acres each, in what is known as Whitney, Idaho. They were the first saints to own land in Idaho.

John and his good friend, Porter Rockwell watched from a distance the massacre of a tribe of Indians on the Bear River. Colonel P. Connor was in charge of the massacre. One of the chiefs, Sagwitch, was shot in the hand, and knowing John was his friend, he went to him for help. Hundreds were slaughtered, men, women and children as they slept.

John, his father, and brothers helped build the first railroad into Idaho, the Northern Utah Railroad. There were seven more children born to John and his wife. John was a pioneer, Indian Scout, teamster, wagon master, father, grandfather of 70 children and great grandfather of 26 children.

Children:

JOHN ALFRED, b. 1863, Franklin, Idaho. D. 1925.
ELIZABETH ESTHER, b. 1865, Franklin, Idaho. D. 1921.
THOMAS WILLIAM, b. 1867, Franklin, Idaho. D. 1915.
RUTH SUSANNAH, b. 1869, Franklin, Idaho. D. 1955.
KARLEEN STANFORD, b. 1871, Franklin, Idaho. D. 1949.
FRANKLIN STANFORD, b. 1872, Franklin, Idaho. D. 1935.
JOSEPH FRANCIS, b. 1874, Franklin, Idaho. D. In first year.
ELLEN FRANCES, b. 1875, Franklin, Idaho. D. 1936.
NEPHI-STANFORD, b. 1878, Cove, Cache, Utah. D. 1883.
ALBERT STANFORD (twin), b. 1879, Cove, Utah. D. 1930.
ALBERTA STANFORD (twin), b. 1879, Cove, Utah. D. 3 months.
JANE (stillborn), b. 1880, Cove, Utah.
PEARL STANFORD, b. 1884. Cove, Utah. D. 19_7.
FAYE STANFORD, b. 1887, Cove, Utah. D. 1969.
LEO STANFORD, b. 1889, Cove, Utah. D. 1946.

Submitted by: Harold Manwaring

WILLIAM COMISH

Born: 20 May 1805, Arbory, Isle of Mann, Great Britain
Parents: John and Margaret Duggan Comish
Died: 16 Dec 1877, Franklin, Franklin, Idaho
Arrived in Valley: 3 Sep 1855, John Hindley Co.

Married: Elizabeth Kegg
Date: 12 Feb 1831, Arbory, Isle of Mann, Great Britain

Born: 22 Dec 1805, Kirk, Rushen, Isle of Mann
Died: 6 Nov 1885, Franklin, Idaho

William joined the Church in 1841. Due to the opposition of his wife's parents, Elizabeth, didn't join until 1848. They wanted to leave for the Valley but finances did not permit at the time. It was decided that William and their oldest daughter, Jane, would go and William would work to earn money to send for the rest of the family. William and his daughter found work in St. Louis, Missouri, where they lived for two years before they were able to send for the rest of the family. Elizabeth and her eight children came immediately. They lived in St. Louis for two more years before they joined John Hindley's Company for the trip west.

They settled in Kaysville, Utah, until they were called to help settle Franklin, Idaho, where they lived the rest of their lives. William was part of the guard in Echo Canyon. He was a farmer all his life, a good man, and good member of the church.

Children:

JANE, b. 11 Oct 1831, Castletown, Isle of Mann. Md. Mr. Ashton.
WILLIAM KEGG, b. Apr 1833, Onchan, Conchan, Isle of Mann.
MARGARET, b. 28 Sep 1834, Onchan, Isle of Mann. Md.
    Mr. Roueche.
ELIZABETH, b. 18 Oct 1836, Onchan, Isle of Mann. Md. Mr.
    Whitaker.
JOHN, b. 9 Dec 1838, Onchan, Isle of Mann. Md. Esther
    Elizabeth Stanford.
ELEANOR/ELLEN, b.30 Dec 1840, Onchan, Isle of Mann. Md.
    Mr. Preece
ROBERT NEPHI, b. 12 Dec 1841. Onchan, Isle of Mann.
JOSEPH, b. 7 Jul 1844, Onchan, Isle of Mann. D. age 8 yrs, St.
    Louis, Missouri.
EMMA, b. 12 Jun 1849, Douglas, Isle of Mann. Md. Mr
    Densmore.

Submitted by: Jacqueline Hyden

JOHN ALAN COMPTON

Born: 23 Jan 1843, Johnson Co., Illinois
Parents: Allen and Mary Bettis Compton
Died: 16 Jun 1912, Thatcher, Box Elder, Utah
Arrived in Valley: Bef. 1865

Married 1st: Mary Elmira Miller
Date: 9 Dec 1865, Salt Lake City, Utah
Born: 10 Sep 1843, Nauvoo, Hancock, Illinois
Parents: Henry William and Elmira Pond Miller
Died: 2 Jan 1882, Beaver, Beaver, Utah

Married 2nd: Matilda Isabell Neibaur

John was baptized in 1861 and remained active in the church all his life. He and his first wife were married in the Endowment House. Their first child was born while they lived in Beaver.

From there they moved to Farmington, Utah and then to Fillmore and then Deseret, Minersville and back to Beaver.

John was a good man who contributed much to the community and church as well as his family.

Children of 1st wife:

WILLIAM ALLEN, b. 8 Apr 1868, Beaver Dam, Utah. Md. 17 Nov 1894, Esther Johnson.
JOHN FRANKLIN, b. 23 Aug 1869, Farmington, Utah. Md. 24 Feb 1892, Lucy Mae Bodily. D. 10 Mar 1947, Los Angeles, California.

MARY ELIZABETH, b. 2 Oct 1871, Fillmore, Utah. Md. 27 Dec 1888, John Thomas Fisher. D. 21 Jan 1949, St. Anthony, Idaho.

JAMES ARNOLD, b. 6 Jul 1873, Fillmore, Utah.

BURTON OLIVER, b. 17 Apr 1876, Deseret, Utah. Md. 28 Oct 1902, Emma Erickson. D. 25 Oct 1950, Salt Lake City, Utah.

SARAH ANN, b. 23 Dec 1877, Minersville, Utah. Md. Frank Hess.

IDA LUCINDA, b. 18 Dec 1879, Horse Shoe Bend, Beaver, Utah.

GEORGE HENRY, b. 2 Nov 1881, Beaver, Utah. D. 7 Sep 1882. Child.

Submitted by: Mary Elmira Miller & Jay Whitmore

GIBSON CONDIE

Born: 14 Jun 1814, Sauchie, Clackmannan, Scotland
Parents: Gibson and Jean Russell Condie
Died: 19 Nov 1892, Salt Lake City, Utah
Arrived in Valley: 1850, John Sharp

Married: Cecelia Sharp (widow of Nathaniel Sharp)
Date: 10 Dec 1844, Clackmannan, Clackmannan, Scotland
Born: 9 Apr 1812, Westfield, Clackmannan, Scotland
Died: 17 Jun 1892, Salt Lake City, Utah

Gibson and his wife were baptized in Scotland in 1848. The Condie's and Sharp were coal miners. In 1848, after their baptism, they sold their possessions and left for America. On the ship, son Nathaniel got sick and was buried at sea.

When they arrived in St. Louis, Gibson obtained work in the coal mines and worked for two years to support his family and save enough to continue on west. In 1850, they joined John Sharp's wagon train.

Gibson and his family settled in the sixth Ward in Salt Lake. A grandson wrote the following," He was a man who was clean both on the inside and outside, who neither looked up to the rich nor down to the poor, too brave to lie, too generous to cheat, who won without bragging, lost without squealing, was considerate of women and children and old people, who was willing to take his share of this world's goods and let other people have theirs."

Stepchildren: (children of Nathaniel Sharp and Cecelia.)

NATHANIEL, b. abt 1831, Clackmannan, Scotland. D. & bur. at sea in 1848.

CECILIA, b.24 Apr 1833, Clackmannan, Scotland. Md. 6 Apr 1853, John Crawford. D. 31 Mar 1892, Manti, Utah.

PETER, b. 1834, Stirling, Glackmanshire, Scotland. D. 1839, Scotland.

JANE, b. 13 Apr 1836, Stirling, Scotland. Md. 11 Jun 1854, Joseph Stacy Murdock. D. 17 Oct 1922, Heber City, Utah.

Children of Gibson and Cecelia:

MARY (twin), b. 29 Oct 1845, Drum Gray, New Monkland, Lanark, Scotland. Md. 6 Aug 1864, James Cowan. D. 1 Jul 1922, Salt Lake City, Utah.

GIBSON SHARP (twin), b. 29 Oct 1845, Drum Gray, Lanark, Scotland. Md. 1st, 8 Nov 1866, Elizabeth Whitaker Hattersley. Md. 2nd, 15 Jan 1880, Esther Palfreyman. D. 9 Feb 1936, Springville, Utah.

PETER, b. abt 1848, New Monkland, Lanark, Scotland. D. Child.

ELLEN, b. 27 Apr 1849, St. Louis, Missouri. Md. Peter John Burt. D. 30 Aug 1931.

ROBERT SHARP, b. 20 Sep 1851, Salt Lake City, Utah. Md. 16 Feb 1873 Harriet Frances Powell. D. 18 Jun 1918, Salt Lake City, Utah.

ELIZABETH ANN, b. 8 Jul 1853, Salt Lake City, Utah. Md. 15 Jul 1872, John Smellie Cowan. D. 9 Oct 1945, Nephi, Juab, Utah.

PETER SHARP, b, 3 Apr 1855, Salt Lake City, Utah. Md. 1st, 28 Aug 1876, Janet Watson. Md. 2nd, abt 1876, Georgina. D. 26 Feb 1939.

THOMAS SHARP, b. 20 Jun 1857, Salt Lake City, Utah. Md. 1879, Margaret Ellen Watson. D. 3 Feb 1951, Salt Lake City, Utah.

Submitted by: Thomas Monson

PHINEAS WOLCOTT COOK

Born: 28 Aug 1819, Goshen, Litchfield, Connecticut
Parents: Phineas and Irene Churchill Cook
Died: 24 Jul 1900, Afton, Lincoln, Wyoming
Arrived in Valley: Oct 1848, 2nd Brigham Young Co.

Married 1st: Ann Eliza Howland
Date: 1 Jan 1840, Michigan
Born: 18 Jun 1823, Stillwater, Saratoga, New York
Parents: Henry Howland
Died: 17 May 1896, Garden City, Rich, Utah.

Married 2nd: Amanda Polly Savage
Date: 18 Dec 1853, Salt Lake City, Utah
Born: 23 Aug 1836, Leeds, Upper Canada, York, Canada
Died: abt 1915, Garden City, Utah

Married 3rd: Catherine McCleve
Date: 18 Dec 1853, Salt Lake City, Utah (Div. 1857)
Born: 17 Sep 1836, Belfast, Down County, Ireland

Married 4th: Johanna Christina Palsson (Pahlson, Polson, Poulson)
Date: 13 Sep 1878, Salt Lake City, Utah
Born: 8 Aug 1845, Malmo, Sweden.
Died: 13 Feb 1929, Afton, Lincoln, Wyoming.

Phineas first heard the gospel in 1844. He and his wife soon joined the Church and moved to Winter Quarters, Nebraska. Two of their children died there. In 1848, they left there to emigrate to the Valley in Brigham Young's second company. He drove one of President Young's wagons. Once they arrived, Phineas was hired to build the first sawmill for Isaac Chase.

Phineas was also a millwright, carpenter, and cabinet maker. In 1850 he was asked to go to Sanpete County, he willing moved his family there and built a saw and grain mill for President Young and Isaac Morley. Three years later they moved back to Salt Lake and he was appointed water master. Brigham Young made him foreman on the building of the Beehive House and supervisor over the building of the Tithing Office. He made some of the first furniture of Utah Pine including the bureau for President Young, which is in the Church Museum. He built many other homes and buildings for the early settlers.

In 1857, he moved to Goshen, Utah, and was bishop for three years. In 1863 he moved his family to Bear Lake Valley to help colonize the area. They stayed in Paris until 1865 when they moved to Swan Creek to build a sawmill and grist mill. They remained in the area for many years. In 1889, at the age of 70, he moved his family to Afton, Wyoming, where he died in 1900.

Children of 1st wife:

CHARLOTTE AURELIA, b. 7 Jan 1841. D. 23 Nov 1847, Winter Quarters.
DANIEL WEBSTER, b. 5 Oct 1842. D. 14 Sep 1844, Ross, Kalamazoo, Michigan.

HARRIET BETSY, b. 28 Oct 1844, Richland, Michigan. Md. 21 Aug 1859, William Randolph Teeples. D. 31 Oct 1933.

ELIZA HALL, b. 9 Oct 1846. D. 12 May 1847, Winter Quarters, Nebraska.

AUGUSSTA PRESUNDA, b. 9 May 1848, Winter Quarters, Nebraska. Md. 25 Dec 1864, Joseph Robert Messervy. D. 26 Sep 1867.

PHINEAS HOWLAND, b. 28 Jan 1850, Salt Lake, Utah. Md. 12 Jul 1869, Elizabeth Hill. D. 5 Oct 1876.

PHEBE IRENE, b. 19 Jan 1852, Manti, Sanpete, Utah. Md. 15 Oct 1867, Byron Harvey Allred. D. 18 Apr 1913.

VULCUM, b. 23 Jan 1854, Salt Lake, Utah. D. 28 Oct 1854, Salt Lake, Utah.

ANN ELIZA (twin), b. 29 Sep 1855. D. 3 Feb 1857, Payson, Utah.

ALONZO HOWLAND (twin), b. 29 Sep 1855. Md. 1st, 14 Nov 1878, Amy Laker. Md. 2nd, 30 Sep 1880, Sarah Edith Laker. Md. 3rd, 14 Jun 1895, Johanne Kirstine Jensen. D. 7 Jun 1933, Salt Lake, Utah.

MARY, b. and D. 31 Dec 1857, Goshen, Utah, Utah.

HENRY HOWLAND, b. 28 Feb 1859, Goshen, Utah. Md. 3 Jun 1880, Genett Calder. D. 29 Mar 1933.

MARTHA, b.and d. 24 Apr 1861, Goshen, Utah.

WILLIAM, b. 19 May 1862, Goshen, Utah. Md. 18 Sep 1885, Sarah Tryphena Bryson. D. 31 Oct 1933, Provo, Utah.

AURELIA, b. and D. 10 Mar 1864, Paris, Idaho.

HYRUM HOWLAND, b. 6 May 1866, Swan Creek, Rich, Utah. Md. 24 May 1888, Annie Catherine Vaterlaus. D. 26 Dec 1918.

Children of 3rd wife:

DAVID SAVAGE,b. 13 Jan 1858. Md. 30 Sep 1880, Lydia Ann Nelson. D. 27 Feb 1924.

ROZALIA (twin), b. 12 Nov 1863, Cedar Fort, Nebo, Utah. D. 13 Dec 1863.

MARY ROZALIE (twin), b. 12 Nov 1863, Cedar Fort, Nebo, Utah. Md. 12 Jul 1883, Hyrum Johnston McCann. D. 29 May 1945.

JOSEPH, b. 4 May 1866, Swan Creek, Rich, Utah. D. 31 Aug 1866.

Child of 4th wife:

JOSEPH WOLCOTT, b. 21 Apr 1855. Md. 1st, 4 Oct 1883, Elizabeth Neibaur. Md. 2nd, Elizabeth Snow Bryson., 30 Sep 1891. D. 25 Feb 1931.

Children of 5th wife:

CARL, b. 25 Sep 1879, Swan Creek, Utah. Md. 10 Sep 1902, Ella Call. D. 24 Dec 1970, Salt Lake City , Utah.

MOSES, b. 21 Nov 1880, Swan Creek, Utah. Md. 25 Feb 1907. D. 14 Feb 1970.

KIB PHINEAS, b. 4 Jul 1882, Swan Creek, Utah. Md. 17 Jun 1903, Addie Dimick. D. 12 Oct 1934.

EMER (twin), b. 18 Aug 1883, Logan, Cache, Utah. Md. 1st, Ella Bell, Md. 2nd Minnie Delfenburg, 17 Nov 1913. D. 24 May 1949.

OMER (twin), b. 18 Aug 1883, Logan, Utah. D. 11 Feb 1885.

PARLEY ABRAHAM, b. 23 Mar 1886, Logan, Utah. Md. 18 Dec 1907, Mae Dimick. D. 19 May 1960.

IDALIA, b. 5 Sep 1889, Logan, Utah. Md. 1st, 15 Nov 1909, Leslie Covey. Md. 2nd, 4 Mar 1964, Cecil A. Roley. D. abt 1985.

Submitted by: Sharon Marcyes

WILLIAM FRANCIS COOK

Born: 4 Aug 1836, Westminster, Middlesex, England
Parent: William and Louisa Malpas Cook
Died: 12 Sep 1914, Fountain Green, Sanpete, Utah

574

Arrived in Valley: 7 Sep 1859, Harton D. Haight (?) Co.

Married 1st: Jane Pearsley
Date: 31 May 1862, Salt Lake City, Utah
Died: Feb 1866, Fountain Green, Utah. (died childbirth)

Married 2nd: Jane Booth
Date: 16 Dec 1866, Salt Lake City, Utah
Born: 25 Jun 1844, Bolton, Lancs, England
Died: 18 Jun 1928, Fountain Green, Utah

William Francis lost his father when he was five years old. His father was a wagoneer and William followed in his footsteps as he grew a little older.

He was baptized when he was 18 years old, in 1854. Two years later he left England with some of the other saints for America. To earn money, he worked for a doctor in New York keeping his horse and carriage in good condition to make his calls. William stayed there three years and saved enough money to travel to Utah.

Upon arriving there, he acquired a yoke of oxen, the only thing he possessed, and he used them to make a living. He helped haul the temple blocks for the Salt Lake Temple. He also hauled timber for firewood for people. One of his acquaintances persuaded William to loan him his oxen to make a trip to Sanpete. When the oxen didn't get back, William made a trip to Sanpete and found the man using the oxen to plow his farm. William ended up living in Fountain Green and spent most of the rest of his life there after his marriage. He was a kind and loving husband, father and friend, and a devoted member of the church.

The only child of his 1st wife died, along with his mother.

Children of 2nd wife:

DAUGHTER, D. at birth, 4 Nov 1867, Fountain Green, Utah.
ELIZA ANN, b.8 Oct 1868, Fountain Green, Utah. D. 13 Oct
    1962. Bur. Fountain Green, Utah.

JOSEPH FRANKLIN, b.26 Aug 1870, Fountain Green, Utah. D. 18 Jun 1931. Bur. Fountain Green, Utah.

GEORGE EDWARD, b. 23 Nov 1872, Fountain Green, Utah. D. 27 May 1952. Bur. Fountain Green, Utah.

THOMAS HENRY, b. 24 Jul 1876, Fountain Green, Utah. D. 27 Apr 1961. Bur. Fountain Green, Utah.

DAVID WILLARD, b. 17 Jan 1878, Fountain Green, Utah. D. 16 Jun 1962. Bur. Fountain Green, Utah.

WILLIAM LESTER, b. 18 Feb 1881, Fountain Green, Utah. D. 5 Jan 1958. Bur. Fountain Green, Utah.

Submitted by: Kermit Cook

FREDERICK COOKE

Born: 17 Apr 1812, Manchester, Lancs, England
Parents: William and Sarah Hilton Cooke
Died: 24 Feb 1895, Spry, Garfield, Utah
Arrived in Valley: about 1852

Married 1st: Sarah Elizabeth Davis
Date: Unknown
Born: 7 Nov 1810, Chester, Cheshire, England
Died: 1879, Utah

Married 2nd: Margaret Hodges Peyton
Date: Shortly after arriving in the valley
Born: abt 1812
Died: three months after their marriage
No known children

Married 3rd: Mary Ann Picton Luke
Date: 13 Jun 1863, Salt Lake City, Utah
Born: 5 Jun 1847, Merthyr Tydfill, Glamorgan, Wales
Died: 12 Dec 1919, Richfield, Utah

Frederick's father died when he was 13 leaving a family of five. The two brothers worked with their grandfather Hilton who was a weaver of woolen cloth, to support the family.

In 1839, Frederick was made police constable in Borough, Manchester, England. He accepted the gospel and was baptized in 1838. He baptized 23 people while he was a constable. In January 1841, he was called on a mission to Wales. He kept a diary of his experiences. His father had been a school master and taught his children well. He returned home in time for Christmas in 1841.

In the spring of 1842, Frederick and his family left for America. He helped work on the Nauvoo Temple until its completion and then left with the first group of saints for the west. They lived in Salt Lake until about 1896 when they were called to help settle Kanab. They were friends to the Indians who helped save their tiny daughter when she was ill. They called him many times to administer to their sick. Frederick recorded in his journals many spiritual experiences he had throughout his life.

The moved to Hillsdale in Garfield county in 1884, and then to Spry near Panguitch. He became blind and died knowing he had been faithful.

Children of 1st wife:

SARAH ANN, b. 12 Jun 1838, Manchester, England. Md. abt
     1855, Joseph Addison Thompson. D. Dec 1915, Provo, Utah.
FREDERICK, b. abt 1840, Manchester, England.
AMELIA, b. abt 1842, Manchester, England. D. abt 1847 on plains.
AMANDA, b. abt 1844, Manchester, England. D. abt 1847 on plains.

Children of 3rd wife:

FREDERICK WILLIAM, b. 17 Apr 1864, Salt Lake City, Utah.
     Md. 1st, abt 1889, Cora Mary Margaret Pinny. Md. 2nd, 1

May 1895, Mary Caroline Robinson. D. 14 Jul 1926, Salt Lake City, Utah.

SARAH ALICE, b. 29 Mar 1866, Salt Lake City, Utah. D. 1869.

DAVID JOHN, b. 6 Apr 1868, Salt Lake City, Utah. Md. 5 Nov 1890, Mary Ellen Mathews. D. 30 Mar 1944, Caliente, Nevada.

JOSEPH WOODBRIDGE, b. 25 Jun 1870, Salt Lake City, Utah. Md. 1st, 17 Apr 1929, Sarah Elizabeth Stevens. Md. 2nd, Mary Ruby Mangum. Md. 3rd, Etta Johnson. D. 8 Nov 1933.

BENJAMIN, b. 28 Jan 1872, Salt Lake City, Utah. Md. Jun 1902, Isabelle Dobson. D. 1 Feb 1956.

MARY ANN, b. 9 Mar 1874, Salt Lake City, Utah. Md. 10 Mar 1889, Richard Robinson. D. 13 Apr 1906, Junction, Utah.

EMMA, b. 12 Jul 1876, Kanab, Utah. Md. 1st, 14 Jul 1894, Oden Goodman Flanders. Md. 2nd, 16 Nov 1903, Thomas James Winn. D. 13 Sep 1943.

ELIZA, b. 16 Dec 1878, Nephi, Utah. Md. 14 Jul 1896, Charles Marion Collins. D. 17 Jun 1955, Salt Lake City, Utah.

Submitted by: Jerry Riggs

EDWARD CORBRIDGE

Born: 10 Jan 1806, Thornley, Lancs, England
Parents: William and Ellen Bolton Corbridge
Died: 8 Jan 1883, Bountiful, Davis, Utah
Arrived in Valley: 29 Aug 1852, John Parker Independent Co.

Married: Alice Parker
Date: 17 Jul 1843, Chipping, Lancs, England

Born: 16 Apr 1820, Chaigley, Lancs, England
Parents: John and Ellen Heskin Parker
Died: 5 Feb 1890, Bountiful, Davis, Utah

Edward had a love of working in the soil all his life. He probably gained it from farming in his youth. In 1837, when the Mormon missionaries came to England, Edward was readily converted and was baptized in 1840. He married Alice in 1843. She and her family had joined the Church in 1838. Four of Edward's children were born in England.

Alice's parents came to America in the first ship chartered for the saints, and settled in Nauvoo where Ellen died. Edward and Alice waited until 1852 to come. They settled for a time in St. Louis, where they buried two of their children.

John Parker, brother to Alice, formed an independent company to get to the Valley. Edward and Alice joined him. Most of the members of the train were relatives of the Parker and Corbridge families.

The first winter, Edward and his family lived in a covered wagon at the mouth of Weber Canyon. The next spring they moved to Bountiful where he farmed. He also helped haul rock with an ox team for the Salt Lake Temple. He spent one summer hauling logs to make lumber for the Bountiful church house. He loved helping others and serving the church and his family.

Children:

WILLIAM HENRY, b. 9 Aug 1844, Chipping, Lancs, England. Md. Emma Howard. Md. 2nd, Olive Cordelia Session.
JOHN JAMES, b. 25 Dec 1846, Chipping, Lancs, England. Md. Caroline Frances Holbrook. Md. 2nd, Maary Horsfield Bretnor. D. 11 Jul 1915, Richmond, Cache, Utah.
MARGARET ELLEN, b. 3 May 1848, Chipping, Lancs, England. D.1851, St. Louis, Missouri.
RICHARD EDWARD, b. 30 May 1850, Chipping, Lancs, England. D. 1851, St. Louis, Missouri.
MARY ANN, b. 12 Aug 1853, Bountiful, Davis, Utah. Md. Benjamin Kirkham.

ALICE ELIZABETH, b. 27 Apr 1855, Bountiful, Utah. Md. James Grace Wood.

ROBERT LAWRENCE, b. 17 Mar 1858, Bountiful, Utah.

GEORGE CHRISTOPHER, b. 7 Feb 1860, Bountiful, Utah.

ISABELL JANE, b. 28 Mar 1862, Bountiful, Utah. Md. Chester Sessions.

Submitted by: Steven Nelson

JOHN JAMES CORBRIDGE

Born: 25 Dec 1846, Chipping, Lancs, England
Parents: Edward and Alice Parker Corbridge
Died: 11 Jul 1915, Richmond, Cache, Utah
Arrived in Valley: 29 Aug 1852, John Parker Independent Co.

Married 1st: Caroline Francis Holbrook
Date: 12 Mar 1871, Salt Lake City, Utah
Born: 21 Oct 1851, Utah Territory
Died: 24 May 1907, Richmond, Cache, Utah

Married 2nd: Mary Horsfield Bretnor
Date: 27 Jul 1910.
Born: abt 1845.

John was just five years old when his parents brought their family to America. They crossed the plains in his uncle's company, along with other members of the extended family. After a cold winter spent living in a covered wagon at the mouth of Weber Canyon, his parents moved their family to Bountiful where

John grew up. They were a happy family and all worked hard to make a success of the farm.

John married the daughter of Caroline Francis Angell, a sister to Brigham Young's wife. Many were the wonderful tales told of life in his home. They lived in Bountiful for awhile and then they moved to Woodruff, Utah, where John was a freighter. They soon moved back to Bountiful where they lived until 1886. John wanted a ranch so they moved to Star Valley, Wyoming, where they lived for a time. Then John moved his family to Richmond, Utah, where they stayed.

They were faithful members of the church and were loved wherever they lived.

Children:

CAROLINE FRANCES, b. 9 Nov 1872, Bountiful, Utah.
ALICE ELIZABETH, b. 8 May 1876, Bountiful, Utah.

Submitted by: Steven Nelson

WILLIAM HENRY CORBRIDGE

Born: 9 Aug 1844, Chippine, Lancs, England
Parents: Edward and Alice Parker Corbridge
Died: 24 May 1904, Layton, Utah
Arrived in Valley: 29 Aug 1852, John Parker Independent Co.

Married 1st: Emma Howard
Date: 14 Feb 1870, Salt Lake City, Utah
Born: 31 Jul 1851, Aston, Warws, England

Parents: Joseph and Ann Shelton Howard

Married 2nd: Olive Sessions
Date: 29 Jan 1880, Salt Lake City, Utah

William Henry came to America with his parents when he was only eight years old. His parents settled first in Bountiful, Utah, in a log home they had built. At the age of 18, William drove a mule team back to Council Bluffs to help bring some of the families to Utah. He made two more trips and then the third summer brought back telegraph wire. He did logging to help in the construction of the Bountiful Tabernacle.

He was musical, learning to play the violin, accordian, and horn. He and some friends organized the first brass band in Bountiful.

In 1865, he enlisted in the U.S. Army and fought in the Black Hawk Indian War. After receiving a bullet wound in the leg, he met and married Emma Howard. In 1880, Bishop John Stoker asked him to accept polygamy and take another wife, which he did with Emma's permission.

In the fall of 1885, he accepted a mission call to Great Britain. Sometime later when the Edmund Tucker Law was passed, he decided to move to Wyoming. He took Olive and her children to Auburn, Star Valley. He was made bishop there and helped construct a new church building.

Emma remained in Utah. In 1889, Olive and her children moved back to Utah, and Emma went to Auburn to be with her husband. In 1890, William decided to move back to Davis County, where they lived in Layton.

William was finally able to devote more time to his beloved music and he bought and learned to play an organ. Emma and Olive were close friends and lived together. Emma lived to be one hundred years and eight months old.

Children of 1st wife:

EMMA ANN, b. 1871. D. 1951.
WILLIAM E., b. 1874. D. 1963.

TAMER (twin), b. 1876. D. 1876. Infant
MATILDA (twin), b. 1876. D. 1876. Infant.
MARY ELIZABETH, b. 1877. D. 1877. Infant.
JOSEPH HENRY, b. 1882. D. 1953.
JOHN THOMAS, b. 1882. D. 1949.
CAROLINE ELLEN, b. 1886. D. 1944.
SAMUEL RAY, b. 1889. D. 1971.
MARY AMELIA, b. 1891. D. 1891. Infant.
LUCINDA MAY, b. 1892. D. 1951.

Children of 2nd wife:

OLIVE ELIZABETH, b. 1881. D. 1959.
PHEBE ALICE, b. 1882. D. 1964.
DAVID WILLIAM, b. 1886. D. 1889. Child
GEORGE LAWRENCE, b. 1888. D. 1958.
ISABELL, b. 1890.
CALVIN DARIUS, b. 1891. D. 1955.

Submitted by: Mark Nichols

ALFRED CORDON

Born: 28 Feb 1817, Liverpool, Lancs, England
Parents: Sampson and Myrah Hampson Cordon
Died: 13 Mar 1871, Willard, Box Elder, Utah
Arrived in Valley: 1 Oct 1851, James W. Cummings, Capt.

Married 1st: Emma Parker
Date: 19 Dec 1836, Burslem, Stafford, England

Born: 24 May 1819, Burslem, Stafford, England
Died: 28 Apr 1898, Willard, Box Elder, Utah

Married 2nd: Emily Maria Pridmore
Date: 21 Mar 1856, Salt Lake City, Utah
Born: 30 Mar 1828, Coventry, Warwick, England
Died: 15 Nov 1894, Willard, Box Elder, Utah

Married 3rd: Rebecca Eleanore Collins–No known children
Date: 17 Dec 1864

Married 4th: Mary Ann Voss
Date: 22 Apr 1865, Salt Lake City, Utah
Born: 2 Aug 1842, Rugby, Warwick, England
Died: 8 Mar 1884, Willard, Box Elder, Utah

Alfred was an apprentice in pottery. His parents were potters also. After his marriage and the death of his first child, he heard of The Church of Jesus Christ of Latter Day Saints and was baptized immediately. He helped spread the gospel through his work while in England. In 1840, Heber C. Kimball urged him to quit his work and become a full-time missionary, which he did.

In 1842 he brought his family to America and settled for a time in Nauvoo. He was called on another mission in 1844 to Vermont. After the martyrdom, the family moved to Burlington, Iowa, where a branch of the church was organized. They had planned to go west with the saints, but Orson Hyde called Alfred on a second mission to England. He did missionary work with many of the twelve apostles when they were there. He returned home and brought his family west.

Alfred dedicated the southwest cornerstone of the Salt Lake Temple in 1853, attended the Brigham City School of the Prophets, and was bishop for 20 years. He kept journals most of his life.

Children of 1st wife:

ELIZABETH, b. Jun 1838, Burslem, England. D. 24 Feb 1839.
GEORGE, b. 1 Jan 1840, Burslem, England. D. 1 Jan 1840.

EDWIN PARKER, b. 7 Oct 1841, Burslem, England. Md. 14 Dec 1867, Sarah Voss. D. 1 Jul 1929, Willard, Utah.

RACHEL ANN, b. 24 Jan 1844, Nauvoo, Illinois. Md. 1st, 24 Jul 1861, William Ward. Md. 2nd, 15 May 1879, Robert W. Herold. Md. 3rd, 4 Nov 1888, Alfred H. Brandow. D. 21 Oct 1911, Willard, Utah.

EMMA, b. 17 Apr 1846, Nauvoo, Illinois. Md. 27 Jan 1865, William Lowe. D. 10 Nov 1935, Willard, Utah.

ALFRED, b. 19 Dec 1847, Burlington, Iowa. D. May 1848, Burlington, Iowa.

ADELAIDE AMELIA, b. 22 Feb 1849, Burlington, Iowa. Md. 25 Dec 1865, George Meears. D. 9 Nov 1914, Salt Lake City, Utah.

MYRA GREEN, b. 25 Sep 1851, Green River, Wyoming. D. Mar 1852.

WINN HENRY, b. 1852, Salt Lake City, Utah. D. 1853, Salt Lake City, Utah.

MARY FRANCES, b. May 1854, Salt Lake City, Utah. D. 1862, Willard, Utah.

CHARLES EDWARD, b. 11 Feb 1856, Brigham City, Utah. D. 1 Dec 1877

ELIZA ALMIRA, b. 23 Feb 1858, Willard, Utah. Md. 8 Jan 1880, Joseph Toombs. D. 8 Jul 1926, Willard, Utah.

SARAH JANE, b. 10 Aug 1860, Willard, Utah. Md. 27 May 1880, Peter R. Shupe. D. 10 Jun 1925, Ogden, Utah.

IDA VICTORIA, b. 2 Oct 1862, Willard, Utah. Md. 10 Nov 1881, David Hubbard. D. 28 Jan 1919, Jerome, Idaho.

Children of 2nd wife:

HARRIET ELIZA, b. 8 Sep 1858, Willard, Utah. Md. 7 Oct 1874, James J. Chandler. D. 21 Nov 1936, Rigby, Idaho.

GEORGE ALBERT, b. 3 Nov 1860, Willard, Utah. Md. 15 Dec 1881, Sally Agnes Call. D. 26 Sep 1944, Idaho Falls, Idaho.

ARTHUR EDMUND, b. 21 Dec 1864, Willard, Utah. Md. 14 Jan 1886, Mary J. Whitaker. D. 23 Jun 1914, Rigby, Idaho.

HORACE HERBERT, b. 28 Sep 1867, Willard, Utah. Md. 5 Apr 1889, Sarah E. Cole. D. 4 Jun 1951, Ogden, Utah.

Children of 4th wife:

RALPH ROLAND, b. 23 Feb 1866, Willard, Utah. Md. 17 Dec
    1885, Annie S. Shumway. D. 28 Jul 1936, Victor, Idaho.
LUCY ELIZABETH, b. 4 Jan 1868, Willard, Utah. Md. 8 Jun
    1887, John Frederick Owens. D. 8 Apr 1890.
PHOEBE ANN, b. 9 Mar 1869, Willard, Utah. D. 11 Dec 1879,
    Willard, Utah.
SALINA GENEVA, b. 6 Jan 1871, Willard, Utah. D. 30 Nov
    1879, Willard, Utah.

Submitted by: Jay Smith

GEORGE COULAM

Born: 26 May 1848, Louth, Lincoln, England
Parents: John Sr. and Sarah Cordon Coulam
Died: 24 Nov 1905, Salt Lake City, Utah
Arrived in Valley: Spring 1849

Married: Elizabeth Horrocks
Date: 27 Dec 1869
Born: 21 Sep 1851, Aughton, Lancs, England
Died: 10 Nov 1934, Salt Lake City, Utah

    George was only nine months old when his parents joined the
Church and started west. His mother became ill in Missouri and
died, leaving her husband and six children.
    Later on the journey, George became ill but was given the

blessing that he would live to grow up. When he was 28, George and some other young men were called to go back to Green River to meet the emigrants.

He and his wife witnessed the driving of the Golden Spike for the railroad. He was called as a guard to Brigham Young, and later for his grave. He also was a policeman, a fireman, and had other civic appointments as well as serving in many religious offices including the Sunday School superintendency.

Later in his life, he was a contractor and builder. He was a faithful husband and father and friend to all.

Children:

ELIZABETH, b. 30 Sep 1871. Md. 16 Nov 1892, Thomas J. Midgley. D. 16 May 1936.

GEORGE, JR., b. 23 Jun 1874. Md. 11 Jun 1902, Estra Ella Jackson. D. 24 Nov 1941.

JOHN, b. 18 Jan 1877. D. Sep 1879.

DANIEL, b. 16 Oct 1879. Md. 6 Jan 1909, Lucille McMaster. D. 27 Nov 1949.

LILLIE MAY, b. 17 Jan 1882, Md. 9 May 1907, T. Albert Hooper. D. 4 Dec 1951.

SARAH, b. 27 Oct 1884. Md. 9 May 1907, Sanford Hedges. D. 26 Dec 1962.

MARY, b. 19 Feb 1887. Md. 20 Apr 1911, Irvin A. Jackson. D. 20 Jul 1937.

ELLEN WRAY, b. 25 Sep 1889. Md. 25 Sep 1912, Arthur John Wood Jr. D. 11 Nov 1982.

CHARLES HENRY, b. 13 Mar 1893. Md. 16 May 1918, Georgia Billings. D. Nov 1977.

GRETTA, b. 25 Dec 1897. Md. 25 Jun 1919, Francis Charles. D. abt 1990.

Submitted by: John Wood

JOHN COULAM, SR.

Born: 2 Aug 1802, Louth, Lincoln, England
Parents: John and Josanna Ward Coulam
Died: 20 May 1877, Salt Lake City, Utah
Arrived in Valley: 1849, Orson Spencer Co.

Married: Sarah Cordon
Date: 1825, England
Born: 14 Feb 1803, Raithley, Lincoln, England
Died: 22 Apr 1849. Buried bank of Missouri River

John joined the Church in England on March 19, 1843. He brought his wife and six children to America. His wife died on the way west and was buried on the banks of the Missouri River.

He was a cabinet maker by trade and he worked with his three sons, who also learned the trade. They worked well together as is shown when the oldest brother, John, was crippled and the other brothers helped him unselfishly.

At John's death, his family and friends honored him for his many virtues. He was a kind and affectionate father, a sincere friend, a loyal and hard working member of the church, and a industrious member of the community.

Children:

JOHN, b. 1 Sep 1826, Louth, Lancastershire, England. Md. 29 Oct 1859, Sarah Jane Orton. D. 16 Oct 1893.
CHARLES, b. 23 Oct 1835, Louth, England. D. 14 Jul 1858.
FANNIE, b. 26 Dec 1838, Louth, England. Md. 19 Apr 1862, John Baker. D. 1 May 1914.

HENRY, b. 13 Mar 1842, Louth, England. Md. 24 Aug 1867, Sarah Bean. D. 5 Nov 1916.

SARAH JANE, b. 19 Jan 1845, Louth, England. Md. 1st,23 Mar 1867, John Heiner. Md. 2nd, 31 Mar 1873, Daniel Heiner. D. 30 Apr 1918.

GEORGE, b. 26 May 1848, Louth, England. Md. 1st, 27 Dec 1869, Elizabeth Horrocks. Md. 2nd, Mary Rasmussen. D. 24 Nov 1905.

Submitted by: John Wood

HEBER CHARLES COX

Born: 14 Jan 1866, Lambeth, Surrey, England
Parents: John and Hannah Stiff Neville Cox Jr.
Died: 7 Dec 1963, Woodruff, Rich, Utah
Arrived in Valley: 15 Sep 1866, William Henry Chipman Co.

Married: Teenie Bowns
Date: 6 May 1896, Salt Lake City, Utah
Born: 16 Dec 1878, Almy, Uintah, Wyoming
Died: 6 Aug 1970, Mendon, Cache, Utah
Buried: Woodruff, Rich, Utah

Heber Charles was born while his parents were waiting word for a ship to emigrate to America. When they got word, Heber, his parents, a sister, and two brothers boarded the ship. His brother Hyrum died and was buried at sea. Heber was six months old when they started across the plains.

Upon their arrival in the Valley, they were assigned to settle in Centerville, Utah, where they lived for four years. Then they moved back to Salt Lake so his father could help haul granite for the Temple.

In 1868, his maternal grandparents arrived in the valley and were asked to help settle Woodruff. Heber and his brother, William, went with them to help. Two years later, Heber's parents moved to Woodruff. Heber got some schooling and was quick to learn. When he was 17 years old, he was awarded a scholarship to the University of Deseret. During the school vacation he returned home and taught school in Woodruff. In 1887 he returned to school to complete his education and graduated.

He taught school for three months and then went to Evanston, Wyoming, for five years. He traveled some and was a volunteer fireman. After his marriage to Teenie, they stayed in Almy for five years, and then he got a job in Carbon County. In 1906, they returned to Salt Lake City where he eventually opened a store. He was also Superintendent of Schools, County Attorney, and held other community positions. He was a bishop and Ward Clerk, stake missionary, and he held other positions in the church. In 1963 he was recognized as one of the last two living Pioneers.

Children:

CHRISTINA MAY, b. 1 Sep 1897, Almy, Uintah, Wyoming. Md. 20 Jun 1917, Frederick Stacy. D. 26 Feb 1981, Bountiful, Utah.

HEBER JAMES, b. 29 Apr 1900, Almy, Unitah, Wyoming. Md. 27 Mar 1930, Gladys Ivy Burrell. D. 2 Dec 1987, Salt Lake City, Utah.

WILLIAM JARED, b. 6 Dec 1902, Castlegate, Utah. D. 6 Oct 1961, Woodruff, Utah. Unmarried.

JOHN GILBERT, b. 14 Sep 1904, Sunnyside, Utah. D. 26 Dec 1992, Ogden, Utah. Unmarried.

MILDRED, b. 12 Jan 1912, Woodruff, Utah. Md. 4 Sep 1930, Edward Cannon South. D. 17 Jul 1982, Logan, Utah

RAYMOND BOWNS, b. 26 Jun 1918, Woodruff, Utah. Md. 1 Dec 1950, Elaine Kennedy. Living (1996)

Submitted by: Marlene Dimond

JOHN COX, JR.

Born: 12 May 1836, Weild, Hamp, England
Parents: John and Ann Baker Cox Sr.
Died: 17 Nov 1915, Woodruff, Rich, Utah
Arrived in Valley: 15 Sep 1866, William Henry Chipman Co.

Married 1st: Hannah (Annie) Stiff/Neville
    (Hannah was always known as Annie. She and her 6 brothers
    and 3 sisters often went by the surname "Neville" instead of
    "Stiff," which was the maiden name of William Stiff's mother).
Date: 22 Aug 1858, South Hampton, Hamps, England.
Born: 19 Mar 1839, Rotherick, Hamps, England
Parents: William and Rachel Jennings Stiff
Died: 28 Feb 1920, Woodruff, Rich, Utah

Married 2nd: Ellen Eliza Akers
Date: 22 Aug 1859, Utah
Born: 23 Jul 1867, London, Middlesex, England
Parents: William and Rachel Stiff Akers
Died: 24 Jul 1921, Ogden, Weber, Utah

    John Jr. and his family were baptized into The Church of Jesus
Christ of Latter Day Saints. When a young man, he joined the
British Navy. It is not known if he went to sea or if he worked in
the large shipyards, but during his service, he learned the carpenter trade.
    After his marriage to Annie, the family had a strong desire to
go to America. They worked and saved, gathered a few belongings, and left. While waiting for a ship in London, Annie had

their fourth child. They had to wait four more months before they left. Their little seven-year-old boy died aboard the ship. Upon their arrival in America, they immediately left for Nebraska, where they purchased a wagon and oxen and supplies and left for the west.

Upon their arrival in the Valley, they were sent to Centerville, Utah, where they settled. Annie's parents emigrated in 1868 and joined them. By 1871, John moved his family to Salt Lake. He worked as a carpenter and hauled logs and granite rocks to help build the temple. In 1873, they were called to help settle Woodruff, Utah, in the Uintah Mountains.

John was active in the affairs of the community and church. He helped construct and operate mills in the area. He ran a creamery for a time. He was bishop and, when polygamy came, he entered that practice. He accepted each call that came to him and did his best. After the Manifesto, Ellen and her children moved to Wyoming with other polygamy wives. John kept close to both wives and their children. He was loved and respected by all who knew him.

Children of 1st wife:

JOHN HYRUM, b. 18 Jul 1859, Southampton, England. D.16 May 1866 at sea.

ELIZABETH ANN, b. 4 Feb 1861, Portsmouth, England. Md. William Henry Lee.

WILLIAM JAMES, b.31 May 1863, Basingstoke, England. Md. Minnie May Bowns.

HEBER CHARLES, b. 14 Jan 1866, Lambeth, England. Md. Teenie Bowns.

ANNIE, b. 8 Dec 1867, Centerville, Utah. Md. Thomas Josiah Timgey.

GEORGE EDWIN, b. 7 Dec 1869, Centerville, Utah. Md. 1st, Vinnie Mangum. Md. 2nd, Carrie Johnson.

ELLEN JOSEPHINE, b. 23 Dec 1871, Salt Lake City , Utah. Md. Byron Arbury Sessions.

MARY LOUISE, b. 1 Mar 1874, Woodruff, Utah. Md. David Dean.

MINNIE AMELIA, b. 311 Jul 1876, Woodruff, Utah. Md. James Richard Stuart.

AGNES ADA, b. 22 Jan 1881, Woodruff, Utah. Md. Scott Aytch Sessions.

JULIA RACHEL, b.22 Jun 1881, Woodruff, Utah. D.2 Jun 1888. Child.

JOHN ALMA, b.13 Dec 1883, Woodruff, Utah. Md. Laura Rosina Godbe/Godby.

Children of 2nd wife:

CHARLES WILLIAM, b.19 Oct 1887, St. Charles, Idaho. Md. Emily Elizabeth Dickson. D. 5 Jul 1962.

WILFORD WOODRUFF, b. 7 Mar 1890, Montpelior, Idaho. D.6 Jan 1906.

RACHEL FANNY, b. 13 Dec 1891, Woodruff, Utah. Md. Ernest Melvin Crouch.

LEONARD HENRY, b. 26 Feb 1893, Woodruff, Utah. Md. Maude Dean. D. 11 Mar 1933.

SARAH EDITH, b. 21 Oct 1894, Woodruff, Utah. Md. James Henry Buck

BARBARA, b. 30 Sep 1896, Woodruff, Utah. Md. 1st, Paul Clifford.

IRVIN JAMES, b.30 Apr 1898, Woodruff, Utah. Md. Elsie Lord.

ARTHUR JABEZ, b. 7 Dec 1899, Woodruff, Utah. Md. Elsie Cornia. D. 7 Oct 1984.

NEWEL, b. 1 Sep 1901, Woodruff, Utah. D. 3 Sep 1901. Infant.

ONEITA RHODA, b. 3 Oct 1902, Woodruff, Utah. Md. Hans Victor Hansen.

OWEN JOHN, b. 24 Jul 1904, Woodruff, Utah. Md. Hannah Cornia. D. 9 Aug 1984.

VERNON LEROY, b. 13 Sep 1906, Woodruff, Utah. Md. Bella Morrow. D. 10 Jan 1939.

THELMA MAY, b. 19 May 1910, Woodruff, Utah. Md. Francis Lowry Wadsworth. D. 19 Oct 1946.

Submitted by: LaVaun Cox

WILLIAM JAMES COX

Born: 31 May 1863, Basingstoke, Hampshire, England
Parents: John and Annie Stiff Cox
Died: 3 Jun 1945, Woodruff, Utah
Arrived in Valley: 15 Sep 1866, William Henry Chipman Co.

Married: Minnie Bowns Hempel
Date: 5 Apr 1911, Salt Lake City, Utah
Born: 23 Apr 1881, Almy, Wyoming
Parents: James and Christina Spowart Bowns
Died: 26 Mar 1959, Woodruff, Utah

William, also known as Billy, left England with his parents and siblings in 1866 for America. His family crossed the plains when he was only three years old. They lived in Centerville for a time.

In 1872, William and his brother Heber moved to Woodruff where they lived in a dugout on the banks of Dry Creek with his grandparents, until his parents moved to Woodruff a year later. After his marriage to Minnie May Bowns, they made their home in Woodruff.

William was active in church and community affairs in Woodruff all his life. He remained close to his parents and assisted them when there was a need. He helped in the construction of the Randolph and Woodrufff canal.

He served for a time as Justice of the Peace in Woodruff. He served a mission in England from 1899 to 1901, was in the high council and held various other positions. He was active in the affairs of the community and a friend to all.

Children, Minnie's first marriage to Mr. Hempel:

NELZINA CHRISTINA INGEBORG, b. 17 Aug 1900, Almy,
Wyoming. Md. 10 Mar 1920,Warren Williard Hooper. D. 10
Oct 1992, Ogden, Utah.
MINNIE MAY CAMILLA, b. 5 Nov 1902, Sunside, Utah. Md.
G.H. Gallineau (Div). Md. 2nd, 20 Jan 1924, Joseph Teel
Farrar. D. 4 Aug 1964, Oakland, California.
LILLIAN, b. 3 Nov 1905, Salt Lake City, Utah. Md. Corless,
Wamsley (Div). Md. 2nd 4 Apr 1943, John Albert Bunderle.
D. 20 Dec 1979, Bountiful, Utah.

Children of Minnie and William:

LYNN WINSTON (twin), b. 4 Jun 1912, Woodruff, Utah. Md. 3
May 1937, Zoe Buck. Living 1996.
WILLIAM EMERSON (twin), b. 4 Jun 1912, Woodruff, Utah.
Md. 1 Jun 1944, Helen Mary Putnam. Living 1996.
ANNIE ESTELLA, b. 31 Dec 1913, Woodruff, Utah. Md. 26
Aug 1931, Orioen Marshall Rima. Living 1996.
MILLICENT ETHEL, b. 13 Feb 1917, Woodruff, Utah. Md. 14
Feb 1936, Dominick Spirito Revelli. Living 1996.
LAVAUN, b. 31 Mar 1922, Woodruff, Utah. Md. 2 Apr 1945,
Zella Pearl Putnam. Living 1996.

Submitted by: Emerson Cox and Patricia Bellamy

JAMES CRAGUN

Born: 26 Jul 1814, Connersville, Fayette, Indiana

Parents Elisha and Mary Osborne Cragun.
Died: 7 Feb 1887.
Arrived in Valley: Unknown

Married: Eleanor Lane
Date: 30 Mar 1836, Boone County, Indiana
Born: 11 Nov 1838, Brandenburg, Mead, Kentucky
Parents: Samuel and Mrs. Lane

James lived in Eagle Village, Boone County, Indiana, after his marriage to Eleanor. About 1842, he moved his family to North Field in Boone County, Indiana.

After joining the Church, they decided to move their family west. Their sixth child was born on the way west along the bank of the Platte River in Iowa. Upon their arrival in Salt Lake, they made their home in the southwest section called Millcreek. They had three more children.

Children:

LYDIA, b. 26 Jan 1838, Eagle Village, Boone, Indiana. D. 23 Jun 1916.
JAMES HYRUM, b. 31 Jul 1840, Eagle Village, Indiana. D. 14 Feb 1919.
THOMAS CALVIN, b. 28 Dec 1843, North Field, Boone, Indiana. D. 23 May 1909.
MARY ELLEN, b. 24 Feb 1844, Boone Co., Indiana. D. 28 Oct 1930.
MELVINA, b. 30 Mar 1847. D. Jun 1847.
ELISHA, b. 3 Aug 1849, along bank of Platte River, Iowa. Md. 22 Feb 1874, St. George, Utah, Marguerite Lawson. D. 3 Apr 1903 Caliente, Lincoln, Nevada.
MARTHA JAMES, b. 3 Mar 1852, Mill Creek, Utah. Md. Isaiah Cox. D. 30 Nov 1932, St. George, Utah.
SARAH JANE, b. 27 Apr 1854, Mill Creek, Utah.
TYRESHA, b. 27 Mar 1857, Mill Creek, Utah. D. 9 Mar 1894.

Submitted by: Woodrow Dennett

GEORGE CRANE

Born: 14 Jan 1832, Yoxford, Suffolk, England
Parents: John and Mary Girling Crane
Died: 18 May 1919, Kanosh, Millard, Utah
Arrived in Valley: 19 Aug 1868, John R. Murdock Co.

Married 1st: Emily Sabey
Date: 4 Apr 1854, England
Born: 29 Jun 1831, Bolnhurst, Bedford, England
Died: Sept 186_, London, England

Married 2nd: Anne Howe
Date: 1 Feb 1868, Chelsea, London, England
Born: 6 Feb 1843, Wick, Glamorganshire, Wales
Died: 2 Jul 1895, Kanosh, Millard, Utah

Married 3rd: Anne Parkinson (Hopkinson) widow–No children
Date: 2 Feb 1899, Fillmore, Utah
Born: 9 Sep 1851, Chatburn, England
Died: Aug 1930, Kanosh, Millard, Utah

George, at a young age, was left alone in England when his parents emigrated to Galt, Canada. It was determined that George should remain behind and complete his apprenticeship as a painter and glazer. In 1854 he married Emily and they lived in London where George worked. When their youngest child was six weeks old, Emily died. George took the children to their grandmother who lived in Bolnhurst. He visited them as often as he was able.

In 1868 he married Anne and immediately made plans to

emigrate to America. He took the children and they sailed on 30 June 1868. Upon their arrival in America, they were given space in cattle cars for their trip west. Each family was allotted space for their beds and to prepare meals. George was made Captain of the Company. When they arrived in Laramie, Wyoming, they were met by prairie schooners and mule teams to complete their journey. They stayed in Salt Lake that winter.

George worked on the Utah Central Railroad and the Union Pacific until the Golden Spike was driven. The next spring, George moved his family to Kanosh, Utah, where he taught school.

In 1879 he was called on a mission to England. He returned home in November 1880. He held many offices in Millard County including county commissioner, president and director of the Kanosh Store, a branch of Z.C.M.I. He acted in plays and organized a dramatic society in Kanosh. He was active in the church and held many positions. He was a friend to Chief Kanosh and spoke at his funeral.

Children of 1st wife:

EMILY ADELINE, b. 6 Jun 1855, Bolnhurst, Bedford, England. Md. 26 Dec 1879, Lorenzo Dow Watson. D. 10 Mar 1933, Cedar City, Utah.

ALICE JULIA, b. 3 Apr 1856, London, Middlesex, England. Md. John Baldwin Roberts. D. 22 Nov 1900, Utah.

FREDERICK HORACE, b. 16 Nov 1857, London, Middlesex, England. D. Dec 1868, Salt Lake City, Utah.

VICTOR OWEN, b. 2 Aug 1859, London, Middlesex, England. Md. Elizabeth Charlesworth. D. 5 Jul 1946, Colorado.

Children of 2nd wife:

MARY ELLA, b. 28 Oct 1868, Salt Lake City , Utah. Md. Dec 1887, William H. Staples. D. 24 Apr 1942, Kanosh, Millard, Utah.

GEORGE GIRLING, b. 24 Jan 1870, Kanosh, Utah. D. 28 Feb 1871, Kanosh, Utah.

ANNIE, b. 11 Feb 1872, Kanosh, Utah. D. 21 Aug 1873.

MAUDE ESTELLA, b. 18 Jun 18785, Kanosh, Utah. Md. 30
   May 1900, James Alexander Melville. D. 25 May 1968, Salt
   Lake City, Utah.
JOHN HOWE, b. 3 Jun 1877, Kanosh, Utah. D.d 7 Mar 1889,
   Kanosh, Utah.
GEORGE AZERIAH, b. 19 Sep 1879, Kanosh, Utah. D. 2 Mar
   1889, Kanosh, Utah.
ETHEL EDNA, b, 26 Oct 1881, Kanosh, Utah. D. 11 Aug 1900,
   Kanosh, Utah.
HARRY MARTIN, b. 7 Jan 1884, Kanosh, Utah. D. 13 Mar 1889,
   Kanosh, Utah.

Submitted by: Naomi Cottam

HENRY CRANE

Born: 12 Apr 1852, Pulham, Norfolk, England
Parents: John L. and Sarah Stannard Crane
Died: 22 Feb 1901, Herriman, Salt Lake, Utah
Arrived in Valley: 28 Sep 1866, Thompson Co.

Married: Jeannette Dansie
Date: 2 Apr 1879, Salt Lake City, Utah

Henry was three when his parents moved their family to
Coldgate, England. His parents taught him to be honest and that
there was a God that he should love and fear. When he was eight
years old, he was apprenticed to a brick mason who demanded
long, hard work. He stayed there a year and then went with a man

who was a bricklayer and spent the next two and a half years learning from him.

In 1860 the family moved to Pulham Market St. Soon they became acquainted with a member of the Church who taught them the gospel. A year later the parents were baptized. The following year, Henry and three siblings were also baptized.

His parents decided to take their family to America. In May 1866, they sold their possessions and left for America. They were welcomed to America by fireworks in the harbor because it was the 4th of July.

At Fort Bridger, Henry's youngest brother died and was buried at the side of the road. They stayed in Salt Lake until 1869, when they moved to Herriman. Henry went to school the first winter and learned to read and write. Most of his livelyhood was gained from farming.

In 1879 he married and continued to live in Herriman where he and his brother James farmed. Henry also hauled ore from the mines in West Canyon, Sandy, Utah. He was a member of the school board, Justice of the Peace, and Postmaster. He filled a mission in Great Britian, was a Stake High Councilman and was a stake missionary. He died of pneumonia along with his brother Will and his mother, Sarah, all within three weeks.

Children:

HENRY JAMES, b. Herriman, Utah.
FLORENCE JEANNETTE, b. Herriman, Utah.
WALTER EARNEST, b. Herriman, Utah.
ALBERT JOHN, b. Herriman, Utah.
ARTHUR WILLARD, b. Herriman, Utah.
JAMES REYNOLD, b. Herriman, Utah.
LILY EDITH, b. Herriman, Utah.
ANNIE MAY, b. Herriman, Utah.
MAYME VIOLET, b. Herriman, Utah.
WILLIAM LAFAYETTE, b. Herriman, Utah.

Submitted by: Roberta Crane

JAMES CRANE

Born: 1 Apr 1831, Penally, Pembrokeshire, South Wales
Parent: Elizabeth Harris
Died: 6 Jul 1886, Herriman, Salt Lake, Utah
Arrived in Valley: 1859, Church Freight Train led by Joseph W.
    Young.

Married 1st: Alice Davis
Date 5 Apr 1858, Iowa City, Iowa

Married 2nd Elizabeth Stewart
Date: 3 Feb 1865, Utah

Married 3rd: Rachel Briggs
Date: 28 Mar 1869

James was placed in an orphanage when he was three weeks old. There were good times and hard times, depending on who was in charge. He finally ran away and went to work for Mr. Watters. He stayed there for seven years.

In 1851, he heard the gospel for the first time and joined the Church. While in England, he served a mission and presided over a branch. It took him until 1856 to raise the money to go to America. James and a friend lived in New York for two years and then joined the Company going west. James signed on as a teamster and his wife did the cooking for 14 of the drivers.

James worked for President Young for a year and a half and then purchased a home in the Sugarhouse area. In 1869, James, his three wives, and three children moved to Herriman, where he farmed. He remained active in the church all his life.

Children of 2nd wife:

JAMES GEORGE.
HEBER STEWART.
WILLIAM ABNER.
ANNIE.
BRIGHAM.
FRANKLIN THOMAS.
MARY ELIZABETH.
FANNIE JANE.

Children of 3rd wife:

ALICE BRIGGS.
CHARLES EDWARD.
REBECCA.
ESTHER.
HYRUM.
SARAH MARIE.
CARRIE.

Submitted by: Evelyn Crane

WILLIAM ROBINSON CRAWFORD

Born: 29 Sep 1842, on an island in the Illinois River, Calhoun
   Co., Illinois.
Parents: John and Marilla Terry Crawford
Died: 29 Oct 1913, Springdale, Utah.
Arrived in Valley: prior to 1862

Married: Carnelia Gifford
Date: 1 Nov 1886, Salt Lake City, Utah
Born: 3 May 1851, Manti, Utah
Died: 15 Apr 1913, Springdale, Utah

William Robinson came to Utah with his mother and siblings. His step father had refused to come. They settled in Draper where his uncle converted and baptized him. After helping his mother get settled, he drove a team and wagon back to Missouri to help other saints get to Utah. The family became one of the first two families to settle Rockville, near St. George.

When he married Cornelia, they made their home in Rockville where five sons were born. In 1879, William bought a farm in Zion Canyon. He built a fine ranch, including a blacksmith shop, carpenter shop, wagon assembly shop, shoe shop, and gristmill.

William remained active in the church and community. He served as the first bishop in the area, was a road supervisor and a member of the school board.

Children:

JOHN ROBINSON, b. 12 May 1871, Rockville, Utah. Md. 15 Mar 1892, Eliza Ellen Hepworth. D. 15 May 1960, Springdale,Utah.

WILLIAM LOUIS, b. 15 Jul 1873, Rockville, Utah. Md. 21 Mar 1909, Mary Jane Bean. D. 14 Apr 1976, Springdale, Utah.

SAMUEL KENDALL, b. 3 Nov 1874, Rockville, Utah. Md. 1st, 30 Sep 1896, Emma Jane Curtis. Md. 2nd Marie Elizabeth Tunnell. D. 25 Jan 1955, Springdale, Utah.

JAMES, b. 10 Jan 1877, Rockville, Utah. Md. 15 Mar 1898, Pauline Spiess. Md. 2nd 15 Jun 1916, Ellen Caroline Crabtree Bean. D. 22 Feb 1968, Springdale, Utah.

DANIEL, b. 25 Mar 1879, Rockville, Utah. Md. 12 Nov 1901, Sarah Sabrina Curtis. D. 11 Dec 1965.

ANNIE, b. 7 Aug 1881, Springdale, Utah. Md. 28 Nov 1901, George Howard Isom. D. 10 Mar 1971, Hurricane, Utah.

JACOB, b. 10 Aug 1883, Springdale, Utah. Md. 30 Nov 1910, Mary Effie Cox. D. 6 Jan 1935.

MARY, b. 19 Apr 1887, Springdale, Utah. Md. 2 May 1905, Marion Fisk Stout. D. 19 Jun 1965.

MARILLA, b. 7 Nov 1888, Springdale, Utah. Md. 1st, 30 Sep 1905, Walter Ruesch. Md. 2nd, 2 Jan 1951, William T. Morris Jr. D. 19 Mar 1969.

EMMA, b. 11 Jul 1890, Springdale, Utah. Md. 23 Mar 1955, Samuel Bell Jr. D. 26 Aug 1970, Cedar City, Utah.

LORA ANN, b. 24 Apr 1892, Springdale, Utah. D. 30 Aug 1893.

JOSEPH, b. 1 Dec 1893, Springdale, Utah. D. 4 Jun 1898.

Submitted by: Fern Crawford

THOMAS CRAWLEY

Born: 10 May 1836/37, Dunstable, Bedford, England
Parents: James and Mary Foster Crawley
Died: 21 Mar 1899, Nephi, Juab, Utah
Arrived in Valley: 15 Oct 1863, Samuel White Co.

Married: Betty/Betsy Ritchie
Date: 4 Jun 1863, Aboard ship "Amazon"
Born: 27 Jul 1841, Forfar, Angus, Scotland
Parents: Samuel and Ann Anderson Ritchie
Died: 16 Mar 1904, Nephi, Juab, Utah

Thomas was the fifth son and child. The family moved to Hemel Hempstead, Hertford, England, when he was young. He was baptized into the Church in 1853.

At the age of 19, Thomas was called on a mission to Belfast, Ireland. He served about seven years, presiding for part of that time. He served from about 1856 to 1863. He met his wife, Betsy, in Ireland. Betsy was baptized in 1857. Thomas, Betsy, and her mother boarded the ship where Thomas and Betsy were married before it sailed.

Their trip across the ocean and to the Valley brought them many experiences, and they were glad when they finally got to Salt Lake. They went to Nephi shortly after arriving. They lived in the Salt Creek Fort until Thomas built them a home.

His occupation was making straw hats. Later he was in the bee business. He remained active in church and community, serving in many positions in both including politics. He died of "heart problems."

Children:

BETSY ANN, b. 25 Feb 1865, Nephi, Juab, Utah. Md. 10 Feb 1881, Hezekiah Carter. D. 17 Feb 1929, Nephi, Utah.

MARY, b. 2 Dec 1866, Nephi, Utah. Md. 3 Apr 1883, Thomas H. Carter. D. 16 May 1923, Salt Lake City, Utah.

ROSE HANNAH, b. 4 Jul 1869, Nephi, Utah. Md. 20 Jun 1898, Alexander George Gourley. D. 16 May 1923, Salt Lake City, Utah.

THOMAS WILLIAM, b. 25 Jun 1871, Nephi, Utah. Md. 16 May 1897, Julia Linton. D. 21 May 1932.

EMILY/EMMLIE, b. 2 Dec 1873, Nephi, Utah. Md. 25 Nov 1908, James Edward Memmott. D. 29 Jun 1958, Orem, Utah.

ISABELLE, b. 4 Dec 1875, Nephi, Utah. Md. 15 Aug 1897, Nephi, Utah. Wallace Mangum. D. 15 Feb 1936, Provo, Utah.

JAMES, b. 18 Dec 1877/8, Nephi, Utah. D. 18 Dec 1877/8. Infant.

JOSEPH McKAY, b. 9 Sep 1880, Nephi, Utah. Md. 7 Jul 1898, Margaret Effie Bird. D. 16 Nov 1943, Provo, Utah.

ELIZA LYDA RITCHIE, b. 25 Dec 1882, Nephi, Utah. Md. 16 Nov 1904, Robert Lomax. D. 18 May 1948, Reno, Washoe, Nevada.

Submitted by:

EDWARD CREER

Born: 3 Nov 1813, Bolton, Lancs, England
Parents: Mathias and Nellie Greenhalgh Creer
Died: 12 Jan 1886, Beaver, Beaver, Utah
Arrived in Valley: 25 Sep 1854, Joseph Fields Independent Co.

Married 1st: Ann Morris
Date: 21 Jun 1835, Chorley, Lancs, England
Born: 27 Dec 1813, Chorley, Lancs, England
Died: 18 Dec 1877, Provo, Utah, Utah

Married 2nd: Mary Radabough–No known children

For many years Edward worked in a factory, becoming acquainted with construction and operation of woolen and cotton mills. After his marriage to Ann, they worked at a factory in Preston, England, he as a spinner and she as a weaver.

In 1837, they met the Mormon missionaries and joined the Church. Edward did much missionary work among the people. To help earn money to go to America, they both worked in the mills while his parents tended the children. By 1847, they were able to leave England for America, along with his mother, four sisters, and his own family of Ann and six children.

They settled for a time in St. Louis where Edward worked in the coal mines. He dug the coal and two of his boys hauled it to market. They worked hard to obtain the funds to go to Utah.

Upon their arrival in the Valley, they settled in Salt Lake City. Edward worked in the temple quarries until 1850, when he and his oldest son William joined the forces to obstruct Johnston's Army. After things settled down, Edward moved his family to

Spanish Fork. He helped erect the adobe walls fortification outside the city. He did much to help in the building up and running of the city government. He helped build mills and worked in them. They moved to Provo, where his wife later died.

He married an acquaintance he had worked with in the mills. After several years they moved back to Spanish Fork and then to Beaver, where he and his wife worked in the St. George Temple. He was always active in the church and in community projects. He was loved and respected by his family and those who knew him.

Children:

WILLIAM, b. 18 Feb 1836, Preston, England. Md. 22 Feb 1858, Sarah Jane Miller Bradley. D. 10 Aug 1900, Spanish Fork, Utah.

ELLEN, b. 7 May 1837, Preston, England. D. 19 Feb 1845, Preston, England.

MARY, b. 22 Feb 1839, Preston, England. Md. 22 Feb 1858, John Banks. D.30 Oct 1875, Spanish Fork, Utah.

WILLARD ORSON, b. 2 Feb 1841, Preston, England. Md. 1st, 13 Dec 1862, Barbara Orther Fergusen. Md. 2nd, 15 Jan 1872, Emma Elizabeth Robertson. D. 4 Jun 1917, Spanish Fork, Utah.

MORMON MATHIAS, b. 3 May 1842, Preston, England. Md. 14 Oct 1876, Marie Wiatt Cables. D. 22 Dec 1909, Spanish Fork, Utah.

JANE, b. 3 Feb 1845, Preston, England. Md. 1st, 11 Sep 1866, (Div) Joseph Horace Skinner. Md. 2nd, Thomas Jones. D. 6 Jun 1917, Spanish Fork, Utah.

ELLENOR ANN, b. 18 Apr 1847, Preston, England. D. 5 Feb 1848.

ROBERT, b. 27 Jan 1849, Gravois, St. Louis, Missouri. D. 22 Nov 1852.

ALICE ANN, b. 9 Oct 1850, Gravois, Missouri. Md. 28 Mar 1868, Llewellyn Jones. D. 18 Sep 1930, Spanish Fork, Utah.

EDWARD, b. 7 Oct 1853, Gravois, Missouri. Md. 1st, 9 Jan 1879, Mary Sophia Davis. Md. 2nd, 10 Sep 1924, Margaret A. Miller. D. 18 May 1928, Spanish Fork, Utah.

SARAH LETTA, b. 13 Dec 1855, Salt Lake City, Utah. D. 18 Dec 1855

ANN, b. 31 Mar 1857, Salt Lake City , Utah. Md. 22 Mar 1874, Owen J.Rowe. D. 9 Feb 1938, Spanish Fork, Utah.

Submitted by: Helen Harris

HENRY CRIDDLE

Born: 14 Mar 1814, Fifehead, Trull, Somerset, England
Parents: William and Mary Turner Criddle
Died: 16 Sep 1866, Pacific Springs, Dakota Territory
Buried: 17 Sep 1866, Antelope Springs, Albany, Wyoming
Arrived in Valley: 1 Oct 1866, Joseph Rawlins Co.

Married: Mary Ann Bull
Date: 22 Jun 1837, West Buckland, Somerset, England
Born: 23 Jul 1813, Hail, Bradford, Somerset, England
Parents: Robert and Elizabeth Trout Bull
Died: 10 Feb 1894, Meadow, Millard, Utah

After Henry's marriage they settled in Taunton, England, where Henry worked as a "Maltster," "Journeyman Brewer" and "Brewer."

In 1856, their son George was baptized, followed by his mother a few months later, and finally Henry's father. Two of Henry's children left for America in 1862. Henry, his wife, and five children left for America in 1866.

After a difficult voyage and journey on the plains, Henry took a chill when he and the other men were forced to hang onto the wagons while crossing an extremely cold river. He developed pneumonia and died and was buried alongside the trail in Wyoming. Mary Ann brought the rest of her family to the Valley where eventually all of them were joined together. She died at the age of 80 years.

Children:

GEORGE, b. 15 Apr 1838, Taunton, Somerset, England. Md. 21 Apr 1858, Mary Ann Lacey. D. 1 Aug 1891, Brigham City, Utah.

WILLIAM, b. 3 Dec 1839, Taunton, England. Md. Selina Hartnell. D. 15 Aug 1917, Taunton, England.

SARAH ANN, b. 21 Oct 1841, Taunton, England. Md. 24 Mar 1863, Thomas E. Spackman. D. 31 Jan 1911, Farmington, Utah.

JANE, b. 1 Nov 1843, Taunton, England. Md. 16 Mar 1867, Henry George Labrum. D. 9 Apr 1923, Meadow, Utah.

ELIZABETH, b. 16 Oct 1845, Taunton, England. Md. 23 May 1870, James Studley. D. 13 Mar 1905, Taunton, England

CHARLOTTE, b. 21 Nov 1847, Taunton, England. Md. 12 Jan 1867, John Gull. D. 7 Jul 1922, Meadow, Utah.

SELENA, b. 28 Feb 1850, Taunton, England. Md. 27 Mar 1867, Joseph Adams. D. 15 Jan 1924, Fillmore, Utah.

ROBERT, b. 9 Aug 1852, Taunton, England. D. 12 Dec 1852, Taunton, England.

CHARLES, b. 22 Jul 1854, Taunton, England. Md. 1st, 6 Jul 1874, Emma Jane Crofts. Md. 2nd, 12 Oct 1911, Harriet Habbeshaw. Md. 3rd (Div), 12 Jun 1880, Dorothy Norwood. D. 16 Jun 1936.

Submitted by: Jerry Steele

CHARLES CRISMON

Born: 25 Dec 1807, ,Christian, Kentucky
Parents: George and Elizabeth Hagler Christman
Died: 23 Mar 1890, Mesa, Maricopa, Arizona
Arrived in Valley: 2 Oct 1847, Jedediah M. Grant Co.

Married 1st: Mary Hill
Date: 6 May 1830

Married 2nd: Elizabeth Hill

Charles will always be associated with the development of the West, particularly with grist mills, saw mills, sugar and silk mills. He joined the Church in its infancy. He said his baptism cured him of a lingering illness.

Brigham Young sent him to New Orleans to help converts that were arriving, to know of the trek going west after the Prophet was martyred. He returned to Nauvoo and obtained the material for a grist mill, which he built in Salt Lake. He ran freight lines that he established during the next 30 years. He helped build the railroad and did much work that helped him to know the West as few men did. He helped in the settlement of many Mormon Colonies, particularly in San Bernardino, California, and later in Southern Arizona.

He became interested in mining and helped discover and develop some of the largest copper and gold fields in the state. He is believed to be the first millionaire in Utah. There were many other businesses he was a part of during his life. He became a rancher in Southern Arizona and was known for his cattle and fine horses.

He was always active in the church and community and held many positions.

Children:

MARTHA JANE, b. 8 Sep 1831.
GEORGE, b. 5 Jul 1833.
JAMES, b. 8 Sep 1834.
ESTHER ANN, b. 27 Nov 1837.
SAMANTHA, b. 27 Mar 1840.
MARY ANN, b. 13 Feb 1842.
CHARLES, b. 13 Jun 1844.
EMILY PRECINDA, b. 18 Jan 1847.
ELLEN, b. 18 Jul 1849.
JOHN FRANKLIN, b. 14 Feb 1852.
CYNTHIA ADELINE, b. 14 Jun 1854.
WALTER SCOTT, b.27 Aug 1856.

Submitted by: Dawn Curtis

ALVIN CROCKETT

Born: 19 Oct 1831, Vinal Haven, Knox, Maine
Parents: David and Lydia Young Crockett
Died: 9 Jul 1902, Logan, Cache, Utah
Arrived in Valley: 19 Oct 1849, Willard Richards Co.

Married 1st: Mary Sophia Reed
Date: 20 Jun 1852, Payson, Utah

Married 2nd: Annie Naomi Peel

Alvin's parents accepted the gospel when Wilford Woodruff first introduced it in Fox Islands on his first mission. Alvin was baptized when he was eight.

In 1841 the entire family traveled to Nauvoo. When the saints left Nauvoo, the Crocketts settled in Davis County, Iowa until 1849 when they left for the valley. President Young sent them to settle Payson. Alvin went with friends to California to find gold, but found very little. He returned to Payson where he met and married the school teacher, Mary Sophia Reed.

In the summer he did mason work and built adobe houses. In the winter he mended shoes and did copper work on tubs, buckets, kegs, barrels, and churns to sell. He was in the military and a friend to the Indians.

In 1860 he moved his family to Logan where he became mayor. He was the first county sheriff and chief of police. He served in many other positions in the community. He was in the high council until his death. He took a second wife and in 1888 was arrested for having two wives.

He helped haul rocks for the Logan Temple, built roads and did anything else needed. He was a loving father and husband, went on two missions for the church, was known for his honesty, and was well respected wherever he went.

Children of 1st wife;

MARY SOPHIA, b. 8 Jun 1853.
ALVIN DAVID, b. 24 Oct 1854.
OZRO OZIAS, b. 29 Nov 1856.
LYDIA LOVARA, b. 21 Oct 1858.
DELIA ANN, b. 21 Oct 1860.
NORA ELLEN, b. 28 Dec 1862.
GEORGE EMER, b. 28 Nov 1865.
WILLIAM JOSEPH, b. 10 Feb 1868.
ROXANA CATHERINE, b. 19 Apr 1870.
HYRUM ENOS, b. 18 Apr 1873.

FRANK WALDON, b. 19 Oct 1874.
HENRY WALLACE, b. 10 Feb 1876.

Children of 2nd wife:

ALTHEA ANNIE, b. 22 Sep 1867.
BARBARA WOOSTER, b. 19 Oct 1869.
DELIA SOPHIA, b. 11 Dec 1871.
JOHN ALVIN, b. 18 Apr 1874.
FRED WALDO, b. 4 Jan 1876.
ELLA SABRA, 6 Nov 1877.

Submitted by: Dawn Curtis

DAVID CROCKETT

Born: 30 Dec 1806, Vinal Haven, Knox, Maine
Parents: James and Elizabeth Brackett Crockett
Died: 12 Apr 1876, Logan, Cache, Utah
Arrived in Valley: 19 Oct 1849, Willard Richards Co.

Married 1st: Lydia Young
Date: 20 Dec 1830, Knox, Maine

Married 2nd: Lucinda Sophronia Ellsworth
Date: 23 Jul 1856

David was baptized in 1840. His wife was baptized a year earlier. David and his family traveled to Kirtland but found the members leaving for Nauvoo, so they joined with them. A few years later they left Nauvoo and went back to Ohio where they farmed until 1849, when they started west.

Brigham Young sent David and his family to Payson to settle. David became the first mayor. While there, he took a second wife. He lived for a time near Ogden and later moved to Logan where he became a leader in the church and community.

Children of 1st wife:

ALVIN, b. 19 Oct 1831.
SABRA ANN, b. 31 Jan 1833.
ROXANNA KATHERINE, b. 26 Sesp 1834.
MELINDA MALLISSA, b. 13 Jul 1836.
LUCINDA COLEHALL, b. 21 Jan 1838.
EDWIN MADSEN, b. 14 Jun 1840.
WILFORD WOODRUFF, b. 9 Jun 1842.
DEBORA ATHENA, b. 12 Apr 1834.
BARBARA YOUNG, b. 5 Jun 1846.
DAVID WILLIAM, b. 13 Mar 1848.
NORMAN VICTOR, b. 14 Mar 1850.
EMER, b. 25 Feb 1852.
ENOS SAMUEL, b. 13 Mar 1855.
LYDIA ANN MANGUM, b. 13 Mar 1856.

Children of 2nd wife:

WILLIAM ALFRED, b. 6 Jan 1858.
LYDIA, b. 18 Sep 1859.
CELESTIA ADELAIDE, b. 19 Apr 1864.
EFFIE, b. 21 Feb 1869.
ATHENIA, b. 9 Feb 1875.

Submitted by: Dawn Curtis

GEORGE CROFT

Born: 17 Jul 1845, Ohio
Parents: Jacob and Amanda Miller Croft
Died: 10 Nov 1888, Provo, Utah
Arrived in Valley: 11 Oct 1856

Married: Letitia Maria Davies
Date: 6 Dec 1869, Salt Lake City, Utah
Born: 31 Nov 1851, St. Louis, St. Louis, Missouri
Died: After 1888, Fillmore, Utah

George and his parents moved to Texas when he was a small boy. His mother and sister were killed in a fall from a horse when he was six years old. He was baptized in 1855 and came to the Valley later with his father.

He helped his father haul rock for the Salt Lake Temple and also helped build the fort in Deseret. He was a miller in Fillmore and a stockman in Fillmore and Deseret. He was a sheriff, and later a contractor on the railroad up Parleys Canyon. He served a mission in Britain in 1882. He died of cancer of the liver.

Children:

GEORGE FRANCIS, b. 3 Oct 1871, Fillmore, Utah. Md. Mary Bur. Conk. D. 20 Sep 1937.
JACOB, b. 27 Jan 1873, Fillmore, Utah. Md. Mary Eliason. D. 16 Apr 1938.
MARY EVELYN, b. 6 May 1875, Fillmore, Utah. D. 15 Aug 1890.
AMANDA, b. 28 Nov 1876, Fillmore, Utah. D. 12 Dec 1955.
THOMAS, b. 27 Jul 1879, Fillmore, Utah. D. 27 Jul 1890.

LEFFEL PEARSON, b. 3 Aug 1882, Fillmore, Utah. D. 14 Feb 1907.

FLORENCE, b. 18 May 1885, Fillmore, Utah. D. 13 Aug 1890.

FRANCIS MARION, b. 13 Nov 1888, Fillmore, Utah. D. 12 Nov 1933.

Submitted by: Merrill Croft

JACOB CROFT

Born: 30 Apr 1808, near Springfield, Clark, Ohio
Parents: George and Mary Critz Croft
Died: 3 Jul 1900, Fillmore, Utah
Arrived in Valley: 11 Oct 1856, Jacob Croft's Co.

Married 1st: Amanda Miller
Date: 22 Jun 1843
Born: 1 May 1827
Parents: Joseph and Hannah Cornog Miller
Died: 8 Jul 1852, Harris Co., Texas

Married 2nd: Sebrina Land Matheny Cropper (widow with 8 children)
Date: Winter of 1854, Texas
Died: 27 Oct 1878, Fillmore, Utah

Married 3rd: Mary Ann Powell
Date: 8 Apr 1861, Salt Lake City, Utah
Born: 16 Sep 1843, London, England
Parents: John and Fanny Chamberlain Powell

Died: 12 Apr 1888, Scipio, Utah

Married 4th: Elizabeth Bean Crouch
Date: 4 Oct 1862, Salt Lake City, Utah
Born: 23 Mar 1804, Washington Co., Tennessee

Jacob, in 1850, moved his family to Harris County, Texas. While there, they were converted to the Mormon Church. Amanda was killed in a fall from a horse.

In 1852, Jacob and his two children decided to go west with the next wagon train from Texas, which left in 1853. However, when they got to Oklahoma, the Indians persuaded him to remain and build two grist mills, which he did. In the meantime he married Sebrina Cropper. They remained in Oklahoma two years before finally leaving for Utah. Upon their arrival in Salt Lake, Brigham Young sent them to settle Fillmore.

He helped in building many mills and other projects, including the settling of Deseret. He moved his family next to Scipio where he operated his flour mill. After Mary Ann died, he took his two daughters and moved back to Fillmore, where he remained until his death.

His help in building many mills, the cattle he ran and the fine horses he raised, helped greatly in the settling of that part of Utah. He donated land for the first cemetery in Scipio. At his funeral, it was said that he lived a long and productive life. He was a friend to not only the people around him, but also to the Indians. He buried four wives and 12 children before he finally died at the advanced age of 92 .

Children of 1st wife:

MARY ANN, b. 22 Feb 1844, Harris, Texas. D. 8 Jun 1844.
GEORGE, b. 17 Jul 1845, Harris, Texas. Md. 6 Dec 1869,
    Letitia Maria Davies. D. 10 Nov 1888.
FRANCES, b. 23 Aug 1847, Harris, Texas. Md. 1853, John
    Felshaw. D. 21 Jul 1914.
MICHAEL, b. 1849, Harris, Texas. D. Unknown
AMANDA, b. May 1851. D. 8 Jul 1852.

Children of 2nd wife: from first husband

WISE.
THOMAS.
LEIGH.
KATE.

Children of 3rd wife:

FANNY MERCY, Md. John W. Callister.
NELLIE DEAN, Md. Clark Reuben McBride.
    This represents 2 of the 9 known children, other childrens names were not provided.

Submitted by: Merrill Croft

BENJAMIN STEPHEN POWELL CROMPTON (Webster)

Born: 30 Jan 1817, Hainsfsord, Norfolk, England
Parents: Stephen and Mary Crompton Powell
Died: 6 Jan 1901, Salt Lake City, Utah
Arrived in Valley: 24 Sep 1862, Homer Duncan Co.

Married 1st: Ann Gladman
Date: 22 Apr 1836, Norwich, Norfolk, England
Born: 18 Apr 1817, St Faiths, Norfolk, England
Died: 18 Dec 1849, East Wyner, Norwich, Norfolk, England

Married 2nd: Emily Rushmer
Date: 26 Sep 1850, Norwich, Norfolk, England (Div. 1863.

Born: 21 Apr 1824, London, England.
Died: 22 Nov 1916, Ogden, Utah.

Married 3rd: Jane Elizabeth Holton
Date: 20 Jan 1865, Salt Lake City, Utah
Born: 15 Dec 1842, Sprowston, Norfolk, England
Died: 3 May 1902, Salt Lake City, Utah

Benjamin was a bootmaker and a shoe store owner. In 1862 he brought his family to Utah where they lived in Salt Lake. He remained active in the church all his life.

After the death of his father, when Benjamin was young, his mother married Mathis Webster. Benjamin took his mother's maiden name when he became a man.

Children of 1st wife:

ELIZABETH, b.14 Jan 1838, Norwich, Norfolk, England. Md. 18 Apr 1863, John Harris Picknell. D. 10 Nov 1932, Salt Lake City, Utah.

ALFRED, b. 29 Dec 1839, Norwich, England. D. 1840, England.

HARRIET ADELAIDE, b. 15 Jan 1841, Norwich, England. Md. 8 Nov 1862, William Henry Hockings. D. 6 Aug 1921, Salt Lake City, Utah.

VIRTUE LEAH, b. 22 Dec 1843, Norwich, England. Md. 31 Jan 1862, Elias Hicks Blackburn (5th wife). D. 28 Nov 1927, Salina, Utah.

MARIAN RACHEL, b. 14 Oct 1845, Norwich, England. Md. 1 Jun 1867, George William Chandler (3rd wife). D. 29 Dec 1909, Ogden, Utah.

KEREN, b. 16 Mar, Norwich, England. Md. 19 Apr 1869, James Goddard. D. 22 Feb 1876, Salt Lake City, Utah.

BENJAMIN STEPHEN, b. 11 Dec 1849, Norwich, England. Left in England with grandparents.

Children of 2nd wife:

GEORGEANNA ELIZA, b. 12 Sep 1852, Norwich, England.

Md. 8 Feb 1869, George William Chandler. (5th wife). D. 7 Jan 1922, Ogden, Utah.

CHARLES WILLIAM, b. 9 Feb 1855, Norwich, England. D. 22 Oct 1860, England.

Children of 3rd wife:

STEPHEN GEORGE, b. 9 Sep 1865, Salt Lake City, Utah. Md. 28 Aug 1894, Gina C. Whittenburg. D. 17 May 1949, Salt Lake City, Utah.

EMELINE ANN, b. 10 Oct 1867, Salt Lake City, Utah. Md. 30 Mar 1887, Joshua Beanland Bean. D. 6 Feb 1888, Salt Lake City, Utah (child birth).

EZRA P., b. Apr 1870, Salt Lake City, Utah. D. Sept. 1871.

MINNENETTA CLARE, b. 12 Mar 1872, Salt Lake City, Utah. Md. 22 Oct 1891, Philip Henry Brooks. D. 22 Oct 1922, San Francisco, California.

ALBERT EDWIN, b. 21 Feb 1874, Salt Lake City, Utah. D. 4 Apr 1874.

ROSEMOND ELVIRA, b. 10 Feb 1875, Salt Lake City, Utah. Md. 8 Oct 1899, David A. Palmquist. D. 22 Mar 1929, Salt Lake City, Utah.

ELIZABETH, b. 4 Apr 1877, Salt Lake City, Utah. D. 8 Apr 1877.

IDA PEARL, b. 27 Jul 1879, Salt Lake City, Utah. Md. 23 Jul 1909, James Pagano. D. 5 Aug 1926, Bingham Village, Utah.

BENJAMIN, b. Nov 1881, Salt Lake City, Utah. D. 17 Mar 1882.

Submitted by: Philip Speck

JOHN CROOK

Born: 11 Oct 1831, Trenton, Lancs, England.
Died: 31 Mar, 1921, Heber, Utah
Arrived in Valley: Fall of 1856, E. B. Tripp Co.

Married: Mary Giles
Date: 6 Sep 1856, Provo, Utah
Born: 13 Apr 1833, Calvertson, Nottingham, England
Parents: William and Sarah Huskinson Giles
Died: 5 Sep 1888, Heber, Utah

John was baptized into the Mormon Church in the spring of 1847. In 1852 he left England for America. He peddled ice upon arriving there, until he left for Utah. He came west with the William Giles family and married their daughter shortly after their arrival in the Valley in 1856.

In June 1859, the west half of Heber was laid out in city blocks and a month later John hauled logs to build a house. When the area was made into a stake, John was chosen as first counselor to Bishop Forman of the Heber West Ward. His main interest lay in music, genealogy and history. He was considered to be one of Wasatch County's best historians. He farmed and raised stock and owned the first red sandstone quarry in the area. He also was choir director for some time.

He and Mary lived in a covered wagon box until John could build them a two room adobe house. Their home was built in the fort for protection from the Indians. Later they built a red sandstone home, which is still standing (1997). John was one of the stalwarts members of the church and community. He lived to be 89 years-old.

Children:

JOHN WILLIAM, b. 9 Apr 1858, Md. Sarah Elizabeth Bond.
SARAH ELIZABETH, b.28 Nov 1859, 2nd child born in Heber.
    Md. John Carlile.
HEBER GILES, b. 18 Ssep 1861. Md. Sarah Matilda Nicol.
GEORGE FRANKLIN, b. 9 Nov 1863. D. 28 Apr 1864, Heber,
    Utah.
MARY JANE, b. 29 May 1865. Md. Jonathan O. Duke.
THOMAS HUSKINSON, b. 25 Apr 1867. Md. 1st, Julie Etta
    Duke. Md. 2nd, Gertrude Bond.
FREDERICK, b. 17 Aug 1869. Md. Minnie M. Lindsay.
JAMES, b. 5 Jan 1872. D. 20 Jan 1872. Child.
MARGARET ANN, Md. 18 Jan 1876, Joseph Callister.

Submitted by: Ralph Carlisle

JOSEPH CROOK

Born: 6 Jun 1823, Chalford, Gloucs, England
Parents: James and Sophia Mason Crook
Died: 8 Jan 1897, Payson, Utah, Utah
Arrived in Valley: 24 Oct 1855, Milo Andrus Co.

Married 1st: Elizabeth Walters
Date: 21 Jan 1845, Cheltenham, Gloucs, England
Died: 26 Jan 1891, Payson, Utah

Married 2nd: Rosina Muellar, German widow–one son.
Died: 17 Jan 1901, Payson, Utah

Joseph came from a large family. His father was a weaver by trade and was well known for his religious and historical tapestries. At the age of 18, Joseph was baptized into the Church. He became a druggist and owned two apothecary shops in England.

When his youngest daughter was born, he sold his drug stores to finance their trip to America and the Valley. They went by rail to Pittsburgh and then by steamboat to Atchison, Kansas, where they joined the Milo Andrus Company. Upon their arrival, they soon moved to Farmington, Davis County, Utah. Five months after their arrival, he got word that his father had died and that his mother and his sister Liza, were leaving England to come to the valley. They came in the Willey Handcart Company. Upon their arrival in Salt Lake, they went to Farmington. His mother died three weeks later as a result of her legs being frozen to her knees.

When Johnston's army came and the saints were asked to move south, Joseph took his family to Payson, Utah. He made a dugout where they lived until he could build a home, that became a hostel or hotel. He and his sons ran an adobe brick yard. They furnished bricks for many homes plus the tithing office, tabernacle, and the first ward. Later he and his sons helped grade the route for the Union Pacific Railroad through Echo Canyon.

Although he was a chemist, he preferred herbs, roots, etc. He had many fruit trees, shade trees, grape vines, and much stock. He helped whenever he was needed and remained active in the church.

Children of 1st wife:

JOSEPH EDWARD, b. 13 Dec 1845, Chalford, Glouc, England.
HYRUM FRANCIS, b. 31 Dec 1848, Chalford, Glouc, England.
BRIGHAM HEBER WILLARD, 29 Sep 1852, Chalford, Glouc, England.
ELIZABETH, b. 6 May 1854, Chalford, Glouc, England.

Children of 2nd wife: Adopted the son of his second wife.

JOHN GOTTLOB FOELL CROOK, b. 9 May 1887, Germany.

Submitted by: Darro Glissmeyer

BENJAMIN CROSLAND

Photograph
not
available

Born: 12 May 1815, Sheffield, Yorkshire, England
Parents: John H. and Nancy Crosland/Croslin/Crossland
Died: 15 Jun 1860, Tooele, Tooele, Utah
Arrived in Valley: bef. 1852

Married 1st: Sarah Hobson–No children
Date: England

Married 2nd: Catherine A. Smith
Date: 14 Jun 1852, Utah

Married 3rd: Jane Gillette
Date: 14 Jun 1852, Utah

Benjamin was born in England and married there the first time. After arriving in the Valley he established a home in Lake Point, Utah. Little is known about this good man and his families except that he married three times and fathered six children. Later they lived in Tooele.

He was active in the church and community and was a good man, husband, and father.

Children of 2nd wife:

JAMES SMITH, b. 14 Apr 1853, Lake Point, Tooele, Utah.
    Md. 1st, 1875, Polly Stringham. Md. 2nd, 10 Feb 1879,
    Hedvig Nielsen. D. 20 Oct 1913, Oakland, California.
SARAH, b. 24 Oct 1855, Tooele, Utah. Md. 6 Sep 1873,

Willard Richard Johnson. D. 3 Jul 1918, Holden, Utah.
JOHN SMITH, b.12 Mar 1858, Tooele, Utah. Md. 25 Oct
   1882, Lillias Smith. D. 12 May 1926, Holden, Utah.
BENJAMIN CROSLAND, b. 15 Feb 1859, Tooele, Utah. Md.
   25 Oct 1882, Amelia Walton. D. 3 Jan 1917, Holden, Utah.

Submitted by: Blaine Wasden

WILLIAM CHARLES CRUMP

Born: 25 Mar 1829, Pontesbury, Shrops, England
Parents: William and Martha Betton Crump
Died: 18 Mar 1904, Herriman, Salt Lake, Utah
Arrived in Valley: 3 Sep 1852, Abraham O. Smoot Co.

Married 1st: Margaret Ann James
Date: 1852, Salt Lake City, Utah
Born: 28 Jun 1826, Lugwardine, Hereford, England
Died: 22 May 1911, Herriman, Utah.

Married 2nd: Sarah Cornick
Date: 7 Nov 1872, Salt Lake City, Utah
Born: 12 Sep 1842, Stoke Abbot, Dorchester, England
Died: Sept 1911, Herriman, Utah

   Charles, as he was known, was the only member of his family to join the church. Shortly after his baptism in 1849, he did missionary work. In February 1852, he left England for America.
   After arriving in Salt Lake where he stayed for about three

weeks, he moved to Taylorsville and he helped build the fort. He was a guard on the south and also on the west side of the Valley during 1953.

When Brigham Young called for 20 families to go to Butterfield Settlement to help settle the area, Charles volunteered. He helped build the fort there and then became a friend to the Indians. They called him Big Chief, even though he was of small stature.

Charles helped in the battle against Johnston's Army. In 1863, he made one of six trips back to Florence, Nebraska, to help bring some of the church's poor to the valley. He remained active in the church all his life, and was ordained a patriarch in 1897.

Children of 1st wife:

MARTHA ELEANOR, b. 6 Oct 1856, Fort Herriman, Utah.
MARGARET MARY, b. 24 Dec 1857, Herriman, Utah.
WILLIAM CHARLES, II, b. 18 Mar 1859, Herriman, Utah.
SARAH ANN, b. 20 Jan 1862, Fort Herriman, Utah.
REYNOLD ALEXANDER, b. 20 Aug 1863, Herriman, Utah.
THOMAS EDWARD, b.17 Jun 1866, Herriman, Utah.
SAMUEL HEBER, b. 24 Dec 1867, Herriman, Utah.
JOSEPH HENRY, b. 21 Sep 1870, Herriman, Utah.
EDWARD, b. abt 1872, Herriman, Utah.

Children of 2nd wife:

SARAH JANE, b. 2 Sep 1873, Herriman, Utah.
BETSY MARINDA, b. 28 May 1875, Herriman, Utah.
LUCY, b. 1 Apr 1877, Herriman, Utah.
MARY, b. 14 Jan 1879, Herriman, Utah.
ELIZABETH ANN, b. 1 Mov 1880, Herriman, Utah.
GEORGE WILLIAM, b. 12 Nov 1882, Herriman, Utah.
MARGARET EMMA, b. 2 May 1885, Herriman, Utah.

Submitted by: Blaine Crump

WILLIAM CUFLEY

Born: 26 Feb 1804, Enfield, Middlesex, England
Parents: William and Susannah Cufley
Died: 8 Mar 1883, Salt Lake City, Utah
Arrived in Valley: 26 Sep 1853, J. Gates Company

Married 1st: Harriet Clark
Date: 12 Jun 1825, St. Andrew Parish, Enfield, England
Born: abt 1804, England

Married 2nd: Jeanette Irvine
Date: abt 1856, Salt Lake City, Utah
Born: 3 Mar 1836, New Monkland, Lanark, Scotland
Parents: William and Janet White Irvine
Died: 2 Jan 1908, Blackfoot, Bannock, Idaho

William worked for Queen Victoria, probably as her gardner and handy man, and was a trusted servant of hers as he was entrusted with the keys to some parts of the palace. When he left for America, she gave him several gifts.

After William joined the Church he felt that he should move his family to join the saints in the Valley. However, his wife Harriet refused to leave or let any of the children go with him. William felt bad to leave his family, knowing he would probably never see them again, but he felt he had to go. It is not known if they got a bill of divorcement. He left in February 1853.

Upon arriving in New Orleans, they sailed up the river to Keokuk where they set out for the valley. William settled in the southeast part of the valley called Pleasant Valley. It was just west of the mouth of Parley's Canyon. Within the next two years he met and married Jeanette Irvine from Scotland. Their first home was a dugout on the south side of Pleasant Valley, but Jeanette was frightened by the Indians so William traded that property for a home on the north side of the hollow at about 20 East. It was called Decker's Fort. They raised their children there.

William probably worked in the Young/Little Mill near their home. He was 32 years his wife's senior, but he was a kind, gentle and loving husband and father. He called Jeanette "his little Scotch Lassie" and loved to watch her sing and dance. He was well liked by everyone and remained strong in the gospel. He later heard that one or more of his sons from his first marriage had gone to Australia and become sheep farmers.

Children of 1st wife:

SUSANNE, b. 19 Sep 1825, Enfield, Middlesex, England.
WILLIAM, b. 10 Jul 1830, Enfield, Middlesex, England.
CAROLINE ANNE, b. abt 1833, Enfield, Middlesex, England.
JOHN, b. 21 Mar 1834, Enfield, Middlesex, England.
RICHARD, b. 23 Aug 1835, Enfield, Middlesex, England.
JOSEPH, b. 17 May 1836, Enfield, Middlesex, England.
HENRY, b. 8 Apr 1838, Engield, Middlesex, England.
HENRIETTA, b. 9 Nov 1840, Enfield, Middlesex, England.

Children of 2nd wife:

MIRIAM "Mamie", b. 27 Nov 1858, Salt Lake City, Utah. Md. 1st, Willis Knapp, 1899 (Div). Md. 2nd, David Dupuis. D. 19 Feb 1948, Salt Lake City, Utah.
LOUISA, b. 7 May 1860, Salt Lake City, Utah. Md. 4 Mar 1880, James Devalson Cummings. D. 20 May 1933, Provo, Utah.
MARGARET, b. Feb 1862, Salt Lake City, Utah. Md. 1881, George A. Askew. D. 1944, Salt Lake City, Utah.

Submitted by: Florence Youngberg

BENJAMIN FRANKLIN CUMMINGS

Born: 3 May 1821, Farmington, Kenebec, Maine
Parents: James and Susannah Willard Cummings
Died: 22 Oct 1899, Salt Lake City, Utah
Arrived in Valley: 21 Sep 1847, Daniel Spencer;s Company

Married 1st: Catherine Hall
Date: 19 Feb 1852

Married 2nd: Mary Jane Yearsley
Date: 27 Apr 1856, Salt Lake City, Utah
Born: 30 Sep 1859, West Chester, Chester, Pennsylvania
Parents: David Dutton and Mary Ann Hoopes Yearsley
Died: 16 Mar 1921, Salt Lake City, Utah

Benjamin Franklin, being a religious boy, readily accepted the gospel, but he wasn't baptized until the next spring, April 1840. His parents joined about the same time. His father moved his family to Nauvoo where they all became active in the church and community.

Benjamin was described by his son as being over six feet tall and 200 pounds. He stood straight, had a light complexion, blue eyes, and curly hair that came out early and left him bald. He wore a full beard. He was well informed, but with little formal education. He was talented in being able to express himself when speaking before an audience or to friends.

His parents died in Winter Quarters leaving Benjamin and his older brother, James, to bring the children west. He was a fine carpenter, was active in the community, serving as county recorder, assessor, sheriff and colonel in the militia. He taught a military school and played fife in the military band.

He was one of the first to be called as missionaries to the Salmon River Mission. In 1850 he ran a ferry at the Platte River for some time. He moved his family to Ogden where he made furniture for the settlers. After the forced move to Provo, upon their return he moved his family to Willard and then to Ogden for a time, and eventually to Salt Lake. After his polygamous marriage to his second wife, he worked in the mill in Parley's Hollow for about six years.

In 1874 to 1879, he served a mission in Council Bluffs. He kept a good journal much of his adult life. He wore buckskin, which he made, most of his life. He had a good sense of humor. He was killed by a boy on a bicycle in his 78th year.

Children of 1st wife:

CHARLOTTE MEHITABEL, b. 8 Jan 1853, Ogden, Utah. D. 11 Jan 1864.
BENJAMIN F., b. 22 Aug 1855.
HORACE, b. 12 Jun 1858, Provo, Utah.
IMOGENE, b. 26 Feb 1860, Willard, Utah.
WILLIAM HENRY, b. Dec 1866, Salt Lake City, Utah. D. next day. Infant.
GEORGE HALL, b. 2 dec 1870, Salt Lake City, Salt Lake, Utah. D. 24 Jul 1927.

Children of 2nd wife:

ANNA ELIZABETH, b. 13 Feb 1858, Ogden, Weber, Utah. Md. 23 Aug 1883, Horace Eldredge. D. 55 Jan 1936, Salt Lake City, Utah.
JAMES DEVALSON, b.30 Sep 1859, Willard, Box Elder, Utah. Md. 4 Mar 1880, Salt Lake City, Utah. D. 9 Jun 1926, Salt Lake City, Utah.
MARY LAVENIA, b. 13 Apr 1862, Ogden, Weber, Utah. D. Young.

Submitted by: Florence Youngberg

LYMAN CURTIS

Born: 21 Jan 1812, New Salem, Franklin, Maine
Parents: Nahum and Millicent Waite Curtis
Died: 5 Aug 1898, Salem, Utah
Arrived in Valley: 22 Jul 1847, Brigham Young Company

Married 1st: Charlotte Alvord
Date: Feb 1834.
Born: 25 Sep 1815, Lockport, Niagra, New York
Died: 9 Sep 1879, Salt Lake City, Utah

Married 2nd: Sarah Wells Hartley
Date: 26 Jul 1862, Salt Lake City, Utah
Born: 10 Aug 1837, Sheffield, Yorks, England
Parents: Samuel and Elizabeth Gill Hartley
Died: 12 Jul 1921, Salem, Utah

Lyman was one of the original nine horsemen sent out as scouts into the Valley on July 22, 1847. He was a member of Zion's Camp, Nauvoo Legion, and a guard over Prophet Joseph Smith and Hyrum's bodies after their martyrdom. He helped to erect the Kirtland and Nauvoo Temples.

Upon his arrival in Salt Lake, he lived there for a time and then was sent to Santa Clara and then Salem to help settle those towns. He was a farmer, logger, stone mason, and ran a saw mill. He planted the first field of cotton in Utah's Dixie. He served a mission to the Southern Indian Mission in 1851.

He helped evacuate the saints out of Missouri after the mob action. He remained active in the church and communities all his life. He helped build irrigation dams and canals in the southern part of the state. He died in Salem, Utah.

Children of 1st wife:

JULIA, b. 7 May 1835, Liberty, Clay, Missouri. Md. 17 May 1853, Alonzo Hazeltine Raleigh. D. 8 Feb 1891.

AMMON, b. 12 Jul 1837, Quincy, Adams, Illinois. D. 22 Jan 1839.

THADDEUS, b. 28 Mar 1839, Quincy, Adams, Illinois. D. 25 Apr 1839.

ADELINE CLARINDA, b. 16 May 1840, Nauvoo, Illinois. Md. 1st, 1 Feb 1857, Peter Mack Elliott. Md. 2nd, George G. Carson. D. 27 Aug 1842.

HENRY, b. 29 Feb 1842, Nauvoo, Illinois. D. 27 Aug 1842.

SAMUEL B., b. 9 Dec 1844, LaCrosse, Wisconsin. Md. 1st, 1867, Lucinda Stewart. Md. 2nd, 20 Jan 1873, Susan Lucretia Gardner. Md. 3rd, 27 Dec 1878, Elizabeth Gardner.

SON, b. 1846, Kegg, Pottawattamie, Iowa. D. 1846.

SON, b. 1846, Kegg Creek, Pottawattamie, Iowa. D. 1846.

CHILD (stillborn), b. 1846, Kegg Creek, Pottawattamie, Iowa.

JOSEPH NAHUM, b. 9 Aug 1847, Kegg Creek, Pottawattamie, Iowa. Md. 1st, 17 Jan 1870, Sarah Diantha Gardner. Md. 2nd, 24 Mar 1881, Marilla Gardner. D.26 Jul 1925.

WILLIAM FREDERICK, b. 14 Jul 1850, On Plains, Nebraska. Md. 24 Dec 1872, Sarah Alice Higgins. D. 3 May 1928.

CHARLES GRANDISON, b. 16 Dec 1852, Salt Lake City, Utah. Md. 1 Jan 1872, Eolia Virginia Killian. D. 8 Mar 1946.

ORSON ELLIOTT, b. 7 Mar 1857, Salt Lake City, Utah. Md. Ellen Atwood.

Children of 2nd wife:

PARLEY PARRY, b. 28 Jan 1858, Salt Lake City, Utah. Md. 22 Sep 1881, Clarissa Cornelia Atwood. D. 28 Feb 1939.

CHARLES, b. 20 Aug 1859, Spanish Fork, Utah. D. 13 Dec 1901.

SARAH LUSINA, b. 22 May 1863, Salem, Utah. Md. 10 Feb 1881, Robert Augustus Snyder. D. 9 Mar 1921.

ELIZA JANE, b. 23 Feb 1865, Salem, Utah. Md. 23 Feb 1885, William Jerome Durfey. D. 31 Jan 1949.

MILLICENT, b. 16 Jun 1867, Salem, Utah. Md. 9 Apr 1888, James Edwin Smith. D. 22 Feb 1965.

EMMA CORNELIA, b. 31 Jul 1869, Salem, Utah. Md. 21 Nov 1889, Charles Hanks. D. 6 Mar 1951.

JOSEPHINE MATILDA, b. 30 Nov 1872, Salem, Utah. D. 26 Jun 1877.

ASA LYMAN, b. 3 Feb 1877, Salem, Utah. Md. 4 Jan 1905, Anne Beatrice LIttlewood. D. 5 Oct 1961.

Submitted by: Melea Allan

HOZEA (HOSEA) CUSHING

Born: 2 Apr 1826, Boston, Suffolk, Massachusetts
Parents: Phillip and Mary C. Rundlett Cushing
    Records say Hosea was adopted by Heber C. Kimball.
Died: 6 May 1854, Salt Lake City, Utah.
Arrived in Valley: 24 Jul 1847, with Heber C. Kimball family

Married: Helen Jennett Murray
Date: 4 Feb 1847, Winter Quarters, Florence, Nebraska

Hosea, while yet a small child, moved with his parents to Hingham, Plymouth, Massachusetts, where he spent his childhood. In 1842, he was sent to Boston to serve an apprenticeship as a ship's joiner and carpenter. He was there until he was 21.

Soon after he arrived in Boston, he heard the elders preach, and after much prayer and study he was baptized. In 1844, he

633

was sent to Hingham, Massachusetts. His parents were very bitter about him joining the church and they disowned him. He was called back to Nauvoo where he helped build the Nauvoo Temple. Shortly after, he was adopted as one of Heber C. Kimball's children.

When the saints left Nauvoo, Hosea drove one of Heber C. Kimball's wagons with one of Heber's wives and children. He married on the trek west and settled in Salt Lake after his arrival. He remained faithful to the church doing all he was asked to do.

When Brother Kimball lost some cattle, he sent Hosea and another man to find them. When they didn't return, Brother Kimball became concerned and looked for them. He found them out by Grantsville where they had been attacked by Indians. The other man was dead but Brother Kimball brought Hosea home and Helen nursed him, but he soon died.

Children:

WILLIAM ELLIS, b. 5 Dec 1848.
HOSEA PHILIP, b. 26 Aug 1850.
SAMUEL ROSWELL, b. 15 May 1853.

Submitted by: Janice Betts and William Davis

AARON EUGENE DANIELS

Born: 1 Aug 1822, Dryden, Tompkins, New York
Parents: Sheffield and Abigail Warren Daniels
Died: 1896, Fort Duchesne, Utah
Arrived in Valley: Here in 1850 Utah Census

Married 1st: Hannah Caroline Rogers
Date: 14 Dec 1845, Nauvoo, Illinois
Born: 20 Mar 1827, Dunkirk, Chattagua, New York
Parents: David White and Martha Collins Rogers
Died: 14 Mar 1915, Salt Lake City, Utah

Married 2nd: Harriet Nixon
Date: 20 Feb 1856, Utah

Married 3rd: Rose Jenson (Indian)
Date: about 1885, Utah

Aaron Eugene was about eight years old when his parents joined the Church. He was baptized at the same time as his parents. Aaron became a trapper and spent his winters trapping on the Provo River. Daniels Creek and Daniels Canyon are both named for him. In 1861 he and his family settled in Wanship, Utah. Aaron built a large building that was used as a mail station. When the stage coach came in, the drivers and passengers could eat and spend the night.

Aaron guided wagon companies across the plains and, along with his wife Rose, worked with the Indians, and taught them how to plant. In his own words, "I have had many varied experiences from the early persecutions and riots in Missouri and Illinois. I guided wagon companies across the plains to Utah. Equally exciting and interesting events happened as I trapped, explored, and prospected throughout the western parts of the United States. I have seen the coming of the wagon trains and the railroads."

Children of 1st wife:

DAVID CHARLES, b. 30 Sep 1846, Polk City, Polk, Iowa. Md. Feb 1876, Elizabeth Lemmons. D. 30 Nov 1904, Provo, Utah.
MARIA EUPHRESIA, b. 26 Nov 1848, Polk Co, Iowa. Md. 31 Aug 1868, George Jefferson Simonds. D. 23 Aug 1919, Boise, Idaho.
LENORA IDA, b. 23 Sep 1850, Salt Lake City , Utah. Md. 1871, William Shaffer. D. 14 Mar 1921.

EUGENE AARON, b. 7 Aug 1851, Provo, Utah. Md. 24 Dec 1874, Martha Melissa Bullock. D. 20 Jul 1953, Atascadero, San Luis Obispo.

HENRY ROGERS, b. 6 Aug 1856, Provo, Utah. D. 26 Oct 1858, Provo, Utah.

LEHI, b. 26 Oct 1858, Provo, Utah. Md. 1879, Delia Lowe.

CAROLINE AMELIA, b. 9 Dec 1860, Provo, Utah. Md. 22 Mar 1883, Charles Frank Mills. D. 24 Aug 1934, Salt Lake City, Utah.

EDWARD F., b. 3 Mar 1864, East Weber, Weber, Utah. D. Nov 1865.

NELLIE MAY, b. 1 May 1866, Salt Lake City, Utah. D. 7 Feb 1868.

LOUIE ROVENIA, b. 13 Jun 1868, Heber, Wasatch, Utah. Md. 20 Dec 1889, Robert John Liddiard. D. 16 Feb 1918, Boise, Ada, Idaho.

ROY ROGERS, b. 5 Feb 1873, Provo, Utah. D. Apr 1882.

Submitted by: Douglas Smith

ROBERT DANSIE, JR.

Born: 5 May 1850, Boxford, Suffolk, England
Parents: Robert Sr. and Charlotte Rudland Dansie
Died: 10 Nov 1920, Salt Lake City, Utah
Arrived in Valley: 5 Oct 1862, Ansel P. Harmon Co.

Married 1st: Roseina Silcock
Date: 22 Mar 1875, Salt Lake City, Utah
Born: 29 Jan 1856, Salt Lake City, Utah

Died: 12 Oct 1879, Herriman, Utah

Married 2nd: Paulina Silcock (sister to Roseina)
Date: 9 Sep 1880, Utah
Born: 4 Oct 1861, Grantsville, Tooele, Utah
Died: 7 Apr 1935, Salt Lake City, Utah

Married 3rd: Christine Madsen
Date: 29 May 1885, Utah
Born: 2 May 1857, Gronfeld, Arks, Denmark

Robert Jr., at age 12, left England for America, with his parents and siblings. While crossing the plains, his mother and youngest brother died at childbirth and were buried in Wyoming. Robert Jr. helped take care of the younger children after the death of their mother, until his father remarried. He was a farmer and stockman. They lived in Salt Lake for awhile and then moved to Herriman, Utah.

Robert was a farmer and stockman. While in Riverton, he was constable for three years. He helped dig the first irrigation ditch from Bingham Canyon. He was in the National Guard and helped in the tithing office.

He was always active in the church. At ward functions, he would lead the crowd by whistling and singing. He was well liked and active in the community as well as the church.

Children of 1st wife:

CHARLOTTE JANE, b. 2 Apr 1876, Herriman, Utah. Md. 28 Apr 1898, David Edward Shelley. D. 16 Mar 1940, American Fork, Utah.
ROBERT MORONI, b. 12 Mar 1878, Herriman, Utah. Md. 17 Aug 1972, Ida Edith Reynolds (by proxy). D. 29 Jan 1904.
ALMA, b. 10 Oct 1879, Herriman, Utah. D. 12 Oct 1879, Herriman, Utah.

Children of 2nd wife:

NICHOLAS THOMAS, b. 6 Sep 1881, Riverton, Utah. Md. 6 Nov 1902, Emma Jorgensen. D. 12 Mar 1912.

ROSEINA HARRIET, b. 7 Oct 1883, Riverton, Utah. D. 23 Oct 1885, Riverton, Utah.

ANNIE LOUISE, b. 29 Sep 1885, Riverton, Utah. Md. 19 Nov 1915, Percil Gates. D. 28 Feb 1932, Salt Lake City, Utah.

MAHONRI MORIANCUMER, b. 1 Sep 1887, Riverton, Utah. Md. 17 Apr 1913, Lillie Estella Starling. D. 25 May 1985, Salt Lake City, Utah.

CHARLES ALFRED, b. 1 Aapr 1889, Riverton, Utah. D. 5 Apr 1889, Riverton, Utah.

EDNA PEARL, b. 20 Nov 1890, Riverton, Utah. D. 8 Dec 1890, Riverton, Utah.

ELECTA HORTENSE, b. 12 Dec 1891, Riverton, Utah. Md. 10 Jun 1912, Allyn Wilbur Lind. D. 16 Jun 1975, Salt Lake City, Utah.

MARY ISABELLE, b. 2 Aug 1894, Riverton, Utah. D. 24 Sep 1908, Riverton, Utah.

CHAUNCEY MILLARD, b. 7 Nov 1896, Riverton, Utah. Md. 19 Sep 1923, Gladys Delilah Hilton. D. 27 May 1969, Salt Lake City, Utah.

ROBERTA SARAHANN, b. 3 Aug 1899, Riverton, Utah. Md. 8 Oct 1924, Samuel O. Jarman. D. 28 Sep 1928, Salt Lake City, Utah.

PERCY JEWEL, b. 26 Nov 1901, Riverton, Utah. D. Feb 1993, Salt Lake City, Utah.

IDA PAULINE, b. 26 Sep 1906, Salt Lake City, Utah. Md. 24 Apr 1929, Earl Ray Peck. D. 25 Aug 1969, Salt Lake City, Utah.

Children of 3rd wife:

JAMES HYRUM, b. 12 Mar 1886, West Jordan, Utah. Md. 16 Jun 1909, Josephine Love. D. 25 Jun 1917, Riverton, Utah.

JOSEPH HENRY, b. 23 Mar 1893, Riverton, Utah. Md. 14 Aug 1944, Ruth Evelyn Huggett. D. 18 Dec 1978, Salt Lake City, Utah.

ENGREE MARIE, b. 2 Nov 1894, Riverton, Utah. Md. 1 Jul
1949, Daniel Otis Corbett. D. 31 Jan 1989, Bountiful, Utah.
ELSIE ROBERTA, b. 8 Jun 1898, Riverton, Utah. Md. 7 Jun
1923, Charles Lewis Knight.

Submitted by: Estella Benson

ROBERT DANSIE, SR.

Born: 5 Feb 1825, Boxford. Suffolk, England
Parents: James and Sarah Chenery Dansie
Died: 12 Oct 1896, Salt Lake City, Utah
Arrived in Valley: 5 Oct 1862, Ansel P. Harmon Co.

Married 1st: Charlotte Rudland
Date: 8 Apr 1849, Boxford, Suffolk, England
Born: 24 Mar 1829, Newton, Suffolk, England
Parents: William and Susan Foster Rudland
Died: 21 Sep 1862, Pacific Springs, Sweetwater, Wyoming

Married 2nd: Jane Wilcox
Date: 12 Dec 1862, Salt Lake City, Utah
Born: 24 Aug 1836, Bristol, Somerset, England
Parents: John and Melissa Hurley Wilcox
Died: 17 Mar 1892, Herriman, Utah

Married 3rd: Sarah Ann Glenn–No children
Date: 14 Sep 1892, Salt Lake City, Utah
Born: 26 Jan 1859, Commerce, Madison, Georgia.

Parents: John and Martha Francis Emily Pool Glenn
Died: 12 Jul 1931, Salt Lake City, Utah

Robert was introduced to the church in 1849 in England. He brought his future wife to hear the missionaries. They knew it was true but she wanted to study more. They were married in April and baptized in October 1849. Their families weren't pleased with their acceptance of the Gospel so they moved to Barking, Essex, England. It was here Robert acquired the trade of gardener.

In 1862 they traveled by boat and then by ox wagon to the Salt Lake Valley. On the way, in Wyoming, Charlotte gave birth to a baby boy following which they both died and were buried in the same grave. Jane Wilcox had come in the same train and feeling sorry for Robert and the children, she went to keeping house for them and ended up marrying Robert.

They lived in Cottonwood and then moved to Bingham Creek. Soon they purchased property in Herriman where Robert and his boys built a nice two story rock house. Being a gardener by trade, he raised all kind of fruit trees and was one of the first to grow alfalfa or lucerne in Herriman. He sent to Paris for the seed.

He served a mission in England in 1879. He was released in six months due to ill health. After his recovery, he formed a community sheep herd. People paid by the month or year for the care of each animal. From this, Robert obtained a large flock of sheep.

He was a bishop and served until his death. He was a man of great faith, and true to his church. He was a friend of the poor and the needy and was kind to everyone.

Children of 1st wife:

ROBERT JR., b. 5 May 1850, Boxford, Suffolk, England. Md. 22 Mar 1875, Roseina Silcock. D. 10 Nov 1920, Salt Lake City, Utah.
ALFRED JOHN, b. 29 Jul 1852, Boxford, England. Md. 12 Jul 1875, Martha Ann Wright. D. 21 Apr 1913.
CHARLES NEPHI, b. 29 Apr 1854, Boxford, England. Md. 6 Jan 1874, Margaret Mary Crump. D. 28 Feb 1926.

SARAH ELIZABETH, b. 9 Apr 1856, Boxford, England. D. 1857, Boxford, England.

SARAH ANN ELIZABETH, b. 6 Jan 1858, Boxford, England. Md. 11 Oct 1878, James Stannard Crane. D. 13 Mar 1945.

WILLIAM HEBER, b. 18 Jul 1860, Boxford, England. Md. 8 Sep 1881, Eliza Jane Wright. D. 5 Jun 1927, Riverton, Utah.

JOSEPH, b. 21 Sep 1862, Pacific Springs, Sweetwater, Wyoming. D. Same day.

Children of 2nd wife:

JAMES WILCOX, b. 15 Nov 1861, Cottonwood, Utah. Md. 28 Dec 1885, Alice Jane Smith. D. 27 Jun 1944.

GEORGE HENRY, b. 31 Jan 1866, Bingham Canyon, Utah. Md. 20 Sep 1893, Sarah Ann Elizabeth England. D. 21 Mar 1935.

FRANCIS HYRUM, b. 26 Jan 1867, Bingham Canyon, Utah. Md. 10 Nov 1891, Eliza Hardcastle Evans. D. 9 Aug 1930.

BENJAMIN WILCOX, b. 23 Ap[r 1868, Herriman, Utah. Md. 6 Feb 1893, Katie Taylor. D. 19 Dec 1941.

ISABELLA JANE, b. 20 Aug 1869, Herriman, Utah. Md. 24 Nov 1897, Zachariah Butterfield. D. 2 Feb 1937.

ELIZA ELLEN, b. 4 Apr 1871, Herriman, Utah. D. 25 Apr 1871.

CHARLOTTE LAMENIA, b. 29 May 1872, Herriman, Utah. Md. 15 Dec 1897, George Wheeler. D. 13 May 1939.

ADA AMELIA, b. 6 Apr 1874, Herriman, Utah. Md. 10 May 1893, George Thomas Webster. D. 13 Jan 1957.

ALMA HALEMAN, b. 4 Dec 1876, Herriman, Utah. Md. 23 Jun 1909, Agnes Ruth Kunz. D. 31 Dec 1963.

ROSENA CLARRISIE, b. 19 Apr 1878, Herriman, Utah. D. 26 Jun 1880.

Submitted by: Estella Benson

DAVID DAVIDSON

Born: 5 Mar 1841 , Burrelton, Perthshire, Scotland
Parents: Thomas Bell and Ann Davidson Davidson
Died: 6 Dec 1865, Logan, Utah (gunshot wound)
Arrived in Valley: 28 Sep 1853, Jacob Gates Co.

Unmarried

David, age 10, along with his parents and older brother Robert, were baptized into the Church in Scotland in 1852. The next year the family emigrated to the Salt Lake Valley. They lived in their wagons in Pioneer Park until a one room log cabin was finished. The following year they completed a two room adobe house.

David served in the militia at the time of Johnston's Army. He and his brother went with Lot Smith's group to Echo Canyon and also served as guards in the city. He was 16 at the time.

Two years later Brigham Young asked David's father to help start the new settlement of Logan. The boys helped build the new homes for the family.

Not much is known of David during the next six years. We do know that in 1865, David was heading a freighting train. He was only 24 but extremely capable. He tried to separate a young boy from another man who was set on teasing the youth. The man pulled out a gun and shot David. Some of the men tried to get him to Logan for help, but it took them two days to reach there. David died a few days later.

Submitted by: Joseph Reed

DAVID DAVIDSON

Born: 1 Aug 1776, Kingsbarns, Fife, Scotland
Parents: Herbert and Mary Bonner Davidson
Died: 28 Jul 1853, on the trail in Wyoming
Came with the Jacob Gates Co.in 1853

Married: Janet Adamson
Date: 11 Nov 1826, Kingsbarns, Fife, Scotland
Born: 2 Jul 1780, Kingsbarns, Fife, Scotland
Parents: John and Isabelle Brown Adamson
Died: 5 Jan 1847, Kingsbarns, Fife, Scotland

David was probably a farmer in Scotland although many in the area were seaman or fisherman. He and his family joined the Church in 1852. When his daughter and her husband decided to emigrate to America, David decided to go with them although he was 76 and a widower. They waited until Ann had her baby before leaving Scotland. Ann's husband was Thomas Bell Davidson.

David and Thomas had prospered over the years, so they were able to purchase all the necessary equipment when they reached Keokuk, Iowa. They joined the Jacob Gates Company to go west. The cause of David's death is unknown. He was buried near the trail and his grave was hidden and covered with stones because of wild animals. It is recorded that it was near the White River in Wyoming. The company was still two months away from the Valley.

Children:

JANET PEARSON, b. 30 Jul 1802, Kingsbarns, Fife, Scotland.

She was the child of Janet's first marriage and was adopted by David. D. 7 Nov 1834.

ANN, b. 7 Jan 1814, Kingsbarns, Fife, Scotland. Md. 26 Jul 1835, St. Andrews, Fife, Scotland. D. 26 Apr 1904, Rexburg, Madison, Idaho.

Submitted by: Joseph Reed

HANS CHRISTIAN DAVIDSON

Born: 28 Mar 1820, Kagnaus, Alsen Island, Denmark
Parents: Hans and Dorothea Catherine Hansen Davidson
Died: 23 Aug 1892, Mt. Pleasant, Utah
Arrived in Valley: 20 Sep 1858, Ivan N. Iverson Co.

Married 1st: Anna Maria Jensen
Date: 2 Nov 1852, Nomack, Denmark
Born: 24 Feb 1828, Nomack, Denmark
Died: 2 May 1886, Birch Creek, Sanpete, Utah

Married 2nd: Anna Dorthea Hansen–No children
Date: 16 Nov 1887

Married 3rd: Karen Marie Nielson–No children
Date: 10 Oct 1869

Married 4th: Johana Marie Nielson–No children
Date 9 Jul 1890

Hans was a surveyor and draftsman in Denmark. After coming to the Valley, he settled in Mt. Pleasant, Utah. He was the first photographer and newspaper editor in Mt. Pleasant. At various times he served as a wagon master in bringing saints to Utah.

He was fluent in English, German and Danish, and had a good education for the times. He created the H. C. Davidson perpetual calendar. He invented the pressure cooker and had several other patents. Besides being active in the church and community, he used his talents in many other ways.

Children of 1st wife:

MARY DIANTHA CATHERINE, b. 22 Feb 1853, Majolli, Denmark. Md. 22 Mar 1875, Niel Peter Nielson. D. 15 Apr 1933, Sigured, Utah.

HANS THOMAS, b. 24 Oct 1855, Majolli, Denmark. Md. 16 Oct 1878, Elizabeth Young Robertson. D. 9 Nov 1920, Millburne, Wyoming.

ELIZABETH, b. 24 Aug 1859, Pleasant Grove, Utah. Md. 1 Jan 1878, Hans phraim Larsen. D. 25 Aug 1947, Spring City, Sanpete, Utah.

LORENZO, b. 31 Aug 1861, Pleasant Grove, Utah. Md. 4 Mar 1887, Anna Louise Peterson. D. 12 Apr 1924, Salt Lake City, Utah.

AMASA, b. 29 Mar 1863, Pleasant Grove, Utah. Md. 12 Jun 1889, Annie Elizabeth Hansen. D. 5 Jan 1930.

SARAH, b. 9 Sep 1864, Pleasant Grove, Utah. D. 20 Mar 1865, Pleasant Grove, Utah.

EPHRAIM MARNING (twin), b. 4 Jul 1866, Mt. Pleasant, Utah. Md. 12 Jun 1888, Hannah Amelia Hjort. D. 24 May 1942, Rexburg, Madison, Idaho.

SARAH (twin), b. 4 Jul 1866, Mt. Pleasant, Utah. Md. 5 Jan 1886 Asa Wilcox. D. 30 Dec 1934, Mt. Pleasant, Utah.

LUCINDA, b. 30 Apr 1869, Mt. Pleasant, Utah. Md. 26 Nov 1886, Neils Wahlin. D. 15 Feb 1949, Salt Lake City, Utah.

JOSEPH, b. 15 Feb 1871, Mt. Pleasant, Utah. Md. Mary Sanstorm. D. 5 Jul 1901.

Submitted by: Lowell Parkinson

HANS THOMAS DAVIDSON

Born: 24 Oct 1855, Maybelle, Alsen Slesvig, Germany
Parents: Hans Christian and Anne Maria Jensen Davidson
Died: 6 Nov 1920, Millburne, Wyoming
Arrived in Valley: 20 Sep 1858, Ivan N. Iverson Co.

Married: Elizabeth Young Robertson
Date: 20 Oct 1876
Born: 12 Jun 1856, Airdie, Lanark, Scotland
Died: 14 Oct 1939, Millburne, Uninta, Wyoming

Hans Thomas walked the entire distance even though his family came with an ox wagon company.

He owned and operated a sawmill in Millburne, Wyoming.

Children:

EMMERY HANS, b. 7 Sep 1880, Mt Pleasant, Sanpete, Utah. Md. 16 Oct 1901, Lennie Cooper Barton. D. 21 Aug 1938.

MAUD ELIZABETH, b. 7 Sep 1882, Mt Pleasant, Sanpete, Utah. D. 19 Oct 1894, Mt Pleasant, Utah.

MARY JENNETT, b. 29 Jan 1885, Mt Pleasant, Utah. Md. 28 Nov 1904, William C. Barton. D. 2 Jan 1937.

DORA ELISE, b. 25 Jul 1887, Beaver, Utah. Md. 22 Oct 1911, Orlando Wayman. D. 4 Jan 1921.

Submitted by: Lowell Parkinson

JOHN McNEIL DAVIDSON

Born: 1 Dec 1852, Kingsbarns, Fife, Scotland
Parents: Thomas Bell and Ann Davidson Davidson
Died: 22 Sep 1912, Central Point, Jackson, Oregon
Arrived in Valley: 26 Sep 1853, Jacob Gates Co.

Married: Harriet Ann Thatcher Holden
Date: 12 Apr 1875, Salt Lake City, Utah
Born: 7 Aug 1850/54, Holden, Fillmore, Utah
Died: 11 Aug 1912, Central Point, Jackson, Oregon

John McNeil left Scotland to travel to the Salt Lake Valley when he was only three months old. His parents joined the Church in 1852. Family legend says that John was named after the missionary that taught or baptized his family. His parents had planned to leave Scotland soon after their baptism, but upon learning that another child was due, they determined to wait. That new child was John. He was nine months old when they arrived in the valley.

In 1860 when John was seven years old, the family moved to a new settlement called Logan in Cache Valley, north of Salt Lake. Little is known of the life of John. He apparently lived most of his life in Logan as that is where his children were born. Later on he apparently moved to Central Point, a few miles northwest of Medford, Oregon, as that is where he and his wife died.

Children:

JOHN HOLDEN, b. 4 Nov 1875, Logan, Cache, Utah. Md. 26 Feb 1902, Rose Elizabeth Stevens. D. 12 Jun 1950.

MARY CATHERINE, b. abt 1877, Logan, Utah. Md. Armine W. Lewis.

ROBERT HOLDEN, b. 3 Aug 1885, Logan, Utah. Md. Nettie Lorraine Stevens. D. 28 Jun 1946.

WILLIAM PRESTON, b. 24 Nov 1887, Logan, Utah. Md. 30 Dec 1908, Florence Bell Bowles. D. 10 Jun 1949.

Submitted by: Joseph Reed

ROBERT DAVIDSON

Born: 31 Jan 1839, Dundee, Angus, Scotland
Parents: Thomas Bell and Ann Davidson Davidson
Died: 23 Dec 1899, Logan, Cache, Utah
Arrived in Valley: 26 Sep 1853, Jacob Gates Co.

Married 1st: Ada Cemantha Hemenway
Date: 8 Nov 1861, Salt Lake City, Utah
Born: 13 Sep 1842, Cheshire, Northampton, England
Parents: Luther Singleton and Elvira Day Hemenway
Died: 12 Oct 1895, Logan, Utah

Married 2nd: Janet Jean Reid McNeil
Date 10 Jun 1880, Salt Lake City, Utah
Born: 14 Mar 1861, Logan, Cache, Utah
Parents: Thomas and Janet Reid McNeil
Died: 12 Mar 1909, Logan, Utah

Married 3rd: Margaret McNeil
Date: 20 Mar 1895

Robert, being the oldest son of Thomas and Ann, joined the Church when his parents did in 1852. He was 13 years old at the time. His parents determined to emigrate to the Valley but waited until after the birth of their sixth child. Robert's maternal grandfather, David Davidson, traveled with his only child's family. He did not survive the difficult trip but died and was buried on the plains of Wyoming.

Upon their arrival in the valley, they lived in Salt Lake until 1860. Their home was similar to others of the time, a one-room log cabin located where the D & R G depot was later built. Robert learned the shoemaker's trade from his father in Scotland. President Young asked him to take charge of the shoeshop in the tithing office, and he continued to teach others the shoemaking trade.

When Johnston's Army came to the valley, Robert and his brother, David, stayed with the militia and later went to Echo Canyon. In 1859, Robert and David went to Cache Valley and built a log home for their family. He became a farmer and taught his sons to be good farmers by buying farmland. As his sons grew older he "put them on the farms," to work and develop them.

Robert was a bishop for 27 years. He was a trustee on the school board and remained active in the church and community all his life.

Children of 1st wife:

HERBERT SINGLETON, b. 22 Oct 1863, Logan, Utah. Md. 26 Feb 1890, Mary Isabelle Littlefair. D. 11 Feb 1941.

ELVIRA DAY, b. 14 Jan 1866, Logan, Utah. Md. 2 Oct 1884, Henry William Ballard. D. 2 Sep 1951.

ANNIE, b. 18 Jun 1868, Logan, Utah. Md. 15 Mar 1893, Julius Charles Wahlen. D. 1 Oct 1952.

ADA CEMANTHA, b.23 Mar 1871, Logan, Utah. Mc 7 Jan 1891, John Ephraim Dahle. D. 15 Mar 1950.

AMY DIANTHA, b. 3 Oct 1873, Logan, Utah. Md. 13 Mar 1895, Lee Preston. D. 16 Jun 1960.

ROBERT, b. 21 Jul 1876, Logan, Utah. Md. 28 Apr 1897, Margaret Swift. D. 1 Apr 1958.

JOHN (twin), b. 9 Mar 1879, Logan, Utah. D. 10 Jul 1879.

ISABELLE (twin), b. 9 Mar 1879, Logan, Utah. D. 9 Jul 1879, Logan.

JESSIE EXILE, b. 1 Aug 1880, Logan, Utah. Md. 30 Mar 1905, Frederick Gibbons. D. 14 Dec 1948.

Children of 2nd wife:

THOMAS McNEIL, b. 16 May 1881, Logan, Utah. D. 20 Oct 1905.

JOSEPH REID, b. 7 Apr 1883, Logan, Utah. Md. 13 Feb 1913, Lillie Dell Chapman. D. 25 Jul 1968.

GEORGE WILLIAM, b. 24 Nov 1885, Logan, Utah. D. 2 Jul 1902.

JANET EXILE, b. 1 Sep 1890, Hyde Park, Cache, Utah. Md. 6 Sep 1911, Francis Wayne Shurtliff. D. 7 Oct 1971.

EDNA MAE, b. 21 May 1894, Franklin, Franklin, Idaho.

Submitted by: Joseph Reed

THOMAS BELL DAVIDSON

Born: 28 Dec 1809, Kilrenny, Fife, Scotland
Parents: Robert and Mary Bonner Davidson
Died: 15 Jul 1876, Logan, Cache, Utah
Arrived in Valley: 26 Sep 1853, Jacob Gates Co.

Married 1st: Ann Davidson
Date: 26 Jul 1835, St. Andrews, Fife, Scotland
Born: 7 Jan 1814, Kingsbarns, Fife, Scotland
Parents: David and Janet Adamson

Died: 26 Apr 1904, Rexburg, Madison, Idaho
Married 2nd: Ellen Hall
Date: 7 Jun 1857, Salt Lake City, Utah
Born: 23 Jan 1822, Manchester, Lancs, England
Died: 5 Nov 1908, Logan, Utah

Thomas Bell's family were seamen. Thomas wanted to go to sea and continue the tradition, but his mother persuaded him to earn a living on land. Two of his older brothers had drowned at sea and she didn't want to lose another son. He learned the craft of shoemaker and did well and soon prospered. His business was in Dundee and after his marriage they continued to live there for a time. After their first two children, they moved to Burrelton and then to Kingsbarns.

Thomas and his wife, Ann, heard the missionaries and joined the church in 1852. They decided to emigrate to the Valley but Ann felt she should wait until after the birth of their sixth child. They finally left in 1853 and crossed the plains with the Jacob Gates Company, along with Ann's father and Thomas's father. Thomas paid the passage for two women who helped Ann with the children. In Wyoming territory, Ann's father died and was buried by the side of the trail.

Upon their arrival, they lived for a time in Pioneer Park and then in a log cabin. Thomas soon was able to provide a two-room adobe home. They didn't have all the comforts they had had in Scotland, but they were happy with the decision to leave Scotland.

They were intelligent, hard working people, and were active in the church. Thomas had brought metal lasts and tools from Scotland to help him establish a shoemaking trade in the valley.

Thomas and his family were asked to help establish Logan. Here he built a shoeshop and tannery. He taught others the trade.

He died as a result of an accident with a team and wagon in the fields.

Children of 1st wife:

JANET, b. 15 Mar 1837, Dundee, Angus, Scotland. D. 15 Jul 1839, Dundee, Scotland.

ROBERT, b. 31 Jan 1839, Dundee, Angus, Scotland. Md. 8 Nov 1861, Ada Cemantha Hemenway. D. 23 Dec 1899, Logan, Utah.

DAVID, b. 5 Mar 1841, Birlton, Perth, Scotland. D. 6 Dec 1865, Logan, Utah.

JOHN, b. 5 Mar 1843, Birlton, Perth, Scotland. D. 21 Jun 1849.

JESSIE, b. 8 Mar 1845, Kingsbarns, Fife, Scotland. Md. 1 Jan 1866, John Abner Cowley. D. 18 Jan 1893, Logan, Utah.

THOMAS, b. 10 Mar 1849, Kingsbarns, Fife, Scotland. D. 18 Feb 1939, Dillon, Beaverhead, Montana.

ANN, b. 26 Oct 1850, Kingsbarns, Fife, Scotland. D. 16 Jan 1863.

JOHN McNEIL, b. 1 Dec 1852, Kingsbarns, Fife, Scotland. Md. 12 Apr 1875, Harriet Ann Thatcher Holden. D. 22 Sep 1912, Central Point, Jackson, Oregon.

ISABELLE, b. 22 Sep 1855, Salt Lake City, Utah. Md. 17 Feb 1885, Logan, Utah. D. 30 Sep 1951, Mesa Maricopa, Arizona. Bur. Logan, Utah.

ANDREW, b. 1 Feb 1858, Salt Lake City, Utah. D. 18 Aug 1858.

JOSEPH EPHRAIM, b. 29 Dec 1861, Logan, Cache, Utah. Md. 8 Oct 1902, Bertha Emily Pond. D. 25 Sep 1945.

Children of 2nd wife:

JAMES HALL, b. 11 Apr 1858, Salt Lake City, Utah. Md. 11 Jan 1888, Sylvia Araminta Bell. D. 15 Feb 1946.

RICHARD HALL, b. 25 Jun 1860, Salt Lake City, Utah. D. 18 Jun 1899.

HYRUM DAVID, b. 2 Jan 1864, Logan, Utah. Md. 3 Apr 1889, Eliza Annie Hawkes. D. 4 Jan 1920.

Submitted by: Joseph Reed

THOMAS DAVIDSON

Born: 10 Mar 1849, Kingsbarns, Fife, Scotland
Parents: Thomas Bell and Ann Davidson Davidson
Died: 18 Feb 1939, Dillon, Montana
Arrived in Valley: 26 Sep 1853, Jacob Gates Co.

Unmarried

Thomas was three years old when he and his parents and two grandfathers, plus two women to help with the children, left Scotland to travel to America and then on to the Valley. Thomas walked most of the way as did most other pioneer children.

His father was asked to help settle Logan after they had been in Salt Lake a few years. After Thomas was old enough, he helped his father farm and develop the property. His father was a shoemaker.

Thomas never married. He operated a freight line between Cache Valley and Montana. The last 40 years of his life, he operated a cattle ranch in Big Hole, Montana. He died at Dillon, Montana, a month before his 90th birthday. He was buried in Logan.

Submitted by: Joseph Reed

EDWARD DAVIES

Born: 15 May 1807, Guiltsfield, Montgomeryshire, North Wales
Parents: David and Elizabeth Davies Davies
Died: 8 Nov 1859, El Monte, Los Angeles, California
Arrived in Valley: Fall of 1849, Orson Spencer Co.

Married 1st: Elizabeth Jasper
Date: 17 Nov 1827, Kinnerly Parish, Shropshire, England
Born: 27 Oct 1808, Kinnerly Parish,Shropshire, England
Mothers name: Martha Jasper
Died: 21 Jan 1890, Los Angeles, California

Married 2nd: Margaret Thomas
Date: 1850, Salt Lake City, Utah
Born: 26 Oct 1827, Llamfihengel, Carmarthen, Wales
Parents: Thomas and Sarah Thomas

Edward was a miller in Wales. After his first marriage, they lived in Kinnerly, England, where their children were born. His wife Elizabeth joined the Church before he did. The rest of the family joined at various times after that. As soon as Edward joined the church, the family decided to emigrate to the Valley. They left England 3 April 1849.

After arriving in the valley, they settled in the Millcreek area of Salt Lake. Edward married his second wife the following year. Because Elizabeth, his first wife, did not approve of the marriage, she took her family and moved to California. They lived in San Bernardino for awhile and then moved to El Monte, California.

Edward worked in a grist mill in the La Puenta area. He was

out delivering his mill products when, it is supposed, he was robbed and killed. He was found dead on the 8 November 1859. He was buried in Los Angeles, California.

Children of 1st marriage:

PHOEBE, b. 10 Oct 1828, Kinnerley, Shrops, England. Md. 20 Jan 1852, Stephen Chipman. D. 13 Nov 1827.

WILLIAM, b. 19 Dec 1830, Kinnerley, Shrops, England. Md. 6 Apr 1851, Mary Ann Raybould (widow of Stephen Wood). D. 4 Jan 1898.

MARY, b. 29 Apr 1832, Kinnerley, Shrops, England. Md. 2 Dec 1850, George Wood (as his 3rd wife). D.27 Feb 1907, Cedar City, Iron Co.,Utah.

ELIZABETH (twin), b. 9 Apr 1836, Kinnerley, Shrops, England. Md. 1856, Jacob Stump. D. 18 Apr 1926.

RUTH (?) (twin), b. 9 Apr 1836, D. Infant.

DAVID, b. 25 May 1838, Kinnerley, Shrops, England. Md. Sarah Ann Martin. D. 10 May 1885.

JANE, b. 28 Jun 1841, Kinnerley, Shrops, England. Md. 7 Nov 1858, Jose Sanchez, (Div). D. 27 Mar 1907.

Children of 2nd wife:

ELIAS, b. 19 Apr 1851, Salt Lake City , Utah. Md. 7 Nov 1872, Lavinie Gaines. D. 28 Sep 1922.

MARTHA, b. 11 Jun 1853, Coal Creek Fort, Iron, Utah. Md. 26 Dec 1871 Seburn Gaines. D. 2 Apr 1937.

CALEB (twin), b. Jun 1856, San Bernardino, California. Md. 1st, 10 Feb 1877, Phebe Brush. Md. 2nd, 12 May 1901, Annie Chapman. D. 11 Jun 1929.

CHILD (twin?), b. Jun 1856, San Bernardino, California. D. Infant.

MARGARET, b. 19 Aug 1859, El Monte, Los Angeles, California. Md. 1st, 20 Aug 1877, Edward Oliver Davies. Md. 2nd, 13 Apr 1896, Marcus Lafayette Bennett. D. 20 Nov 1928.

Submitted by: June Danvers

DAVID DAVIS

Born: 19 Feb 1829, Glenmorganshire, So. Wales
Died: 1858, Bountiful, Davis, Utah
Arrived in Valley: Sep 1854

Married 1st: Margaret Price
Died: Wales

Married 2nd: Ann H. Davis
Date: 25 Dec 1853, Wales
Born: 5 Mar 1823, Pendairm, Glamorganshire, So. Wales
Parents: Henry and Ann Lewellyn Davis

David was introduced to the gospel in South Wales. His first wife died shortly after receiving the gospel. David remarried in 1853. He and Ann, a member of the church, left Wales for America, where they crossed the plains. David was listed on the shipping records as a collier, age 23. Ann was listed as being 30. Ann was apparently crippled in her feet which caused her to walk on the side of her feet. She walked most of the way across the plains.

Upon their arrival in Salt Lake, they went on north to Bountiful or Sessions as it was then called, where they built a small one-room house. Ann sewed to help earn money, and she also grew potatoes.

A daughter was born in 1855, and a son in 1858. Two weeks after the birth of their son, David died at the age of 28. He had been a miner in Wales and his chest had been crushed in the mine. After coming to Salt Lake, his chest had started to heal, but he finally died as a result of the problem.

Children:

MARY ANN, b. 26 Sep 1855, Bountiful, Utah.
SON, b. 1858, Bountiful, Utah.

Submitted by: Darwin L. Salisbury

DAVID W. DAVIS

Born: 25 Aug 1810, Brokenog, Brecknock, So. Wales
Parents: William and Ann Price Davis
Died: 5 Apr 1889, Logan, Cache, Utah.
Arrived in Valley: 1854, wagon and team by themselves.

Married 1st: Mary Rosser
Date: abt 1837, Memoth, So. Wales
Born: 3 Feb 1838, Memoth, So. Wales
Died: 5 Sep 1854, California

Married 2nd: Ann H. Davis (widow–David Davis)
Born: 5 Mar 1823, Penderyn, Memoth, So. Wales
Parents: Henry and Ann Lewellyn Davis Davis
Died: 22 Oct 1883, Logan, Utah

David and Mary were baptized in 1846 and emigrated to America in 1847. They settled in Pennsylvania where David worked in the coal mines.

In 1853, they started to cross the plains to the Valley but because of a late start, they wintered at the Platt River. They crossed in a wagon by themselves. In the spring they went on to California where Mary died. David moved back to Utah in the fall of 1855 and located in Farmington. Later, in 1859, he moved to Smithfield in Cache Valley.

David went to purchase some pigs and met Ann whom he married. They lived in Logan, Utah. Life was hard but Ann weathered it all, even the loss of two children. She helped all who needed help and lived her religion as best she could. She had been previously married to David Davis, a collier, who died in 1858.

Children of 1st wife:

MARY ANN, b. 3 Feb 1838, Memoth, South Wales.
ANN, b. 18 Jun 1840, Memoth, South Wales. D. 5 Jan 1845,
    Brecknookshire, So. Wales.

Children of 2nd wife: (2 Children by 1st husband)

AMELIA JANE, b. 19 May 1860, Logan, Utah. Md. 11 Dec 1879.
    D. 29 Apr 1940.
ELISABETH ANN, b. 28 Aug 1862, Logan, Utah. Md. 19 Oct
    1878. D. 16 Sep 1903.
WILLIAM HENRY (twin), b. 16 Aug 1866, Logan, Utah. Un-
    married. D. 10 Jun 1875, diphtheria.
CATHERINE MARGARET (twin), b. 16 Aug 1866, Logan, Utah.
    Unmarried. D. 23 May 1875, diphtheria.

Submitted by: Darwin Salisbury

EDWARD WILLIAM DAVIS

Born: 1 Feb 1794, London, Middlesex, England
Parents: William and Elizabeth Davis (Whales)
Died: 1 Oct 1878, Salt Lake City, Utah
Arrived in Valley: 2 Sep 1852, Abraham O. Smoot Co.

Married: Sarah Drabble
Date: 13 Jan 1822.
Born: 16 Jan 1802, England
Died: 29 Oct 1876, Utah

Edward William was a weaver of silk and cloth. After he joined the Church, he emigrated with his family to the Valley. He settled in Salt Lake.

Children:

SARAH ANN, b. 1823, England. D. 13 Oct 1842.
EDWARD WILLIAM, b.18 Nov 1826. Md. 1st, 22 Apr 1852, Sarah Elizabeth Hyder. Md. 2nd, 26 Feb 1857, Jemima Nightingale. D.10 Sep 1896
LYDIA, b. 15 Jul 1828. Md. 15 Oct 1852, George Benjamin Wallace. D. 8 Mar 1869.
HANNAH, b. 4 May 1830. Md. 15 Oct 1852, George Benjamin Wallace. D. 5 Feb 1896.
SAMUEL, chr 24 Nov 1840.
MARTHA, b. 9 Jan 1834. Md. 15 Oct 1852, George Benjamin Wallace. D. 7 Oct 1913.
THEOPHILUS, b.1835/36.
JOSIAH, b. 29 Oct 1838.

THEOPHILUS, b. 20 Sep 1841.

Submitted by: Junith Roberts

ELISHA HILDEBRAND DAVIS, JR.

Born: 7 Feb 1850, near Kanesville, Pottawattamie, Iowa
Parents: Elisha Hildebrand and Mary Ann Mitchell Davis
Died: 10 Dec 1937, Lehi, Utah, Utah
Arrived in Valley: 1 Oct 1852, Uriah Curtis Company

Married: Sarah Ellen (Lelly) Stewart
Date: 30 Jan 1871, Salt Lake City, Utah
Born: 2 Feb 1847, Keokuk, Lee, Iowa
Parents: Charles and Sarah Ann Roberts Stewart
Died: 14 Dec 1932, Lehi, Utah, Utah

Elisha Hildebrand, Jr., was born while his parents and family were on their way west to the Valley. Three months later in June, the family left in the Uriah Curtis Company. The family lived in various parts of the area wherever his father could obtain work as a miller. Later on he enjoyed sharing memories with his family.

He received the average education for the times, including a boarding school in Draper, Utah. While furnishing wood for his family, he gathered extra, which he gave to the school to help pay his tuition. During his life time, he bought and sold horses and cattle. He also farmed. When he was 16, he enlisted with a group of men to fight the Black Hawk Indian War.

After his marriage they moved with the family to Lehi where they lived on his father's farm in a one room log home. A year later he had saved enough to purchase an entire city block, which he later traded for property so he could build a home.

He was a good speaker and was chosen "Orator of the Day" at a celebration. He loved missionary work and in August 1889 was called on a mission to the British Isles. He served two more missions, one in Provo and one in Alpine-American Fork areas.

He held many church positions and spent much time tracing his ancestral lines.

Children:

ELISHA STEWART, b. 26 Feb 1872, Lehi, Utah. D. after 1932.

CHARLES ASHWELL, b. 2 Dec 1874, Lehi, Utah. D. 1 Sep 1875, Lehi, Utah.

PEARL ELLEN, b. 8 Aug 1876, Lehi, Utah. Md. 1st, 3 Mar 1927, James William Bone. Md. 2nd, 14 Apr 1932, Alfred John Broomhead. D. 21 Mar 1956, Salt Lake City, Utah.

ALPHONZO LEROY, b. 26 Aug 1878, Lehi, Utah. Md. 6 Feb 1902, Nellie Helena Powers. D. 26 Jan 1963, Lehi, Utah.

SARAH ANN (Sadie), b. 27 May 1880, Lehi, Utah. Md. 17 Aug 1910, Oliver Leach Kittinger. D. 17 May 1972, Salt Lake City, Utah.

MYRTLE IOWN, b.26 Apr 1882, Lehi, Utah. D. 25 Aug 1888, Lehi, Utah.

RUBY, b. 26 Aug 1884, Lehi, Utah. Md. 20 Jan 1909, John William Stoker. D. 19 Nov 1969, Salt Lake City, Utah.

ARREVA ADDA, b. 12 Sep 1887, Lehi, Utah. Md. 1st, 20 Feb 1913, James Earl Armitstead. Md. 2nd, 26 Aug 1944, George William Morris. D. 28 Jan 1968, Salt Lake City, Utah.

CHELTONA RISPA (Chelta), b. 9 Feb 1890, Lehi, Utah. Md. 28 Jun 1916, Alexander Brown. D. 19 Nov 1972, Lehi, Utah.

OREN DAVID BLACKHURST, (They took him in and raised him He was four years old and they were 50.)

Submitted by: Golden Buchmiller

ELISHA HILDEBRAND DAVIS, SR.

Born: 22 Oct 1815, West Township, Columbiana, Ohio
Parents: Isaac and Edith Richards Davis
Died: 31 Jul 1898, Lehi, Utah, Utah
Arrived in Valley: 1852, Uriah Curtis Co.

Married: Mary Ann Mitchell
Date: 25 Dec 1846, London, Middlesex, England
Born: 19 Oct 1822, London, Middlesex, England
Parents: Robert and Sarah Hunt Mitchell
Died: 14 Sep 1892, Lehi, Utah, Utah

Elisha Hildebrand was named after early family members. Hildebrand was his paternal grandmother's surname. His parents were Quakers. Elisha was not only a farmer but a grain miller.

In 1838, Joseph Smith did missionary work in Ohio, and Elisha's parents and some of his sisters joined the Church. Elisha joined a little later in 1838. After being ordained an Elder in January 1839, he left on a mission with the elders. He served in Pennsylvania and also New Jersey. While on the mission, his family moved to Nauvoo where he met them after his mission. In 1841 he was called on another mission to Connecticut. After that mission he was called to England where he served until 1846.

Upon his release, he married Mary Ann Mitchell while in London. They sailed for America and upon their arrival found that both his parents had died. They spent a winter at Winter Quarters where Elisha worked at a grist mill. In 1848 they returned to Kanesville, Iowa, where they lived for three years. They left for the Valley in 1852. Upon their arrival, they stayed for awhile in Salt Lake and then moved to Ogden and then Bingham and finally to Bountiful. Later they moved to Lehi where he ran a mill. He farmed as well as doing milling. He served another mission in Iowa and Illinois. Sometime before he died, he became interested in genealogy and did a lot of research and wrote a short biography.

Children:

MARY ANN MINERVA, b. 31 Oct 1848, Council Bluff, Iowa. D. 2 Sep 1939, Lehi, Utah

ELISHA HILDEBRAND JR., b. 7 Feb 1850, Council Bluff, Iowa. Md. 30 Jan 1871, Sarah Ellen Stewart. D. 20 Dec 1937, Lehi, Utah.

SARAH AGNES, b. 21 Mar 1852, Keg Creek, Pottowattamie, Iowa. Md 25 Dec 1871, Charles Hopkins Karren. D. 23 Oct 1922, Lethbridge, Alberta, Canada.

ORINDA JANE, b. 14 Apr 1855, Bountiful, Utah. Md. 25 Apr 1878, Dilbert Hyrum Allred. D. 20 Jan 1934, Lehi, Utah.

GEORGE EDWARD, b. 4 Feb 1857, Bingham Fort, Weber, Utah. Md. 1st, 8 Jun 1882, Harriet Martha Brown. Md. 2nd, 25 Jan 1905, Mary Ann Boone. D. 26 Nov 1914, Lehi, Utah.

ALPHONZO MITCHELL, b.19 Feb 1859, Lehi, Utah. Md. 18 Nov 1880, Martha Ann Winn. D. 8 Sep 1927, Salt Lake City, Utah.

EDITH RICHARDS, b. 17 Dec 1860, Lehi, Utah. Md. 1st, Banks Smith, (Div). Md. 2nd, 7 Aug 1902, Henry W. Sadler. D. 1 Oct 1904, Lehi, Utah.

SABINA ANN, b. 9 Dec 1862, Lehi, Utah. Md. 1st, 10 Mar 1884, Albert Henry Candland. Md. 2nd 11 Jun 1907, James Weeden McDaniel. D. 4 Mar 1939, Alhambra, Los Angeles, California.

Submitted by: Golden Buchmiller

GEORGE DAVIS

Born: 8 Dec 1833, Norchard, Hartlebury, Worcs, England
Parents: James and Elizabeth Goodwin Davis
Died: 14 Jun 1903, Perry, Box Elder, Utah
Arrived in Valley: 24 Oct 1854, William A. Empley Co.

Married 1st: Mary Ann Sparks
Date: 27 Dec 1852, Claines, Worcs, England
Born: 10 Dec 1832, Worlds End, Worcs, England
Parents: George and Hannah Lake Sparks
Died: 2 Jul 1905, Dingle, Bear Lake, Idaho

Married 2nd: Alice Eliza Goody
Date: 24 Feb 1865, Salt Lake City, Utah
Born: 12 Sep 1854, Barking, Essex, England
Parents: Henry and Mary Wiltcher Goody
Died: 28 Mar 1933, Perry, Box Elder, Utah

George was a very spiritually-minded young man and when he heard the missionaries, he knew the gospel was true, in spite of all his parents said.

His parents made him an apprentice in carpentering and the wheelwright trade to try to disuade him from the Church. He did well in the trades but at the age of 14 he joined the church. He went to live with friends until his parents softened and then he returned home.

After his marriage they left for America, arriving in Salt Lake in October 1854. They stayed in Salt Lake for a time while George worked for the church in his trades. He was in the Echo Canyon problems.

After his release from this, they moved to Lehi where he hired someone to run the farm while he returned to Salt Lake to help Brigham Young and the church.

He married his second wife and he moved both families to Clarston, Cache, Utah, where they lived for several years. In 1875 they moved to Perry, Box Elder, Utah. While here he held several positions in the church and was called on a mission to England in 1900. After a successful mission of 26 months, he returned home. His health began to fail and he developed typhoid fever and never recovered.

Children of 1st wife:

ARTHUR NEPHI, b. 10 Sep 1876, Three Mile Creek, Utah.
    Unmarried. D. 17 Oct 1894.

Children of 2nd wife:

WILLIAM HENRY, b. 2 Feb 1866, Lehi, Utah. Md. 16 Dec 1885,
    Mary Elizabeth Young. D. 24 May 1929.
ALICE MARY, b. 9 Jan 1868, Lehi, Utah. Md. 13 Sep 1883,
    Isaac Thorne. D. 19 Jul 1907.
SAMUEL ARTHUR, b. 5 Jan 1870, Lehi, Utah. Unmarried. D.15
    Nov 1889. HERBERT JOHN, b. 10 Apr 1872, Clarkston,
    Utah. Unmarried. D. 14 Nov 1889.
LOUISE JANE, b. 14 Dec 1874, Clarkston, Utah. Md. 18 Dec
    1895, Hyrum Thorne. D. 26 Aug 1917.
ELIZABETH ANN, b. 9 May 1877, Three Mile Creek, Utah,
    Md. 19 Dec 1900, David Rees Morgan. D. 17 Jul 1959.
EMMA ELLEN, b. 21 Oct 1879, Three Mile Creek, Utah. Md.
    25 Oct 1899, Willard Facer. D. 20 Aug 1934.
SARAH ELIZA, b. 20 Jan 1882, Three Mile Creek, Utah. D.11
    May 1883.
GEORGE ALMA, b. 30 May 1884, Three Mile Creek, Utah. D.22
    Sep 1890.
PARLEY ERNEST, b. 16 Jan 1887, Three MIle Creek, Utah.
    Md. 16 Jan 1907, Marie Jacobsen. D. 21 Aug 1942.

JONATHAN, b. 13 Mar 1891, Three Mile Creek, Utah. Md. 28 Aug 1911, Mabel Miller. D. 8 Jan 1961.

Submitted by: Enoch Thorne

THOMAS WILLIAM DAVIS

Born: 10 Apr 1828, Tredegar, Momouthshire, England
Parents: David and Mary Leishon Davies
Died: 5 Aug 1892, Huntington, Emery, Utah
Arrived in Valley: 1861

Married 1st: Ann Thomas
Place: England

Married 2nd: Sophia Caroline Vickery
Date: 1861, Youngstown, Ohio
Parents: Arthur and Caroline Lang Vickery
Born: 24 Jul 1844, No. Molton, Devonshire, England
Died: 20 Apr 1919, Huntington, Emery, Utah

Thomas William joined the Church in England. Whether his wife Ann died in England is not known. He arrived in Youngston, Ohio, where he married his second wife in 1861. They crossed the plains with his wife's parents and their children.

Not much is known of the family. They apparently lived in Rush Valley, Tooele County. where their first child was born. They moved to Holden, Millard County, where they lived until about 1889, and then moved to Huntington, Emery County where their last two children were born. Thomas died in Huntington.

Children of 2nd wife:

MARY ANN, b. 15 May 1867, Rush Valley, Utah. Md. 24 May 1883, William Harrison Burgess. D. 22 Jan 1942.

ESTHER, b. 7 Feb 1869, Holden, Utah. Md. 13 Mar 1889, Owen Winnie Guymon. D. 7 May 1926.

DAVID THOMAS, b. 10 Feb 1872, Holden, Utah. Md. 23 Dec 1896, Adeline Precinda Hill. D. 21 Apr 1958.

ROSE HANNAH, b. 23 Dec 1874, Holden, Utah. Md. 23 Dec 1896, George Richard Hill. D. 10 Jun 1964.

GEORGE ARTHUR, b. 25 Jul 1876, Holden, Utah. Md. 7 Jan 1915, Patience Hope (Pat) Nielsen. D. 20 Sep 1955.

ELIZABETH, b. 25 Jul 1876, Holden, Utah. D. 1877.

SUSAN CAROLINE, b. 28 Sep 1878, Holden Utah. Md. 13 Dec 1901, Charles McEwen. D. 27 Jan 1963.

FANNY MAY, b. 13 Nov 1884, Holden, Utah. Md.13 Jun 1901, Charles Saxton. D. 3 Jan 1958.

JAMES, b. 1 May 1889, Huntington, Utah. D. 8 Oct 1889.

JANET (JENNY), b. 1 May 1889, Huntington, Utah. Md. 26 Oct 1912, James William (Jim) Nielsen. D. 11 Apr 1972.

Submitted by: Kent Davis

MEREDITH DAWSON

Born: 4 Apr 1844, Ruabon, Denbigh, Wales
Parents: Joseph and Francis Meredith Dawson

Died: 18 Jun 1928, Henefer, Utah
Arrived in Valley: John R. Murdock or S.A. Wooley Company

Married: Ann Bird
Date: 19 Dec 1873, Salt Lake City, Utah
Parents: Ann Shill Bird, widow
Died: 23 Dec 1938

Meredith lost his mother when he was 16. His father remarried and brought his family to America. They crossed the plains with either the John Murdock or Samuel Wooley Company.

Meredith was a strong and ambitious young man. He helped haul freight from Montana to Salt Lake. He was a minute man guard and helped dig the first irrigation ditch in Kamas, Utah. He helped fight the Indians. His father helped him construct a rock house. Later he borrowed money and sent for his sister and her family who still lived in Wales. He built her a home near him.

His children and grandchildren loved him because he played with them and helped them. He and his wife always had room at their table for one more person. In later years he sat in his rocking chair and told children stories of the past. He remained a strong member of the church and community.

Children:

FRANCIS ELIZABETH, b. 20 Dec 1874, Henefer, Utah. Md. Benjamin Hopkins.
HYRUM JOSEPH, b. 25 May 1877, Henefer, Utah. D. Aug 1877, Henefer, Utah.
ANNIE GOLDING, b. 15 Jun 1878, Henefer, Utah. Md. Amos Dearden.
JESSIE THRUSA, b. 17 Jun 1881, Henefer, Utah. Md. Heber Charles Henefer.
MEREDITH ANDREW, b. 16 Oct 1883, Henefer, Utah. Md. Ellen Toone.
OSCAR ELMER, b. 2 Jul 1886, Henefer, Utah. Md. Helena Matilda Saxton.

ORSON STEWART, b. 30 Ap 1889, Henefer, Utah. Md. Bernice Davis.

JESTON BIRD, b. 5 Apr 1892, Henefer, Utah. Md. Sadie Marie Danks.

ELSIE MAUD, b. 29 Jun 1895, Henefer, Utah. Md. Horace Hilman Richins.

Submitted by: Renee Call

ABRAHAM DAY

Born: 24 Sep 1817, Winhall, Windham, Vermont
Parents: Abraham and Hannah Sawyer
Died: 28 Apr 1900, Lawrence, Emery, Utah
Arrived in Valley: 20 Nov 1851, Abraham Day Co.

Married 1st: Elmira Bulkley
Date: 16 Jun 1838, Rutland, Tiago, Pennsylvania
Died: 24 Dec 1905, Castle Dale, Emery, Utah

Married 2nd: Charlotte Catherine Broomhead (Melland)
Date: 30 Nov 1851, Salt Lake City, Utah
Dicd: 26 Sep 1872, Mt. Pleasant, Sanpete, Utah

Abraham was the third male in this line to bear this name. His father died when he was only one year old. By the time he was 16 he started to work on his own. There was not another man in the village who could beat him at chopping wood. He was baptized shortly before his marriage to Elmira. He lived for a time in

Nauvoo where he worked on the Nauvoo Temple. He started west with his family in 1846 and joined the Mormon Battalion.

Upon his arrival in California, he and his brother-in-law, Newman Bulkley, stopped at Sutters Fort to have their horses shod. They arrived in the Valley 16 October 1847. They stopped long enough to obtain provisions and then left on the return trip to find their families. It took three years for Abraham to get provisions and equipment to bring his family to the Valley.

There was a young girl staying with his family and she came west with them and became his second wife 10 days after their arrival.

They settled in Springville, Utah. He was a millwright and served as mayor. In 1860 he moved his families to Mt. Pleasant, Utah. Later he moved to Lawrence, Emery County, until his death.

Children of 1st wife:

JOSEPH SMITH, b. 7 Sep 1839, Exter, Scott, Illinois. Md. 1st Mary Anderson. Md. 2nd, Petrena Bertleson. D. 26 Apr 1902.
MELINDA JANE, b. 27 Oct 1840, Barry, Pike, Illinois. D. 18 Aug 1843.
HARRIET, b. 17 Jul 1842, Nashville, Iowa. D.5 Aug 1843.
AMELIA, b. 6 Aug 1843, Montrose, Scott, Iowa. D. 6 Aug 1843.
ELMIRA JENNETTE, b. 7 Apr 1846, Montrose, Iowa. D. 7 Mar 1883.
EZRA JONAS, b. 11 Jul 1847, Council Bluffs, Iowa.
JULIETTE, b. 18 Oct 1848, Council Bluffs, Iowa. Md. 25 Mar 1866, Henry Bohne. D. 27 Dec 1916.
ALICE, b. 22 Feb 1850, Council Bluffs, Iowa. Md. 26 Feb 1872, Walter Christopherson. D. 15 Dec 1925.
ABRAHAM NELSON, b. 14 Feb 1852, Salt Lake City, Utah. Md. 1st, Mary Rowe. Md. 2nd, Elizabeth Jane Staker. D. 31 Jan 1917.
LAURA ANN, b. 6 Jun 1853, Springville, Utah. Md. 5 Jan 1873, Ole Nielsen Tuft . D. 2 Sep 1924.
IRA ALFRED, b. 14 Feb 1855, Springville, Utah. Md. 29 Dec 1877, Polley Ann Noakes. D. 7 Mar 1933.

EDWIN SUMMERS, b. 25 Jan 1857, Springville, Utah. Md. 14 Feb 1884, Maria Josephine Johnson. D. 9 Sep 1939.

ELLA LEANORA, b. 22 Mar 1859, Springville, Utah. D. 24 Nov 1861.

ALBERT ARLINGTON, b. 27 Aug 1861, Mt Pleasant, Utah. Md. 25 Jan 1887, Emmer Jene Loveless. D. 1 Nov 1918.

Children of 2nd wife:

DORA ELMIRA, b. 21 Aug 1852, Springville, Utah. Md. 28 Nov 1870, John Gustovus Johnson. D. 28 Jul 1934.

ALBERT DEMASONS, b. 10 Dec 1853, Springville, Utah. D. Oct 1854.

HERBERT STEVENS, b. 11 May 1855, Springville, Utah. Md. 8 Mar 1877 Mary Mahetible Wilcox. D. 9 Apr 1933.

ELI AZARIAH, b. 23 Sep 1856, Springville, Utah. Md. 1st, Eliza Jane Staker. Md. 2nd Elvira Euphrasia Cox. D. 23 Nov 1943.

BENJAMIN FRANKLIN, b. 12 Dec 1857, Springville, Utah. D. Jul 1860.

HANNAH FLAVILLA, b. 5 Dec 1859, Springville, Utah. Md. 1 Nov 1876, Andrew Emerson Smith. D. 2 Apr 1945.

EPHRAIM ARTHUR, b. 27 Jan 1862, Mt. Pleasant, Utah. Md. 1889, Mary Jane Gartrell. D. 12 Sep 1954.

HARRIET ANNE, b. 27 Dec 1863, Mt Pleasant, Utah. Md. 27 Oct 1880, James Henry Wilcox. D. 12 Sep 1902.

GEORGE WILLIAM, b. 7 Sep 1865, Mt. Pleasant, Utah. Md. 17 Nov 1886, Elizabeth Ellis Staker. D. 14 Apr 1901.

HARRY HAZELTON, b. Mar 1868, Mt. Pleasant, Utah. D. Mar 1868.

MARY ELLEN, b. 10 Aug 1870, Mt Pleasant, Utah. Md. 1st Joseph Prouse and four more. D. 6 Jan 1946.

JOSEPH ABRAHAM, b. Nov 1871, Mt. Pleasant, Utah. D. Jul 1874.

Submitted by: Lamar Day

FINITY DAYBELL

Born: 11 Mar 1814, Millthorpe, Aslackby, Lincolnshire, England
Parents: Samuel and Rebecca Ham Daybell
Died: 25 Oct 1897, Charleston, Wasatch, Utah
Arrived in Valley: William S. Warren Company 19 Jul 1864

Married: Mary Draper
Date: 9 Feb 1841, Falkingham, Lincolnshire, England
Born: 6 Jan 1820, Haceby, Lincolnshire, England
Parents: Richard and Ann Green Draper
Died: 2 Sep 1899, Heber, Wasatch, Utah

Finity went to work early in his life as did most young children. In 1844 he met the Mormon missionaries. Finity accepted the gospel but it took a little longer for Mary. They were baptized in August 1844. Mary had a fear of the ocean but it left her after they were baptized. It took them 20 years before they were able to save enough money to emigrate to the Valley due to an accident when Finity splintered a bone in his shoulder. Mary supported the family until Finity was able to resume working.

In 1863 Susan left, being only 15 at the time. In Salt Lake she found a family to live with. The next year, the remaining members of the family, who had not married or died, left for America. After their arrival here, it was suggested that they move to Charleston (Heber), Utah, and live in Joseph E. Taylor's house until they could manage a home. They lived there until Brigham Young told every one to move during the Black Hawk Indian War. They moved to Heber but still had problems with the Indians.

All their family finally arrived from England. After the war, the entire family moved back to the Provo area. Finity died of a stroke when he was 82. He was a good man with much hard luck, who lived and cared for his family to the best of his ability.

Children:

ROBERT DAYBELL (PUDLER), b. 2 Jul 1842, Pointon, Lincolnshire, England. Md. 26 Dec 1864, Agnes Ann Bancroft. D. 16 Aug 1866, Lost North, Platt River, Nebraska.

GEORGE DAYBELL, b. 14 Sep 1844, Pointon, Lincolnshire, England. D. 2 Mar 1847, Pointon, Lincolnshire, England. Child.

ANN DAYBELL, b. 17 Apr 1846, Pointon, Lincolnshire, England. Md. 3 Aug 1863, William Webster. D. 3 Feb 1924, Charleston, Wasatch, Utah.

SUSAN DAYBELL, b. 5 Aug 1848, Pointon, Lincolnshire, England. Md. 3 May 1866, John Pollard. D. 12 Nov 1932.

SARAH DAYBELL, b. 9 Mar 1850, Pointon, Lincolnshire, England. Md. 28 Jan 1867, George Thomas Giles, Heber City, Wasatch, Utah. D. 11 Apr 1942, Heber City, Wasatch, Utah.

GEORGE DAYBELL, b. 2 Aug 1852, Pointon, Lincolnshire, England. Md. 16 Nov 1876, Sarah Ann Carlile. D. 4 Aug 1913, Charleston, Wasatch, Utah.

ELIZABETH DAYBELL, b. 9 Jul 1856, Pointon, Lincolnshire, England. D. 11 Jan 1855, Whittington, Derbyshire, England.

WILLIAM DAYBELL, b. 23 Feb 1858, Whittington, Lincolnshire, England. Md. 12 Nov 1877, Annie Price. D. 29 Nov 1945, Heber, Wasatch, Utah.

MARY DAYBELL, b. 15 Jun 1860, Whittington, Lincolnshire, England. D. 17 Jun 1860, Whittington, Lincolnshire, England.

Submitted by: Reah Diamond

WILLIAM DAYBELL

Born: 24 Feb 1858, Chesterfield, Derbyshire, England
Parents: Finity and Mary Draper Daybell
Died: 29 Nov 1945, Heber, Utah
Arrived in Valley: 4 Oct 1864, Capt Warren's Co.

Married lst: Annie Price
Date: 12 Nov 1877, Utah
Parents: James and Ann Price
Born: 21 Jun 1858, Ludlow, Shropshire, England
Died: 14 Feb, 1920, Heber, Utah

Married 2nd: Hannah Jensen
Date: 21 Apr 1920, Utah
Parents: Lars Jensen and Anne Helene Pettrsen
Born: 4 Oct 1863, Roken, Norway.
Died: 4 Mar 1947, Heber, Utah

William's family emigrated to America and the Valley when he was six years old. He always remembered walking beside his father as they crossed the plains. After their arrival in the valley, where they stayed for several weeks, they moved to Joseph E. Taylor's farm in Charleston (Heber Valley). Later William bought this farm.

William learned to read from the Book of Mormon. He had a little schooling during January, February, and March for which his father paid $3.00, sometimes it was in money, but mostly in produce. As he grew up, he was able to provide a good living for his family as a dairy farmer.

He went on a mission for two years to Tennessee after he was married. He remained active in the Church all his life. He was a bishop, member of a high council and patriarch. He was also active in the community, holding the position of county commissioner, trustee of school board, president of a canal company and other positions.

Children of 1st wife:

JOHN WILLIAM, b. 6 Aug 1878, Charleston, Utah. Md. Jessie Fowers. D. 26 Feb 1948, Garfield, Utah.

MARY ANN, b. 5 May 1880. Md. Moronie Moulton. D. 20 Mar 1848, Salt Lake.

JAMES FINITY, b. 5 Jul 1882, D. 25 Sep 1882, Charleston, Utah.

PHOEBE ELIZABETH, b. 8 Dec 1883. Md. John W. Simmons. D. 9 Dec 1921, Charleston, Utah.

JOSEPH FRANKLIN, b. 1 Sep 1888, Charleston, Utah.Md. Hilda Dahlman. D. 1 Sep 1970, Salt Lake.

MYRTLE, b. 31 Aug 1890, Charleston, Utah. Md. Archie Boren. D. 19 Feb 1981, Pleasant Grove, Utah.

VIOLET B., b. 5 Oct 1892, Md. Heber J. Simmons. D. 8 Jul 1955, Midway, Utah.

LULA, b. 24 Oct 1894 Md. Earl N. Carlile. D. 21 Jul 1987, Heber, Utah

SON (stillborn), b.12 Apr 1897, Charleston, Utah. D. 12 Apr 1897.

ERNEST, b. 15 Mar 1899, Charleston, Utah. Md. Ednal Clyde. D. 8 Sep 1968, Magna, Utah.

WARREN, b. 19 Jun 1901, Charleston, Utah. Md. Thelma Leak. D. 9 Jan 1986, St. George, Utah

Submitted by: Melvin Carlile

JOHN WESLEY DEAL

Born: 18 Oct 1822, Pasquotank County, North Carolina
Parents: Daniel and Ruth Wilcox Deal
Died: 12 Aug 1887, Springville, Utah, Utah
Arrived in Valley: 2 Sep 1850, Aaron Johnson Company

Married: Eliza Crandall
Date: 28 Oct 1901, Springville, Utah, Utah
Born: 10 Jun 1816, Villinova, Chtg., N.Y.
Died: 27 Mar 1901, Springville, Utah, Utah

John Wesley was a man of infinite good humor. As a young man, he spent much time on the Mississippi River as a flatboatman. His trade was that of stonecutter, which trade he made good use of in Nauvoo helping build the temple.

He was one of the first to settle in Springville, Utah. He was in charge of digging the first ditch to irrigate the area. He had the first lime kiln in Springville and also made bricks.

The youth loved to gather in his home. He was loved and respected by everyone and remained faithful to the church.

Children:

DANIEL EDGAR, b. 2 Dec 1845, Quincy, Adams, Illinois. Md. 22 Aug 1870 Sarah Daphne Hamblin. D. 23 Sep 1911.
MARY ELLEN, b. 3 Oct 1845, Quincy, Adams, Illinois. Md. 15 May 1864, Thomas Lowell Mendenhall. D. 30 Jun 1910, Springville, Utah, Utah.
JOHN WESLEY, b. 16 Oct 1847, Quincy, Adams, Illinois. Md. Azalia M. Spafford. D. 19 Feb 1918.

LAURA FRANCES, b. 20 Nov 1849, Quincy, Adams, Illinois. D. 3 Oct 1858, Springville, Utah, Utah.

ROMANZO ALGERNON, b. 3 Feb 1852, Springville, Utah, Utah. Md. 24 Jan 1876. Helen Marzella Maycock. D. 28 Aug 1903.

STEPHEN OLIVER, b. 16 Feb 1854, Springville, Utah, Utah. D. 24 Feb 1877.

THEODORE MONROE, b. 29 Dec 1855, Springville, Utah, Utah. Md. 20 Mar 1895, Eunice Christean Blanchard. D. 5 Oct 1917.

LUCIAN DELANCY, b. 29 Jul 1858, Springville, Utah, Utah Md. Ruth E. Coats D. 13 Jun 1918.

Submitted by: Royal Oakes

ALFRED DEGREY

Born: 12 Mar 1831, West Bromwich, Staffordshire, England
Parents: John and Maria Brooks DeGrey
Died: 27 Aug 1885, Salt Lake City, Utah
Arrived in Valley: Capt. Loveland's Company on 15 Aug 1868

Married: Ann Maria Raybold

Alfred's father was a tailor and his wife helped him. After his father's death, Alfred, although young, quit school to work in the iron works near his home. They lived near an uncle who taught Alfred how to blow glass. About this time, the family met the missionaries. His mother and sisters were later baptized. When the family decided to emigrate to the Valley, Alfred remained in

England. He married and 10 years later was baptized.

He and his wife finally decided to come to America. They arrived in 1868. They stayed in Salt Lake and Alfred got work at a quarry in Cottonwood Canyon, cutting stone for the temple. Later he worked at a foundry owned by the Utah Central Railway. He became quite skilled in the art of casting tools from brass.

He died suddenly at home. He was never very active in church or community, but was well respected and liked by everyone.

Children:

JOHN, b. 18 Oct 1856, Netherton, Worcestershire, England.
ALFRED, b. 26 Jul 1859.
SAMUEL, b. 2 Nov. 1861, Dudley, England. Md. Maria Jarman
 D. 6 Dec 1945.
MARIA, b. 17 Feb 1865.
SELINA, b. 17 Mar 1866.
ELIZABETH (LIZZIE,) b. 30 Apr 1868.
SARAH, b. 27 Nov 1873 Md. James Olsen.
LUIE, b. 31 Jan 1875 Md. Al Pitts.

Submitted by: Thais DeGrey

SAMUEL DEGREY

Born: 2 Nov. 1861, Dudley, England
Parents: Alfred and Anna Maria Raybold Degrey
Died: 6 Dec. 1945, Salt Lake City, Utah
Arrived in Valley: Capt. Chester Loveland Co. on 20 Aug 1868

Married: Maria Jarman

Samuel and his parents and siblings came to America with others who had joined the Church. They took the train west as far as Laramie, Wyoming, where they joined a wagon train.

Upon their arrival in the Valley, they were taken to the home of the Henry Aldous Dixon family where they stayed until Alfred, Samuel's father, was able to obtain a place for them to live. It was some years after their arrival in the valley that Samuel was finally baptized. Samuel lived with his sister, Maria, in Provo for a time.

After his marriage, they continued to live in Salt Lake where they raised their family. Samuel was a religious man but never active in the church. He backed the church in all it did and attended occassionally. He was always a willing donator and helped those in need. He was honest and upright in all his dealings and well liked by all.

Samuel was a blacksmith by trade, but after coming to the valley he worked in the Sugar factory in Sugarhouse. Later he worked for the Denver and Rio Grande Railroad and later on The Shortline.

Children:

ALFRED, b. 24 Dec 1889, Salt Lake City, Utah.
MAY, b. 1 May 1892 D. 17 May 1894, Salt Lake City, Utah.
SIDNEY, b. 20 Jan 1889, Salt Lake City, Utah.

Submitted by: Thais DeGrey

FREEBORN DE MILL

Born: 3 Mar 1795, Plattekill, Ulster, New York
Parents: Garrett and Magdelena Emigh (Known as Lanah Amey)
    De Mill
Died: 23 Jan 1881, Manti, Sanpete, Utah
Arrived in Valley: 21 Sep 1848, Capt. Stoker Co.

Married 1st: Anna Knight
Date: 11 Mar 1819, Colesville, New York
Born: 5 Mar 1804, Halifax, Windham, Vermont
Parents: Joseph and Polly Peck Knight, Sr
Died: 22 Jul 1878, Manti, Sanpete, Utah.

Married 2nd: Lunette Janette Richardson
Date: 3 May 1856

Children of 1st wife:

MARIA, b. 12 May 1820, Colesville, Broome, New York. Md.
    22 Apr 1841, Daniel Buckley Funk. D. 25 Mar 1889,
    Sterling, Sanpete, Utah.
ORPHA, b. 24 Dec 1822, Colesville, Broome, New York. Md.
    1843, Perry Davis. D. 29 Oct 1846.
LORA ANN, b. 2 Jun 1828, Colesville, Broome, New York. Md.
    1848, Samuel Kendal Gifford. D. 6 Apr 1870.
OLIVER, b. 30 Mar 1830, Colesville, Broome, New York. Md.
    Emily Almira Beal.
ADELIA, b. 29 Sep 1832, Low Township, Jackson, Missouri.
    Md. 1863, John Prichard Squire. D. 17 May 1917

ELIAS, b. 12 Jan 1838, Far West, Caldwell, Missouri. Md.
   Melvina Wingate. D. 21 Jul 1905.
LOVINA ESTER, b. 13 May 1843, Nauvoo, Illinois. Md. 1859,
   John Alma Beal. D. 13 Mar 1880.

Submitted by: Howard Hardy

HANS DENISON (DINESEN)

Born: 20 Jul 1824, Gjentofte, Copenhagen, Denmark
Parents: Rasmus and Ingar Marie Monson Dinesen
Died: 13 Jan 1904, Manti, Utah
Arrived in Valley: Oct 1853, John Forsgren Scandinavian Group

Married: Johanne Christofferson
Date: 22 Nov 1846, Copenhagen, Denmark
Died: 28 Jul 1880, Manti, Utah

Hans, while working on a neighboring farm, met his future
wife. After the birth of two children and the death of one, he was
called to participate in the war of 1849.

After the war, he heard of Joseph Smith and shortly after,
joined the Church. They sailed on the first ship that carried Scandinavian emigrants. When they reached St. Louis, his mother,
who had come with them, died.

After reaching the Valley, they determined to go on to Manti
where the other members of the company had decided to settle. It
was extremely difficult but they perservered. Hans helped with
the erection of three temples, Salt Lake, St George, and Manti.

Children:

RASMUS, b. 1847. D. soon after birth. Copenhagen, Denmark.
JENS, b. 10 Jan 1849. Copenhagen, Denmark.
KIRSTINE, b. 3 Sep 1851. D. 10 Sep 1851. Infant.
EPHRAIM MONARCH, b.11-12 Mar 1853, aboard ship outside
    New Orleans, Louisiana.
HANS, JR., b. 29 Jul 1856, Manti, Utah.
JOSEPH, b. 16 Mar 1860, Manti, Utah.
JOHANNA, b. 8 Jan 1863, Manti, Utah.
HYRUM, b. 6 Jan 1865, Manti, Utah.

Submitted by: Mardene Denison

DANIEL QUIMBY DENNETT

Born: 27 Dec 1808 Hollis, York, Maine
Parents: John F. and Jane Woodward Dennett
Died: 10 Mar 1872, Rockville, Washington, Utah
Arrived in Valley: 1847, Mormon Battalion

Married 1st: Elizabeth Robinson

Married 2nd: Lucy Ann Newell Very
Date: 30 Jun 1851, Salt Lake City, Utah
Born: 12 Jun 1818, Boxford, Essex, Massachusetts
Parents: Jonathan and Susan Peabody Very
Died: 5 Jan 1876, Rockville, Washington, Utah

Not much is known about Daniel's early life. He was baptized in 1833. He then went to Kirtland and worked on the temple for two weeks. In 1846 he left Nauvoo and joined the Mormon Battalion and served one year, then went on to Salt Lake.

He played the fife in the Nauvoo Legion Band. He and his family lived in Salt Lake City and were active in the ward. He was quite talented and frequently sang solos in the meetings.

Children:

DAVID ALMA (twin), b. 23 Oct 1851, Salt Lake City, Salt Lake, Utah. D. Oct 1914. Unmarried.

DANIEL AMULEK (twin), b. 23 Oct 1851, Salt Lake City, Salt Lake, Utah. D. bef. 1860. Unmarried.

JOHN FABYAN, b. 10 Oct 1853, Salt Lake City, Salt Lake, Utah Md. 18 Apr 1872, Rockville, Washington, Utah, Rebecca Alvira Fisk Stout. D. 5 Feb 1933, Rockville, Washington, Utah.

CHARLES, b. abt 1856, Provo, Utah, Utah. D. bef. 1860. Unmarried.

LUCY JANE, b. 1859 in Provo, Utah, Utah. Md. 28 Mar 1876, John N. Curtis, D. 16 Dec 1891, Alameda, Alameda, California

Submitted by: Woodrow Dennett

DANIEL DENSLEY, SR.

Born: 29 Jul 1826, English Combe, Sumerset, England
Parents: George and Nancy Ann Tipney Densley
Died: 19 Feb 1910, Bluffdale, Salt Lake, Utah
Arrived in Valley: Sep./Oct. 1866

Married 1st: Sarah Beech
Date: 26 Dec 1851, Walsall, Staffordshire, England
Died: 19 Feb 1910, Bluffdale, Salt Lake, Salt Lake

Married 2nd: Harriet Shaw Berthea Flamack (Div.)
Born: England

Daniel, as a young man in England, worked in the coal mines in Walsall. He joined the Church in 1863 and Sarah joined in 1864. They left England in 1866 for America. Sarah was pregnant during the trip west. They had four other children with them. Upon their arrival in Salt Lake, they stayed for a time with Heber C. Kimball, who had stayed in their home in England.

In 1898, Daniel returned to England on a mission. He was an avid genealogist and took his results to the temple. He was known for his kindness to others and for his generous nature. He was honest and upright in his dealings. He hauled ore from Lark to the Sandy City Smelter to earn a living. He died in Bluffdale, Utah.

Children of 1st wife:

SAMUEL, b. 23 Mar 1853, England. D. Jul 1894.
ANN, b. 19 Nov 1854, England. D. 15 Oct 1919.
DANIEL (first), b. 28 Mar 1856, England. D. Feb. 1857. Child.
DANIEL (second), b. 28 Feb 1858, England. D. 13 Dec 1930.
SARAH, b. 28 apr 1861, England. D. Oct 1863.
GEORGE, b. 18 Dec 1863, England. D. Oct 1863(?).
MARY, b. 7 Nov 1864, England D. 29 Aug 1921.
WILLIAM JOHN, b. 6 Nov 1866, Utah. D. 12 Mar 1954.
JOSEPH (HENRY), b. 5 Feb 1870, Utah. D. 19 Aug 1883.
MOSES (twin), b. 21 Mar 1873,Utah. D. 10 May 1952.
AARON (twin), b. 21 Mar 1873, Utah. D. 27 Apr 1948.
THOMAS, b. 10 Jul 1875, Utah. D. 7 Aug 1883.
ESTHER, b. 14 Feb 1878, Utah.

Submitted by: Elva Merkley

HENRY WATERS DESPAIN

Born: 28 Sep 1847, Calhoon Co., Illinois
Parents: Solomon Joseph and Ruth Amelia Newell DeSpain
Died: 6 Dec 1925, Joseph City, Navajo, Arizona
Arrived in Valley: David H. Cannan Company, 16 Aug 1861

Married 1st: Grace Provis
Date: 15 Mar 1869
Born: 2 Mar 1853, Africa
Died: 13 Feb 1919, California

Married 2nd: Joanna Matilda Erickson
Date: 4 Jun 1854, Sweden
Died: 23 Jan 1929, New Mexico

Henry Waters was the father of 20 children. They lived in Granite, Utah, where Henry quarried stone. He spent some time as a policeman in Salt Lake City. He was called to help settle Northern Arizona in 1876, at Sunset, Arizona.

He was a farmer, dam-builder, carpenter, butcher, shoemaker, and hunter. He was in charge of the tannery at Mormon Lake, Arizona. He was a missionary to the Indians from 1879 to 1883. They called him "Jedda BE-AY" by the Indians because he wore a buckskin shirt. He spent much time doing temple work.

Children of 1st wife:

HENRY WATERS, b. 17 Jul 1872. Md. 22 Dec 1891, Elizabeth
Tanner. D. 18 Feb 1957.

MELVINA LOUISA, b. 23 Oct 1874. Md. 15 Feb 1898, Robert
　Morris. D. 9 Mar 1958.

JOSEPH RICHARD, b. 5 Jun 1877. D. 21 Oct 1882. Child.

DAVID SYLVESTER, b. 17 Sep 1879. Md. 1st 2 Sep 1903, Sarah
　Adaline Freeman. Md. 2nd 11 Jul 1907, Rozalia Gillespie. Md.
　3rd Jan 1936, Clara (Mosely) Sutcliffe. D. 26 May 1961.

ANNIE (twin), b. 7 Feb 1883. Md. 28 Jan 1903, Thaddeus Orren
　Mossman. D. 28 Feb 1960.

ALVIN (twin), b. 7 Feb 1883. Md. 7 Jul 1904, Ida Willis, D. 17
　Jun 1952.

AARON NEWELL, b. 11 Jun 1885. D. 6 Jul 1886. Child.

GRACE ADORA, b. 18 Jul 1887. Md. 1st. Albert Henry
　Thompson. Md. 2nd Francis Lynn.

LOIS ELIZABETH, b. 11 Nov 1889. Md. Herbert Harry Osmer.
　D. 4 Dec 1964.

MARY AMELIA, b. 23 Feb 1892. Md. 1st Charles William
　Newby. Md. 2nd. Mr. Wright.

WILLIAM CLYDE, b. 28 Oct 1894. Md. Sadie. D. 5 Sep 1950.

ROBERT SAMUEL, b. 29 May 1897. Md. 1st Etheline Carolyn
　Haggle. Md. 2nd 21 Sep 1944, Edith Haggle. D. 26 Apr 1956.

LAWRENCE MELVIN, b. 30 Nov 1899. Md. Thelma. D. 23
　Feb 1956.

Children of 2nd wife:

JOHN LYCURGUS, b. 4 Oct 1880. Md. 1 Oct 1902, Maren Adele
　Bushman. D. 8 Dec 1971.

MARY SOPHIA, b. 8 Oct 1882. Md. 10 Oct 1940, James Willie
　Richards. D. 15 Jul 1940.

AMELIA CHRISTINA, b. 29 Jun 1885. Md. 2 Jun 1909,
　William Arthur Tenny, Jr. D. 25 Jan 1978.

ELECTA DRUCILLA, b. 8 Oct 1887. Md. 15 Aug 1910, John
　Andrew Turley. D. 25 Aug 1981.

EMMA OCTAVA, b. 12 Oct 1889. Md. 1st. 3 Jun 1914, Henry
　Marvin Beckstead. Md. 2nd. 3 Oct 1935, Angus "Q"
　Beckstead. Md. 3rd 31 Aug 1953, Clarence Monroe Beckstead.
　D. 23 Aug 1972.

ALBERT OSCAR, b. 9 Oct 1893. Md. 30 Jul 1919, Caroline
    Arthur Nelson. D. 21 Jul 1972.
FRANZ HENRY, b. 10 Jul 1896. Md. 21 Sep 1921 Leona Smith.
        D. 16 Jul 1955.

(The last seven children, belonged to Edwin Lycurgas
Westover. As he was dying, he requested that Henry marry his
widow. The children retained the surname of Westover.)

Submitted by: Junith Roberts

SOLOMON JOSEPH DESPAIN

Born: 3 Dec 1823, Lauderdale Co., Alabama
Parents: Soloman and Nancy Bell Despain
Died: 17 Feb 1895, Thatcher, Graham, Arizona
Arrived in Valley: David H. Cannon Company, 17 Aug 1861.

Married 1st: Ruth Amelia Newell
Date: 30 Jun 1842
Born: 21 Sep 1822, New York
Died: 20/21 Aug 1901

Married 2nd: Susan Dean
Date: 17 May 1862, Utah
Born: 17 Nov 1843
Died: 5 Feb 1922, Utah

Married 3rd: Charlotta Albertina Lundstedt
Date: 28 Mar 1881, Utah

Born: 25 Feb 1857
Died: 23 Jul 1940, Arizona

Solomon Joseph was always active in the Church, being in the church when he was in Illinois. He went on a mission to Arkansas in 1853.

When he came to Utah, he settled at the mouth of Little Cottonwood Canyon. He homesteaded in Granite in 1862. He was postmaster and Justice of the Peace in Granite. He was the first bishop of Granite. He fathered 27 children. He moved to Arizona in 1886, and settled in Thatcher, Arizona.

Children of 1st wife:

SOLOMON, b. 9 Apr 1843, D. 9 Apr 1843. Child.
WILLIAM JOSEPH, b. 9 Apr 1843. Md. 1st 8 Jul 1864, Ann Hill. Md. 2nd 4 Sep 1874, Sarah Catherine Egbert. D.29 A??? D. 29 Apr 1918.
HYRUM SMITH, b. 7 May 1846. Md. 9 Aug 1870, Ruth Amelia Griffith. D. 17 Apr 1904.
HENRY WATERS, b. 28 Sep 1847. Md. 1st 15 Mar 1869, Grace Provis. Md. 2nd. 21 May 1879, Joanna Matilda Erickson. D. 6 Dec 1925.
EDWIN SYLVESTER, b. 27 Mar 1849. D. 9/18 Aug 1951. Child.
ORSON AUGUSTUS, b. 8 Mar 1851. Md. 1st 4 Dec 1871, Janette Russell Livingston. D. 11 Nov 1927. Md. 2nd 17 Oct 1876, Catherine Cameron (Div).
AMANDA CAROLINE, b. 6 Dec 1853. Md. 24 Jun 1874, Solomon Avery Wixom. D. 23 Jan 1928.
DORA MELVIA, b. 27 Feb 1856. D. 14 Sep 1858. Child.
ELLA EUGENIA, b. 27 Aug 1858. Md. 30 Jan 1879, John Boyce. D. 8 Jan 1936.
DAVID ALVIN, b. 1 Sep 1861. Md. 26 Jan 1887, Luella Miranda Butler. D. 28 Dec 1936.
OSCAR NEWELL, b. 7 Nov 1836. Md. 1st 4 Jan 1888, Lizzie Adelle Boyce. Md. 2nd 30 Jan 1938, Effie Mae Welch. D. 28 Mar 1946.

CLARA LOUISA, b. 24 Jun 1877. Md. 15 Feb 1883, Andrew
   Wilson Thomson. D. 26 Jun 1910.

Children of 2nd wife:

MARTHA ELIZA, b. 23 Feb 1863. Md. 27 Sep 1878, William
   Thompson. D. 16 Apr 1899.
LEWIS EDGAR, b. 28 Sep 1864. Md. 20 Feb 1889, Hannah Eliza-
   beth Anna Butler. D. 25 Apr 1948.
EFFIE ELZINA, b. 23 Nov 1866. Md. 1st 11 Dec 1889, Frederick
   Summerfield Cowley. Md. 2nd Henry Pymm. D. 22 Dec 1924.
GEORGE FRANCIS, b. 21 Sep 1869. Md. 20 Sep 1899, Pru-
   dence Georgia Butler. D. 14 May 1946.
ANNA LAURA, b. 1 Sep 1871. Md. 20 Feb 1895, Alva John
   Butler. D. 6 Jul 1939.
CHARLES ROY, b. 5 Nov 1873. Unmarried. D. 9 Mar 1900.
DE BART, b. 17 Sep 1875. Md. 21 Sep 1899, Bertha Minnie
   Kener. D. 25 Dec 1957.
FRANK PARLEY, b. 2 Sep 1878. Md. 1st 5 Nov 1897, Margaret
   B. Butler. Md. 2nd Leah Lovena Clayson. D. 15 Jan 1948.
ANGUS RAY, b. 28 Dec 1880. Md. 11 Sep 1912, Emily Kate
   Tucker. D. 9 Jul 1949.
IDA ETHEL, b. 12 Dec 1883. Md. 28 Mar 1906, Ephriam Amos
   Jensen. D. 29 ec 1965.

Children of 3rd wife:

MARK LORENZO, b. 22 Jan 1882. Md. 12 Oct 1906, Mary
   Emma Cluff. D. 28 Feb 1965.
WALTER GUSTIVE, b. 17 Nov 1883. Md. 3 Apr 1912 Clarissa
   Clyde Birdno. D. 14 May 1958.
LOTTA PEARL, b. 21 Nov 1885. D. 13 Mar 1886. Child.
INA PAULINE, b. 7 Apr 1887. Md. 1st 4 Jan 1911, James Will-
   iam Haws. Md. 2nd Guy L. Wilson. Md. D. 17 Aug 1956.
FRANCIS OTTO, b. 10 Aug 1889. Md. 1st 23 Dec 1923, Dor-
   othy May Cass. 2nd 16 Sep 1946, Marie Elizabeth Collins.
   D. 1958.

Submitted by: Junith Roberts

JOHN COOK DEWEY

Christened: 12 Jan 1831, Stroxton, Lincolnshire, England
Parents: Thomas (Unknown) and Eliza Dewey
Died: 8 Oct 1895, Deweyville, Box Elder, Utah
Arrived in Valley: Moses Daley's Company on 28 Sep 1853

Married 1st: Mary Allen
Date: 23 Apr 1854
Parents: Jude and Mary Allen Nicholas Allen
Born: 18 Apr 1838, Parma, Caugha, Ohio
Died: 23 Aug 1911

Married 2nd: Harriet May
Date: 11 Feb 1857, Salt Lake City, Salt Lake, Utah
Parents: George and Hannah Hobson May
Born: Jul 1834
Died: 18 Sep 1887, Deweyville, Box Elder, Utah

John joined the Church when he was 17 and was disowned by his parents. He left England in September 1850 for America. He spent the winter in New Orleans and then went to St. Louis. He stayed until May 1853, when he was hired to drive a team across the plains. Upon his arrival in the Valley, he settled in Bountiful.

He helped guard the city when Johnston's army came. He married twice in polygamy. He was musical and led the choir for nine years in Bountiful. In 1864 he moved his family to Empy Springs, later called Deweyville, Utah. He was a bishop, farmer, postmaster, school master, Justice of the Peace, and friend.

He was a good father and husband. He was faithful in all his callings and was loved and respected by all. He died of stomach cancer and jaundice.

Children of 1st wife:

MARY ELIZA, b. 9 Mar 1855, Bountiful, Davis, Utah. Md. 10 Oct 1872, William Walter Howard. D. 24 Nov 1928, Deweyville, Box Elder, Utah.

MARTHA MATILDA, b. 7 Feb 1857, Bountiful, Davis, Utah. Md. 27 Dec 1875, Marion Alexander Lish. D. 20 Jan 1941, Deweyville, Box Elder, Utah.

JOHN CYRUS, b. 12 Apr 1859, Bountiful, Davis, Utah. Md. 24 Jan 1878, Sarah Annie Child. D. 21 Mar 1948.

EUNICE ELLEN, b. 10 May 1861, Calls Fort, Box Elder, Utah. Md. 23 Dec 1880, Orville Rensseler Child. D. 7 Feb 1944.

EMILY JANE, b. 11 May 1863, Calls Fort, Box Elder, Utah. Md. 23 Dec 1880, James Samuel Lindsey. D. 18 Jun 1890.

JUDE LEHI, b. 21 Oct 1865, Deweyville, Box Elder, Utah. D. 4 Oct 1866.

HORACE ANDREW, b. 1 Oct 1867, Deweyville, Box Elder, Utah. D. 26 Aug 1889.

JOSEPH IRA, b. 13 Jan 1870, Deweyville, Box Elder, Utah. Md. 4 Jul 1889, Emma Tricha Lindsey. D. 2 Mar 1943.

SARAH MARETTA, b. 20 Nov 1873, Deweyville, Box Elder, Utah. D. 10 Apr 1874.

LETTIE ANN, b 28 Jul 1875, Deweyville, Box Elder, Utah. Md. 12 Apr 1898, Chester Frederick Campbell. D 25 Sep 1955.

CHARLES JESSE, b. 23 May 1879, Deweyville, Box Elder, Utah. Md. 1st, 8 Oct 1903, Mary Ceneth Chidester. Md. 2nd 22 Feb 1909, Constant Ann Eggleston. D 30 Mar 1953.

LOIS EDNA, b. 31 Oct 1881, Deweybille, Box Elder, Utah. Md. 7 Jun 1911, Lester Hyrum Peirson. D. 9 Oct 1946.

EDWARD RILLEY SPIKINGS, (Adopted) b. 4 Mar 1883, Oxford, Idaho. Md. 24 Feb 1902, Maude Elizabeth Priest. D. 14 Dec 1918.

Children of 2nd wife:

GEORGE CARLOS, b. 23 Dec 1857, Bountiful, Davis, Utah. Md. 22 Mar 1876, Susan Emma Chidester. D. 2 Sep 1930.

WILLIAM ALFRED, b. 28 Jun 1861, Calls Fort, Box Elder, Utah. Md. 20 Jan 1882, Eunice Jane Shurtliff. D. 12 Dec 1943.

HANNAH ELIZABETH, b. 1 Sep 1863, Calls Fort, Box Elder, Utah. Md. 20 Nov 1880, Almond Francis Loveland. D. 20 Jun 1938.

JAMES ERNEST, b. 12 Jun 1866, Deweyville, Box Elder, Utah. Md. 23 Jan 1889, Matilda Bailey. D. 23 Jun 1945.

HARRIET ADELAIDE, b. 27 Dec 1868, Deweyville, Box Elder, Utah. Md. 23 Jan 1889, Robert Nathanial Gardner. D. 3 Apr 1954.

THOMAS EZRA, b. 24 Feb 1871, Deweyville, Box Elder, Utah. D. 19 Jan 1877.

ALMA (Twin), b. 28 Jan 1874, Deweyville, Box Elder, Utah. D. 28 Feb 1874.

AMELIA (Twin), b. 28 Jan 1874, Deweyville, Box Elder, Utah. D. 20 Apr 1874.

Submitted by: Bessie Barnes

JOHN DICKSON

Born: 24 Aug 1781, Cambridge, Washington, New York
Parents: David & Sarah Dickson
Died: 1860, American Fork, Utah, Utah
Arrived in Valley: 1852

Married: Mary Henderson

Date: 1810, Probably in Cambridge, Washington, New York
Born: 11 Apr 1785, Cambridge, New York
Parents: David & Mary Henderson
Died: 1851, Kanesville, Pottawattamie, Iowa

John's ancestors were some of the first settlers in the 1600's. After his marriage to Mary, they moved to Canada where their children were born. They apparently lived in several towns in Ontario, Canada, as evidenced by where their children were born.

John and Mary started west but Mary died in Kanesville, Iowa. John took his children and went on to the Valley. They settled in American Fork, Utah where he died at the age of 79.

Children:

JOHN, b. 17 Oct 1811, George, Ontario, Canada.
MARY, b. 25 Apr 1813, George, Ontario, Canada
BILLA, b. 8 Mar 1815 , Elizabeth, Upper Canada. Md. 10 Apr 1837, Mary Ann Stoddard. D. 31 Jan 1878, Richville, Morgan, Utah.
DAVID, b. 28 Jan 1817, Elizabeth, Ontario, Canada. Md. 27 Jun 1837, Nancy Stevens. D. 11 Aug 1903.
ALBERT, b. 11 Sep 1820, Elizabeth, Ontario, Canada. D. 28 Jul 1837.
SARAH, b. 5 Aug 1822, Leed Co., Upper Canada. Md. 1873, John Myers. D. 14 Dec 1870, Mountain Spring, Lincoln, Nevada
MARTHA, b. 20 Aug 1825, Elizabeth, Ontario, Canada. D. 26 Jun 1826.
STEWART (STUART), b. 14 Jun 1827, Twp. York, Upper George, Canada. Md. 27 Aug 1849/50, Mary Jane Champlin. D. 18 Dec 1911, Chesterfield, Bannock, Idaho.
CHILD, b. abt 1829.

Submitted by: L. Hoffman

STEWART (STUART) DICKSON

Born: 14 Jun 1827, Twp York, Upper George, Canada
Parents: John and Mary Henderson Dickson
Died: 18 Dec 1911, Chesterfield, Bannock, Idaho
Arrived in Valley: 1852

Married: Mary Jane Champlin
Date: 27 Aug 1849/50, Austin, Fremont, Iowa
Born: 20 May 1830, Brooklyn, Susquehana, Pennsylvania
Parents: William Sesson and Mary Ring Champlin
Died: 1 Nov 1906, Chesterfield, Bannock, Idaho

Stuart and his wife supposedly joined a handcart company and came west in 1852. However, the handcart companies didn't start until 1856.

After their arrival in the Valley, they moved to Lehi where they made their home. Later they moved to Brigham City where their fifth child was born. While he was small, they moved to Richville in Morgan County, where the balance of their eight children were born.

Later they moved to Woodruff in Rich County. When they grew older, they moved to Chesterfield, Bannock, Idaho, where Mary Jane died at the age of 76, Stuart lived to be 84. They were active in the church all their lives. Stuart was a shoemaker.

Children:

WILLIAM STUART, b. 23 Aug 1851, Keinsville, Pottawattamie, Iowa. D. 14 Jun 1892.

MARY SOPHRONIA, b. 7 Aug 1853, Lehi, Utah. Md. 26 Aug 1877, Orson Shipley. D. 30 Jun 1944, Chesterfield, Carribou, Idaho.

SARAH MARIA, b. 10 Nov 1855, Salt Lake City, Utah. Md. 9 Dec 1872, Chester Call. D. 12 Jun 1935, Chesterfield, Bannock, Idaho.

ADELAIDE AVILDA, b. 9 Nov 1858, Centerville, Davis, Utah. Md. 15 Apr 1880, Ezekiel Lee. D. 18 Jan 1940, Idaho Falls, Bonneville, Idaho.

ANN, b. 1859.

ALBERT HENRY, b. 8 May 1861, Brigham City, Utah. Md. 18 Dec 1893, Ellen Bryson. D. 26 Feb 1929, Woodruff, Rich, Utah.

SAMANTHA JANE, b. 4 Apr 1863, Richville, Morgan, Utah. Md. 15 Apr 1880, Daniel Carter Cornia. D. 4 Jan 1922, Brigham City, Utah.

LUCY HELEN, b. 23 Apr 1866, Richville, Utah. Md. 3 Apr 1884, Peter Carlos Cornia. D. 8 Jun 1893, Woodruff, Rich, Utah.

JOANNA SUSANNA, b. 6 Jul 1869, Richville, Utah. Md. 5 Dec 1889, Charles Lee. D. 18 Feb 1905, Iona, Bonneville, Idaho.

Submitted by: L. Hoffman

HENRY ALDOUS DIXON

Born: 14 Mar 1835, Grahamtown, South Africa
Died: 4 May 1884.
Arrived in Valley: Capt. Martin's Co. on 15 Sep 1857

Married 1st: Sarah DeGrey

Date: 27 Jan 1865
Nine children born to Sarah.
Married 2nd: Mary Smith
Date: 13 Apr 1869
Seven children born to Mary.

Submitted by: Mary Ella Getts

WILLIAM WILKINSON DIXON

Born: 14 Nov 1818, Bothel, Cumberland, England
Parents: William and Ann Wilkinson Dixon
Died: 10 Jun 1891, Harrisville, Utah
Arrived in Valley: 7 Oct 1850

Married: Sabra Lake
Date: 16 Aug 1842, Geneva, Scott Co., Illinois

Children:

HENRY, b. 2 Jun 1843. Md. 13 Nov 1871, Amelia Jane Garner.
     D. 29 Jul 1908.
HARVEY, b. 12 Sep 1844. Md. 1st 7 Mar 1870, Kittie Evalin
     Pritchett. Md. 2nd 6 Mar 1876, Susan Elizabeth Harmon. D.
     2 Jul 1906.
EMMA JANE, b. 1 Sep 1846. Md. 30 May 1863, Dudley Chase.
     D. 20 Aug 1863.
LYDIA ANN, b. 22 Oct 1848, d. 2 Dec 1853 at 5 years of age.
MARY LUCY, b. 12 Apr 1850. Md. 17 May 1869, Cyrus Rawson.
     D. 5 Nov 1882.

ELECTA PHILOMELIA, b. 2 Jun 1852. Md. 8 Feb 1870, Lyman
  Stoddard Skeen. D. 28 Apr 1891.
ESTHER ANN, b. 22 Mar 1854, D. 18 Nov 1865 at 10 yrs of age.
WILLIAM JAMES, b. 26 Jan 1856, D. 6 Sep 1862 at 6 yrs of
  age.
SABRA ELIZABETH, b. 24 Oct 1857, D. 7 Dec 1865 8 yrs of
  age.
BAILEY, b. 20 Nov 1859, D. 24 Nov 1865 at 6 yrs of age.
SARAH ELLEN, b. 1 Oct 1862. Md. 26 Jun 1879, Charles D.
  Brown. D. 23 Jan 1824.
DUDLEY, b. 26 Jan 1864. D. 26 Jan 1864.
JOHN LAKE, b. 27 Jan 1865. D. 15 Mar 1872 at 7 yrs of age.
RILEY GEORGE, b. 9 Nov 1866. Md. 22 Dec 1886, Mary Ann
  Taylor. D.29 Sep 1918.
ALFRED, b. 3 Jan 1869. Md. 15 May 1901, Ida Ellen Harris. D.
  10 Aug 1937.

Submitted by: Roger Rawson and Belva Moyle

ABRAHAM DONE

Born: 3 Mar 1853, Staley Bridge, Hartshead, Lancs., Eng.
Parents: John and Sarah Barker Done
Died: 13 Jun 1937, Provo, Utah, Utah
Arrived in Valley: 24 Oct 1855, Milo Andrus Company

Married lst: Elizabeth Annie Robinson
Date: 22 Jun 1875
Died: 5 Aug 1938, El Paso, El Paso, Texas

Married 2nd: Louisa Mathilda Wilhelmine Haag
Date: 18 Nov 1900
Died: 14 Jul 1965, Tucson, Pima, Arizona

Married 3rd: Ellen Precinda Moffett
Date: 5 Jun 1903
Died: 3 Aug 1975, Ogden, Weber, Utah

Abraham left little record of his early life. Shortly after the marriage of his parents, they heard and accepted the gospel. They were advised to emigrate to America as soon as possible, which they did by help from the Perpetual Emigration Fund. They took their two small children and Abraham's grandmother, Ann Hancock Done.

After they arrived in the Valley, they settled in the Little Cottonwood area southeast of the city. Abraham's father had worked in factories in England and was not familiar with farming, so times were very difficult. They lived in Springville for a while and then moved to Moroni.

Abraham was baptized while they were living in Moroni. He learned early how to help on the farm. He also took an apprenticeship in a carpenter shop and became very proficient. Later, Abraham and his father and brothers purchased a saw mill up Payson Canyon.

Abraham was called on a mission to the Southern States and while there contracted malaria. Because of his health he was released before the end of his mission.

He and his wife were determined to live the complete gospel, so Abraham took two more wives over the next three years. He loved the gospel and as long as his health permitted, he remained active in the church and also in the community. He died from a stroke in Provo, Utah.

Children of 1st wife:

ARTHUR JESSE, b. 15 Mar 1876.
EDITH JEMIMA, b. 5 Mar 1879.

ABRAHAM, b. 19 Feb 1881, died at 1 yr.
JOSEPH FRANKLIN, b. 13 Jan 1883.
MARY BRENTNALL, b. 18 Feb 1885.
EVA SARAH, b. 4 May 1887.
ETHEL CHOLERTON, b. 15 Sep 1889.
ROBINSON PARKES, b. 27 Jan 1892.
JEDDE BARKER, b. 11 Aug 1894, died at 3 yrs.
HEBER JOHN, b. 8 Apr 1896.
ABRAM WILFORD, b. 5 Oct 1898, died at 3 yrs.

Children of 2nd wife:

RICHARD HAAG, b. 2 Sep 1901.
WILLIAM JARED, b. 12 Sep 1903.
MARBA, b. 9 Aug 1906.
OTTO, b. 21 Nov 1906.
BETH, b. 17 Feb 1908.

Children by 3rd wife:

REED, b. 15 Mar 1904.
OLIVE, b. 13 May 1906.
LEO, b. 21 Dec 1907, died at 4 yrs.
BERNARD, b. 18 Nov 1909.
LEOLA, b. 12 Jan 1912.
AMMON, b. 1 Mar 1914.
PEARL, b. 12 Dec 1891.
HORACE, b. 9 apr 1921.
OWEN EMMETT, b. 4 Jul 1924.

Submitted by: Ross Haws

GEORGE DONE

Born: 18 Mar 1834, Stockport, Cheshire, England
Parents: Abraham and Ann Hancock Done
Died: 14 Sep 1906, Smithfield, Cache, Utah
Arrived in Valley: Oct 1853, Captain Wheelock's Company

Married: Alice Smith
Date: 9 Sep 1858, Smithfield, Utah

George was just 15 months old when his father died, leaving his mother to raise their children alone. She took care of the home, her children, and took her boys with her when she went to work in a factory. George learned to work at a young age.

In 1852, George and his older brother accepted the gospel and were baptized. Within six months they left for America. Upon their arrival in the Valley, George was hired by a Mr. Griffiths his first day. He and his brother worked and saved their money for two years to send for their mother, their brother John and his family, and to pay off their emigration debt.

Five years after his arrival in the valley he married Alice Smith, who later obtained her certificate and became a midwife.

George and his family settled in Smithfield. He had a love of music and purchased an organ for his home. He was choir director, and he held other leadership positions in the church and community until his death.

Children:

MARY, b. 18 Sep 1859.

ALICE, b. 14 Jan 1862.
SARAH ANN, b. 23 May 1864, D. at age 2.
MARIA, b. 25 May 1866.
GEORGE, b. 5 Sep 1868.
JAMES, b. 16 Mar 1873. D. at age 4.
JOHN, b. 5 May 1875, D. at age 4.
DONNA JANE, b. 17 Nov 1877.
BERTHA ELEANOR, b. 11 May 1880.
NATHAN, b. 22 Mar 1883.
LILLIAN, b. 10 Nov 1886. D. at birth.

Submitted by: Vickie Prows

JOHN DONE, SR.

Born: 28 Jan 1826, Chesterton, Wolstanton, Staffs., England
Parents: Abraham and Ann Hancock Done
Died: 12 Jul 1901, Payson, Utah, Utah
Arrived in Valley: 24 Oct 1855, Milo Andrus Company

Married 1st: Sarah Barker
Date: 15 Feb 1852, Ashtounder, Gine, England
Died : 27 Nov 1886, Payson, Utah, Utah

Married 2nd: Ellen Barker
Date: 26 Oct 1889, Manti, Sanpete, Utah

John's father died when he was nine years old. John went to work in a coal factory to help support the family. He was unable to attend school until he got a little older. He took every effort to gain an education thoughout his life. When he was 18, he learned to play the violin and became a fine musician. He later purchased an organ for his family. He became one of the leading musicians in Payson. Two of his little boys learned the violin and played with him on many occasions. He was the church organist for many years.

John, his mother, and two brothers joined the Church in 1852. They were advised to emigrate to the Valley. Due to lack of funds, his two brothers, James and George, went first and then worked to help John and the rest of the family emigrate.

When they arrived, they settled in Little Cottonwood. John spent one winter helping guard the valley when Johnston's army came. When he returned, he moved his family to Springville, where they lived until the fall of 1859 when they moved to Moroni. Later they moved to Payson where John invested in a saw mill with his sons. He loved the gospel and was active in doing what he could. He died of kidney disease.

Children by 1st wife:

ABRAHAM, b. 3 Mar 1853.
ELIZABETH ANNE, b. 27 Jun 1854.
GEORGE HENRY, b. 29 Jun 1857.
MARY JANE, b. 5 Jul 1859.
JOHN, b. 11 Aug 1861.
SARAH ELLEN, b. 9 Sep 1863. D. at 19 mo.
WILFORD (twin), b. 10 Dec 1865. D. at 21 mo.
WILLARD (twin), b. 10 Dec 1865.

Submitted by: Ross Haws and Lynn Ottesen

CHARLES MADISON DONELSON

Born: 12 Sep 1823, Hilliard, Knox, Ohio
Parents: John and Eleanor Bell Donelson
Died: 7 Mar 1893, Salt Lake City, Salt Lake, Utah
Arrived in Valley: Sept 1850, Ed Richardson's Company

Married: Caroline Carson Jolley
Date: 1 May 1850, Harris Grove, Iowa
Born: 15 Nov 1832, Weakley Co., Tennessee
Parents: Reuben Manning and Sarah Pippin Jolley
Died: 13 Feb 1895, Salt Lake City, Salt Lake, Utah

Charles Madison, as a young man, was employed on an early steamship on the Mississippi River. While working there, a friend converted him to the Church. He had met Caroline and when the time came to go west, he asked her to marry him and go with him to the Valley.

Upon their arrival in Salt Lake, they determined to settle in Battle Creek (Pleasant Grove). After the birth of their first child, they moved to Palmyra and then to Spanish Fork. In 1862, they were called to help settle Dixie but soon returned to Salt Lake where they operated a rooming house.

Charles was handy with tools. He made a loom for carpet weaving on which his wife wove their first carpet. He also started one of the first lumber yards in the valley. He made many things welcomed by the people. He went on a mission to Tennessee from 1882-1883. He was a doorkeeper in the old Salt Lake Theatre for many years and sometimes assisted in small parts. He was an expert chess and checker player.

People loved and respected him and he loved people. He remained active in church and community all his life until he died.

Children:

SARAH ELENOR, b. 10 Jul 1852, Pleasant Grove, Utah. Md. 1st, William Goforth, Salt Lake City, Utah.Md. 2nd, John Graham Coltrin, 16 Sep 1886. D. 5 May 1935, Salt Lake City, Utah.

CHARLES MADISON, b. 31 Jan 1854, Pleasant Grove, Utah., Md. Susannah Bell McAllister, 19 Oct 1873. D. 20 Feb 1922, Los Angeles, California.

JOHN REUBEN, b. 5 Dec 1855, Salt Lake City, Utah. Md. Angeline Aldous, 2 Aug 1874. D. 25 Nov 1917, Salt Lake City, Utah.

WILLIAM THOMAS, b. 13 Feb 1858, Salt Lake City, Utah. Md. Annie Haich, 27 Mar 1880. D. 10 May 1880, Salt Lake City, Utah.

CAROLINE MARIAH, b. 7 Apr 1860, Salt Lake City, Utah. Md. Ezra Oakley Best, 25 Sep 1882. D. 27 Jan 1941, Salt Lake City, Utah.

MARY JANE, b. 7 Apr 1862, Salt Lake City, Utah. Md. Jessie T. Burbidge, 22 Dec 1881. D. 1 Aug 1916, Salt Lake City, Utah.

ELIZA ANN, b. 18 Jul 1864, Salt Lake City, Utah. D. 26 Nov 1881, Salt Lake City, Utah.

NANCY LAURA, b. 5 Feb 1867, Salt Lake City, Utah. Md. John Brown Burbidge, 13 Mar 1887, in Logan, Utah. D. 7 Mar 1951, Salt Lake City, Utah.

JOSEPH SAMUEL, b. 30 Nov 1869, Salt Lake City, Utah. Md, Emily Williamson, 30 Nov 1893. D. 24 Nov 1950, Los Angeles, California.

Submitted by: Beverly Moore

ROBERT HUGHES DOWDLE

Born: 6 Apr. 1830, Moulton, Lawrence, Alabama
Parents: Robert and Sarah Ann Robinson Dowdle
Died: 27 Oct 1907, Franklin, Franklin, Idaho
Arrived in Valley: U. S. Government Freight Wagon, Summer
    1849

Married 1st: Henrietta Messervy
Date: 27 Mar 1857, Santaquin, Utah, Utah
Born: 20 Mar 1836, St. Heliers, Jersey, Channel Islands
Died: 20 Jul 1919, Teton, Fremont, Idaho

Married 2nd: Janet Lowe
Date: 3 Oct 1869, Salt Lake City, Utah
Born: 20 Apr 1852, Muirhead, Fife, Scotland
Died: 26 Apr 1893, Cove, Cache, Utah

Married 3rd: Allison Hamlin
Date: 26 Jun 1856 (Div.)

Robert Hughes was always proud that he was born on the day the Church was organized. He was proud of his membership in the church and filled every calling well. He was an Indian Scout and interpreter. He was a carpenter and farmer. He was active in the community affairs, including the position of constable and Justice of the Peace.

When Robert was about 13, his family moved to Jackson County, Mississippi. A year later they moved to King Creek, Pontotoc, Mississippi. While they were in Jackson County they met the missionaries and learned of the Book of Mormon. His parents were so impressed with the church that they were baptized within a few days, with the children following closely behind.

In 1846, the family determined to gather with the saints. Because they were very poor, a man by the name of Jefferson Jones offered to help them, if they would let him go with them. They started their journey in 1847. They arrived at Council Bluffs where they remained for a time. In September 1847, his father died, leaving a wife and seven children.

In the spring of 1848, when the saints were preparing to move west, some of them, including Robert and his family, returned to the Iowa side of the Missouri River to try to get things they would need to go west. In May 1852, they finally made their start west.

Upon their arrival in the Valley, they settled in Santaquin where his brother had previously gone. Robert married in 1858, and then in 1860 they moved to Franklin, Utah, now called Franklin, Idaho. He married again in the practice of polygamy.

Shortly before his death, he moved to Preston, Idaho, to be near some of his family. He was much loved by everyone.

Children by 1st wife:

ROBERT, b. 16 Nov 1858, Santaquin, Utah, Utah. D. 18 Nov 1858.
JOSEPH, b. 16 Jul 1859, Santaquin, Utah, Utah. D. 16 Jul 1859.
JOHN, b. 6 Aug 1860, Franklin, Idaho. D. 6 Aug 1860.
HENRIETTA JANE, 25 Jul 1861, Franklin, Idaho. D.26 Oct 1936.
SARAH ANN, b. 15 Jun 1863, Franklin, Idaho. D. 1 Feb 1922.
ELVIRA, b. 29 Apr 1865, Franklin, Idaho. D. 1 Jun 1879.
WILLIAM ROBERT, b. 4 Feb 1867, Franklin, Idaho. D. 6 Feb 1867.
ANNIE ELIZABETH, b. 22 Dec 1867, Franklin, Idaho. D. 13 Jun 1936.
HUGH JOSHUA, b. 9 Jan 1870, Franklin, Idaho. D. 13 Oct 1921.
LOUISA, b. 2 Nov 1872, Franklin, Idaho. D. 14 Nov 1910.
MORONI JEROME, b. 4 Jan 1874, Franklin, Idaho. D. 1 May 1879.

Children of 2nd wife:

THOMAS, b. 18 Nov 1870, Cove, Cache, Utah. D. 18 Nov 1870.
ELIZA, b. 13 Apr 1872, Cove, Utah. D. 18 Apr 1872.
JAMES, b. 24 Jun 1873, Cove, Utah. D.24 Jun 1873.
ELLEN ESTHER, b. 4 Feb 1874, Cove, Utah. D. 4 Feb 1874.
MARGARET, b. 13 Jan 1876, Cove, Utah. D. 13 Jan 1876.
ETHELAND, b. 21 Nov 1879, Cove, Utah. D. 9 Jul 1977.
ROSELLA, b. 31 May 1881, Cove, Utah. D. 26 May 1974.
JOHN ALVIN, b. 9 Aug 1883, Cove, Utah. D. 23 Jun 1922.
NELLIE, b. 11 Jun 1885, Cove, Utah. D. 20 Dec 1980.
LAVONIA JANETTE, b. Mar 1887, Cove, Utah. D. 17 Mar 1887.
ROBERT HAZEN, b. 25 Feb 1888, Cove, Utah. D. 12 Mar 1977.
ORVILLA, b. 20 Jun 1890, Cove, Utah. D. 1890.
ANIA, b. 1 May 1891, Cove, Utah. D. 28 May 1891.
MARY, (twin) b. 31 Jan 1892, Cove, Utah. D. 31 Jan 1892.
JANE, (twin) b. 31 Jan 1892, Cove, Utah. D. 31 Jan 1892.
MARTHA LEAH, b. 13 Apr 1893, Cove, Utah. D. Jan 1894.

Submitted by: Veldon Hodgson

JAMES DUKE

Born: 21 Dec 1827, Albany, Albany, New York
Parents: Jonathan Oldham and Mary Stone Duke
Died: 20 May 1892, Wallsburg, Wasatch, Utah
Arrived in Valley: 22 Sep 1850, Pace's 100

Married 1st: Almira Moore
Date: 10 Oct 1851, Provo, Utah, Utah
Born: 21 Feb 1836, Pomfret, Chautauqua, New York

Parents: Ethan Allen and Sarah Webber Moore
Died: 23 Apr 1922, Vernal, Uintah, Utah

Married 2nd: Margaret Jane Carter.
This was a sealing only, no issue and she never lived with him.

Married 3rd: Mary Murry Murdock
Date: 3 Oct 1868, Salt Lake City, Salt Lake, Utah
Born: 20 May 1852, Kansas City, Kansas
Parents: John Murray and Ann Steele Murdock
Died: 20 Dec 1917, Heber, Wasatch, Utah

James was a third generation member of the Church. His grandfather, Robert Stone, was the first member in 1838, followed by his daughter, Mary Stone Duke. The family of Jonathan and Mary Stone Duke moved to Nauvoo in 1841, where James was baptized in 1841. They determined to move west with the saints but were delayed for a time because of Jonathan's illness. In May 1850, the family finally left.

James learned the trade of brick masonry from his father. He was called to help in an exploration trip to Parowan and later he helped construct a fort there. He and his wife helped settle Heber City, Utah. He helped build some of the general authorities homes and worked on many church buildings and forts. He was also a farmer and rancher. He enjoyed taking part in dramatics, was a fiddler at the dances, and was active in the church and community activities.

Children of 1st wife:

JAMES MOORE, b. 12 May 1853, Provo, Utah, Utah. Md. 23 Aug 1875, Mary Lille Allred. D. 14 Jan 1911.
ALMIRA JANE, b. 5 Aug 1855, Parawan, Iron, Utah. Md. 26 Dec 1875, Moses Moroni Mecham. D. 4 May 1894, Jensen, Uintah, Utah.
ETHAN ALLEN, b. 23 Sep 1857, Salt Lake City, Utah. Md. 22 Jul 1880, Martha Jane Parcell. D. 24 Feb 1932.

ROBERT STONE, b. 21 Feb 1860, Provo, Utah. Md. 15 Jul 1886, Margaret Elizabeth Vanausdal. D. 12 Apr 1930.

JOHN CALVIN, b. 16 Mar 1863, Heber City, Utah, Md. 25 Nov 1886, Lurany Jane Ross. D. 10 Mar 1920.

JOSEPH MORONI (twin), b. 8 Mar 1868, Heber City, Utah. Md. 23 Dec 1887, Emily Jane Nisonger. D. 18 Jan 1899.

HELAMAN (twin), b. 8 Mar 1868, Heber City, Wasatch, Utah. Unmarried. D. 4 Mar 1898, Wallsburg, Wasatch, Utah.

MAHONRI MORIANCUMAR, b. 30 Apr 1870, Heber City, Wasatch, Utah. Md. 24 Jul 1893, Wilmurth LaMaude Wall. D. 25 Mar 1933.

LAMONI ROY, b. 24 Jan 1873, Wallsburg, Wasatch, Utah. Md. 28 Nov 1901, Lucinda Charlotte Nye. D. 29 Oct 1936.

BERNICE GERTRUDE, b. 19 Jan 1875, Wallsburg, Wasatch, Utah Md. 1 May 1896, George Albert Thomas. D. 22 Jan 1917.

SARAH PHEGENIA, b. 22 May 1877, Wallsburg, Wasatch, Utah. Md. 10 Apr 1895, James Provost. D. 27 Jun 1930.

Children by 3rd wife:

JONATHAN MURDOCK, b. 9 Sep 1869, Heber City, Wasatch, Utah. Md. 24 Jul 1891, Christina Kennedy Lindsey. D. 4 Oct 1942, Heber City, Wasatch, Utah.

MARY ANN, b. 14 Apr 1871, Heber City, Wasatch, Utah. Md. 23 Feb 1892, Robert Mitchell Simpson. D. 20 Dec 1914, Logan, Cache, Utah.

JANET, b. 26 Mar 1873, Heber City, Wasatch, Utah. Md. 5 Sep 1900, Arthur Emmanuel Hansen. D. 11 Nov 1940.

LILLIAN, b. 21 Mar 1875, Heber City, Wasatch, Utah. Md. 24 Jul 1893, Arch Shanks. D. 23 Feb 1940.

JOHN MURRAY, b. 15 Jan 1878, Wallsburg, Wasatch, Utah. D. 14 Nov 1878, Heber City, Wasatch, Utah.

ARCHIBALD KERR, b. 25 Oct 1878, Heber City, Wasatch, Utah. D. 6 Nov 1880.

JAMES MONROE, b. 2 Jul 1881, Heber City, Wasatch, Utah. Md. 26 Jun 1906, Mary Alice Pinnock. D. 27 Jan 1907.

THOMAS T., b. 13 Dec 1883, Heber City, Wasatch, Utah. D. 6 Nov 1884.

Submitted by: Lena Bartholomew

JONATHAN OLDHAM DUKE

Born: 31 Aug 1807, Derby, Derbyshire, England
Parents: James and Mary Oldham Duke
Died: 29 Dec 1868, Provo, Utah, Utah.
Arrived in Valley: Pace's 100 Wagon Train, 22 Sep 1850

Married 1st: Mary Stone
Date: 30 Dec 1828
Born: 1 Sep 1805, Derby, Derby, England.
Parents: Robert and Sarah Cartwright Stone
Died: 22 Jun 1890, Heber City, Wasatch, Utah

Married 2nd: Sarah Thompson
Date: 19 Oct 1855, Provo, Utah, Utah.
Born: 19 Mar 1836, Hull, York, England
Parents: George and Jane Goldthorpe Thompson
Married 2nd: Charles Henry Emmons
Date: 14 Nov 1870

Married 3rd: Martha Thompson
Date: 3 Dec 1855
Born: 10 May 1840, Hull, York, England
Parents: George and Jane Goldthorpe Thompson

Died: 23 Jul 1916, Provo, Utah, Utah.

Jonathan was bound as an apprentice to learn the mason business. He didn't marry until he was 22. They remained in England for about six months before leaving for America. They remained in Albany, New York, for two years and then moved to Jefferson County, New York; but they soon returned to Albany where they remained for 10 years. His wife visited her parents in Brooklyn and accepted the Church. Jonathan was baptized a few weeks later.

He helped with the building of the Nauvoo Temple and was sent on a mission from Nauvoo to Delaware, but at the end of two months was called home because of the martyrdom of the Prophet Joseph.

They left Nauvoo at the urging of the mob and settled in Pisgah for three years before starting west in 1850. Upon their arrival in the Valley, Jonathan went south to Provo where he built their home. He and his family remained active in the church, and he became the first bishop of the Provo First Ward. He was a major in the Silver Gray Company and was Justice of the Peace.

Children by 1st wife:

JAMES, b. 21 Dec 1829, Albany, New York. Md. 1st, 10 Oct 1851, Almira Moore. Md. 2nd, Margaret Jane Carter. Md. 3rd, Mary Murry Murdock. D. 20 May 1892, Wallsburgh, Wasatch, Utah.

SARAH JANE, b. 14 Nov 1832, Oswego, Oswego, New York. Md, 1 Aug 1851, James Smith. D. 15 Jan 1890.

JOHN, b. 28 Nov 1834, Albany, Albany, New York, Md. 1st, Mar 1857, Martha Vance Young. Md. 2nd, Mary Jones D. 4 Nov 1919.

ROBERT STONE, b. 14 Apr 1837, Albany, New York. Md. 1st, 9 Mar 1857, Anna Ross Young. Md. 2nd, 11 Nov 1872, Rachel Horrocks. D. 13 Jun 1923.

MARY ANN, b. 3 Mar 1842, Nauvoo, Hancock, Illinois. D. Aug 1842.

JONATHAN MORONI, b. 23 Oct 1844, Nauvoo, Illinois. Md, 13 Jul 1867, Sarah Gold Montgomery. D. Aug 1887.

Children by 2nd wife:

CHARLOTTE, b. 30 Sep 1856, Provo, Utah. Md, 1872, Dominicus Carter. D. 4 Apr 1921.

GEORGE JONATHAN, b. 25 May 1858, Provo, Utah.Md 1st, 26 Oct 1881, Sarah Temperance Meacham. Md. 2nd, 12 May 1921, Olga Jensen. D. 25 May 1858, Provo, Utah, Utah.

SARAH ANN, b. 9 Jan 1860, Provo, Utah. Md. 1st,9 Jul 1875, Jonathan Gledhill (Div). Md. 2nd, 31 Dec 1889, Issac Brigham Smith.

THOMAS WILLIAM, b. 23 Apr 1862, Heber City, Wasatch, Utah.Md 1st, 15 May 1885, Leah Pauline Smith. Md. 2nd, 12 Mar 1937, Pearl Smith Merrill. D. 19 Jan 1948.

ELIZABETH, b. 9 May 1864, Provo, Utah, Utah.Md. 26 Oct 1881, Jonathan James Meacham. D. 19 Oct 1919, Provo, Utah.

ALMIRA (twin), b. 1 Apr 1866, Heber City, Wasatch, Utah. Md. 1st, Richard George Harrison, 25 Jan 1888, Provo, Utah, Utah.Md. 2nd: 8 May 1907, Halma James VanWagener Smith. D. 13 Feb 1948, Vernal, Uintah, Utah.

MARY (twin), b. 1 Apr 1866, Heber City, Wasatch, Utah. D. 14 Sep 1866, Heber City, Wasatch, Utah.

HEBER, b. 19 Aug 1868, Provo, Utah, Utah. Md. 21 Jan 1889, Elizabeth Agnes Boardman. D. 9 Dec 1948, Provo, Utah, Utah.

Children by 3rd Wife:

MARY ANN, b. 21 Dec 1857, Provo, Utah. Md, 15 Nov 1875, Alma Brown. 7 Aug 1944, Provo, Utah.

CHARLES THOMPSON, b. 24 Apr 1860, Provo, Utah, Utah.Md, 26 Jul 1883, Emily Williams. D. 7 Aug 1940, Salt Lake City, Utah.

JANE, b. 23 Aug 1862, Provo, Utah. Md, 16 Feb 1887, Thomas Alexander Meldrum. D. 9 Dec 1941, Provo, Utah, Utah.

HYRUM, b. 23 Nov 1864, Heber, Wasatch, Utah. Md, 10 May 1886, Eleanor Ann Farrer. D. 5 May 1935, Provo, Utah, Utah.

JOSEPH, b. 23 Nov 1864, Heber City, Wasatch, Utah.Md, 4 Sep 1885, Lucy Jane Harrison. D. 20 Sep 1933, Provo, Utah.

ALMA, b. 3 Jan 1866, Provo, Utah. D. 18 Aug 1868.

Submitted by: Lena Bartholomew

ROBERT STONE DUKE

Born: 14 Apr. 1837, Albany, New York
Parents: Jonathan Oldham and Mary Stone Duke
Died: 16 Jun 1923, Heber City, Wastach, Utah.
Arrived in Valley: Capt. James Pace Company, 1850

Married 1st: Annie Ross Young
Date: 6 Mar 1857, Provo, Utah, Utah
Died:14 Jan 1926

Married 2nd: Rachel Horrocks
Date: 11 Nov 1872, Salt Lake City, Utah
Died: 24 Apr 1942, Provo, Utah, Utah

Children by 1st wife:

ROBERT, b. 1857.
ADOLPHIA, b. 1860.
ANNA LENORA, b. 1862.
MARY MIRANDA, b. 1864.
FRANCIS, b. 1866.
LAWRENCE BRIGHAM, b. 1870.
RODA MATILDA, b. 1872.
ALMA, b. 1874.

WILLIAM WADE, b. 1876.
MARTHA JANE, b. 1878.

Children by 2nd wife:

MARY ANN, b. 1875.
ADELIA, b. 1877.
ROBERT ROGER, b. 1878.
EMILY JANE, b. 1881.
LYMAN, b. 1885.
BETSY, b. 1889.
KATY LENHART, b. 1890.

Submitted by: Donna Bell

JAMES DUNCAN

Born: 5 Feb 1828, Green End, Lanark, Scotland
Parents: James and Mary McLaughlin Duncan
Died: 4 Jan 1912, Meadow, Millard, Utah
Arrived in Valley: James W. Bay Wagon Train, 13 Aug 1852

Married: Jennett (Janet) Snedden, Pennsylvania
Date: 1852
Parents: David and Christine Lyle Morris Snedden
Born: 21 Apr 1830, Passover, Scotland
Died: 28 Jul 1914, Meadow, Millard, Utah

Children:

MARY JANET, b. 15 Apr 1854, Fillmore, Utah.Md. J. M. Stewart, 22 Dec 1873.

JAMES JR., b. 26 Feb 1857, Fillmore, Utah.Md. A. J. Beckstrand, 7 May 1879.

DAVID, b. 4 Feb 1859, Meadow, Utah.Md. 1st: Stott, 8 Dec 1880, Md. 2nd: Gallaway, 4 Jan 1888.

JOHN, b. 7 Jan 1861, Meadow, Utah.Md. A. Prisbey, 20 Jun 1883.

CHRISTENA, b. 24 Nar 1863, Meadow, Utah.Md. H. A. Larson, 26 Sep 1880.

ELIZABETH EMMA, b. 8 Feb 1866, Meadow, Utah.Md. J. M. Stewart, 21 Dec 1883.

ADAM, b. 3 Feb 1868, Meadow, Utah.D. Mar 1868, Meadow, Utah.

RICHARD, b 8 Feb 1869, Meadow, Utah.Md. A. M. Martin, 12 Apr 1889.

GEORGE, b. 27 Aug 1871. D. as child, Meadow, Utah.

Submitted by: Dayle D. White

ALBERT JOSEPH ORSON DUNCOMBE

Born: 8 Apr 1858, Wolverhampton, Staffordshire, England
Parents: Joseph and Elizabeth Glover Duncombe
Died: 24 Oct 1902, Salt Lake City, Salt Lake, Utah.
Arrived in Valley: Capt William S.S. Willis Company, 1 Nov 1865

Married: Mary Alice Mackay
Date: 12 Jan 1882, Salt Lake City, Salt Lake, Utah.
Parents: Thomas Sloan and Charlotte James Mackay
Died: 4 Jul 1940

Albert Duncombe was the youngest of 15 children, six of whom died young. His father, Joseph Duncombe, was baptized in the Church 27 November 1848 in Westbromwich, Staffordshire, England. One month later, Albert's mother became a member. Some of the older children were already settled in Utah when they departed for America in 1865 on the ship "Belle Wood." Albert was seven years old at the time.

They joined other saints in Nebraska to outfit for the journey to Utah and left with the William S. S. Willis Company by ox team. The family walked most of the way and settled in the Valley. The family took up homesteads and farmed.

Albert married Mary Alice Mackay and took over his father's farm and also got into the sheep business. Later, Albert homesteaded land with a partner near Evanston, Wyoming. Albert raised thoroughbred horses, cattle and sheep, and the ranch became one of the largest sheep and cattle ranches in the area.

His wife and children always spoke highly of Albert. He was meticulous about recording family events in the Bible, and helped his daughter Daisy in genealogy work. He was honest, industrious, intelligent, and always provided well for his family.

Albert died in 1902 at age 44. Although his property later produced much oil, because Albert had become partners only on a handshake, his family never received any money from it. His wife was pregnant at the time of his death.

Children:

MARY ALICE DUNCOMBE, b. 6 Jul 1882 Md. James Brown, Jr., 23 Dec 1910 D. 11 Mar 1973, Evanston, Wyoming.

DAISY ELIZABETH DUNCOMBE, b. 22 Dec 1883, Unmarried. D. 4 Sep 1962, Salt Lake City, Utah.

CHARLOTTE "BIRDIE" EDNA DUNCOMBE, b. 31 Dec 1885, Md. John Earl Guest, 8 Jul 1912. D. 10 Apr 1956, Salt Lake City, Utah.

JOSEPH THOMAS DUNCOMBE, b, 4 Apr 1888 Md. Rene Melissa Swift, Jan 1913 D. 14 Jan 1929, Price, Utah.

LULU LOREENE DUNCOMBE, b. 25 Sep 1890 Md. Sherman Granter Freeze, June 1916 D. 18 Sep 1972, Murray, Utah.

WILLIAM CLIFFORD DUNCOMBE, b. 19 Jun 1893 D. 7 Dec 1902, Ogden, Utah

DENSLOW B. DUNCOMBE, b. 15 Mar 1896 D. 12 Feb 1897, Evanston, Wyoming.

JENNIE GERTRUDE DUNCOMBE, b. 29 Dec 1897. Md. Joseph Isaac Williams, 31 May 1917 D. 2 Aug 1974, Evanston, Wyoming.

ULVA LUCILLE DUNCOMBE, b. 4 Jul 1900 D. 12 Mar 1918, Salt Lake City, Utah.

MARGUERITE ALBERTA DUNCOMBE, b. 8 Mar 1903, Md. Dave R. Silvers, 3 Oct 1925 D. 16 Mar 1987, Salt Lake City, Utah.

Submitted by: Louise Williams Champneys

SAMUEL EAMES

Born: 16 Aug 1790, Bristol, Glooucester, England
Parents: William and Mary Eames
Died: 15 Oct 1868, Plain City, Utah
Arrived in Valley: Aug 1868, Chester Loveland Co.

Married: Nancy (Ann) Castree
Date: Jan 1817, Much Dewchurch Parish, Hereford, England
Christened: 16 May 1796, Much Dewchurch Parish, Hereford, England
Mother: Elizabeth Castree

Samuel, at the age of three, was placed in the home of uncle

Samuel Watkins, a stonemason, who lived in Orcop, Hereford, England. Under his uncle's guidance, Samuel learned the trade of mason. Several of the houses he built there still stand.

Samuel, Nancy, and some of their children were converted to the Church in about 1840, and they opened their home to the missionaries to hold meetings. Their desire was to immigrate to America but Nancy died before they were able to leave. Samuel, by careful saving, was able to periodically send some of his adult children to America. He also donated to help others.

Finally, in 1868 after 30 years of waiting, he left England with his son and their family. They road the train to Wyoming, where they joined a company and completed their journey.

Less than two months after his life long dream was fulfilled, Samuel died at the age of 78.

Children:

JAMES, b. 1817, Hereford, England. Md. Mary Lloyd. D. 1880.
JOHN, b. 1819, Hereford, England. Md. 1st, Sarah Elizabeth
    Powell. Md. 2nd Hannah Jenkins. D.1869, Plain City, Utah.
WILLIAM, b. 1823, Hereford, England. Md. Mary Lloyd. D.
    1850.
MARY ANN, b. 1828, Hereford, England. Md. John Carver. D.
    1870, Utah.
HENRY, b. 1831, Hereford, England. Md. Emma Beecroft. D.
    1869, Plain City, Utah.

Submitted by: Jay Burrup

ANDREW CAMPBELL EATCHEL

Born: 2 Oct 1834, Hopewell, Bedford, Pennsylvania
Parents: Adam Edward and Agnes Eatchel
Died: Nov 1898, Murray, Salt Lake, Utah
Arrived in Valley: 1862, Lewis Brunson, Capt. Independent Co.

Married: Sarah Ann Lloyd
Date: 25 Sep 1855, Alleghany, Alleghany, Pennsylvania
Died: 1878, Salt Lake City, Utah

Andrew Campbell was a Stationary Engineer by trade. After joining the Church, Andrew and his family immigrated to the Valley in 1862. It was an independent company. Most of the 212 saints were from Great Britain and Germany and were the first company to arrive that year.

Andrew and his family lived in Union Fort for many years. Later, Andrew was able to purchase property on what is now known as 33rd South in South Salt Lake. He built a home there. Ten months after the birth of their last daughter, Sarah Ann died. An aunt of Sarah's came to the house and helped care for the children.

Andrew never remarried. He raised hay that he sold to Fort Douglas. He died at the home of his son, George, in Murray.

Children:

DAUGHTER, b. abt 1856, Pennsylvania. D. Infant.
WILLIAN ANDREW.
THOMAS CAMPBELL.

CHARLES EDGAR.
GEORGE DONALD.
FRANK MEYERS.
CLARA EMILY (died 10 months old 1878).
AGNES ANNETTA GOUGH. (Adopted.)

Submitted by: Bud Eatchel

THOMAS ECCLES

Born: 11 Apr 1819, Wilton, Chorley Parish, Lancashire, England
Parents: James Bennet (Bennett) Eccles and Ann Ranvian
Died: 8 Apr 1859, Pinto, Washington, Utah
Arrived in Valley: 30 Nov 1856, Edward Martin Handcart Co.

Married: Alice Hardman
Date: 6 Aug 1843, Dean Parish, Lancashire, England
Born: 5 Nov 1821, Harwood, Bolton Parish, Lancashire, England
Died: 12 Jul 1883, Pinto, Washington, Utah

Thomas was baptized a member of the Church in 1841 by John Nightingale in Bolton, England.

Thomas was working as a weaver in a cloth making and printing factory. While working in the factory he met Alice Hardman and they married.

Thomas was a crofter (tenant farmer) and continued as a cloth printer after they were married. Thomas had already accepted the gospel and Alice was baptized in May 1847.

Thomas and his family emigrated 18 May 1856. They first

traveled to Liverpool where on 25 May 1856 they sailed on the "Horizon" for America in a group of 856 church members. They arrived in Iowa City, Iowa and joined the Handcart Company of Edward Martin who had also been their leader aboard ship. It has been said that Thomas was one of the captains in the Handcart Company. The Company left for the west on 28 July 1856 with 575 people, 146 handcarts and 7 wagons. Neither ship or handcart company records list their second daughter, Margaret, and no death records have been found. She probably died in England. Her baptism and endowments have been done, so she must have lived to age eight or older.

After arriving in the Valley, they stayed in Salt Lake City for five months after which Brigham Young sent them to colonize the Virgin River Valley. The family arrived in Santa Clara, Utah, on 3 May 1857. This colonization was the forerunner to the "Cotton Mission." Thomas became a farmer.

The family lived in the home of David Wilson Tullis. The Eccles had lived there a year and a half when Thomas became very ill with an appendicitis. David Tullis had just left for Parowan and Thomas died the same day. He was buried before David returned. Thomas was the first man who died and was buried in Pinto, Utah. His death was a blow to the entire family.

In early 1861, David married Alice in a civil ceremony in Pinto, Utah. Their only child, Thomas E. Tullis, was sealed to her first husband with David acting as proxy. Wanting an eternal family of his own, David married Alice's daughter Martha, probably in April 1863.

Thomas was a stalwart man who devoted his life to the church, his wife and family. He sacrificed and endured much in order that Zion could be established.

Children:

MARY ANN, b. 6 Sep 1844, Bolton Parish, Lancashire, England. Md. 27 Oct 1866, Richard Smith Robinson, Pinto, Washington, Utah. D. 19 Jul 1906, Provo, Utah, Utah.
MARGARET, b. 1845 (age 6 in 1851 census), Bolton Parish,

Astley Bridge, Sharples, Lancashire, England. D. date and
place unavailable.

MARTHA, b. 1 Jun 1847, Bolton Parish, Lancashire, England.
Md. 27 Aug 1863 (or Apr), David Wilson Tullis, Washington
Co., Utah, Sealed in Endowment House, Salt Lake City, Utah,
29 Aug 1863. D. 18 May 1915, Newcastle, Iron, Utah.

ALICE JANE, b. 28 Oct 1857, Santa Clara, Washington, Utah.
Md. 9 Mar 1882, David Cameron, St. George, Washington,
Utah. D. 23 Jun 1926 Panguitch, Garfield, Utah.

Submitted by: Leilani Grange

ESAIAS EDWARDS

Born: 10 Apr 1812, Pike Co., Missouri
Parents: Andrew and Anna Buckalew Edwards
Died: 8 Jun 1897, St. George, Utah
Arrived in Valley: 5 Oct 1848, Amasa Lyman (left wagon train
early to go on and obtain grazing for his animals.)

Married 1st: Elizabeth Campbell
Date: 27 Aug 1831, Quincy, Adams, Illinois
Born: 21 Jul 1814, Blount Co., East Tennessee
Died: 6 Apr 1845, Nauvoo, Hancock, Illinois

Married 2nd: Sarah Catherine Gibbs
Date: 27 Apr 1845, Nauvoo, Hancock, Illinois
Born: 26 Mar 1823, Ontario, Upper Canada
Parents: Cornetia Boyce (father died shortly after her birth)

Died: 29 Apr 1847, Iowa

Married 3rd: Belinda Miles
Date: 24 Oct 1847, Council Bluffs, Iowa
Born: 14 Jul 1827, Athens Co., Ohio
Parents: Thomas and Sally Seager Miles
Died: 11 Apr 1890, Millville, Cache, Utah

Married 4th: Ann Nuttall
Date: 23 Jun 1873, Utah
Born: 15 Oct 1838, Totington Township, England
Parents: William Nuttall
Died: 11 May 1909, Utah

Esaias was considered an educated man because he could read, write and do arithmetic. He contributed much to the early days of the Church and Utah. He built his own home and for many years made furniture, spinning wheels, beds, etc., for the people. He also built many mills including one in Nauvoo.

About 1838, Esaias found some unfortunate Mormons camped in the snow, had compassion for them and invited them to his home. He rented them some property and a house. The man, Alexander Williams, conversed freely about the gospel. Not long after this, Elizabeth became very ill. Mr. Williams gave her a blessing and she was healed. She and Esaias went down to the river and were baptized. Shortly after, in 1839, Esaias and Mr. Williams were called on a mission to the South where they served in Illinois, Kentucky and Tennessee. Esaias later served another mission in Galena.

After his first mission, he moved his family to Nauvoo. Shortly after the birth of their sixth child, Elizabeth died. Upon going to Heber C. Kimball for advice, he was told to give the baby to Sister Thomas Bennett to raise and told to take another wife. His second wife died shortly after the birth of their first child, who also died.

He decided to start west. They experienced many problems on the way but eventually made it to the Valley. He kept good records of the things he did. He married twice more. They stayed in Salt Lake for two years before moving to Tooele in 1850. In 1857 he and Belinda moved to Cache Valley.

In 1873 he married for the fourth time. Two years later he was called to help settle St George. Belinda refused to go, so he took his fourth wife and her daughter and two of his sons. He settled on a farm with fruit trees. He was always sad that he didn't have the rest of his family with him. He worked in the temple and did much for the growth of the West with the mills he built and other work he did. He held positions in the community and also the church.

Children of 1st wife:

SARAH ANN, b. 28 Aug 1832, Quincy, Adams, Illinois. Md. 7 Mar 1847/8, Thomas Algar/Alger. D. 18 Jul 1903, Eagar, Apache, Arizona.

GEORGE WASHINGTON, b. 8 Jul 1834, Adams Co., Illinois. Md.22 Apr 1855, Electa Jane Lee. D. 18 Sep 1882, Panaca, Lincoln, Nevada.

POLLY ANN, b. 25 Oct 1836, near Quincy, Adams, Illinois. Md.24 Jul 1851, Franciss Wilson Gunnell. D. 26 Dec 1862, Wellsville, Cache, Utah.

LOUISA JANE, b. 21 Jul 1839, Quincy, Adams, Illinois. D. 22 Feb1846, Nauvoo, Illinois.

THOMAS ANDREW, b. 22 Aug 1842, Nauvoo, Illinois. D. Jul 1843, Nauvoo, Illinois.

ELIZABETH RACHEL, b. 14 Sep 1844, Nauvoo, Illinois. Md.22 Nov 1862, Ephraim Edgar Ellsworth. D. 19 Feb 1878, Whitney, Oneida, Idaho.

Child of 2nd wife:

ESAIAS, b. 18 Oct 1846, Nauvoo, Illinois. D. 23 Jul 1847, Iowa.

Children of 3rd wife:

JOHN ALLEN, b. 1841, (Adopted 10 Oct 1852)

OLIVE. b. 14 Nov 1848, Salt Lake City, Utah. Md.7 Feb 1867, Durias Clinton Bishop. D. 22 Apr 1883.

EMMA JANE, b. 2 Jun 1850, Salt Lake City, Utah. Md.24 Jun 1867, Francis Joseph Sadlier. D. 12 May 1936, Burnt Fork, Sweetwater, Wyoming.

JULIAN, b. 17 Apr 1852, Tooele, Utah. D. 19 Dec 1858, Tooele, Utah.

ARMILDA, b. 8 Sep 1854, Tooele, Utah. D. 5 Nov 1858, Tooele, Utah.

ISAAC, b. 25 Jan 1857, Tooele, Utah. D. 18 Oct 1915.

DAVID, b. 31 Mar 1859, Millville, Cache, Utah. D. 28 Sep 1931.

ZEBULON, b. 4 Jun 1861, Millville, Utah. Md. 7 Jun 1904, Catherine Rebecca Hill. D. 24 Sep 1924, Vernal, Uintah, Utah.

CAROLINE, b. 11 May 1863, Millville, Utah. D. 14 May 1872.

ANDREW, b. 15 Sep 1865, Millville, Utah. Md.12 Oct 1892, Emma Elizabeth Hamblin. D. 12 Mar 1945, Provo, Utah.

JESSE, b. 20 Sep 1867, Millville, Utah. D. 28 Sep 1867, Millville, Utah.

Submitted by: Mella Bedell

PHILLIP EDWARDS

Born: 24 Dec 1833, Clayton, Sussex, England
Parents: John and Harriet Cheesman Edwards
Died: 14 Jan 1908, Charleston, Wasatch, Utah
Arrived in Valley: 3 Sep 1860, James D. Ross Handcart Co.

Married: Mary Simmons
Date: 10 Feb 1860, Clayton, Sussex, England

Phillip was baptized into the Mormon Church in 1856 at the

age of 23. After his marriage to Mary, they decided to leave for America and the Valley to be with the saints.

After arriving in New York, they traveled to Nebraska and joined the handcart company there. Because of an extreme case of arthritis, he had to ride in the wagon most of the way. They lived in Salt Lake until 1883, when they moved to Charleston, Utah.

Up to that time, Phillip owned and operated the first slaughter house in Salt Lake where Fort Douglas now sits. He was also a farmer until he could no longer work because of the pain and crippling effect of his arthritis.

Children:

LUCY S.
ELLEN.
MARY ELIZA.
EMMA MIRIAM.
ALICE MATILDA.
PHILLIP WILLIAM.
GEORGE HENRY.
JOHN OLIVER.
JOSEPH PARLEY.
ORSON DANIEL (adopted).

Submitted by: Thais DeGrey

HOWARD EGAN

Born: 15 Jun 1815, Tullemore, Kings County, Ireland

Parents: Howard and Ann (Betty) Meade Egan
Died: 15 Mar 1878, Salt Lake City, Utah
Arrived in Valley: 24 Jul 1847, Brigham Young. (Howard was
    Captain of the 9th and 10th groups)

Married: Tamson Parshley
Date: 1 Dec 1838, Salem, Massachutes
Born: abt 1824
Married: (age 14 years and 4 months when married)

Howard came with his father and six other children to the Canada in 1823, after the death of his mother when he was eight. His father left one child in Ireland with relatives. His father died while in Canada. Howard joined the navy for 10 years before returning to America and settling in Salem, Massachusetts.

He helped the exodus to Salt Lake by making three trips. He was a messenger who carried the earnings of the Mormon Battalion back to the church leaders. He was a trailblazer, overland stage and mail agent, and took part with the pony express. He remained active in the church all his life. He filled several missions within the United States and was active in the Nauvoo Legion and police.

Children:

HOWARD R., Md.19 Nov 1847, Amanda Andrus. D. 17 Mar 1916.
RICHARD ERASTUS, Md.1844, Mary Minnie Fisher. D. 21 Apr
    1918.
CHARLES JOHN, b. 28 Mar 1844. D. 1845.
HORACE ADELBERT, b. 12 Aug 1847. D. 24 Mar 1862.
WILLIAM MOBURN, b.13 Jun 1851. Md.7 Feb 1886, Ruth
    Nichols. D. 15 Apr 1929.
IRA ERNEST, b. 5 Feb 1861. Md.24 Aug 1881, Emma Moss. D.
    13 Dec 1933.

Submitted by: Mardene Denison